To Virginia

Preface

The basic aim of this book is functional in that it is concerned with orienting the material to the student's present and future needs. However, in direct contrast to most functional textbooks, this book has as its basic premise that, ideally, marriage and family relations may be studied through examination of the extensive historical and scientific material available on the subject. In other words, the student can better understand his needs and values if he is acquainted with a considerable amount of data on socialization, role taking, and other processes. At the same time, the institutional aspects of the family are emphasized. The approach of this book is consequently both psychological and sociological. The critical importance of socialization is indicated in Chapter 5, where the subject is approached in the context of the individual's development, and again in Chapters 17 and 18, in which the socialization process is analyzed from the parent's point of view. The interactionist position expressed in the book is fundamental, as is the viewpoint that marriage and family cannot be understood apart from the other social institutions that shape the personality. Also, in view of the majority of research findings cited here and the interests and backgrounds of the readers, the book may be said to have a middle-class bias.

This textbook may be used by students who have had no previous courses in sociology and psychology, although such a background could be helpful. A glossary is provided as an aid to students for whom certain terms may be unfamiliar. The wide coverage of materials in this book enables the instructor to include only those chapters he considers relevant to his interpretation of the course.

My interest in the subject of the family dates from my courses with Harvey J. Locke at the University of Southern California. I wish also to acknowledge my debt to certain major researchers and theorists of the family, most notably to William M. Kephart, Clifford Kirkpatrick, Talcott Parsons, and Robert F. Winch.

Specifically, I wish to thank Robert R. Bell for his critical comments, and especially Bernard Farber and Shirley Clark, who reviewed the entire manuscript. James R. Frakes was largely responsible for the choice of extracts from literature. I am grateful to Miss Nancy Unger for the selection of the illustrations, and to Francis J. Quirk for the drawings in Chapter 14. I am also deeply indebted to Mrs. Carol Levine, Miss Roberta Cook, and to my wife, Virginia L. Williamson, for their editing. The typing of the manuscript was primarily the work of my wife and Mrs. Dorothy N. Frye. Most of all, I wish to thank the members of my family for their patience in enduring my absorption in the manuscript.

ROBERT C. WILLIAMSON

October, 1965

Contents

Part I INTRODUCTION: THE SOCIAL SETTING   1

   Chapter One Marriage and the Family in America Today   3
   Chapter Two The Historical Fabric of Marriage and the Family   23
   Chapter Three The Contemporary Setting of Marriage and
                 Family Life   43
   Chapter Four Marriage Variations in Mid-century America   71

Part II PREMARITAL PATTERNS   99

   Chapter Five Prologue to Maturity   101
   Chapter Six Differences in Sex Roles   141
   Chapter Seven Dating Patterns   165
   Chapter Eight Premarital Sex Behavior   193

Part III PRELUDE TO MARRIAGE   221

   Chapter Nine Love and the Romantic Quest   223
   Chapter Ten The Selection of a Mate   249
   Chapter Eleven Society, Law, and Marriage   279
   Chapter Twelve The Threshold of Marriage   301

Part IV RELATIONS IN MARRIAGE   321

   Chapter Thirteen Roles, Personality Dynamics, and the
                 Adjustment Process   323
   Chapter Fourteen Sex Adjustment in Marriage   355
   Chapter Fifteen The Family and the Economy   383
   Chapter Sixteen Becoming Parents   417
   Chapter Seventeen Parental Roles   453
   Chapter Eighteen Problems in Parent-Child Relationships   475

Part V   CONFLICT, CRISIS, AND DISSOLUTION   495

    Chapter Nineteen   Marital Conflict and Family Crises   497
    Chapter Twenty   Bereavement, Separation, and Divorce   525
    Chapter Twenty-One   Marriage and Family Counselling   565

GLOSSARY   581

APPENDIX   587

NAME INDEX   599

SUBJECT INDEX   609

Part one

Introduction:
The Social Setting

What is the meaning of marriage and family institutions? Why do we in our culture prefer the small, so-called *nuclear* family, that is, a family consisting of the parents and immediate children, rather than the *extended* family found in some parts of the world? Why are we monagamous? Are American marriages different from others? Marriage can be more meaningful if these questions are answered. Consequently, this section introduces the broad perspective of marriage and the family: its significance in our society, its background in Western history, the institutions that interact within the home today, and the varied types of marriage in the United States.

Chapter one

Marriage and the Family in America Today

All tragedies are finish'd by a death,
All comedies are ended by a marriage.
      Byron, Don Juan, *III, 1821.*

    The American family is not a dying institution. It already has been strengthened by new forces. Although in addition to stresses within the kinship structure, it is subject to multiple strains from other institutions (e.g., occupational structure which interferes in many ways with stable family life), higher birth rates, and renewed emphases on family values attest to the continued tenacity of this basic social unit.
    Robin M. Williams, Jr., American Society: A Sociological Interpretation *(second edition), Alfred A. Knopf, New York, 1960, p. 85.*

    The ancient trinity of father, mother, and child has survived more vicissitudes than any other human relationship. It is the bedrock underlying all other family structures. Although more elaborate family patterns can be broken from without or may even collapse of their own weight, the rock remains. In the Götterdammerung which otherwise science and overfoolish statesmanship are preparing for us, the last man will spend his last hours searching for his wife and child.
    Ralph Linton, "The Natural History of the Family," in Ruth N. Anshen (ed.), The Family: Its Function and Destiny *(revised edition), Harper and Row, New York, 1959, p. 52.*

Group of Figures by Milton Hebald
Courtesy of the Bronx Municipal Hospital Group—Ernie Pile, Photographer

More than nine out of ten Americans at some time in their lives are married. For practically all of us, marriage is the universal "great adventure." No single day has the emotional impact of a wedding day. With the possible exception of a birthday, no other event has the same significance in an annual round of rituals as the wedding anniversary. Part of this feeling stems from tradition. The rites of the wedding, from the presentation of the ring to the throwing of rice, came from classical civilizations of more than two thousand years ago. But the glorification of marriage is reinforced by the stimuli that pervade our twentieth-century urban culture: glamorous advertisements in magazines featuring a smiling couple surveying their latest time-purchase; the romantic literature of the magazine serial; the sagas of the wide-angle screen. Anatole France once said that we would never fall in love, if someone had not told us about it. He was describing, in a commonplace way, what sociologists for the past fifty years have called the *socialization* process. Our cultural pattern conditions us to the idea that some day we will be married. Marriage becomes one more test of conformity, but far more positive motives impel us to marriage.

What are most of us looking for in marriage? Motivation is never simple, and important decisions in life are generally complicated. Yet there are some basic motives that explain the attraction of marriage, whether most of us realize them or not. Marriage is regarded as the most acceptable means of realizing the maximum personality enrichment and growth. For one thing, it involves the intimate exploration of another's personality and the enhancement and security that this exploration may give. Only in marriage do most individuals find an opportunity to express in any mature sense their emotional and sexual needs. In marriage, especially with the addition of children, one can enjoy the satisfaction of creativity and the other values of family life. Some people may marry for social acceptance: to fulfill the expectation of their peers and enjoy the status that society confers on the married. In the competitive employment market being married is a distinct advantage, at least for the male, especially in regard to positions of prestige. There are many other reasons for marrying, and we shall discuss them later in Chapter 12.

MARRIAGE, FAMILY, AND SOCIAL SCIENCE

Despite this universal commitment to marriage, it has not been studied by many. With the exception of two or three nineteenth-century scholars, only since the turn of the century have sociologists studied in any systematic fashion this basic part of human living. Moreover, until the last three decades little empirical research was conducted in such critical areas as mate selection or marital adjustment.

One basic reason for this lack of study has been the relative lag in the development of the social, or behavioral, sciences. Sociology, which has assumed much of the responsibility in studying marriage and related institutions, was coined as a term in 1837 but did not constitute a department in any university of the United States until the 1890's. Other social scientists, particularly psychologists and anthropologists, gave only limited attention to marriage before the turn of the century, or more specifically, before World War I. Similarly, the home economist only recently has become interested in the subject.

Although marriage and the family are universal institutions, they are not automatic behavior patterns; and even though the majority of the world's population marries and stays married, ubiquity should not discourage investigation. An explanation for this fact, according to one popular viewpoint, is that any intelligent individual can make a mature judgment at any juncture of behavior merely by using common sense. After all, exponents of this opinion say, a careful student of human nature, even without formal training, may solve his marital or other personal problems by observation of others. In addition, there is trial and error; and where this does not suffice, the young person may seek general counsel from friends.

It is presumptuous to deny that there is some value in this approach. However, the history of science is replete with instances where common sense has failed to provide a scientific answer or, in most instances, to solve basic human problems. Friendly advice generally is inadequate to determine personal planning in marriage, vocational, or other problem areas. Yet the daily newspaper is a testimonial to the attempts to resolve emotional conflicts and all kinds of personal problems by "advice-to-the-lovelorn" columns and other forms of pseudopsychology.

True, some persons are more astute than others in profiting from experience; a certain degree of logic or wisdom is gained through intelligent trial and error, but a more systematic and empirical viewpoint is necessary. This book offers few generalizations that cannot be documented by findings based on controlled observation, case studies, or other dependable methods of investigation. Marriage is no exception to the canon of applying the scientific method, although it is possible that something more than the scientific method is relevant. This "something more" consists of emotional and romantic responses along with common sense, which may not always be the products of the scientific method. Scientific method can enlighten decisions during marital interaction, but cannot necessarily replace certain affectional insights.

A serious factor governing reluctance to approach the study of marriage and the family in a scientific frame of reference is the fear of most societies, including our own, to investigate any ritualized behavior pattern. This hesitation to look objectively at our cultural heritage is universal and probably can be explained by the widespread conservatism of man. He finds security in his time-proved habits; the familiar is psychologically more reassuring than the new or unusual. Marriage, with its roots deep in the past, its religious sanctions, and its significance for many aspects of our existence is even less subject to scrutiny than most institutions.

This is not to imply that marriage can or should be detached from emotion, or even from romantic ecstasy. Yet the increase in the divorce rate over the last seventy years constitutes one justification for a detached viewpoint. Family institutions can be approached from many perspectives: religious, educational, economic, biological, psychological, sociological, etc. In this book, our approach to these perspectives is as scientific as possible. Our present-day society frequently tends to objectify some of the more sacred aspects of living; for example, certain religious groups recently have moved toward clinical and counselling techniques in handling marital difficulties.

WHY STUDY MARRIAGE AND THE FAMILY

The scientific method rests on the actuarial premise that predictions in science apply to the group rather than to the individual. There is evidence to indicate that education beyond the secondary level is favorable to marital adjustment.[1] Although it is thought that enrollment in a course on marriage is positively correlated with marital happiness, thousands of happy marriages existed before the works of Freud, Kinsey, or dozens of other books on marriage appeared. We do not claim that happy marriages depend on the candidates' successfully mastering the relevant undergraduate course, although clearly systematic information can be enlightening.

The scientific study of marriage is all the more relevant at college age because many young people marry, or at least select a spouse, while in college. One cynic has quipped that the major purpose of college is to provide the shy teenager with a mate or fulfill the last stage of the socialization process: getting married. The college environment does provide one of the few opportunities in life to be among contemporaries at a highly advantageous period. The undergraduate is likely to have more varied social opportunities than he will ever have again.

A review of various evaluations of marriage courses in colleges revealed that more than 80 per cent of the students had found value in the courses.[2] According to those investigations that included a married sample, the course proved helpful to these couples. Still other studies involving students who had taken the course (as compared to "controls" who had not) showed understanding of roles and the ability to identify with others as results of the course. It is unlikely that these favorable reports were simply rationalizations since adjustment tests and inventories were used.

Let us now summarize the reasons for systematically studying marriage and family relations:

1. Those individuals who apply empirically tested principles to their marriage are more adequately adjusted. This book stresses that this kind of intellectual preparation before marriage provides a wider set of alternatives available to the partners. Individuals entering marriage without this knowledge depend almost entirely on trial and

---

[1] Lewis M. Terman, *Psychological Factors in Marital Happiness*, McGraw-Hill, New York, 1938, pp. 187f; also, Harvey J. Locke, *Predicting Adjustment in Marriage*, Holt, Rinehart and Winston, New York, 1951, p. 346.

[2] E. M. Duvall, "How Effective Are Marriage Courses?," *Journal of Marriage and the Family*, 1965, **27**, 176–184.

error, are inclined to follow norms blindly, and experience more difficulties in their married life.

2. For a variety of reasons, in the past there has been reluctance to
investigate the more adequate norms of family life.

3. What knowledge has been derived about marriage and the family
from surveys, interviews, and other types of investigations rarely has
been applied by the general population partially because of lower
standards of education, the feeling that marriage depends more on
intuition or common sense, and because of the difficulty in communicating scientific knowledge to them.

4. The purpose of this book, and of family-life education in general,
is to make available information to insure more satisfactory marital
and family relations.

Generally, our society has been moving toward a more scientific
approach to human events. Not only has the number of books and
courses available in marital or family education increased, but the
emphases have also shifted. For instance, a textbook on marriage and
the family published in 1934 focused on understanding the biology of
heredity, reproduction, and sex; whereas an analysis of three present-
day texts shows the focus to be on better mate selection and more
companionable and competent marriages.[3] Today we regard marriage
as an experience in interpersonal relations, which constantly can be
improved. The present outlook is that marriage and family relations
can be approached in terms of flexibility and change.

THE QUESTION OF DEFINITIONS

Marriage appears to be as old as human life itself. No society is
without this institution, however varied the patterns may be. In the
broadest sense, *marriage* can be defined as a relatively permanent
sexual union implying a number of interlocking statuses and roles.
This definition differs for every society, since marriage, like all culture,
is conditioned by time and place. The urban world of the twentieth
century, especially, has given marriage a new meaning. Marriage also
has different significance for the farmer or the accountant, for teenager

[3] Reuben Hill, "The American Family of the Future," *Journal of Marriage and
the Family,* 1964, **26,** 20–28.

or octogenarian, for liberal Congregationalist or orthodox Jew, for Frenchman or Navaho.

The family may be defined as a marriage with the addition of progeny; in other words, the family refers to a limited social system composed of two individuals and their offspring. In a more complete sense the *family* may be constituted of persons united by ties of marriage, blood, or adoption, who generally share a household, interact with each other, and maintain a common culture.[4] In fact, more than a generation ago Burgess defined the family as a "unity of interacting personalities."[5] Within the definition of family we must distinguish between the *nuclear* or conjugal family, composed of the immediate family, and the *extended* or kinship-oriented family still found within non-Western cultures. This book uses the term, "family," to mean the modern nuclear family. However, we have both ceremonial and affectional relations with our cousins and grandparents, so we still have occasional trappings of extended families.

The family and religion are the only two social institutions "formally developed" in all societies.[6] For all cultures the family represents a set of definite practices and rules with rewards and punishments; without these controls, the society could not be maintained. We may, in fact, define either marriage or the family in terms of its functions. The functions of marriage are to some extent the functions of the family, as the one with the addition of children becomes the other. First, a society to endure must reproduce its members; this is the primary function of the family from the viewpoint of society's needs.[7] Second, the infant and child must become a functioning member and acquire the cultural norms of his society, through the socialization process. Third, social control, particularly of the sex urge, is most feasible through some form of marriage. Fourth, there are miscellaneous functions. Perhaps the most important is the process of conferring status, or placing the family member in his proper location within the social structure. There are also various institutional functions. Marriage is,

[4] Ernest W. Burgess, Harvey J. Locke, and Mary M. Thomes, *The Family from Institution to Companionship* (Third Edition), American Book Company, New York, 1963, p. 2.

[5] Ernest W. Burgess, "The Family as a Unity of Interacting Personalities," *The Family*, 1926, **7**, 3–9.

[6] William J. Goode, *The Family*, Prentice-Hall, New York, 1964, p. 4.

[7] Robert F. Winch, *The Modern Family* (revised edition), Holt, Rinehart and Winston, New York, 1963, p. 16.

among other things, an economic arrangement in which the husband is responsible for supporting the wife, who in turn is expected to be a good homemaker. Religious and recreational functions exist as part of marriage and the family for all cultures. However, we take our own culture for granted and perceive our own institutions as more fitting and just than those of other societies. In any case, the three basic functions—reproduction, socialization, and social control—are found universally within marriage, though these functions and roles may be implicit for most individuals.

Just as there are different functions of marriage, there are also very distinct types of marriages throughout the world. There are two general forms: singular and plural, or *monogamy* and *polygamy*. In practice, monogamy is the preferred type (as much by necessity as for any other reason), since in most societies neither the sex ratio nor the economy permits the luxury of a second wife. Even in the numerous societies that practice *polygyny*, or plurality of wives, only the wealthier members can afford more than one wife. *Polyandry*, or the plurality of husbands, exists, as far as we know, in not more than two tribes of the world: the Todas and the Marquesas.[8] A fourth form, *group marriage*, whereby several men may be married to several women, has been observed, but it generally remains as an incidental or special form within a society adhering to one of the three conventional systems of matrimony. Our own society, with it Hebrew-Greek-Roman heritage, has been strongly monogamous, and cases of rapid, successive divorces and marriages sometimes reported in Reno, Las Vegas, or Hollywood are even today somewhat unusual.

Anthropologists have described the commitment of some societies to *endogamy*, marriage within the group, or *exogamy*, marriage outside the group. In fact, all societies are both endogamous and exogamous to some degree. Statistically speaking, we marry within our race, nationality group, religion, class, educational level, and locality. By law, in more than twenty states we must marry outside certain kinship ties, namely the first cousin, and in some religious groups marriage is not sanctioned within the third degree of kinship.

Marriage results from a culturally defined need supported by a system of rewards and punishments. The universal desire for marriage represents what the psychologist calls a social motive. Beginning with

[8] Clellan Ford and Frank Beach, *Patterns of Sexual Behavior*, Harper and Row, New York, 1951, p. 109.

Aristotle, and until the first decade of this century, marriage or mating was defined as an instinctual need. Courtship, love-making, the desire to be a parent were considered variations of this so-called inborn drive system. Indeed, all deep-seated human behavior was considered by philosophers and scientists to be the product of a given number of instincts, the precise number of which was always a subject of controversy. With the repudiation of the instinct doctrine, marriage as a form of social behavior has been explained as *learned response*. Behavior is learned in the framework of the cultural heritage in which the individual happens to be born, and in which he acquires his particular set of actions as patterned by a specific family group, peer group, or community. His specific needs and experiences operate as a dynamic factor in combining his inherited tendencies with the diverse stimuli of his environment. Finally, although its form varies greatly from society to society, marriage is a universal institution because all cultures prescribe it as an expected behavior pattern. Apparently, it meets the need of the vast majority of individuals in all societies. In our social order, for instance, it is an exceptional person who can find his maximum psychological wellbeing or personality integrity outside of marriage.

CHANGING NORMS OF COURTSHIP AND MARRIAGE

One of the more remarkable transformations of our time is the revolution in the folkways and mores of courtship and marriage. This change in the roles of men and women began with the Industrial Revolution, but its full effects were not apparent for more than a century later. In the process of mobility and urbanization that arrived at the end of World War I, a number of factors upset the traditional norms of love-making and marriage. These included the breakup of religious orthodoxy, the rise of new sciences, the economic employment and enfranchisement of women, radically new leisure-time pursuits, and a multitude of inventions, from the automobile to contraceptives.

COURTSHIP IN THE TWENTIETH CENTURY. To our grandparents at the turn of the century, initiative in love-making in the sense of serious courtship, including kissing, was reserved for the fiancé. The young man who appeared twice consecutively with the same girl at the church supper implied matrimonial intentions on his part, and was expected to approach the young lady's father to formalize the event. In small-town America, the behavior of young people was carefully scrutinized lest there be "hanky-panky." Recreation was confined largely to the parlor or the church social. In the urban centers, social life might extend to the well-supervised high school "prom." Possibly a "shirt-tail" relative or one of the gang occasionally encouraged the younger male to "sow his wild oats"; however, all women, except for the few who had "fallen," were held on a pedestal in the untarnished purity their role had commanded for some centuries. In theory, sex could exist only in marriage, but for those males who were impatient there were clandestine sources. Yet, the middle-class ideal was a genteel courtship followed by the "holy bands of matrimony."

By the 1920's, or a little earlier, a new mode of premarital and marital patterns had emerged. Individual dating became the usual social relationship among unmarried adolescents and adults. For the moment, we may say that this new behavior was characterized by a term popularly known as the "romantic complex." Psychologically, the romantic complex implies a tendency to gloss over reality with the result that the love-relationship is ecstatically idealized, and the physical appearance of the loved one assumes immense importance. Along with this romantic veneration is what Waller called the "rating-dating complex." [9]

With this new approach came a whole set of cultural elements: for example, a high verbal art of concealment and the "fast line." This verbal charm is not without its function and the dating-courtship process is one of trial-and-error learning. It represents a movement of ego expansion, conquest and defense, and other social skills. The girls must be appealing and yet self-protecting; the young male is acquiring something between exploitive sex appeal on one side, and maturity of affection on the other.

THE NEW SEX BEHAVIOR. While the romantic complex was changing the relationship between the sexes in their dating and courtship practices, other influences were transforming the physical relationships between them. Perhaps some historians would assert that the romantic strain inevitably ushered in a set of changes in the sex mores. Although the chain of cause and effect is too complex to analyze precisely, the romantic complex, together with a number of other urban factors, undoubtedly sped along the revolution in sex mores.

[9] Willard Waller, *The Family*, Cordon, New York, 1938; also, "The Rating and Dating Complex," *American Sociological Review*, 1937, 2, 727–734.

The aftermath of World War I is usually cited as the beginning of the new mores. The decade 1910 to 1920 was a transition to this redefinition of the sexual outlook of the new generation. The war itself brought home more than two million men from the trenches in France with somewhat different cultural viewpoints than they had previously and in a mood for change. The war saw the emergence of the new woman too, who became employed more often in the office, factory, and the field. The Nineteenth Amendment of 1920 gave women the right to vote on a national scale. This new legislation emphasized the redefinition of women's status.

In the so-called "Flapper Age" of the 1920's, women militantly expressed the right to bob their hair, wear trousers, and even more daring, to smoke cigarettes. The still more adventurous entered into overt sex relationships with ardent male admirers. In other words, the double standard was weakened but certainly not destroyed. Women were no longer set in two rigid categories of good and bad. Dating was less carefully chaperoned than it had been before World War I. Kissing became a more casual matter, and new terms like "necking" and "petting" joined the common vocabulary. While coitus on a premarital basis was, and is, disfavored by the majority of the population, old or young, the very fact that it could exist before marriage for a middle-class girl was in itself a revolution.

Basically, the new behavior of the 1920's has continued with certain variations until the present. Yet this sex revolution has not drastically affected the taboo on premarital sexual intercourse. For example, while perhaps 50 to 70 per cent (the figure depends on the study selected) of college males have experienced premarital sex relations, the number of contacts is limited for many to only one or two experiences. For the woman, the picture demonstrates even more dramatically the retention of conventional patterns. According to the study of Kinsey and his colleagues, less than 20 per cent of college women report sexual intercourse, and in those cases most frequently with only one partner.[10] Another study finds that only 13 per cent of college women have experienced sex relations.[11] It appears that for the middle

---

[10] A. C. Kinsey, W. B. Pomeroy, C. E. Martin, and P. H. Gebhard, *Sexual Behavior in the Human Female,* W. B. Saunders Co., Philadelphia, 1954, pp. 295, 330, and 336.

[11] Winston Ehrmann, *Premarital Dating Behavior,* Holt, Rinehart and Winston, New York, 1959, pp. 141–142.

and upper-middle class at least, marriage is the preferred setting for sex experience.

CHANGES IN THE FAMILY RELATIONSHIP. Together with a redefinition of courtship and premarital practices has come a drastic change in the institution of marriage itself. Much of this revolution has been a product of the immense cultural change in Western society. The processes of political democracy, industrialization, and urbanization have inevitably transformed marriage, especially during the last sixty years. This change of the socio-economic order has completely altered the status and role of women. At one time the home was a self-contained economic unit with a number of crafts occupying the wife and other members of the family. Today, practically all production is industrialized. No less than one-third of married women are gainfully employed outside the home.

In addition to the loss of certain economic functions, the change in recreation has also affected marriage patterns. Whereas at one time the home was the focal point in leisure activities, the present generation has turned to the sports arena, the bowling alley, the drive-in theater, and the dance hall. The suburban middle-class wife finds absorbing community activities: attending PTA meetings, serving as den mother, being chairman of the country club "garden beautiful" committee, baking cookies for the camp fund drive for underprivileged children. Among these activities must be sandwiched, only too often, the essential do-it-yourself chores. Economic security is focused, more than before, on the gratification that may be enjoyed outside ever-shorter work hours.

The home has drifted away from religion, and although there has been some revitalization of the church in recent years, the overall amount of time and energy that the average American family devotes to religion has been progressively diminishing for nearly a century. At one time, the typical American considered family Bible reading as an indispensable part of the daily round of activities. Today, the middle-class parent provides for the religious orientation of his children, but it is likely to be outside the home, and generally is a casual part of the socialization process.

Several of the functions once held by marriage and the family have been transferred to other institutions. The state, particularly, has taken over some of the diverse roles that the family once monopolized. Care of the aged, of the mentally and physically ill, social-security benefits, and the variety of unemployment and health insurance programs have shifted the ultimate responsibility of the individual to resources outside the family. The function of socialization now rests partially with the agencies of formal education, from the nursery school to the postgraduate programs. The child has a number of opportunities in the classroom and playground to develop his personality. Visits with his class to the school doctor, local dairy, city council, or a butterfly chase relieve his parents of duties they once had. Nevertheless, the parents themselves retain the major responsibility in the child's basic personality formation, his ethical training, and the provision for his general welfare.

Despite the various changes within the family, such as its centrifugal tendencies, its high mobility—both in terms of geography and in the desire for status advantages—and its loss of functions to the state and other institutions, the family has not lost all of its traditional functions. There are still relations between the nuclear family and its extended kinship system, as the degree of mutual aid between parents and their married children indicates.[12] A study of Buffalo, New York housewives indicated that neither upward mobility nor geographic distance greatly disturbed the network of extended family relationships.[13] However, our family relationships are based on affection and companionship rather than the less voluntary roles of the traditional extended families of previous centuries.

In the twentieth century we have accepted individuality and personality growth both in the husband-wife and parent-child relationships; this topic is discussed in Chapter 17. The marital relationship is one of "commitment" rather than coerciveness.[14] Some of our institutional ties have been shifted, and not suspended: for example, if a member of the family is cared for in a state hospital, the family's responsibilities are altered, not terminated. The emphasis of social security for the elderly, and community interest in establishing senior citizens' facilities, permits enriched family or marital ties. Grandparenthood can be enjoyed by all three generations involved, but on a more relaxed basis now. This is true since the economic and health

[12] Marvin B. Sussman and Lee Burchinal, "Parental Aid to Married Children: Implications for Family Functioning," *Marriage and Family Living*, 1962, **24,** 320–333.

[13] Eugene Litwak, "Geographic Mobility and Family Cohesion," *American Sociological Review*, 1960, **25,** 385–394.

[14] Bernard Farber, *Family: Organization and Interaction*, Chandler Publishing Co., San Francisco, 1964, pp. 296–302.

problems of this age group are at least partially solved by the intervention or cooperation of the state, or our economic institutions, not least of which is the insurance company. Even the Church, although it lacks the deep universal significance it held two or three generations ago, still remains a vigorous unit for a sizeable number of our citizens and persists, as with other institutions, in a more flexible or voluntaristic relationship to the individual.

The change in marriage and the family has been described as a movement away from behavior based on institutional demands and conformity toward relationships marked by affection, companionship, and the maximum expression of each personality.[15] In contrast to a hundred years ago, biological and economic pressures have relatively less effect on our decision to marry. A young person of the 1960's may fare better financially by not marrying, and undoubtedly remain in a more advantageous position economically by not having the responsibility of a home; yet Americans continue to marry now for psychological advantages. Only in the marital relationship is it possible to enjoy maximum affectional expression and explore sex relations with delicacy, subtlety, and privacy. Moreover, despite the economic and other sacrifices that children are likely to cause, married couples consider parenthood a major goal of marriage. In the long-term trend, the size of the average family has diminished from 5.7 in 1790 to 4.7 in 1900, and 3.65 in 1960.[16] However, there was an increase from the early 1940's to the 1960's, which means that for most people no home is complete without children. Whereas it was unusual to find more than two children per family in the Great Depression period, parents with four children are not uncommon today.

The advantages of marriage are indirect and subtle in social prestige, in emotional security, and in fulfilling needs of the community. The young man who is upwardly mobile in the social, political, or economic world probably will move further if married. Ample evidence demonstrates that he is likely to have better mental health and higher longevity. While woman seems to be the more durable creature, married or unmarried, she too prefers the marital role, however much she may combine it with other activities and roles.[17]

[15] Burgess, et al., *op. cit.*

[16] Bureau of the Census, *Current Population Report,* Series P. 20, No. 88, Nov. 17, 1958, and Bureau of the Census, *Statistical Abstract of the United States,* Government Printing Office, Washington, D.C., 1965, p. 38.

[17] Lamar T. Empey. "Role Expectations of Young Women Regarding Marriage and a Career," *Marriage and Family Living,* 1958, **20**, 152–155.

Summing Up.   Despite a generally growing marriage rate in contemporary Western society, the more pessimistic writers and sociologists have questioned the survival of marriage and the family itself. For example, Zimmerman has charted a downward course of the family since the Justinian Code in the last days of the Roman Empire.[18] In a more popular tone, the German philosopher Keyserling once described marriage as "a tragic state of tension." [19] Many observers have portrayed marriage, or at least the American variant, as a fragile relationship caught in the frenzy of urban life. They claim divorce is only one of several symptoms of the centrifugal tendency away from the home. The secularization of marital values is another dangerous trend. To what degree can these criticisms of marriage be assessed?

On the *negative* side, American marriage appears to be in a precarious state. One marriage out of four ends in divorce.[20] The causes of this marital instability are complex. The mobility of modern life is a central factor; at no time in history have as many people moved both horizontally and vertically. This movement places a strain on marriage, since there is inevitably some disorganization with the lack of residential mooring, conflicts in values, attitudes, and social relationships. The constant movement up and down (mostly up) the social scale is not conducive to enduring friendships or stable associations with relatives. The world itself is constantly in change and threatened by a number of tensions. To the Victorian world there was some permanency to values and traditions, however fallacious they may have been. Even the closed-class system, by which one was born, lived, and died in his social class, offered a stability to family life. Today the individual finds himself under many pressures, internal and external, so that marital life is frequently subordinated to other goals.

Many other causes of marital and family conflict have been suggested ranging from the breakdown of religion to the adverse effects of the mass media (motion pictures, television, radio, and the press).

---

[18] Carle Zimmerman, *Family and Civilization,* Harper and Row, New York, 1947.

[19] Count Herman Keyserling, *Marriage,* Harcourt, Brace, New York, 1926.

[20] Marriage and divorce rates in 1946 were 16.4 and 4.3, respectively, and in 1964, 8.5 and 2.2. The 1946 divorce rate was unduly high because of the large number of war marriages that were dissolved. Actually, it is difficult to obtain a valid divorce rate, as the marriages and divorces cannot be accurately compared for the same year. United States Department of Health, Education and Welfare, Public Health Service: *Monthly Vital Statistics Report, Annual Survey for 1958,* Part I, March 12, 1959, also Bureau of the Census, *op. cit.,* p. 63.

There are also role conflicts which develop from institutional demands made on individuals. The modern home, even when overtly intact, presents a picture of constant tension as a result of the involvements of urban life. Business competition, "keeping up with the Joneses," and the social obligations of suburban living may disrupt marital harmony.

Sociologists disagree as to whether the vast changes in marital and family behavior constitute a loss or simply a modification of functions. Speaking of the change in the American family, Parsons says:

> It has also resulted in the transfer of a variety of functions from the nuclear family to other structures of the society, notably the occupationally organized sectors of it. This means that the family has become *more specialized than before,* probably more specialized than it has been in any previously known society. This represents a decline of *certain* features which traditionally have been associated with families; but whether it represents a "decline of the family" in a more general sense is another matter; we think not. We think the trend of the evidence points to the beginning of the relative stabilization of a *new* type of family structure in a new relation to a general social structure, one in which the family is more specialized than before, but not in any general sense less important, because the society is dependent *more* exclusively on it for the performance of *certain* of its vital functions.[21]

Marriage is at present more voluntarily selected than in the past, because it offers a number of invaluable functions psychologically and socially. Marriage today probably offers more specific roles and functions than it did in the last century. Can the marriage and family relationship be distributed in so many different directions and still be considered a healthy, solidified unit? Those who argue the downfall of modern marriage maintain that the negative aspects outweigh the favorable ones.

On the *positive* side more Americans are marrying than ever before, more than nine-tenths of them and at an increasingly earlier age. Over 70 per cent of divorced individuals remarry, indicating that they do not regard the institution itself a failure but look for a more satisfying union with some other mate.

There are more sociologists who are optimistic about the future of marriage than pessimistic.[22] They consider that marriage is stronger today than ever before in terms of its psychological bonds. Marriage is

[21] Talcott Parsons and Robert F. Bales, *Family, Socialization and Interaction Process,* The Free Press of Glencoe, A Division of Collier-Macmillan, New York, 1955, pp. 9–10.
[22] Burgess, et al., *op. cit.*

no longer held together by its institutional demands but rather by the need for affection and the attainment of maturity, which is to love and to be loved. The reason for divorce is that our standards of marriage are much higher than they were in the past. The freer social relationships that permit divorce are indicative of the voluntary nature of the marital bond. And, in contrast to the past, various counselling facilities exist to work out some of the tensions that develop in marriage.

The widely dispersed interests of the married couple today are not necessarily evidence of a decline in the marriage relationship; rather, they indicate the commitment of the husband and wife to the community and the larger society. One widely cited study shows a statistically significant positive relation between marital adjustment and the couple's participation in the community.[23] Another indicates that employment of the wife outside the home does not adversely affect the marital relationship.[24] Despite the scattered involvements of married people, they do feel that their roots are in the home and that the marriage itself is a principal, integrating factor in their lives. Although there is much mutual criticism of each partner in modern marriage, it is this freedom to express one's individual tendencies that gives marriage its tone and variety. There are perhaps as many kinds of marriages as there are husbands and wives. It becomes a challenge to harmonize oneself with another individual into a working relationship. In any case, courtship and marriage cannot follow an inflexible pattern, for they represent a dynamic process of personality growth. In this process of personality change, the knowledge of other people's experiences can be illuminating. For this reason, studying marriage can make the learning process more systematic.

THE ORGANIZATION OF THE BOOK.   A broad perspective of the problems of marriage and the family is given here. To understand the family, we must be aware of the larger social milieu in which it develops. Similarly, we cannot understand the full significance of the pattern of today's marriage without knowledge of the past. The broad outlines of the Western marriage-family institution are presented in Chapter 2. Chapter 3 discusses the question of leisure and recreation, the

[23] Ernest W. Burgess and Leonard S. Cottrell, Jr., *Predicting Success or Failure in Marriage*, Prentice-Hall, Englewood Cliffs, 1939, as reprinted in Robert F. Winch and Robert McGinnis (eds.), *Selected Studies in Marriage and the Family*, Holt, Rinehart and Winston, New York, 1953, pp. 465–471.

[24] Harvey J. Locke and Muriel Mackeprang, "Marital Adjustment and the Employed Wife," *American Journal of Sociology*, 1949, **18**, 536–538.

significance of the school, church, and the state in this interlocking relationship with the family. Chapter 4 presents certain cross-sectional approaches to the marriage institution as it functions in the present-day United States, with emphasis on given cultural types and problem areas of the family—including the tendency toward a younger age at marriage, campus marriages, and employment of the wife.

Part Two begins with the evolution of the individual from infancy to adolescence. It is impossible to understand courtship and marriage without exploring certain aspects of the theory and development of personality. The remaining chapters of the book deal with the various stages of premarital life, the expectations and problems of marriage, and the roles of parents.

This book presents interaction and role behavior as the context in which our marital and family life may be best conceptualized, whether in reference to our values and goal expectations, or to the practical realities of day-to-day living. Implicit in this approach is the awareness that an understanding of marriage and the family is dependent on both a psychological and sociological frame of reference. The emphasis on the development of the individual, particularly from childhood, as a preparation for adolescence and adulthood is presented in Chapter 5 and again in Chapter 17, in which the parents' tasks and responsibilities are stressed. Life events—whether they consist of dating, courtship, marriage, or parenthood—cannot be detached either from our own psychological past or from society.

Supplementary Readings

Burgess, Ernest W., Harvey J. Locke, and Mary M. Thomes, *The Family from Institution to Companionship* (third edition), American Book, New York, 1963. The early chapters present a contemporary perspective on marriage and the family.

Burgess, Ernest W. and Paul Wallin, *Engagement and Marriage,* J. P. Lippincott, Philadelphia, 1953. A statistical, longitudinal study of engaged couples and their subsequent marriage.

Cavan, Ruth S., *American Marriage, A Way of Life,* Thomas Y. Crowell, New York, 1959, Chapters 1 and 2. An overview of the social bases of modern marriage.

Christensen, Harold T. (ed.), *Handbook of Marriage and the Family,* Rand McNally, Chicago, 1964. Chapter 1 presents some critical viewpoints to our subject.

Christensen, Harold T., *Marriage Analysis* (revised edition), The Ronald Press, New York, 1958. Chapters 1–3 outline the scientific approach to marriage and its significance in the United States today.

Kephart, William M., *The Family, Society and the Individual*, Houghton Mifflin, Boston, 1961. Chapters 1 and 3 treat marriage and the family in a cross-cultural setting.

Kirkpatrick, Clifford, *The Family as Process and Institution* (second edition), The Ronald Press, New York, 1963. Chapter 1 offers conceptualizations and theoretical models for the study of our subject.

Marriage and Family Living, February 1957, **21** (The National Council on Family Relations) reports a family conference on various facets of marriage and sex from a research aspect.

Nickell, Paulena and Jean Muir Dorsey, *Management in Family Living* (third edition), John Wiley and Sons, New York, 1959. Chapters 1 and 2 relate to marriage and family, values and goals in decision-making in marital experience.

Nimkoff, Meyer F. (ed.), *Comparative Family Systems*, Houghton Mifflin, Boston, 1965. Parts 1 and 2 provide a systematic approach to family forms and their significance for society; Part 4 examines present and future change in the family.

Ogburn, William F. and Meyer F. Nimkoff, *Technology and the Changing Family*, Houghton Mifflin, Boston, 1955. Possibly the best work regarding the influence of technology on the present and future of marriage and family.

Parsons, Talcott and Robert F. Bales, *Family, Socialization, and Interaction Process*, The Free Press of Glencoe, A Division of Collier-Macmillan, New York, 1955. An analysis of the family as a small group applying various patterns of interaction to the larger society.

Sussman, Marvin B. (ed.), *Sourcebook in Marriage and the Family* (second edition), Houghton Mifflin, Boston, 1963. Part I offers six readings on the modern family.

Waller, Willard, *The Family: A Dynamic Interpretation* (revised by Reuben Hill), Holt, Rinehart and Winston, New York, 1951. An insightful approach to courtship, dating, and marriage. Chapter 1 places the family in its appropriate social setting.

Winch, Robert F., *The Modern Family* (revised edition), Holt, Rinehart and Winston, New York, 1963. Chapter 1 establishes a theoretical frame of reterence for studying the family.

Chapter two

The Historical Fabric of Marriage and the Family

The man is not of the woman, but the woman of the man. Neither was the man created for the woman; but the woman for the man.

I Corinthians *II, 8–9, c. 55.*

Marriage, to tell the truth, is an evil, but it is a necessary evil.

Menander, Fragment, *c. 300* BC

Marriage was not instituted by man, but by God.

Pope Leo XIII, Arcanum divinae sapientiae. *February 10. 1880.*

If ever two were one, then surely we;
If ever man were loved by wife, then thee;
If ever wife was happy in a man,
Compare with me, ye women, if you can.
I prize thy love more than whole mines of gold,
Or all the riches that the East doth hold.
My love is such that rivers cannot quench,
Nor aught but love from thee give recompense.
Thy love is such I can no way repay;
The heavens reward thee manifold, I pray.
Then while we live in love let's so persevere
That when we live no more we may live ever.

Anne Bradstreet, To My Dear and Loving Husband, *1678.*

Sunday Morning in Front of the Arch Street Meeting House, Philadelphia
by Pavel Petrovitch Svinin
Courtesy of The Metropolitan Museum of Art, Rogers Fund, 1942

The American family has roots in some three thousand years of history. For example, our wedding ceremony is a complex of rites that largely developed from Near Eastern sources well before the birth of Christ. The major bases of Western marriage are male dominance, monogamy, nuclear family grouping, and individual personality functioning. These tenets, with the possible exception of the last, were derived from classical sources: Hebrew, Greek, and Roman. Christianity contributed limited sex expression and emphasis on family loyalty and affectional bonds. Out of this cultural Gestalt, especially as found in Anglo-Saxon or English institutions, emerged American patterns, representing regional variations tempered by a frontier existence. An understanding of this background is essential to assess and appreciate the meaning of modern marriage.

ANCIENT HERITAGES

HEBREWS AND PATRIARCHALISM. The early Hebrews were an intricate set of pastoral tribes, woven into a nation following their escape from Egypt under the leadership of Moses, presumably in the thirteenth century before Christ. Since Hebrew history covers an enormous range of time and territory, it is difficult to make generalizations that are valid for all phases of development, especially in view of tribal and social class variations. Hebrew society as portrayed in the Old Testament was predominantly a *patriarchal* social system. Marriages were arranged by the father, and compensation in the form of a gift had to be made to the bride's family. Consent by both parents was considered essential; however, children deferred to their parents in the matter of matrimony. According to Talmudic law, the legal age for contracting marriage was set at puberty: twelve for the female and thirteen for the male. Although the father might arrange for the marriage of the daughter before she reached puberty, the contract would be invalid unless she consented.[1]

While Mosaic law regarded the distinction between betrothal and nuptials as an arbitrary one, these two ceremonies together constituted a kind of engagement period. Betrothal consisted of an agreement between the families, generally supported by monetary benefits. The nuptials were performed about a year later and included a ceremony

[1] Willystine Goodsell, *A History of the Family as a Social and Educational Institution*, Macmillan, New York, 1923, pp. 58–59.

consisting of a banquet and a procession to the home of the groom, followed by a benediction. Essentially, Hebrew marriage was a family or civil affair. Even the presence of a priest or rabbi was discretionary.

The basic pattern of Western marriage was set by the Hebrews. The betrothal and nuptials were under relative control of the family. The rather restrictive attitudes on sex and marriage had considerable influence in later Christian thought. Somewhat unique to the Hebrew conception was the intense group loyalty; hence most marriages took place within the tribe, although *exogamy* was possible. The emphasis in marriage, as in much of the ancient world, was on continuance of the family line of which procreation and assurance of property rights were essential elements. The *levirate,* the practice in which the widow was expected to marry the husband's brother, served to insure issue of the family. Concubinage was prevalent and perhaps reflected the procreative desires of the Hebrews, as demonstrated in the words of Sarah, the childless wife of Abraham: "Behold now, the Lord hath restrained me from bearing: I pray thee, go in unto my maid; it may be that I may obtain children by her." [2] But for the Hebrews plural wives were comparatively rare. Monogamy, though considered the established system, was not held as rigidly sacred as it was in later cultures. Divorce was a means of dissolving the marriage according to Deuteronomy. However, this privilege belonged predominantly, although not exclusively, to the male. The divorce rate probably was not high except for a few periods of Hebrew history. Public opinion generally opposed divorce; Malachi, a book of the prophets, in particular warned against it. Adultery was strictly condemned by the Hebrews. One reason for this was that inheritance rights had to be protected. Also, the institution of marriage was apparently strengthened in that a number of deviant sexual practices became increasingly disapproved in the later periods of Hebrew history.[3]

THE GREEKS: MONOGAMY REAFFIRMED. On the surface the Greek outlook on marriage was somewhat similar to that of the Hebrews. If anything, patriarchal control was even more entrenched. Yet by the Periclean and post-Periclean ages, the harsher aspects of male dominance were undoubtedly liberalized. In a society in which affectional ties were minimal, marriage designed for procreation was even more

---

[2] Genesis, 16:2.

[3] Panos D. Bardis, "Family Forms and Variations Historically Considered," in Harold T. Christensen (ed.), *Handbook of Marriage and the Family,* Rand McNally, Chicago, 1964, pp. 420–421.

emphasized than by the Hebrews. Of course, mate selection was a prerogative of the father. However, in contrast to Hebrew customs, there is no evidence that the spouse-to-be could challenge the father's authority on his decision. Nor was there the relatively stern moral code of the Hebrews, except for the propitiation of the gods, which was essentially an amoral act. The marriage ceremony itself, nonetheless, had religious significance. As with most Western culture, a distinction was made between the betrothal, marked by a dowry, and the nuptials or wedding ceremony.

As Nash points out, the Greek family was more urbanized and, if anything, more monogamous than the Hebrew family, at least by the Periclean age.[4] To secure continuance of the family name, concubinage occasionally was practiced; for if there was no issue from the legitimate wife, the child of a concubine became legal heir. A variation of the levirate was also permitted in which the widower married a close relative of the late wife for the purpose of providing heirs to the family. Divorce was possible for the male on two grounds: infertility (any infertility was ascribed to the female) and adultery. It was most unusual for a wife to secure a divorce. She had to prove that her husband had endangered the welfare of his family tradition. Property arrangements also made divorce anything but a casual occurrence for either sex.

Generalizations are difficult, as can be observed in the differing status and treatment of children. In Homeric times the child was vital because of his economic significance in a pastoral and agricultural society. Relations between parents and children were close and affectionate. On the other hand, brutalization of children in Sparta is mentioned by Aristotle. In Athens, a more aristocratic society, the child was important for reasons of family status, but abandonment of an unwanted child (usually the female) did not necessarily constitute a crime. Upper-class children were almost entirely reared by slaves. In Athens the socialization process was very different for the two sexes after the age of seven; whereas Spartans provided general social training for both boys and girls.[5]

ROME—RISE AND DECLINE OF MARRIAGE SYSTEM. In certain respects the patriarchal pattern of the ancient world reached its climax

---

[4] Arnold S. Nash, "Ancient Past and Living Present," in Howard Becker and Reuben Hill (eds.), *Family, Marriage and Parenthood* (second edition), D. C. Heath and Company, Boston, 1955, p. 95.
[5] Bardis, *op. cit.*, pp. 428–433.

in ancient Rome. However, it is difficult to generalize about marriage and the family as they functioned in several centuries of Roman history. The succession of Republic, to Empire, to its disappearance had far-reaching effects on the institutional fabric of that society. The absolute power of the father over his children was known by the phrase *patria potestas*. The counterpart of this power over the wife was termed *manus* (hand). The male son escaped his father's control by marriage; the daughter was simply transferred from the will of the father to that of the husband. In a sense, marriage and the family had less religious significance than it did in Greece, but although it remained a family or civil affair, it was something of a "training school" for the state.[6] In accordance with characteristic Roman stoicism, marriages might be contracted for political reasons, but certainly not for romantic ones.

Roman society, even compared to the Greek, became exceedingly stratified, which was reflected in its marriage system. In fact, there were two general varieties of marriage. The regular marriage (*matrimonium justum*) generally was reserved for marriages between patricians. Here, the father's authority was expressed in its ideal form. The irregular marriage (*matrimonium injustum*) was confined to the lower ranks, and did not confer the honor of Roman citizenship. Privileges regarding the family property were also somewhat reduced in this last type, and the ceremonies attending the marriage were simplified. On the other hand, within the patrician class, marriage was an event involving the entire extended family.

Marriage ceremonies also differed according to social class; the most elegant was the *confarreatio*, which included eating the ceremonial cake, attending certain sacrificial rites, an elaborate procession to the residence of the husband (accompanied by ribald songs and other festivities), and carrying the bride across the threshold. Another more simplified ceremony was the *coemptio* in which a fictitious sale was made with the transfer of a coin, perhaps symbolizing the bride price of a former period.[7] The ceremony of the lowest rank was the *usus*, the most frequent form for the plebeians. In a way, this mode of marriage anticipated what we call *common-law marriage.* If vows were exchanged between a man and a woman, and she remained in his

---

[6] Nash, *op. cit.,* p. 98.

[7] Stuart A. Queen, Robert W. Habenstein, John B. Adams, *The Family in Various Cultures,* J. B. Lippincott Company, Philadelphia, 1961, p. 165.

house for a year—not absenting herself more than three nights in succession—she came under his *potestas*.

As Rome extended her empire and prospered, marriage and family mores degenerated. The concept of *pater potestas* was drastically altered. Marriages and divorces increasingly became matters of convenience. The Punic Wars, which decreased the male population, further hastened some of these changes. During the era of the Empire, divorce was possible on a number of grounds beyond the conventional one of adultery, such as "making poison, drinking wine, and possibly counterfeiting housekeys." [8]

As Nash comments on the status of marriage in the Empire,

Parallel to these revolutionary changes was a disclination to marry at all. This of itself was indicative of the plight into which the empire had fallen at the height of its military power. Ancient family ideals no longer served to challenge the practices of a generation to whom a decline in moral standards was simply a matter of course. Marriage was no longer regarded as a matter upon which the dignity and honor of the state ultimately depended. Both men and women, following only the personal gratification of their own desires, chose illicit affairs rather than marriage with its legal and moral and civic responsibilities. In short, marriage tended to disappear to such an extent that Julius Caesar initiated a series of rewards as an incentive to the adoption of the marital state. But the canker had eaten too far into the fabric of Roman society. The sickness was too deep for financial inducement, direct or indirect, to have a profound effect. Augustus Caesar soon realized that Rome faced a crisis not only in her attitude towards marriage but also in her economic life and in her political ideals.[9]

In other words, marriage became a markedly individualized affair. Adultery, abortion, and homosexuality were frequent. Zimmerman describes the decline of the Roman family as one from a *trustee* to an *atomistic* family; that is, the transition from a patriarchal to the fractionalized nuclear family.[10] This decline may be compared to the transition of the familistic unit of, for example, the Middle Ages to the individualistic family of today. In whatever way Roman society disintegrated, the fundamental character of the family, patricentric monogamy, was not altered. The Western marriage system was not

---

[8] *Ibid.*, p. 169.

[9] Nash, *op. cit.*, pp. 99–100.

[10] Carle C. Zimmerman, *Family and Civilization*, Harper and Row, New York, 1947, Chapters 14–16. He believes also that the Greek family passed through a similar series of stages, Chapters 11–13.

disturbed by the political, social, and military events of the fourth and fifth century except as it was influenced by Christianity.

CHRISTIANITY AND WESTERN EUROPE

EARLY CHRISTIANITY: A NEW ORIENTATION. The Christian heritage was partially a product of Hebrew thought but had some unique aspects. First, the teachings of Jesus emphasized the universal brotherhood of man with the implication that marital practices were essentially the same at all social ranks; this was not the case for most of the classical Mediterranean societies, including the Hebrews. Second, monogamy was even more important than in the Hebrew society. Third, both Jesus and Paul preached the necessity of celibacy. Physical pleasures, including sex, were not deemed worthy of the good life. In particular, sexual activities either before or outside of marriage were condemned. Chastity became almost the highest virtue to which man could aspire. How much of this position was a result of Paul's reaction to the profligacy of Greek and Roman society is debatable.

As implied here, the early Christians did not basically interfere with the marriage procedure of the Empire, at least not during the first three centuries of the Empire. The betrothal and marriage folkways remained. Marriages were freely contracted by the two parties involved, although parental consent was highly desirable. Some practices that the Romans had not taken very seriously became more important, for example, categories of kinship with whom marriage was outlawed. Both *consanguinity* (blood relationship) and *affinity* (relatives by marriage) were considered unacceptable, even if prospective mates were related as remotely as "the seventh degree." [11] Compared to the ideology of most of the ancient world, Christian marriage was intended more for the benefit of the offspring, and considerable attention was directed to the welfare of children. The Church Fathers denounced abortion, infanticide, and the sale of children. By the time of Constantine, traffic in children for slavery became unlawful, except for the poorest of classes.

Marriage for the early Christian leaders, like loyalty to the state, was secondary, at least in theory, to devotion to God and to Christian principles. If this subordination of the family was detrimental to its significance, the stress on spiritual, and possibly on affectional, values

[11] Queen, et al., *op. cit.*, p. 188.

tended to strengthen marital relations. Religious orthodoxy became enmeshed with marital fidelity. As a progressively greater segment of the Roman population and officials adopted this new faith, the ideal of monogamy inevitably gained and paternal authority lessened.[12]

CONTINUITY AND CHANGE: THE MIDDLE AGES. Christianity as formulated by the Church Fathers, encountered in the Europe of the early Middle Ages an environment that was not entirely friendly. The Germanic tribes, for instance, had been accustomed to wife capture, which was superseded by wife purchase at the time of the Roman decline. This practice continued as late as the tenth century in what today are Britain, Germany, and Scandinavia.[13] Most marital matters were under the control of a system of extended kinship (the *maegth* or *sib*). Marriage, at this time, might be described as a kind of collective-bargaining situation between extended families.

The ancient distinction between betrothal (*bewedung*) and nuptials (*gifta*) was retained by the Germanic peoples, including the Anglo-Saxons. Gradually these ceremonies took on religious, as well as economic, significance. Between the seventh and tenth centuries the practice of bestowing a "morning gift" by the husband on the day after the wedding appeared. With this gift the husband acknowledged his satisfaction with the marriage. Optional at first, this gift became compulsory, and both the morning gift and bride-price (*weotuma*) had to be stipulated in the marriage contract at the time of betrothal. In feudal society with its rigid stratification, the ceremonies and requirements concerning marriage were determined by rank. No serf, for example, could marry outside his manor without permission of his lord and the payment of a fee.[14] In spite of the opposition of the Church, marriage in the upper ranks could be contracted on a consanguineous basis in order to consolidate holdings.

After the Norman conquest marriage was managed increasingly by the Church. For instance, in the early Middle Ages there had been many common-law or clandestine marriages not formalized by the Church. Between the fourth and twelfth centuries, the Church came to officiate at all marriages. By the twelfth century the marriage ceremony was recognized as one of the seven sacraments of the Roman Catholic

---

[12] Nash, *op. cit.*, p. 103.

[13] Goodsell, *op. cit.*, p. 189.

[14] Richard A. Schemerhorn, "Family Carry-Overs of Western Christendom," in Becker and Hill, *op. cit.*, p. 107.

Church.[15] At the conclusion of the Council of Trent in 1563, marriage was regarded as an indissoluble union presided over by an officiant of the Church. Divorce was not permitted since the Church Fathers from the beginning of the Christian era had forbidden it. However, "separation from bed and board" was permitted by canon law for reasons of adultery, heresy, or cruelty of one of the partners. In addition, annulment could also be arranged by papal authority on certain grounds. Fundamentally these remain Catholic principles.

In the late Middle Ages and in the Renaissance, marriage and family norms changed. The Crusades, which hastened the rise of trade and commerce culminating in the development of cities, brought about accumulation of wealth and the advent of an affluent burgher class that sought new luxuries. In this period corruption by the clergy, not to speak of the remaining population, reached incredible proportions. The sale of indulgences became a travesty to canon law. Moreover, the Troubadours lyricized a new theme, in which love was detached from marriage. These changes, combined with incipient urbanization, hardly strengthened the family. One change was the rise of the home, or guild, factory system in which apprentices lived in dormitories. Another was the decreasing supervision of apprentices by their families. These minors became an unsettled group in the towns of the late Middle Ages and Renaissance periods. But the event that perhaps most fundamentally disrupted the social world, including the institution of marriage, was the Protestant Reformation in the sixteenth century.

THE PROTESTANT REFORMATION AND THE CIVIL CONTRACT. With the revolt of Martin Luther in 1519, a new ideology began to dominate large portions of Western Europe. There had been "heretical" or reform movements before his time, but none achieved Luther's success. Other variations of Protestantism were advocated by John Calvin and John Knox, whose teachings differed somewhat from Lutheranism. Out of the Reformation came the notion that marriage was a civil contract rather than a sacrament; divorce was thus possible in theory and in practice. Luther firmly disagreed with the Catholic Church on the rights of the clergy to marry, and he himself married a former nun, Katherine von Bora. Protestantism subscribed to the notion of celibacy

[15] George Howard, *History of Matrimonial Institutions,* as cited in Clifford Kirkpatrick, *The Family as Process and Institution* (second edition), The Ronald Press New York, 1963, pp. 109–110.

but not to the point of excluding the clergy from matrimony. Parenthetically, the issue of marriage for the clergy was under fire in some quarters during the Middle Ages and is still debated by some segments of contemporary Catholicism.

Considerable controversy surrounded the acceptance of the theory that marriage is determined by human beings rather than divine ordinance. Absolute divorce rather than the "separation from bed and board," the Catholic approach, was grudgingly accorded legitimacy. In fact, the dispute concerning divorce was one of the factors leading to the Council of Trent. The issue was particularly confused in England, where Henry VIII had broken with the Roman Catholic Church. The Church of England, however, did not accept the Protestant viewpoints on a number of issues, including marriage. The Marriage Act of 1653, passed during the Cromwellian period, temporarily solved the problem. It required a civil ceremony although banns had to be published in the church. If either party was under twenty-one years of age, parental consent had to be secured. The ceremony itself consisted of a simple exchange of vows. With the Restoration, the Church of England returned to a version of canon law that underwent considerable readjustment later in the American colonies.

Divorce was strongly disapproved even though legally feasible. Divorce suits were rarely granted, and remarriages were all but impossible and of questionable validity. Through Parliament it was permissible to sue for divorce on the grounds of incapacity or refusal to have sex relations, adultery, and cruelty.[16] Naturally, the cost was prohibitive to all but the wealthiest segments of the population. This situation was not altered until 1857, and only in 1937 was divorce available to the majority of the British people.

SOME TRADITIONAL AMERICAN PATTERNS

The New World was a more fluid environment than feudalistic and stratified European societies. America originally was settled by individuals protesting the social and religious order they had left, and this situation affected certain marital and family regulations. Moreover, survival itself placed a premium on family life. The vastness of the land required an expanding population; from the point of view of

---

[16] Queen, et al., *op. cit.*, pp. 264–265.

both society and the individual, children were an economic asset. This was true to some extent in Europe, but the drive to be married was more urgent in the new wilderness overseas.

The variation of sects and geographic regions created diversity in family culture. In addition, national and religious differences in background and purpose influenced family behavior. The development of American marriage and family norms is usually divided into three geographic areas: New England, the Middle Colonies, and the Southern Colonies.

NEW ENGLAND. The Puritan-Calvinist ideology inevitably gave an austere stamp to the New England family. Paternal authority was clearly ordained; however, the wife, by her economic role in frontier society, enjoyed slightly higher status than she had known in England. There were few women in the colonies. Courtships were brief by present standards; and as with most of America until the beginning of the twentieth century, a young man was not likely to be seen twice with the same young woman unless there were serious intentions. Calhoun writes of the intensity of courtship in early New England:

> Love and marriage at first sight brought romantic interest to the wilderness life where existence without home connections offered no attraction to serious men. In more than one instance a lonely Puritan came to the door of a maiden he had never seen, presented credentials, told his need of a housekeeper, proposed marriage, obtained hasty consent, and notified the town clerk, all in one day. On one occasion a bold fellow removed a rival's name from the posted marriage notice, inserted his own, and carried off the bride. After his death she married the first lover. Another Lochinvar kidnapped a bride-to-be on the eve of marriage.[17]

Compared to the old world, courtship was relatively unchaperoned. The freedom from certain rigid traditions, and the spaciousness and rugged living demanded by frontier life did not allow either the finesse or supervision known in Europe. *Bundling* arose in the early eighteenth century as a makeshift courtship device: a young couple might sit or lie in the same bed, usually fully clothed, to carry on conversations, often without illumination of candles. This custom was practiced extensively, and persisted in both New England and the Middle Colonies until the late eighteenth century. At about the time

[17] Arthur W. Calhoun, *A Social History of the American Family*, Vol. 1, Barnes and Noble, New York, 1945, p. 52.

of the French-Indian War and War of Independence, bundling began to disappear.

The relative freedom of young people to carry on their love-making was not without penalties. According to the records of one New England church (Groton), between 1761 and 1775 the parents of roughly one-third of the children being baptized publicly confessed to illicit sex relations before marriage.[18] Ecclesiastical courts dealt with a series of sex delinquencies, both premarital and marital.[19] Ironically, the Puritans objected to the Catholic confessional; but their own confessional treatment of sex problems was of larger scale and incidentally served as a gratuitous identification with the sins of others.

Marriage was regarded as a civil contract, although religious authorities still officiated at the ceremony. Marriages occurred well before the age of twenty, especially for women. The basic pattern of marriage of the Cromwellian period was adopted: (1) notification by banns was posted; (2) parental consent was necessary for those under age; (3) the ceremony was performed by a justice of the peace or a similar official; and (4) the marriage was registered.[20] Interracial marriages and marriages between relatives were prohibited, including some thirty grades of kinsmen and in-laws. Common-law marriages, in which the man and woman made their own vows, were recognized and continued into the frontier of the nineteenth century, and are still recognized in certain states today.

Although not frequent, dissolution of marriage was possible to a degree unknown in Europe, but practices varied among the individual colonies. The legal framework favored the male, as it did in most aspects of marriage; for example, grounds in Massachusetts included adultery by the wife, desertion, and cruelty (notwithstanding the husband's right to impose physical punishment on his wife—with discretion, however). Remarriage was generally possible in the Northern Colonies.

THE MIDDLE COLONIES. The Dutch colonists of New York, according to Calhoun, held a more lenient viewpoint than the New Englanders on courtship, marriage, and the upbringing of children, be-

[18] Queen, et al., *op. cit.,* p. 286.

[19] George L. Haskins, *Law and Authority in Early Massachusetts,* Macmillan, New York, 1960, pp. 183–184.

[20] Kirkpatrick, *op. cit.,* p. 122.

cause of less harsh living conditions and traditions of the burgher class in Holland.[21] But male dominance was firmly entrenched, and the roles of women and children were nearly as unattractive as those of their northern neighbors. Courtship was a more lengthy, formalized process than in New England. Marriage in the Middle Colonies was fundamentally a civil affair. For the Scotch-Irish who came to Pennsylvania by the thousands in the early eighteenth century, marriage was initiated by reading the banns on two successive Sundays, followed by a ceremony in the bride's home. On the next Sunday the couple appeared in church in festive attire.[22]

Quaker marriages always have been a variation within American culture. The Society of Friends stressed an inward spirituality and cooperativeness, and consequently family life reflected this "inner light." The Friends' belief in internalized controls, in addition to their own experience with arbitrary rule in England, made for democratic values in all aspects of their living.

Attitudes on sex, courtship, and marriage were strict but without the harshness of the Puritans.[23] Mate selection was confined to members of the Meeting or local society of Quakers. In fact, it appears that a marital candidate had to pass the scrutiny of the Meeting. Some impatient Friends would not defer to the exogamy of their group, and looked elsewhere for marriage.[24] Marriage was regarded in most respects as an individual question. Consequently, there was a minimum of civil, religious, or parental control by the standards of Colonial America.

In the Middle Colonies, marriage, or at least premarital sex practices, occasionally occurred on an interracial basis. In some colonies there were severe penalties attached to miscegenation as well as to a number of unconventional behaviors. Although the religious groups of the Middle Atlantic on the whole were more tolerant than the Puritans, this was only by a matter of degree. Some sects, for example the Brethren and the Dunkers, followed unique folkways and mores identified with courtship and marriage. Others, notably the Amish, still exist in large numbers with a culture distinctly their own.

[21] Calhoun, *op. cit.*, p. 153.
[22] *Ibid.*, p. 207.
[23] Manford H. Kuhn, "American Families Today: Development and Differentiation of Types," in Becker and Hill, *op. cit.*, p. 140.
[24] Calhoun, *op. cit.*, p. 200.

Divorce was no less objectionable to the New Yorkers than to the New Englanders, although it existed in both areas. On the other hand, Pennsylvania in the Great Law of 1682 provided for divorce for "the spiritual cause." Divorce for the Quakers and Moravians was extremely rare; and for the Scotch-Irish, it was all but outlawed, except when such a grievous crime as adultery was involved.

THE SOUTHERN COLONIES. The practices of the North were considerably modified in the South, despite their common Anglo-Saxon heritage. Most important, the Cavalier background of the settlers and the more temperate climate of the South encouraged a freer approach to life, at least in the upper classes. Moreover, the highly stratified and rigid nature of the society necessitated class or caste exogamy. The slaves were a class of virtual untouchables, although this did not prevent a certain degree of miscegenation and of confusion to family stability. The diversity of crops and problems of agricultural economy, the social and racial structure, and the expanding frontier produced heterogeneity in marriage and family mores. Norms were different for the plantation family, the frontier planter, the bondsman, and the slave.

The Southern outlook was more paternalistic than that of the Middle Colonies, and the double standard was highly entrenched. The code of chivalry glorified the purity of womanhood, but left the male free to pursue both white and Negro partners. Religiously the Church of England dominated during the colonial period, except in Maryland, which was predominantly Catholic. In certain areas religious practices were relatively relaxed; for example, marriages were occasionally performed by an unordained minister.[25] In Virginia, Cavalier sentiment far outweighed Puritan ideology.

Queen points out that mate selection in the South, as in most of the colonies, was influenced both by romantic and practical considerations.[26] For one thing, the male settlers of early Virginia sent for women from England to become bondservants, who in many cases later became their wives. In much of the South marriages were restricted according to a complex set of laws concerning consanguinity. Approximately thirty varieties of kinship were designated as inappropriate. Laws on miscegenation hardly affected the informal unions, and more than one plantation owner had a concubine. Unions between bondsmen

[25] Calhoun, *op. cit.*, p. 260.
[26] Queen, et al., *op. cit.*, p. 293.

and the Negro slaves may have been encouraged for the purpose of multiplying the number of available slaves.

The mode of family living differed greatly from the Middle and Northern colonies. The plantation families lived in almost self-contained empires reminiscent of the estates of Roman nobility and medieval Europe. Gracious living probably encouraged romanticism as well as chivalry, and in segments of this aristocracy the choice of a mate assumed enormous social and economic importance. Generally, religion never had the intense significance in the functioning of the family that it enjoyed in the North. In fact, marriage was essentially a civil contract in most of the Southern colonies. In the more remote areas of the South, common-law marriages were far from unknown. Divorce was practically nonexistent, but annulments as well as dissolutions by mutual consent were recognized, with the occasional granting of alimony by a court.

THE NINETEENTH CENTURY AND A NEW AMERICAN CULTURE.   The culture surrounding marriage in America was influenced by the following factors during the period of national growth: (1) a broad base of American Protestantism, especially as developed in evangelical faiths such as Methodism and Baptism; (2) continued immigration which, among other things, favored a male ratio; (3) a sinuous line of frontier and settlement producing a somewhat unstable family life; and (4) the emergence of industrialization and urbanization. These influences interacted; for instance, the shortage of women as much as the presence of a frontier was calculated to break the feudalistic, patriarchal social system. Certainly the rise of cities changed courtship and marriage patterns.

In the nineteenth century a tradition of individualism, at least as compared to some aspects of European culture, was developing. This was possible because of a quasifrontier, higher literacy standards, and the absence of rigid cultural molds. Freer choice in marital selection and romantic overtones in courtship, along with more equalitarianism between the sexes strengthened the independent nuclear family. This more individualistic way of life was partially encouraged by the stream of immigration that brought to American shores some thirty million people from the period of the 1820's to the beginning of World War I. These immigrants came at first from Western Europe, but during the 1880's they came predominantly from Southern and Eastern Europe and represented a variety of nationalities, sects, and cultural standards. Immigrants also arrived from the Near East and from Latin

America, especially in the twentieth century. Consequently, our landscape came to be dotted by clusters of Scandinavian family culture in Minnesota; Mexican and Chinese variations in Texas and San Francisco; as well as remnants of a folk culture in pockets of the Appalachians.

Cultural variations are not exclusively foreign in origin; some are religiously or philosophically inspired. The Mormons were persecuted for a polygamous system; that aspect of their culture has disappeared, and the religion has been identified with strong family-oriented values. Various socialistic experiments such as Brook Farm, New Harmony, and notably the Oneida community, have colored the history of American family behavior by their collective living and sharing of common facilities.

In comparing the American family with its European antecedents, it cannot be forgotten that the colonists were religious dissenters, at least in the Northern and Middle Colonies. Consequently, there was a Protestant, or largely Puritan, outlook in New England, with a number of highly diversified sects in the Middle Atlantic area. The Southern area was more traditionalistic, with marked class distinctions. As Kuhn points out, the Southern aristocracy stands in sharp contrast to the equality-minded Society of Friends.[27] The New England colonists in some respects were intermediate between these two types in regard to stratification.

We have emphasized some of the differences that exist in American marriage and family behavior; but there is still a communality in Western culture. The emphases on monogamy, patriarchal authority, and inheritance rights provide a continuous cultural heritage when compared with certain non-Western family patterns. Zimmerman carries this similarity further in his insistence on a historical cycle during which Greece, Rome, and the United States have undergone a decline in family stability.[28]

Our contemporary American family has freedom and selectivity in the choice of a mate, an extensive repertory of roles, an emphasis on smooth and comfortable socialization, and a general commitment to nonauthoritarianism.[29] These tendencies are rooted in a Judeo-Chris-

[27] Kuhn, in Becker and Hill, *op. cit.,* pp. 145–146.
[28] Zimmerman, *op. cit.*
[29] Ruth Benedict, "The Family: Genus Americanum," in Ruth N. Anshen (ed.), *The Family: Its Function and Destiny* (revised edition), Harper and Row, New York, 1959, pp. 53–64.

tian past, and are combined with certain discontinuities of the
European cultural system. However, the American family as compared to its classical and European antecedents is deeply committed to
a nuclear family. In this connection Parsons notes that our system of
property inheritance differs from English Common Law in that we
prefer to give equal shares to each child in contrast to the primogeniture system which has a built-in protection to family continuity and
wealth.[30] These preferences for a nuclear unit and a basically democratic family pattern were in part adaptations to the newer interpretation of Christianity and social ideology by Puritans, Quakers, and
other sects, especially in the frontier setting.

Supplementary Readings

Anshen, Ruth (ed.), *The Family, Its Function and Destiny* (revised edition), Harper
and Row: New York, 1959. The first of the book contains some significant
material on marriage and the family in non-Western cultures.

Aries, Philippe, *Centuries of Childhood*, Alfred A. Knopf, New York, 1962. A
history of the role of children in European society.

Bardis, Panos D., "Family Forms and Variations Historically Considered," in Harold
T. Christensen (ed.), *Handbook of Marriage and the Family*, Rand McNally,
Chicago, 1964, pp. 403–461. A complete treatment of the ancient family.

Becker, Howard, and Reuben Hill (eds.), *Family, Marriage and Parenthood* (second
edition), D. C. Heath, Boston, 1955. Part One is an excellent treatment of
the history of the subject by various authors.

Bell, Robert R., *Marriage and Family Interaction*, The Dorsey Press, Homewood,
Illinois, 1963. Chapter 2 is a valuable assessment of the Puritan system.

Blitsen, Dorothy R., *The World of the Family*, Random House, New York, 1963.
A comparative study of family structure, contrasting such diverse areas as
Scandinavia and Italy, Russia and Israel, and the Chinese and Moslem worlds.

Calhoun, Arthur W., *A Social History of the American Family*, Barnes and Noble,
New York, 1945. Now also available in paperback, this large work is the most
complete source on marriage from colonial times to the nineteenth century.

Goodsell, Willystine, *A History of Marriage and the Family* (revised edition), Macmillan, New York, 1934. A particularly good work on the ancient and medieval
periods.

Kenkel, William F., *The Family in Perspective*, Appleton-Century-Crofts, New
York, 1960. Especially adequate histories of Hebrew, Roman, and New England
marriage systems.

[30] Talcott Parsons, "Social Structure of the Family," in Ruth N. Anshen, *op. cit.*,
p. 249.

Kephart, William M., *The Family, Society, and the Individual*, Houghton Mifflin, Boston, 1961. Chapters 4–8 are presentations of European and American patterns.

Kirkpatrick, Clifford, *The Family as Process and Institution* (second edition), The Ronald Press, New York, 1963. Chapter 5 traces the history of marriage in the Western world, with special reference to the problem of the Church.

Queen, Stuart A., Robert W. Habenstein, and John B. Adams, *The Family in Various Cultures*, J. B. Lippincott, Philadelphia, 1961. Ancient family systems as well as the Anglo-Saxon heritage are described.

Westermarck, Edward, *The History of Human Marriage*, Allerton Book Co., New York, 1922. An authoritative record although occasionally the author makes a debatable statement.

Zimmerman, Carle C., *Family and Civilization*, Harper and Row, New York, 1947. A pessimistic and subjective theory on cycles of family culture in the Western world.

Chapter three

The Contemporary Setting
of Marriage and Family Life

Although it seems likely that the nuclear family has never carried out totally the religious function and is incapable of being religiously self-sufficient, it has carried on worship and the religious instruction of the young, especially under conditions of isolation. With the reduction in isolation and the rise of specialties that accompany urbanism, worship and religious instruction appear to become less frequent activities of family life.

> *Robert F. Winch,* The Modern Family *(revised edition), Holt, Rinehart and Winston, New York, 1963, p. 150.*

A modified ideology favoring male dominance still appears to be accepted by most American families. However, this is not entirely inconsistent with the employment of the wife, provided her position is lower than her husband's in the occupational hierarchy and yields a smaller portion of the family income.

> *F. Ivan Nye and Lois W. Hoffman,* The Employed Mother in America, *Rand McNally, Chicago, 1963, p. 5.*

The first fact about the modern family may be taken to be that the family institution is still a going concern, and a vital one. True, it is no longer, as in a society built on blood relationship, either the central structure or (as with the New Mexican Pueblos today) an emerging line of structure which has already outrivaled the clan and already threatens the dominance of the ancient religio-political organization. Neither is the family in our own culture any longer a hearth in which reproduction, education, half and more of economic and social life, and much of government and religion all are centered into going ways of life and thought.

> *Karl N. Llewellyn, "Education and the Family," in Ruth N. Anshen (ed.),* The Family: Its Function and Destiny *(revised edition), Harper and Row, New York, 1959, p. 328.*

Cliff Dwellers by George Bellows
Collection of the Los Angeles County Museum of Art

Young married people find themselves in a complex social environment that is in an almost constant state of flux. Change has been too rapid for us to assess its meaning. Crises are commonplace in our world of international or national tensions, psychological or physical handicaps, financial or occupational pressures.

In addition, we are confused about the meaning of society itself. What are our relationships to each other and to our social institutions? How has the style of living varied over the last century and a half? How do the mass media of communication influence the home? How do certain institutional variables affect marriage? How do the school, state, and church interact with the family? How do these various social influences compete for the allegiance of the individual and the family? And most important, how have these phenomena, institutional and otherwise, altered in the twentieth century? This chapter attempts to answer these questions, and to describe the social climate surrounding marriage and family relations today.

SCIENCE, INVENTION, AND THE NEW SOCIETY

During the last few centuries Western society has been moving historically in a pattern variously identified as *Gemeinschaft and Gesellschaft* (see Glossary), sacred-secular, mechanistic-organic, universalistic-particularistic, and folk-urban. In these dichotomies, the *Gemeinschaft* is a rural or traditional society with a more rigid kinship-oriented social order, and the *Gesellschaft* is an urban, rationalistic, dynamic, modernistic, ever-shifting secular world. These divisions, as with most explanatory concepts, tend to oversimplify a highly complicated social fabric, but they offer some plausible hypotheses and explanations for the recent changes in the Western family. Frequently, the change has been characterized as of one moving from the family as a nonvoluntaristic institution to one of socialization combined with individualization. In other words, marriage and the family have become nuclear and form a household based on affection and mutually advantageous companionship.

Let us turn to a discussion of the definition of marital and family norms. The reasons for these norms may be found in the following factors:

1. The emergence of science in the seventeenth and eighteenth centuries, and its advances in the nineteenth century, made possible not

only novel processes of production, but also a new conception of the universe. Printing (developed about 1450) provided a means of spreading scientific theories and helped to shatter the ignorance of a sizeable portion of the population.

2. The discoveries, explorations, and colonizations offered a challenge to Western Europeans, and furnished a new environment in which folkways and mores were readjusted to a different set of conditions. The marriage and family system of the United States developed as a modification in European, and, predominantly English, patterns, adapted to the colonial milieu and frontier situation that existed for nearly three centuries.

3. The Industrial Revolution, as the result of developments in science and invention, set in force new modes of production. More than previous historical events, these new economic techniques altered the home and ultimately reduced its scope drastically. By the middle of the nineteenth century the migration of the work force from domestic handicrafts to the factory meant a work week of perhaps seventy hours, or two-thirds of the waking hours, for most family members. This daily exodus from the home led to the replacement of many other functions, ranging from the making of clothes and furniture to the baking of bread.

4. With industrialization came urbanization. The concentration of individuals in urban areas was a product of the Neolithic revolution, followed by a number of higher-level urban cultures in the classical Mediterranean world. Especially after the Civil War the city increasingly loomed on the landscape as industry and commerce spread. The middle class flourished. Socio-economic changes, the specialization of labor, and increasing literacy changed man's perspective.[1]

Today 72 per cent of the population of the United States is urban according to the Census Bureau, which designates an "urban place" as one having a population of 2,500 or more. Well over a third of the population are inhabitants of the true metropolises, those cities of a million or more, including inner and outer suburbias.

However, even for that declining minority of Americans we label as rural, the effects of urban life have penetrated with near-staggering effects. In fact, part-time and full-time farmers and their family mem-

[1] Alvin Boskoff, *The Sociology of Urban Regions,* Appleton-Century-Crofts, New York, 1962, pp. 22–30.

bers constituted a total of some thirteen million people in 1964,[2] or 6.8 per cent of the population, a mere fraction of their ratio of 1900, not to speak of 1800. Yet these citizens encounter urban encroachments that would have seemed extremely strange to the common man of Andrew Jackson's or even Theodore Roosevelt's time: television, drive-in movies and banks, credit financing, a metropolitan press, as well as an elaborate display of mechanical gadgetry. For all practical purposes, the country dweller has most of the amenities of his distant city cousin, and a few hours on superhighways bring the remote rural population to the metropolis. The farmer is consequently subject to some of the standardizations, regimentations, and symbolizations of the city, although the degree to which he accepts or rejects these influences is not certain.

5. Equally critical are far-reaching changes in transportation and communication, which are related to the process of urbanization. Constriction of the boundaries of space and time are possibly among the most profound changes of the last century; ideas as well as people can travel with speed and ease. Including his work and recreation, the average American probably travels more than 10,000 miles a year and, for some, this mobility extends beyond national borders. However, travel itself does not guarantee the expansion of mental frontiers. Nor does the lack of geographic mobility necessarily create ignorance. This mobility has had its effects on the family, both in regard to the separation of its members and in their reassembly.[3] The dispersal of the family unit or its individual members for whatever reasons, is equalized by their reunions, at least temporarily. These reunions are often for ceremonial purposes such as weddings, funerals, or annual Christmas festivities.

6. A number of economic changes have occurred in recent history. First, a highly involved money economy has altered the social relations of man in respect to the process of production, distribution, and consumption of goods. Accompanying this rationalization in industrial process has been a loss of economic functions for the family institution. The standard of living has risen from one generation to the next. A display of purchasable items beyond the reach of yesterday's elite has

[2] Bureau of the Census, *Statistical Abstract of the United States*, Government Printing Office, Washington, D.C., 1965, p. 614.

[3] Clifford Kirkpatrick, *The Family as Process and Institution* (second edition), The Ronald Press, New York, 1963, pp. 127–128.

given the average man in our present-day culture an inevitable materialism, although different from the materialism of our ancestors, who were primarily concerned with next day's meal. That so many of the objects and activities of our contemporary world carry a dollar sign has had definite implications for our sense of values. It is not that economic concepts and realities did not exist for the men of Washington's or Jackson's time; it is only that these values have been so irrevocably transformed.

THE DRIFT TOWARD SECULARISM.   Scientific innovations and consequent changes in industrialization and urbanization, along with their peripheral effects, have changed the quality of social relations. The ways in which human beings interact have been transformed, in turn influencing family behavior. The fundamental changes in social relations may be summarized:

1. Rationalized and scientific norms have tended to replace traditional responses. When a person marries, he must have a blood test and fulfill other bureaucratic requirements; he plans his family size and spacing with the help of scientific rules and devices; he brings up his children with the aid of psychiatric authorities. We are reasonably accustomed to adopting changes in the material culture but not in the ideational culture. A new method of street paving will be adopted more readily than basic innovations in the school curriculum.

2. Role segmentalization and flexibility characterize our secular urban culture. The shift from the simpler folk or rural cultures to our metropolitan and corporate world calls for a wide repertory of response. A teenage girl may have to learn calculus during the school year, spend the summer on a job as life-guard, or stay at home acting as a mother-surrogate to a younger sister. She must be the "life of the party," cajole father into buying her a new wardrobe, and then accept the routine of household chores. We are trained by our peers to manipulate implicitly our various roles, to play a sophisticated "front" to the senior-class scion of an upper-class family, and an evening or two later present a "folksy" appearance to the boy from back home. Our role repertory includes the expected loyalties or commitments to family, church, school, and employer. The female role is especially vulnerable to conflict, and is discussed further in Chapter 6. However complex the roles of single life, marriage increases role tensions; the succession of roles includes husband, father, breadwinner, "do-it-yourselfer," and community leader, or wife, mother, hostess, Sunday

school teacher, and chauffeur. Research literature indicates that women are more flexible than men in role changes.[4] Consequently, responsiveness of women to various types of innovations as reported in recent studies of suburbia is not surprising.[5]

3. The quality of emotional involvements has become more casual. In a rapidly moving world where geographic dimensions are diminished and class boundaries are shifting for many individuals, interpersonal relations are not the same as they were for the more static society of the nineteenth century. In our contemporary, highly bureaucratized society, we are seemingly compelled to treat human beings as means to ends rather than ends in themselves. In other words, our contacts are fleeting and casual and, consequently, we frequently look upon other people as conveniences. In contrast, in the rural or *Gemeinschaft* type of society we are in contact with a limited number of people, to whom we have a more lasting and personal attachment. Today the careful cultivation of the proper "image" is only one aspect by which the individual maintains, in Parsons' words, "affective neutrality," as opposed to "affectivity." [6] In other words, we learn to control expression of feeling and to exhibit a more subtle type of responsiveness to the people who surround us. Although we make more friends than our grandparents did, at least a few of these associations represent strong affectional ties.

4. Along with the processes of secularization, role manipulation, and emotional restraint has come the blurring of moral judgments. This is not to say that we presently lack a moral perspective, but it has shifted from a more absolutist, universal position to something resembling a sliding scale. Any society is dependent on the structure and texture of its moral norms. As Parsons says, "Moral standards constitute, as the focus of the evaluative aspect of the common culture, the core of the stabilizing mechanisms of the system of social interaction." [7] The gradation of moral judgments, that has been apparent in sex behavior, tends both to clarify and complicate moral

[4] Mirra Komarovsky, "Functional Analysis of Sex Roles," *American Sociological Review*, 1950, **15**, 508–516; also her *Women in the Modern World, Their Dilemmas*, Little, Brown, Boston, 1953.

[5] David Riesman, "Styles of Response to Social Change," *Journal of Social Issues*, 1961, **17**, 78–92.

[6] Talcott Parsons and Edward A. Shils, *Toward a General Theory of Action*, Harvard University Press, Cambridge, 1954, p. 80.

[7] Talcott Parsons, "The Superego and the Theory of Social Systems," in Talcott Parsons, Robert F. Bales, and Edward A. Shils, *Working Papers in the Theory of Action*, The Free Press of Glencoe, A Division of Collier-Macmillan, New York, 1953, pp. 13–28.

decisions, for example, the twilight of the "double standard" as we shall see in Chapter 8. The mass media reflect this transition in morality. The Hollywood screen presents the "good-bad" girl, the heroine with the low-cut neckline who is addicted to mild alcoholic indulgence and may have an illicit affair, but who is essentially faithful to the man of her choice.[8] The child is confused as he watches on television a kaleidoscope of figures: the cowboy shooting it out with a rustler; the policeman apprehending a criminal, both justifying violence, without distinguishing the source of their power. Certain fuzzy lines of morality have been with us throughout history, but the exposure of novel varieties to mass audiences, juvenile and adult, is essentially new. What is acceptable conduct is occasionally too intricate a discrimination for the mass public to make, or possibly even for a professional philosopher. The blurring of sharp boundaries on questions of right and wrong does often emphasize the complexity of moral events, although many persons use this intricacy to justify any course of action. (The reverse may occur when conventional morality is upheld when convenient; a presidential candidate may be rejected because he is divorced.) One aspect of the indefinite quality of moral standards is that money or the market place becomes the final arbiter. Expediency (any action is justified by its goal) or the bandwagon (everybody is doing it) are the rules. These slogans of practical ethics are not original but our century has championed them.

5. Conformity has taken on added significance. According to some critics, there is an almost frantic search for the "image," the necessity for being within the style of the times. This concern with propriety or social approval is hardly new, however. Conformity is a psychological process whereby social living is possible. However, it may be so reinforced in the individual through a system of reward and punishment that the response can be learned too well. Crutchfield, among other social psychologists, has demonstrated in the laboratory the enormous pressure of group judgment on the individual even when the judgment is a false one.[9] Riesman, in more impressionistic terms, describes the individual as adhering to one of three types of behavior or to combinations of the three: "tradition-directed," where the person is

<hr/>

[8] Martha Wolfenstein and Nathan Leites, *Movies—A Psychological Study*, The Free Press of Glencoe, A Division of Collier-Macmillan, New York, 1950.

[9] Richard S. Crutchfield, "Conformity and Character," *American Psychologist*, 1955, **10**, 191–198; also "Personal and Situational Factors in Conformity to Group Pressure," *Acta Psychologica*, 1959, **15**, 386–388.

unreflective, mores-oriented in his action; "inner-directed," where he behaves on the basis of internally arrived at norms; and (for the twentieth-century man in particular) "other-directed" man, whose motives are derived from his sensitivity to approval by his peers.[10] In other words, we have our antenna focused on the anticipated applause of the group; we must be in atune with the latest song, the newest dance, the most fashionable coiffure, and cite the most acceptable and witty commentator on current events.

The mass media of our age aimed at a secularized urban audience only facilitates this new style of conformity. Marital decisions are derived from the woman's page or what the 10 A.M. family-counsellor-turned-TV-performer says on the subject. Reference to group or authority judgment is not unusual, but the fact that five million housewives may listen to the same program on how to reduce family tensions reveals a startling change in our society. A few secular segments of society are, if anything, *less* conformity-bound than in the past, but never before have such vast opportunities awaited the enterprising innovator who is determined to change inner or outer behavior in a given direction. The succession of fads and cults is a testimonial to the commercial success of these ventures.

LEISURE, RECREATION, AND THE MASS MEDIA

We have described how urbanization, together with "mass society," has altered every institution in our society. Let us now look at some of the changes in our institutions, recreation, education, government, and religion, and attempt to determine how these have affected the individual in his family setting.

Leisure in the modern world is signified by the relief from drudgery facilitated by a shortening of work hours. Yet some critics have questioned whether modern man has genuine leisure given the many distracting obligations our socio-economic universe contains.[11] Many suburbanites spend so much time commuting that their work time will not be appreciably lessened until a breakthrough, such as the thirty-hour or four-day week, is adopted. Moreover, we may question the appropriateness of the term "recreation" to describe what occurs in

---

[10] David Riesman, *The Lonely Crowd*, Yale University Press, New Haven, 1950.
[11] Harold L. Wilensky, "The Uneven Distribution of Leisure: The Impact of Economic Growth on Free Time," *Social Problems*, 1961, 9, 32–56.

off-hours; although in the broad sense any activity that is a change from the working hours qualifies as recreation, regardless of the action and effects on the individual. Recreation has been defined as "activity voluntarily engaged in during leisure and primarily motivated by the satisfaction or pleasure derived therefrom." [12] From a functional viewpoint leisure time or recreational activities may be divided into the following categories:

1. *General socialization.* Our basic social activity consists of visiting neighbors, friends, or relatives for games, dancing, conversation, or the exchange of ideas, and even of recipes, etc.

2. *Voluntary associations.* Principal among these are fraternal organizations, which represent a large, although slightly declining, segment of American social and recreational life. Other variations of voluntary associations are garden clubs, community welfare councils, veterans' organizations, and labor unions—even though their functions are not entirely recreational. Leisure-time activities centering about the church or school, such as square dancing or the bowling team, are a kind of voluntary association for recreational purposes and an adjunct of another institution, that is, educational or religious.

3. *Commercially sponsored diversion* (or as in the case of the solitary drinker or solitaire player, nonsocialization). Bars, nightclubs, dance halls, and related enterprises flourish because recreation is most welcome as an escape from the home. Money also can become a means of demonstrating status or the limits of an individual's incentives and resources. For most middle-class members, attendance at these establishments is probably a part of dating or becomes a subsidiary form of recreation, as in festivities, such as anniversary celebrations. For less integrated individuals without social moorings, and usually without a family unit, bar-hopping and the like is a most available outlet.

4. *Athletic activities.* Sports and related outlets constitute still other areas of revitalization. Here, especially, a distinction is made between what is *passive* and what is *active* recreation. That is, the observers and the participants.

5. *Hobbies and "do-it-yourself" movements.* These have become especially popular in the post World War II years. Stamp collecting, photography, and poetry composition are clearly distinguished from, for

---

[12] Charles K. Brightbill and Harold D. Meyer, *Recreation: Text and Readings,* Prentice-Hall, Englewood Cliffs, 1953, p. 50.

example, paneling the den or reupholstering the chairs. The high cost of personal services may be a stimulant to a vast set of household hobbies. This financial motive does not prevent the "do-it-yourself" urge from being a hobby.

6. *Entertainment.* Most of us derive our major satisfaction from spectator types of cultural and entertainment activities: the theater, concert hall, literature, and most widely, the mass media.

It is to the mass media that most individuals and, consequently, most families commit the major part of their "free" time. In addition, the mass media are related to other forms of recreation, since we may find inspiration for creativity, exposure to travel, knowledge of sports, etc., in the mass media. Finally, the material and symbols of mass media have an inescapable relation to the home, whether it is the motion picture, television, or books and newspapers.

THE MOTION PICTURE. Motion picture attendance has declined from its peak of 1946, when the average American went to the movies more than twice a month. The first wave of universal television exposure showed that by the early 1950's box-office receipts had been more than cut in half. The mid-1950's witnessed some return to the movie theater, but even so, more than a third of the nation's 17,000 movie theaters and drive-ins have been operating in the red.[13] Motion-picture production has been reduced to less than half of its early postwar production rate. The audience continues to be youthful (the average age being under twenty-five), and consequently has an above average educational level, in view of increased school and college attendance of recent years. Among adults, high school and college background is more highly correlated with higher movie attendance than is lower education,[14] whatever Hollywood producers may have considered to the contrary. The price of admission is undoubtedly a factor in the more frequent attendance by the middle to upper class, as opposed to lower class, a finding not confined to the United States.[15] Both sexes attend on an approximately equal basis.

Movies have a more than academic relationship to the institution of

[13] *Statistical Abstract, op. cit.,* p. 843; cf. also, "Hollywood Save the Flowers," *The Saturday Review,* March 1958, 11–13.

[14] Leo A. Handel, *Hollywood Looks at Its Audience,* University of Illinois Press, Urbana, 1950, p. 106.

[15] Robert C. Williamson, "Some Variables of Middle and Lower Class in Two Central American Cities," *Social Forces,* 1962, 41, 195–207.

marriage and the family. First, the factor of mate selection itself has been sketched out as the simplified "love at first sight" or a super-hedonistic viewpoint in many motion pictures. Moreover, marriage itself receives a variety of treatments in the American motion picture. While the movie medium does not pretend that the cases it portrays are necessarily typical of the American milieu, the casual observer might easily judge that infidelity and pervading conflict are endemic to the American household. This attitude would not be surprising if the screen focuses on a random, almost flippant entry into marriage as normal. These criticisms are in themselves not decisive, since the movies have a right to use the deviate as legitimate material. The basic criticism is of the concentration on the vagaries of love-making and courtship, with the tacit assumption in films that the whole problem of life is in *getting* married. The adolescent observer is often more astute in judgment than the level of the screen instrument assumes him to be.

From another viewpoint, the screen industry has presented problems in censorship, voluntary or coercive. In the early 1920's film companies realized that unless some covenant were adopted, the standards of behavior presented on the screen might lead to anarchy and certainly to harsh governmental controls. Consequently, the Hays office (Production Code of the Motion Picture Association of America) reigned over such problems as the length of hemline or the use of colloquial terms. The drift away from conventional studio production by the late 1950's brought up the problem anew as the independently or foreign-made film became more imaginative in its techniques. Ultimately, this experimental attitude required court decisions. An important breakthrough occurred in June 1959, when the Supreme Court reversed a New York State board's finding that *Lady Chatterley's Lover* was outside "moral bounds." The Supreme Court maintained that the film was within acceptable limits of what might be considered "free speech." [16] This decision has permitted freer access to "problem films" —whether on drug addiction, race relations, or civil liberties—and a more sophisticated conversational level. Liberalization has been abetted by a more mature viewpoint on the part of producers, distributers and the public.

Motion pictures raise certain problems for parents about their children's exposure to them. The solution in most foreign countries has been

[16] Arthur Knight, "Lady Chatterley's Lawyer," *The Saturday Review,* July 25, 1959, p. 25.

to demarcate age categories for which films are intended and to penalize the theater manager for nonadherence to these codes. The American tradition of individual freedom leans away from this restriction. Strictly adult movies are labeled so that the responsibility for such decision is placed on the parent. Despite the disadvantages this solution may have, it appears the most sensible. There are numerous "family movies," yet many of these are not appealing to all age levels. Certain spectacle films stress their supposed attractiveness for the entire family.

TELEVISION—THE WUNDERKIND OF THE MASS MEDIA. Since its proliferation at the end of the 1940's, television has dwarfed all other mass media in effects if we combine the number of sets and total viewed hours for the American public. The number of television sets increased from 10,000 in 1946 to 3,000,000 in 1950, to 49,000,000 households or (considering multiple sets in the same household) to 56,000,000 sets in 1962.[17] Some 90 per cent of the population own sets, and it is estimated that people use their sets upwards of five hours a day on the average.[18]

Several aspects of television (and these generalizations apply also to radio), are relevant to its effects. First, it enters the privacy of the home, and consequently public control over its material is of a more sensitive nature than with the motion picture medium. Second, the fact that in most homes viewing occupies a large portion of the later afternoon and evening hours means that the home becomes oriented to the demands of the program schedule. Dinner must be completed in order to make room for a particular program, perhaps one of dubious distinction. Standardization of time habits as well as family conflicts over the program preferences would seem strange to pre-radio and pre-television society. Third, a pseudoaudience effect is stimulated by the familiar techniques of live or taped audience applause and an intermittent reminder from the announcer that neighbors, friends, and relatives are listening. Several major urban areas of the country have attempted to respond to mediocre programing by promoting noncommercial educational television, provided funds were forthcoming from private or institutional sources. However, the fact that less than one per cent of the population tuned into the educational stations in the Boston area

[17] Clara T. Appell, "Television Viewing of the Pre-School Child," *Marriage and Family Living*, 1963, 25, 311–318.

[18] Raymond A. Bauer and Alice H. Bauer, "America, Mass Society and Mass Media," *Journal of Social Issues*, 1960, 16, p. 34.

points to the feasibility of educational television in only a half dozen or so urban areas of the country, at least in the near future.[19]

Television as well as movies face the question of ethical values. Most conspicuous of the problems is the array of violence on the living-room screen. One survey indicated no less than 3,000 acts of violence were shown during one week of programs.[20] While this report dates from the early 1950's and the wave of violence has subsided slightly since that period, the display of crime and delinquency has invited considerable criticism. Part of the problem has been the tendency of children to confuse fantasy and reality.[21] Some authorities maintain that only the disturbed child and adolescent are directly stimulated by this material. The child who is unduly aggressive, withdrawn, or tends to live in a fantasy world may be influenced by this violence. Continued emphasis on, and governmental support of, mental hygiene movements may be a more fruitful method of tackling the problem than direct censorship of the television screen. In fact, voluntary controls by producers have had some moderate success in the 1960's.

Finally, television may affect family relationships directly, primarily through its effect on children. There is increasing indication that television is used as a pacifier or tranquilizer of children.[22] In a large-scale survey it was found that roughly 75 per cent of parents thought their children gained more from television than they lost. On the favorable side they mentioned both the educative value and its distractive or "baby-sitting" values, although there were misgivings about its display of violence and inhibitive effects on homework.[23] One earlier report points to television viewing as a relief from frustration, utilized more by upper-middle class children than by upper-lower class children. When other activities were presented to the child the tendency to view television was reduced.[24]

Few can question television's ubiquitousness in the life of contem-

[19] Ithiel de Sola and Barbara Adler, "Educational Television: Is Anyone Watching?" *Journal of Social Issues,* 1962, **18,** 50–61.

[20] Bauer and Bauer, *op. cit.,* p. 20.

[21] Wilbur Schramm, Jack Lyle, and Edwin B. Parker, *Television in the Lives of Our Children,* Stanford University Press, Stanford, 1961, pp. 161–168.

[22] Leo Bogart, "American Television: A Brief Survey of Findings," *Journal of Social Issues,* 1962, **18,** 36–42.

[23] Gary A. Steiner, *The People Look at Television,* Alfred A. Knopf, New York, 1963, pp. 82–91.

[24] Eleanor E. Maccoby, "Why Do Children Watch Television," *Public Opinion Quarterly,* 1954, **18,** 239–244.

porary man. In a New York study, one-half of the families reported watching programs while eating meals, and 87 per cent of the respondents were involved in other activities concurrently with television. For both adults and children, work and play may be combined with viewing.[25] Finally, there is need for a more intensive survey of the question of program control and public education, at all age levels, in program selectivity.[26]

MASS MEDIA AND THE FAMILY.   Voluntary controls appear to have made some headway in mass media. For instance, the Comics Magazine Association of America has provided some improvements in the material of that medium.[27] Violence, overt sex symbols, and stereotyping of supposed inferiorities (religious, racial, physical, etc.) in people have been lessened. However, any upsurge in the tastes of the public seems to rest with an improvement in educational level.

The American public is exposed to mass media, but there is also an "embedding process," namely, the public as individuals "work through" the newspapers, magazines, television, and radio material and communicate to their acquaintances and neighbors. In other words, personal influence appears to be more effective than mass media in inducing change in behavior.[28] Consequently, the home has special significance, because it provides the environment in which the greatest amount of receptivity to news and similar content takes place. We are told that the family has discovered a new unity as it sits in front of the television screen. Although there is some interpersonal stimulation and a mutual receptivity to the common image on the screen as interpreted occasionally by conversation, considerable intrafamilial conflict occurs regarding program choice. It is too soon to determine the ultimate effects of mass media on the home; but as a common focus of attention and a primary source in determining values, it is likely that television has added more cohesion in the home than it has removed.[29] The same is no doubt true for radio. Or rather, despite their passivity, these media have given a central pivot of values in the home, though perhaps below the desirable qualitative level. Also desirable

[25] Appel, *op. cit.*

[26] Schramm, *op. cit.*

[27] Otto N. Larsen and William R. Catton, Jr., *Conceptual Sociology*, Harper and Row, New York, 1962, p. 48.

[28] Elihu Katz, "Communication Research and the Image of Society; Convergence of Two Traditions," *American Journal of Sociology*, 1960, **65**, 435–440.

[29] Steiner, *op. cit.*

from the viewpoint of the sociologist is the mass media's effort to present the data of scientific studies in marriage and the family rather than the pedestrian, journalistic presentations of certain paperbacks, and of the "advice to the lovelorn" syndicated columnist. Some middle ground can be found between the technical research report and the "souped up" rendition in the press, radio, and television.[30]

EDUCATION AND THE FAMILY

One of the significant aspects of the school and the family is that both share a number of the same functions: socialization of the young, preservation of the cultural pattern, and conferment of status. These functions are found universally in human society, and are necessary if culture is to have continuity. In preliterate societies the family or kinship group performs the entire task, and there is no formal educational institution. In our society the educative process is usually more formalized and controlled than is the family. In other words, the diverse basis of the educational institution permits change with greater facility than does the family. Its purveyors also are selected with more formalized discrimination: the criteria for selecting a teacher in the public school can be more stringent than those for a marital candidate. For a number of reasons society has a bureaucratized and readily controllable organization by which the younger generation may be prepared for their tasks of worker, citizen, and a number of other status-role situations, including that of family member.

In any case, with the universalizing, lengthening, and diversifying of the educational system, the family has had many of its more intimate functions extended to the school. In our society the nursery school and day-care center have performed part of the socialization process in recent years. Moreover, at the other end of the process, that is, late teens and early twenties, formal education has been extended.

At one time the economic institution recruited the young person in his late teens, but he is now partially lost to both the economic and the family institutions. As explained in the first pages of this chapter, society also has become sufficiently complex that while the family has lost ground in its commitment of the individual, it has gained in education. The average individual of the eighteenth century was an

---

[30] Harold T. Christensen, *Handbook of Marriage and the Family*, Rand McNally and Company, Chicago, 1964, pp. 978–980.

illiterate peasant or frontiersman. Today with much of education free, universal, compulsory, and encouraged from nursery school to university, the family has often been interpreted as a relatively residual institution. However, the school has not replaced the family. Instead, the two agencies, family and school, are collaborating in the task of socialization. In this respect the American school demands of its students a more total commitment than is true of most other Western cultures.[31]

With present-day secularization, education has been necessarily moving toward transmitting a more intricate set of skills so as to enable the individual to perform more adequately in this changing world. As a person enters the higher grades, he must be taught how to perform in a bureaucratic society, that is changing from an industrial to an atomic or space age, and yet at the same time he must be able to verbalize the values of an ancient culture. As one recent appraisal of education expressed the function of education, "The perspective we hold is that of the school as a transitional institution in which the process of education gradually separates the young from the family and locality and prepares them to join the great corporate systems and to establish their own independent nuclear families." [32] Historically, one major shift in education was the progressivism of John Dewey, together with Francis Parker, William Kilpatrick, and Boyd Bode. For these educators the old system was regarded as a mechanical process in which the individual was trained to respond in the classroom with ritualized parcels of memorization. What was needed, preached this new credo, was a more creative approach to life. Dewey insisted that the individual must be considered as an end and not merely as means to an end. The whole self or personality was the function of education. Emphasis in the schoolroom shifted to motivation and to eliciting a felt need for learning. The individual child had to be stimulated to learn. In addition, education was linked to democracy. The mature individual would contribute to reform and social change. In the end Dewey's principles in practice, if not in theory, led to excesses, and by the late 1940's strong countertendencies were in operation. Still, after the decline of progressivism, the humanization of education did not disappear.

[31] Jesse R. Pitts, "The Structural-Functional Approach," in Christensen, *op. cit.*, p. 114.

[32] Solon T. Kimball and James E. McClellan, Jr., *Education and the New America,* Random House, New York, 1962, p. 39.

Dewey had correctly perceived that socialization was a process shared by the school and home.

GENERATIONAL APPROACHES AND CONFORMITY. Parents have the final responsibility of managing and safeguarding the local school. However, in most communities indifference, especially among the lower class, and preoccupation with various obligations in the middle and upper-middle groups prevent active participation in the task of coordinating with the teacher and administrator. A study in New London, Connecticut indicated that less than 30 per cent of the citizenry were perceived by the interviewees as "taking enough interest in the city's high schools." [33] Probably the suburbs have a more enviable record for interest in this problem. One problem in the relationship between the public and the school system is the role of special interest groups who often subvert the general public from the essential issues, as was the case during the 1950's in Levittown, a postwar suburb on Long Island.[34] A large number of parents aligned themselves in two factions regarding the role of the schools in the community, including the expansion of the physical plant and the question of progressivism in the methods and content of the teaching program. In this contest personalities and the indirect influences of ethnic and religious factors were visible. In line with the political climate of the times, progressivism and liberalism were interpreted as communism.[35]

Society as it operates on the school system, through the family, regards the indoctrination of status advantages as indispensable; although in both the family and school, status appears more as a latent function than a manifest one. We consider skill socialization as the primary reason for sending the younger generation through the educational system. But in addition to the acquisition of occupational and social skills, upward mobility becomes a major motive, albeit only partially conscious.

Certainly in our schools great stress is placed on conformity and competitiveness.[36] The schoolroom and playground become another arena in which the family's status is tested. The study of the Midwest-

[33] Frederic W. Terrien, "Who Thinks What About Education?" in Robert R. Bell (ed.), *The Sociology of Education*, The Dorsey Press, Homewood, Illinois, 1962, p. 15.

[34] William M. Dobriner, *Class in Suburbia*, Prentice-Hall, Englewood Cliffs, 1963, pp. 113–118.

[35] *Ibid.*, p. 138.

[36] Robin Williams, Jr., *American Society: A Sociological Interpretation*, Alfred A. Knopf, New York, 1961, pp. 296f.

ern community, Elmtown, points to the degree to which the status system affects the clique structure in order that adolescents may be socialized along appropriate class lines. Dates, dances, and betrothals all reflected the five social classes of this Illinois town.[37] More recent evidence indicates that peer groups, which gradually replace influence of the family constellation, create a prestige system based on a combination of family socio-economic status, athletic achievement, leadership, and—to a differential extent—academic achievement, not to mention a few minor variables such as car ownership.[38] There was marked variation in this scheme among the nine communities studied. The parents were especially vulnerable in the more affluent Chicago suburbs and in a working-class suburb; least disturbance was found in a lower-class, smaller factory city and in a more traditional farming and middle-class retail community.[39]

THE UPSURGE OF HIGHER EDUCATION. One of the revolutions of the 1960's seems to be the growth of collegiate education. College populations are predicted to double almost each decade from the present number of four million.[40] In other words, as the population advances—if present rates of growth continue—by nearly 20 per cent per decade, the number of students is growing at possibly twice that rate, because of the greater emphasis placed on college education and the younger average age of population due to the high birth rates of the postwar years. Young people now enter college in numbers comparable to those that entered high school in the years after the turn of the century. Unquestionably this tendency means a higher rate of literacy, a vast reservoir of skills for the nation's economy, upgrading of tastes, and, in terms of the family, an increased dependency in the extension of the school years. It may be hoped that in the present context, the expansion of higher education will develop a more insightful and sophisticated public of marital partners. However, according to some observers, by tapping the middle and lower mental abilities of the population, some strains are placed on the college program. There will be either a large attrition rate or some colleges will have to lower their standards. The quality of colleges varies now, but there is an increased danger of proliferating mere "diploma mills."

[37] August B. Hollingshead, *Elmtown's Youth: The Impact of Social Classes on Adolescents*, John Wiley, New York, 1949.
[38] James S. Coleman, *The Adolescent Society*, The Free Press of Glencoe, A Division of Collier-Macmillan, New York, 1961, Chapter 7.
[39] *Ibid.*, p. 138.
[40] *Statistical Abstract, op. cit.*, p. 110.

Not least relevant in this expansion of higher education is the matter of family budgeting, unless there are appropriate state college or university facilities in the region. Other relevant aspects of the trend toward universal higher education, such as the campus marriage, are mentioned in Chapter 4.

THE EXPANDING ROLE OF GOVERNMENT

In the drift of events from the semifolk culture of the last century to the corporate, urban culture of the mid-twentieth century, sociologists have stressed the importance of expansion of governmental bureaucracies. Despite the laments of a number of articulate individuals and groups, this process has been inevitable. From the viewpoint of a family sociologist, the shift in the relationship of the state means that the functions once reserved for the family are now shared with governmental authorities: for example, unemployment insurance, now handled by state and local resources, the care of mental illness, and largest of all, the federal social security system. This depersonalization, or "defamilization," has generally supported the nuclear family, with responsibility for the aged and the infirm, for instance, now in the hands of the state. As in the relationship of the school and the family, there is a tendency for the state to provide the means by which the family can better carry out its traditional functions, with the responsibility for certain maintenance functions in the hands of governmental agencies, such as that of social security. Through these facilities family members may more adequately meet the psychological demands placed upon them, for example, socialization of aged parents now residing at a rest home, which is made possible by social security benefits. In other words, since the young couple know they will not be required to support their parents, they can act more spontaneously with them on an equal level, unlike the frustrating situation of the past when caring for the elderly was almost universally regarded as an unavoidable burden.

We look to the state for security from international tensions and threats in an age marked by the anxiety of thermonuclear war.[41] Governmental structure and processes assume bewildering significance as compared to their place in the nineteenth century. Certainly, no

[41] An analysis of the effect of nuclear war threat on the adjustment of children is found in Bernice T. Eiduson, "A Study of Children's Attitudes Toward the Cuban Crisis, *Mental Hygiene*, 1965, **49**, 113–125.

other institution can demand such commitment from the individual.

In a broad sense, the marriage and family institution overlaps with the governmental in a number of legal aspects. In addition to the stipulations regarding monogamy, there are other contractual relationships established. Family authority is under governmental supervision, such as the behavior of parents toward their children, the juvenile court procedure, and compulsory registration as in military service. The school receives its authority from the state. In some respects, court decisions may also rest on uncodified mores as in the disposition of the child to the mother in divorce cases, or "unwritten law" by which a man defines the "sanctity of the marriage bed." Increasingly, though, the tendency is to utilize written law as the authority of social action.

Most individuals in our society are not aware of the increasing dependence of the family on the state. Yet millions of mothers have obtained the Children's Bureau publication on infant and child care. In comparison with Canada and many European countries, the relationship of family and government in the United States is more potential than actual. Although the opponents of socialized medicine may wish otherwise, the idea of governmental aid to lower-class or older-age families in regard to their health needs is presumably only a question of time, as demonstrated by the recent passage of the Medicare Bill. Parents of the future may look to public agencies to resolve their problems in fertility control or of infertility. With the rate of population growth in the United States at 1.8 per cent per year, it may be necessary to enter into more active programs of this type. Family counselling services are also available for various problems, and the high rate of divorce (one out of five marriages) is likely to call for further expansion in this area.

THE FAMILY AND POLITICAL SOCIALIZATION. One aspect of the relationship of the family to the younger generation is the degree to which political coloration is determined by the family as opposed to other influences. Newcomb, in a study of Bennington College during the 1930's, demonstrated the tendency among students to become politically liberated between the freshman and senior years.[42] Follow-ups have not detracted from this generalization.[43] Research indicates that students of "ivy league" institutions, more than those at large state-

[42] Theodore M. Newcomb, *Personality and Social Change*, The Dryden Press, New York, 1943.

[43] Harold Webster, Mervin Freedman, and Paul Heist, "Personality Changes in College Students," in Nevitt Sanford (ed.), *The American College*, John Wiley, New York, 1962, pp. 811–846.

supported universities, exhibit this change toward liberalization. College youth display more conformity toward the political viewpoint of their parents when the latter have enjoyed moderate control over them; the greatest change in these young people is associated with either parental strictness or a *laissez faire* attitude.[44] In a Cambridge, Massachusetts, sample, 58 per cent of the college graduates changed to some extent from the political outlook of their parents, but only 28 per cent of those who did not graduate from high school changed.[45] At the same time, once out of college, there was a tendency of young people to drift toward the Republican fold, at least in the postwar world of relative prosperity.[46]

THE "NEW" RELIGION

The relation of religion to marriage and the family is complex; in Chapter 2 we noted some of the relationships between these two institutions in the historical evolution of marriage. Religion and the family offer a basis for comparison, because religion, more than other social institutions, is associated with emotional depth and reverence. Both religion and kinship relationships may represent highly intimate experiences. We may have other personal experiences such as attending a sports event, signing a contract, or volunteering for army service, but these evoke a totally different feeling from the emotional impact of, for example, baptism or marriage. Yet, unlike the world of our medieval forebears, we do not have the kind of commitment toward the church that we must have toward the family constellation. In fact, the close integration that religion imposes on other institutions in some cultures of the world is less conspicuous in contemporary Western society.

The United States is regarded as a religious nation, however secularized it has become. In the 1957 special census of individuals 14 years or older, there were 78 million Protestants (the largest denominations among these were Baptists, 23 million; Methodists, 16 million; Lutherans, 8 million). In this same census Roman Catholics numbered

[44] Eleanor E. Maccoby, Richard E. Matthews, and Anton S. Morton, "The Family and the Political Behavior of Youth," *Public Opinion Quarterly,* 1954, **18,** 23–39.
[45] *Ibid.*
[46] Ernest Havemann and Patricia S. West, *They Went to College,* Harcourt, Brace, New York, 1952.

30 million, and Jews, 4 million.[47] Other types of Catholics possibly constitute 2 million. In addition, there are perhaps 15 million Americans who have a given religious preference, largely Protestant, but who are not active members. Even for those who are church members, the maintenance of overt religious ties is subject to great variation. In a survey of married couples in Los Angeles, 50 per cent of the non-Catholic sample went to a church a maximum of two times a year, with the remainder averaging attendance of more than once a month.[48] Age affects religious participation. Individuals practicing Judaism tend to be older; Catholics, younger; and Protestants are intermediate in age. Jews are almost entirely urban, as are 80 per cent of Catholics, while almost half of Protestants are rural.[49]

In terms of the total transition of religion, the revolution of the last century has seen the decline of orthodoxy. This change began with the intellectual Renaissance in Europe in the seventeenth and eighteenth centuries, and reached its culmination in this century. The causes are clear, as mentioned at the beginning of this chapter: science, industrialization, urbanization, and mobility, among others. In the home these changes are especially evident in the liberation of women. With this shift has also appeared a religious pluralism by which the three principal faiths are functioning in relative harmony. Protestantism is divided into perhaps ten major branches, in addition to many other splinter camps; Judaism into Orthodox, Conservative, and Reformed; Catholicism is occasionally caught in a conflict of conservatives and liberals, and is tinged with some of the effects of Protestantism: emphasis on morality and practical Christianity. Although the social message is implicit in Catholicism, it is less evident in nations such as Spain, Colombia, Peru, and Ireland where only one religion exists. This effect is in contrast to, for example, France and Germany, which have a more functional type of Catholicism. It may be added that Protestantism has a lack of momentum in areas like Scandinavia, where it is practically the only faith.

[47] Bureau of the Census, "Religion Reported by the Civilian Population of the United States: March 1957," *Current Population Reports: Population Characteristics*, no. 79, Government Printing Office, Washington, D.C., 1958.

[48] Robert C. Williamson, *Socio-Economic Factors and Marital Adjustment in an Urban Setting*, Ph.D. dissertation, University of Southern California, 1951.

[49] David O. Moberg, *The Church as a Social Institution*, Prentice-Hall, Englewood Cliffs, 1962, p. 33.

THE RELATION OF THE CHURCH TO MARITAL AND FAMILIAL PATTERNS. In a number of respects the church influences family behavior. On a premarital basis the religiously identified tend to be less promiscuous than those with no religious affiliation. According to Kinsey, devout Catholics and Orthodox Jews had particularly low indices of premarital sex relations.[50] However, religion was not as critical a determinant as social class. In a southern University campus it was found that roughly 84 per cent of the strongly religious students opposed premarital sex relations as opposed to only 16 per cent of the nonreligious ones.[51] To what degree these attitudes are ascribable to parental moral values or to the effect of church participation cannot be known.

Parental expressions about child rearing also point to familial loyalties in regard to religion, and parental determination is well documented. Over 80 per cent of adolescents and postadolescents studied retained the religion of both their parents, and in the case of mixed parents the tendency was to accept the religion of one of the parents, which was twice as likely to be that of the mother.[52] A Florida study pointed to higher religious activity in families with children, residential stability, and an unbroken marital situation. (Death was more of a deterrent to religion than divorce.)[53] Religious rites in the home have shown a decrease. For instance, it was found that 70 per cent of Protestant families still observe grace before meals, although only 5 per cent hold family worship ceremonies.[54]

As we can see, there are a number of interrelationships between religion and the family. The question of whom we marry is highly influenced by religious belongingness, as we shall see in Chapter 10. Many studies point to religious identification as being statistically associated with marital adjustment. In a study of the attitudes of 2,654 college students, a close association was revealed between the religiosity and happiness of their parents, although there were differences among the three groups. The Jewish subjects rated their parents

[50] Alfred C. Kinsey, Wardell B. Pomeroy, and Clyde E. Martin, *Sexual Behavior in the Human Male,* W. B. Saunders Co., Philadelphia, 1948, pp. 483–487.

[51] Jean Dedman, "The Relationship between Religious Attitude and Attitude toward Premarital Sex Relations," *Marriage and Family Living,* 1959, **21,** 171–176.

[52] Howard Bell, *Youth Tell Their Story,* American Council on Education, Washington, D.C., 1938.

[53] Sarah F. Anders, "Religious Behavior of Church Families," *Marriage and Family Living,* 1955, **27,** 54–57.

[54] Roy. W. Fairchild and John Wynn, *Families in the Church: A Protestant Survey,* Association Press, New York, 1961, p. 184.

as happier and less religious than did Protestants and Catholics.[55] However, the least happiness for the parents' marriage was reported by students from homes with no religious identification. It is possible that some bias operated in these judgments; that is, perhaps respondents inclined to be religious may also perceive their parents as being happier.

Religion does offer a rationalizing and ritualistic sanction to marriage and family functioning. The belief in religious concepts is one means of providing the individual with a sense of purpose in his life, and his identification with religious groups offers a medium of socialization within the community. Worship and the festivities in connection with religious holidays such as Christmas, Easter, Hanukkah, and Yom Kippur are interrelated with family solidarity. Frequently, religious subcultures determine the family attitude in response to a crisis. Farber found that Protestant parents were least reluctant to permit institutionalization of a handicapped child, whereas Jewish parents were most resistant to the idea, Catholics assuming an intermediate position.[56] Family solidarity is apparently most intense among minority-group religions, particularly if discrimination or persecution has been a factor.

Most important in this contemporary period, religious organizations have become service-oriented. The three principal faiths in the United States offer a number of family services: pastoral counselling, psychological services (including marital guidance), family life education, and social and economic attention to special problems and groups ranging from the effects of racial discrimination to the welfare of migratory laborers.[57] Extensive publications are circulated by various church groups in respect to these problems.

There is some controversy regarding the status of religion in America today. Membership figures indicate that churches are growing in membership at a more rapid rate than the population in the postwar years.[58] Yet there is a question as to the degree of commitment

[55] Judson T. Landis, "Religiousness, Family Relationships, and Family Values in Protestant, Catholic, and Jewish Families," *Marriage and Family Living*, 1960, **22**, 341–347.

[56] Bernard Farber, *Family: Organization and Interaction*, Chandler Publishing Co., San Francisco, 1964, pp. 433–435.

[57] Muriel W. Brown, "Organizational Programs to Strengthen the Family," in Christensen, *op. cit.*, pp. 855–859.

[58] Moberg, *op. cit.*, pp. 38–39.

these numbers represent. In no way is the membership increase comparable to the revivalism and consequent church growth of the 1890's, when Dwight L. Moody evangelized a highly fervid religious faith after having abandoned his Congregationalism for a combination of social gospel and fundamentalism. What characterizes the present era is a secularized religion in which the laity regards religion not as a preparation for salvation but as an attempt to rationalize one's philosophy in an age of anxiety and prosperity. According to one survey, the average churchgoer regards theology as highly tempered with scientific or modernist concepts.[59] While perhaps few Americans would accept the notion attributed to Jane Russell that God is a "livin' doll," the religious books that have been best sellers over the last fifteen years indicate that a tranquilizing brand of religion has attracted a large reading public. For one or two popular theologians of television fame, religion is a kind of insurance policy, a philosophy to guarantee success, or a technique to insure marital tranquility. It is not our purpose to dispute the humanized philosophy but rather to point to how profoundly our conception of religion has shifted over a half century.

Despite this shift, for most people family and religion are closely related. In our own country three principal faiths have operated in parallel fashion, and present trends indicate that this relative coalescence is unlikely to disappear.[60] Churches are today divided into the conservative—whose orientation is toward Biblical doctrine and reward in a future life—and the liberal—oriented to the needs of man in the present life—"redemptive fellowship" and social service.[61]

This chapter sketches both the social setting surrounding modern marriage and the mass media which are important in determining our values regarding marriage and the family. Despite criticism of motion pictures and television, for instance, there is today more frankness and honesty than at any time in the history of these media. But in view of the complex urban quality of our culture these standards still lag. In view of increased commerciality at all levels of society, we are caught in considerable norm confusion. These problems often provide a fallacious environment in which two individuals marry and attempt to ad-

[59] Fairchild and Wynn, *op. cit.*
[60] Will Herber, *Protestant, Catholic, Jew,* Doubleday and Co., Garden City, 1955.
[61] Luther G. Baker, Jr., "Changing Religious Norms and Family Values," *Journal of Marriage and the Family,* 1965, **27,** 6–12.

just. The socialization of our children is made more difficult because of the values purveyed.

Supplementary Readings

Bailyn, Lotte (ed.), "The Uses of Television," *The Journal of Social Issues,* 1961, **18,** 1–96. The Society for the Psychological Study of Social Problems. Case studies in television, including data from both Britain and America.

Bell, Robert R. (ed.), *The Sociology of Education,* The Dorsey Press, Homewood, Illinois, 1962. A compilation of readings on the climate of education today.

Bensman, Joseph and Bernard Rosenberg, *Mass, Class and Society,* Prentice-Hall, Englewood Cliffs, 1963. Chapters 11 and 12 provide a critical commentary on the arts and their relationship to society.

Christensen, Harold T. (ed.), *Handbook of Marriage and the Family,* Rand McNally, Chicago, 1964. Chapter 2, "The Institutional Approach" by John Sirjamaki and Chapter 13, "Family and Community in Urban-Industrial Societies," by John Mogey are relevant to the contemporary social setting of marriage and the family.

Elliott, William Y. (ed.), *Television's Impact on American Culture,* Michigan State University Press, East Lansing, 1956. Although somewhat dated, there are some good chapters on educational television.

Farber, Seymour M., Piero Mustacchi, and Roger H. L. Wilson, (eds.), *Man and Civilization: The Family's Search for Survival,* New York: McGraw Hill, 1965. A discussion by a number of theorists of the institutional aspects of the family in the contemporary world.

Kimball, Solon T. and James E. McClellan, Jr., *Education and the New America,* Random House, New York, 1962. This book is one of the most adequate overall treatments of the educational institution in the United States.

Kirkpatrick, Clifford, *The Family as Process and Institution* (second edition), The Ronald Press, New York, 1963. Chapters 4–6 treat the social setting of the American family system.

Moberg, David O., *The Church as a Social Institution,* Prentice-Hall, Englewood Cliffs, 1962. Even though some of Moberg's conclusions are controversial, it is a solid work on religion in America.

Neumeyer, Martin H. and Esther S., *Leisure and Recreation* (third edition), The Ronald Press, New York, 1958. This sociological approach covers both the private and public aspects of the subject.

Riesman, David, *The Lonely Crowd,* Yale University Press, New Haven, 1950. Available in pocket book, this impressionistic treatment of the "other-directed man" has become a classic.

Steinberg, Charles S., *The Mass Communicators,* Harper and Row, New York, 1958.

The author presents a highly readable account of the mass media, public relations, and assorted problems.

Whyte, William H., Jr., *The Organization Man*. Simon and Schuster, New York, 1956. This best-seller, now in paperback, is a critique of bureaucracy, suburbia, and our present-day culture.

Williams, Robin M., Jr., *American Society: A Sociological Interpretation* (revised edition), Alfred A. Knopf, New York, 1961. Chapters 7–9, and 11 are highly relevant since they provide a critical discussion of the social institutions introduced in this chapter.

Winch, Robert F., *The Family* (revised edition), Holt, Rinehart and Winston, New York, 1963. Chapters 4–6 give a brilliant treatment to the institutions and social setting of the family.

Chapter four

Marriage Variations in Mid-century America

"Do you have any girl friends?" Francis asked.

"I'm engaged to be married," Clayton said. "Of course, I'm not old enough or rich enough to have my engagement observed or respected or anything, but I bought a simulated emerald for Anne Murchison with the money I made cutting lawns this summer. We're going to be married as soon as she finishes school."

"We're going to have a large family," Clayton said. "Her father's a terrible rummy, and I've had my hard times, and we want to have lots of children. Oh, she's wonderful, Mr. and Mrs. Weed, and we have so much in common. We like all the same things. We sent out the same Christmas card last year without planning it, and we both have an allergy to tomatoes, and our eyebrows grow together in the middle . . ."

John Cheever, "The Country Husband," reprinted in Fiction of the Fifties, *Herbert Gold* (ed.), *Farrar, Straus and Giroux, New York, 1961, pp. 145–146. (First published in* The New Yorker, *1954.)*

If I am right, the problem that has no name stirring in the minds of so many American women today is not a matter of loss of femininity or too much education, or the demands of domesticity. It is far more important than anyone recognizes. It is the key to these other new and old problems which have been torturing women and their husbands and children, and puzzling their doctors and educators for years. It may well be the key to our future as a nation and a culture. We can no longer ignore that voice within women that says: I want something more than my husband and my children and my home."

Betty Friedan, The Feminine Mystique, (W. W. Norton Company), *New York, 1963, p. 27.*

My Family Reunion by Louis Bosa (1950. Oil.)
Collection of the Whitney Museum of American Art, New York;
Gift of Mr. and Mrs. Alfred Jaretzki, Jr. (42½ x 62)

In any complex society such as ours, status and roles are patterned according to a number of cultural and institutional variables. The corporate urbanistic society described in Chapter 3 permits a diversification of styles in marriage. In fact, the attractiveness of marriage itself seems to depend on the social climate of the times. Individualistic, occupational, and social roles provide extensive coloration. American culture is one of considerable heterogeneity: ethnic strains contribute greatly to the diversity of marital patterns in this country. Consequently, this chapter attempts to present some subcultures that the individual might encounter in marriage. We can look at marriage more objectively, in a wider frame of reference, if we are acquainted with certain variations in the marriage pattern. The configuration of marriage is in part a product of the social situation in which the individual finds himself. Notably, at the middle of the twentieth century millions of young people are on the campuses of colleges and universities or in military service. And, most important, modern woman is faced with the choice of career or marriage or with combining and integrating the two alternatives. Before assessing these problems let us look at some statistical trends.

NEVER SO YOUNG NOR SO MANY

An Even Lower Age at Marriage.   A greater percentage of Americans marry, and at earlier ages, than do people of almost any culture of the world. One of the few exceptions is India, where 90 per cent of the women are married before they are 20 years of age.[1] Another exception is Germany, where 93.2 per cent of the males (in the age group of forty-five to forty-nine) were married in 1951, a phenomenon growing out of the postwar female surplus.[2] In the United States there has indeed been a decrease in the age at marriage since roughly before the turn of the century. The proportion of single males aged fifteen or over has been declining steadily from 42 per cent in 1890 to less than 25 per cent in 1950; for women of the same age group the rate of decline has been from over 30 per cent to 18 per cent during a comparable period.[3]

[1] Paul H. Jacobson, *American Marriage and Divorce*, Holt, Rinehart and Winston, New York, 1959, p. 75.
[2] William J. Goode, *World Revolution and Family Patterns*, The Free Press of Glencoe, A Division of Collier-Macmillan, New York, 1963, p. 49.
[3] Jacobson, *op. cit.*, p. 35.

Several factors are involved in the trend toward younger marriages. First we have an impatient, hedonistic attitude. Our individual goal has become pleasure and happiness, or at least the pursuit of these goals seems worthwhile. The desire to become married is sufficient reason to justify the act. This pleasure-oriented motivation was probably always present, but it is more outspoken today. More significantly, we look at life in terms of "adjustment," and for some people this means happiness. Clinical psychology, and the neo-Freudian insistence on affectional security and the desirability of a feeling of purpose, have been central to our belief in marriage as a means of mature adjustment. Second, the philosophy of deferred gratification by which sex is postponed until marriage has some relationship to upward mobility as well as to the ideology of an equalitarian personal happiness.[4] Marriage, like socio-economic success, becomes a principal goal in life. The decline of prostitution to a small fraction of what it was at the turn of the century is related to this situation, the end of the double standard, and the increase in formal education, literacy standards, and the psychological sophistication of love. Third, increased prosperity, with the resultant higher standard of living, has made possible a younger marriage age. Fourth, middle- and upper-class parents are more willing to support their adult children both for higher education and for early marriage. The admission by educational institutions of married college students after World War II is also relevant. Fifth, two world wars and the Korean episode to some extent postponed marriages for some millions of individuals, but the overall effect of modern war is a "Why wait?" if not a "devil-may-care" attitude. Whether age at marriage will continue to drop, remain stabilized, or even advance slightly cannot be known. The recent trend toward specialization and professionalization of skills might prevent marriage age from dropping further.

A phenomenon receiving considerable attention in recent years has been the teen-age marriage. Contrary to popular opinion, marriages at high school age are not increasing significantly.[5] However, marriages earlier than 19 years of age are more frequent than they were before

---

[4] Louis Schneider and Sverre Lysgaard, "The Deferred Gratification Pattern: A Preliminary Study," *American Sociological Review*, 1953, **18**, 142–149.

[5] Lee G. Burchinal, "Trends and Prospects for Young Marriages in the United States," *Journal of Marriage and the Family*, 1965, **27**, 243–254. See also Vladimir De Lissovoy and Mary E. Hitchcock, "High School Marriages in Pennsylvania," in the same issue, pp. 263–265.

World War II. It is usually the females who marry young. For example, at age 17 in 1960 12 per cent of white females were married in contrast to 1.9 per cent of the males, the rate for Negroes being slightly higher. Some factors associated with youthful marriages include lower socio-economic background, lower intelligence scores, lower educational attainment, and particularly premarital pregnancy. It is estimated that from one-third to more than one-half of teen-age marriages involve a premarital pregnancy.

SOME VARIATIONS IN AGE AT MARRIAGE. Educational level affects age at marriage in two directions. The high school graduate marries younger than those who represent the two extremes of the educational continuum. Urban individuals with only an elementary school background marry later than those who have been to high school or college. Individuals with more than four years of college tend to marry later than those with lower educational attainments. In regard to the occupational status of the husband, the variation between the median age at first marrige was 22.9 for laborers to 25.4 for managerials and professionals.[6] Thus even for the less educated, the age at marriage is higher than the age at which an average college graduate completes his education. In any case, the gap in the marriage rate is smaller than the difference in education attained.

Age differences between mates vary with the age of the individuals concerned. At 20, the man marries a year below his age; and at 25 he prefers a bride three years younger. The gap is five years for a man of thirty-one, and the disparity is 8 years by the age of fifty. For the girl of eighteen, the groom is, on the average, 3.7 years older; the difference is 2.3 years at twenty-one; and at twenty-eight years narrows to only 1.6 years, and widens again after age thirty.[7] At increasing age levels, more women tend to be married than do males, because usually women marry below men in age. This differential is erased by the age of forty.[8]

SOCIAL CLIMATE AND THE MARRIAGE RATE. The degree to which historical events, particularly war, can effect the marriage rate is illustrated in Table 4.1. The low rate of marriage during World War I was

[6] Paul C. Glick, *American Families*, John Wiley, New York, 1957, pp. 115–118.
[7] Jacobson, *op. cit.*, p. 63.
[8] Donald J. Bogue, *The Population of the United States*, The Free Press of Glencoe, A Division of Collier-Macmillan, New York, 1959, p. 224.

Table 4.1

MARRIAGE RATES, WAR, AND THE ECONOMIC CYCLE *

YEAR	HISTORIC EVENT	MARRIAGES PER 1000 POPULATION
1860	Pre-Civil War	9.3
1863	Civil War	7.7
1866	Recovery	9.6
1874	Depression	8.6
1913	Pre-World War I	10.5
1917	American entry	11.1
1918	Full participation	9.6
1920	Recovery	12.0
1929	Prosperity	10.1
1932	Depression	7.9
1938	Pre-World War II	10.3
1942	Early war period	13.1
1944	Full participation	10.5
1946	Recovery	16.2
1963		8.8†

* Paul E. Jacobson, *American Marriage and Divorce,* Holt, Rinehart and Winston, New York, 1959, p. 21; *Statistical Abstract of the United States,* Bureau of the Census, Government Printing Office, Washington, D. C., 1964, p, 84.

† The comparatively low rate in 1963 was largely a result of the disproportionate population at marriagiable age, or in their lower twenties.

not equalled again until the depression in 1932.[9] In both world wars the rate rose during the military preparations prior to our entry, and fell as the men were concentrated on foreign battlefields, only to surge to new heights after the war was ended. A similar three-phase shift occurred in the birth rate. It was not until 1948 that the birth rate receded, although not to its prewar level.[10] Other factors besides war, prosperity, and depression influence the marriage rate, for example, the psychological atmosphere. Perhaps the pleasure-seeking trend of the 1920's, with its permissive attitude toward intimate dating and sex mores, may have made marriage less inviting.

[9] Jacobson, *op. cit.,* p. 22.
[10] Bogue, *op. cit.,* p. 300.

ETHNIC AND CULTURAL PATTERNS

In the heterogenous society of the United States, marriage and family life—both structurally and functionally—assume the pattern of a given culture or subculture. Historical backgrounds, as mentioned in Chapter 2, are influential even today. Immigration, especially, has left an imprint. In addition, social class barriers impinge on regional and ethnic norms. We can obtain a richer perspective of marriage patterns in the United States if we are acquainted with the variability of subcultures in regard to family life. With the tendency toward a common culture in American society, these differences are becoming less marked from decade to decade. In this section we examine only three variants: Negro, Italian, and Mormon family types as representations of racial, national, and religious subcultures, respectively.

THE AMERICAN NEGRO FAMILY. One-tenth, or approximately nineteen million, of the United States population in 1960 was Negro. The marriage and family mores of the Negro differ somewhat from those of the white. First, the Negro tends to marry younger, and, as compared to whites, a higher percentage marry during the child-bearing years. A markedly higher percentage of Negro marriages are terminated, mainly by separation. Earlier in this century temporary unions without legal or religious sanction were fairly common among rural Negroes in the South and were found among the migrants to Northern cities, a movement that began in sizeable numbers during World War I.

Traditionally, in the plantation system of the South the family approached a matriarchal culture. Some matriarchalism was a carry-over from African cultures. A more important factor was the greater mobility of the male as compared to the female. Also, the plantation owners were desirous of high fertility of slaves and consequently avoided liaisons productive of offspring, legitimate and illegitimate, whether by white or Negro males. Frequently under these conditions a matricentric type of family pattern developed, because the father was either absent, unknown, or both.[11] Even today, in some segments of rural and urban Negro culture, the mother is either the dominant or only

[11] E. Franklin Frazier, *The Negro Family in the United States,* The University of Chicago Press, 1939.

sustaining adult influence the children know. In 1957, for example, 20
per cent of all nonwhite families had a female head; whereas in white
households the figure was approximately 10 per cent.[12]

Other variations in the Negro family structure may still be found in
parts of the South. There is the small patriarchal family, a hangover
from the slavery period by which certain male Negroes "owned" their
own families.[13] In other words, the Negroes who were freed before the
end of the Civil War purchased the freedom of their families, and maintained a patriarchal family culture, somewhat in imitation of the
white aristocracy by whom they were owned or for whom they had
worked. In addition, in the Negro culture, evidence of the extended
family system still exists in the tendency to adopt legitimate or illegitimate offspring such as grandchildren, nephews, nieces, or even more
distant relatives. The necessity of living at the economic margin and
in an older, dilapidated, and sometimes larger home may make for
multiple family relations. With the migration of the Negro to the
northern cities, an increasing occupational mobility has permitted
more differentiation and sophistication of interpersonal relations
within the family.

The family without a male household head has declined markedly
in urban areas. Frazier observed significant variation of family
demography within the zones of the city. For instance, in 1930 the
percentage of married Negroes fifteen years or older increased from
roughly 50 per cent within Harlem to 62 per cent in the outer
fringe.[14] In the decades since 1930 the general pattern still obtains but
has shown a high percentage of married in all zones.[15] Yet Negro marriage and family life have been affected by discrimination, an inadequate economic base, impoverished housing, and a lack of predictable
norms in interpersonal relations. These factors have caused many
Negroes to fall into the lower economic classes. The instability and
dissolution of lower-class families has been well documented.[16] Even

[12] Bogue, *op. cit.*, p. 282.
[13] E. Franklin Frazier, *op. cit.*,
[14] E. Franklin Frazier, *The Negro in the United States* (revised edition), Macmillan,
New York, 1957, p. 326.
[15] Bureau of the Census: *Census of Population and Housing: Census Tracts, 1960,
New York*, U.S. Government Printing Office, Washington D.C., 1962, pp. 366f.
[16] St. Clair Drake and Horace R. Cayton, *Black Metropolis: A Study of Negro
Life in a Northern City*, Harcourt, Brace, and Company, New York, 1945, pp.
585–586.

in the middle class sensitivity to disadvantages suffered on a racial basis becomes a point of tension in marital family relations. Yet in many cases the family is the only protection the individual knows. According to Frazier, the middle-class Negro builds up, as a compensatory mechanism, a protective system for his children to reduce the hostility, either open or disguised, they encounter in the white world.[17] The unpredictability of his social universe makes it difficult for the Negro to establish consistent norms in his general socio-economic behavior or in his marital relationships.

The mode of life in the professional and managerial segments of the Northern urban Negro population, and in certain Southern cities, is similar to that of the white. Although there are differences in the standard of living, the Negro's percentage of increase in real wages has been advancing at about the same rate as for the white.[18] Consequently the new Negro lower-middle class has been able to attain higher educational and occupational levels. Unquestionably, a more integrated family pattern has emerged. Although traditionally much of Negro middle-class family life has been oriented around church activities, the growing number of voluntary associations have introduced new norms, and indirectly have strengthened the family. The civil rights movement, in particular, has developed a sense of pride and achievement operating in the direction of reducing personal and social disorganization. After a transitional period of perhaps a generation or two, Negro family patterns may be in no way distinguishable from those of the white. Only class, and perhaps regional differences, will remain to give differential texture to family norms and roles, as is true for whites.

SECTARIANISM AND THE FAMILY: THE MORMONS. Mormon marriage, perhaps the only polygynous system in modern Western culture, has never failed to evoke interest. The religion was initiated in the 1830's by Joseph Smith, who wrote the *Book of Mormon* by "Divine Revelation." Soon after, the practice of plural wives appeared, especially as exemplified by Brigham Young, who became leader of the religion following the martyrdom of Smith. Polygamy became known as "The Principle" and was practiced by a minority, particularly the Mormon elite. The system was officially renounced by the Mormon church in 1890 at the time Utah was being considered for statehood. Since that

[17] E. Franklin Frazier, *Black Bourgeoisie,* Collier Books, New York, 1962, p. 184.
[18] Bogue, *op. cit.,* pp. 656-658.

time polygamy has appeared only in isolated parts of Southern Utah and Northern Arizona.

The justification for polygamy was found in the Old Testament, which recounted the case of Abraham and his concubines and a similar history on the part of other Hebrew patriarchs. When polygamy was practiced, it is doubtful that more than 7 per cent of the Mormon male population enjoyed this privilege, and of this group probably two-thirds had at most two wives.[19] Restraining influences toward polygyny were constituted by a lack of available females and a monogamous background from which the Mormons had arisen. In addition, although the marriage system was defended by both the men and women, there was not complete agreement in the Mormon community about its validity—especially in the 1870's and 1880's, when Utah was awaiting statehood.

In the hierarchy of Mormon marriages the position of favorite wife, or *wife-headship,* generally fell to the first wife. In some instances residence for all the wives was within the joint household. A more frequent and less tense arrangement was the separate household. On the whole, the traditional monogamous culture from which the Mormons came was hardly compatible with a harem-like institution. Polygyny was inevitably a difficult adaptation to the Western system. As Kuhn points out:

> The larger society sanctioned the dyad as a model or ideal of marriage interaction. But the critical interaction going on in the Mormon polygynous family was frequently of the unstable triadic sort; for example, the relation among the husband, the last-wife-married, and the wife-before-the-last; or the relation among husband, youngest wife, the next youngest wife; or that among husband, most physically attractive wife, and next most physically attractive wife; or that among husband, most fertile wife, the next most fertile wife; or that among three dominant wives, when the husband was of a weak sort or preoccupied with other matters.[20]

In explaining the hierarchical character of the marriage system a distinction was made between *celestial* and *secular* marriages, and a combination of the two. The priority of the first wife was attributable

[19] Thomas F. O'Dea, *The Mormons,* The University of Chicago Press, 1957, pp. 138–139, 246.

[20] Manford H. Kuhn, "American Families Today: Development and Differentiation of Types," in Howard Becker and Reuben Hill (eds.), *Family, Marriage, and Parenthood* (second edition), D. C. Heath and Co., Boston, 1955, p. 161.

to the theory of celestial marriage, namely marriage for eternity (performed only in the Temple), as opposed to secular marriage for a lifetime. Each form could exist without the other, as when a widow married a man already with a wife. The widow was still married celestially to her first husband, and her new spouse had his first wife. Celestial marriages could be arranged for a person who had died. In fact, converting one's ancestors to Mormonism was desirable. Consequently, Salt Lake City, because of the labors of a church society, contains possibly the best genealogical library in the world. Civil marriages for Mormons were, and are, only for a life-time. Under present monogamous conditions most marriages are considered both celestial and secular.

In an attempt to assess the quality of the Mormon polygyny, Young, on the basis of historical documents, has analyzed 175 marriages of which 53 per cent could be labeled "highly successful" or "reasonably successful," 23 per cent as having "considerable conflict" and/or "severe conflict," the remainder being of insufficient evidence to permit a classification.[21] In addition, he found a high correlation between economic status and polygyny.

Mormonism today is a religion that has made the transition from a rejected sect to a highly respected denomination, and one that is presently well assimilated within the American culture. Self-sufficiency for the Mormons is combined with a belief in group support. For instance, the religion demands maximum commitment of the individual to the religion. Thrift and tithing are expected, and provide the religious institution and the community with extensive resources for any individual or group crisis.

The Mormon concept of marriage and the family points to sacredness in family continuity, as the concern with ancestors indicates. There is strong church control over the activities of the individual and family; alcohol and stimulants (tea, coffee, and tobacco) are outlawed, divorce is tabooed (only 2 per cent of devout Mormons, that is, those married in the Temple, were divorced among the parents of one university sample).[22] Birth control is specifically discouraged. Although urbanization has tended to reduce the birth rate, it is apparently the

[21] Kimball Young, *Isn't One Wife Enough?*, Holt, Rinehart and Winston, New York, 1954, pp. 56–57.
[22] Philip R. Kunz, "Mormon and Non-Mormon Divorce Patterns," *Journal of Marriage and the Family*, 1964, **26**, 211–212.

highest for any religious group, and the widespread growth of Mormonism in recent decades is apparently more attributable to fertility than to conversion.

As a final note, an individual who marries a practicing Mormon (or who marries a devout member of a number of other denominations), must either convert or develop a considerable understanding of the other person's religion, as well as be willing to adjust to certain habit systems. Similarly, when the more faithful person marries an agnostic or "free-thinker," the same requirements are in order. Whether a harmonious relationship can be worked out depends on the flexibility of the two individuals.

IMMIGRANT PATTERNS: THE ITALIAN TRADITION.   With the exception of the German immigrants, Italian immigration to the United States has been the largest single flow from any nation. Roughly five million Italians have come to this country since 1820, when the first accurate records on immigration were kept. Most of this immigration occurred during the period from the late 1870's to the advent of World War I. At present, the majority of Italian-Americans are second or third generation. Let us discuss the Italian family as it exists in the homeland.

The Italian family, like those of most of Latin Europe, represents a more stable structure than the American family. The majority of those Italians who immigrated to the United States are of rural or semirural origin, notably from the southern part of their country. The pattern is basically patriarchal with rigid designation of sex roles. Courtship and marriage selection have been stiffly regulated by the parents with the advice of other kinsmen. Marriage age is generally older than in the United States. Until 1940 it hovered between the ages of twenty-seven to twenty-eight years for men and twenty-three to twenty-four for women. In the postwar years it has become twenty-nine and twenty-five, respectively.[23] Generally a dowry is expected, although in the cities this system is breaking down. Marriage as a sacrament of the Church is indissoluble. However, unlike the true extended family system, the young couple once married constitutes a nuclear family with separate residence.

Childbirth, as with all major life events, is an occasion for a sacred ceremony. In fact, the female's major role in addition to keeping her husband happy is to bear children. Until recently the Italian family

[23] Corrado Gini and Elio Coranti, "The Family in Italy," *Marriage and Family Living,* 1954, **16**, 350–361.

was a fairly prolific one; the average number of children per family dropped from 4.3 at the beginning of the century to 2.6 in 1950.[24] The effects of industrialization and urbanization on the Italian family have been similar to those in other countries. Socialization is strenuously enforced by the father, and indirectly controlled by the total kinship system. The interlocking of the total family may have interesting effects.

Each nuclear unit competes with the others for a larger and better share of the resources of the extended family. Such things as inheritance from grandparents or unmarried aunts and uncles, or access to desirable positions, are not strictly determined by law or tradition. There is room for personal influence over the distribution of family benefits, and children are often an important means to this end. They are likely to be encouraged to learn to manipulate a variety of people quite early in life. A favored grandchild or niece or nephew not only has an ally with whom to resist parental pressure on occasion, but he or she builds up a power position in both the nuclear unit and the extended family organization. The advantages such a child brings to the nuclear family give him or her a limited equality with elders that is a foreshadowing of adult relationships in these societies.[25]

The Italian family life cycle is different in meaning from its counterpart in this country. The Italian grandparents contribute to family continuity rather than becoming superfluous entities. The grandfather continues to work the land until physically unable. The doting grandmother has her young charges, permitting her a sense of importance as well as freeing her daughter or daughter-in-law for other household duties and allowing for further procreativity. The discontinuities known to our culture rarely exist in these families. Despite the poverty of an overpopulated landscape and two world wars, the Italian family offers its members a protective atmosphere not especially familiar to urban Americans. At the same time, the drift toward urbanism and *Gesellschaft* (see Glossary) has affected Italy. Consequently, the family life of Milanese and Florentines may be more like that of Chicagoans than of rural Sicilians. A relatively common culture has diffused throughout the Western middle-class world.

When we examine the changes experienced by the Italian family in its adjustment to the United States, we encounter three stages: initial

---

[24] *Ibid.*, p. 359.
[25] Dorothy R. Blitsen, *The World of the Family*, Random House, New York, 1963, p. 157.

contact, conflict, and accommodation.[26] The first is illustrated in the transplanting of the family from its position in the Old World; although new ways of life are experienced, there is no break in the solidarity of the family. The second stage is reached when the children begin to question the traditional values of behavior patterns; third, accommodation occurs when memories of the "Old Country" recede into the background, the second generation has adapted itself to the new ways, and has to a considerable extent carried the older generation along with these newly acquired cultural traits. Assimilation is achieved when the second or third generation becomes indistinguishable from the American population, living in a non-Italian neighborhood and enjoying the amenities and mobility of other Americans. Yet, frequently, Anglo-Saxon biases tend to identify Italians as laborers by occupation, as members of a minority religion, and as having foreign names.

In family norms the second generation becomes gradually integrated with the prevailing New World culture. Accommodation and assimilation are indicated by a number of factors: increasing power of the female, decreasing control of the father over the general conduct of the family members, conflict concerning the freedom of the daughter's dating habits, and elimination of the dowry. In fact, status and roles of family members may be in a gradual transition for the several decades after the migration of the original family to America. For instance, the daughter-in-law, if she is of a traditional American background, is regarded at first as being subordinate to the family, which becomes for her a conflict situation, with her independence marking an accommodative stage.[27] The independence of the woman generally involves a lengthy process of accommodation. A number of other adaptations take place, such as the growing infrequency of family celebrations.

This portrait of the Italian family is presented as another example of the adjustments encountered in marrying into cultural enclaves. Among other things, the individual may have to adapt to the behavior of an extended family system as well as to modifying his religious viewpoint. If he is accustomed to the permissive atmosphere of the American home, he may experience mild cultural shock when confronted with

---

[26] Paul J. Campisi, "The Italian Family in the United States," *The American Journal of Sociology*, 1948, **53**, 443–449.
[27] *Ibid.*

the exhortations of the in-laws that the young married couple appear weekly for dinner with reciprocal invitations expected. Also, it may be anticipated that he will provide financial support in case of a family crisis. At the same time, he may find the European-oriented family offers a relatively solid refuge against the world.

THE MARRIED COLLEGE STUDENT

Another type of marital situation found in the United States today, and one of the striking changes on the university and college campuses of the country, is the married student. This tendency for college students to get married became conspicuous about the time of World War II, continued into the postwar era, and was again reaffirmed during the Korean War. The postwar prosperity that permitted part-time jobs, particularly among the urban commuter-type institutions, furthered this tendency. Apparently the early wartime student marriages were a general response to the heightened emotionality; although there were a few student marriages even before the war. In the fall of 1941 a study of campus marriages at the University of Washington indicated that a number of these partners were from somewhat disoriented home situations and divorced parents. In some instances the marriage had been kept secret from the parents to insure continuance of monthly payments. The study demonstrated at least two characteristics of collegiate marriages: financial strain with the threat of termination of studies, and a close cooperation of the two partners in household duties.[28]

In 1959 a study was made of 203, or 10 per cent, of the married couples at the University of Arizona and of a control group of noncollege married couples matched on age, education, and estimated socioeconomic status of parents.[29] This study indicated that only 35 per cent of the college wives were full-time homemakers. Yet, unlike the University of Washington students, the men were not able to contribute their help to home duties—particularly child care—because of their study regime. In some instances the control group was more involved in household duties than was the student sample. It should be noted that the student sample had a lower birth rate: 56 per cent had children as

[28] Svend Riemer, "Marriage on the Campus of the University of Washington," *American Sociological Review*, 1942, **7**, 802–815.

[29] Victor A. Christopher, Joseph S. Vandiver and Marie N. Krueger, "The Married College Student," *Marriage and Family Living*, 1960, **22**, 122–128.

against 86 per cent of the controls. Yet the number of anticipated children was appreciably higher for the students, possibly another indicator of the trend toward increased procreation among the more educated population.

The level of living was definitely restrained in the college sample. The student married couples were more reluctant to become involved in installment buying. However, despite the more meager standard of living, television and high fidelity radio sets were more prevalent. Television was considered a pleasant distraction for the wife while the husband was studying, and it was also used as a mechanical baby sitter.

Most of the married students looked on marriage as a stabilizing influence and as providing companionship. They believed that marriage combined with college encouraged cooperative adjustment to one another's roles. On the negative side, there was the nearly overwhelming problem of financial hardship, insufficient time, the responsibilities connected with "beginning too early," the limiting of social life, and the arrival of children before they were desired. Apparently one positive aspect of the students' marriage was the close association with other college couples.

Consequently there are several problems in college marriages that have not been resolved, notwithstanding the advantages in companionability, affectional stability, and sex enjoyment. First, such marriages signify the end of dating and wide sociability between the sexes. Most campus marriages, if we except the graduate students and the veterans, have been contracted before the age of twenty-one. This figure is below the average marriage age in the United States, especially as it relates to the socio-economic stratum of the majority of college students. One possible rationale of college marriages is that for many of our urban middle-class population, marriage traditionally has occurred nearly ten years above the age of sexual maturity. Marriage is a definitive psychological and social act. Yet an early marriage often introduces a permanent union before the young adult is ready.

Possibly the most severe problem for campus couples is financial pressure. Parents take a more protective attitude toward their college-age children if they remain single. The father is especially reluctant to support a son-in-law. Students are themselves divided on this problem of parental responsibility. A survey among single students in 1957 revealed that half the men and two-fifths of the women thought parents should continue support in case of marriage of their student sons and daughters.[30] Compared with the prewar period, parents have restructured their attitude concerning financial obligations, including support of unplanned grandchildren. Mutual aid between the two generations is not new, but early marriages have tended to reinforce this cultural habit, especially in view of the postwar prosperity. Moreover, as an aid to college students at the graduate level, considerable funds exist for research assistantships and the like, but are less available for undergraduates, except for the usual campus jobs or employment in the urban community—not always available in a small college town.

Time pressures and the distribution of labor imposed by a college marriage may be more stringent than those in the normal marriage. If the wife is working, the husband generally is expected to perform some of her traditional chores. If there are children, the husband is subjected to additional strain, because presumably he is working as well as studying. In any case, the wife is generally forced to spend many hours on her own. However, the problem of the husband studying does not seem to be a major one. In a sample of California male students, married and single, matched on age and other variables, marriage more often raised rather than lowered grade averages. Such improvement was more marked for majors in social science and education than for those in the natural sciences or humanities. The research raises the hypothesis that in certain subjects the commitment required by the individual may be greater than in others. Consequently the emotional security marriage brings may be dissipated in the more exacting disciplines. Students in the natural sciences were found to marry younger than those in the social sciences and humanities, a finding possibly explained by the comparative absence of women in these curricula. Perhaps the male finds marriage the proper means by which to secure companionship with the opposite sex.[31]

For all married people there is the inevitable problem of unplanned children, or even the financial and time pressures of those that are planned. The unanticipated arrival of infants in the early married years may be frustrating both emotionally and economically to the young parents. In a Purdue University veteran-student sample of persons married on

---

[30] Judson T. and Mary G. Landis, *Building a Successful Marriage* (third edition), Prentice-Hall, Englewood Cliffs, 1958, p. 189.

[31] Ralph Schroder, "Academic Achievement of the Male College Student," *Marriage and Family Living*, 1963, 25, 420–423.

the average of four years, 34 per cent of the pregnancies were planned.[32] Two-fifths of the respondents asserted that the presence of children had aided their adjustment, one-fifth held the opposite opinion, and two-fifths were neutral or divided in their opinion. Fifty-eight per cent of the sample were satisfied with having children as early as they did. However, the pressure of children was found to be a deterrent to the husband's study regime.

Modern man asks, "Is it better to have a family early or late?" The energy level of parents is higher if they are under twenty-five instead of over thirty, but the financial resources are generally lower. In any case, we tend to rationalize whatever course of behavior we have chosen.

In summary, campus marriages are probably a permanent aspect of college life. The higher percentage of individuals attending college, indulgent parents, and the relatively plush postwar job market have produced this relatively new marital type. Recent evidence (at least at one Midwestern liberal arts college) regarding satisfaction with housing, economic conditions, and the study situation supported the adjustment of the married student versus the single student.[33]

Whatever the merits of the arguments, married college students apparently accept their situation. When the Purdue sample was asked whether their status as students had aided or disturbed their marriage adjustment, 28 per cent replied positively, 32 per cent negatively, and the other 40 per cent indicated that their student status had no effect on their abilities to adjust to their new roles. In this sample, the childless couples were more inclined to favor the married student role.[34] Campuses are now at least improving the residential situation for married students, although such attentions have been primarily directed toward the graduate student rather than the undergraduate.

THE EMPLOYED WIFE

The working wife has become a commonplace part of our society. The budgetary requirements of the present-day marital relationship,

[32] Harold T. Christensen and Robert E. Philbrick, "Family Size as a Factor in the Marital Adjustments of College Couples," *American Sociological Review*, 1952, **17**, 306–312.

[33] Laurence L. Falk, "A Comparative Study of Problems of Married and Single Students," *Journal of Marriage and the Family*, 1964, **26**, 207–208.

[34] Christensen and Philbrick, *op. cit.*, p. 310.

the stimulus value of consumer items, and the relative ease in house-keeping because of modern appliances, all conspire to keep the wife in the employment market until the arrival of the first child—and occasionally thereafter. In this respect, Western society contrasts markedly with some others (for example, the Arabic world) in which employment of the wife is considered undignified. In 1940 an eighth of American wives were in the labor force, the rate increasing to one-fifth in 1950 and approaching one-fourth in the early 1960's.[35] Presumably, today at least 55 per cent of all working women are wives, in contrast to only 30 per cent before World War II. These figures are even more impressive when we realize that in March 1965, one-third of the labor force in the United States was composed of women, approximately 26 million out of a total of 76 million.[36] The employment of women reaches its peak between the ages of thirty-five and forty-five with a plateau of extensive employment from ages twenty-five to fifty-four, the period of highest commitment to household duties but also before marked physical decline sets in.[37] Postwar prosperity, temporarily interrupted by the recessions of 1949, 1958, and 1962, provided reasonably ample job opportunities for women. Approximately one-third of these women have chosen clerical positions, with the next largest group being factory workers.

THE FEMININE ROLE AND OCCUPATIONAL OUTLETS. As we shall see, a woman experiences difficulties in crystallizing her definition of her role or roles in our society. Kirkpatrick suggests that there are six courses of action open to the college-trained woman.[38] First, there is the career woman, who prefers to remain single; or if she marries, it is as a purely incidental event. This role is most developed by women whose success is sufficient to outweigh the disadvantages of spinsterhood and childlessness.

Second, "marriage-maternity-homemaking" is the other extreme from the career woman, and the most universal pattern for wives. Here homemaking and parenthood are regarded as a career. The principal problems for these women are monotony and the lack of intrinsic reward.

[35] Glick, *op. cit.*, p. 90.

[36] *Statistical Abstract of the United States,* Bureau of the Census, Government Printing Office, Washington, D.C., 1965, p. 217.

[37] F. Ivan Nye and Lois W. Hoffman, *The Employed Mother in America,* Rand McNally, Chicago, 1963, p. 15.

[38] Clifford Kirkpatrick, *The Family as Process and Institution* (second edition), The Ronald Press, New York, 1963, pp. 444–466.

The suburban wife has become relatively famous for her discontent with maternal duties and the urge to return to a career as the study of one Montreal suburb testifies.[39]

Third, the "low-fertility-companion" path is another alternative, and implies subordination of the woman to her husband or at least to one who regards his wife's role as contributing happiness to their lives and possibly having one or two children. In some instances a married couple may operate a business enterprise together, in which case the marriage has economic overtones. The wife of a writer, a diplomat, or an executive often relieves her husband of as many household and familial duties as possible. She may become a kind of social director. One study of executives' wives showed an outline of duties as summarized in the wives' responses, in which they indicated the following as desirable features: (1) to take care of the house and children; (2) to manage so that the husband gets some of her time; (3) to keep the home running smoothly and to be able to entertain; (4) to participate to some extent in civic and social affairs.[40]

Fourth, the "low-fertility-marriage-plus-career" outlet, in comparison to the pure career type, presupposes marriage and possibly a child. This woman perceives marriage and career as having equal utility, the emphasis depending on the disposition and age of the woman and the adjustability of the husband. In a Florida study of career-oriented women versus traditional homemakers, it was found that given occupational models, that is, teachers and professors, were important in the choice of a career; whereas the noncareer women were more influenced by conformity and security motives.[41] Although not all of the population regard children as necessary for a happy marriage, the scarcity of infants for adoption is evidence that most married couples find an exclusively career-oriented wife not the ideal solution.

Fifth, the "fertile-marriage-plus-partial-career" combination points to a purely subordinate type of professional relationship that is calculated to be most satisfying, or least dissatisfying, to the college-trained woman. The woman's commitment is relative to her life situation,

[39] John R. Seeley, R. Alexander Sim, and Elizabeth W. Loosley, *Crestwood Heights: A Study of the Culture of Suburban Life,* Basic Books, New York, 1956, pp 178–179.

[40] Margaret L. Helfrich, "The Generalized Role of the Executive's Wife," *Marriage and Family Living,* 1961, **23**, 386.

[41] Richard L. Simpson and Ida H. Simpson, "Occupational Choice Among Career-Oriented College Women," *Marriage and Family Living,* 1961, **23**, 377–383.

which varies with age. Her work, if any, outside the home is confined to a part-time arrangement during the early years of motherhood. Possibly civic, church, or charity activities constitute a semicareer. In this connection a study of Los Angeles highschool seniors suggests that girls look forward to career roles that are "eminence-" or "culture-oriented" (that is, intrinsic rewards); whereas boys look to more extrinsic rewards, such as monetary considerations.[42] The college-trained woman often looks forward to returning to the career for which she was educated. The most frequent reason for a wife's employment is apparently financial pressure. In one study, 48 per cent of a sample of 2,700 wives ascribed their desire to work to this motive.[43] The early years of the marriage and children's adolescent period are logical points for shifting emphasis to the career role.

Sixth, the "fertile-marriage-plus-full-career" option remains the most challenging and, if successful, can be the most satisfying. However, the demands of modern living make this combination nearly impossible except for the most vigorous. With the help of an energetic grandmother or an organized household, some women are able to have three or more children and still maintain a forty-hour work schedule. Teaching is possible as a career for this type, since schools generally have a generous policy on maternity leaves and the school schedule is similar for both mother and children.

A woman at the crossroads must consider the negative feeling about the working wife. The employed single woman is accepted without conflict, whereas the dual role of the married woman, especially with children, has been regarded with some ambiguity on the part of the public.[44]

In this connection significant changes have occurred in the class complexion of working mothers. At one time the employed mother was mainly associated with the lower class. Today, according to the National Industrial Conference Board, in homes of $7,000 to $10,000 yearly income, 41 per cent of the wives work; in homes having $10,000 to $15,000 yearly income, 42 per cent of the wives work. In 1961 the

[42] Ralph H. Turner, "Some Aspects of Women's Ambition," *American Journal of Sociology*, 1964, **70**, 271–285.

[43] Marion G. Sobol, "Commitment to Work," in F. Ivan Nye and Lois Hoffman, *The Employed Mother in America*, Rand McNally, Chicago, 1963, p. 49.

[44] William J. Goode, *After Divorce*, The Free Press of Glencoe, A Division of Collier-Macmillan, New York, 1956, p. 209.

proportion of wives employed decreased precipitously in homes where income was above \$15,000 and below \$7,000.[45]

THE FACTOR OF CHOICE AND THE DIVISION OF POWER. In many cases a girl is not certain about the alternatives (just outlined) at the time she finishes college or enters marriage. Yet most girls seem to choose marriage rather than a career. In a 1953 study of a sample taken from a state college in Washington, 8 per cent of the girls preferred a simple career to marriage, 80 per cent were marriage-oriented, and the remainder were uncertain of their feelings.[46] However, in the highschool sample just discussed, girls made their decisions about an occupational field earlier than boys, and in college at least as early as the males did. Seventy-five per cent of the girls in the Washington state sample stated that they preferred work "involving relationships with people," whereas the boys were more inclined toward working "with things." In a study of 27 mobile or career-oriented women, and 33 who were nonmobile, results imply that the mobile women were lonely, socially nonadjusted individuals. Childhood was marked by poorer relations with their parents and symptoms of personal unhappiness.[47] In certain occupational areas such as journalism, law, medicine, and scientific research, latent homosexual tendencies may be present in certain career women. However, since ideal adjustment is rare, it is unfair to stereotype the career-woman as maladjusted. Recent evidence, although somewhat fragmentary, indicates that the career woman remains unmarried due to accidental inability to find a mate rather than because of any given personality pattern.[48]

A fundamental question remains about how women decide between a career and marriage and, second, how the decision to work affects the divisions of tasks within the home and the equilibrium between the two sexes. Research points to cultural factors (for instance, religion) as determining career choice and the husband-wife relationship. A study of 178 Catholic college girls revealed a tendency to choose marriage over a career when certain given situations obtained: low socio-eco-

[45] Nelson N. Foote, "New Roles for Men and Women," *Marriage and Family Living*, 1961, 23, 325–329.

[46] LaMar T. Empey, "Role Expectations of Young Women Regarding Marriage and a Career," *Marriage and Family Living*, 1958, 20, 152–155.

[47] Evelyn Ellis, "Upward Social Mobility among Unmarried Career Women," *American Sociological Review*, 1952, 17, 559–563.

[48] Carol N. Doty and Ruth M. Hoeflin, "A Descriptive Study of Thirty-Five Unmarried Graduate Women," *Journal of Marriage and the Family*, 1964, 26, 91–94.

nomic status, low academic scores, and low educational aspirations. Religion as a fourth factor in these results, at least in the lower socio-economic group, affected positively the orientation toward marriage. Girls rating high in religiousness tended to project their viewpoint onto future husbands; namely, they believed the male desired homemaking as the proper female role.[49] These findings bear out the generalization that the less secure woman is likely to plan on marriage as a solution to her problems.

A study of middle-class suburban housewives stressed the importance of the husband's feelings regarding the wife's choice of employment, especially when children were involved. Other factors influencing her selection of employment were: performance before marriage in an occupation requiring higher education or special training, continuance of employment after marriage, sharing child care and household tasks with the husband, and the children being of school age.[50] In other words, husband-wife interaction and various incentives determine her readiness for a career. Employment in lower socio-economic classes apparently hinges on economic necessity.

One of the suppositions regarding wives with careers has been an equalitarian power structure as opposed to the patriarchal or male-dominated type of marital relationship. In a Michigan study, samples included working wives and wives who had not been employed for a year or more. Both groups were nearly identical in background, socio-economic class, religion, and length of the marriage. On investigation the two samples were found to have an equalitarian type of marital relationship. Proportionately, the husbands of employed wives performed more housework in the number of hours they actually worked, but it is doubtful that they accomplished more, because often in households where the wife is employed, chores are reduced to a minimum.[51]

Automation is displacing large numbers of workers engaged in routine, clerical, and manual tasks leading to reduced employment and

---

[49] John Kosa, Leo D. Rachiele, and Cyril O. Schommer, "Marriage, Career, and Religiousness Among Catholic College Girls," *Marriage and Family Living*, 1962, **24**, 376–380.

[50] Mildred W. Weil, "An Analysis of the Factors Influencing Married Women's Actual or Planned Work Participation," *American Sociological Review*, 1961, **26**, 91–96.

[51] Robert O. Blood, Jr. and Donald M. Wolfe, *Husbands and Wives: The Dynamics of Married Living*, The Free Press of Glencoe, A Division of Collier-Macmillan, New York, 1960, pp. 55–72.

shorter hours found for both sexes. Women without special training may have difficulty finding employment. However, the shortened work week for the husband may favor his assumption of a greater role in household duties, enabling a larger ratio of qualified women to enter the employment market. These changes probably will further increase the democratization of the power structure within the home.[52]

THE EMPLOYED MOTHER AND THE CHILD. Although this topic is discussed in Chapter 17, some examination of children's adjustment when the mother works outside the home belongs in this context.

Extensive arguments have focused on the effects of the mother's employment on the child.[53] The popular literature has been unmistakable regarding the dangers to the child's personality adjustment and for his potential delinquency. In reality, sociological and psychological research has not supported this negative conjecture.

An exhaustive examination of young children whose mothers were employed, in regard to possible physical symptoms, anxiety reactions, and other maladjustive indices revealed no negative effects.[54] In a sample of 130 southern women who were largely college-trained, several tests (Children's Apperception Test, Thematic Apperception Test, General Home Standards from the Child Guidance Survey, etc.) disclosed a normal adjustment both on the part of the children and their working mothers. Affiliation and achievement feelings were healthy for the children of elementary school age and above.[55]

Adolescence often has been cited as the period when the child is most vulnerable to the effects of the working mother. Neurosis, school truancy, unsavory sex activity, and juvenile delinquency all are supposedly correlated with the results of maternal neglect. Research literature indicates no ill effects of mothers' employment on the adolescent or on the younger child. For example, a study of urban and rural adolescents in the state of Washington revealed no conspicuous neurotic symptoms in children of working mothers. Neither affectional

---

[52] Robert O. Blood, Jr., "Long-Range Causes and Consequences of the Employment of Married Women," *Journal of Marriage and the Family,* 1965, **27**, 43–47.

[53] James H. S. Bossard, *The Sociology of Child Development* (revised edition), Harper and Row, New York, 1954, pp. 282f.

[54] Lee G. Burchinal and Jack E. Rossman, "Relations Among Maternal Employment Indices and Developmental Characteristics of Children," *Marriage and Family Living,* 1961, **23**, 334–340.

[55] Kathryn S. Powell, "Maternal Employment in Relation to Family Life," *Marriage and Family Living,* 1961, **23**, 350–355.

relations toward the mother nor educational achievement suffered, and part-time employment of the mother is apparently beneficial to the adjustment of the adolescent girl.[56] Even in the case of broken homes the working mother did not produce unfavorable results. The only exception was delinquency, which was to a small but significant degree statistically related to employment of the mother.[57] We cannot assume from this study that there is no adverse relationship between maternal employment and childhood and adolescence personality functioning, but the surveys are not able to detect one.

Another study points to similar results in urban and rural environments. Four hypothetical areas were tested regarding the behavior of the adolescent son and daughter: (1) amount of household work performed, (2) social activities, (3) academic performance, and (4) discipline and other personal relations within the family. Although there was some difference between the urban and rural samples, the results indicated no clear-cut negative effects as a result of the mother's employment.[58]

Undoubtedly more data is desirable to determine to what degree nonmeasured or nonobservable factors are operating in the adjustment of the children or adolescents. It also appears that the personality of the mother more than the fact that she is working is a determinant in her child's adjustment.

This chapter has surveyed several of the marriage patterns found in the United States. In a national culture marked by a variety of ethnic strains, religious and occasionally utopian experimentation, divergent rates of rural and urban development, and—most important—the presence of a class system, marital roles inevitably vary. In addition, marital and familial patterns are affected by differences of age, education, and occupation, historical processes and events—such as the recent expansion of higher education—combined with a younger age of marriage. Most incisive has been the impact of two world wars and the cycles of depression and prosperity. However, no matter what the national circumstances, the woman must make major decisions. She is

[56] Elizabeth Douvan, "Employment and the Adolescent," in Nye and Hoffman (eds.), *The Employed Mother in America,* Rand McNally, Chicago, 1963, *op. cit.,* pp. 142–164.

[57] F. Ivan Nye, "Employment Status of Mothers and Adjustment of Adolescent Children," *Marriage and Family Living,* 1959, **21,** 240–244.

[58] Prodipto Roy, "Adolescent Roles: Rural-Urban Differentials," in Nye and Hoffman, *op. cit.,* pp. 165–181.

required to choose between marriage, motherhood, and a career or in rare instances she may combine these goals.

In this chapter we have cited a number of research studies regarding marital roles as associated, for instance, with the married college student, with the employed wife and mother, and the effects on relevant family members. It is clear that a single research investigation seldom provides conclusive evidence; however, findings, if based on replicated studies, can be the basis of valid generalizations. We must be especially cautious in our interpretation when we are told that married college students are enthusiastic about the arrival of their children, or that husbands approve of the employment of their spouses. The findings may be valid, but on the other hand, the response may be to a loaded question, and the subject may be trying to find a rationalization for his conduct. This question as to the validity and consistency of the testing instrument and the interviewing situation is examined in the appendix.

Supplementary Readings

Becker, Howard and Reuben Hill (eds.), *Family, Marriage and Parenthood* (revised edition), D. C. Heath, Boston, 1955. Chapters 5, 24, and 25 are most relevant to the topics of contemporary marital patterns.

Frazier, E. Franklin, *The Negro Family in the United States,* The University of Chicago Press, 1939. The classic statement of a minority type of family culture.

Friedan, Betty, *The Feminine Mystique,* W. W. Norton, New York, 1963. A psychologist-journalist maintains that the contemporary household-orientation of the woman needs drastic revamping.

Gans, Herbert J., *The Urban Villagers: Group and Class in the Life of Italian-Americans,* The Free Press of Glencoe, A Division of Collier-Macmillan, New York, 1962. The Italian-Americans of the West End of Boston; Chapter 3 treats family relationships.

Hunt, Morton M., *Her Infinite Variety: the American Woman As Lover, Mate, and Rival,* Harper and Row, New York, 1962. An impressionistic account with some interesting insights in the best style of this contributor to the New Yorker.

Jacobson, Paul H., *American Marriage and Divorce,* Holt, Rinehart and Winston, New York, 1959. An excellent account of statistical trends.

Kirkpatrick, Clifford, *The Family As Process and Institution* (second edition), The Ronald Press, New York, 1963. Chapters 7, 16, and 17 treat the changing climate of marriage and particularly the problem of women and careers.

Komarovsky, Mirra, *Women in the Modern World: Their Education and Their Dilemmas,* Little, Brown, Boston, 1953. Probably the best treatment in one volume of the role conflicts of twentieth-century woman.

McKinley, Donald G., *Social Class and Family Life,* The Free Press of Glencoe, A Division of Collier-Macmillan, New York, 1964. An intensive empirical study of the status subculture's effect on family life and socialization.

Nye, F. Ivan and Lois W. Hoffman (eds.), *The Employed Mother in America,* Rand McNally, Chicago, 1963. A collection of articles, mostly the results of empirical studies.

Ogburn, William F. and Meyer F. Nimkoff, *Technology and the Changing Family,* Houghton Mifflin, Boston, 1955. The impact of our present-day material culture on marriage and the family, including the problem of the working wife.

"The Woman in America," *Daedalus,* 1964, **93,** no. 2, 577–803. Articles on the question of sex equality, working and professional women, and the problem of accommodation of women to our culture, including portraits of Jane Addams and Eleanor Roosevelt.

Winch, Robert F., *The Modern Family* (revised edition), Holt, Rinehart and Winston, New York, 1963. Chapters 6, 11 and 12 are most pertinent to the texture of modern marriage and its roles.

"Women and Work," *Marriage and Family Living,* November 1961, **23,** no. 4, 325–387. This issue is in the same vein as the Nye and Hoffman volume.

Young, Kimball, *Isn't One Wife Enough?,* Holt, Rinehart and Winston, New York, 1954. The author, a noted sociologist and grandson of Brigham Young, discusses the documents regarding Mormon polygyny.

Part Two
Premarital Patterns

Part Two examines the spectrum of behavior patterns that exists prior to marriage. Chapter 5 explores the question, "What made us the way we are?" What events that took place in infancy, childhood, and adolescence have left permanent traces? It introduces significant questions regarding development of the individual during the first eighteen or twenty years of life until he is on the brink of the serious courtship that is to be followed by marital and family responsibilities. Chapter 6 discusses sex roles from the physical and psychological standpoints, and follows the matter of sex identity introduced in Chapter 5 into adolescence and adulthood. In Chapter 7 we investigate dating, how it relates to the individual, and its broader significance in our society. The question of premarital sex practices is explored in Chapter 8.

Chapter five
Prologue to Maturity

Children have more need of models than of critics.
Joseph Joubert (1754–1824), Pensées, *No. 261.*

All women become like their mothers. That is their tragedy. No man does.
That is his.
Oscar Wilde, The Importance of Being Earnest, *Act One, 1895.*

Both the forcing of children and the fear of forcing them were inadequate
substitutes for the long, careful watchfulness, the checking and balancing and
reckoning of accounts, to the end that there should be no slip below a certain
level of duty. . . . They had that wistful charm, almost sadness, peculiar to
children who have learned early not to cry or laugh with abandon; simple
regimentation and the simple pleasures allowed them. They lived on the
even tenor found advisable in the experience of old families of the Western
world, brought up rather than brought out.
F. Scott Fitzgerald, Tender is the Night *(revised edition), cited by
permission of Charles Scribner's Sons, 1951, p. 275.*

Crabbed age and youth cannot live together;
    Youth is full of pleasure, age is full of care;
Youth like Summer morn, age like Winter weather;
    Youth like Summer brave, age like Winter bare
Youth is full of sport, age's breath is short;
    Youth is nimble, age is lame;
Youth is holt and hold, age is weak and cold;
    Youth is wild, and age is tame.
Age, I do abhor thee; youth I do adore thee.
Shakespeare (?), The Passionate Pilgrim, *XII, 1599.*

The childhood shows the man, as morning shows the day.
John Milton, Paradise Regained, *Book IV, line 220.*

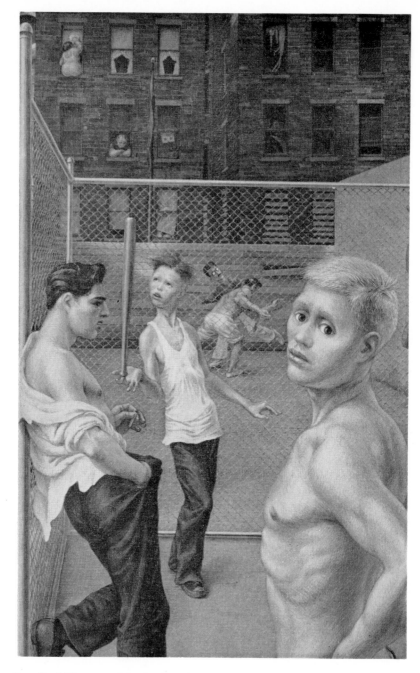

Detail of *Playground* by Paul Cadmus
Courtesy of the Midtown Gallery, Collection of Mr. Merrick
Lewis—Geoffrey Clements, Photographer

It is generally accepted that the experiences of infancy, childhood, and adolescence are fundamental in determining adult personality structure. Success in marriage is determined in large part by the psychological events of these critical years. In many marital adjustment studies, several items were found to be predictive of marital happiness: child-parent relationship, kind of discipline, and the memory of childhood as a happy experience.[1] Clinicians, as well as sociologists, have traced the origins of marital problems back to the critical years of childhood. As with any intricate interrelationship of human personalities, no point-to-point correlation can be made. That is, there are some happy marriages following an unhappy childhood, but statistically the advantage lies with a happy home environment. Divorce has been shown to occur where individuals have had either severe or very relaxed childhood discipline.

This chapter first examines the personality concepts centering around the theories of Freud and his revisionists. Personality is a product of genetic components [2] and the critical influences of environment, particularly of early social relationships. In this chapter we look specifically at infancy for its possible later effects.

The discussion of childhood is introduced to determine the range of parental behavior and its influence. Certain aspects of the parent-child relationship are deferred to Chapter 17, where they are discussed in detail. One important area of the child's socialization is the acquisition of self and sex identity, which is also examined here. Some parental omissions and excesses have enormous consequences for the child's psychological development: rejection, overprotection, overpermissiveness, domination, and ambivalence. Adolescence, the more advanced stage of socialization, presents a number of problems in the search for identity, independence, and maturity. The physical changes along with the challenging equilibrium between the parental orbit

[1] Lewis M. Terman, *Psychological Factors in Marital Happiness,* McGraw-Hill, New York, 1938, pp. 225f.; Ernest W. Burgess and Leonard S. Cottrell, Jr., *Predicting Success or Failure in Marriage,* Prentice-Hall, New York, 1939; Harvey J. Locke, *Predicting Adjustment in Marriage,* Holt, Rinehart and Winston, New York, 1951, pp. 107–111.

[2] Although it is impossible to present a complete list of relevant literature here, perhaps as significant as any research is the work of Kallman on identical and fraternal twins separated at, or shortly after, birth and the subsequent effects on personality, particularly at the onset of mental illness. See F. J. Kallman, "The Genetics of Mental Illness," in S. Arieti (ed.), *American Handbook of Psychiatry,* Basic Books, New York, 1959, Chapter 8.

and the demands of the peer group make adolesence an interesting, if perplexing, period.

CONFLICTING PHILOSOPHIES OF PERSONALITY DEVELOPMENT

In the last fifty years two theories of child psychology have come into conflict. Our grandparents were firmly educated in a Darwinian, partly Calvinistic, world that held to an inflexible discipline in child rearing. This stoical training had the support of the ancient civilizations, and more than two thousand years of Western culture. In its early twentieth-century form, the disciplinarian viewpoint stressed infant and child conformity to various preordained habit systems, rigid feeding schedules, and the avoidance of coddling. Even caressing and kissing were held in restraint. During the 1920's came a shift to the more permissive, affectionate child-rearing procedures, which reached a climax in the 1940's. This change was examined by Wolfenstein in a study of bulletins on child rearing published in 1910 and later years by the Children's Bureau.[3] Increasingly, the editions reflected a philosophy toward more spontaneity and relaxation in training practices. Literature on child rearing through the 1930's stressed extensive expression of love and affection toward the infant. During the last decade or two the pendulum has been swinging back to a more conservative attitude.[4] These styles in child rearing are apparently the result of shifts in psychological theory, together with a social situation that varies with depression or prosperity, peace or war, etc.

THE FREUDIAN APPROACH

Inevitably any book on courtship and marriage involves some aspects of psychoanalytical theory. The questions, why we love, whom we marry, or the development of our basic personality needs are included in one Freudian, or what has come to be known as the neo-Freudian, viewpoint. This theory, which originated with Sigmund Freud before the turn of the century, has enormous implications for the nature of emotions and relationships between the sexes. Probably

[3] Martha Wolfenstein, "The Emergence of Fun Morality," *Journal of Social Issues,* 1951, **7,** 15–25.

[4] Benjamin W. Spock, *Baby and Child Care* (revised edition), Pocket Books, New York, 1957.

no single individual in modern history has affected our outlook on human behavior, on psychological conflict, and on the significance of infancy and childhood in personality formation as much as Freud. It is too soon for a final evaluation of his theory; however, its significance and influence have been far-reaching.

THE BASIC DOCTRINE. Basic in the Freudian structure is the division of the self, or personality, into three fundamental areas: *id, ego,* and *superego.* The id is the vast unconscious, animalistic, primitive substructure of the self and is motivated by the powerful driving force, *libido.* Freud considers the ego as the conscious, perceiving, organizing aspect of the personality. The ego generally refers to what is commonly known as the *self.* The superego emerges as a consequent of various forceful agencies of social control. The dynamic, ruthless control of libidinal desires by society is best demonstrated by toilet training during infancy. Unconsciously, and sometimes consciously, the superego is in constant warfare with the id, and the ego has amongst its tasks the maintenance of an equilibrium between these two contradictory forces. So firm is the control by the superego in most individuals that only the upper reaches of the id appear in conscious thought and behavior. Through dreams sleep permits a momentary escape for repressed material originating within the id, but even this kind of expression is very limited because the *censor* operates to prevent much freedom. The censor is a mechanism of the superego to protect consciousness from the deeper recesses of the id.

In attempting to understand the development of personality in the early years, Freud theorized that there are three stages: the oral, anal, and phallic. These are based on *erogenous zones,* the more critical areas of the body in which physical pleasure is experienced and which are directly or indirectly sexual in nature. According to Freud these stages (as well as most psychological development) are instinctual. This point has led to considerable controversy. For the first year the infant is *oral* in his needs and gratification; sucking is the primary expression at this time. This period, like successive stages, is never completely outgrown and lingers on in the unconscious. The *anal* stage, also localized in an erogenous zone, emerges when bladder and bowel training commence. The third stage, the *phallic,* or *genital,* is more directly sexual. The infant or young child, now in his fourth and fifth year, becomes aware of his genitalia. Even before this stage, some libidinal drive is apparent in his responsiveness to sexual stimulation.

For instance, erection among male infants is not uncommon in the first years of life. Another development during this phallic stage is the *Oedipus complex,* the unconscious desire of the son to destroy the father in order to capture the mother's love. (A similar mechanism, the *Electra complex,* occurs with the daughter who forms an intense attachment to the father.) Later this attachment weakens as the boy accepts the *reality principle,* a kind of expedience rule, as opposed to the *pleasure principle,* the tendency toward gratification of his diffuse sex urge. He begins to identify more with the father and to accept his traditional sex role. During this phallic phase other problems arise to complicate the child's adjustment. The boy develops an unconscious *castration complex,* the fear that he will be robbed of his masculinity. The girl suffers from *penis envy,* the beginning of her protest against male preeminence. Guilt and anxiety have now become motivating forces in the unconscious life of the individual.

Following this series of stages in infancy and early childhood, a *latency* period begins at about the age of six. The phallic stage has consequently given way to an undifferentiated phase during which the libido is relatively quiescent. Gradually, this stage becomes homosexual in character, largely at the unconscious level, although overt relations are not infrequent in childhood. Finally at puberty, heterosexuality emerges as the end result of sexual development. There may, nevertheless, be a *fixation* at any one of these general levels: the autoerotic (which includes both the oral and anal), the Oedipal, and the homosexual. There are also more serious maladjustments that may occur. For instance, marriage may be impossible for the individual who is psychologically wed to his mother. This person has never quite made a satisfactory transition to higher stages of development. Or there may be a *regression,* a moving back, from one level to a lower one. Failure in marriage may be followed by a return to autoerotic practices or experimentation with homosexuality. Freudians maintain that these stages remain with us at the unconscious level throughout most of our lifetime.

EVALUATION.   It seems fair to attempt some assessment even of this fragmentary account of Freud's theory. First, we must recognize the immense value it has been to psychiatrists, clinical psychologists, and marital counselors in understanding both neurotic and normal behavior. Moreover, Freud pioneered a territory at a period when society was frightened by any mention of behavior that went beyond the delicacy and idealism of Lord Tennyson. Freud offered a remarkable approach for the psychological and social sciences, and a conceptual tool for literature and the arts.

On the negative side, from a scientific viewpoint Freud was unnecessarily dogmatic in insisting on a unicausal theory, namely, that genital or sexual causes were for all practical purposes the only ones responsible for personality dynamics. It was partly his own training as a medical practitioner, in addition to the Darwinian flavor of his era, that led him into his narrow biological determinism. His particular brand of instinctivism, as exemplified in the inevitability of given stages of development, seems dated in view of the development of psychology and sociology of the last generation.

Further criticism of Freud's doctrine has been directed to the rigidity of his system of cause and effect. In it there can be no chance event. All thoughts, dreams, slips of the tongue, losses of personal objects, tripping in the street, are in some way associated with the libido. For example, the loss of a wedding ring can only mean that the person wishes himself unmarried. For dreams there is an elaborate symbolism, which for most scientists still lies on the margin of the scientific. The rigidity of Freud's pattern of analogies or models is illustrated in his statement that all girls desire to obtain male genitalia, or that the origin of competitive behavior among males, as one classical Freudian put it, was derived from competition among young boys in urinating.

Disturbing in the Freudian viewpoint is the difficulty in testing his hypotheses cross-culturally. Freud's experiences were limited to his upper-middle class Viennese patients. This was not a random sample of the population, and represented clinical cases derived from referrals. In addition, his sample reflected a national and class culture. More important, some of his theories, such as infantile sexuality, were considered valid before testing, but when tested they have not been supported. One example of this situation is Freud's theory that the oral, anal, and phallic stages remain with us into adulthood was not supported by a lengthy questionnaire study in a college sample.[5] As we shall see later in this chapter, Sewell's study of a sample of Midwestern children comparing infantile reactions with later personality

[5] Charles A. Barnes, "A Statistical Study of the Freudian Theory of Levels of Psychological Development," *Genetic Psychological Monographs*, 1952, 45, 105–174.

patterns discovered no evidence supporting the Freudian theory of sexual development.[6] This is not to say that the empirical research developed has disproved the Freudian thesis, but support has been in terms of individual case histories rather than large-scale data. Perhaps the theory has been most useful as a springboard from which the revisionists have related the concepts to individuals operating at different age levels in a variety of social situations.

THE SOCIAL INTERACTIONIST AND THE NEO-FREUDIAN REVISION. Concurrently with the emergence of Freudian theory arose another viewpoint of child development and the acquisition of personality. Two sociologists, Charles Horton Cooley [7] and George Herbert Mead,[8] more than any others, pointed to social factors in the emergence of personality. The individual is inevitably part of a group and assumes personality and a self through a dynamic interrelationship with others; in other words, it is the reciprocal relations of give-and-take that humanize the individual. The *primary group* is especially critical in the acquisition of personality and the self: the relations of the child with his parents, siblings, and later with the peer group— his playmates in the neighborhood and school. The children in the sandbox building castles, the family sharing gifts from the Christmas tree, the third-grade class working together on a multiplication problem, are all part of this group experience by which personality is acquired. *Role playing,* too, is a major process in the socialization of the child. The boy playing locomotive engineer or the eight-year old girl who pretends she is an adult by wearing mother's high heels are both part of the identification process by which we become adults. *Identification* is another basic mechanism in the parent-child or the child-sibling relationship. It refers to the emotional involvement of one person with another, the tendency to take the role of another person, or "feeling-in" (empathy) with another. The close personal interaction within the family is an ideal setting for this process. The child acquires his motives and emotional behavior through interaction with others; by this process he identifies with their roles, values, and problems. This interactional theory portrays an ever-changing rela-

---

[6] William H. Sewell, "Infant Training and the Personality of the Child," *American Journal of Sociology,* 1952, **58,** 15–59.

[7] Charles H. Cooley, *Human Nature and the Social Order* (revised edition), Charles Scribners, New York, 1922.

[8] George H. Mead, *Mind, Self and Society,* The University of Chicago Press, 1934.

tionship between the parent and child, between the individual and his social environment.

In the Freudian camp itself, there was growing discontent with the classical formula among certain psychoanalysts, who have come to be known as neo-Freudians. They attempted to eradicate the narrow stress on organic and instinctual factors, and substituted an interactional viewpoint. Among these was Karen Horney, who sees socio-cultural influences shaping the child and adult, and conceives of libidinal attachments as more responsive to environmental stimuli than did Freud.[9] Another was Harry Stack Sullivan who like Freud posits a theory of stages, but one in which the child moves into progressively higher levels of social relations.[10] Sex is largely a learned response and appears only toward puberty, much of it sublimated. Even needs arising from biological origin are transformed into social motives, such as aggression, protection, and the like. Anxiety plays a role in the socialization process; acquiring maturity depends on the presence of authority figures whether parent, teacher, policeman, or captain of the football team.

Neither the Freudian (classically analytical approach) on one side nor the neo-Freudian (newer analytical thought) on the other have been throughly presented in this discussion, yet it is evident that both offer many insights into the dynamics of personality. The neo-Freudian and the interactionist approach have been particularly useful, since these hypotheses are framed in a manner which makes it possible to test the relationship between early behavior and adult personality.

Parsons has provided a theoretical system by which certain Freudian concepts can be helpful in understanding the socialization process.[11] According to him, oral dependency is extended into love dependency. Identification is particularly rooted in the close relationship of mother and child. Consequently the mother's role may be considered an *expressive* one providing nurturance to the child. This expressive role essentially administers to the id or pleasure-seeking aspect of the self.

[9] Karen Horney, *The Neurotic Personality of Our Time,* W. W. Norton, New York, 1937.

[10] Harry S. Sullivan, *The Interpersonal Theory of Personality* in H. Perry and M. Gamal (eds.), W. W. Norton, New York, 1953.

[11] Talcott Parsons and Robert F. Bales, *Family, Socialization and Interaction Process,* The Free Press of Glencoe, A Division of Collier-Macmillan, New York, 1955, pp. 67–94.

In contrast, the role of the father is labeled as an *instrumental* one and is associated with the superego. Conformity needs are superimposed on the id so that we may become members of society. The identification process, which began with the mother, is extended to the father and eventually to the siblings. The ego plays the active role in adopting and integrating these needs, a self-centered nurturance and a more socially oriented conformity. With the internalization of various roles there emerges the "hall of mirrors" personality, largely built on the principle of the ego, in which the self intermingles with many other selves. The social self or ego thus began with the infant's dependency on the mother. Of course, in the long run the mother plays an even greater role than the father in the child's socialization including acquisition of conformity.

INFANCY: THE BASIC PATTERNS

It is in this background of rival theories of biological determinism and social interaction that infancy and its potential for adult behavior must be assessed. Is the infancy period a determining factor for later emotional adjustments? Are adolescent and adult patterns of affection and hostility determined by the regime of breast feeding, weaning, toilet training, amount of caressing, kind of play activity, and other types of experience?

MATERNAL VERSUS NONPERSONAL INFANT CARE. There has been controversy as to the degree of personal attention infants require during the first year. Reports from animal studies show that a basic need exists among a number of animals for direct physical contact, whether animal or human; they especially need maternal stimulation. One typical investigation studied rats that were petted for ten minutes a day for a three-week period during their weaning period. The results were positive for both physical growth and emotional stability; there were fewer fear responses observed than with the nonpetted group.[12] Even more conclusive results have been forthcoming with the studies of young monkeys and their urge for "contact comfort." [13] Animal research must always be applied to human beings with caution, but

[12] O. Weininger, W. J. McClelland, and R. K. Arima, "Gentling and Weight Gain in the Albino Rat," *Canadian Journal of Psychology*, 1954, **8**, 147–151.

[13] Harry F. Harlow, "The Nature of Love," *American Psychologist*, 1958, **13**, 673–685.

these studies do suggest that strong mothering is a basic need for the
infant.

Spitz presented one of the more dramatic studies of infant rearing in
her comparison of two institutions in Latin America.[14] A foundling
home and a nursery were matched for nutrition, medical care, and
certain other variables; but in one institution the infant and mother
were kept together, and in the other there was little or no personal
attention given to the infant. In comparing rates of development, illness, and mortality, it was found that no mother lost her infant in the
nursery; whereas in the foundling home, without maternal care, 37 per
cent of the infants died during the two-year observation period. Moreover, emotional adjustment and intellectual development lagged considerably for the infants in the foundling home. Ribble reached the
same conclusions in a study of some 600 infants in New York with a
follow-up in Berlin. She found that affectional deprivation had
enormous effects on nutrition, physical health, and aftereffects were
noted for years.[15]

Another study points to the psychological deprivation of children
of from fifteen to thirty months of age who were assigned to residential
institutions. The psychological stages exhibited by the infants included rejection of substitute parents, followed by a second stage of
withdrawal and inactivity, and third, a period of social detachment
and intense involvment with material things such as toys. If several
mother substitutes were removed successively the children appeared to
become permanently preoccupied with impersonal objects, and were
reluctant to commit themselves to personal relationships.[16] Bakwin, as
a result of a lengthy study with institutional infants, reached the
following conclusions:

Infants under six months of age who have been in an institution for some
time present a well-defined picture. The outstanding features are listlessness,
emaciation and pallor, relative immobility, quietness, unresponsiveness to
stimuli like a smile or a coo, indifferent appetite, failure to gain weight prop-

[14] René A. Spitz, "The Role of Ecological Factors in Emotional Development in
Infancy," *Child Development,* 1949, **20**, 145–155.

[15] Margaret Ribble, *The Rights of Infants,* Columbia University Press, New York,
1943.

[16] J. Bowlby, "Separation Anxiety," *International Journal of Psychoanalysis,* 1960,
41, 80–113, as reported by Edward Z. Dager, "Socialization and Personality Development in the Child," in Harold T. Christensen (ed.), *Handbook for Marriage and the
Family,* Rand McNally, Chicago, 1964, p. 770.

erly despite ingestion of diets which, in the home, are entirely adequate, frequent stools, poor sleep, an appearance of unhappiness, proneness to febrile
episodes, absence of sucking habits.[17]

Not all psychologists agree with these statements about the critical
effects of mothering. Orlansky, in reviewing the literature presented,
points to the casual observation, noncontrolled experimental design,
and lack of validation in clinical reports. He feels there is no direct
relationship between infant feeding, various training disciplines, and
later behaviors. In an examination of certain preliterate cultures he
finds, as an example, that Navaho infants may meet excellent standards in mother-child relationships but still demonstrate adult anxiety.[18] Much of the material that touches on this field appears to have
been written with the intention of proving Freud right or wrong.
While Ribble probably exaggerates the necessity of showering love on
the child, her general principle regarding the necessity of affectionate
warmth is correct. Emotional security has its origins in the first year of
life, although possibly at that age it is too soon to assess its exact
significance.

The collectively oriented *kibbutz* (cooperative society) of Israel
offers an interesting comparison. The infant is placed in a nursery
during the early months with the mother visiting for nursing as well as
for other socialization activities. The infant and child have intimate
physical and emotional contact with nurses and teachers quite as much
as with parents. In other words, warmth and affection may be transmitted by individuals other than parents.[19]

SOME SPECIFIC TRAINING PRACTICES. Until this point our remarks
about infancy and later traits have been fairly general. Let us examine
more specific events and behaviors in infancy to determine what significance they may have in later personality development. A number
of theorists claim the birth process is itself traumatic and affects the
personality of the individual. A few writers go further and assume that
there are significant psychological events during the prenatal period
which have predictable effects for adulthood; but (except for heredity
and a few provable congenital factors), this viewpoint is confined to the

[17] Harry Bakwin, "Emotional Deprivation in Infants," *Journal of Pediatrics,* 1949,
35, 512–521.

[18] Harold Orlansky, "Infant Care and Personality," *Psychological Bulletin,* 1949,
46, 1–49.

[19] Melford E. Spiro, *Children of the Kibbutz.* Harvard University Press, Cambridge, 1958.

pseudoscientific. We are concerned only with areas of interaction and discipline that are presumably related to later experience.

Nursing or breast feeding has been stressed by clinicians as giving the infant affection and security and as being a precaution against later anxiety.[20] One study found a positive relationship existing between early breast feeding and adjustment in late adolescence in a sample of college students.[21] The proponents of breast feeding also maintain that the nutritional value of the mother's milk is superior, since it is sterile and thus avoids exposing the infant to the microorganisms found in the animal product. It is safer to be fairly modest in claims for breast feeding. Breast feeding probably has most value for the mother in fulfilling a maternal need with marked individual variation. Symbolically, the mother's offer or refusal of the breast to the infant may be to him a kind of acceptance or rejection. However, there has been no scientific evidence to prove that actually the infant can distinguish between the breast and the bottle.

The weaning process also has led to considerable controversy. Clinicians hypothesize that weaning is orally frustrating to the infant and may give rise to anxiety. The evidence from studies in our own society shows that weaning leaves few residual psychological effects.

Toilet training is significant because of its implications for sexual development. It also concerns and is related to Western concepts of cleanliness. According to the psychoanalytical (or Freudian) interpretation, the middle-class parents' interest in this function may result in the child's compulsiveness, miserliness, self-consciousness, or introversion.[22] The anti-Freudian might point out that stress on bowel training could have just the opposite effects; compensatory behavior whereby the child might become a lackadaisical, spendthrift extrovert! Approaching the problem from a maturational instead of psychoanalytical viewpoint, the success of toilet training depends on the development of certain sphincter muscles. Overly eager parents are more likely to create negativistic attitudes than to speed up the process of acquiring acceptable bathroom habits. The more casual approach may have the advantage of allowing the infant a feeling of naturalness

[20] Ribble, *op. cit.*

[21] A. Maslow and I. Szilagyi-Kessler, "Security and Breastfeeding," *Journal of Abnormal and Social Psychology*, 1946, 41, 83–85.

[22] M. Huschka, "The Child's Response to Coercive Bowel Training," *Psychoanalytic Medicine*, 1942, 4, 301–308.

and objectivity. Although any psychological process is complex, it is possible that unhealthy attitudes about sex are in part a result of compulsive parents endowed with a puritanic zeal about toilet cleanliness.

From these various interpretations one conclusion may be drawn: there is no specificity in the pattern of behavioral practices and the affectional or emotional responses of the infant and child. On the other hand, there is evidence that warmth and security are necessary for the infant. The natural tendency of most mothers in Western culture (and in a number of preliterate societies) has been to provide a responsive environment. Aside from the mother's own inclination to care for her young, the culture itself generally rewards maternal protectiveness. During her own infancy and childhood, the daughter acquires these responses from observing her mother.

In interpreting the specific infant behaviors and their relation to personality, there is no explicit evidence to support a Freudian theory. In a study by Sewell, mentioned earlier in this chapter, 162 children of native-born American parents were compared in terms of infant training, which was revealed through interviews with the mothers. The results were correlated with personality tests and ratings of mothers and teachers. While no test is final concerning the relationship of infant experiences with later behavior, the design of the Sewell study is a strong recommendation for its significance. On the basis of the research he concludes:

1. The personality adjustments of the children who were breast fed do not differ from those of the children who were bottle fed.

2. The personality adjustments of the children who were fed on a self-demand nursing schedule do not differ significantly from those of the children who were fed on a regular schedule.

3. The personality adjustments and traits of the children who were weaned gradually do not differ significantly from those of the children who were weaned abruptly.

4. The personality adjustments and traits of the children whose introduction to bowel training was late do not differ significantly from those of the children whose induction was early.

5. The personality adjustments and traits of the children whose introduction to bladder training was late do not differ from those of the children whose induction was early.

6. The personality adjustments and traits of the children who were not punished for toilet training accidents do not differ significantly from those of the children who were punished.

7. The personality adjustments of the children who slept with their mothers during infancy do not differ significantly from those of the children who did not sleep with their mothers.

8. The personality adjustments and traits of the children whose infantile security index scores are favorable do not differ significantly from those of the children whose scores are unfavorable.

9. The personality adjustments and traits of the children whose toilet training factor scores are favorable do not differ significantly from those of the children whose scores are unfavorable.

10. The personality adjustments and traits of the children whose feeding-training factor scores are favorable do not differ significantly from those of the children whose scores are unfavorable.[23]

Less than 5 per cent of the total chi squares (a statistical test for significance) that were attempted proved to be significant. In other words, the attempt to find the Freudian formula in infancy failed. Again, the results should not be considered definitive, but the evidence simply has not supported the Freudian hypothesis.

Perhaps no empirical test can be devised for measuring the subtle effects of infant behavior or for testing Freudian concepts in general.[24] However, there would be universal agreement that the concept of *instinctual* stages must be abandoned completely. For example, the Oedipus complex has been rejected for a more variable concept, known by the neo-Freudians as the *Oedipal tendency* referring to the emotional bond between mother and son without the sense of inevitability implied by the original Freudian doctrine.

Many psychoanalysts have pointed out the significance of infancy; psychiatrists as well as research-oriented psychologists and other social scientists must now track down the questions and answers that can be studied systematically. From the evidence to date, we conclude that specific behavior patterns are probably not crucial in determining personality traits or heterosexual conduct, but the feeling of being loved as an infant has profound effects later in life.

CHILDHOOD: THE PERSONALITY TAKES FORM

During childhood the basic structure of the personality assumes shape. The child's relations to his parents and siblings dominate the

[23] William H. Sewell, *op. cit.* Reprinted by permission of the University of Chicago Press.
[24] George Simpson, "Empiricism and Psychoanalysis in the Sociology of the Family," *Marriage and Family Living,* 1957, **19**, 382–385.

early period of his adolescence. In this section we are concerned with the aspects of the child-parent relationship that have most importance to adjustment in later life. We are also interested in the process of sex identification, the degree to which the child assumes the personality characteristics associated with the male or female roles.

There is no sharp break between infancy and childhood. Child psychologists perceive stages, but they are arbitrary and vary a good deal among various children. The parent may be able to see no end to each phase, and perhaps has little recollection of the details of a past period. Some parents cling almost neurotically to a particular childhood stage; for example, the mother who cannot see her son in long pants. Conversely, some fathers, in perhaps a zealous form of identification, might demand that a son assume an adult role long before he is ready.

As with infancy, there are various philosophies of childhood. Parents are confronted with a variety of programs and panaceas on child rearing in the Sunday supplement and current professional literature. The intellectual confusion concerning how to be a parent is further compounded by the demands of urban living and commitments in the social and economic worlds. The mother and father of today find all too little time to devote to their children or home life in general. Parents struggle to be faithful and understanding to their children, and at the same time to compete for a constantly higher standard of living or the acquisition of a number of prestige symbols. The result is that parents frequently arrive at a somewhat feverish compromise between parenthood and their other obligations.

The child, too, is baffled by the diverse identifications, interests, and loyalties with which he is confronted. He is confused by his relations with his parents, who may have different emotional approaches or preconceived roles, and probably have varying attitudes about definitions of limits for the child. His siblings present still a different problem. There may be competition among the siblings for securing approval of the parents; this is known as *sibling rivalry*. However, the positive significance of siblings as agents of socialization outweigh any negative aspects of sibling rivalry.[25] We may ask whether the small family, rather than the large, is more adequately suited to the socialization needs of the child or whether social interaction is more satisfying in

[25] Donald P. Irish, "Sibling Interaction: A Neglected Aspect in Family Life Research," *Social Forces*, 1964, 42, 279–288.

one or the other. There is no satisfactory answer to this question, although a suggestion is found in a study of 256 Midwestern fifth-grade children in which the child with one or two siblings was in some respects better integrated than his peer in large families.[26] Siblings may act as effective models or teachers for each other. They may also reduce the egocentrism and sensitivity often identified with the only child.[27] However, considerably more research is needed in the area of sibling relationships, and their absence, to determine their precise contribution.

The *peer group,* such as that composed of neighborhood children or classmates, presents a whole new set of situations often accompanied by stresses. In addition, each teacher exercises some influence and alters in some way the intricate patterns of personality. By the time the youngster is in school the mass media are already impinging on his nervous system. The motion picture and television screen are major conditioning agents in the life of the child. By prepuberty the peer group has become more influential than the parents in the life of the youngster. Probably the mass media are more influential than the school in many instances. From all these influences emerge the emotional predispositions and value systems that someday will determine the kind of dating experiences and choice of mate the individual eventually makes. The structure of the marriage has its roots in childhood and is further formed in adolescence. Children are as varied as their communities and subcultures. The remote farm community, the Western mining town, the crowded urban slum, or spacious semirural suburb all produce a different set of experiences in childhood. There are also tremendous differences among lower-, middle-, and upper-class families. However, in this chapter we are concerned with questions of development that are found regardless of subculture. First, how does the child assume a meaning of the self and particularly in terms of sex roles, that is, masculinity and femininity? Second, what are some of the maladjustments that are likely to occur in the family setting? Third, and related to these, what kinds of affectional and emotional experiences influence his later heterosexual relations and the pattern of his marriage?

[26] Glenn R. Hawkes, Lee Burchinal, and Bruce Gardner, "Size of Family and Adjustment of Children," *Marriage and Family Living,* 1958, **20,** 65–68.

[27] James H. S. Bossard and Eleanor S. Boll, *The Sociology of Child Development,* (third edition), Harper and Row, New York, 1960, pp. 89–111.

SEX IDENTITY.   One important part of early socialization is the sex identification of the child. According to Freudian theory the father functions in an instrumental role. The male child eventually will be called on in adulthood to serve the economic needs of the family and to play the traditional role of household head. His role in Western culture includes the notions of aggressiveness and dominance; the girl tends slightly toward passivity and docility. However, in contrast to the traditional pattern of Western Europe, our family structure is more equilitarian and less father dominated.

As with other types of socialization, parents arrange the sex typing by rewarding and punishing behavior that respectively elicits or inhibits the acquisition of the proper sex role. Boys are encouraged in masculine activities and choice of toys; girls identify with motherly duties in the maternal care of their dolls. The child's identification with the parent influences his learning of the appropriate role. In a study of kindergarten boys no significant role identification was found in their relation to the mother; however, the boys who saw their father as more rewarding and nurturant formed stronger identification with them than the boys who were more neutral in their perception.[28] The child apparently identifies or *assimilates the role* of the individual with whom he has most interaction. The mother demonstrates an expressive role or "love-oriented techniques of control" to both children; whereas the father is expressive toward the daughter, but more demanding or instrumental in relation to his son. To provide adequate sex identity for his son, the father must in some way combine the expressive role with the instrumental or demanding one.[29] At the same time, the mother who usurps the instrumental or dominant role of the father may, as we shall learn, later encounter difficulties in her son's adjustment.

Generally our culture is more rewarding of the masculine rather than the feminine role. Research studies reflect this bias; first, males become proportionately more strongly identified during their development with the masculine role than females do with feminine roles.[30] Second, girls prefer and identify with the role of the opposite sex more

[28] Paul Mussen and Luther Distler, "Masculinity, Identfiication and Father-Son Relationships," *Journal of Abnormal and Social Psychology,* 1959, **59,** 350–356.

[29] Miriam M. Johnson, "Sex Role Learning in the Nuclear Family," *Child Development,* 1963, **34,** 319–333.

[30] David B. Lynn, "A Note on Sex Differences in the Development of Masculine and Feminine Identification," *Psychological Review,* 1959, **66,** 126–135.

than boys do. This difference may be explained in the clearer prerogative and power enjoyed by the male in our culture. His role is more
clearly structured: the father goes to work every morning, whereas the
mother may have many roles. It is a mistake, however, to oversimplify
the nature of sex identity since ethnic, religious, and class subcultures
impose their own differentiation.[31] The lower-class or "blue collar"
worker, for example, is likely to provide different images for sex roles
than the middle-class worker. Whatever the conditions of learning and
their final effects, the acquisition of sex roles, which begins in early
childhood and continues into adolescence, has marked impact on the
young person's interest and readiness for serious courtship and
marriage.

POSSIBLE MALADJUSTMENTS IN THE PARENT-CHILD RELATIONSHIP

PARENTAL REJECTION. A serious maladjustment may develop for
the child who has been, or thinks he has been, rejected. *Rejection* may
be defined as the withholding, in this case by the parent, of attention,
affection, or psychological and moral support from the child. It may or
may not be deliberate and, similarly, can be severe or mild. Perhaps
all parents reject their progeny to some degree, because, psychoanalyti-
cally, love and hate alternate with each other—at least at the unconscious level. Systematic and intense rejection has serious consequences
for the child. He may develop a hostile and apathetic attitude toward
the world in his social relations as well as confused feelings toward the
opposite sex. A child's starvation for affection may lead him to a
desperate search for friends resulting in immature or even unsavory
relationships. Like other unfortunate psychological environments, rejection may lead to the so-called "weak personality"—a lack of "ego
strength." Many individuals who are excessively dependent on others
are reacting to rejection. In the history of known rejected children are
such reactions as fingernail biting, enuresis (bedwetting), nutritional
problems, and a number of psychosomatic disorders.[32]

According to clinicians, some of the causes of rejection are subtle,

[31] Georgene H. Seward, "Sex Identity and the Social Order," *The Journal of
Nervous and Mental Disease*, 1964, **139**, 126–136.

[32] Hyman S. Lippman, *Treatment of the Child in Emotional Conflict*, McGraw-
Hill, New York, 1956. pp. 104–105.

indirect, and generally unconscious. One principal cause, of course, is simply that the parents do not really want the child. An unplanned first child may create resentment if the couple finds it difficult to accept this disruption in their adult routine. A third or fourth child may, in the parents' view, make the family too large. Some parents may reject a child because his sex is "wrong"; this is especially likely where there have been a number of children of similar sex. Children are very resourceful in detecting these subtle signs of rejection. In some cases the child may imagine the parents are rejecting him simply because of his misinterpretation of parental treatment. (The middle-class parent of today has considerable anxiety about the problem of rejection, and may make superhuman efforts to avoid this accusation.)

Another variation of rejection can be seen in the parents' preference for a particular child because he realizes their aspirations to a greater degree than his siblings. Often the child is expected to fulfill unaccomplished dreams of the parent, who cannot give up this unrealistic image he has created for the child. A parent may reject his child for a trait that in some way resembles an unattractive characteristic in the mate. Again, this thought may be entirely at the unconscious level. The woman who has become a "man hater" because of her experience in marriage may reject her son in subtle ways. Or one parent may be jealous of the love and attention that his mate gives to the child, and consequently may reject the child. It is not easy for many individuals to give and receive love in a mature, nonegocentric fashion.

OVERPROTECTION. At the other extreme of rejection is overprotection. The child is kept in overly close relationship with the parents. This situation may result from exaggerated attachment to the child, and is usually attributed to the behavior of the mother rather than the father. Again, the causes are inextricably complex. Overprotection may arise from exuberant affection with some inability to regard the child in a detached position. While the parent must be warm and accepting to a child, at the same time he must permit some independence in his behavior and emotional life. Some parents have a constant neurotic anxiety, an almost continuous fear reaction about the child's welfare. This type of parent constantly imagines dire tragedies that may befall the child. The only child or the handicapped child is more likely to be subject to this affectional intensity. In some instances the overprotective parent is unconsciously rejecting the child, while the conscious manifestation, out of some obscure guilt feelings, becomes overprotection. This situation involves a psychological compensation for an initially unwanted child. The mother who has an infant unexpectedly during or approaching the period of menopause may feel guilty for her initial rejection and show exaggerated concern for his welfare as he grows up. Marital problems may also enter into the process of overprotection: the parent who rejects or is rejected by the spouse may develop an excessively deep attachment to the child.

One aspect of overprotection is the tendency toward "Momism." This term, popularized by Philip Wylie,[33] refers to the excessive attachment between mother and child. The son is especially vulnerable as a result of the overly feminized world he inhabits and the craving the mother has for male companionship. It is related to the Oedipal tendency, but is more of a situational motive; the mother feels her own security is insured by looking after the welfare of her son. Often it is the result of her own egocentric or narcissistic needs and is most likely to occur when the father is a passive type.[34] "Smother-love," as this emotional tie has been labeled, is less frequent than it was a generation ago, because considerable attention has been directed to the problem in recent years by mental hygienists, child welfare agencies, and the popular literature.

The overprotected and indulged child cannot reach maturity without some painful readjustment. His life is dominated by the search for his own pleasure, which does not help him to prepare for marriage. Overprotection may be a more common threat to the child than rejection because of a number of factors: the cult of affection so characteristic of our age, the progressively smaller size of the family, and the hazards of modern urban life.

The rejected child may be in a better position to adjust than the overprotected one. Affectional and emotional starvation in many cases may drive the rejected child to form warm, personal relationships. However, the ability of the overprotected individual to enter successful courtship and marriage is blocked at times by his pursuit of self-gratification. Since he has never known mature person-to-person relationships, the emotional involvement of adult love is a difficult learning or adjustment process for him as he has only a limited capacity to identify with another person. Occasionally this type of individual be-

[33] Philip Wylie, *A Generation of Vipers*, Holt, Rinehart and Winston, New York, 1942.
[34] Lippman, *op. cit.*, p. 144.

comes fixated at a low level of romantic attachment such as in the case of homosexual tendencies. For these reasons affectionate protectiveness in the home is the ideal norm. The extreme of overprotection is probably as undesirable as its opposite, rejection.

PERMISSIVENESS AND OVERPERMISSIVENESS. The problem of independence is central to child rearing. Parents have to set limits to the conduct of the child. At what rate and to what extent can children be permitted to make decisions? How is the middle course to be followed between arbitrary discipline by the parents and free experimentation by the child and adolescent? Philosophies and trends have moved in both directions during the last half century. The extremes are both well known: the overdisciplined child who lacks spontaneity and security, and the individual who has never known the frustration of having been told "no." Possibly the second is a more frightening possibility than the overdisciplined child. Research studies of the socialization process are not altogether consistent but they indicate that more harm may be done by too firm a control than by permitting some degree of spontaneity in the child's behavior.[35]

Permissiveness is a relevant variable in sex education. The child who is allowed to discuss sexual and other biological processes in a natural setting is less likely to develop blocks and fears in this area. It is believed that a permissive attitude toward toilet functions, masturbation, and curiosity about sex diminishes the possibility of sex conflicts in adulthood. There are limits to this question of permissiveness, however, especially in the critical years of adolescent sex behavior. The definition of conduct must be arrived at in realization of the background and needs of both generations. A parent's code of ethics and conception of standards of conduct have to be transmitted to the child and adolescent. Decision making here depends on a number of factors. Certainly, the latitude of sexual attitudes and behavior for both parents and their offspring are broader than they were in the Victorian and post-Victorian periods.

INDECISION AND TENSION IN THE HOME. One characteristic of the well-adjusted home is parents who are reasonably consistent in temperament. Parents have responsibility for the emotional climate in the

[35] Daniel R. Miller and Guy E. Swanson, *Inner Conflict and Defense,* Holt, Rinehart and Winston, New York, 1960; Albert Bandura and Richard H. Walters, *Adolescent Aggression,* The Ronald Press, New York, 1959, and *Social Learning and Personality Development,* Holt, Rinehart and Winston, New York, 1963.

home. In other words, the child should feel consistently wanted, even though punitive action may be taken on occasion. Even more important than this stable emotional atmosphere, is for the child to be able to feel he lives in a predictable world. He must know when to expect his meals, when he may play with his friends, and what the sanctions are for certain infractions. He should feel that he is treated the same as his siblings. Thus, the democratically oriented home involves reciprocity of roles and ready identification with other members of the family. In the ideal home there is sharing of experiences among the members and ability to see age levels in an objective frame of reference. A recent study indicated, for example, that the authoritarian father was more of a threat to the child's adjustment than the overprotective mother.[36] Just as serious is the problem of the parent who can never reach a decision, who constantly vacillates in his conduct toward the child.

Where some homes are marked by indecision and fluidity, others are characterized by a constant pattern of tension. In some homes wrangling and vituperation are daily events. The fact that 51 per cent [37] of divorces involve children suggests that many children have known months or possibly years of tension in the home, and are then caught in the frustration and other problems following the divorce. However, one study of several hundred adolescents concluded that the children of divorced parents experienced fewer psychosomatic difficulties, fewer tendencies toward antisocial behavior, and often better relations with their parents than those with unbroken but tension-ridden homes.[38] Even among children who are caught in the tension of a divorce there is considerable variation in the effects this traumatic experience has on their personalities. According to one investigation, the degree of unhappiness suffered by children from broken homes was inversely related to the age of the child at the time of the divorce. For one child under eight, the divorce seemed to have a minimum of frustration. Another factor was the degree of interparental tension before the divorce. Less unhappiness was experienced when there was a remarriage and an adjustment made to the new parent. Most serious

[36] Donald R. Peterson, et al., "Child Behavior Problems and Parental Attitudes," *Child Development,* 1961, **32,** 151–162.

[37] William M. Kephart, *The Family, Society and the Individual,* Houghton Mifflin, Boston, 1961, p. 631.

[38] F. Ivan Nye, "Child Adjustment in Broken and in Unhappy Unbroken Homes," *Marriage and Family Living,* 1957, **19,** 356–361.

was the problem of losing contact with the father.[39] Undoubtedly, divorce produces much unhappiness in children, but clinicians maintain that the principal source of anxiety is emotional conflict in the family structure rather than in the event of divorce itself. More harm is probably done to children by the unbroken but constantly conflict-ridden marriage than by many marriages drifting toward dissolution or those already dissolved.

HOSTILITY AND AGGRESSION.   Hostility may be a form of rejection as in the case of the child who rejects his parents, his siblings, or possibly society in general; some hostility is present in all persons. However, it is the degree to which it is controlled or sublimated that determines our effectiveness in life. To what extent can our hostile feelings be directed along constructive or harmless channels, such as into sports and other forms of competition and interpersonal rivalry? The expression of hostility can have many forms; withdrawal and rejection are only two of these. In some cases the hostile person feels incompetent to compete with those about him. Of course, the actions of the withdrawn or seclusive person may be a result of many different causes, of which hostility would be only one. Other hostile types include the child who is suspicious, carries a grudge or gets a good "mad" spell for several days at a time. In this category is the disruptive, violent child and menacing adolescent.

Hostility is sometimes accompanied by aggression, which refers to overt (or covert) expression of hostility toward oneself, objects in the individual's world, and particularly to other individuals. A normal level of aggressiveness is desirable, and especially for boys is frequently highly prized—finding its sanctioned outlet in sports, the business world, and in the conquest of a mate. Lack of aggression is illustrated in the shy, retiring individual who is deficient in "ego-strength." Equally serious is the uncontrolled aggressiveness, which, like most personality disturbances, is generally traceable to childhood.

The basic cause of aggression is frustration according to the now classic approach of the Institute of Human Relations at Yale University.[40] While this theory has been subject to some controversy, it has been supported for the most part. One study among adolescents

[39] Judson T. Landis, "The Trauma of Children When Parents Divorce," *Marriage and Family Living*, 1960, 22, 7–13.

[40] J. Leonard W. Doob, Neal E. Miller, O. Hobart Mowrer, Robert R. Sears, and J. Dollard, *Frustration and Aggression*, Yale University Press, New Haven, 1939.

showed aggression to have been the result of frustration resulting either from rejection by the parents or from sufficient disturbance of the normal dependency relation between the child and his parents.[41] Undoubtedly, aggressiveness as a result of frustration depends on a number of factors: the consistency of parental discipline, the emotional security provided by the parents, relations with siblings, and a number of other situational factors—including type of school and neighborhood associates. Another large-scale investigation suggests that aggressive behavior directed against the parents should be held in check, and that permissiveness itself must have certain bounds.[42] However suppression of the child generally has more risk than allowing relatively free reign. The final answer is in the personality of each child.

Frustration depends in large measure on how the child perceives a situation. It is also possible for a child to develop unrealistic attitudes from insufficient exposure to frustration. The term *frustration tolerance* describes the level of disappointment and thwarting an individual can support. Aggression in a child frequently is traceable to parents who have not prepared the child to accept the inevitability of conflict and frustration. Somehow mothers are more successful in handling frustration and aggression in girls than in boys, possibly because, as one source asserts, boys are less able to identify with the mother.[43]

Punishment is inevitably related to the question of frustration and aggression. The use of punishment, whether judged in such different settings as maze experiments with animals in the psychological laboratory or in the complexities of disciplines within the home, has been found to have certain problems in training. In the words of Sears and his associates, "It is ineffectual over the long term as a technique for eliminating the kind of behavior toward which it is directed." [44] Punishment must be explained to the child as being related to the infraction, and should, if possible, follow closely on the punishable act so as to be understood in relation to the act. The parents' philosophy on

[41] Albert Bandura and Richard H. Walters, *Adolescent Aggression,* The Ronald Press, New York, 1959, p. 32.

[42] Robert R. Sears, Eleanor E. Maccoby, and Harry Levin, *Patterns of Child Rearing,* Harper and Row, Evanston, 1957, pp. 267–269.

[43] Robert R. Sears, "Identification as a Form of Behavioral Development," in Dale Harris (ed.), *The Concepts of Development,* University of Minnesota Press, Minneapolis, 1958.

[44] Sears, Maccoby, and Levin, *op. cit.,* p. 484.

permissiveness is a critical factor in determining the use of punishment.

The long-term trend has been away from excessive punitiveness. One of its most serious disadvantages is that punishment inhibits the learning of a more adequate response, and may interfere in the identification process with the parents. This problem is especially serious as regards the young child, and even with an older one excessive punishment may lead to habit rigidity.[45] (Habit rigidity may be an adequate or inadequate response depending on the life situation: the assembly line worker or the man who wants to stay with his wife under any or all circumstances may find inflexibility worthwhile, whereas adjustability might be more appropriate for the man who finds his wife different from what he had expected before the marriage.) Extrapunitiveness on the part of the parents occasionally leads to complete passivity or, more often, hyperaggression on the part of the child. Hyperaggression may not always be undesirable, as illustrated by the prize fighter or the social reformer. Parents hope to direct the normal aggressive tendencies of children into constructive channels.

Today among the middle class there is a residual attitude which exhorts "good children" to refrain from activity that might appear undignified or improper. This attitude is a throwback to the post-Victorian period. Proper conduct implies essentially nonviolent and nonaggressive activity. The girls especially have been trained to preserve a "lady-like" appearance under all circumstances. Of course, in the lower class there has been more freedom to express overt feelings; street fights and direct, vigorous sexual conquests are not uncommon in lower class neighborhoods. Moreover, where the Western frontier condition has had some effects, aggressiveness has enjoyed more social approval. From the viewpoint of the psychologist, repression of legitimate and normal aggression is emotionally unrealistic. In other words, the frustration-aggression hypothesis may operate in reverse: the repressed aggression may lead to frustration. Self-respect can function adequately only when there is the freedom to express justifiable anger. The histories of patients with peptic ulcers, migraine headaches, and other psychosomatic disorders demonstrate the need for free emotional expression. Hostility and aggression must be permitted, but when their

[45] John P. Seward, "Learning Theory and Identification: II. "The Role of Punishment," *Journal of Genetic Psychology*, 1954, **84,** p. 204, as cited in John Aldous and Leone Kell, "A Partial Test of Some Theories of Identification," *Marriage and Family Living*, 1961, **23,** 15–19.

expression is excessive, the causes should be discovered and some means found for rechannelizing this pent-up energy.

CONCLUSIONS: AFFECTION, ANXIETY, AND THE EGO.   For the child, as for the adult, the question is, "To what degree has some relationship been worked out between hostility and affection?" These two deep-seated emotional patterns have to be incorporated into a reasonably stable ego structure. Too frequently, popular lectures and articles on mental hygiene take the position that there is a certain, almost stereotyped, formula for arriving at adjustment. On the contrary, everyone finds his individual adjustment within the delicate juncture of his heredity, early environment, and the complex set of experiences he has during a lifetime. Much behavior is forced on an individual by chance events. In fact, there is something arbitrary in all that happens to us: who our parents are, what the neighborhood is like, and who happens to be the third-grade teacher.

The child inevitably comes to know anxiety: disappointments, frustrations, the inability to understand the mysteries of sex, the failure to compete adequately with siblings or with the norms of society—in his peer group, the school class, and the larger world outside. A number of emotional conflicts are in store for the child. He may be torn between his mother and father because of underlying libidinal elements or simply by the clash of roles and loyalties of everyday living. As the child enters adolescence he comes to the realization that he cannot bring to completion all his dreams and ambitions. In other words, only with some degree of fear and anxiety is the individual in contact with reality.

According to Freud, the coherent or integrating structure throughout life, including childhood, is the ego. We maintain the integrity of the ego (self) by incorporating a variety of experiences into our consciousness and unconscious. Through this kaleidoscope of stimuli, together with all the identifications with other individuals, there emerges a self-conception. As Winch points out, we have an ideal or ideal self, an "ego-model," which is derived from our parents in addition to many other sources. This ego model is constantly undergoing change as the child increases the range of his identifications, his emotional reactions, attitudes, and values.[46] The child, to varying degrees,

[46] Robert F. Winch, *Mate Selection: A Study of Complementary Needs,* Harper and Row, New York, 1958, p. 80; also his *Identification and Its Familial Determinants,* Bobbs-Merrill, Indianapolis, 1962, pp. 1f.

lives in a dream world. The self is merged with the primary group of which he is so intimately a part. This is poignantly expressed by a young girl on the threshold of adolescence, in Carson McCullers' play, *Member of the Wedding*, frustrated from accompanying her "ego ideal," an older brother who is being married. She is speaking to a younger playmate:

Frankie.   I tell you I know I'm going. It's like I've known it all my life. To-morrow I will tell everybody.
John Henry.   Where?
Frankie (dreamily).   After the wedding I'm going with them to Winter Hill. I'm going with them after the wedding.
John Henry.   You serious?
Frankie.   Shush, just now I realized something. The trouble with me is that for a long time I have been just an "I" person. All other people can say "we." When Berenice says "we" she means her lodge and church and colored people. Soldiers can say "we" and mean the army. All people belong to a "we" except me.
John Henry.   What are we going to do?
Frankie.   Not to belong to a "we" makes you too lonesome. Until this afternoon I didn't have a "we," but now after seeing Janice and Jarvis I suddenly realized something.
John Henry.   What?
Frankie.   I know that the bride and my brother are the "we" of me. So I'm going with them, and joining with the wedding. This coming Sunday when my brother and the bride leave this town, I'm going with the two of them to Winter Hill. And after that to whatever place that they will ever go. (There is a pause.) I love the two of them so much and we belong to be together. I love the two of them so much because they are the *we* of me.[47]

ADOLESCENCE: THE SEARCH FOR IDENTITY

Adolescence is the threshold of adulthood or, at least, the transition period between childhood and adulthood. Generally, adolescence refers to the period that begins at the onset of puberty (about age twelve to thirteen) and ends at roughly age eighteen to twenty-one when physical changes are complete, and some degree of psychological independence and maturity has been reached. Puberty begins earlier for girls than for boys by a year and a half, more or less. The critical significance of adolescence results from the confrontation by the adult-to-be with some major problems; choice of vocation, preoccupation with sex, and the selection of a marital partner. The period of adolescence might be labeled as *anticipatory socialization*—the final preparation for the status and roles of adulthood. This "launching stage" will set the tone of the adolescent's career and marriage. A self-conscious type of adolescent socialization is especially characteristic of middle-class youth.

This period of the growth process has been identified with "storm and stress" in Western society. Somehow the physical changes combined with deep psychological problems have made adolescence a not altogether comfortable time. Throughout childhood there is a world of semireality in which daydreams are a normal part of existence. Gradually, adulthood emerges; the world of reality is forced on the maturing child by a set of physical, emotional, social, and intellectual events. This self-consciousness, so characteristic of our Western culture version of adolescence, became particularly romanticized in the literary and artistic movements of Europe and the United States during the nineteenth and twentieth centuries, and is comparatively absent in certain preliterate cultures. Even less advanced societies demonstrate marked variation from one culture to another. There is, for instance, a natural outlook in Samoa and certain Oceanic cultures as opposed to the Manus of New Guinea, where a kind of Puritanism toward sex has been reported.[48] In some of the preliterate societies, definitions of behavior are more specific than in ours, and situations more simple; the individual is not caught in the maze of conflicting models, and so experiences less role conflict. This is not to imply that the situation is necessarily less demanding for teenagers of other societies, but it is more clear-cut. The Hopi child and adolescent in Arizona grows more naturally from childhood to adulthood than does our teenager who is trying, in his repertory of roles, to find his way out of the demands of such pressures as school grades, access to the family car, and certification of his popularity rating. Primitive society offers more specific, ritualized signposts; for example, the puberty rites that formally prepare the adolescent for the adult functions that lie ahead.

Among the various problem areas of adolescence are a number of changes inferring potential crises. Growing up, of course, is more diffi-

---

[48] Margaret Mead, *Coming of Age in Samoa,* William Morrow, New York, 1928, and *New Lives for Old,* William Morrow, New York, 1956.

cult for some than for others. For the adolescent, even more than for the child, there are more conflicting loyalties, more complicated situations in which he must act. In any case, his first adjustment in adolescence is to the complex set of physical changes.

PHYSICAL CHANGES. The most visible aspect of early adolescence is the body change that takes place. First is the spurt of growth that predates adolescence. It appears in girls earlier than in boys, and there is a period in which the height of females exceeds that of males. The growth curves level off at about fifteen years for girls and about seventeen for boys.[49]

Puberty itself is the most dramatic change during adolescence. The changes are more complete for the girl with the menarche, initiating into her life the new phase of menstruation. The average age for the first menstruation is thirteen years, with cultural and subcultural variations. The first ejaculation appears for the average male at approximately fourteen years. Another criterion of the onset of puberty is the appearance of pubic hair which Kinsey reports occurs for males at 14.4 and for the females at 12.3 years of age. There are changes in the endocrine system in both sexes prior to and during puberty when the hormones (androgens for the males and estrogens for the females) increase at about age thirteen and twelve, respectively.[50] In addition to the direct sexual changes, secondary sex characteristics appear: the growth of pubic and axial hair, changes in body contour, and deepening of the voice—particularly in the male. These changes are likely to cause a mixture of emotions for the teenager, some self-consciousness, uneasiness, and even pride. He is troubled by the varying rates of growth, differing amounts of body hair, facial blemishes, occasionally falsetto voice, and other unfavorable comparisons he may make with members of the peer group. The boy may be concerned with a sense of losing something of himself in seminal emissions, or the girl may have been frightened by various meanings associated with menstruation. These physical adjustments are more difficult if the adolescent has not been prepared for them. In many homes these occurrences are considered improper topics for conversation, and are an inviolable

[49] Alfred C. Kinsey, et al., *Sexual Behavior in the Human Male*, W. B. Saunders, Philadelphia, 1948, p. 184; for the female, Kinsey, 1953, p. 131.

[50] Leonard Carmichael, *Manual of Child Psychology* (second edition), John Wiley, New York, 1954, presents a summary of the many physical changes in adolescence.

mystery. In some cases the school may help, but discussion of these topics is usually late in the educational process, if at all.

ADOLESCENCE AND SOCIETY. In our society the adolescent is caught in the dilemma of reaching physical maturity several years before he enjoys adult social status. The older generation retains the key positions and roles. In preliterate societies high status is assigned to the elderly (and to a greater extent than with our culture); yet adolescents attain marital and adult occupational roles at puberty. In some instances, participation in certain adult functions comes before puberty. On the other hand, in the more complex societies the adolescent remains in a subordinate position, frequently with a confused set of statuses and roles until he is more mature. To many observers it is incomprehensible that in the United States a citizen is not privileged to vote until twenty-one, but may be subject to military service at eighteen. Regarding the confused status of the adolescent in a Midwestern community, Hollingshead says:

> Elmtown's culture does not provide any community-wide procedures to help the adolescent define himself as an adolescent in the transition from child to adult. Of course, there are no rites or ceremonies, such as are found among many preliterate people, to signify the end of childhood and the beginning of adulthood. But what is more important, the culture has developed very few substitutes; so neither adults nor adolescents have group-wide conventions to guide them in their definitons of what to expect from either youth or adult. Moreover, the culture has few definitions either relative to the borders or divisions within the period called adolescence. Consequently, both age groups function in an ill-defined no-man's-land that lies between the protected dependency of childhood, where the parent is dominant, and the independent world of the adult, where the person is relatively free from parental controls. This no-man's-land is a place where the maturing person works out the extremely important developmental tasks of freeing himself from his family, making heterosexual adjustments, selecting a vocation, gaining an education, and—for a considerable percentage of young Elmtowners—establishing a home of his own.[51]

This circumscribed status is particularly true with regard to sex behavior. The average age at marriage in the United States is twenty-three for the male and twenty for the female, six or seven years after the onset of puberty for both. Marriage usually comes at a still later age for young people planning business and professional careers. Dur-

[51] August B. Hollingshead, *Elmtown's Youth: The Impact of Social Classes on Adolescents,* John Wiley, New York, 1949, pp. 148–149.

ing this inevitable gap between puberty and marriage there is confusion as to what course to follow: should the young person abide by the traditional norms of the parents or enjoy the experimentation of some of the members of the peer group? Neither course seems satisfactory.

It seems ironic that the adolescent finds himself with such undefined status, since this age level represents the highest energy level and in some respects the highest mental and physical capacity of a person's lifetime. For certain segments of the population intelligence scores are higher in adolescence than at later testings.[52] Kinsey reports that the highest number of sexual "outlets" for the middle class (largely in the form of nocturnal emissions or masturbation) occur at the ages of eighteen and nineteen.[53] This physical factor coupled with the social controls that the adolescent encounters, inevitably means a conflict situation.

THE FAMILY SETTING. The difficulty that develops between parents and adolescents is possibly physiological, since the rhythm of bodily movement in the adolescent lends itself to adaptability, youthful change, and exuberance. More important, though, are the psychological and social changes. The older generation is more security-conscious, less adaptable to new modes of behavior, and with increasing years is inclined to look backward rather than forward. Moreover, as Kingsley Davis points out, there is "little explicit institutionalization of the steps of parental authority." [54] There is no standardized procedure in our society by which phases of adolescence lead to adulthood. There are no defined limits of parental authority on one side or adolescent decision making on the other. Frequently, the parent and the adolescent become involved in a power struggle which becomes an end in itself.

To what degree does the relationship between the husband and wife affect the adjustment of the adolescent? In a study of the parents of 287 nonfarm high school boys in Wisconsin, Strauss found four psychological climates within marriage: husband dominant, wife dominant, equalitarian or autonomous, and interspousal conflict. Although the findings are seldom final in regard to a complex psychological study of this type, the results of the research pointed to better adjustment

[52] Clifford T. Morgan, *Introduction to Psychology*, McGraw-Hill, New York, 1956, pp. 394–395.

[53] Kinsey, *op. cit.*, pp. 219–221.

[54] Kingsley Davis, "The Sociology of Parent-Youth Conflict," *American Sociological Review*, 1940, 5, 523–534.

(using, among other indices, school grades, and anxiety level) of the adolescent in an equalitarian regime. The most difficult adjustment was associated with the mother in the dominant role or in a conflict situation.[55]

FAMILY STYLES. Parent-adolescent relations, like the psychological world of childhood as seen by the adult, have been interpreted according to different philosophies. There again exists the problem of deciding between the permissive, the rigid, and the middle-of-the-road attitudes. Some parents approach parenthood as a learning experience in which the child or adolescent is to be treated as a distinct personality, an approach much in contrast to the conception of the juvenile's having to adjust to rigid standards of conduct. In recent years the youth-oriented viewpoint has been bolstered by the writings of neo-Freudians and others. Yet the conflict between two ideologies is inevitable. For many parents, the problem of the adolescent invites a firm, determined attitude, threatened as they are by loss of control and the increasing independence of the teenager. The young person in our society is trapped between the differing rates of socialization of two generations, whose cultures in all probability are undergoing tremendous change. Parents find themselves distressed by fears of all sorts of dangers, from traffic hazards to sex stimulation, and any number of forces that attract the youngster away from the home. They find the adolescent drifting away from the home, and the control parents once held during childhood is no longer effective. Frequently parents feel any attitude other than a rigid one may lead to disaster.

Another point on which philosophies of discipline conflict is the need to strive toward achievement and status versus the consumption theme that Wolfenstein identified as "fun morality." [56] In a more exhaustive study of family styles in the Detroit area, Miller and Swanson discovered two "ideal types" (the *enterpreneurial* and the *bureaucratic*), or two norms by which other family regimes might be investigated.[57] Both of these orientations might be described as middle class, urban, and relatively successful in meeting the social expectations of the period. The entrepreneurial emphasized personal

[55] Murray A. Strauss, "Conjugal Power Structure and Adolescent Personality," *Marriage and Family Living*, 1962, **24**, 17–25.

[56] Martha Wolfenstein, "The Emergence of Fun Morality," *The Journal of Social Issues*, 1951. **7**, pp. 15–25.

[57] Daniel R. Miller and Guy E. Swanson, *The Changing American Parent*, John Wiley, New York, 1958.

achievement in terms of status expectations: the child must demonstrate advancement toward success goals, that is, acquisition of elimination control at an early age, taking swimming lessons when the boy next door does, having superior grades, going to the right college, and finding the proper professional pursuit. In this "individualistic, institutional, or entrepreneurial" family, self-control in the young person is interpreted as his having upward mobility as his goal. The adolescent's own desires must be subordinated to the needs of the family and its future.

In contrast to this "success-oriented" family, is the bureaucratic or companionship-oriented family in which accommodation is stressed. In this family, values are oriented to equalize sharing of roles, enjoyment of leisure-time activity, general exploration of "other directedness" and affection—the tendency to regard family values in terms of love and related themes. Inspiration for this viewpoint has come from the large-scale organization in which teamwork is emphasized and individual motives are deferred to the general good. The family then reflects this camaraderie, and the ideal becomes personal adjustment rather than success. On the whole, the bureaucratic, welfare-type of family seems to be supplanting the enterpreneurial type. However, they are both models that may be combined in the same home. The success theme may be idealized for the older sibling and a decade later the trend may shift to a more relaxed tempo. In some families, both become concurrent ideals: the image of success and at the same time, proper development of recreational activities in which personal striving and competition may be reduced.

THE ADOLESCENT DILEMMA. Implicitly or explicitly the adolescent finds himself in the following conflicts:

He is, particularly, caught in the dilemma of making proper choices for the sake of the family. He must not let the family down; yet his own preferences perhaps do not include the "right" girl, or his peers are not those his mother and father might choose—all of which is a fairly familiar theme in present-day fiction and screen entertainment.

The adolescent finds a confusion of standards that are to be maintained. He is caught in conflicting role behaviors; he must compete one moment and be accepting and affectionate another, both with his siblings and the out-group. Some of his precarious status is related to the fact that he belongs in this transitional period between the institutional family and the companionship-equalitarian type. A study of both rural and urban Louisiana high school students suggests that the urban group's expression of marriage and the family is winning out, but that traditionalism still exists. The majority of the boys still think of their adult roles as the breadwinners, and the girls think of themselves as homemakers.[58] Role definitions are blurred for all members of society, but at least the question of status is clearer for the adult. The teenager has the added disadvantage of being neither child nor adult, and both his present role norms and those projected for the future are confused.

Certainly the adolescent experiences anxiety in approaching his role in sex behavior. It is significant that authorities themselves do not agree on what the role of the parent or the adolescent ought to be.[59] For the adolescent, the choice between freedom and authority is frustrated in the supposed reality that "everyone is doing it," and, as the alternative, anticipating the penalties that society exacts for transgressions against the moral code. These difficult problems—the adolescent's attempts to find the right niche, of meeting both the demands of the peer group and his parents—are caught in vignettes in a short story by Herbert Gold:

I learned contempt for my cousins, the submissive ones, who worked so that they could spend dimes like grownups instead of nickels in the Chippewa Lake slot machines. No amount of labor could harden their gluey hands. Irwin had flat feet, a mustache at fourteen because his mother did not tell him to shave, the habit of standing too close when he talked, and, as luck would have it, a talent for projecting his bad breath with such accuracy that any customer's sales resistance must have died in the first whiff. Later he learned to brush his tongue, shave his armpits, sprinkle himself with Johnson's Baby Powder, and rinse his mouth with spearmint mouthwash. Anything for a client. He gave up his soul, a pulpy one at that, which resided in the crevices of his teeth.

Bernie, Narcissus Gaynesbargh the Go-getter, developed an artist's pure love for illness, hospitals, and operations. He saved up enough—"All by his lonesome," bragged Aunt Sarah—for an operation which joined his ears more cunningly to his head. "Clark Gable can let himself go, he's a big man already, but not my Bernie," his mother proudly recounted. "Today he looks a million —stand frontways Bernie! And how tall is your Daniel?"

"*They* will marry nice rich girls from New York City, you'll see," my mother

[58] Marie S. Dunn, "Marriage Role Expectations of Adolescents," *Marriage and Family Living*, 1960, 22, 99–104.

[59] Lester A. Kirkendall, O. Hobart Mowrer, and Thomas Poffenberger, "Sex Education of Adolescents: an Exchange," *Marriage and Family Living*, 1960, 22, 317–331.

threatened me. Later both took Marital Engineering courses, one at Miami University and the other at Cornell, and it paid, because Bernie married a nice rich shoe business from Hartford and Irwin married a wholesale Divan & Studio Couch, a steady thing.[60]

THE PARENT-ADOLESCENT RELATIONSHIP. In his relations with the teenager, the parent can be more realistic if he first attempts to identify with the adolescent. The adult, with a less active physiological makeup, is likely to forget the robust drives and emotions of adolescence. Second, parents must find some means of communication. Intimate talks with teenagers are sometimes difficult to introduce and carry through, but if there has been a solid psychological base in childhood, the generational chasm can be bridged. Discussion may center on a whole gamut of issues from homework to dating arrangements, from career choices to political ideology. The parent may have to be ingenious to win the adolescent's confidence in broaching some of these questions. Third, the parent must find some middle ground between permissiveness and strict discipline; no formula can be applied to all cases. A familiar example is time limits on dating, which must be decided with some consideration of the individual and the situation. The twelve o'clock deadline may be preferred by the parent, but two o'clock may be the reality for a number of reasons: it is Saturday night, there was a flat tire, there was a long wait at the drive-in, and the date was appealing. Fourth, perhaps the parent's difficulty in this process is to attain some degree of detachment despite an intense ego-involvement with the teenager. This is an even more difficult task for the parent during the offspring's adolescence than during childhood or infancy. Fifth, the parents must be expected—along with the community, the church, and the school—to solve some of the social problems of our times. Many adolescents are disturbed by the threat of nuclear warfare and international chaos that presents a constant picture of tension and anxiety.

INDEPENDENCE AND THE SELF. In Shakespeare's "Seven Ages of Man," the adolescent has his particular set of roles. In a sense, he is more isolated, since he is a member of a number of groups but yet not really part of any. As Kirkpatrick says, "He is marginal with respect to the child culture and the adult culture, and hence occupies a wavering

[60] Herbert Gold, "The Heart of the Artichoke," reprinted in *The Hudson Review Anthology*, Random House, Vintage Books, New York, 1961, pp. 124–125. Copyright © 1960 by Herbert Gold and used with the permission of the publishers, The Dial Press, Inc.

intermediate position. In another sense he is peripheral with respect to three cultures, namely, the private culture of his particular family, the culture of his companion group, and the community culture of adults." [61] The adolescent himself lives in a subculture related to the class structure, the economic order, and yet is not completely a part of any. We have already mentioned his ambiguity in the political and military sphere.

The adolescent is characterized by a distinctive life of his own. It is apparent that he can be moved emotionally and stimulated intellectually as perhaps is true in no other age period. His penchant for idealistic and utopian causes is great. Long ago it was pointed out that the most prevalent age for religious conversion is in early and mid-adolescence. But most important is the adolescent's peer group. This fact cuts across class lines, and is true for all adolescents. How these groups and experiences affect the thirteen- or eighteen-year-old depends on the class setting, other subcultures, and the youngster's resources.

The self-image of the adolescent becomes more individualized and structured than it was in childhood. He has his identifications: the hero of the athletic field, the senior class queen of the prom, the screen idol of last Friday night's movie. His self includes all that is his world: his car, his bowling score, or the latest hair style. The most persistent ego-involvements appear to be in the sexual area: adjustments to menstruation for the girl, to seminal emissions for the boy, to the intricacies of heterosexual love. Gradually, in mid- or late teens the difference between physical sex and romantic love usually begins to become strikingly apparent. With these deep emotional and sexual preoccupations, guilt and anxiety are sometimes inevitable, but this is a transitional phase, and a mature sex outlook is the goal of nearly all. Possibly a majority of today's generation is accomplishing this goal, with the educational and guidance program of present-day culture.

Adolescence is the most important period of socialization or resocialization after childhood. If the ingredients in personality structure are outlined in childhood, the detail and coloring are effected in adolescence. Adolescence is characterized by the beginnings of courtship. As Parsons puts it, "Adolescence, in this sense, is practically defined by the awakening of a different order of interest in persons of opposite sex, an interest which includes sensitivity to specifically sex-categorized

[61] Clifford Kirkpatrick, *The Family as Process and Institution* (second edition), The Ronald Press, New York, 1963, p. 268.

qualities, beauty and "charm" for example in girls, and an undercurrent, which may emerge into overtness at any time, of erotic attraction." [62]

Supplementary Readings

"American Adolescents in the Mid-Sixties," *Journal of Marriage and the Family,* 1965, **27**, 139–276. The articles range from sex education and teen-age marriages to volunteerism in the Peace Corps.

Bain, Read, "Producing Marriageable Personalities," in Howard Becker and Reuben Hill (eds.), *Family, Marriage, and Parenthood* (second edition), D. C. Heath, Boston, 1955. A discussion of personality factors in marriage.

Bee, Lawrence S., *Marriage and Family Relations,* Harper and Row, New York, 1959. An interesting introduction to personality and psychosexual development is found in Chapters 2–5.

Bell, Robert R., *Marriage and Family Interaction,* The Dorsey Press, Homewood, Illinois, 1963. Chapters 13 and 14 stress the interactionist approach to the childhood and adolescent "launching stage."

Bernert, Eleanor H., *America's Children,* John Wiley, 1958. Possibly the most complete sociological study of children in recent years.

Blos, Peter, *On Adolescence: A Psychoanalytical Interpretation,* The Free Press of Glencoe, A Division of Collier–Macmillan, New York, 1962. A well-documented study, with both case studies and examples from literature.

Bossard, James H. S. and Eleanor S. Boll, *The Sociology of Child Development* (third edition), Harper and Row, New York, 1960. Part Two is a presentation of the roles and interaction within the family.

Coleman, James C., *Personality Dynamics and Effective Behavior,* Scott Foresman, Chicago, 1960. Chapter 3 is a most adequate treatment of some of the problems of psychological development.

Coleman, James S., *The Adolescent Society,* The Free Press of Glencoe, A Division of Collier-Macmillan, New York, 1961. A study of the value climates and adolescent folkways of nine Midwestern high schools.

Dager, Edward Z., "Socialization and Personality Development in the Child," in Harold T. Christensen (ed.), *Handbook of Marriage and the Family,* Rand McNally, Chicago, 1964. This survey of the findings of many research studies on typical and atypical home environments has maximum relevancy to this chapter.

[62] Talcott Parsons and Robert F. Bales, *Family, Socialization, and Interaction Process,* The Free Press of Glencoe, A Division of the Collier-Macmillan Company, New York, 1955, p. 126.

Green, Arnold W., "The Middle-Class Child and Neurosis," *American Sociological Review*, February 1946, 11, 31–41. A now classic statement of children caught in the competitive social order.

Hollingshead, August B., *Elmtown's Youth*, John Wiley, New York, 1949. The study of adolescents and their dating in the class system of a Midwestern town.

Kirkendall, Lester A., et al., "Sex Education of Adolescents: An Exchange," *Marriage and Family Living*, November 1960, 22, 317–332. Some problems in the sex attitudes of adolescents.

Kirkpatrick, Clifford, *The Family as Process and Institution* (second edition), The Ronald Press, New York, 1963. Chapters 9–11 are a keenly analytical discussion of the problems of infancy, childhood, and adolescence.

Miller, Daniel R. and Guy E. Swanson, *The Changing American Parent*, John Wiley, New York, 1958. A study of norms of parent-child relationships in a Detroit sample.

Peterson, James A., *Education for Marriage* (second edition), Charles Scribner's Sons, New York, 1964. Chapters 4–6 state an intelligent, neo-Freudian viewpoint on the psychological problems of growing up.

Seidman, Jerome M. (ed.), *The Adolescent: A Book of Readings*, Holt, Rinehart and Winston, New York, 1953. Part Two, "Growth and Development," contains articles on physical, mental, and personality growth.

Whiting, Beatrice B. (ed.), *Six Cultures: Studies in Child Rearing*, John Wiley, New York, 1963. Part Six, "The New Englanders of Orchard Town, U.S.A.," is a careful study of socialization in our culture; the other parts deal with less advanced cultures.

Winch, Robert F., *The Modern Family* (revised edition), Holt, Rinehart and Winston, New York, 1963. Chapters 12–16 offer a sophisticated treatment of the psychodynamics of sexual development.

Chapter six

Differences in Sex Roles

Men have broad and large chests, and small narrow hips, and more understanding than women, who have but small and narrow chests, and broad hips, to the end they should remain at home, sit still, keep house, and bear and bring up children.

>   *Martin Luther,* Table-Talk, *DCCXXV, 1569.*

Tommy.   No, that's my point. All animals are the same, including the human being. We are male animals, too.

Michael (stares at him, bewildered).   You said—

Tommy.   Even the penguin. (His voice shows emotion as he thinks of the penguin.) He stands for no monkey business where his mate is concerned. Swans have been known to drown Scotties who threatened their nests.

Michael.   I don't think so.

Tommy.   There it is, in us always, though it may be asleep. The male animal. The mate. When you are married long enough, you become a mate— think of the sea lion for a minute.

Michael.   All right.

Tommy.   His mate is lying there in a corner of the cave on a bed of tender boughs or something. (Turns to Michael for confirmation.) Is that all right, "tender boughs?"

Michael.   Yeah!

Tommy (illustrating by gesture, a great seal, or eel).   Now, who comes swimming quietly in through the early morning mist, sleek and powerful, dancing and whirling and throwing kisses?

Michael.   Joe Ferguson.

Tommy.   And what do I do?

Michael.   You say, "Hello."

Tommy (in self-disgust).   The sea lion knows better. He snarls. He gores. He roars with his antlers. He knows that love is a thing you do something about. He knows it is a thing that words can kill. You do something. You don't just sit there. (Michael rises.) I don't mean you. (Michael sits.) A woman likes a man who does something. All the male animals fight for the female, from the land crab to the bird of paradise. They don't just sit and talk. They act. (He removes glasses and blinks owlishly around.) I hope I have made all this clear to you. Are there any questions?

Michael.   No, sir.

>   *James Thurber and Elliott Nugent,* The Male Animal, *Act II, Scene 2, Copyright 1940 by James Thurber and Elliott Nugent. Reprinted by permission of Random House, Inc.*

Throughout history, the more complex activities have been defined and re-defined, now as male, now as female, now as neither, sometimes as drawing equally on the gifts of both sexes, sometimes as drawing differentially on both sexes.

Margaret Mead, Male and Female *(Mentor Book), William Morrow and Company, New York, 1949, p. 277.*

. . . she would try to get herself between him and the punishment which, deserved or not, just or unjust, was impersonal, both the man and the boy accepting it as a natural and inescapable fact until she, getting in the way, must give it an odor, an attenuation, and aftertaste.

Because she had always been kind to him. The man, the hard, just, ruthless man, merely depended on him to act in a certain way and to receive the certain reward or punishment, just as he could depend on the man to react in a certain way to his own certain doings and misdoings. It was the woman who, with a woman's affinity and instinct for secrecy for casting a faint taint of evil about the most trivial and innocent actions. . . .

It was not the hard work which he hated, nor the punishment and injustice. He was used to that before he ever saw either of them. He expected no less, and so he was neither outraged nor surprised. It was the woman: that soft kindness which he believed himself doomed to be forever victim of and which he hated worse than he did the hard and ruthless justice of men. . . .

William Faulkner, Light in August, *Random House, Modern Library Edition, New York, 1932, pp. 146–147. Condensed from William Faulkner,* Light in August, *Copyright 1932 and renewed 1959 by William Faulkner. Reprinted by permission of Random House, Inc.*

Daughters of Edward D. Boit by J. S. Sargent
Courtesy of Museum of Fine Arts, Boston

Although roles in interpersonal behavior may arise from a number of sources, this chapter treats roles as they emerge from sex differences. We first discuss some of the physical differences between men and women. Following this we explore some of the differences in mental traits and personality to determine the degree to which they are attributable to biological, cultural, or psychological experiences. The relation of the two sexes may be clearer if we understand certain cross-cultural comparisons including the tradition of sex roles within Western societies. Finally, we analyze within our own society certain role conflicts that emerge from sex differences.

THE BIOLOGICAL HERITAGE

THE SEX RATIO AND LONGEVITY.   It is well known that women live longer than men. They are hardier even before birth. At conception the proportion of males to females is 120 males to 100 females. There is higher probability of miscarriages for the male fetus, and this ratio drops to approximately 105.5 males at birth. Roughly 25 per cent more males than females die during the first year of life. By adulthood the sexes balance each other; but from birth to old age the advantage lies with the female. For whites, the life expectancy of the male is 67.3, of the female, 73.6; for nonwhites it is 61.2 and 65.9, respectively. This differential longevity may be attributed to the varying rates in metabolism and other biochemical processes, to the varying resistance to disease, and to the different kinds of occupational hazards men and women encounter.

BODY SIZE AND STRENGTH.   Men are on the average 5 inches (or 9 per cent) taller, and 30 pounds (or 25 per cent) heavier than women. The male skeleton is more heavily constructed with larger muscles attached to the framework. Male body lines are straighter, more stockily built, and the legs are straighter. The woman has more curvature to her body, and has a wider and shallower pelvis that is adapted for child-bearing. Her legs are more "V-shaped." The rate of growth varies between the two sexes. The girl exhibits the most rapid rate of growth between ages ten and fifteen, and the boy between fourteen and eighteen years. Similarly, boys demonstrate more impressive muscular strength and skillful coordination. Of course, as with human traits in general, there are marked individual differences so that between the

sexes we encounter overlapping curves of normal distribution. Inevitably, this variation makes for feelings of both pride and awkwardness, superiority and inferiority, in both sexes.

REPRODUCTIVE AND SEXUAL FUNCTIONS. The most significant physical differences between man and woman are in their reproductive
capacities. Yet men are capable of generating reproductive cells at a
prodigiously higher rate than women. A man may produce some 100
million spermatozoa daily from the mid-teens until physical decline in
the mid-forties, and a man still may be fecund at seventy or, in a few
cases, at eighty. Women, on the other hand, ordinarily produce one
ovum every 27 or 28 days within the childbearing ages of fourteen to
forty-five, or in some instances a few years beyond. The beginning and
end of the fertile period, the onset of menstruation, and menopause
are all abrupt and dramatic in the female.

Menstruation itself poses a particular role behavior for the female.
The dominance and occupational preeminence of men in most cultures have been justified by the temporary disability of women for a
part of each month. In some primitive cultures she may be isolated
ritualistically from the group during her menstrual period. Western
society too, has fostered, at least until recently, a number of mythical
ideas. Various ills, obscure psychological tendencies along with certain
taboos, were ascribed to the menstrual process. In reality, research
indicates that little serious disturbance to the mental and social life
occurs during this four- to five-day period. Occupational skills, sports,
and most activities may be continued. Seward tested certain psychological reactions by means of electrical shock, and found no relation
between menstruation and depressive reactions. Neither the psycho-
galvanic response, a test for emotional tension, nor tests for breathing
and muscular tension produce significantly different reactions during
the menstrual period.[1] Research indicating genuine anxiety or
introvertive reactions during this hormonal process may result from a
cultural tradition. Perhaps the mother has warned her daughter that
this is a critical period, and that certain psychological conditions may
be expected. However, the girl who enters puberty with an objective
attitude is unlikely to experience feelings of weakness, depression, and
conflict in regard to menstruation.

SEXUAL NEEDS. The sexual needs of the two sexes differ to some

---

[1] Georgene H. Seward, "Psychological Effects of the Menstrual Cycle on Women
Workers," *Psychological Bulletin,* 1944, **41,** 90–102; see also Terese Benedek, *Psychosexual Functions in Women,* The Ronald Press, New York, 1952.

degree, although it is not easy to separate biological aspects from psychological and cultural factors in this function.[2] Men are more regular and predictable in their sexual needs than women, who are influenced more by indirect stimuli, are overtly attracted to sex earlier, and are more intense in their sexual interests. For the male, the number and variety of outlets exceeds the female's: a larger percentage of males over a greater number of years are systematically interested in sex relations, or at least report a higher number of sex "outlets." The orgasm experience also varies for the two sexes. In the male, it is expressed directly by ejaculation, compared with the more subtle, less visible, internal response in the woman.

The sexual threshold for the male is usually lower than for the female allowing him to be more easily aroused than the woman. The stronger male sex drive depends on many variables. Learning may be partially responsible. The male is usually the initiator of coitus, and plays the aggressive role in almost all societies. The success of the sexual act depends on the male's erection, which is necessary to effect coitus.

Part of the comparative hypersexuality of the male rests on the fact that his genitalia are external to the body; whereas the female sex organs are internal and more complex. Culture has, in fact, elaborated this biological scheme. Society particularly emphasizes modesty and protection for the female, whereas the male is generally encouraged in his quest for sexual adventure.

However, in reference to differences between the sexes, we must be cautious about attributing too much to the physical. For example, in sex relations both men and women have certain cerebral controls. The human male may voluntarily prolong his orgasm, a capacity unknown to the animal. The psychological influences on menstruation have already been mentioned. Finally, it is interesting to note that from both physiological and psychological viewpoints reproduction among men and women is not always "genetically" compatible.[3] The process of conception may be delayed by certain "hostile" factors within the genital area, which is explained in Chapter 16. Reproductive ability differs between the sexes because of physical and mental variables.

[2] Ira L. Reiss, *Premarital Sexual Standards in America,* The Free Press of Glencoe, A Division of Collier-Macmillan, New York, 1960, pp. 22–25.

[3] Jesse R. Pitts, "The Structural-Functional Approach," in Harold T. Christensen (ed.), *Handbook of Marriage and the Family,* Rand McNally, Chicago, 1964, pp. 57–59.

PSYCHOLOGICAL DIFFERENCES

It is a gross error to consider the differences between men and women as entirely physical. Certain psychological conditions exist that make for separate subcultures for men and women. Some caution should be considered in discussing sex differences. Statistical curves overlap; in all mental and physical differences, some women surpass some men. Some assumed differences have never existed or what differences there may have been are grossly distorted. More than one hundred years' struggle to achieve sex equality has been only partially successful in removing these prejudices.

MENTAL TRAITS. Without exception it has been found that men and women are equal in intelligence scores. However, in certain areas of intelligence women surpass men, and only 40 per cent of the boys reach or surpass the median of the girls' verbal scores.[4] Girls also learn to talk one or two months before boys, and apparently retain this advantage. Women are generally more accomplished in tests for perception, and are more sensitive to social relationships. Part of the superiority of women seems to disappear toward maturity. Men are noticeably superior to women in mechanical and mathematical operations. However, in all characteristics, the averages between the two sexes are not far apart.

PERSONALITY TRAITS. Men and women show differences in their interests and values. For example, in the Allport-Vernon test for values, the girls tend to concentrate on esthetic, religious, and social values; while men concentrate on economic, political, and theoretical values. The Strong Vocational Interest Blank finds men high in the mechanical, athletic, outdoor, and mercantile areas, while women are high in artistic and literary activities, with such occupational fields as clerical tasks, social work and teaching. Again, there is considerable overlapping of scores. Sex differences have been revealed in an eaves-dropping study of conversations in streetcars, campus walkways, theater lobbies, and other public places: men were oriented toward money, business, and sports; women, toward clothes, personalities, and social events.[5]

---

[4] Anne Anastasi and John P. Foley, Jr., *Differential Psychology* (revised edition), Macmillan, New York, 1949, p. 614.

[5] *Ibid.*, pp. 665–66.

The most farreaching study of sex differences is the Terman and Miles test for interests and attitudes.[6] Ratings were given according to the degree of masculinity and femininity associated with given activities. There was a clearly bimodal distribution with scores ranging from +220 to −219, the average being +52.6 for males and −70.7 for females. Occupational groups displayed various averages. For example, among the males, college athletes showed higher ratings than music students. Women M.D.'s and Ph.D.'s were less feminine than women music students. Male homosexuals had an average of −20, more feminine than women college athletes (−14), but more masculine than most women. Generally, with increased education there was more resemblance between the sexes. In any case, the only legitimate interpretation is that certain differences are cultural and not biological in origin.

THE ENVIRONMENTAL PROPS. Sex typing has become a fundamental part of the socialization process. Certain cultures even more than our own insist on rigid roles for the two sexes. In Japan there is a tradition of deference to the male with insistence on strong, aggressive trends with the role of the female a subservient and docile one. Other societies, too, have operated on the basis of a rigid demarcation of the divisions of mankind. The German Third Reich assigned authoritarian, almost sadistic norms to the male and self-depreciating, semimasochistic roles to the female.

Our own culture has been more lenient and less structured. Yet there are certain norms or expectancies for each sex, as explained in Chapter 5. When childhood begins, dress, games, and verbalization remind the youngster of his sex. During later childhood a determined effort is made to maintain specific behavior patterns identified with each sex. The parents are concerned if Johnny does not exhibit the proper aggressive tendencies or if he is playing with dolls beyond the fourth or fifth year, or if Kitty is too "tomboyish." The child increasingly selects his friends among his own sex group, and by the preadolescent period is militantly championing his or her own sex. Adolescence brings increasing espousal of the personality reactions of one's own sex, and erotic interest becomes distinctly heterosexual. At that time the youngster is obliged to make certain vocational choices within the kinds of occupational activity proper for each sex. There has, in fact, been a

[6] Lewis M. Terman and Catherine C. Miles, *Sex and Personality*, McGraw-Hill, New York, 1936.

long history of identification with various employment models, such as when Junior plays "engineer," or the playroom becomes a doll infirmary with Jane as nurse and Bobby as doctor.

This process of sex typing is largely cultural and psychological, as implied, with biology playing a negligible role. The indoctrination of sex roles is complicated, however, by the matriarchal character of our society. Mothers are the decisive agent in the child-rearing pattern. Although this maternal dominance has been counteracted in recent years, the child continues to be largely influenced by a female both at home and at school. In this feminized realm the boy often lacks satisfactory male ego-models, and may develop a passive reaction to the world or strive toward a compensatory reaction. Parsons refers to this reaction as "compulsive masculinity," a kind of overcompensation to escape the feminine environment and approval.[7] The hyperaggressive boy, who has a predilection for street gangs, and rough-and-tumble behavior both reflect such needs. He may also become disinterested in the classroom, because conformity in that setting constitutes meeting feminine approval. To varying degrees this overtly vigorous activity gives way to more conforming behavior as the boy moves into adolescence, because at this age he begins to be interested in approval by the opposite sex as opposed to his previous desire to escape it. The rewards of academic success as a means for preparing his vocational future also become a major part of his value system.

Much confusion may result from what might be considered the "wrong" models. Perhaps the boy has a preference for his mother over his father, or the girl may find her father's personality more congenial than her mother's. The boy may find some interests or abilities that are clearly identified as feminine more to his liking than those of his own sex. In a survey by *Fortune* only 3.3 per cent of males reported that they had once wished they were a girl; whereas 25.2 per cent of females had once expressed a desire to belong to the opposite sex.[8] Corroborative of this preference is a finding that the qualities judged to be masculine by both male and female college students are also those qualities they judge to be feminine.[9]

To some observers, Western culture has tended to differentiate sex

[7] Talcott Parsons, "Certain Primary Sources and Patterns of Aggression in the Social Pattern of the Western World," in Patrick Mullahy (ed.), *A Study of Interpersonal Relations*, Hermitage, New York, 1949, pp. 269–296.

[8] "The Women in America," *Fortune*, 1946, **34**, 5–14.

[9] John P. McKee and Alex C. Sheriffs, "Men's and Women's Beliefs, Ideals, and Self-Concepts, *American Journal of Sociology*, 1959, **64**, 356–363.

roles too rigidly, which imposes strain on the necessity to conform to an inflexible mold. Certain preliterate societies permit a more relaxed sex typing. Although there has been some improvement over the last half century in this respect, a strong emphasis remains on the separateness of the two sexes. Margaret Mead has some pertinent remarks on the subject of culture and sex roles:

> Externally at some given period of history and in some set of social arrangements it may often look as if one sex gained and the other lost, but such gains and losses must in the end be temporary. To the extent that women are denied the right to use their minds, their sons suffer as well as their daughters. An over-emphasis on the importance of virility will in the end make the lives of men as instrumental as an over-emphasis on their merely reproductive functions makes the lives of women. If our analysis is deep enough and our time-perspective long enough, if we hold in mind all the various possibilities that other cultures hint at or fully embody, it is possible to say that to the extent that either sex is disadvantaged, the whole culture is poorer, and the sex that, superficially, inherits the earth, inherits only a very partial legacy. The more whole the culture, the more whole each member, each man, each woman, each child will be. Each sex is shaped from birth by the presence and the behavior of both sexes, and each sex is dependent upon both. The myths that conjure up islands of women who live all alone without men always contain, and rightly, some flaw in the picture. A one-sex world would be an imperfect world, for it would be a world without a future. Only a denial of life itself makes it possible to deny the interdependence of the sexes.[10]

Of course, there is much individual variation in sex identification which depends on the outlook and definitions of the parents. Some parents have no clear direction in the formation of attitudes about adult roles and expected sex models. There may be a casual drifting of behavior in both sex and age norms in some homes; whereas definite standards of conduct and personality traits may characterize the parental regime in others. Undoubtedly, the more sophisticated parent of today is moving toward a permissive consensus on attitudes toward sex characteristics. With higher educational standards the question of what is masculine and feminine no longer has the significance it did a century ago.

THE ROLE OF CULTURE

SEX ROLES IN NON-WESTERN SOCIETIES. The meaning of male and female in our society becomes more significant if we look at the prob-

---

[10] Margaret Mead, *Male and Female,* William Morrow, New York, 1949, p. 368.

lem in some less advanced societies. As anthropologists have frequently pointed out, we are culture-bound. We see masculinity or femininity in a certain frame of reference that has been conditioned in Western society along the norms formed by the ancient civilizations, and further influenced by historical events of the last two thousand years. As we have discussed, there are biological, psychological and environmental factors influencing the sex roles. Overwhelming evidence indicates that the prevailing values of a society, the nature of the socialization process, and the institutional framework all fashion our outlook toward sex. Culture determines the definition of manhood and womanhood and the degree of flexibility in these sex roles. Sex roles, whether defined physically or culturally, represent a wide gamut of expected behaviors.

A comparison of three New Guinea tribes made by Margaret Mead reveals the degree to which culture can form sex and personality.[11] The Arapesh are a group of people in which both sexes are inclined to cooperation, docility, and passivity. There is no sharp distinction between the roles of the two sexes. On the other hand, their neighbors, the Mundugumors, are violent and competitive, and both sexes react aggressively in sex relations. However, most remarkable are the Tchambuli, who demonstrate specifically defined roles for men and women. The men are passive, almost coquettish, concerned with domestic and artistic pursuits. The women are more vigorous, and are concerned with the energetic and productive enterprises of the tribe; incidentally, these women assume the initiative in sex relations. Apparently because of contrasting social and marital roles, along with transvestism in certain ceremonials, homosexuality is not infrequent. Yet the Arapesh and Mundugumor show a lack of ambivalence and confusion in sex roles.

In regard to sex roles and the possibility of sexual inversion, less strain is found in a society with a minimun of contrast between the sexes. One of the reasons for a relatively high amount of homosexuality in our society is considered to be the tight adherence demanded by certain norms of sex identification. At the same time, there has been a serious confusion about the traits and roles attached to one sex. In reality, some 60 per cent of the known societies permit homosexual practices under certain conditions; although few of the world's socie-

[11] Margaret Mead, *Sex and Temperament in Three Primitive Societies,* William Morrow, New York, 1935.

ties deliberately encourage this pattern.[12] One institutionalized role is the *berdache* found among some of the Southwest Indian tribes of the United States. In this role the male may dress and assume some of the behaviors of the female. The status of the individual is in no way enhanced by this choice, but he is not necessarily relegated to low status. In some societies, a female who may feel more congenial to the heavier pursuits of the male occupation may enjoy the berdache in reverse. In both cases of the deviant male or female, the status may in certain societies be higher than that of the conventional female or male of the society; although this second situation occurs more rarely.

Groups from the South Pacific offer cultural variations of the sex role. The Samoan culture presents a gradual and easy initiation into sex relations. The parents encourage, within limits, adolescent experimentation. Sex is regarded as a pleasure, and consequently taboos are minimal. In contrast, the Manus, until recently, looked at sex as a necessary evil and a pursuit that should be grudgingly subordinated to the more significant goals of life, such as social and economic success. Marriages are arranged by the parents, and thus the "romantic" or erotic interest characteristic of Samoan adolescence is unknown. For the Manu, secrecy surrounds almost every aspect of sex. For instance, the male remains unaware of woman's menstruation beyond the fact that it does occur at puberty.

Still different is another Pacific culture, the Marquesans, who have a plurality of males. Situated in volcanic islands, this culture suffers not only from a low ratio of women to men (for which there is no reliable explanation) and a shortage of food supply, but from a relatively high anxiety level attributable to various factors, particularly competition in mate selection. Moreover, there is some marked interpersonal hostility, which is not surprising in view of their background of head-hunting. Sex is a more important value as hostility and aggression become curtailed, because of the close conditions under which Marquesans must live. Sex also seems to be a compensatory activity for eating. Sex becomes more strained in competition for wives combined with rivalry among the women for securing access to the most prestigeful households. In other words, cultivation of sexual activity is raised

---

[12] Clellan S. Ford and Frank A. Beach, *Patterns of Sexual Behavior*, Harper and Row, New York, 1951, p. 130.

to the dominant value of life as a result of the blocking of some other social motives.[13]

The cultures of some of these Pacific peoples emphasize the arbitrary quality of marriage roles in society. *Modal personality* (the personality that represents the norm or ideal for a given society) is the product of institutional factors that are shaped by history and geography. Yet, despite exceptions like the Tchambuli, sex differences have a suggestion of universality. The majority of cultures throughout the world reward the physical strength and aggressiveness of the male, and reduce the woman to a menial and passive role. Her occupations, however, may be quite varied. In most societies, she is the agriculturist, often performing fairly heavy duties. Menstruation and childbearing set limits to her vocational potential, and certain occupations—military, hunting, and fishing—are almost universally reserved for the male. Still, many marriage roles are infinitely colored by the culture. For instance, coital practices are as varied as the number of societies themselves, in addition to individual preferences.

SEX ROLES IN WESTERN SOCIETY

The equalitarian nature of contempory sex roles is remarkable when considered in historical perspective. Woman has undergone a long uphill struggle. In this section we briefly review her status and role in the Hebrew, Greek, and Roman worlds, then discuss the Christian influence, the Middle Ages, and the Renaissance. A new stream of thought during the period of the Reformation extending to Colonial America and the nineteenth-century frontier, concludes this historical portion. In attempting to explain the development of the institution of marriage, we must consider the total culture, which has contributed to its formation. No event can be detached from any other.

THE CLASSICAL MEDITERRANEAN. As we discussed in Chapter 2 regarding the institution of marriage, Western life begins with the Hebrews and Greeks. The Hebrew woman was held to a position of relatively low status in certain respects. She was confined mostly to the home, was forced to be veiled in public, could not enter commercial life, and could not inherit property. Marriage did not basically change her status; it simply conferred the power of the father over the daugh-

[13] Abram Kardiner, *The Individual and His Society*, Columbia University Press, New York, 1939, pp. 197–250.

ter to that of the husband over his wife. Part of this low status also is attributable to the system of polygyny which prevailed in early Hebrew history. However, the Hebrew woman did have limited divorce rights with which she might obtain in divorce roughly equivalent status to the male. In later Hebrew history her role improved somewhat as the prophets exhorted for a more just treatment of all human beings. Essentially, the Hebrew woman did not attain any perceptible degree of freedom, although she was undoubtedly valued for her homemaking and companionship.

Similarly, Greek culture conferred little status on the female. As we noted in Chapter 2, the Greeks had an entirely patriarchal viewpoint. Women were not educated in any worldly skills and were confined to the home. With marriage arranged by the parents, followed by the kind of social seclusion that Athens demanded of its women, relations between the spouses must have been anything but affectionate. While Greek marriage was monogamous, prostitution flourished. The widespread indulgence in homosexuality indicates that heterosexual love was very limited judging by what we consider love to be today. Any perspective on heterosexuality is limited by the culture, but from our viewpoint the Greeks seem immature in their fixation at the homosexual level. The low status of women was both cause and effect of this homosexual or bisexual interest.

Sparta was slightly more generous to its female citizens. Both sexes underwent rigorous training at an early age, and social relations were freer than in Athens. Furthermore, women could direct domestic activities with more freedom and initiative than they could in Athens. Plato was impressed by the status Sparta gave its women and in *The Republic* advocated complete sex equality. Yet Spartan culture scarcely provided an ideal social system, and homosexuality was practiced even more flagrantly than in Athens.

In Rome women fared a little better. In the Republic she remained in an inferior position, but in the Empire men were occupied with the conquest and administration of a vast area, and for practical reasons women were permitted some liberation. As we mentioned earlier (Chapter 2), loss of manpower as a result of the Punic Wars against Carthage was an important factor in making women independent. With the late Empire, bureaucracy (including slavery) grew to unprecedented proportions. A single household, for example, might include a thousand slaves. Consequently, the wife might be given considerable responsibility in the management of the household. By this time marriage had become a fairly weak institution; divorce was possible and other signs of instability were common. Goodsell compares the status of woman and the general decline of marriage and childbearing in Imperial Rome with equivalents in modern America:

> This matron of the Imperial period has far more in common with the emancipated American woman of the twentieth century than with her country woman of the early Roman Republic. . . . As the rights of Roman women were gradually extended after the Punic Wars, in an age when the wealth and culture of Rome were steadily increasing and the stern patriarchal ideas were dying out, so have the rights of American women been extended and their disabilities lessened, due to much the same causes.[14]

EARLY CHRISTIANITY AND THE MIDDLE AGES. Concurrently with the fall of Rome came the spread of Christianity, which offered a different perspective on relations between the sexes. Women themselves were considered a hazardous temptation, and were reduced in status even by Roman terms. However, they did enjoy some minor gains in that the rule of abstinence, in theory at least, applied to men as well as women. Also, the Christian interdict on divorce allowed the woman some protection, but in practice, essentially a double standard existed.

The Middle Ages offered women the choice of marriage or the nunnery. Religious retreat proved to be a refuge in some instances, especially for the more able who might become scholars or overseers of abbeys and thereby attain high status. For most of the female population during the thousand years between the decline of Rome and the Renaissance, life was a dreary prospect with marriage forced on the girl by her family, followed by a completely patriarchal family pattern.

There was one suggestion of escape. Romanticism in the form of chivalry arose during the twelfth century. The *minnesingers* of Germany and the troubadours of Southern France spread a cult of idealization of love and the glory of womankind. One aspect of the chivalry movement was the training of pages and *demoiselles* in specific roles whereby sons and daughters of knights were sent to the castles of the nobility. With the institutionalization of the chivalry movement, romanticism was an apotheosis of physical beauty and ecstatic love, directed, of course, toward someone other than one's

[14] Willystine Goodsell, *A History of Marriage and the Family* (revised edition), Macmillan, New York, 1934, pp. 154–155.

spouse! Chivalry led to slightly higher status of women, although this change had little effect on the population at large.

THE RENAISSANCE AND THE REFORMATION. By the late Middle Ages, women had attained some degree of prestige or independence through the increase of wealth and the dowry system. Moreover, the rise of Platonism in the Renaissance increased the status of women. To the girl of sixteen, married by parental arrangement, the thought of celestial love made the present more endurable. In its more advanced form the cult preached that love and marriage were reconcilable. Despite some enlightenment during the Renaissance, the double standard continued. Of course, as in all times, the wives of the upper classes enjoyed more privileges than the males of the lower strata, but among her peers in social class woman was the inferior.

The Reformation raised woman's position in certain respects. Marriage became a civil affair which indirectly offered certain protection to the wife. It attempted also to apply equal moral standards to both sexes.

COLONIAL AND NINETEENTH-CENTURY AMERICA. The Colonial period was imbued with Puritanism, and retained a harsh patriarchal outlook, but it is unwise to generalize for all the thirteen colonies. The woman in the South enjoyed somewhat more freedom than her sister in the North partially because of both the employment of slave labor and the less rigorous climate. However, in the colonies English common law considered woman as having neither economic nor civil rights and remaining substantially the property of her husband. On the positive side, the husband was responsible for the support of his wife, who had inheritance rights to his property. Most overt forms of maltreatment were illegal. It is reported that many marital relationships were affectionate and that despite hardships, they were not unlike some of our marriages of today. Certainly, the frontier existence enhanced the prestige of the wife in her ability to maintain a home under adverse circumstances.

The American and French revolutions anticipated a new definition of human rights. Possibly even more important, industrialism and urbanization during the nineteenth century produced a number of changes in the relationships between sexes. Growing humanitarianism in the cities called for a feminist movement and the first "Woman's Rights" Convention was held in Seneca Falls, New York, in 1843.

Beginning with the 1840's, feminism grew into a major social movement climaxed by certain political changes for woman in the twentieth century. Meanwhile, woman's status was only partially advanced by the industrial revolution in the economic "liberation" it offered. Although economic opportunities were a chance at independence, the question of whether her well being was really furthered in view of the long hours in monotonous factory conditions still remained. The result of this social, political, and economic movement was that woman attained near equality in the eighty years from Jacksonian democracy to the Nineteenth Amendment of 1920.

Our historical survey indicates that woman has fought an uphill battle for her position in a society which has cultivated freedom for only a century and a half. Certainly the status of either sex or the relationship between the sexes depends on the total social situation of any age. A severe disaster—economic, international, or otherwise— might cause a shift in the role of woman in any society. We may recall the startling change of the woman's role in the Soviet Union. From a highly subordinate status in the Czarist period, she has moved to a position of equality at practically all levels, including the right to employment in any occupational category. We may also consider the varying position of women in Germany from the pre-World War I Empire to her liberation in the Weimar Republic of the 1920's, her downgrading in the Third Reich, and her rising to new heights in postwar Germany. These events were not due to chance alone. The position of the postwar German woman reflects the loss of manpower during the war, her role in the economic world, loss of the male household head, and ideological changes. Possibly even more dramatic is Japan, where there has been a sharp upgrading of women since World War II.

PROBLEMS IN SEX ROLES TODAY

With few exceptions, the human being takes the other sex much for granted. Men find difficulty in fathoming the depths of the "woman's psychology." She cannot completely understand man's interests. Both sexes insist on some exclusive world, as evidenced by the fact that many men and women join lodges, bowling teams, luncheon clubs, etc. This separateness of the sex roles appears absolute and sacred.

Despite the overlapping scores on interest, attitude, and value tests, or the growing coalescence of male and female with higher education, there remains a separate subculture for each sex. The man may retreat into his world of politics, sports, and machines; the woman into the labyrinth of fashion, personalities, and social events. In this cultural indoctrination of interests and roles, a fairly rigid sex typing of occupations is acquired early in life and demonstrates the need for conformity. It was found that the responses of elementary school girls exhibited preferences for certain adult sex roles corresponding to what they considered the socially approved models rather than their personal preferences. They accepted as the norm the majority of adults' roles they perceived. Most of the subjects expressed a liking for the traditional types of occupations for men and women.[15]

We have stressed in this chapter the discrimination that women have experienced throughout history. They are restricted to certain occupations often with lower salaries and limited promotional opportunities. Woman's roles of childbearing and child rearing limit her potential for the business and professional worlds. For the male who is well entrenched in the power structure it is easy to rationalize that the woman is hardly worth the investment, whether for a Ph.D. candidacy or for the head supervisor of an office staff. She may, however, occasionally find herself in a favorable bargaining position. She has periodically used wartime to advance her cause by serving in an emergency function and retaining some of this upward mobility after the crisis has passed.

We cannot concentrate entirely on the negative side of feminine status and role. Statistically, women are less prone to suicide, alcoholic and drug addiction, psychotic disturbances, or, most emphatically, criminal behavior. A woman may stand up under stress better than the male, as reports of the London bombings during World War II indicate. Also, she has certain economic and legal advantages. She can expect financial support whether it is a Saturday night date or the entire expense of marriage. Most life insurance policies name the wife as beneficiary. She enjoys more leniency in treatment by the courts.

ROLE CONFLICTS. The eighty-year struggle from 1860 to the 1920's created compensatory activity by women to attain equality. The almost compulsive desire to imitate men exhibited by some women was probably inevitable. However, today many women find themselves

---

[15] Ruth E. Hartley and Armin Klein, "Sex-Role Concepts among Elementary School-Age Girls," *Marriage and Family Living*, 1959, 21, 59–64.

liberated, but with nowhere to go. They are still caught in the basic conflict of career versus marriage. One study indicated that the college girl prefers matrimony and maternity, but still looks forward to five or ten years of a career.[16] Besides this ambivalence about career and marriage, the modern young lady finds herself in an uncertain world fraught by international disaster. With the possibility of military service for the husband and the potentially tragic implications of that situation, it is not unwise for the wife to have a career to fall back on.

The male, too, is uncertain in his own sex role. There has been a shift in the past three generations from the male as supreme agent in the domestic scene to a kind of equalitarian role that modern marriage implies. This new definition of his role is found in the economic world as well. The man is competing with women in business and professional life; at home he often thinks of himself as a partner. Even his children may see him as a cross between an intermittent companion and a malevolent authority. For some men this situation of equality or near-equality is not so appealing as the dominant position their grandfathers knew. The frustrated male, for that reason, seems to be more subject to psychosomatic disorders; he has, for instance, well over half the peptic ulcers of today, whereas before 1900 this distinction belonged to women. For the majority of men and women, however, role adaptability can be learned even though it is not an easy task. The arrival of women to power in what was once a man's world has changed the image of both sexes toward each other. If there is hostility on both sides, it is of a different quality than existed a generation or two ago.[17]

SIGNIFICANCE FOR COURTSHIP AND MARRIAGE. The relations of young people have profited enormously from the equalization that has developed between the sexes in recent decades. Separate worlds may still exist for men and women, but there is a more frank and honest relationship between them. Increased harmony between the sexes has seen concurrent development of more self-respect for the individual. The most significant shift has probably been the weakening of the double standard. A recent study of 11 university campuses revealed that only 6 per cent of the sample could justify a man's indulgence in

[16] LaMar T. Empey, "Role Expectation of Young Women Regarding Marriage and a Career," *Marriage and Family Living*, 1958, **20**, 152–155.

[17] David Riesman, "Two Generations," *Daedalus*, 1964, **93**, 711–735.

premarital sex relations and still deny the same privilege to a woman.[18] No longer are women placed in two categories: the "pure and the "fallen." The popular image, at least in some subcultures, is something akin to the "good-bad" girl, which has been noted as a recurrent theme in films.[19]

The college girl today finds her role confused, since she is confronted with a number of possible models. A variety of culturally acceptable roles are available to her ranging from the clinging-vine type to the sport partner, from the sexual companion to the mother-sister substitute, from the languishing beauty to the fellow helper. In marriage she may combine all of these. A young woman is especially caught in the dilemma of knowing that even the man of the twentieth century expects her to be the subservient mate on more than one occasion, and that the conception that beauty is more important than brains may still persist. Komarovsky found this conflict quite frequently among college girls. On dates they had to cultivate a kind of role behavior that was often not their own preference. Examples of this behavior were seen in the enterprising girl assuming an apologetic or depreciating attitude about high grades or the girl portraying a helpless, dependent attitude toward the male.[20] Although these reactions may not be typical of all girls, they suggest at least that the problem of role conflict exists. Part of the question of masculinity and feminity and their definitions depends on the sample selected.

As we have already mentioned in Chapter 1, for many the basic problem is whether or not to marry. In our present society there is an internal debate for some young people of both sexes as to whether more advantage may be gained by remaining single, at least for a while. This is another example of conflict or indecision imposed by the freedom of choice in our society. Our great grandparents were permitted little selectivity. Their roles were more rigidly circumscribed. For us today each role offers a multiplicity of subrole behaviors prescribed by our sex membership, role as boyfriend, husband, or father; girlfriend, wife, or mother. Each role may involve a number of decision points about the pattern of behavior expected in our family relation-

[18] Rose K. Goldsen, Morris Rosenberg, Robin M. Williams, Jr., and Edward A. Suchman, *What College Students Think,* Van Nostrand, New York, 1960, p. 95.

[19] Martha Wolfenstein and Nathan Leites, *Movies: A Psychological Study,* The Free Press of Glencoe, A Division of Collier-Macmillan, New York, 1950.

[20] Mirra Komarovsky, "Cultural Contradictions and Sex Roles," *American Journal of Sociology,* 1946, 52, 184–189.

ships, study, work, church, and any other social responsibilties we have.

It is in marriage itself that sex roles become the most complex. We can see that in this relationship male and female subcultures have to be intricately interwoven. The husband must understand the deep affectionate needs of the wife. The wife must accept her husband's desire for male companionship, despite whatever differences in sexual needs may exist. Sex differences are further complicated by the fact that both partners bring to their marriage a subculture that has been conditioned by family members, in addition to an accretion of role expectations acquired from peer groups, books, and religion. It has been demonstrated that if the mother has been nurturant, indulging, and permissive, her son may find his marriage somewhat traumatic if his resourceful and autonomous wife insists on making the decisions. On this general problem a recent study on the dynamics of marital interaction concludes:

For example, husbands and wives approach a given situation from different role perspectives, i.e., their roles represent a sexual division of labor. Ideally, these sex roles are interlocking to the point where interaction process within marriage and the family can operate smoothly. However, due to several cultural factors, conflicts of interest can easily replace role reciprocity. For example, a marital conflict in a culture like our own may result from, among other things, social change, where the transition from largely ascribed to achieved roles makes sex prerogatives in various situations less clear. Accompanying this, subcultural differences between males and females may produce incompatible value orientations between the spouses. Also, it must be remembered that husbands and wives are the representatives of two separate kinship organizations whose background and orientation may not always coincide. This list of sources of conflict is not offered as exhaustive, but is suggestive of major origins.[21]

We may conclude that the recognition of differences between man and woman, the ability to vary roles, the capacity to treat courtship and marriage as a learning experience will be of enormous advantage in marriage. Learning to be an adult means being able to adjust to new situations and new roles. The development of mature heterosexual love is partially an experiment in living.

[21] Jack V. Buerkle, Theodore R. Anderson, and Robin F. Badgley, "Altruism, Role Conflict, and Marital Adjustment: A Factor Analysis of Marital Interaction," *Marriage and Family Living*, 1961, **23**, p. 25.

Supplementary Readings

Bowman, Henry A., *Marriage for Moderns* (fifth edition), McGraw-Hill, New York, 1965. Chapter 1 presents the physical and mental differences between men and women.

Christensen, Harold T., *Marriage Analysis* (second edition), The Ronald Press, New York, 1958. Chapter 7 analyzes the traits and attitudes that separate the two sexes.

"Images of Women in Society," *International Social Science Journal*, 1962, 14, no. 1, pp. 7–174. Several cross-cultural presentations of modern woman.

Kirkpatrick, Clifford, *The Family as Process and Institution* (second edition), The Ronald Press, New York, 1963. Chapter 7 is a brilliant study of the role of women in our society. See also Chapter 17 on marriage versus career.

Komarovsky, Mirra, *Women in the Modern World: Their Education and Their Dilemmas*, Little, Brown, Boston, 1953. A distinguished work on the role conflicts of the college educated woman.

LeMasters, E. E., *Modern Courtship and Marriage*, Macmillan, New York, 1957. Chapters 22 and 23 are an insightful discussion of sex differences.

Mead, Margaret, *Male and Female*, William Morrow, New York, 1949. If occasionally overspeculative, Mead writes well of an anthropological and psychological approach to sex differences.

Montagu, Ashley, *The Natural Superiority of Women*, Macmillan, New York, 1956. A very readable if not too well documented account of the "superior sex."

Scheinfeld, Amram, *Women and Men*, Harcourt, Brace, New York, 1943. A readable comparison of sex differences.

Seward, Georgene H., *Sex and the Social Order*, McGraw-Hill, New York, 1946. Chapters 9, 10, and 15 are a well-documented study of psychological and cultural differences.

"The Woman in America," *Daedalus*, 1964, 93, 577–803. Nine outstanding articles on woman in the contemporary world.

Chapter seven
Dating Patterns

I discovered that nobody wanted me to go with Molly Bingaman. My friends
. . . never talked to me about Molly, and when I brought her to their parties
gave the impression of ignoring her, so that I stopped taking her. Teachers
at school would smile an odd tight smile when they saw us leaning by her
locker or hanging around in the stairways. . . .

Molly's parents disapproved because in their eyes my family was virtually
white trash. It was so persistently hammered into me that I was too good for
Molly that I scarcely considered the proposition that, by another scale, she
was too good for me. . . .

While Molly protected me from the Bingaman side of the ugliness, I con-
veyed the Dow side more or less directly to her. It infuriated me that nobody
allowed me to be proud of her. I kept, in effect, asking her, Why was she stupid
in English? Why didn't she get along with my friends? Why did she look so
dumpy and smug?—this last despite the fact that she often, especially in intimate moments, looked beautiful to me. I was especially angry with her
because this affair had brought out an ignoble, hysterical, brutal aspect of my
mother that I might never have had to see otherwise. I had hoped to keep
things secret from her, but even if her intuition had not been relentless, my
father, at school, knew everything. Sometimes, indeed, my mother said that
she didn't care if I went with Molly; it was my father who was upset. Like a
frantic dog tied by one leg, she snapped in any direction, mouthing ridiculous
fancies—such as that Mrs. Bingaman had sicked Molly on me just to keep me
from going to college and giving the Dows something to be proud of—that
would make us both suddenly start laughing. . . . In her desperate state she
would say unforgivable things to me even while the tears streamed down her
face. I've never seen so many tears as I saw that winter.

Every time I saw my mother cry, it seemed I had to make Molly cry. I developed a skill at it; it came naturally to an only child who had been surrounded all his life by adults ransacking each other for the truth. Even in the
heart of intimacy, half-naked each of us, I would say something to humiliate
her. We never made love in the final, coital sense. My reason was a mixture
of idealism and superstition; I felt that if I took her virginity she would be
mine forever. I depended overmuch on a technicality; she gave herself to me
anyway, and I had her anyway, and have her still, for the longer I travel in
a direction I could not have taken with her, the more clearly she seems the
one person who loved me without advantage. I was a homely, comically ambitious hillbilly, and I even refused to tell her I loved her, to pronounce the

word "love"—an icy piece of pedantry that shocks me now that I have almost forgotten the context of confusion in which it seemed wise.

John Updike, "Flight," in Pigeon Feathers and Other Stories, *Alfred A. Knopf, New York, 1962 (Crest Paperback Edition, 1963, pp. 52–54).*

Now he would have liked a girl if she had come to him and not wanted to talk. But here at home it was all too complicated. He knew he could never get through it all again. It was not worth the trouble. That was the thing about French girls and German girls. There was not all this talking. You couldn't talk much and you did not need to talk. It was simple and you were friends. . . . He did not want to leave Germany. He did not want to come home. Still, he had come home. He sat on the front porch.

Ernest Hemingway, "Soldier's Home," from In Our Time, Charles Scribner's Sons, New York, 1958, pp. 92–94. Copyright 1925, Charles Scribner's Sons, renewal copyright 1953, Ernest Hemingway.*

Croquet Scene by Winslow Homer
Courtesy of The Art Institute of Chicago; Friends of American Art Collection

D ating has become one of the most fascinating phenomena of the twentieth century. For all practical purposes it did not exist prior to this century, or even before the 1920's. It is a peculiarly American invention; although there are suggestions of such behavior in North-Western Europe and in certain other urbanized areas of Western culture, dating has a style and scope that developed in the rapidly changing American milieu. It is one aspect of American life that most Europeans, at least until recently, have regarded as strange; they look at American dating behavior as frivolous, capricious, and heavily tainted with commercialism.[1] The American conception of dating, however, is quite different. For example, the young person who does not date, even in high school, is regarded as a nonconformist or even a social reject. The percentage of young people who date has increased steadily over the past generation, and the age at which they begin has become ever lower. Data suggest that even preadolescents are caught up in this surge for romantic adventure.[2] Dating and courtship in their elaborate rituals reflect the feverish pace of the mid-century: the desire to fill every minute with the search for new experience. But despite all the trappings, there is the apparent need for and expression of affection and security. As marriage has become a popular goal for young people, its prelude—dating—becomes almost their prime preoccupation.

Dating and courtship procedures like most other behaviors, are learned through trial and error, imitation, and other types of experience. Inevitably there are rewards—often very high ones—and there are risks. Fortunately for most people, dating, which is essentially socialization with the other sex, becomes a pleasurable pursuit.

In this chapter we first examine the basic motivation in dating. Next we determine the meaning that dating has for different age and sub-cultural levels and the degree of commitment individuals feel in the experience of dating. We then proceed to the problem of dating as the basis of mate selection or what has been conventionally known as "courtship." Finally, the question of obstacles or conflicts in dating and how they may be resolved is examined.

[1] For some documentation on the European image of American dating, see Robert F. Winch, *Mate-Selection, A Study of Complementary Needs,* Harper and Row, New York, 1958, Chapter 14.

[2] Carlfred B. Broderick and Stanley E. Fowler, "New Patterns of Relationships between the Sexes among Preadolescents," *Marriage and Family Living,* 1961, **23,** 27–30.

MOTIVES FOR DATING

Most behavior is traceable to a complex of motives, and dating is no exception. Although the most obvious motive is that a young person is attracted to a member of the opposite sex, other factors exist, including:

RECREATION. Dating is an enjoyable pastime. Mass media and advertising are oriented to enjoyment as an end in life. The popular songs of today express the pleasure theme of dating as well as its more erotic aspects.

CONFORMITY AND STATUS. Teenagers are more sensitive to the judgment of the peer group than are adults. In fact, no one can escape the pressure of the social group, or is it necessarily desirable that he should. Studies indicate that roughly 90 per cent of high school students are dating by the senior year. Consequently, only a very exceptional individual is not caught up in the tide. It appears that in some high schools and colleges the individual's status, as well as the social hierarchy in general, is largely structured on a competitive scheme of dating. The young person's prestige depends on being seen with the queen of the junior class, with the athletic star, or the nearest possible equivalent. Dating, then, is a means of ego-enhancement. For the noncollege dater, the regime is less complex, although conceivably any large organization, such as the young adults of the local church, may have on a minor scale its version of a status structure. Still, studies indicate that noncollege young people date less than the campus population.

PERSONALITY GROWTH AND MATURITY. A major reason for dating, unconscious though it may be, is the preparation it offers for adulthood, the give-and-take in relation to another person. Still more important, it is one avenue of acquiring identification and the ability of role playing, that is, to take the role of the other person. Individuals begin to lose some of the feeling of self-importance. Dating is a succession of personal involvements and it can be interpreted as an elaborate form of trial and error, which becomes a basis for marital interaction. Dating may be considered the cause and result of what Foote and Cottrell call "interpersonal competence." [3] Competence connotes skill,

[3] Nelson N. Foote and Leonard S. Cottrell, Jr., *Identity and Interpersonal Competence*, The University of Chicago Press, 1955.

power, and tact. It develops opportunity to observe one's effect on another person, and to test one's sensitivity to the range of personalities met not only in dating but in other facets of life.

EMOTIONAL EXPLORATION. Dating is a major learning experience involving the opposite sex. The intricacies of love-making and new ranges of emotional experience are challenges. There is, too, the acquisition of a "line"—a perfection of conversational skill—which is not to be minimized as an experience in dating, although more serious dating tends to play down this kind of verbal finesse. The learning becomes generally more refined as the person becomes more deeply involved in the dating relationship.

MATE SELECTION. Dating for most young people is in some sense a prelude to marriage. Surveys, at least in colleges with a male majority, indicate that girls date more frequently than boys, and undoubtedly one reason for this frequency is their hope for an earlier marriage. It is this unfolding experience with the opposite sex that crystallizes attitudes about the kind of mate one is looking for. Mate selection in the college period has one major drawback in that students frequently do not wish to become involved in courtship so early in life. Yet serious dating at this time is functional since the student is among his contemporaries, who are likely to share common values and goals.

Teenage marriages are often premature, for they cut short the period in which the individual may have the opportunity to come into contact with a broad range of marriage candidates and learn to perceive the more subtle psychological nuances of the opposite sex. On the other hand, those who date in later years—over ages thirty or thirty-five—and those who have voluntarily or involuntarily remained single may encounter another obstacle. At this age the number of candidates is distinctly limited.

Dating gives the individual an opportunity to enjoy the companionship of the opposite sex and the "romantic cult," of which we shall say more in Chapter 9. Even casual dating affords some degree of affectional security and a feeling of normality that cannot be found by retiring to the peer group of one's sex or by remaining a "lone wolf." A study conducted some years ago pointed to the lack of emotional adjustment of nondaters in secondary school and college.[4] Those who dated indicated more self-confidence and revealed higher scores in

[4] M. F. Nimkoff and Arthur L. Wood, "Courtship and Personality," *American Journal of Sociology*, 1948, **53**, 263–269.

various adjustment areas. The scores on adjustment were based on the Bell Adjustment Inventory with the limitations of paper-and-pencil tests of personality. Yet results suggest that the failure to get to know the opposite sex may have unfavorable effects on personality growth. Preparation for courtship and later marriage is sharply curtailed.

DATING PATTERNS

The classical picture of dating was presented by Willard Waller a generation ago: "Dating is not true courtship, since it is supposed not to eventuate in marriage, it is a sort of dalliance relationship." [5] Dating in many colleges is, or at least was, influenced by this "rating and dating complex." This complex represents a hierarchy of statuses and values. The potential date is rated according to his or her social standing, which may consist of the availability of a car, prestige as a dancer, and what might be called *campus visibility*. For both sexes the scheme is highly competitive. In the experience of the date itself this competitiveness continues in the form of the "line," a contest in which both partners display a verbal sophistication which may have little to do with their real feelings or intentions. According to Waller, both individuals are regulated by the "principle of least interest," the continuation of the relationship depending on the person who has the lesser degree of ego-involvement in the affair.

Undoubtedly the Waller presentation had, and perhaps still has, a basis in fact. Although his much-cited paper was published in 1937, it referred to a study of life on the campus of Pennsylvania State College during 1929–1930, the twilight of the raucous 1920's, before the somber world of economic and international anxieties had dimmed the social whirl of the college and university student. For example, Robert Blood in a questionnaire survey of the University of Michigan in 1953 found that for both sexes the personality traits most desired in their dating partners were considerateness, pleasantness, neatness, sense of humor, dependability, intelligence, and naturalness. These criteria were more important than the Waller traits of twenty-five years before. Blood retested the Waller hypothesis and found that a "competitive materialistic rating complex" governed casual dating. Yet to say that the rating complex is "dysfunctional in relation to mate selec-

[5] Willard Waller, "The Rating and Dating Complex," *American Sociological Review,* 1937, **2**, 727–734.

tion, seems to be questionable at every point so far as its applicability to 1953 Michigan undergraduates as a whole is concerned." [6] Blood did find, in a later study, somewhat varying norms in regard to the kind of individual desirable for a casual as against a serious date, but the essential characteristics showed little difference. There were some discrepancies between the two sexes in the ratings of what constituted a desirable date: both the men and the women agreed that essentially they were interested in basic qualities like human relations, emotional maturity, affectionateness, and intelligence. Interestingly enough, respondents judged that the college population as a whole stressed the more materialistic aspects of dating, such as "going to popular places" and "willingness to drink socially," but considered this a superficial outlook. Although concern with popularity was the image most students had of their peers, results showed that the more serious outlook was fairly universal.[7]

EARLY ADOLESCENT DATING. Young people vary greatly in the kind of dating they do, including the age at which they may begin. For most individuals dating has been reported to begin in high school, although a sizeable minority, if not a majority, now commence at least a mild degree of socializing in junior high school. In fact, according to one study, 45 per cent of the boys and 36 per cent of the girls maintain that they began dating in the fifth grade or at ages ten and eleven.[8] More than half the juvenile sample claimed there had been some kissing in late childhood. In Elmtown, a Midwestern town studied in 1942, approximately 20 per cent of the girls and 15 per cent of the boys reported dates during the fourteenth year, or the terminal junior high period, with a good deal of awkwardness and self-consciousness in these initial dates. Hollingshead noted an increase of dating through high school, the clique structure becoming a dominant factor in dating experience. In upper high school years the "steady date" was more the pattern.[9]

The clique influence was also found by Coleman in his study of nine different high schools in the Midwest. Within a given high school, girls

---

[6] Robert O. Blood, "A Retest of Waller's Rating Complex," *Marriage and Family Living,* 1955, **17,** 41–47.

[7] Robert O. Blood, "Uniformities and Diversities in Campus Dating Preferences," *Marriage and Family Living,* 1956, **18,** 37–55.

[8] Broderick and Fowler, *op. cit.*

[9] August B. Hollingshead, *Elmtown's Youth: The Impact of Social Classes on Adolescents,* John Wiley, New York, 1949, pp. 223f.

in the upper years dated from roughly twice to three times a week depending on the clique to which they belonged. Dating at all levels, but especially in the upper class, depended on the individual's popularity in athletics, dress, leadership, as well as clique position. Social class was also important: girls from working-class families dated more than boys from that class, whereas in an upper-class suburb there was more equality, undoubtedly reflecting the tendency in the lower class toward earlier marriage.[10]

With the increase of dating during the later high school years, there comes improvement in self-confidence, more elaborate verbal interplay and sophistication, and increased physical contact. Particularly for the adolescent who is not college oriented, high school courtship assumes considerable importance. A study of six Connecticut high schools demonstrated a wide variation between those seriously thinking of marriage qualities and those mainly involved in dalliance behavior. The dating aspirations of the high school student responded to a number of factors in his environment and peer group. Among the results were various findings such as: girls were generally more date-conscious than boys, Protestants and Catholics more active than Jews, although churchgoers were significantly less frequent in their dates than those of low church attendance. Those of urban background were slightly more oriented to dating than those of rural areas, although the students from rural areas were less inclined to dalliance dating once the individual became a dater. The most significant differences were obtained among those youngsters who were more psychologically and socially prepared for marriage, as was true for the girls versus the boys, or for the later high school years as opposed to the earlier.[11]

Individuals who date early also find dating more rewarding. There seems to be positive correlation between the enjoyment of the first date and later "heterosexual socialization."[12] Lowrie, in a study of high schools in three cities of middle-size population in Ohio, Texas, and California, found that early dating was more likely to occur among the following groups: (1) children, especially girls, of the older Anglo-Saxon population in contrast to more recent foreign origin; (2)

[10] James S. Coleman, *The Adolescent Society,* The Free Press of Glencoe, A Division of Collier-Macmillan, New York, 1961, pp. 198f.

[11] Jerold S. Heiss, "Variations in Courtship Progress among High School Students," *Marriage and Family Living,* 1960, **22,** 165–170.

[12] John R. Crist, "High School Dating as a Behavior System," *Marriage and Family Living,* 1953, **15,** 23–27.

daughters of parents with some college training; (3) children, especially daughters, from small rather than large families; (4) students from homes of higher economic and social status; and (5) students in the South or Texas. The age at which girls begin dating, he also found, is more sensitive to various social factors and changing conditions than that for boys. Early dating was found to occur in homes that were permissive, liberal, and in those parts of the population studied, more adaptable to change, where there perhaps has been a social climate and parent-adolescent relationship offering guidance, understanding, and some direction.[13]

Parental opposition is a familiar problem in relation to dating. Several issues divide parents concerning teenagers and the question of dating. One of these is the first date. In one study, half the boys—although only a third of the girls—had to secure permission for the first date. Both the number of dates permitted per week and the time limits posed some intense conflict. Difficulties arose, especially, between parents and daughter regarding the choice of a boyfriend and her degree of acquaintance with him. There were also disagreements about the kinds of activities encompassed by the date. Homes differed to a marked degree on the freedom of discussion about the dating experience.[14]

Another general problem that the high school student is likely to encounter is the decision about "going steady." This behavior pattern has been increasing over several years and seems now a persistent pattern in teenage culture. The question remains whether going steady at the high school level is a prelude to informal engagement or simply "making time," since this type of relationship offers the male certain sexual advantages that might border on exploitation of the opposite sex.[15] There is evidence that the high school "steady" daters are more inclined to marry each other if they do not go on to college, whereas dating is more of a dalliance relationship for those who continue their education.[16] In any case, steady dating might be a test of

[13] Samuel H. Lowrie, "Early and Late Dating: Some Conditions Associated with Them," *Marriage and Family Living*, 1961, **23**, 284–291.

[14] Paul H. Landis, "Research on Teen-Age Dating," *Marriage and Family Living*, 1960, **22**, 262–267.

[15] Robert D. Herman, "The 'Going Steady' Complex: A Re-examination," *Marriage and Family Living*, 1955, **17**, 36–47.

[16] Ira L. Reiss, "Sexual Codes in Teen-Age Culture," *The Annals* of the American Academy of Political and Social Science, 1961 (November), **338**, 53–62.

conformity, a better means of delving deeper into the intricacies of personality than random dating. Even at the high school level it appears that the quest for security includes the steadiness of something akin to a semipermanent love experience.

There are undoubtedly certain characteristics for which the young person is looking in a date, despite the steadiness of relationship. High school students, in one study, considered the following characteristics as foremost in a date: physical and mental fitness, dependability, pride in appearance and manners, appropriateness of speech and action, pleasantness and a sense of humor, considerateness, and maturity.[17] A sample of Purdue University students also rated these same traits as important in their criteria for dates.[18] Studies of high school dating suggest that the basic pattern for most adolescents is largely structured by the experiences of this age level.

According to research findings, then, early dating may prove rewarding, but on the whole, we are not yet ready to assess the ultimate significance of this phenomenon. It seems presumptuous to consider certain dating characteristics as an inflexible goal for all teenagers.

COLLEGE DATING

For most the culmination point of dating comes during the college years or about age 20–24. At least the experience is likely to be richer than in the high school period, because at this age the individual has reached a higher level of maturity. For some there is a feeling of finality in college dating. They are more aware of where they are going, are more mature intellectually, socially, emotionally, and sexually. In other words, marriage becomes something other than a remote possibility; nearly a fifth of college undergraduates are married. Moreover, dating at this age is more discriminating than it was earlier and somewhat less sensitive to the pressures of the peer group.

Dating is universal: less than 2 per cent of the college population are believed to be nondaters, although the frequency may vary from two to five times a week to that many times a year. In one survey it was discovered that the preferred frequency was once to twice a week for 46 per cent of the men and 37 per cent of the women. Roughly 20 per

[17] Harold T. Christensen, *Marriage Analysis* (second edition), The Ronald Press, New York, 1958, pp. 239–243.
[18] *Ibid.*

cent of the sample reported dating one or two times a month. The next most popular pattern was dating more than twice a week. Finally, 23 per cent of the women, but only 17 per cent of the men, dated less than once a month or in a few cases not at all during their college careers.[19] These differences can be accounted for by differences in amount of interest, motivation, finances, study pressures, and (especially for the girls) the availability of dates. Although not typical, some college surveys indicate that girls tend to date less than boys. In certain college environments the girl may find her social status suffering more by dating the "wrong" boy (one who is not accepted by her peers) than by not dating at all. For example, dating in sororities may operate along clique lines.

Young people consider romantic reasons the most important criteria for dating. As shown in Table 7.1, when asked their reasons for dating,

Table 7.1

MOTIVES IN HIGH SCHOOL AND COLLEGE DATING

	Boys (N = 782)	Girls (N = 813)	Total (N = 1595)
COURTSHIP-ORIENTED RESPONSES			
Affection	27.2%	24.8%	25.9%
Select mate	13.9	15.7	14.9
ADJUSTMENT-ORIENTED RESPONSES			
Learn to adjust	8.5	13.2	11.0
Gain poise or ease	20.3	25.4	23.0
RECREATION-ORIENTED RESPONSES			
Fun	8.1	8.0	8.0
Social outlet	12.9	11.1	11.9
Prestige	3.1	1.3	2.2
Neck	6.0	0.5	3.1

Note: High school sample was roughly two-thirds of total sample. Adapted from Samuel H. Lowrie, "Dating Theories and Student Responses," *American Sociological Review,* 1951, **16,** 334–340.

more than 40 per cent of one high school and college sample responded in terms of romantic or affectional motivation, not to be

[19] Ruth S. Cavan, "Dating and Selection of a Mate" in Ruth S. Cavan (ed.), *Marriage and Family in the Modern World,* Thomas Y. Crowell, New York, 1960, p. 129.

separated from courtship interests. The other two principal areas of motivation were personality adjustment and socio-recreational impulses. In analysis of the college sample, as opposed to the high school group, the college group were found to be more interested in the romantic, affectionate, or possibly recreational aspects, and less interested in the learning phases, since they were more mature. Of course, it is difficult to assess the validity of reasons or motives given in a questionnaire study, but the pattern of responses appears to be plausible. However, it is likely that the effect of conformity needs and the peer group might be somewhat greater than was realized by the respondents.

Whatever the motivation, in general the two sexes are apparently attracted or alienated by differing characteristics. Christensen found sex differences between the two partners influenced what they expected their dates to be like or specific qualities in the opposite sex that were problems on dates. Most criticized in male behavior were (in declining order): "telling off-color jokes," not knowing when to say "good night," insisting on "too much necking or petting," and being "disrespectful of the opposite sex." The five traits most criticized in the girl were (in declining order): being "artificial in dress and manners," "asking stupid questions or making silly remarks," being "too cold emotionally," lacking "life and energy," and "wanting expensive things and favors." [20] The male and female subcultures are clearly visible in the two biases: the female complaints might seem incomprehensible to her male partner since these traits are considered "feminine" in our informal culture. Undoubtedly any comparison of qualities that the two sexes might look for in dates or marriage is influenced by the age of the persons involved, their images of what the ideal date should be, availability of dates, and the social and recreational climate of the atmosphere in which they date.

The seriousness of the particular dating situation also influences the rating of certain traits. Some of the less frequently mentioned traits might prove to be more difficult in the long-run, "going steady" process. In any case, in terms of the Christensen traits, men were described as "loud," "overly self-assured," "never offering compliments or thanks," and "too staid and conventional." Among the less critical items in the girl were "late in calling or being ready for dates," "too dependent on others," and "prudish regarding sex and morals." Re-

[20] Christensen, *op. cit.,* p. 237.

peatedly mentioned as a source of conflict between the two sexes is the question of sex itself, as we shall see in Chapter 8.

SUBCULTURES AND DATING

Culture markedly affects the style of dating. For instance, a Norwegian, as compared to an American, usually expects the girl partner to contribute to the financing of the date, tends to be more cautious about his sexual behavior in the initial period of the dating relationship, but freer in the more serious phase of courtship.[21] In Scandinavia, and perhaps central Europe, if there is mutual attraction with genuine affection and some possibility of marriage, sex relations between two young adults are not unexpected. Even within the United States there are cultural differences in dating practices. However, mass media and the ease of communication have generally reduced extreme regional differences.

Certain subcultures are also conditioning agents in dating and courtship. Of these we have selected class belongingness and religion for discussion.

The *class structure* is generally regarded by sociologists as the most important subculture influencing personality. Whether a person is French, Russian, American, or Bantu, the class into which he is born determines the type of home he lives in, whom he meets—and to a remarkable extent—whom he marries. Elmtown, the Midwestern community we have already discussed, might appear to the casual observer as a pleasant, democratic, one-class town. Yet the dating system of the adolescents was highly influenced by the adolescent's position within the five-class strata. In Hollingshead's study, 61 per cent of the dates of the interviewees belonged to the same social class, 35 per cent to an adjacent class, and only 4 per cent from a nonadjacent class. The Elmtown male tended to date and marry girls who were below him in class to a greater extent that the female did. Class also influenced the frequency of dating. The upper-middle class had the highest number of dates, and the lower-lower class the smallest number. The lower classes were inclined to select their dates outside of the school environment.[22]

---

[21] William Simenson and Gilbert Geis, "Courtship Patterns of Norwegian and American University Students," *Marriage and Family Living*, 1956, **18**, 334–338.

[22] Hollingshead, *op. cit.*, pp. 227–232.

The status system of daters within a college environment depends on many factors, of which the social class of the family is only one. A study of 8,200 students of Iowa State University demonstrated that campus prestige depended on the political power of the residence group, including the elaborateness of its parties and dances, the individual's participation in college athletics and other activities, along with such diverse features as the potential of spending money, access to or possession of automobiles, and miscellaneous factors, such as grades and personality traits. How much the individual's original class position affected this scheme cannot be known, but undoubtedly it enjoyed some influence. Being a member of a fraternity (and to a lesser extent a sorority) was a positive factor in the ability to obtain dates, both in a quantitative and qualitative sense. Similarly, the extent of participation in campus activities generally was a positive factor.[23]

Much of the literature on class stratification stresses the influence of class on the degree of physical intimacy. According to one source which interprets social class in terms of educational and occupational level, lower-class members indulge in more premarital sex relations.[24] Ehrmann found that males tend to date below themselves in social class as a means of finding a more willing sexual partner; thus women are more likely to have more direct physical experience when dating a male above them in social class. However, in Ehrmann's study there was more intimacy within the social class than outside it.[25]

Religious identification also influences the choice of dating partners and, to some extent perhaps, behavior on dates. Kirkpatrick and Caplow found in their Minnesota study that Protestants and Jews were more endogamous in their courtship behavior, that is, dated more within their own group, than did Catholics.[26] The Protestant pattern can be attributed to the fact that they form the religious majority in the United States. The preference of Jews for dating within their group may be explained by the in-group feeling of their parents, as well as by some rejection by the out-group. Catholic girls

---

[23] Everett M. Rogers and A. Eugene Havens, "Prestige Rating and Mate Selection on a College Campus," *Marriage and Family Living*, 1960, **22**, 55–59.

[24] Alfred C. Kinsey, Wardell B. Pomeroy, and Clyde E. Martin, *Sexual Behavior in the Human Male,* W. B. Saunders, Philadelphia, 1948, pp. 295 and 349.

[25] Winston Ehrmann, *Premarital Dating Behavior,* Henry Holt, New York, 1959. pp. 144–156.

[26] Clifford Kirkpatrick and Theodore Caplow, "Courtship in a Group of Minnesota Students," *American Journal of Sociology*, 1945, **51**, 114–125.

were more disposed to date non-Catholics, because the goal of marriage was stronger than their religious ethnocentricity, and their position was not so marginal as the Jew. Since this study was conducted in 1945, results may not be entirely valid in view of the emphasis on intergroup living in the years following World War II. A more recent survey in the Midwest revealed that boys generally had more favorable attitudes than girls toward crossreligious dating and marriage. More religious tolerance was expressed by lower- and middle-status individuals than by upper-class members. High school students were more tolerant than college students, possibly because the serious aspects of dating were relatively remote. Intense religious participation also made the individual more resistant toward interreligious dating and courtship. The general principle operating in the degree of tolerance is the amount of pressure on the individual. People date in correspondence with the norms of their *reference groups,* the groups to which they turn for their values, attitudes, and ethical standards. The more deeply the individual is involved with a given group, the more sensitive he is to making his choice in line with group approval, and the more the girl he courts and marries must conform to his total motivational system.[27] There seem to be characteristic styles of dating depending on the religious background of the individual. In a study at Temple University it was found that Protestants engaged in more steady dating than Jews; at least "going steady" and engagement occurred later than in the Jewish group. Catholics apparently included sex relations in their going-steady relationships to a greater degree than the other two religious groups. However, the limited size of the sample (410 total, of which only 160 were male) precludes any hasty generalizations.[28]

In a study of students from six Philadelphia colleges and universities, the tendency toward going steady for Protestants and toward earlier dating for the Jewish girls (12.8 years for their first date, or more than a year earlier than for Protestants and Catholics) was corroborated. Generally, the men showed fewer differences among the three religious groups. It appears that in large urban universities dating is often with off-campus individuals. Furthermore, in the high school population there is an

[27] Lee G. Burchinal, "Membership Groups and Attitudes toward Cross-Religious Dating and Marriage," *Marriage and Family Living,* 1960, 22, 248–253.

[28] Robert R. Bell and Leonard Blumberg, "Courtship Intimacy and Religious Background," *Marriage and Family Living,* 1959, 21, 356–360.

observable tendency for the two sexes to attend different educational institutions. Consequently, generalizations may not apply equally to both sexes within a particular religious or ethnic group.[29]

Parenthetically, it may be added that in a study of international dating at the University of Michigan, religious identification influenced the attitudes toward dating of foreign students. Protestants were generally less prejudiced against dating foreign students than active members of the other two faiths, but inactive Catholics and Jews were more liberal than either active or inactive Protestants.[30]

DATING AND MATE SELECTION

COURTSHIP AS PROCESS. There is no clear-cut difference between dating and courtship. In the earlier writings, following Waller, it was popular to describe marriage-oriented dating as courtship, but the postwar tendency has been to refer to the entire process of premarital dating as a courtship continuum.[31] The term courtship has become somewhat academic but still characterizes the more serious side of dating. Historically it has had different meanings depending on the cultural environment of the period. Merrill has designated five stages in our American tradition. One was the "colonial stage," in which Old World patterns persisted and the parents were the dominant individuals in the selection process for the younger generation. Two, the "rural stage," as found along the frontier and farm, held to strict codes and the commitment to marriage on the basis of a few meetings. Three, the "town stage," in the mid- and late nineteenth century brought industrial America to a more relaxed, spontaneous kind of courtship— although premarital mores did not allow any sexual digressions. Virginity for the female was still absolute. Four, the "metropolitan stage," dominated the 1920's and 1930's with a new sexual freedom and the triumph of experimental dating as opposed to traditional courtship. Five, there was the security stage of the postwar period.

[29] Robert C. Williamson, "Dating, Courtship and the 'Ideal Mate': Some Relevant Subcultural Variables," *Family Life Coordinator*, 1965, **14**, 137–143.

[30] Robert O. Blood, Jr. and Samuel O. Nicholson, "The Attitudes of American Men and Women Toward International Dating," *Marriage and Family Living*, 1962, **24**, 35–41.

[31] Lee G. Burchinal, "The Premarital Dyad and Love Involvement," in Harold T. Christensen (ed.), *Handbook of Marriage and the Family*, Rand McNally, Chicago, 1964, p. 624.

Steady dating and courtship today have reached some compromise of the pre-World War I pattern and the hedonistic philosophy of the 1920's. Although there is much variation, the ideal for most young people is early marriage, and the motive for marriage is affectional security.[32]

THE PROBLEM OF COMMITMENT. In any analysis of the process of mate selection, Farber regards dating as a series of involvements rather than as a sifting of prospective mates.[33] In other words, in our concept of dating today, the end is enjoyment, the exploration of another's personality, and, incidentally, mate selection. Unquestionably one aspect of this dating is symbolic of the liberation from parental influence. Males perhaps more than females find in a serious dating process emancipation from the parent and adopt a more critical viewpoint toward their parents' marriage.[34] For both sexes the dating-courtship continuum represents a process of love involvements leading to a more total socialization process which for most people is marriage. Each possible mate is part of a testing experience so as to improve interpersonal techniques and not only from a manipulative viewpoint, but more frequently to acquire a more sensitive and sophisticated set of personality responses. In any case, the extension of the dating concept from the idea of narrowing the field of prospective dates, to the new one of a limited series of affectional relationships has provided more rationalization of sexual liasons. Hand in hand with this rationalization has been the realization that there is no one and only true mate; consequently that there is less need to preserve feminine virginity— although sexual relationships are reserved more generally for only the deepest relationships, which are discussed further in Chapter 8.

It is difficult to say at what point our courtship patterns shifted in this direction. Undoubtedly the 1920's and 1930's were a transitional period between the pre-World War I dating-courtship as a prelude to marriage and the present type of relationship that is found within the middle class, dating as a means of personality growth, emotional and perhaps physical exploration, and the search for a marital partner. Perhaps, as Farber suggests, our dating and courtship, at least our

[32] Francis E. Merrill, *Courtship and Marriage,* Holt, Rinehart and Winston, New York, 1959, pp. 109–110
[33] Bernard Farber, *The Family, Organization and Interaction,* Chandler Publishing, San Francisco, 1964, pp. 160–163.
[34] Charles W. Hobart, "Emancipation from Parents and Courtship in Adolescence," *Pacific Sociological Review,* 1958, **6,** 25–29.

going steady, socializes us into a state of "permanent availability" as a marriage partner throughout life. Permanent availability refers to the tendency of the basic needs of an individual to change within a lifetime. Consequently, availability to change, or flexibility, continues into the marriage with the expectation of a constant process of personality adjustment reminiscent of the courtship stage. With blockages of the adjustment capacity of the two personalities, dissolution of the marriage could occur. In other words, the socialization aspects of courtship are prolonged into marriage.

RANDOM DATING VERSUS STEADY DATING.   It is an oversimplification to maintain that there are two types of dating, random or casual, on one hand, and serious or steady on the other. Perhaps there are three main possibilities: the *random* or competitive date, the *noncommitment steady* date, and the *commitment steady* date. Which of these types a person becomes involved in depends on several factors.[35] Individuals function along a somewhat sliding continuum. Random dating continues to be the preferred system for the early high school period and for those of any age who are finding their way through the perplexities of the other sex, and this type of dating may be divided between those who completely or partly play the field.[36] As has been suggested, random dating "serves as the point of least resistance to enter or reenter the system." [37] It remains the preferred system possibly for the psychologically insecure and those who have least ego involvement. Such dating may or may not serve those whose interest in dating is primarily sexual. It is in random dating that the "line" has its most eloquent development. The degree of subterfuge is also at its maximum, and both partners can end by giving so little of themselves that each may remain a mystery to the other. Yet this subtle relationship may actually constitute the essence and real satisfaction of dating, because the dalliance function is most useful in the early stages of dating.

Steady Dating.   This type of dating has become more and more the standard practice, even in high school.[38] In the university freshman

[35] Ernest A. Smith, *American Youth Culture,* The Free Press of Glencoe, A Division of Collier-Macmillan, New York, 1962, Chapter 8.

[36] Robert D. Herman, "The 'Going Steady' Complex: A Re-examination," *Marriage and Family Living,* 1955, **17,** 36–40.

[37] E. E. LeMasters, *Modern Courtship and Marriage,* The Macmillan Company, New York, 1957, p. 124.

[38] Charles W. Cole, "American Youth Goes Monogamous," *Harpers Magazine,* 1957, **214,** 29–33.

sample tested by Herman, no less than 77 per cent were found to have gone steady with at least one person. The going-steady pattern became increasingly prevalent through the college years. However, in this group it appeared to be mainly a dalliance relationship. The advantages of steady dating are several. First, a dependable date is assured. The "steady" will be available for the Wednesday night movie, the football game, or the Saturday prom. There is a psychological security in knowing the individual better, in being able to predict behavior of the partner, and in feeling some degree of affection that is not likely with more casual dating. In purely random dating the individual must constantly make intricate adjustments, and concentrate on making a favorable impression because of the more competitive interpersonal behavior. In steady dating the techniques of discussion and compromise are usually less harassing. It permits a more complete socialization process. Students report that in dating of the same person regularly the learning experience is more mature, and there is more to be gained by becoming well acquainted with a few personalities than by exploring an almost infinite number of dates. The student also discovers the range of his psychological resources in the opportunity to pursue the give-and-take of an affectionate relationship with the opposite sex.[39] It is, functionally speaking, a preparation for marriage itself.

Many students solve the problem of random versus steady dating in a compromise of the two: *the random-going-steady* system.[40] This arrangement refers to a series of "going-steady" relationships, each of which lasts several weeks or even several months. Although going steady may provide maximum security, it also has its risks. First, going steady obviously limits acquaintance with other date prospects. Second, it may also commit the pair beyond their psychological or social readiness. They may not have played the field long enough to understand the gamut of dating possibilities. Third, sexual problems may arise for which the couple is not ready. Fourth, there is usually parental opposition, especially among the high school group. On the other hand, the random date has its liabilities; there is the danger that the norms and values of the date may be very different from what is anticipated. Unpleasant situations arise from the gulf that can exist between two people, and conflicts are especially probable in the area of sex, particularly because of the more narrow restrictions on the

[39] Herman, *op. cit.*

[40] LeMasters, *op. cit.*, p. 124.

girl's behavior. These calculated risks are part of any dating situation, but the casual date is likely to be more fraught with unpredictables.

For various reasons, young people choose both forms of dating, and both may demand a maximum of psychological resources and emotional control. It is entirely possible that the young person may feel the need to seek professional guidance, for example, from the school counsellor.

PINNING AND ENGAGEMENT.   A relatively new phenomenon has developed in the postwar period: the quasiengagement arrangement known as *pinning*. The boy attaches his fraternity or dormitory pin to the girl, an act which represents a major commitment in the going-steady process. It may represent a state of being "engaged to be engaged" or actual engagement.[41] In some cases, the term *chained* supersedes being pinned, when the sorority and fraternity pins are put together on a chain indicating that a marriage date is set. The fact that these campus symbols are used may be an indication of social solidarity and status within the campus environment as much as a matrimonial commitment. As with an engagement, the girl may pass out candy, the boy cigars, and the event may appear in the social column of the campus newspaper. An Iowa State College survey found that pinning followed class or status lines. It was significantly more frequent for the high-status fraternity member to be pinned to the high-status sorority girl. The boy might pin below his status level, but for the girl to do so was socially inappropriate.[42]

Engagement is discussed more thoroughly in Chapter 12, but here we are concerned mainly with the way pinning, or similar arrangements, represent an opportunity to deepen the relationship and to make some of the adjustments that will be called for in marriage. Engagement is a transitional state as is dating and courtship. It is a public announcement that two individuals are serious about their intentions. It is an opportunity for the marital situation to be viewed in a comparatively public setting. All other competitors are excluded from courtship.

SOME DEEPER INVOLVEMENTS.   Courtship means that two individuals are developing into a single unit, a process that becomes even more intimate and involved in marriage itself. The sociologist is necessarily interested in the individual's capacity to assume the role of the other, because the success of courtship and marriage depends on this ability.

[41] *Ibid.*, p. 151.
[42] Rogers and Havens, *op. cit.*

To what degree can disagreements and awareness of differences exist, still allowing the relationship to be a healthy, on-going affair.

Individuals in love have the advantage of some degree of enchantment that facilitates togetherness. Burgess and Wallin discovered that 46 per cent of the men and 34 per cent of the women among their engaged sample reported a situation of mutual personality attraction and interest on their first meeting. However, a smaller group, about a sixth of the sample, stated that they were attracted to each other on the first meeting but it was mainly physical attraction.[43] Most experience the feeling of exclusiveness and the emergence of a love relationship. In the Minnesota study there were sex differences; the male, at least in the early phases, was more inclined to a feeling of dalliance, the girl found the idea of marriage a more agreeable or even pressing prospect. When asked about the development of their affectional relationship, both sexes mentioned a tendency for the feeling of exclusiveness to grow from one love affair to the next. Yet men were more inclined to experience worry, confusion, jealousy, criticism, dislike of their partners' friends, and they were more inclined to have the feeling of being trapped. Among other items, women stated some uncertainty about the future and less frequently admitted giving-in.[44]

Unquestionably the strength of the courtship relation is found in the degree of empathy that the couple shows. Empathy is a partial product of what an individual brings to a situation and the characteristics of the situation itself. As we saw in the preceding chapters, the ability to understand the other's viewpoint and role is a product of knowledge gained over a decade or two of interpersonal reactions along with a person's own emotional development. The boy who wants to stay out until two o'clock in the morning when the girl has strict limits is an example of how a given situation may affect both their role perceptions. Much of our enjoyment of courtship depends on the degree of ego satisfaction it gives us. Moreover, our culture has trained us to look at the dyad (twosome) relationship as particularly satisfying: we are geared to expect an emotional satisfaction from it. The socialization process normally provides us with the means of an *einfühlung*, or identification for others. This intermingling of two personalities gives the warmth and security that love comes to mean.

Evidence indicates that there is a rise and fall of mutual under-

---

[43] Ernest W. Burgess and Paul Wallin, *Engagement and Marriage*, J. P. Lippincott, Philadelphia, 1953, pp. 160–162.

[44] Kirkpatrick and Caplow, *op. cit.*

standing and agreement and disagreement at successive stages of courtship.[45] These fluctuations in empathy may be explained as resulting from moods, environmental circumstances, or the accommodation process that inevitably unfolds as two people come to know each other. Hesitations, doubts, and anxieties probably accompany any deep feeling of love.

The college atmosphere permits a more leisurely and low-pressured environment in which two young people may explore the gamut of warm interpersonal responses. The romantic atmosphere of college life, away from some of the realities of the world, is in contrast to the pressures that arise in marriage: economic problems, child-rearing, and the like. Mutual understanding and empathy begin in the courtship stage and continue through the adjustment phases of marriage.

BREAKUP AND READJUSTMENT IN DATING. A problem of the courtship process is the emotional upheaval of breakup. Most young people have had a love affair or engagement previous to the one that leads to marriage. In breakups some individuals report a slow upward growth of love and affection with quite erratic moods. Other partnerships experience a gradual buildup and an ebbing away when the relationship is about to terminate or there may be entirely cyclic "ups" and "downs" depending on the moods and emotional experiences of the two lovers. These cycles may continue into the readjustment process following the breakup.[46]

The Kirkpatrick and Caplow [47] study demonstrated that the cause of breakup was attributable to a number of factors. The principal one of these was mutual loss of interest, which was admitted by about half (46.9 per cent) of the men and more than a third (38.1 per cent) of the women. About a third of the women and a sixth of the men claimed they lost interest because of their attraction to another person, with a third of the men and a sixth of the women stating that their partner had become interested in someone else. It appears that the girl is more in demand or more popular, a condition undoubtedly ascribable to the predominantly male population of the average college. Friends and parents were mentioned, more by the female, as a contributory cause of the breakup. In explaining the differences leading to the

---

[45] Charles W. Hobart, "Disagreement and Non-empathy during Courtship: A Restudy," *Marriage and Family Living*, 1956, **28**, 317–322.

[46] Clifford Kirkpatrick, *The Family as Process and Institution* (second edition), The Ronald Press, New York, 1963, pp. 307–313.

[47] Kirkpatrick and Caplow, *op. cit.*

drifting away, there was strong evidence of moral self-justification in regard to the question of whether one individual was more or less honest than his mate. Both sexes considered themselves more straight-forward than the partner at the ratio of nearly two to one. The reactions following the end of the love affair varied from being hurt to a feeling of indifference, relief, satisfaction, or some combination of these without any pronounced sex difference. At the same time, nearly a third of the males and a fourth of the females spoke of dreaming or of day-dreaming about the partner. The tendency was to remember pleasant rather than unpleasant characteristics about the former mate, which is generally true of all reminiscence. About half of the sample maintained that they did not recover from the affair for several weeks or even several years; the other half appeared to have made an almost immediate readjustment.

PROBLEMS OF DATING AND COURTSHIP

The study of dating and courtship has revealed some fascinating aspects of American folkways. For the young American it is a world rich in psychological rewards yet fraught with various interpersonal and emotional obstacles. As Parsons has noted, courtship is probably more *achieved* than *ascribed* behavior—a distinction resulting from the individual's own initiative and accomplishments as opposed to his inborn heritage.[48] As a people we are very conscious of social success and failure. Caught in this race for a happy love relationship and the expected meetings of young men and women, what are some of the problems?

One problem at any age of mate-seeking is how to find a date. There are no prescribed folkways in our culture for securing a partner; much of this behavior is necessarily trial and error. First, who should be selected—the girl at the corner, a blind date? How should the first date be initiated? What about succeeding dates and the possibility of steady dating?

For many there is the question of attractiveness—physical or social. Our culture tends to place an extremely high reward on physical beauty, and the mass media have elevated this quality to a major value orientation. But we should also mention that, for example, in France

---

[48] Talcott Parsons, *The Family, Socialization and Interaction Process*, The Free Press of Glencoe, A Division of Collier-Macmillan, New York, 1955, p. 127.

and Italy, the heroine is not always a contemporary Venus de Milo. Also, modern Hollywood's standards have been somewhat modified, although the viewer is still occasionally bewildered when he sees a heroine with freckles or a hero with eye glasses. The lack of reality on the movie and television screen is not the most propitious atmosphere in which to prepare for courtship and marriage.

PARENTAL OPPOSITION. A problem the young person may encounter in dating is parental disfavor. One survey revealed that of the male sample, 49 per cent of fathers and 79 per cent of mothers were opposed to their youngster's dating habits. Comparable figures for the girls were 68 and 97 per cent.[49] Kirkpatrick and Caplow found the father inclined to be more of a problem to the daughter than to the son or more than the mother is to either son or daughter, which they felt indicated a sort of Electra complex in operation.

The adolescent is caught between peer-group culture and parental pressures. The question of hours and the choice of candidates are the two most debatable points. Crist in a study of high school dating found two possible regimes: "parent-adolescent democratic control" (a give-and-take orientation), and less frequently reported, "parental authoritarian control." Parents in this study generally restricted the behavior of daughters more than sons, and students low in socio-economic status were under more scrutiny than those of higher status. Generally girls had more complete discussions with their parents on topics ranging from emotional development to sex behavior.[50]

SUBCULTURAL OBSTACLES. The young person is also caught in the various conflicts imposed by his socio-cultural environment. The study of Elmtown graphically posed the question of dating in terms of class, and the barriers within the high school social structure of this Mid-western community are quite as imposing as those found in urban universities. In fact, educational institutions run the gamut of social status; compare the Ivy League university with the downtown evening college. Even within a single institution there may be tremendous variation of social position.

Similarly, religion complicates the dating situation. Although these differences are less pronounced than they were a generation ago, the forces of family tradition, group loyalties, religious preferences, and

[49] Alan Bates, "Parental Roles in Courtship," *Social Forces*, 1942, **20**, 483–486.
[50] John R. Crist, "High School Dating as a Behavior System," *Marriage and Family Living*, 1953, **15**, 23–28.

ideology and ritual were more potent than today. Political differences and other kinds of belongingness may also enter the dating picture.

We have seen in this discussion of dating that it is an activity pursued for its own sake, and yet is one of the ultimate symbols of growing up. Its variety and subtlety make it difficult to discuss scientifically, because dating is an individual matter. However, information in this chapter suggests that some order or generalizations can be made nevertheless. First, both sociologically and personally, the magic process of dating and courtship has its various functions. Courting behavior varies with the subcultures that surround the individual, whether economic, geographic, or ideological.

Aside from the sociological and psychological aspects, we are interested in the question of personal involvement in the process. How does each of us identify ourselves and our own brand of self-expression in becoming acquainted with and emotionally attached to the other sex? Despite experiencing some of the problems raised in this and succeeding chapters, the individual does find his way through the maze of dating. Still, for both the casual dater and the more serious dater this ritual in the game of love is likely to be a little heady, and he or she may suffer in the struggle for love, belongingness, and status. Nevertheless, despite its imperfections as compared to the relative security of traditional systems of courtship known to our ancestors, the more informal and romantic selection process of contemporary America is likely to continue. Over some parts of the world parental controls are breaking down and young people are continually more insistent about whom they shall see socially and whom they shall marry. But only in America does the cult of romantic individualism have its peculiar values and folkways in dating. For most young people this comparative freedom is a satisfying experience.

Supplementary Readings

Bee, Lawrence S., *Marriage and Family Relations,* Harper and Row, New York, 1959. Chapters 7–9 are a readable discussion of some historical and recent developments in courtship.

Blood, Robert O., Jr. *Marriage,* The Free Press of Glencoe, A Division of Collier-Macmillan, New York, 1962. Chapter 2 describes various studies of college courtship.

Burchinal, Lee G., "The Premarital Dyad and Love Involvement," in Harold T. Christensen (ed.), *Handbook of Marriage and the Family*, Rand McNally, Chicago, 1964. A nearly complete listing of research studies systematized into a meaningful statement.

Burgess, Ernest W., Harvey J. Locke, and Mary M. Thomes, *The Family* (second edition), American Book, New York, 1963. A documented study of some of the problems of adolescent and post-adolescent dating is found in Chapter 12.

Coleman, James S., *The Adolescent Society*, The Free Press of Glencoe, A Division of Collier-Macmillan, New York, 1961. The social structure of high school students' dating is among its features.

Ehrmann, Winston, *Premarital Dating Behavior*, Holt, Rinehart and Winston, New York, 1959. While Ehrmann is interested in sexual behavior primarily, his monograph furnishes significant findings about dating in general; also available in paperback edition.

Hollingshead, August B., *Elmtown's Youth*, John Wiley, New York, 1949. This classic study of high school youth in a Midwestern town deserves reading for the folkways of intra- and interclass dating.

Kirkpatrick, Clifford, *The Family as Process and Institution* (second edition), The Ronald Press, New York, 1963. A very analytical and documented study of the subject is found in Chapter 12.

LeMasters, E. E., *Modern Courtship and Marriage*, Macmillan, New York, 1957. Part Two is an insightful statement of our topic, and like Cavan, is exceptionally easy to read.

Merrill, Francis E., *Courtship and Marriage*, Holt, Rinehart and Winston, New York, 1959. A sociologist critically examines the diverse roles associated with courtship in Chapters 6–10.

Smith, Ernest A., *American Youth Culture: Group Life in Teenage Society*, The Free Press of Glencoe, A Division of Collier-Macmillan, New York, 1962. An analysis of dating, cliques, gangs, and other interesting phenomena.

Sussman, Marvin B. (ed.), *Sourcebook in Marriage and the Family* (second edition), Houghton Mifflin, Boston, 1963. Chapter 2 has a number of selections on such topics as the rating complex, frequency of dating, etc.

Waller, Willard, *The Family, A Dynamic Interpretation*, Holt, Rinehart and Winston, New York, 1951 (revised by Reuben Hill). Chapters 6, 8, 9, and 10 are most relevant to the psychology and sociology of dating and courtship.

Winch, Robert F., *The Modern Family* (revised edition), Holt, Rinehart and Winston, New York, 1963. Chapter 20 treats dating in a profound psychological fashion.

Chapter eight
Premarital Sex Behavior

Climbing the darkened stairs, feeling the maleness in him, the maleness that was denied, hushed, denounced, hedged in, scourged, damned, condemned, and used, feeling the excess that overflowed rancidly, burning acidly all through his blood and settling finally in his throat, a thick acidulous phlegm, feeling all that, he did not wonder that so many men woke up suddenly to find that they were married. But if you weren't, there was only one thing left to do.

> James Jones, From Here To Eternity, *Scribner's, New York, 1951.*
> *Copyright 1951 by James Jones.*

I had decided to allow no room in the universe for something which shamed and frightened me. I succeeded very well—by not looking at the universe, by not looking at myself, by remaining, in effect, in constant motion. Even constant motion, of course, does not prevent an occasional mysterious drag, a drop, like an airplane hitting an air pocket. And there were a number of those, all drunken, all sordid, one very frightening such drop while I was in the Army which involved a fairy who was later court-martialed out. The panic his punishment caused in me was as close as I ever came to facing in myself the terrors I sometimes saw clouding another man's eyes.

> James Baldwin, Giovanni's Room, *New York, The Dial Press, 1956.*
> *Copyright © 1956 by James Baldwin. Reprinted by permission of*
> *The Dial Press, Inc.*

Morality in sexual relations, when it is free from superstition, consists essentially of respect for the other person, and unwillingness to use that person solely as a means of personal gratification, without regard to his or her desires.

> Bertrand Russell, Marriage and Morals, *Allen and Unwin, London,*
> *1929.*

Moralities sooner or later outlive themselves, ethics, never: this is what the need for identity and for fidelity, reborn with each other seems to point to.

> Erik H. Erikson, Youth, Change and Challenge, *Basic Books, New*
> *York, 1963.*

The Lovers by Bernard Perlin
Collection, The Museum of Modern Art, New York. Purchase.

A compelling problem regarding premarital sex relations confronts most young people: "Should I or shouldn't I?" "To what degree should I give way to impulse or at what point should I set limits?" We have already mentioned the marked discrepancy between the age of sex maturity and modal age for marriage. We have also pointed to the confusion of sexual practices and ideological conflicts regarding premarital ethics. Mores reflect time and place, and in our society no behavior pattern is static. We are living in a time when standards of conduct are probably in greater flux than at any other period in history.

Moreover, in addition to the lack of precision about what his or her sex code should be, the young person finds that, after all, it is the individual who must decide. There is essential disagreement regarding personal codes, and in an age of individualism there are no absolutes. The decision about a course of action is partially conditioned by (1) the individual's own primary needs, as defined by heredity and other biological factors; (2) the cultural-social environment defined by his parents and teachers on one side, and his peer group on the other; (3) the particular situation of the moment; and (4) the other party, who has a specific personality, sensitivity of response, and complex needs and attitudes.

In arriving at decisions regarding a mode of conduct, the individual is caught in an age or generational difference. His parents and he may take different stands on the issue of premarital sex or perceive the situation from a different viewpoint. The parent often reflects the viewpoint of his own parents or attitude of his generation. There is a great gulf in outlook on sexual habits between those born before 1890 and those born after 1900.[1] Added to this generational conflict is the problem of sex roles. The double standard permits a greater latitude for men than for women. However, neither has clear-cut standards or norms of behavior to follow on a date. The models vary from an idealized movie version to the strictest interpretation of Judeo-Christian ethics.

In view of this confusion of standards, it is difficult to present a scientific viewpoint of the problem of premarital sex mores. Various

---

[1] Lewis M. Terman, *Psychological Factors in Marital Happiness*, McGraw-Hill, New York, 1938, pp. 321–323. For a discussion of this generational difference see Ira L. Reiss, *Premarital Sexual Standards in America*, The Free Press of Glencoe, A Division of Collier-Macmillan, New York, 1960, pp. 75–80.

motives are relevant to this question. In reality, any statement of conviction in this area can only be beliefs, which may or may not be founded in empirical evidence. Without overanticipating our discussion of these two goals, we should point out that the case for premarital restraint and an objective outlook are not mutually exclusive. However, let us first look at the various outlets available to the young person.

Both biology and culture emphasize the goal of heterosexual interests. However, for either internal or external reasons not all individuals find it possible to realize this potential. Since Biblical times, human beings have had varied sexual interests suggesting that heterosexuality is by no means a universal norm.

AUTOEROTICISM. Kinsey [2] indicates that the major outlet for the young male is masturbation; more than 90 per cent of the male population practice this technique in the upper teens. In fact, 69 per cent of college-educated males reported masturbation during their married lives.[3] Of the female interviewees, 62 per cent admitted having masturbated, 58 per cent to the point of orgasm; although, as with the male, the figures varied with age, marital status, education, and other factors. Masturbation represents the largest outlet for the male (about 60 per cent) until marriage; for the female, 52 to 90 per cent, as determined by educational level. Masturbation is widespread for both sexes despite the traditional gloom, if not psychopathic despair, associated historically with the practice. Even today, many individuals look on it as a neurotic or infantile behavior pattern. For most individuals masturbation may be regarded as a transitional or substitute form of activity, and there is little reason to fear the initiation or continuance of this behavior. Still, the question arises as to why certain adults persist in this habit when other sources of sexual satisfaction are available. In some cases the individual has not graduated into sufficient heterosexual desire, or masturbation indirectly fulfills another sexual urge. Generally, masturbation is a substitution for heterosexual activity. Its intermittent continuance into marriage in the male indicates such factors as his relatively stronger sex desire or perhaps the unavailability of his wife during illness, menstruation,

[2] Alfred C. Kinsey, Wardell B. Pomeroy, and Clyde E. Martin, *Behavior in the Human Male*, W. B. Saunders, Philadelphia, 1948, pp. 500f.

[3] Alfred C. Kinsey, Clyde E. Martin, Wardell B. Pomeroy, and Paul H. Gebhard, *Sexual Behavior in the Human Female*, W. B. Saunders, Philadelphia, 1953, p. 142.

late phase of pregnancy and the postpartum period, etc. In most instances the individual experiences some fantasy, heterosexual or homosexual, directed toward a real or mythical individual. Masturbation also has occasional narcissistic overtones. Although it is hardly likely to be emotionally satisfying, this practice reduces tension and frustration to some extent, and except for excessiveness or compulsion there is no reason to consider it in any way pathological. If masturbation exists during marriage, it will become a very secondary activity.

HOMOSEXUALITY

For purposes of this textbook, homosexuality is defined as a specific sexual or genital contact between members of the same sex. Without a precise definition, the term includes any contact activities—social, athletic, or others—between two members of the same sex. Consequently, homosexual is not a very useful label. Still other implications of the term refer to the tendency to identify with or assume some of the characteristics of the opposite sex or to be emotionally attracted to the same sex, neither of which in itself implies a sexual contact or even a conscious interest that could be called physical. The same person may or may not manifest all of these characteristics: he could prefer to be with members of his own sex, resemble the opposite sex, and be attracted to and cohabit with members of his own sex.

Some distinctions are immediately suggested: there are *overt* (or active) and *latent* homosexuals. Perhaps 2 to 4 per cent of the population might be described as overt, although Kinsey indicated that approximately a third of the male sample had, at one time or another, indulged in this outlet, and in many cases, on only one or two occasions. In other words, the confirmed homosexual is a small fraction of those who experiment in this direction. The latent group are those with repressed homosexual tendencies and might be designated as 2 to 4 per cent of the population. If we accept a bisexual theory of human nature (that human beings have characteristics of both sexes), the estimate might go much higher. Another distinction can be made between the *confirmed* homosexual and the *fortuitious* homosexual. The second refers to the individual who utilizes this outlet as purely substitutive because his environment restricts him to contacts with only his own sex. This type of homosexual might be found in, for example, the armed forces, prison, or other similarly limiting settings or popu-

lations. Once this individual is restored to his normal milieu, the homosexual behavior generally disappears unless he has, by his activities,
acquired definite homosexual needs. As implied, a considerable percentage of the population straddle the fence, not quite certain where
their real tendency lies. It will be recalled that of the 37 per cent of the
Kinsey population that reported at least one homosexual experience
after the beginning of adolescence, the greater number were, at the time
of the study, adjusted to heterosexual experience.[4] It is possible that
some degree of identification with members and characteristics of the
same sex, as well as with those of the opposite, may conceivably be one
of many factors propitious to marriage adjustment. Terman found that
his male respondents who had admitted a mild degree of homosexual
tendencies were as well adjusted in marriage as those who had no similar
feelings.[5]

The confirmed homosexual has no easy solution to his problem. He
often finds himself isolated from society at large and becomes part of
certain in-groups. Such a person may suffer in the employment market,
and find other kinds of penalties levied against him. These sanctions
are often unrealistic and even inhumane from either a psychiatric or
scientifically ethical viewpoint. Society is a harsh arbiter in the matter
of sex deviance. The homosexual almost inevitably experiences some
feelings of inadequacy irrespective of the sophistication he may display
publicly. And in later years, once the glamour of youth and early
adulthood has vanished, his adjustment becomes even more difficult.[6]

Homosexuality is not necessarily confined to men. Although almost
as many women may be homosexually inclined as men (19 per cent
report a homosexual outlet by age thirty), the problem for men is more
serious.[7] First, our culture is more condemnatory toward the male
homosexual, and the penalties for infractions are higher. Two women
may live together with no or little adverse social reaction. Women may
demonstrate overt affection which is accepted as being within the
range of normalcy. However, our culture strongly condemns the overt
demonstration of close emotional responses between two men. Second,

[4] *Ibid.*

[5] Terman, *op. cit.*, pp. 342–346.

[6] Extreme examples of the culture and social relationships of the male homo-
sexual are found in Maurice Leznoff and William A. Welsey, "The Homosexual
Community," *Social Problems,* 1956, 4, 257–263; and Albert J. Reiss, Jr., "The
Social Integration of Queers and Peers," *Social Problems,* 1961, 9, 102–120.

[7] Kinsey, et al., *op. cit., Female,* p. 453.

partly because of its severe repression, male homosexuality once expressed appears to be stronger and more resistant than female homosexuality to therapy and reeducation. Although the question of sex differences and response to therapy needs more investigation, this tendency may be plausible in view of the higher vulnerability of the male toward neurotic and psychotic disorders and personal disorganization. Third, the male homosexual is likely to be more overtly maladjusted in regard to potential relationships with the opposite sex and marriageability, because generally he is the one to take the initiative in sex relations, and completion of the act depends primarily on him. On the other hand, homosexual tendencies of the female are less of an obstacle since she assumes the more passive role in sex relations.

The causes of homosexuality are as diverse as its forms of expression. Chapter 5 outlined some of the complex psychological situations during infancy and childhood that complicate the adjustment of the child: parental rejections or overprotection, overpermissiveness, gross emotional inconsistencies, excessive standards of discipline, compulsive concern with cleanliness, particularly the problem of toilet training—all of which may inhibit a normal attitude toward sex. Not uncommon among homosexuals is a history of abnormally strong identification with or attachment to the parent of the opposite sex. There are also parents who unconsciously develop images of the child as a member of the opposite sex, and who may therefore dress the child in attire of the sex that was really desired.[8] They are usually unaware of the direction that personality and behavior in their son or daughter takes in adulthood.

Another factor in the causes of homosexuality is the possibility of traumatic or unwholesome experiences in the adolescent years, such as failure to interact with members of the opposite sex. More important is the initiation into homosexual activity by some older individual; once introduced to the behavior pattern, an individual may find it satisfying and thus become fixated, especially if the pattern is supported by latent tendencies. Thus, it is a combination of the early psychological environment with the individual's later definition of the situation that causes him to behave in this way. Many clinicians feel

---

[8] Daniel G. Brown, "Psychosexual Disturbances: Transvestism and Sex-Role Inversion," *Marriage and Family Living*, 1960, 22, 218–227. Although Brown is interested in transvestism (the tendency to adopt dress of the opposite sex), the causes of this phenomenon are not unlike those associated with homosexuality itself and transvestism is, of course, found in a large percentage of homosexual individuals.

that later events are secondary in causational significance to the social-psychological climate that surrounds the infant and child in the home.[9] Unwittingly, thousands of parents, by indifference, naïvete, negligence, or their own neurotic predisposition have made all but inescapable the development of a homosexual son or daughter.

In most cases, latent or mildly overt homosexual tendencies are within the range of normal behavior, can be helped, or completely sublimated with psychological assistance. To the confirmed homosexual, in contrast, psychiatric attention can do little but reduce the guilt and anxiety which he may feel, or prepare him to accept his homosexuality unless the motivation of the individual permits broader social adjustment.

NECKING AND PETTING

A large proportion of premarital sex activity today, especially in the middle and upper-middle classes, includes a variety of intimacies that fall short of actual sexual intercourse. These behavior patterns are commonly referred to as necking and petting. Necking is fondling or kissing, excluding manipulation of the breasts or gential areas. Although any clear-cut distinction is unwarranted, petting generally implies exploration and stimulation in direct contact with the skin, especially below the waist. Kinsey tends to deal with necking and petting under the term, "heterosexual petting," and finds that over 90 per cent of all males and over 80 per cent of all females are involved in premarital petting.[10] Some varied reactions to the phenomenon of necking among college populations are found in Table 8.1. The male usually initiates these petting episodes; however, the more intimate love-making does not occur without some cooperation from the female, passive though it may be. In this relationship, as in coitus itself, verbal communication is frequently less important than gesture, facial expression, and innuendo. The way a girl moves her hands, arms, or shoulders, for example, can tell her partner something about how far he may proceed. Certainly necking and, for all practical purposes, petting are an inherent part of the ritual of courtship, an enjoyable

[9] Victor W. Eisenstein (ed.), *Neurotic Interaction Marriage,* Basic Books, New York, 1956, esp. Chapters 4 and 7; also Irving Sarnoff, *Personality Dynamics and Development,* John Wiley, New York, 1962, pp. 322–336.

[10] Kinsey, et al., *op. cit., Male,* p. 37, and *Female,* p. 234.

Table 8.1

SOME RESPONSES BY COLLEGE BOYS AND GIRLS TO QUESTIONS ON SEX MORES, FROM SELECTED STUDIES *

	Boys Agreeing	Girls Agreeing	Differ- ence
Christensen, 234 students at University of Wisconsin, 1939.[1]			
Approve "mild necking or petting for pre-engagement period."	53.6%	14.5%	39.1%
". . . for engagement period"	90.9	83.9	7.0
Approve "heavy necking or petting for pre-engagement period"	7.3	0.0	7.3
". . . for engagement period"	30.0	12.1	17.9
Smith, 602 students at X college, 1950.[2]			
"Girl must neck to be popular"	44.0	15.0	29.0
"Girl must pet to be popular"	21.0	4.0	17.0
Reiss, 187 students in a New York college, 1959,[3]			
"when individual feels strong affection for the partner"	86.8	81.3	5.1

* Adapted in part from Warren Breed, "Sex, Class and Socialization in Dating," *Marriage and Family Living*, 1956, **18**, p. 138.

[1] Harold T. Christensen, *Marriage Analysis*, The Ronald Press, New York, 1950, p. 226.

[2] William M. Smith, Jr. "Rating and Dating: A Re-Study," *Marriage and Family Living*, 1952, **14**, 312–31.

[3] Ira L. Reiss, "The Scaling of Sexual Permissiveness," *Journal of Marriage and the Family*, 1964, **26**, pp. 190–191.

characteristic of the American behavior pattern. The comparison of 1939 and 1950 results with 1959 findings suggests some liberalization of opinion regarding petting and also a diminishing of the double standard. However much it may represent a sublimated act, much of the participation in this activity depends on the degree of psychological intimacy and on operation of certain values and attitudes, as is indicated in Table 8.1.

Undoubtedly, cultural differences adhere in the matter of premarital relations. A survey conducted among students in Utah,

Indiana, and Denmark demonstrated that there was a cultural continuum in the degree of premarital intimacy permitted.[11] The more
religious atmosphere and closer social control of the Utah student was at
one end and the more permissive attitude of the Scandinavian at the
other, with the Midwestern in an intermediate position. As with most
studies, the women were more restrictive in all three cultures in insisting upon a love relationship. Although these questions were directed
as much to coitus as to petting, the same basic sex difference obtained.
Generally, the Midwestern norms were closer to the Western results
than to the Scandinavian. The Scandinavian student is more conservative than the American in insisting on a deeper psychological relationship before he would be willing to engage in intercourse, and is less
promiscuous but more intimate and monogamous.

Religion, education, and social class are all variables in the individual's response to petting. Middle-class girls are especially sensitive, for
instance, to the risks of petting and more likely to resist the advances
of the boy. The girl is vulnerable and concerned about her reputation
in the peer group. Her desirability to the male is not enhanced by
being tagged an habitual petter. Ehrmann's data reveal that the male
may also feel some guilt about petting, especially with females in
whom he is seriously interested. "The degree of physical intimacy
actually experienced or considered permissible is among males *inversely* related and among females *directly* related to the intensity of
familiarity and affection in the male-female relation." [12]

EFFECTS OF PETTING.   One aspect of petting is the possible feeling of
unpleasantness and guilt on the part of the girl as a result of the boy's
insistence on heavy petting. A study of nearly 300 girls at a Midwestern university campus found that more than half (55 per cent) were
offended at least once during the academic year by some aggressive
male act. A fourth of these offenses involved attempted intercourse;
the remainder were attempts at petting, both above and below the
waist. More than half of these erotic intimacies occurred in going-
steady relationships or in the engagement period. Emotional reactions

[11] Harold T. Christensen, "Cultural Relativism and Premarital Sex Norms,"
American Sociological Review, 1960, **25,** 31–39; and Harold T. Christensen and
George R. Carpenter, "Value Behavior Discrepancies Regarding Premarital Coitus
in Three Western Cultures," *American Sociological Review,* 1962, **27,** 66–74.

[12] Winston Ehrmann, *Premarital Dating Behavior,* Holt, Rinehart and Winston,
New York, 1959, pp. 269–270.

of the girl varied among anger, guilt, and fear.[13] While there is a differential reaction according to age and sex, individual variations are equally marked. According to Ehrmann's university survey, men generally have idealistic notions more in theory than in reality, or are more inclined to go beyond the standards they have set up. Both sexes are also more liberal in the code they hold for the peer group than for themselves, which again suggests that considerable conflict surrounds sexual behavior. Ehrmann reported guilt feelings for both sexes in petting, although, of course, to a lesser extent than in coitus. Both men and women appear to have a "sliding scale" as to when certain kinds of sexual intimacy are inappropriate, but the girls are inclined to reserve quasisexual responses for a genuinely romantic aura or strong affectional involvements.[14]

Petting has been criticized from two opposing viewpoints: that it does not go far enough or that it goes too far. A recent critic asserts that petting, in its attempts to retain a "technical virginity," is completely fallacious. Instead of this "petting with affection," a phony, teasing effort at satisfying both morality and physical desires, a person might as well throw off his inhibitions and enjoy an affection-oriented intercourse![15] This viewpoint would be plausible except for the fact that human culture is often fashioned of small but important differences, and that in the ritual of petting some compromise is found between a Victorian past and a Freudian present. Or it may be, as one observer implies, that petting and necking become an interesting way to kill time on a date.[16]

In sharp disagreement with this permissive attitude is the criticism made by parents and the clergy of the close physical contact in present-day dating. From the more liberal pulpit, necking and petting have been intellectually justified in a total love relationship as a prelude to marriage. Much of the significance of petting depends on variables of age, background, and the personality factors that the two individuals bring

[13] Clifford Kirkpatrick and Eugene Kanin, "Male Sex Aggression on a University Campus," *American Sociological Review*, 1957, 22, 52–58.

[14] Robert L. Karen, "Some Variables Affecting Sexual Attitudes, Behavior, and Inconsistency," *Marriage and Family Living*, 1951, 21, 235–239.

[15] Ira Reiss, "The Treatment of Premarital Coitus in 'Marriage and the Family' Texts," *Social Problems*, 1957, 4, 197–200.

[16] O. Hobart Mowrer, "Sex Education of Adolescents," *Marriage and Family Living*, 1960, 22, 322–324.

to the situation. It goes without saying that what is acceptable to the boy of twenty-three might not be for the girl of eighteen, in addition to a number of more subtle differences between two people. Moreover, the two participants bring different levels of emotional involvement to their dating. It is usually not difficult to make a decision about whether to accept or reject necking, because this behavior is within the approved code of conduct. From the viewpoint of the young person, with the combination of an attractive companion, soft music and moonlight, necking would just come naturally. The more critical decision may have to be made about petting, which has a marginal status within our codes of behavior.

PREMARITAL SEX RELATIONS

THE KINSEY PICTURE. Of the total male population that Kinsey examined, 68 per cent had experienced premarital coitus by age eighteen; 77 per cent by age twenty-two; and 92 per cent by age thirty-eight. However, for those men with at least one year of college, the figures were considerably reduced: 31 per cent had experienced premarital coitus by age eighteen; 49 per cent by age twenty-two; and 67 per cent by age thirty-eight.[17] These percentages clearly point to the "deferred gratification pattern" typical of the upward mobile middle class.[18] This means that the middle-class young American sublimates his sex desires and defers total gratification until he feels sufficiently secure in the socio-economic sphere to attempt direct sexual experimentation. Sexual intercourse tends to be postponed until marriage or until a quasimarital situation exists.

The females in Kinsey's study distributed themselves in opposite fashion from the males on premarital intercourse; however, if we control for age, the educational level operates as it did for men. Between the ages of sixteen and twenty, 38 per cent of the elementary school group, 32 per cent of the high school, and 18 per cent of the college-educated groups had experienced premarital coitus.[19] Beyond these years the educational level had progressively less influence, and after age twenty women were not differentiated according to the years of

[17] Kinsey, et al., *op. cit., Male,* p. 550.
[18] Louis Schneider and Sverre Lysgaard, "The Deferred Gratification Pattern: A Preliminary Study," *American Sociological Review,* 1953, **18,** 142–149.
[19] Kinsey, et al., *op. cit., Female,* pp. 293–295.

school completed. On the other hand, the differential effects of education continued to influence the male's behavior until the age of marriage. Whether this finding, in regard to the female is valid, remains to be investigated in further research.

Since much of the discussion has revolved about the Kinsey findings, let us digress to assess the importance of this vast survey. The various volumes of the Kinsey report are cited, since they represent the largest and most penetrating study of sex behavior yet conducted. Nonetheless, there have been a number of criticisms, such as the following:

First, the tone of the study is almost purely physiological. Kinsey, as a biologist, stressed the term "outlet" and minimized the psychological and social aspects of sex. Although his purpose was to amass statistical data as a prelude to further study, we must approach his findings with this limitation in mind.

Second, the composition of the sample, despite its size (12,000 males and 8,000 females) has certain defects. Principally, criticism has been directed to the disproportionate number of volunteer subjects, which means that the sampling is not random. We can easily understand the difficulty of securing a probability or random sample; yet the question remains as to whether the inquiry attracted a large number of sex deviants, exhibitionists, individuals atypically interested in sexual phenomena, or the very conventional. Considering the high rate of homosexual admissions, for example, certain authorities have suspected, rightly or wrongly, bias in the sample. The female population was weighted toward the upper-educated group with only a relatively small sample of the less educated.

Third, the interviewing and statistical techniques have occasionally been found wanting. For instance, the interviewer would place the burden of denial on the interviewee in questions such as, "When did you begin such and such activity?" Kinsey's concern that the subjects would tend to withhold information proved perhaps less serious than the possibility that they reported more than had existed.[20]

THE PATTERN OF PREMARITAL SEX BEHAVIOR. Most studies have presented results similar to those of Kinsey. For the college male the percentages have run from 51 per cent, in a 1938 sample, to various postwar surveys varying from 41 per cent to 68 per cent. Ehrmann

[20] William G. Cochran, Frederick Mosteller, and John W. Tukey, *Statistical Problems of the Kinsey Report*, American Statistical Association, Washington, 1954, pp. 72-79.

found that war veterans were more "experienced," 57 per cent compared to 47 per cent for nonveterans. Percentages for the college female are equally diverse, from 7 per cent to 26 per cent, with rapidly ascending figures if noncollege or postcollege populations are included. Burgess and Wallin observed that of 47 per cent of females reporting premarital intercourse, roughly a third (35 per cent) was confined to the future spouse.[21] It appears that the differential rate of the two sexes is partially attributable to a large number of males finding sexual satisfaction with a smaller number of nonpeer-group females. The college male frequently turns to off-campus stamping grounds; in a very few cases, this includes prostitution.[22] The girl seeks to improve her status by dating above her class as she perceives some possible mobility by purveying sexual favors. Or the male feels that he cannot offend his social equal or superior. These class differences have less effect with the advancing age of the female. Besides education and social class, religion for both sexes was found to have considerable influence when the devout, the moderate, and the inactive are compared. Less difference is visible among the three principal religious faiths: Catholic, Jewish, and Protestant.[23]

As suggested, regional, national, or cultural differences are critical in premarital intimacies. Christensen's Danish sample was less inclined to random dating and less anxious to introduce coitus on the basis of casual dating; yet, once a couple became involved in a serious relationship, coital activities appeared earlier than with the two American samples and were enjoyed more thoroughly in the sense that less negative aftereffects were reported for the following day. The Midwest (Indiana) sample, again, was intermediate between the Danish sample and the Western (Utah) ones, although closer to the second.[24]

Most significant in the Kinsey studies was the factor of educational level and occupational class, with the higher levels inclined to reject coitus and select more sublimated "outlets" (masturbation, petting to

[21] Ernest W. Burgess and Paul Wallin, *Engagement and Marriage,* J. P. Lippincott, Philadelphia, 1953, p. 331. See also Ehrmann, *op. cit.,* pp. 33–34 for a summary of these studies.

[22] Lester A. Kirkendall, "Circumstances Associated with Teenage Boys' Use of Prostitution," *Marriage and Family Living,* 1960, **22**, 145–149.

[23] Kinsey, et al., *op. cit., Male,* pp. 477–479, and *op. cit., Female,* 304–307.

[24] Christensen and Carpenter, *op. cit.;* also, Harold T. Christensen and George R. Carpenter, "Timing Patterns in the Development of Sexual Intimacy," *Marriage and Family Living,* 1962, **24**, 30–35.

climax, etc). Homosexuality followed somewhat the same pattern, but the high school group, or lower-white collar, represented a somewhat higher incidence of this type of behavior than the elementary school group, and a markedly higher incidence than the college-trained sample.[25] Generally, on the urban-rural axis, the city male had the widest outlets available to him. Up to twenty years of age, 55 per cent of city boys have experienced premarital coitus compared to 47 per cent of farm boys.

The data emphasize particularly the critical influence of educational level on attitudes concerning premarital coitus. First, sex differences in responses are less noticeable for college-educated samples than for noncollege samples. In other words, the double standard is more rejected among the better educated. Reiss conducted an elaborate study in which attitudes toward sexual permissiveness were scaled with kissing at one end of the continuum, petting representing an intermediate area, and full sexual relations at the other end. He found considerably more liberal responses among a college and high school (junior and senior year) students sample than in a national adult sample, as Table 8.2 indicates. Within the national and school samples Negroes were more liberal or permissive than whites; however, race differences were less conspicuous than educational or age differences. To a marked extent students accepted the criterion of love and affection as necessary in both petting and intercourse; whereas the adult sample was less interested in that distinction, but was more inclined to consider kissing, petting, and intercourse as emphatically separate types of behavior. The double standard was largely rejected by both adult and student samples, which undoubtedly reflects a long-term trend toward a more liberal approach to sex relations. In addition to age factors, individuals varied within either the racial or sex groupings according to their frequency of church attendance or the degree of romantic attitudes.[26] Negro males generally held the freest attitudes and white females the most conventional.

LIBERALISM VERSUS CONSERVATISM. There are possibly two essentially different standards in premarital sex conduct. First, there is the *double standard,* the traditional Western heritage. Essentially, this is

---

[25] Kinsey, et al., *op. cit., Male,* Chapter 10.

[26] Ira L. Reiss, "The Scaling of Premarital Sexual Permissiveness," *Journal of Marriage and the Family,* 1964, **16,** 188–198; see also "Premarital Sexual Permissiveness among Negroes and Whites," *American Sociological Review,* 1964, **29,** pp. 688–698.

Table 8.2

PERCENTAGE AGREEMENT WITH ITEMS ON PREMARTIAL SEX
BEHAVIOR IN A NATIONAL SAMPLE AND IN A HIGH SCHOOL
AND COLLEGE SAMPLE *

	NATIONAL SAMPLE		SCHOOL SAMPLE †	
	Behavior for		*Behavior for*	
	Males	*Females*	*Males*	*Females*
KISSING ACCEPTABLE BEFORE MARRIAGE				
1. When engaged to be married	95.3	95.0	97.5	98.5
2. When in love	93.6	93.3	98.9	99.1
3. When feels strong affection for partner	90.2	88.1	97.2	97.8
4. When does not feel particularly affectionate toward partner	58.6	50.1	64.2	55.2
PETTING ACCEPTABLE BEFORE MARRIAGE				
5. When engaged to be married	60.8	56.1	85.0	81.8
6. When in love	59.4	52.6	80.4	75.2
7. When feels strong affection for partner	54.3	45.6	67.0	56.7
8. When does not feel particularly affectionate toward partner	28.6	20.3	34.3	18.0
FULL SEXUAL RELATIONS ACCEPTABLE BEFORE MARRIAGE				
9. When engaged to be married	19.5	16.9	52.2	44.0
10. When in love	17.6	14.2	47.6	38.7
11. When feels strong affection for partner	16.3	12.5	36.9	27.2
12. When does not feel particularly affectionate toward partner	11.7	7.4	20.8	10.8
	(N = 1,390)	(N = 1,411)	(N = 811)	(N = 806)

* Adapted from Ira L. Reiss, "The Scaling of Premarital Sexual Permissiveness,"
Journal of Marriage and the Family, 1964, **26**, 188–198.

† The five educational institutions represented were a white Virginia college,
white Virginia high school, white New York college, Negro Virginia college, and a
Negro Virginia high school.

the concept that the male is free to enjoy sexual pleasure with an as-
sortment of available women, but expects the girl he marries to preserve her virginity. Ideally, according to the double standard, there exist two species of women, the pure and the fallen. Traces of this for-

mula from the Latin world can still be found in the Anglo-Saxon male, who clings to the double standard as a simplified approach to combining his sex life with the later roles of marriage and the family. The "hero" of a contemporary satirical novel reflects a not atypical attitude on his male status and the two kinds of women we have described according to the double standard.

Even though I am trying to keep this on a high literary plain, I feel it is obligatory at this point that I go into the matter of my past experience with women. For reasons which will become clear to the intelligent reader, I'm sure.

As I formerly mentioned, there are these two *un*-professional ladies of ill repute I happen to know at home. One is Marge and the other is Susie. Despite their already ruined reputations, I refuse to mention their last names. I'm not a cad, for gosh sakes! On the other hand, I'm not a prude either. What I mean to say is, I'm just a normal nineteen-year-old fellow, with normal appetites and all that, and these girls (at home) are always calling me up anyway. Don't get me wrong—I certainly don't go with either one of them. As previously mentioned, Barbara is my girl, and she's a very high-minded girl too. I wouldn't *touch* Barbara. I'm not that type. As a matter of fact, we may marry some day. But marriage, for me, and also for Barbara, is in the future, so as I've already mentioned, there are these two girls at home, whom I occasionally date. I mean, *go out with.* I can't really consider them *dates,* for gosh sakes'.

What I'm driving at is this: Both of them consider me the best lover in town. I don't mean to brag, but they do. They're constantly telling me they do, and they've been telling me this for some time now. And I'm fully aware that the reason they feel this way—even though they run with any number of other fellows, being the sort they are—is that I'm far from unendowed physically. Also, I know how to handle myself in the backseat of our family Chevy. Though, again I must emphasize, I'm not trying to brag. I'm only stating the facts, the hard cold facts. And as for my being loose enough to run with these two, I must mention that I do not wish to enter wedlock, especially with such a fine girl as Barbara, completely naive about such important matters as the techniques of love-making.[27]

Ehrmann, in the studies we have mentioned, found that the male interviewees holding to a double standard had a higher rate of premarital coitus (80 per cent as opposed to the 63 per cent of the single-standard males).[28] However, the double standard is apparently less and less a part of the value system of today's young people. A survey of ten university campuses throughout the United States revealed that 29

[27] Robert Gover, *One Hundred Dollar Misunderstanding,* Grove Press, New York, 1961, pp. 43–44. Copyright © 1961 by Robert Gover.

[28] Ehrmann, *op. cit.,* p. 191.

per cent of the students considered premarital relations "never justified" for men, and 38 per cent said "never justified" for women, implying that the majority felt a single standard should be applied and that sexual intercourse might be possible under specified conditions.[29]

The *single standard* can be represented by three positions: hedonistic, discretionary, and ultraconservative. The hedonistic approach is illustrated by the individual who believes that sex should be completely free and that love and affection are not necessary, although these emotions are desirable, at least from the feminine viewpoint. The discretionary standard accepts sexual intimacies when there is a deep emotional relationship and states that time and place, along with other factors, determine the acceptance or rejection of intercourse. Last, the conservative or ultraconservative categorically rejects sex relations until marriage, which is the official religious position and the usual preference of parents. In addition, each of these theories varies according to individual acceptance in principle, practice, or both. It has been mentioned that often a person has a more exacting code for himself than for his peer group.

Glassberg, generalizing from his professional clinical experience, states that heterosexual activity may be the result of self-centered needs, such as physical gratification, reassurance of maleness (or femaleness), conformity to group norms, or compensation for affectional deprivation. Such activity also may result from "other-person-centered needs," such as the desire to fill the affectional demands of the partner.[30]

PREMARITAL INTERCOURSE AND CONSEQUENCES IN MARITAL ADJUSTMENT. A primary question in regard to premarital sexual intimacy is the degree to which the individual's future marital adjustment may be affected. The research results are not altogether consistent regarding this relationship. Some studies have revealed a higher orgasm adequacy on the part of the wife if she has had satisfying premarital sex relations, but this thesis has been questioned by still other research. Terman found that virginity was associated with marital happiness but not to the point of statistical significance.[31] Burgess and Wallin found that engagements tended to be broken with significantly greater

[29] Rose K. Goldsen, Morris Rosenberg, Robin M. Williams, Jr., and Edward A. Suchman, *What College Students Think*, D. Van Nostrand, Princeton, 1960, p. 95.

[30] B. Y. Glassberg, "Sexual Behavior Patterns in Contemporary Youth Culture—Implications for Later Marriage," *Journal of Marriage and the Family*, 1965, **27**, 190–192.

[31] Terman, *op. cit.*, pp. 325–330.

frequency when sex relations had occurred. Regarding adjustment in marriage they found "no meaningful association." [32] In another study of a sample of married women, 58 per cent stated that initial sex relationships within marriage benefited somewhat from premarital experience. However, virginal wives reported arriving at successful sex adjustments during the honeymoon; so whatever positive effects may have been gained were only minimal.[33] It appears that satisfactory sex adjustment is effected if there is a good marriage. The effects of previous sexual relations are questionable.

Using a different approach, an analysis of scores on a marital adjustment prediction test for 400 university women revealed a negative relationship between adjustment scores and extensive physical intimacies: petting above and below the waist, and especially sexual intercourse. If anything, the study most clearly reveals a statistical association of quasineuroticism between the entry into sex relations before marriage and the adjustment score, because the items constituting the scale were various indices of maladjustment.[34] On the whole, intercourse before marriage seems to be surrounded with both negative and positive interpretations.

PLEASURE PHILOSOPHY, MORAL ARGUMENTS, AND AFFECTIONAL SEXUAL NEEDS

Scientific inquiry into premarital sexual behavior is difficult, since emotional reactions run high. A biology professor was dismissed a few years ago from a major Midwestern university because he wrote an article for the university newspaper in which he advocated sexual intercourse for "sufficiently mature individuals" who could engage in it without social consequences and without violating their own codes of morality and ethics.[35] Whether the professor was correct or not is a matter of personal opinion, but the violent reaction of the university administration can be interpreted as a barometer of the sensitivity of public opinion in the area of sex relationships.

[32] Burgess and Wallin, *op. cit.*, Chapter 12.

[33] Eugene J. Kanin and David H. Howard, "Postmarital Consequences of Premarital Sex Adustments," *American Sociological Review*, 1958, 23, 556–562.

[34] William R. Reevy, "Premarital Petting Behavior and Marital Happiness Prediction," *Marriage and Family Living*, 1959, 21, 249–255.

[35] *Bulletin* of the American Association of University Professors, 1963, 49, p. 26.

Even among professionals in the field of sociology there is no agreement between the positions of conservative or traditional and liberal or experimental, as occasional discussions in the literature of marriage and family demonstrate. In this book we avoid direct moral statements and permit the reader to arrive at his own judgments by presenting as scientific an approach as possible. The question of sexual morality is discussed in terms of the liberal position and the conservative.

THE LIBERAL POSITION. Adherents to this point of view stress individualism and personal pleasure. They feel since sex is intended for enjoyment, there should be no impediment to its pursuit. Necking and petting are only half-way substitutes, and the true satisfaction is love-oriented intercourse: "permissiveness with affection." If the individual is less hampered by emotional and normative needs, he will choose "permissiveness without affection." [36] In reply to this hedonistic viewpoint we can point out that there is no scale on which happiness or even pleasure can be assessed. Furthermore this course may be difficult to pursue, because, as already discussed, women have largely negative reactions toward cohabitation with the male in view of the persistence of a double standard and the risks that the woman takes in premarital relations.

Second, the liberal viewpoint holds that sex relations are biologically desirable, especially for the male, to release tension, and that health may be impaired if inhibition is attempted; petting is only a provocation. This argument is rejected by medicine and psychiatry. Although the inability to realize sex expression may be frustrating for whatever physical tension may be involved, nocturnal emissions or masturbation have been the traditional outlets. Much of the rationalization for prostitution was the supposed necessity for physical release for the male, but statistics suggest that prostitution is disappearing, at least in its previous form. For a minority of young men, relations with prostitutes has persisted more as an experimental adventure, often in response to peer-group pressure, rather than because of compelling sex drives.[37]

Third, if premarital intercourse is permitted, the liberal argument continues, it will minimize unsavory sexual outlets, that is, masturbation, prostitution, and homosexuality. According to this argument, with a frank admission of the necessity of premarital sex relations,

[36] Reiss, *op. cit.* (1960), Chapter 6.
[37] Kirkendall, *op. cit.*

society can concentrate on the free circulation of information about contraception and precautions against venereal disease. In other words, with sex freedom and full access to information, anxiety and neurotic behavior will be reduced, since there will no longer be the negative attitude individuals had in the past.

This viewpoint assumes a rather simplified notion of human motivation. It also appears that masturbation, homosexuality, and even prostitution meet the needs of certain individuals for long periods of time. As a deterrent to homosexuality this viewpoint disregards the fact that there are a number of bisexuals, and, if we accept the theories of Freud and the statistics of Kinsey, we can say that nearly all human beings are basically ambivalent in this respect. In any case, with the increase of premarital sex relations over the last two generations, there has been no evidence that the practices of masturbation and homosexuality have declined.

A fourth reason for free sexual relations, as seen from this point of view, is that marriage tensions will be reduced since both partners will enter marriage already satisfied, and there will not be the curiosity to experiment further. Moreover, the husband will be more sophisticated in his techniques, and the wife will indulge in marital coitus with more enthusiasm. With less inhibition and the happy inevitability of freer sex relations and elimination of the double standard, the wife would be more capable of orgasm. Of course, the complete argument would apply only if a single standard were in operation. In reply, it should be noted that there is no evidence that sex relations with others make subsequent marriage more satisfying. In fact, in some cases, the individuals who are promiscuous before marriage are least faithful afterwards.[38] We have already discussed the dubious effect of previous practice on sexual relations after marriage. Sex techniques can be as satisfactorily acquired in marriage as prior to marriage. No one has ascertained what degree of marital happiness depends on sexual adjustment; we discuss this question in Chapter 14.

THE CONSERVATIVE POSITION. The moralist or conservative viewpoint of sex behavior raises other arguments:

First, the conservative notes, there is loyalty to certain institutional structures or groupings such as the family, school, church, or specific peer group associations. It is hardly a valid argument to reject sex experience simply because of one's parents or peers. However, it is not

[38] Kinsey, et al., *op. cit., Male*, pp. 354–357.

a viewpoint to be entirely dismissed. In a university woman's sample, "family training" was mentioned by 71 per cent of the respondents as the principal reason for refraining from sex relations. In a similar study, 61 per cent indicated that "sorrow of the parents if discovered" was the underlying reason.[39] A number of surveys point to the effect of religious belongingness on premarital sex mores. An "honor code" system operates on a few campuses whereby the student's respect for the college itself is a contributing deterrent to sexual license. Whether these institutional controls are a valid argument for continence depends on a person's value structure; Western society has depended on such loyalties for centuries.

A second argument is that the theory of sexual gratification often fails to comprehend that personal responsibility and sensitivity to the needs of others is inconsistent with the pursuit of physical pleasure. Ideally, it might be possible to arrive at a "person-centered" sexual relationship, but unfortunately too many other variables become involved: the threat of sexual failure, fear of what other people will say, worry about pregnancy, etc. Where marriage is contemplated these problems may be minimized, but then another problem is encountered. For most young people, marriage cannot have the same meaning if physical indulgences are equally available before the nuptial ceremonies have taken place.

A third point cited by the conservatives is that our society still adheres to something resembling a double standard. The male may behave more independently of society; the female bears the greater risk. Virginity prior to marriage is still respected. For both sexes, but particularly for the girl, premarital relations means there are the threats of an illegitimate child, abortion, or a forced marriage. In the United States about one birth in twenty is illegitimate. In a sample of more than 2,000 unmarried white women, nearly 500 (18 per cent) had had a pregnancy before marriage, and 15 per cent of those were second pregnancies.[40] Roughly three-fourths of premarital pregnancies are estimated by the Kinsey staff to result in abortions. We need hardly dwell on the emotional trauma and financial costs resulting from this kind of experience.

[39] Lemo D. Rockwood and Mary E. N. Ford, *Youth, Marriage and Parenthood*, John Wiley, New York, 1945, pp. 52–53.
[40] Paul H. Gebhard, Wardell B. Pomeroy, Clyde E. Martin and Cornelia V. Christensen, *Pregnancy, Birth and Abortion*, New York, Harper-Hoeber, 1958.

In the United States about one out of five marriages is preceded by conception, as compared to the Danish rate of one out of three.[41] The modal time of conception for pregnancy marriages in the United States is two months prior to marriage; in Denmark, five months. There is evidence in our culture that premarital pregnancies are more likely among the young since they are less informed about contraceptive methods, and among the lower socio-economic groups, because more sexual relations are reported in these groups. Premarital pregnancies are also more probable in economic depression periods because of lengthy courtships. Pregnancy-induced marriages are usually civil rather than religious.[42] The forced marriage has about twice the risk of divorce as the normal marriage, and the divorce is secured in relatively brief time after the marriage.[43] These findings were generally confirmed by Lowrie in a large scale Ohio sample, which also showed that premarital pregnancies occured in relation to marked age differentials. The groom was usually significantly older than the bride. Other factors included limited education and little or no religious training, especially on the part of the bride.[44]

THE DIFFICULTY OF MORAL DECISIONS. The dilemma surrounding moral questions, including the difference in generational viewpoints in the area of premarital sex, is contained in the following excerpt from a contemporary novel:

. . . Suppose she just said, "Daddy, I meant what I said—I'm truly sorry—the sorriest I know how to be." Yes, that was better. Keep it simple and unhysterical.
And her father would say, "What is it you're sorry about—becoming pregnant or having intercourse?"
"Well," she would say, trying to dodge, "they sort of went together. I'm just sorry about the whole thing—"
"Suppose you hadn't become pregnant—would you still be sorry?"

[41] William J. Goode, "Family Disorganization," in Robert K. Merton and Robert A. Nisbet (eds.), *Contemporary Social Problems*, Harcourt, Brace and World, New York, p. 97.
[42] Harold T. Christensen, "Studies in Child Spacing: I—Premarital Pregnancy as Measured by the Spacing of the First Birth from Marriage," *American Sociological Review*, 1953, 18, pp. 53–59.
[43] Harold T. Christensen and Hanna H. Meissner, "Studies in Child Spacing: III—Premarital Pregnancy as a Factor in Divorce," *American Sociological Review*, 1953, 18, pp. 641–644.
[44] Samuel H. Lowrie, "Early Marriage: Premarital Pregnancy and Associated Factors," *Journal of Marriage and the Family*, 1965, 27, 48–56.

That was the clinker and she might as well be ready for it. She would look down at the floor for a minute and then back up. "Shall I be honest?"

"That might be helpful, yes."

"It'll also complicate things."

"Yes," he would say, groping for an aphorism, "that's one of honesty's drawbacks."

"Okay. If I weren't pregnant, I wouldn't be sorry—no. That's the honest answer." And she would look aside. "I guess you're not overjoyed at that, either."

"You wanted to have intercourse?"

"Yes—I wanted to."

"No one took advantage of you?"

"No—no one did."

He would nod and pretend he understood but his anger would creep through. "Why, Robs—couldn't it wait?"

"Not as long as I would have had to—no."

"You're not expecting to be an old maid, are you?"

"Not exactly."

"Then why couldn't it wait?"

And she would gather herself together for the major effort. "Daddy, will you try to understand if I tell you? I mean will you really listen instead of just going through the motions?"

"All right."

She would give a small, thankful nod and then say, "Daddy—the thing is that everything's different now—I mean from when you were my age. I wasn't there or anything so I can't be sure. But that's what I think from everything I've read and heard. Kids now are tired of being kids. I mean it's just a pain. Kids know the score now when they're very young. They know about sex and about liquor and about money—and about being part of a screwed-up world that they're going to be handed. And they know that everything's happening at about a thousand miles a second and that the whole damn earth can blow up the next minute. And if it doesn't, then we'll fly to the moon someday or some kookie planet. Who ever heard of that when you were a kid? And all that put together means—well, it means you have to *do* everything and *see* everything and *be* everything—you know, because the world's too exciting to miss. It's not good enough any more just to be told you shouldn't do this and you can't do that. We *want* to do them—we *want* to try them—and as soon as we can. To hell with being a kid if you have to sit with a rattle, all cooped up in a pen. It's not enough any more to say to a girl she shouldn't go to bed with a boy because it's not nice. That's like telling a little kid the sky is blue because it's not red. Maybe she wants to go to bed and find out for herself. Maybe she thinks it'll be terrifically exciting. Maybe she thinks living dangerously is the only way that makes sense if the bombs may go off any minute. And what's wrong with that? Saying nice girls just don't want to go to bed before they're supposed to—that's no answer. Of course they want to—they've always wanted to. They just never used to dare. And that's the whole point—now kids are daring. Well, so what? What's so bad about that? Okay, sure—I can think of one thing. They can become pregnant—if they're dumb, the way I was—or get diseased. But what's that got to do with the rightness or wrongness of it all?"

He would follow her very closely and then wait for a while very thoughtfully after she was done. And then he would say, "So you think the only thing you did wrong was to get pregnant?"

"See, I can tell already—you don't understand. You think what I said was just dreadful—"

"No, Robs I'm just trying to be sure I got your message right. Is that it? Getting pregnant was wrong—but that's all?"

"Okay—that's about it, yes."

"And you're not ashamed?"

"No, I'm not ashamed—I'm sorry. I tried to explain that."

"Are you proud, then?"

"No—I'm not proud. Don't you see—it doesn't have anything to do with being proud or being ashamed—"

"What *does* it have to do with, Robs?"

"With—well, with everything I said—with being alive and loving to be and—and—well, mostly that."

"I see," he would say, not seeing at all. "And now that you've had a taste of it, do you think you'd like to try it again—I mean after this thing is cleared up?"

She would have to think about that for a moment. "Well—not right away necessarily, no. It wasn't much fun, actually."

"But you think it probably could be, if you had more practice and were careful about it—is that it?"

"Well, no—not exactly. I didn't mean that."

"What other conclusions can I draw from everything you said, Robs?"

"Look, if you're worried that I'm a nymphomaniac in training or something, just forget it. I'm not—I'm not anything like that. I mean being excited to find out what it's like is one thing. And maybe trying it once in a blue moon under very special circumstances, maybe that's a possibility. But I'm not looking to make it a hobby or anything."

"That's just the trouble, though, don't you see, Robs? It could turn into one. And it's not a very pleasant hobby. And as far as your little analysis of the new generation goes, I don't buy your conclusions. They sound to me like a nice, neat excuse to ignore the rules—by deciding they're phony and worthless. That's just not so, Robs. You're preaching moral anarchy. And if that's what you're really cooking up, that generation of yours, you might as well cash in your chips right now. It may be true, the way you say—someone's going to hand you a mighty screwed-up world one day soon. But you're not going to straighten it out by tearing all the rules up and saying to hell with it, let's just have a ball."

And she would have to nod and forget about rebutting.[45]

[45] Richard Kluger, *When the Bough Breaks,* Doubleday, New York, 1964, pp. 285-288. Copyright © 1964 by Richard Kluger. Reprinted by permission of Doubleday and Co.

There is scientific evidence that extensive premarital coitus is of questionable satisfaction to the individual. The fact that the majority of college young people disclaim it is a convincing argument. One of Ehrmann's male interviewees expressed himself as follows: [46]

. . . I am trying to find out what the girl is like. If she goes too far—that is, beyond kissing—I don't think much of her. If she would do that, particularly on a first or second date, she would do it to anyone. . . . Sometimes I go back [to these girls who went farther than he thought they should], but only after a long wait and when I am hungry again.

Or another:

. . . I don't want to try too hard to have sexual intercourse with the girl I love. If she gave in, then I'd think she had done it with others.

A not atypical reaction of a girl is:

. . . The sole reason for not having sexual intercourse with the boys I have loved is moral. I have had the desire to go that far with many boys, but I have completely suppressed it. . . . I believe that the reason that most girls want virginity is because it is the only thing they have. Once they lose it, sexual intercourse doesn't make any difference.

Another girl says:

. . . The amount of pleasure in intercourse is not as high as in activities just short of intercourse. I suppose the reason is that I feel slightly guilty and immoral when I have intercourse.

For many young people, the dividing line between going "too far" and remaining within moral bounds was the waist. Caressing the breasts, inside or outside the clothing, could also be a major decision. In any case, each individual had to set his limits.

In summary, we may refer to Reiss, who has outlined four positions: double standard (sex relations permitted for the male but not the female), abstinence, permissiveness with affection, and permissiveness without affection.[47] His advocacy of sexual freedom with affection has certain coherent arguments (i.e., the graduate student who must defer marriage until the completion of his degree). Yet the problem remains for most college students, who must decide on the role of the individual and his image of himself and of society. Age, personality, and experience determine the individual's choice of conduct. We could argue that our

[46] Ehrmann, *op. cit.*

[47] Ira L. Reiss, *Premarital Sexual Standards in America,* The Free Press of Glencoe, A Division of Collier-Macmillan, New York, 1960.

final decision is in fact not a free decision, because of these internal factors, but this text is not the place to debate free will and determinism. For most middle-class young people the meaning of the love relationship will in the long run be more important than sexual needs, *per se* if these two complex motives or feeling complexes can be dissociated.

Supplementary Readings

Bell, Robert R., *Marriage and Family Interaction*, The Dorsey Press, Homewood, Illinois, 1963. Chapters 7 and 8 are a sound discussion of premarital sex and dating.

Bernard, Jesse (ed.), "Teen-Age Culture," *Annals*, American Academy of Political and Social Science, November 1961, vol. 338. The most relevant article is Ira L. Reiss, "Sexual Codes in Teen-Age Culture," but the others are equally worthwhile.

Blood, Robert O., Jr., *Marriage*, The Free Press of Glencoe, A Division of Collier-Macmillan, New York, 1962. Chapter 5 is a well-documented review of some of the sexual problems of dating.

Christensen, Harold T., *Marriage Analysis* (second edition), The Ronald Press, New York, 1958. Chapters 8 and 9 are clear presentations of our subject with particular reference to the Kinsey report.

Ehrmann, Winston, "Marital and Nonmarital Sexual Behavior," in Christensen, Harold T. (ed.), *Handbook of Marriage and the Family*, Rand McNally, Chigago, 1964, pp. 585–622. Changes in sexual behavior, well documented, are placed into a coherent structure.

Ehrmann, Winston, *Premarital Dating Behavior*, Holt, Rinehart and Winston, New York, 1959. The analysis of results of dating and sex among University of Florida students deserves reading—now available in paperback edition.

Ellis, Albert, *The American Sexual Tragedy*, Twayne Publishers, New York, 1954. An engrossing account of our sex mores by an eminent marriage counsellor.

Geddes, Donald P. (ed.), *An Analysis of the Kinsey Reports*, Mentor, New York, 1954. This paperback presents many viewpoints, pro and con, on the famous sex survey.

Kardiner, Abram, *Sex and Morality*, Bobbs-Merrill, Indianapolis, 1954. Freud, Kinsey, and heavy anthropological data make for interesting interpretations by a psychiatrist.

Kephart, William M., *The Family, Society, and the Individual*, Houghton Mifflin, Boston, 1961. Chapters 12 and 13 are an objective assessment of premarital sex problems including, among other things, the viewpoint of the religionist.

Kirkendall, Lester A., *Premarital Intercourse and Interpersonal Relationships*, Julian Press, New York, 1961. A theoretical and empirical study of sexual liaisons with both casual and more deeply involved partners.

Lantz, Herman R. and Snyder, Eloise C., *Marriage,* John Wiley, New York, 1962. Chapter 8 is written with considerable psychological insight.

Martinson, Floyd M., *Marriage and the American Ideal,* Dodd, Mead, New York, 1960. Chapters 14 and 15 explain, with the aid of tables and bibliographic sources, some of the dilemmas facing young people.

Reiss, Ira L., *Premarital Sexual Standards in America,* The Free Press of Glencoe, A Division of Collier-Macmillan, New York, 1960. A well-thought out evaluation of the choices confronting young people although with a bias toward free sex expression. The first three-fourths of the book definitely merits reading.

Simpson, George, *People in Families,* Thomas Y. Crowell, New York, 1960. Chapters 4–6 present with some psychoanalytical overtones the subjects of dating, courtship, and premarital sexuality.

Sorokin, Pitirim, *The American Sex Revolution,* Porter Sargent Publisher, Boston, 1956. A highly subjective treatment with considerable historical allusion by a controversial sociologist.

Part three
Prelude to Marriage

Part Two discussed young people on the threshold of adulthood grappling with the problems of dating and courtship. Part Three deals more directly with adulthood. Chapter 9 examines the emotion of love and the romantic impulse from the psychological and social viewpoints. The significance and impact of this emotion is enormous. Chapter 10 focuses on the mate-selection process. Shall we marry someone different or like ourselves? There are supporters of both viewpoints, from the perspectives of the layman and professional. Yet for some people the question is even more fundamental: "Where shall I find someone to marry?"

Chapter 11 presents the legal aspects of marriage and their significance to society. Chapter 12 is concerned with the ultimate decision to marry, engagement (formal or nonformal), and the marriage ceremony itself.

Chapter nine

Love and the Romantic Quest

Of her whose gentle will has changed my fate,
And made my life a perfumed altar-flame;
And over whom thy darkness must have spread
With such delight as theirs of old, thy great
Forefathers of the thornless garden, there
Shadowing the snow-limb'd Eve from whom she came.
> *Alfred Tennyson*, Maud: A Monodrama, *Part One, XVIII, iii, 1855.*

This Can't Be Love

This can't be love because I feel so well—
No sobs, no sorrows, no sighs.
This can't be love; I get no dizzy spell;
My head is not in the skies.
　My heart does not stand still; just hear it beat!
　This is too sweet to be love.
This can't be love because I feel so well,
And yet I love to look in your eyes!
> *Richard Rogers and Lorenz Hart*, The Boys from Syracuse. *Copyright © 1938 by Chappell and Co., Inc. Reprinted by permission of copyright owner.*

The loved object is simply one that has shared an experience at the same moment of time, narcissistically; and the desire to be near the beloved object is at first not due to the idea of possessing it, but simply to let the two experiences compare themselves, like reflections in different mirrors. All this may precede the first look, kiss, or touch; precede ambition, pride or envy; precede the first declarations which mark the turning point—for from here love degenerates into habit, possession, and back to loneliness.
> *Lawrence Durrell*, Justine, *Dutton, New York, 1957. Used by permission.*

The Brown Sweater by Raphael Soyer (1952. Oil.)
Collection of the Whitney Museum of American Art, New York (50 x 34)

Ours has been called by some, the Age of Love.[1] This happy characterization of our century is not without considerable foundation. The innuendo and sheer weight of the erotic theme in advertising, the adulation awarded the movie heroine, and the rhapsodic outpouring of the popular ballad all adequately document the importance of romantic love in our culture. But more important is the behavior of man himself during the middle of the twentieth century: he covers more distance, sees more people, and falls in love more frequently than previous generations. A study of three generations of Ohio women demonstrated that the number and length of dates, as well as the number of suitors, had steadily increased so that dating was a richer emotional involvement than it was at the turn of the century.[2]

Western man for over two thousand years has tried to define love without success, but there is general agreement that it is a central focus of life. Burgess and Wallin discovered that 80 per cent of the males and females they studied considered that love is indispensable to any marriage.[3] Love has had a variegated history in Western culture, even in the last century or so. Neither the preliterate nor most of the more complex cultures are committed to love as an institution as we are in our day. The fact that our contemporary society has detached itself from kinship groupings has been an enormous factor in promoting the emotion of love. Husbands and wives are free to love each other without serious interference or competition from kin. Adolescents are given wide range in their activity, and as Goode points out, "Love may be viewed as a mechanism for filling the gap left by the decline of arranged marriages. Young people who in another marriage system would be pushed into marriage by their elders are motivated to marry because of love." [4]

In this chapter we attempt to analyze the emotion of love and its components. After an introduction to the romantic movement we shall examine the psychological foundations of love. However much love depends on an innate capacity, it is a learned response. As a complex response, the bases for development of love in the individual involve his

[1] Morton M. Hunt, *The Natural History of Love,* Alfred A. Knopf, New York, 1959, Chapter 10.

[2] Marvin R. Koller, "Some Changes in Courtship Behavior in Three Generations of Ohio Women," *American Sociological Review,* 1951, **16,** 336–370.

[3] Ernest W. Burgess and Paul Wallin, *Engagement and Marriage,* J. B. Lippincott, Philadelphia, 1953, p. 394.

[4] William J. Goode, *The Family,* Prentice-Hall, Englewood Cliffs, 1964, p. 39.

familial and social relationships, childhood, and late adolescence. The last part of the chapter is devoted to the question of defining love and classifying its different types of expression. Finally, the question of love and emotional maturity provides a prelude to the subject of mate selection and marital happiness. The specific antecedents of our contemporary definition of love began with the Romantic Movement.

THE ROMANTIC HERITAGE

The romantic urge has an elaborate history that goes beyond the limits of this chapter. It probably first appeared with the Greeks in their enthusiasm for esthetics in general and human physical perfection in particular.[5] Most cherished were the *hetaire,* who served as companions to the male, and enjoyed a less submerged position than the wives. The homosexual was significant in the Greek scheme of romantic values, however inappropiate that sentiment may seem today.

The medieval cult glorified a psychic love, but gradually this ethereal relationship assumed more direct physical expression by the advent of the Renaissance. Love had a Platonic conception in its emphasis on romance as a communication with the divine. According to de Rougemont, the medieval Tristan legend defined the romantic theme in its ultimate sense.[6] Both Tristan and Iseult, the wife of King Mark, had been given a love potion. Their love followed the formula: love is essentially tragic and not capable of realization in marriage. Love represents a conflict between themselves and society. The essence of the true romantic quest, as expressed in the classical Tristan myth, is being in love with love. As a matter of fact, the two lovers were almost perpetually separated, and in some masochistic fashion joy was found in the absence of the loved one.

Romanticism became an ecstatic relationship in the Renaissance, generally outside of marriage and remained confined to the upper classes. The pattern shifted slightly by the end of the eighteenth century or certainly by the Victorian age; and the essential ingredients of romantic love were: absence of the lover and consequent pain,

---

[5] F. Muller-Lyer, *The Evolution of Modern Marriage,* Knopf, New York, 1930, p. 59.

[6] Denis de Rougemont, *Love in the Western World,* Pantheon, New York, 1956.

insistence on purity of women and at least an idealized purity of men, and the dissociation of sex and love. However hollow and artificial this Victorian image may have been, the concept was widely accepted. Marriage may have been a happy relationship for perhaps as large a percentage of the middle and upper classes as the percentage that might be labeled "happy" today. In support of nineteenth-century practical philosophy, the poetry of Tennyson and Browning as well as their own marriages would imply that the sentimental basis of human relations had its merits.

In the twentieth century, romantic love is off to new heights. Never before in history has so large a proportion of people enjoyed love both personally and vicariously. We can conjecture that the depth of love is as great as in the Romantic and Victorian periods. One aspect of it today is the pristine and idealistic love of youth. The ingredients of the romantic cult have been extended beyond the medieval and Victorian molds. This may be seen in the product of the world media of today. The romantic impulse has been linked to the ultimate goal of marriage; in fact, the eighteenth-century novelist, Samuel Richardson, is credited with having proclaimed that love is indispensable in marriage.[7] But in the moral transformation of romanticism the mystical components have remained, for example, the suddenness of the erotic attack, "like a bolt out of the blue." Also today, idealization still implies a total absence of defects on the part of the beloved. Consequently, if one is not handsome or beautiful, an assemblage of products—from sapphire-tinged rouge to the bikini—are provided to conjure up a near facsimile of physical perfection.

ROLE OF THE MASS MEDIA. Literature has been a traditional source of the romantic epic and idealized love; this is still true today. An analysis of short stories in two popular magazines covering the periods of 1911–1915 and 1951–1955 demonstrated that the lovers in literature resembled the Nordic image: the men were tall, solid, and muscular with firm, clearly etched features and blue or gray eyes. The heroines were equally classic. The analysis indicated a shift in preference for lovers of diverse hair color in the early period, to the preference for blondes in the second period. In the later period there was a beginning of the love relationship as an "anonymous encounter," the brevity of acquaintance of the lovers, and the now formalized type of

[7] Hugo G. Beigel, "Love: Courtly, Romantic, and Modern," *American Sociological Review*, 1951, **16**, 326–334.

courtship.[8] At this time too, love was even more spontaneous, somehow vaguely akin to a flash of lightning or a mystical visitation.

The motion picture industry has for the last half century presented the contemporary classical portrait of romantic love as we have described it. During this period in motion picture history, love relationships tended to occur with maximum spontaneity, yet each relationship took place in a permanent state of enchantment, however brief, and usually concluded with a fairy-tale ending. The romantic fallacy lingers on in other respects, such as in the frustrated-love situation or the lost opportunity; for example, the two loved ones just missing each other at the airport was occasion for comedy in the American film according to a content analysis made during the late 1940's. In contrast to the American scene, one study indicated that the British or French movie was more likely to regard as tragic the situation of two lovers unable to find each other.[9] Movies sometimes become the world of escape for those who dream of that perfect love, and who have not been able to realize their dream for any number of reasons. The Hollywood romantic formula reached its apogee in the 1920's with Rudolph Valentino. It is impossible to determine to what degree the public has accepted this idealized account of love, but there is more than a grain of truth in the frequently cited passage by Linton, which was written at the height of the movie industry's success:

All societies recognize that there are occasional violent emotional attachments between persons of the opposite sex, but our present American culture is practically the only one which has attempted to capitalize these and make them the basis for marriage. Most groups regard them as unfortunate and point out the victims of such attachments as horrible examples. Their rarity in most societies suggests that they are psychological abnormalities to which our own culture has attached an extraordinary value just as other cultures have attached extreme value to other abnormalities. The hero of the modern American movie is always a romantic lover just as the hero of the old Arab epic is always an epileptic. A cynic might suspect that in an ordinary population the percentage of indviduals of the Hollywood type was about as large as that of persons able to throw genuine epileptic fits. However given a little social encouragement, either one can be adequatly imitated without the performer admitting even to himself that the performance is not genuine.[10]

[8] R. W. England, Jr., "Images of Love and Courtship in Family-Magazine Fiction," *Marriage and Family Living*, 1960, 22, 162–165.

[9] Martha Wolfenstein and Nathan Leites, *Movies: A Psychological Study*, The Free Press of Glencoe, A Division of Collier-Macmillan, New York, 1950.

[10] Ralph Linton, *The Study of Man: An Introduction*, Appleton-Century-Crofts, New York, 1936, p. 175.

Variations of the romantic love ideal also are found in the radio and television serials. Content analysis of a series of daytime programs revealed their emphasis on romantic values as a means of assuring permanence and success to the marriage relationship.[11]

The world of popular music offers one of the more fascinating panoramas of the love emotion. Romanticism is seen in a variety of moods: ecstasy is expressed by such lines as, "Is this dream a perfect dream that we can share?" or "I love you more than Jambalaya Creole shrimp and crawfish pie"; the plaintive note is struck by "Your love is all I'm needing" or "For you my love I'd do almost anything"; or the near-tragic, "I'm afraid that you'll get careless, and someone will steal a kiss" or "Give me your love instead of all those heartaches . . . why must you make me cry?" [12] The reader can no doubt supply numerous variations from the latest harvest of jukebox creations. This musical background adds to the romantic coloration of courtship, and consequently serves an important function.

THE CULTURAL VARIABLE. The romantic heritage seems to have been confined largely to recent Western culture, reaching its apotheosis in twentieth-century America. It might be helpful to survey pre-literate culture for documentation on this point.

The South Sea Islanders might be the most suited to the romantic approach or the individualistic love emotion. Samoans, for instance, consider limited sex experimentation and erotic feelings to be among the central values in their culture; monogamy is highly revered. Poetry and music also are among the esthetic backdrops of Samoan society. However, they do not fulfill our expectation of romanticism, because young people are reared in a naturalistic atmosphere—close to birth, death, and other life processes—and the sense of mystery that is present in the romanticism of Western culture does not exist in the same way. As Margaret Mead points out, boys and girls constitute classes rather than individuals, and consequently there is no specialization of affection. The Samoan girl never tastes the rewards of romantic love as we know it, nor does she suffer as the old maid who has appealed to no lover or found no lover appealing to her, nor as the frustrated wife in a marriage which has not fulfilled her high de-

[11] Leonard S. Cottrell in Paul Lazarsfeld, *Radio and the Printed Page,* Duell, Sloan, and Pearce, New York, 1940, pp. 55–58, as cited by Robert F. Winch, *The Modern Family,* Holt, Rinehart and Winston, New York, 1952, p. 387.

[12] Donald Horton, "The Dialogue of Courtship in Popular Songs," *American Journal of Sociology,* 1957, **62**, 569–578.

mands.[13] In other words, in cultures where traditional economic and kinship needs govern the choice of marriage mates, romantic notions are at best marginal.

Evidence indicates that most of the Western world now has largely accepted the romantic cause. One student has ventured the opinion that the "romantic love value complex" probably belongs only to the United States, Western Europe, Polynesia, and the European nobility of the eleventh and twelfth centuries; however, love as the basis for marriage is considerably more universal than most sociologists and anthropologists have assumed.[14]

Subcultures also have extensive influence on the romantic quest. We have discovered that human beings are usually endogamous—dating included—according to race, religion, and social class. The subculture of religion in our quasisecular age is less significant than a century ago; yet in stricter Protestantism, more devout Catholicism, and Orthodox Judaism some restrictions are found governing whom, and under what conditions, the young person may date. Romanticism is generally favored in the city over the rural environment, and there is still some flavor lent to courtship and romance by ethnic traditions.

Social class is of special significance since the techniques of love-making are conditioned by class. The romantic appeals in our society exerted by such diverse influences as costume jewelry, the coffee house, the opera foyer, or soft music, all respond to class orientation. It has been hypothesized that even the pictorial representation of romantic love in advertising or modeling in the fashion magazine has a class bias. As Winch suggests, there is the "advertising smile" of the lower class by which the young lady on the billboard says "Come buy my product," which somehow is linked with eros itself. On the other hand, we have in the upper class the "deadpan" look providing the contrast between sophistication and vulgarity.[15]

THE BALANCE SHEET.   What is the net result of the romantic outlook on twentieth-century Western culture? Many experts feel it is indispensable as a means of making a smooth transition in the early years of marriage—the softening reaction in courtship and beyond. Others feel that it is a major cause of divorce.

[13] Margaret Mead, *From the South Seas,* William Murrow and Company, New York, 1939, p. 221.

[14] William J. Goode, "The Theoretical Importance of Love," *American Sociological Review,* 1959, 24, 38–47.

[15] Robert F. Winch, *op. cit.* (1952 edition), p. 380.

For example, in the heightened emotional atmosphere of the war period, and more occasionally in the years since, newspaper accounts like the following indicate that the romantic vision is still with us:

On Monday Corporal Floyd H. Jackson, 23, and the then Mary Ella Skinner, 19, total strangers, boarded a train at San Francisco and sat down across the aisle from each other. Jackson didn't cross the aisle until Wednesday, but his bride said, "I'd already made up my mind to say yes if he asked me to marry him." "We did most of the talking with our eyes," Jackson explained. Thursday the couple got off the train in Omaha with plans to be married. Because they would need the consent of the bride's parents if they were married in Nebraska, they crossed the river to Council Bluffs, Iowa, where they were married Friday.[16]

Another approach to this question is found in an analysis of students' reports of their experiences. Farber reaches the conclusion that chance plays a major role in the process of falling in love. An "event or series of events defines the cross-sex individual as someone who is unique and whose relationship must be maintained." Phrases like "falling out of love and in again," and "suddenly it hit me" suggest an interesting factor, that is, all love leading to marriage seems to have some romantic aspects.[17] Chance may enter into the definition and redefinition of the relationship that occurs in the act of being in love: the music which is played, who else appeared on the scene that day, the resemblance of the boyfriend to a devoted uncle or to a high school date. Romanticism is uncontrolled and is largely irrational, but its aura is almost essential in courtship and marriage.

To what degree romantic love influences marital roles is still a moot point. An analysis of 210 married couples representing something of a cross-section of Los Angeles revealed that one of several factors related to marital adjustment is euphoria. This factor was based on the subjects' response to such items as "never having wished he or she had not married" or rating one's own marriage as "very happy."[18] It appears that for some marital partners a honeymoon rhapsody lingers on into the marriage, which is somewhat deeper than the romantic cult, but romance can hardly fail to add coloration to this mood. However this type of account is becoming increasingly less frequent. Young college people

---

[16] San Francisco *Chronicle*, as cited in Hunt, *op. cit.,* p. 365.

[17] Bernard Farber, *Family: Organization and Interaction*, Chandler Publishing Company, San Francisco, 1964, pp. 347–348.

[18] Harvey J. Locke and Robert C. Williamson, "Marital Adjustment: A Factor Analysis Study," *American Sociological Review*, 1958, 23, 562–569.

today, as did their predecessors, have come to realize that marriage is more than a promissory note made in the glamour of flowers-down-the-aisle and in the spirit of champagne punch of the wedding reception, or in the elopement to Las Vegas. No marriage could conceivably be made without the romantic cushioning, but "starry-eyed" romance has seldom guaranteed its success or permanency.

SOME PSYCHOLOGICAL BASES OF LOVE

When the social scientist discusses love, the burden of proof falls on him; he is attempting to approach empirically a delicate area. However, psychologists and psychiatrists have a part to play, and we believe the scientific viewpoint is useful, and frequently intriguing. The behaviorist John B. Watson set off a revolution in psychology during the 1920's by insisting that emotions were basically physical responses. Love, given the same status as fear or anger as an innate reaction pattern, was labeled as a slightly higher-level term for lust, a physical reaction of tumescence and detumescence. All further developments of this emotion were considered simple conditioning—largely verbal —of the original emotion and drive. At the same time that the behaviorists were propounding their theories, providing the intellectual justification for hedonistic self-expression, variations of this ideology were conceived by a group of psychoanalysts in Vienna. However opposed these two streams were, they managed to coalesce in their effects; the Freudian import has remained the more permanent of the two. Neither love, marriage, art, nor literature, have been precisely the same since. And, it may be added, both orientations have provided interesting outlooks even in the present. Harlow, for example, has demonstrated in the laboratory that one basic type of love, the infant love for the mother, originates in "contact comfort," since his experiments with cloth- and wire-covered "mothers," which were constructed for the study, indicated that the "cloth mother" offers for the infant monkey more attractiveness as surrogate than the "wire mother." [19] Perhaps the experiment is more instructive in terms of the possibilities it suggests for studying the bases of love than for providing a definitive answer to what love is. According to the naturalistic explanation of love, from the first positive conditioning toward the mother, in terms of contact comfort and because she gives food in the first months of

[19] Harry Harlow, "The Nature of Love," *American Psychologist*, 1958, 12, 673–685.

life, we learn to enjoy other people because of conditioning; they become substitutes for the mother or other family members who have administered to our primary needs. In later years this social learning becomes linked to the satisfaction of sexual and psychosexual needs associated with the opposite sex. As we have already discussed, many events determine who the chosen individual will be. Although this behaviorist approach is useful, the emotion of love is more intricate than the conditioning theory presumes. Love is more than need gratification.

In contrast to either romantic or behavioristic theories, love may be considered a social relationship. Reiss has suggested that love depends on a social psychological process whereby the individual enters into interpersonal relationships, or a condition of "rapport." After a certain level of ease, intimacy, and empathy has been reached in the individual's relation to another person, a second process called "self-revelation," develops (Figure 1). This stage grows out of and is reciprocal

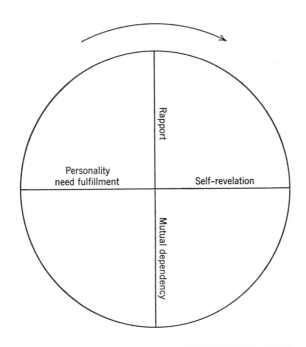

FIGURE 1 GRAPHIC PRESENTATION OF THE
WHEEL THEORY OF THE DEVELOPMENT OF
LOVE.

with certain interpersonal behaviors or interdependent habit systems: conversation, necking, or even more intimate relationships. When these habitual expectations are not fulfilled, pain, loneliness, and frustration may be experienced. The habit systems constitute a third stage called "mutual dependencies," and are largely culturally determined but have individual psychological overtones. Fourth, there emerges a "personality need fulfillment" from the preceding stages, which becomes the need for establishing rapport. This theory of Reiss rests on a certain circularity.[20] In any event, the direction that love may assume depends on the shaping of the individual by cultural, social, and personal circumstances.

SELF-LOVE AND THE PROJECTION OF THE EGO IDEAL.   From the viewpoint of one psychoanalyst, Theodor Reik,[21] love is a kind of escape from oneself. It is a projection of the "ego ideal" onto another individual, whether real or nonexistent. For this process to occur, Reik assumes an erotic or quasierotic relationship to have taken place with the parent or parents, particularly with the mother. This love was always insecure: separation anxiety is a constant threat for the infant and child. Thus, the socialization of the child is at the heart of the problem. The child whose wants are completely satisfied, which is practically impossible, would not experience love; therefore probably no one is completely incapable of love. However, among a certain number of adults this capacity has not been developed in the formative years. The following case about a student, John J., who was unable to focus his emotional potential or his affective capacity on another individual, illustrates this point:

His early history revealed a narcissistic yet masochistic mother, who had neurotically entered a marriage calculated to bring her unhappiness. She consequently bestowed all her available love and affection on John, her only child. The father was wealthy and physically handicapped because of an injury. He was ambivalent and distinctly remote in his relationship to wife and son. John in his late adolescence and early adult years wavered between homosexual and heterosexual relations. At about the time he completed dental school he married (through a forced pregnancy) a girl somewhat below himself in social class and intelligence, after having passed up a number of more appealing candidates. Although the marriage was workable for some time, after

[20] Ira L. Reiss, "Toward a Sociology of Heterosexual Love Relationship," *Marriage and Family Living*, 1960, **22**, 139–145.
[21] Theodor Reik, *A Psychologist Looks at Love*, Farrar and Rinehart, New York, 1944.

three or four years it became too threatening to him, and severe anxiety as well as psychosomatic symptoms appeared, accompanied later by alcoholism.

For perhaps all individuals the predominant love is that of the self. In a slightly different vein than Reik, Symonds [22] indicates that there are at least two self-loves. One is based on parental acceptance, where love is experienced by the child as outgoing, warm, and satisfying. The other type of self-love derives from parental rejection, forcing the child to depend on some kind of artificial self-gratification. Through fantasy he contructs an image of self-glorification. He may become antisocial or aggressive in his attempt to force others to accept his narcissism. In this type of situation, the individual is likely to develop an "anaclitic love," a love based on using another individual to propitiate his own self-regard. A person's fear of losing his self-regard may unconsciously drive him into an almost predatory type of love. The wife of an alcoholic, no matter how consciously she wants his recovery, may wish his dependency to continue and also (although unconsciously) his alcoholism.[23]

A more obvious example of this anaclitic or narcissistic type of love is seen in the highly dependent, anxiety-ridden individual—the "clinging vine." Another is a boy who dates because of the ego and stability needs it satisfies or the girl who collects boy friends. We often encounter the same basic variations of personality dynamics in a politician, actress, or an athletic hero. There is a narrow balance between what is normal self-love and what is neurotic self-glorification. This second type of person may appear to be integrated and poised, or filled with anxiety about finding a person on whom he can be dependent or who can cling to him; or he may also be the martyr type or the perfectionist.

PARENTAL AND PEER MODELS. The ego ideal becomes an important means of completing the self. From the early years, as George Herbert Mead and Robert Hooton Cooley pointed out, there is a socialization process by which the individual develops multiple selves and becomes part of the larger social world. He identifies with others and becomes a social human being through this process. The alter-ego becomes patterned after the parents, other individuals who surround him in

[22] P. M. Symonds, *The Dynamics of Human Adjustments*, Appleton-Century-Crofts, New York, 1946.
[23] Thelma Whalen, "Wives of Alcoholics," *Quarterly Journal of Studies on Alcohol*, 1953, 14, 632–641.

the household, his peer group, and a succession of models. This process gradually evolves throughout middle and late childhood and early adolescence. Ego ideals are frequently patterned after models of one's own self—what we often call "hero worship." With puberty and social and cultural emphasis, experienced by the person at this time, interest is transferred to the opposite sex.

In Chapter 5 we mentioned parental roles in the formation of the Oedipal tendency (or the Electra complex). Much of the ego ideal is formed by a projection of the parent of the opposite sex. The son selects some of his mother's traits if the mother-son relationship has been satisfying, but he may have a very different ego ideal if the relationship with the mother has been defective. The dynamics operating between ego, libido, and super-ego justify again the injection of a Freudian note into the discussion. The idealized behavior is a product of the super-ego in that certain actions are incorporated and some rejected. The perceiving, striving self or ego gropes toward another individual whom a person wishes to emulate, or who is needed in some way as a model for self-completion, whether he represents something very different from a person's own personality organization or is in some way similar. Because of the cultural mold, if not for biological reasons themselves, the individual finds a member of the opposite sex necessary for his own sense of completion. Much of the ecstatic pleasure we encounter in the love relationship is the sense of integration—this magic *Gestalt* discovered by two individuals who have become one. Love may depend on complementary needs, a theory we shall examine in the next chapter in connection with mate selection.

LOVE AND HATE: THE PROBLEM OF AMBIVALENCE. The Freudian scheme is concerned with a number of problems that would take us beyond the discussion of love. However, the problem of love and its counteremotion, hate, is not irrelevant and is one point on which the psychoanalytic theory has some apparently valid insights. In the psychological unfolding of the first years of life the individual is caught in the confrontation of conflicting sources of both positive and negative influences, for example, the indulging mother and the controlling father, or other variations of this situation.

The life and death instincts become the bases of love and hate, the constructive and destructive forces surrounding the individual. However unproved this theory is, there is clinical evidence that these emotions are not so remote from each other, considering the complex affective life of the unconscious. We certainly have a mixture of emotions, love and probably hate ourselves and our parents, and even the one we choose to marry, however hidden these feelings are from ourselves.

For the adolescent, love becomes a structured life goal. At the same time he becomes dimly aware of the anxiety associated with this emotion. He is threatened with its loss. Love can diminish, or, if a person's unconscious fears and more vulnerable defenses are attacked, may be changed to hate.[24]

NATURE AND TYPES OF LOVE

EROS AND AGAPE. The Greeks conceived of two loves, ecstatic love (*eros*) directed to one person, and selfless love (*agape*) expressed toward all people, which the Christian era developed. In the "four-wishes theory" of W. I. Thomas, human motivation was reducible to four categories or wishes: security, recognition, new experience, and response. The last named includes outgoing relationships to other people, both the affiliative desires as well as the deep-seated erotic responses. In the ultimate sense, there is some relationship between eros and agape; both constitute the wish for response, but the emotional components of the two are very different. At least there is evidence to indicate that marital adjustment, which is our conventionalized expression for eros, may be related to an agape-like social sensitivity. Terman discovered a relationship between marital adjustment and interest in humanitarian motives (care of the aged, of children, etc.).[25] However, the quality of emotional experience and the factor of sex make love motives and humanitarian motives different in quality.

CLASSIFICATION SCHEMES OF THE LOVE RELATIONSHIP. The definitions of *eros* and *agape* lead us into the discussion of other kinds of love. From the Freudian and neo-Freudian viewpoints, love may be tinged with sadism and masochism, the tendency to inflict suffering on the loved one or the unconscious gratification of suffering at the hands of the other individual. This theory is documented in clinical literature. Freudian theory also cites other abnormal variations of the love

[24] Harry Stack Sullivan, *The Interpersonal Theory of Psychiatry*, W. W. Norton, New York, 1953; especially relevant to the discussion of adolescence and heterosexual love.
[25] Terman, Lewis M., *Psychological Factors in Marital Happiness*, McGraw-Hill, New York, 1938, pp. 32, 149.

relationship: fetishism (abnormal attention to a specific object), zoophilia (excessive devotion or attraction to animals), voyeurism (delight in visual imagery), exhibitionism (self-display), and others. These are, according to Freud, associated with the libido and are in some way present in every human being. However, there is some question about whether the universality claimed by Freud for these mechanisms can be empirically supported.

Sensual or erotic love may be contrasted with platonic love; romantic love might be compared to the pedestrian love that makes up the everyday habit system of marital relations for many people. There are also parental and filial types of love, which have helped to shape our love relationships to the opposite sex. Nor can we omit the influence of the effect of siblings in the brother-sister type of love. All love has these components in varying degree. It is impossible to determine precisely where love and friendship begin and end. Similarly, love for one individual may be a substitute for loving someone else. The kind of communication love represents is constantly changing even though the basic bond is enduring. If love is a habit system, it also represents a dynamic flow of events in which all our many emotions, motives, values, and experiences form a *Gestalt* (constellation of emotions). In our system of monogamy this *Gestalt* is relatively permanent, because our culture and most others have found that human society can function only with relatively stabilized amorous relationships between man and woman. This durability of the *erotic* (in the Greek sense) relationship, of course, provides the individual with a maximum of emotional security.

A DEFINITION OF LOVE

Most college students have a fairly specific idea of what love means.[26] In a questionnaire survey more than 80 per cent thought they knew what love is or were certain about its meaning; the girls were a little more secure in their belief than the boys.[27] Love means very different things to different people, and this meaning changes in time. Two different definitions, having varying emphases, are seen in the following quotes. The first is Winch's psychological definition:

[26] An interesting discussion and classification of the varieties of love is found in Erich Fromm, *The Art of Loving*, Harper and Row, New York, 1956.

[27] William M. Kephart, *The Family, Society, and the Individual*, Houghton Mifflin, Boston, 1961, p. 321.

Love is the positive emotion experienced by one person (the person loving, or the lover) in an interpersonal relationship in which the second person (the person loved, or love-object) either (1) meets certain important needs of the first, or (2) manifests or appears (to the first) to manifest personal attributes (beauty, skills, status) highly prized by the first, or both.[28]

The second is a more idealistic definition by Magoun, which emphasizes the developmental potential of love:

Love is the passionate and abiding desire on the part of two or more people to produce together the conditions under which each can be and spontaneously express his real self; to produce together an intellectual soil and an emotional climate in which each can flourish, far superior to what either could achieve alone.[29]

INFATUATION AND LOVE. A perennial problem for the individual in our culture is to decide, "Is it love or merely a passing emotional involvement?" Infatuation seems to be especially frequent among younger girls. A study of 500 girls in 19 colleges revealed a tendency for love to be more lasting and more "monogamous," whereas infatuations were short lived and more pluralistic or simultaneous.[30] It appears that a rhapsodic falling in love occurs in only a minority of the population. As judged by the responses in the Burgess and Wallin engaged-and-married sample, less than 25 per cent stated they were "head over heels" in love, whereas most of the remainder said they were "very much so," and only 6 or 7 per cent responded that they were "somewhat or mildly in love." [31]

Falling in love is explained as a "cardiac-respiratory" theory by Folsom, which underlies the romantic complex:

What does it feel like to be "in love"? If one has the sexual, the oral, and the dermal feeling all together toward another person, is he in love with that person? If you are a thoroughgoing introspector, you will find that something else is necessary. To be physiological . . . an element of breathlessness is necessary. "In-loveness" implies catching of the breath, a deep sigh, a feeling about the heart, as if it had stopped, followed by palpitation or rapid beating, a feeling akin to fear. Shivering and trembling sometimes accompany these reactions. Then there is the *thrill* reaction, which may be a kind of muscular trembling, or a circulatory disturbance. Introspection localizes it in the chest,

[28] Winch, *op. cit.*, (1963 edition), p. 579.
[29] F. Alexander Magoun, *Love and Marriage*, Harper and Row, New York, 1948, p. 4.
[30] Albert Ellis, "A Study of Human Love Relationships," *Journal of Genetic Psychology*, 1949, **75**, 61–71.
[31] Burgess and Wallin, *op. cit.*, p. 170.

abdomen, and arms; it seems to involve a sudden increase of energy due possibly to liberation of endocrine hormones into the blood.[32]

The experience of love belongs to that class of emotion that is on the surface disturbing to the physical organism, but in reality seems to be tonic, namely *les grands chocs,* in the definition of the French psychologist Dumas. Whether this emotional upset is truly love or not depends on many factors, but once the individual has had a sample, it becomes a yardstick by which other involvements can be measured. Although happy marriages have been made without strong emotional involvement, and unhappy ones with it, the accompanying zest it adds to love is one of the highpoints of courtship and the prelude to marriage.

Whether these heart palpitations are love or infatuation is still a question to be answered. The individual can distinguish between the two by certain critieria: (1) When physical aspects of the relationship are all important or seem to be the predominant focus of the attraction, infatuation is probably the more accurate term. (2) Conflict is more persistent in infatuation and seems to overshadow the pleasurable aspects of the relationship. (3) Real love grows, and if the early effects are upsetting, the individual stabilizes his feelings toward the other person.

IDEALIZATION AND LOVE.   Romantic love has carried with it an aura of idealized adoration. Waller asserted that fantasy is intrinsic to being in love, as compared with loving a person, which makes for a more realistic bond. And "Since fantasy is much less effective than the appropriate physical behavior as a means of relieving physical tensions, there must be a great deal of this fantasy and it must occupy consciousness almost completely. . . . Upon the innate basis of the overvaluation of the sex object, our culture has built a whole structure of extreme attitudes and behavior." [33] Because Waller's assertion of an innate basis of romanticism seemed dubious, Burgess and Wallin were led to test the relationship of romanticism to marriage. Several items of their test were concerned with whether the romanticism of courtship is followed by disillusion after marriage. First, happiness ratings of the subjects in the year after marriage were higher than in the year of dating, courtship, and engagement. Second, ratings of the fiancé as

[32] Joseph Kirk Folsom, *The Family,* John Wiley and Sons, New York, 1934, p. 75.
[33] Willard Waller, *The Family, A Dynamic Interpretation* (revised by Reuben Hill), Holt, Rinehart and Winston, New York, 1951, pp. 123–124.

opposed to those of the spouse, were not significantly different (before and after marriage): ratings of "good looking" as compared to "very good looking," which were applied roughly 3 to 1 to the fiancé by the female, and 5 to 1 to the fiancée by the male, did not significantly change after marriage. Third, ratings of personality traits that might be considered unfavorable did not differ before and after the marriage. The only significant difference in the reverse direction was that changes or improvements in certain habits and attitudes were desired after marriage that had not been anticipated before marriage, but this postmarital shift may have been more a product of living together than a process of deidealization.[34] As one critic has shown, accepting the Reik thesis that insecurity leads to "falling in love," much of the idealization of the other party arises from one's own self-depreciation and the necessity to compensate by means of perfecting the chosen individual.[35]

Strauss in another study revealed that the ego ideal or conception of the ideal mate had marked effects on the choice of a mate. Only 19 per cent of the men and 26 per cent of the women studied brushed aside the ideal mate as being of marginal importance. It appears that many of the ideal-mate images are patterned after a parent (cases in which the parental model is accepted) or a parent in reverse indicating in some case ambivalence in their relationship. Strauss found that 73 per cent of his sample mentioned personality resemblances between the ideal and the parent and 59 per cent noted indicated physical similarities. About one fifth of the group also mentioned that their conceptualization of the ideal spouse was fulfilled in the choice of spouse or fiancé.[36] We can see from the results of these studies that courtship and engagement are trial-and-error situations in which a remarkable amount of adjustment takes place. Any preconceived notion of what the mate should be may encumber the process of really learning about each other.

THE PARENTAL MODEL. As we have seen, idealization and rigidity in the selection of a mate may be a problem. In the following two case studies the limitations imposed by selection or rejection of a parental model are apparent:

[34] Burgess and Wallin, *op. cit.*, pp. 214–243.

[35] Robert F. Winch, *op. cit.*, pp. 267–370.

[36] Anselm Strauss, "The Influence of Parent-Images upon Marital Choice," *American Sociological Review*, 1946, 11, 554–559; also "The Ideal and the Chosen Mate," *American Journal of Sociology*, 1946, 52, 204–298.

Dorothy's father had died when she was twelve years old and she was devoted to his image. Her mother remarried and the stepfather, unlike the father, was unpermissive, remote, and enjoyed less social status than his predecessor. As the years passed, Dorothy enshrined further the image of her perfect father. Upon entering marriage, she unconsciously designed her husband's roles to emulate the now almost legendary traits of her father, against which her husband rebelled.

Louise was adopted at high school age from an economically underprivileged family where the father was an alcoholic and the mother an insecure, slightly hostile personality. The daughter on being adopted into a middle-class, professional home was given the requisite training for a high-level academic career in chemistry. The condition for adoption was that she would break definitively with her former family, a decision about which she had some later guilt feelings. Being physically attractive and having a charming personality, she had a succession of suitors, but it was difficult for her to adjust to deeply involved personal relations and she rejected several marriage offers. Finally a particularly persistent individual some years older than she succeeded where others had failed, and after an extremely quiet marriage ceremony she attempted "the great experiment." The husband entered the role in the dependent relationship he had formed during courtship, and Louise gradually formed a pattern of destroying him as a father-substitute. After the marriage was terminated, with the aid of therapy she was able to move to a more mature relationship with men, although even then it was questionable whether she would be able to develop the capacity for love that marriage would require.

In investigating the selection of a mate, and the effects of parent and sibling relationships, we may return to the hypothesis dealing with the effect of the parent of the opposite sex. We cannot determine to what degree Oedipal tendencies may operate. The individual may react toward or away from this cross-parent. This problem is especially crucial for the boy, since he is necessarily forced to spend considerable time with the mother, with whom a fairly potent emotional reaction is likely to develop. Although the girl also finds herself in this close relationship with the mother, less risk seems to be involved. In the equalitarian or matricentric home of our culture, the mother has the vital role, whereas previous generations looked to the male as the important figure. The father was, after all, the arbiter of values in the home, and controlled its destiny including the selection of matrimonial mates for his children. Whether this patriarchal pattern tended to produce greater idealization of the father than is true today cannot be known. In any case, evidence from clinicians and marriage counsellors leads us to believe that the chosen mate is partially a parent surrogate for all of us. If we accept the theory that love is completion of the self, the most obvious model is the parent.

LOVE AS A COMPLEX SOCIAL MOTIVE

So far we have attempted to present some definition of love and how it may be distinguished from other kinds of emotional experience. What is its motivational and emotional base? Although this complex problem cannot be resolved in a page or two, the following bases are suggested:

1. The enjoyment of another person. Courtship, love, and marriage express man's affiliative desires.

2. The emotions of tenderness, loyalty, and adoration are all somehow related and expressed in love, both eros and agape.

3. The sex impulse itself, which depends on glandular functioning but also on much else in the socio-cultural conditioning process.

4. The motives of acquisition and exclusiveness. The most simple anthropological history indicates that courtship and marriage are intimately related to the property system of a people. Even in our society the individual reacts to his progress in a love involvement partly with the realization that he has something that belongs to him.

5. A sense of pride, mastery, and achievement directly or indirectly operates in love-making. Status desires are apparent here as they are in some of the other clusters of motives in the drive to love.

6. Conventionality and conformity. Falling in love is the "proper" thing to do at almost any age about thirteen, and reaches a modal point in the twenties.

7. Esthetic needs are met in love as art, poetry, and certain aspects of the commercial world indicate. This aspect of love is apparently present even in cultures quite remote to the romantic complex.

8. The desire for change. Not only is love itself a novel experience, but it offers the possibility to share new experiences. But this desire for change can be detrimental as well as beneficial to sustained love and martial adjustment.

In all these variables the role of culture and subcultures cannot be overemphasized. Yet most of the bases we have mentioned operate on a universal basis, because social motives themselves have a complex cau-

sational base developing from man's own biosocial nature or the similarity of human situations over the world. In other words, however
private and unique each love may be to the individual, he may be
certain that some of the same psychological events are operating in
others.

MATURITY AND LOVE

The decision about when to marry is a function of a person's level of
maturity. Certainly maturity largely depends on age, and divorce data
only emphasize the risk of marriages for the young person under
twenty or twenty-one, especially the male.[37] Educational and economic readiness are equally crucial. However, in this context we are
more concerned with personality maturity. For instance, what emotional and temperamental factors are central to an individual's potential happiness and success in marriage? Can a person detach himself
from the usual subjectivity in viewing his social world? Can he identify sufficiently with another individual so that he is able to acquire
the requisite emotional roles for marriage?

There is considerable documentation on the importance of personality factors for marriage success. Terman found in his sample of 792
couples in the California area during the 1930's the following items to
be positively correlated with marital happiness: stable emotional
mood; cooperativeness; lack of obsessions, compulsions, and depres-
sions; orientation and interest in the world about one;[38] as well as a
number of other factors which are discussed in Chapter 13 on the
dynamics of marriage adjustment. Other studies (Burgess and Cottrell, Locke, Winch) have corroborated the relationship between non-
neuroticism and marital adjustment. This is not to say that the neurotic is unable to make a marital success, but simply that lack of
personal and social adjustment places special strain on the intimate
and sustained process of two people living together. In some cases it
appears that emotional immaturity or ego deficiency may drive individuals into marriage, as indicated in Martinson's sample of post-high
school students, in which two samples of males, one marrying early
and the other marrying later, were compared. The data showed, using

[37] Thomas P. Monahan, "Does Age at Marriage Matter in Divorce?" *Social Forces*,
1953, **32**, 81–87.
[38] Terman, *op. cit.*, pp. 142ff.

scores on the Bell Adjustment Inventory, that early marriages may be symptomatic of emotional inadequacies.[39] Among the principal categories of marital adjustment are:

1. Emotional Warmth. An individual must find some middle point in the continuum of emotional involvement between the extremes of excessive hostility and affectional indifference. Affection or even neutrality is not possible for certain individuals whereas controlled hostility or a lack of deep hostility is a manageable emotional experience. Of course, every person needs to have the means of working off interpersonal tensions, because either conscious or unconscious hostility will produce various neurotic symptoms.

2. Personality Integrity and Freedom from Guilt and Anxiety. Personality integrity makes possible, in the words of Allport, "more efficient perception of reality and more comfortable relations with it." [40] Again we are dealing with relatives, and the individual completely free from anxiety would be inhuman. However, the individual chronically suffering from indecision, compulsive and obsessive thoughts, and wide fluctuation of mood places strain on himself and his marriage partner. At the same time, the emotional security that marriage offers has, for many persons, reduced much of their loneliness, self-doubts, and feelings of inadequacy. Here, again, counselling can often bring the individual to a realization of how internal or external some of these problems are.

3. Empathy and Role Flexibility. Some individuals seem devoid of the capacity to project themselves into the feelings of others or may be too insensitive to the emotional needs or values of others to be a responsive partner in any serious undertaking. They succeed in marriage only by a learning capacity that enables them to reeducate their own perceptual and emotional processes.

Thus the question of love and maturity is arbitrary and depends on an individual's reaction tendencies, his definition of the situation, and his ultimate objective in life. Nor can we forget that the love relationship is today colored by many romantic overtones. As we stated earlier in this chapter, romanticism is not *necessarily* dysfunctional in our

[39] Floyd M. Martinson, "Ego Deficiency as a Factor in Marriage—A Male Sample," *Marriage and Family Living*, 1959, **21**, 48–52.

[40] Gordon W. Allport, *Pattern and Growth in Personality*, Holt, Rinehart and Winston, New York, 1961, p. 280.

society or perhaps any society. In this connection a study of a college
sample showed no significant statistical relation between responses on
a scale for romanticism and a scale of emotional maturity.[41] These
results imply at least as far as any ordinary testing instrument can
determine, that romantic attitudes can accompany both maturity and
immaturity.

Maturity or adjustment frequently can be helped forward with the
aid of various testing instruments and particularly through counselling. It is, of course, not to be inferred that inadequate marriages
are necessarily the result of immaturity, or that two individuals contemplating marriage should perform a daily catechism on what
constitutes maturity. Marriage does not mean the same things to all
people, and there is no precise formula for marital adjustment.

However, there is evidence that love is the basic prerequisite for a
good marriage. A number of individuals marry on the basis of affection in the hope that a stronger relationship will develop. This probably has happened innumerable times in cases of the "rebound." It is
seldom that love toward one individual cannot be transferred to
another. The ultraromantic belief that perfect love is to be found with
that "one and only" person is today a caricature. In fact the emotional
basis of love has, if anything, been exaggerated. Love is a complex
commodity that can be cultivated and nourished out of the total
resources of the individual, emotional *and* intellectual. There may
emerge a maximum degree of freedom and yet integration of tastes,
habits, and values. This synthesis constitutes the profound experience
of love—and marriage.

Supplementary Readings

Becker, Howard and Hill, Reuben (eds.), *Family, Marriage, and Parenthood.* D.
   C. Heath, Boston, 1955. Chapter 6, by Read Bain and Chapter 7, by Joseph K.
   Folsom are relevant to the question of love and maturity.

Blood, Robert O., Jr., *Marriage,* The Free Press of Glencoe, A Division of Collier-
   Macmillan, New York, 1962. Chapter 4 discusses the development, varieties, and
   crises of love.

Burgess, Ernest W. and Wallin, Paul, *Engagement and Marriage,* J. B. Lippincott,
   Philadelphia, 1953. Chapters 3–7 describe the results of their study of engaged

[41] Dwight G. Dean, "Romanticism and Emotional Maturity: A Further Exploration," *Social Forces,* 1964, **42**, 298–303.

and married couples with regard to the premarital aspects of love and its ideali-zation.

de Rougemont, Denis, *Love in the Western World*, Pantheon, New York, 1956. The Tristan legend and what it represents from the Middle Ages to Hollywood.

Hunt, Morton M., *The Natural History of Love*, Alfred A. Knopf, New York, 1959. A delightfully written account of the subject from the Greeks to the present.

Magoun, F. Alexander, *Love and Marriage*, Harper and Row, New York, 1948. Chapters 1–4 represent a very insightful presentation of love and the prepara-tion for marriage.

Martinson, Floyd M., *Marriage and the American Ideal*, Dodd, Mead, New York, 1960, Chapters 6–11. A well-written account of romance and love and the area of the author's research, ego-deficiency.

Merrill, Francis E., *Courtship and Marriage,* Holt, Rinehart and Winston, New York, 1959. Chapters 3 and 10 present in well-documented fashion the questions of romantic love, the ego-ideal, and parental image.

Reik, Theodor, *A Psychologist Looks at Love,* Farrar and Rinehart, New York, 1944.

Reik, Theodor, *Psychology of Sex Relations,* Farrar and Rinehart, New York, 1945. A psychoanalyst gives a nonorthodox interpretation of the problem.

Waller, Willard, *The Family, A Dynamic Interpretation* (revised by Reuben Hill), Holt, Rinehart and Winston, New York, 1951. However subjective, this account remains one of the more penetrating analyses of the love relationship (Part 3).

Winch, Robert F., *The Modern Family* (revised edition), Holt, Rinehart and Winston, New York, 1963. Chapters 18–20, brilliantly state some bases of the psychology of love and courtship, including the theory of complementary needs.

Chapter ten
The Selection of a Mate

The first retainer
he gave to her
was a golden
wedding ring.

The second—late at night
he woke up,
leaned over on an elbow
and kissed her.

The third and the last—
he died with
and gave up loving
and lived with her.

> *Robert Creeley, "A Marriage," from* For Love: Poems, 1950–1960, *Scribner's, 1962. Copyright © 1962 Robert Creeley.*

Man scans with scrupulous care the character and pedigree of his horses, cattle, and dogs before he matches them; but when he comes to his own marriage he rarely, or never, takes any such care.

> *Charles Darwin,* The Descent of Man, *Chapter 21, (1871).*

The concept of the family, the concept of class, and perhaps elsewhere the concept of race, appear as manifestations of the same intolerance toward variety, the same insistence on uniformity.

> *Philippe Aries,* Centuries of Childhood, *Alfred A. Knopf, New York, 1962, p. 415.*

The Quilting Party by an unknown artist
Courtesy of the Abby Aldrich Rockefeller Folk Art Collection,
Williamsburg, Virginia

Sooner or later almost every American reaches that fateful moment in which he enters marriage. However, the question is often *whom* to marry rather than *when* to marry. Some individuals find a surplus of prospective partners; others have difficulty or can find no one. But always we wonder, "Is this the right one?" We may know the answer intuitively, but it is likely that we undergo some pained introspection anyway. According to divorce statistics, at least a tenth of the population make the wrong decision.

ATTITUDE FORMATION IN MATE SELECTION. In this ordeal of choosing a life partner, we are caught between a number of cross-pressures. Throughout our formative period we have been subject to the influence of parents and relatives. Increasingly, through our teens, peers determine our ideas about *what* and *whom* we are looking for in marriage. We also behave within an institutional framework such as the "Y," classroom, church, each with its proliferation of groups. Largely through these groups we construct a set of norms that determine the character of our courtship and marriage. Not least in this process of coloration is the effect of our mass society with its communication and entertainment media. However, more important than these secondary group contacts and commercialized media are the primary group associations of the home and the peer group.

The significance of various sources of attitudinal formation in mate selection was studied from a sample of 492 college and noncollege subjects in the Los Angeles area who were asked to rate in importance certain sources of their attitudes regarding love and marriage.[1] The results revealed that women, more than men, were influenced by their relationships with their mother, dating experiences, and their father, in that order. For the men the only "important" influences were dating experiences and the role of the mother. Other influences downrated by both sexes were: books and magazines, relatives, friends, teachers, and least in importance was the mass media. It is not surprising that parental influences were significantly more important for women than for men in view of the close relation of a girl to her parents. A possible explanation for the men placing more stress on dating experiences (although the difference was not statistically significant) is that their behavior is more variable, less guided by a set of rules, than women's.

Whatever the external pressures of parents, friends, or other associa-

[1] Robert C. Williamson, "Values and Subcultures in Mate Selection," unpublished research.

tions, we are influenced by our own internal needs, our personality structure. A person's personality structure is derived from: (1) a set of inherited capacities or tendencies to react in a given fashion, (2) the accumulation of stimuli or experiences, and (3) the momentary situation in which he finds himself. The personality structure involves a set of needs that shapes the image of whom we wish to marry. The complexity of these needs and values is reflected in the almost contradictory impulses guiding our marriage choice as seen in some common aphorisms, such as, "You marry in your own group" (endogamy), "Like marries like" (homogamy), "Like marries unlike" (heterogamy), and "We marry someone the opposite of our parents." Moreover, it is difficult to distinguish between the conscious and unconscious in the psychological process of mate selection. Choosing a life partner is possibly the most complicated event of a lifetime and, along with the choice of a career, the most critical one. The two contradictory poles—endogamy and homogamy at one end and heterogamy at the other—are prevailing themes of mate-selection studies. In understanding the terminology used here, we must realize that endogamy or homogamy may be: (1) enforced, as is the case for some religious groups; (2) a "function of opportunities," the place where one happens to meet, the neighborhood for example, and (3) normative, or similarity desired in values and interests.[2]

THE PRESSURE OF THE IN-GROUP: ENDOGAMY

PROPINQUITY OR NEIGHBORHOOD.   Possibly the basic truism in regard to mate selection is that we marry the geographically closest candidate. The most definitive study on this subject was performed by Bossard in Philadelphia in 1931; he concluded, on the basis of some 5,000 marriage licenses, that "Cupid may have wings, but apparently they are not adapted for long flights."[3] Roughly one-sixth of the applicants lived within a block of each other, one-third lived within five blocks, and more than half resided within twenty blocks of one another. This propinquity hypothesis by Koller was also tested for the years 1938 and 1946 in Columbus, Ohio. Unlike the Philadelphia sur-

[2] Alan C. Kerckhoff, "Patterns of Homogamy and the Field of Eligibles," *Social Forces*, 1964, **42**, 289–297.

[3] James H. Bossard, *Marriage and Family*, University of Pennsylvania Press, Philadelphia, 1940, pp. 79–92; also "Residential Propinquity as a Factor in Marriage Selection," *American Journal of Sociology*, 1932, **37**, 219–224.

vey, Negroes were eliminated from Koller's sample, because they were not able to move about the city as freely as whites, and, if included, would be a source of bias. Combining the two years, a total of 51 per cent of some 2,000 cases chose a mate within fourteen standard city blocks.[4] Residential nearness has been found to operate especially among lower socio-economic groups in New Haven, Connecticut, Nashville, Tennessee, and Madison, Wisconsin, although not to the identical extent. Propinquity is undoubtedly intermeshed with various factors such as social class, ethnic status, age levels, and differential opportunity.[5] Most people's activities are oriented around local facilities—educational, religious, recreational, etc. In fact, some parents select their residential area with a view toward the quantity and quality of potential mates: namely, the social class they prefer as sons- and daughters-in-law. One especially perceptive parent selected as a residential area a flat rather than hilly terrain, because the rectangular street pattern of the level area provided an address that could be found more readily by prospective suitors for his eighteen-year-old daughter! The quest for a suitor is generally not so thoroughly planned by parents, but it is obvious that the location of a home is a factor that contributes to the final decision of who is to be married into the family.

RACIAL HOMOGENEITY. Americans are highly endogamous by race. In fact, approximately thirty states prohibit varieties of ethnic intermarriage. Traditionally the Southern and borderline states have placed severe legal and moral barriers against white-Negro marriages, and the Western states to a lesser extent outlawed white-Oriental marriages. Conspicuous progress of interethnic and international relations in the postwar years seems only recently to have affected the area of marital selection. Since World War II there has been a grudging toleration of Japanese-American marriages as a result of military service. Possibly resistance has lessened toward, for example, Mexican-American intermarriage.

Apparently much of the opposition to cross-racial marriages originates in: (1) fear reactions based on pressures from either relatives or peer groups, (2) concern with future social status and occupa-

[4] Marvin R. Koller, "Residential and Occupational Propinquity," *American Sociological Review*, 1948, 13, 613–616.

[5] For a theoretical discussion see, Alvin M. Katz and Reuben Hill, "Residential Selection: A Review of Theory, Method, and Fact," *Marriage and Family Living*, 1958, 20, 27–35.

tional security, and (3) the consequences of such a union to the off-spring. Undoubtedly, those who marry in this unconventional arrangement are prepared to accept to some degree the conflict society has about miscegenation and related themes of racial purity.

Strauss's study, made during the late 1940's in the Chicago area, of a sample of some forty servicemen married to Japanese women, indicated that the several kinds of marital strains and stresses involved are not radically different from what racially endogamous marriages involve. In Strauss's sample the girl was separated from her family and had broken with her cultural milieu. Perhaps she was less likely to place emphasis on career mobility of her husband. In some cases he himself did not desire advancement or a shift to civilian employment. There were also strains in relationships with the husband's family. In other words, the majority of difficulties were those that might occur in any marriage.[6] A similar note of comparative harmony was found in mixed marriages in Hawaii during the late 1920's. It was suggested by this study that these marriages might be subject to no more discord than the ethnically pure marriages, especially in a culture marked by diverse ethnic groups.[7]

In this country the most disfavored, and usually infrequent, marriage is the Negro-white marriage. It is significant that most sexual relations between whites and Negroes, particularly in the South, involve a white male and Negro female and preclude marriage. This particular combination results from a caste relationship by which the so-called superior member of society, in this case the white and the male, may initiate the sexual act.[8] The fact that marriages involving a Negro male and a white female are several times more frequent than those of white males and Negro females raises some interesting interpretations. For one, the woman has less freedom than the man in the choice of a mate. Moreover, the middle- (or upper-) class Negro male may frequently select a lower- (or middle-) class white woman, which is in keeping with the tendency of the male to marry downward. It would not be fitting, for example, for a wealthy female to marry a Negro, since it would deprive the male of his customary function of

[6] Anselm L. Strauss, "Strain and Harmony in American-Japanese War-Bride Marriages," *Marriage and Family Living*, 1954, **16**, pp. 99–106.

[7] Romanzo Adams, *Interracial Marriage in Hawaii*, Macmillan, New York, 1937.

[8] Robert K. Merton, "Intermarriage and the Social Structure: Fact and Theory," *Psychiatry*, 1941, **4**, 361–364, as reprinted in William J. Goode (ed.), *Readings on the Family and Society*, Prentice-Hall, Englewood Cliffs, New Jersey, 1964, pp. 56–64.

breadwinner.[9] With a more fluid social situation today, marriages between the races may not always involve a socially superior husband. In fact, homogamy is increasingly observable.[10]

A study of 50 Negro-white marriages in Philadelphia, containing 44 white brides and 6 white grooms, indicated that social pressure was severe.[11] The white partner and the children produced by the union became part of the Negro society, and there was occasional loss of employment for the white spouse. Inasmuch as the white partner was already separated or alienated from his family and community ties, the marriage was not necessarily a traumatic affair. There appeared to be a fair degree of harmony between the mates. One problem in judging the validity of this study is the youthful ages of the marriage partners. (Twenty-eight years was the median age at the time of the interview.) A follow-up is desirable to determine the ultimate success of these marriages. With a sizeable portion of second marriages among this group, possibly a degree of maturity may have operated in the decision to marry. The sample also contained only those who would cooperate with the researcher, and consequently some bias may have been involved. The Philadelphia study implies that individuals entering this kind of marriage enjoy heterogamy: religious diversity was as apparent as the racial variation.

Do whites and Negroes look for different values in marriage? A study of a Southern Negro college found high interest in the partner's concern for stable marital family relations and in the area of personality traits of the marital candidates. On the other hand, there apparently was somewhat less interest in "moral norms," and the family background than would have been expected with a white sample.[12] On the other hand, another study, made in Los Angeles, found no essential difference between the Negro and white samples regarding what they accepted or rejected as traits in a prospective mate. If anything, the Negroes were more desirous of upward mobility, which included the wife working.[13]

[9] *Ibid.*

[10] Todd H. Pavela, "An Exploratory Study of Negro-White Intermarriage in Indiana," *Journal of Marriage and the Family,* 1964, **26**, 209–211.

[11] Joseph Golden, "Patterns of Negro-White Intermarriage," *American Sociological Review,* 1954, **19**, 144–147; also "The Negro-White Intermarried in Philadelphia," *American Sociological Review,* 1953, **18**, 177–183.

[12] Joseph S. Himes, "A Value Profile in Mate Selection among Negroes," *Marriage and Family Living,* 1954, **16**, 244–247.

[13] Williamson, unpublished research.

Some assessment of the students' attitudes toward the idea of inter-racial marriage may be revealed by their attitudes regarding dating persons of other races. Among the reasons listed by a white student sample for avoiding persons of other races were: loss of reputation and status, disapproval by relatives, possibility of marriage with conse-quent discrimination in the job and housing markets, along with un-happiness of the children produced by such a marriage.[14] How realistic these fears may be is suggested by certain emphases in research in this area. Summarization of a number of research studies over the 1950's reveals three principal areas of discontent. Discrimination in the economic world, social ostracism, and personality conflict of the two individuals concerned.[15] Contradictory evidence from some recent research on the matter of interethnic marriages points to minimal ten-sion in white-Negro marriages.[16] Certainly there is a research hiatus concerning the personality adjustment of children of mixed marriages. Eventually investigations may be forthcoming on this point.

It appears that intermarriages are increasing in number. A recent study in Los Angeles covering the years from 1948–1959 points to a tripling of the rate during this ten year period.[17] However, white-Oriental outnumbered Negro-white marriages in proportion to their respective population.[18] Members of ethnic minorities are very likely to look to other minority groups for their mates, as demonstrated, for instance, by Mexican-Chinese marriages. No doubt, improved ethnic relations as well as the growing urbanization of our society are factors in this increase of certain types of mixed marriages.

Among candidates most likely to enter into mixed marriages are those from a city environment, homes marked by a stressful parental situation, and individuals who have been married before.[19] It appears that particularly those individuals discontented with the status quo are among the candidates for interethnic marriages. Youth, rebellious-

[14] Larry D. Barnett, "Students' Anticipations of Persons and Arguments Opposing Interracial Dating," *Marriage and Family Living,* 1963, **25,** 355–357.

[15] Larry D. Barnett, "Research On International and Interracial Marriages," *Marriage and Family Living,* 1963, **25,** 105–107.

[16] Pavela, *op. cit.*

[17] John H. Burma, "Interethnic Marriage in Los Angeles, 1948–1959," *Social Forces,* 1963, **42,** 156–165.

[18] Larry D. Barnett, "Interracial Marriage in California," *Marriage and Family Living,* 1963, **25,** 424–427.

[19] Barnett, *op. cit.,* 1963, p. 107.

ness, and participation in the academic and artistic worlds are further predisposing factors.[20] Thus, mixed marriages may be based on different motives. In some instances a mixed marriage may result from failure in finding a mate among the in-group and preference for the out-group. Mate selection in this instance may symbolize or express the desire for change.

Even in Hawaii, where interethnic marriage is more frequent than in continental United States, intermarriage may express attitudes of rebellion toward a person's own in-group and the idealization of the other ethnic group, as a study of mixed marriages at the University of Hawaii showed.[21] The sample was composed of married individuals who were possibly homogamous in personality or shared a rebellious background, but who were culturally heterogamous. In this type of marriage, adjustment came after a "difficult process in which the participants got to know each other as individuals rather than as stereotypes." [22]

RELIGIOUS INTERMARRIAGE. On a quantitative basis the interfaith marriage looms somewhat larger than the interracial in American culture, but this depends on time and place. In reality, the vast majority of marriages are endogamous by religion. For example in a study made in New Haven, Connecticut, 91 percent of the marriages involved a partner of the same religious affiliation. The percentages varied: Jews (97 per cent), Catholics (94 per cent), and Protestants (74 per cent). The differences in endogamy are accounted for by the "relative intensity of in-group sanction on the individual in the three religious groups." [23]

In contrast to the findings in New Haven and other ethnically stratified communities, there are reports of increasing religious exogamy. In Thomas's study of 132 Catholic parishes over the East and Middle West, there were roughly 30,000 mixed marriages of which approximately 40 per cent were not sanctioned by the Church. Perhaps

[20] Lee G. Burchinal, "The Premarital Dyad and Love Involvement," in Harold T. Christensen (ed.), *Handbook of Marriage and the Family*, Rand McNally, Chicago, 1964, p. 648.

[21] Linton Freeman, "Homogamy in Interethnic Mate Selection," *Sociology and Social Research*, 1955, **39**, 369–377.

[22] *Ibid.*, p. 375.

[23] August B. Hollingshead, "Cultural Factors in the Selection of Marriage Mates," *American Sociological Review*, 1950, **15**, 619–627.

30 per cent of all Catholic marriages are mixed as determined by a 1950 count of half the dioceses of the United States.[24] Generally, the rate of mixed marriage is in inverse ratio to the proportion of Catholics in the population. According to one survey, the lowest rate of cross-religious mariage is in New England—22 per cent in a population that is 47 per cent Catholic. The highest rate is in the South Atlantic states where the population is 5 per cent Catholic, and interfaith marriages are approximately 50 per cent.[25] Thus, communities in the Northeast, such as New Haven, must be seen in the light of their ethnic composition. In less divisive communities mixed marriages are more prevalent, especially among the middle and upper classes. Moreover, they are more frequent for the sons and daughters of mixed marriages. Consequently, the increasing upper mobility and secularism of our day implies an increase of interreligious marriages.[26]

Nevertheless, religious authorities, whether Protestant, Catholic, or Jewish, do not welcome mixed marriages. From the official clerical viewpoint, Catholics consider exogamy as threatening to the welfare of the Church. Part of this opposition is from a tradition, especially that developed at the time of the Protestant Reformation. The Church's position is also influenced by its status as a minority group in the United States. However, the discouragement of mixed marriages has led to formidable burdens being placed on the two partners, especially the non-Catholic one. In order for the marriage to be valid for the practicing Catholic the ceremony must take place in the Catholic church; a civil ceremony has no validity in the eyes of the Church. The non-Catholic must agree to sign at least three pledges: (1) to respect or not to interfere with the "free exercise of the Catholic party's religion"; (2) to permit the baptism of the children; and (3) to educate the children as Catholics. None of these pledges are legally binding on the individual, because they conflict with freedoms guaranteed by the Constitution of the United States. If the non-Catholic (or the Catholic) were to break the pledge, the marriage could be declared fraudulent by the Church and would be in theory subject to annulment. How strictly these rules are interpreted, or whatever additional restrictions (such as birth control) might be applied, depends on the

[24] John L. Thomas, "The Factor of Religion in the Selection of Marriage Mates," *American Sociological Review*, 1951, **16**, 487–492.

[25] Harvey J. Locke, Georges Sabagh, and Mary M. Thomes, "Interfaith Marriages," *Social Problems*, 1957, **4**, 333–340.

[26] Thomas, *op. cit.*

local priest or bishop. There appear, however, to be suggestions of liberalization at present. At the time of the Ecumenical Council in 1962 and in succeeding years there were rumors of a more flexible policy in regard to interfaith marriages.

Divorce statistics reveal that in mixed marriages in which the wife is Catholic there is less risk involved than those with a Catholic husband.[27] The most sensitive aspect of the interfaith marriage is the religious education of the children, and this function in our culture is traditionally allocated to the mother. A non-Catholic husband is less affected than a non-Catholic wife by the demands of the Church, and considerable tension may develop in the marriage. Another source of friction may be the pressure of in-laws and their sensitivity about the religious training of their grandchildren.

As regards Jewish-Christian marriages we may note that some liberalization in exogamy among Jews has been apparent during the last few decades.[28] Yet the rate of mixed marriages is lower for the Jewish group than for Protestants and Catholics. Jews appear to be less willing to marry outside their faith than are members of other religions or those with no religion. Only 41 per cent of one college sample of Jews stated their acceptance of a non-Jew in marriage.[29] One complicating factor is the division of Jews into Orthodox, Conservative, and Reformed. The Reformed group is least opposed to mixed marriage, and the Orthodox are most opposed. In fact, because of the rigid dietary rules, marriages between the Orthodox and non-Orthodox can lead to many problems. The Jewish male more often than the female marries outside his religion or culture.[30] The explanation for this behavior lies in the particularly close control or more intimate family interdependence the Jewish girl encounters in Western culture as opposed to the wider mobility of the male.

There are probably different degrees of parental control during courtship and mate selection among the various religious groups. At least in one study, made at Temple University, Catholic and Jewish

[27] Judson T. Landis, "Marriages of Mixed and Non-Mixed Religious Faith," *American Sociological Review*, 1949, **14**, 401–407.

[28] Milton L. Barron, *People Who Intermarry: Intermarriage in a New England Industrial Community*, Syracuse University Press, 1946, p. 180.

[29] Judson T. Landis, "Religiousness, Family Relationships, and Family Values in Protestant, Catholic, and Jewish Families," *Marriage and Family Living*, 1960, **22**, 341–347.

[30] Barron, *op. cit.*, p. 186.

mothers were more rigid about their daughters' behavior during the "launching stage" than were Protestant and nonreligious mothers. Jewish mothers in particular were reported to be in greater conflict with their daughters on courtship than were those of other religious groups.[31]

The rate of intermarriage for Jews can be affected by a number of variables. A recent study of Washington, D.C. showed that secular education, a professional as opposed to mercantile type of occupation, and especially the nativity were critical factors. For the first generation only 1 per cent intermarried, as against a rate of 10.2 per cent for native born of foreign parentage, and 17.9 per cent for native born of native parentage. With the increase of intermarriage only half of the children tended to be brought up in the Jewish religion.[32]

As is true for Catholic-Protestant marriages, in Gentile-Jewish marriages a major problem may be the determination of the religion of the children. Judaism, like Protestantism, makes no formal or quasi-legal demands on the individual regarding the child's religious instruction. Yet the cultural context of Judaism often results in feelings of conflict in respect to in-group and out-group so that exogamous individuals along with their children are regarded as deviants.

The pros and cons of mixed marriages have been discussed often. There is little doubt that as a part of the various strains exerted by marriage, religious differences can be one more source of friction. Relatives and peer groups look on interfaith unions as invalid and inappropriate. Often guilt, anxiety, and hostility result for those who so marry. The divorce rate has been reported in one study to be higher for mixed marriages than nonmixed ones: only 5 per cent of Catholic and Jewish marriages had ended in divorce or separation, 8 per cent of Protestant marriages, 15 per cent of mixed Catholic-Protestant, and 18 per cent of the marriages in which the partners were without religious affiliation.[33]

Despite these factors we have cited, in our secular age sharp religious

[31] Robert R. Bell and Jack V. Buerkle, "The Daughter's Role During the 'Launching State,'" *Marriage and Family Living*, 1962, **24**, 384–388.

[32] Erich Rosenthal, "Studies of Jewish Intermarriage in the United States," *American Jewish Year Book*, Jewish Publication Society of America, New York, 1963, pp. 3–53.

[33] Landis, *op. cit.* (1949); cf., Loren E. Chancellor and Thomas P. Monahan, "Religious Preference and Interreligious Mixtures in Marriage and Divorce in Iowa," *The American Journal of Sociology*, 1955, **61**, 233–239.

differences are beginning to wane. Marriage adjustment studies show a minimum of tensions resulting from religious differences and conflicts (albeit that these were generally in nonmixed marriages) as compared with other areas, for example, affectional, economic, and recreational.[34] A recent study of Canadians over a three-decade period points to liberalization regarding Jewish-Gentile and Protestant-Catholic marriages.[35] Although we do not have as elaborate a study for the United States, there is little doubt that the same phenomenon is occurring. Except for "forced" marriages, the majority of individuals entering an interreligious union have to some extent accepted the idea of cultural variability or a kind of respect for the differences between themselves and their mates. We are also in an age of transition where interfaith cooperation is stressed. A college survey revealed that more than half the respondents questioned expressed willingness to marry outside their faiths, and a sizeable minority of these stated they would at least consider changing their religion.[36] While these verbalizations of intent are hardly a valid test of the individual's later overt behavior, they do indicate a changing climate in religious outlook.

Whatever the problems of mixed religious marriages, the most successful are individuals whose religious commitment is minimal. A liberal Catholic married to a liberal Methodist may have fewer problems than a liberal Episcopalian married to a fundamentalist Baptist. Also, two Catholics may have difficulty in marriage if one subscribes to a rigid interpretation of birth control and the other ignores the Church doctrine on this point. In other words, it is more *whom* we marry outside our faith rather than simply marrying outside it that counts. Differences in intelligence, education, class, and family background could well be the more critical factors in this question of divergence.[37]

OTHER SIGNPOSTS OF ENDOGAMY. Besides racial and religious differences, other factors operate in the direction of endogamy. One of these is *nationality*. The mobility of our age raises the question of an

---

[34] Harvey J. Locke, *Predicting Adjustment in Marriage: A Comparison of a Divorced and a Happily Married Group*, Holt, Rinehart and Winston, New York, 1951, pp. 76–79, 338.

[35] David M. Heer, "The Trend of Interfaith Marriages in Canada, 1922–1957," *American Sociological Review*, 1962, 27, 245–250.

[36] Landis, *op. cit.* (1960).

[37] Sheila A. Selfors, Robert K. Leik, and Edward King, "Values in Mate Selection: Education versus Religion," *Marriage and Family Living*, 1962, 24, 399–401.

increased rate of marriages across national lines. Historically, large-scale immigration to the United States with its high male sex ratio favored the marriage of a native American woman to a European-born male; even more frequent was the immigrant's marriage to a second generation American. However, on the whole, the "melting-pot" concept may be more of an ideal than a reality.

In recent years wartime and military occupation have encouraged some American males to marry abroad. The international mobility of our age, including such assistance programs as the Peace Corps, may increase further cross-national marriage. The growing number of foreign students on American campuses may in time further shift our traditional endogamy, but although cross-national dating occurs with fair frequency on some campuses, at present it seems not to assume matrimonial expectations.[38]

Endogamy by *social class* has been documented by a number of sociological studies.[39] The Middletown, Elmtown, and Yankee City studies offer poignant testimonials regarding difficulties imposed by class barriers, which are greater in a small town than in a metropolis.

Controversy persists about whether the social class system is becoming more rigid or less. Increasingly we encounter the notion that we live in a mobile age with expanding educational institutions. A study of Columbus, Ohio census tracts revealed distinct homogamy by social class (based on residential areas as measured in terms of property values along with educational and occupational medians). If anything, there was a statistically downward shift of marriages between individuals from widely divergent residential areas from about one-fourth to roughly one-fifth during the generation of 1933 to 1957–58.[40] The postwar prosperity as compared with the depression does not seem to have obliterated the class system within this particular city.

The major consideration in cross-class marriages is the high degree of cultural involvement marriage implies. The girl who marries into the upper or upper-upper class finds herself misplaced socially and culturally. She is cut off from friends and relatives, and in addition,

---

[38] Robert O. Blood, Jr. and Samuel O. Nicholson, "International Dating Experiences of American Women Students," *Marriage and Family Living*, 1962, **24,** 129–136.

[39] The list of corroborative studies is too vast to list, but one example is August Hollingshead, *Elmtown's Youth: The Impact of Social Classes on Adolescence,* John Wiley, New York, 1948.

[40] Simon Dinitz, Franklin Banks, and Benjamin Pasmanick, "Mate Selection and Social Class: Changes During the Past Quarter Century," *Marriage and Family Living*, 1960, **22,** 348–351.

must acquire a distinctly new set of behavior patterns. For the husband who marries upward, the situation is still worse, because the sensitivity of the male about providing the major (if not the total) economic base of the family makes his position in such a situation psychologically untenable. Similarly, the upper class member of either sex who marries downward may experience isolation and conflict. Again, as with any cultural difference in marriage, strain is introduced in what is already a delicate balance. Social class is regarded as an important subculture —certainly more critical than religion for most Americans. Marrying outside one's social class can be a difficult challenge.

Education and occupation are other subcultures which are intermeshed with our social status system. Educational endogamy between marriage partners has been reported in a number of studies,[41] and education equality is suggested as a positive factor by research on marital adjustment.[42] Similarity of occupational background has also been documented. Richard Centers' urban sample of seven occupational groups included the following classes: executive, professional, small business, white collar, skilled manual, semiskilled, and unskilled. He found a tendency among men from the higher occupational groups to marry downward and for those from the lower to marry upward. Thirty-three per cent of sons of business executives obtained fathers-in-law of the same category, whereas 67 per cent married downward, but generally only to the adjacent category. For those in the unskilled category, 75 per cent married upward and 25 per cent remained with spouses of the same background. In most occupational categories couples married within the same stratum. Again, availability is an obvious explanation. When the subjects married into a different level, it was the immediately adjacent stratum. Men were more likely to marry below themselves than were the women.[43]

LIKE MATES LIKE: HOMOGAMY

AGE AND MARITAL STATUS. The median age at which men marry is 23.1 years; the age for the girl is 20.5 years. In fact, the male's

[41] Paul H. Landis and Katherine H. Day, "Education as a Factor in Mate Selection," *American Sociological Review*, 1945, **10**, 558–560; cf. Robert C. Williamson, "Selected Urban Factors in Marital Adjustment," *Research Studies*, State College of Washington, 1953, 237–241.

[42] Among others, G. V. Hamilton, *A Research in Marriage*, Albert and Charles Boni, New York, 1929.

[43] Richard Centers, "Marital Selection and Occupational Strata," *American Journal of Sociology*, 1949, **53**, 530–535.

median age at first marriage is roughly three years older than of the female.[44] Median ages for college students are 26 and 24 years, respectively. According to New Haven data, the discrepancy between men and women increases until age 50, after which it diminishes.[45] Other studies suggest that the age discrepancy, which is less than two years before 20, broadens until the late thirties and then recedes.

There has been extensive discussion about the effect of age and age differences on the predictability of marital adjustment. Marriages made before the age of 20, especially as regards the male, were found to be distinctly risky.[46] There are no really consistent findings. Locke found the happiest marriages were those where the spouses were of equal age or the man was three to four years older than the wife. Terman found no significant or consistent relation between age at marriage and subsequent happiness. Even the women being several years older than the man had no inimical effect.[47] Obviously the matter of age is related to other factors. If the girl is happily married to the man fifteen years older than herself, the apparent father-figure might be precisely what she is looking for. Nor is her husband necessarily objecting to the youthful-looking bride. He may even like the father role implied by this kind of marriage.

The man who marries an older woman may have some advantages, popular prejudice notwithstanding. In terms of longevity it makes sense because women are expected to live approximately six years longer than men. Certainly the shibboleth that the male must be older in order to insure male domination needs revamping. No sociological study indicates that "wife older" marriages necessarily have a negative outcome. The one well-supported generalization that can be made about age in regard to marriage concerns the risk factor associated with marriage before the age of twenty. With this exception age can be regarded as the most arbitrary aspect of marriage.

Individuals tend to marry predominantly within their own marital status: the single marry the single; the divorced, the divorced; and the widowed, the widowed.[48] This trend is especially noticeable in

[44] Statistical Abstract of the United States, Bureau of the Census, Government Printing Office, Washington, D.C., 1965, p. 64.

[45] Hollingshead, *op. cit.*

[46] Locke, *op. cit.*, pp. 101f.

[47] Lewis M. Terman, *Psychological Factors in Marital Happiness*, McGraw-Hill, New York, 1938, pp. 183f.

[48] Charles E. Bowerman, "Assortative Mating by Previous Marital Status," *American Sociological Review*, 1953, **18**, 170–177.

younger people, that is, until the mid-thirties, but persists to a decreasing degree in later decades. The tendency toward assortative marriage on the basis of marital status began at the beginning of the century. Variations also occur in the rate of this kind of endogamous marriage for single, divorced, and widowed according to conditions of peace or war, depression or prosperity.[49]

Investigation of the relationship of previous marital status to present marriage has been made showing considerable divergence of results. A reasonably safe prediction is that for a man to marry a widow carries no risk. Neither does marriage to a divorced woman, but marriage to a male divorcé shows the results are slightly less satisfactory, actuarially speaking. However, the subject of intermarital-status marriage needs further investigation. Certainly predictions are not always valid as applied to individual cases. The question is better phrased if we ask what led to the divorce in a particular instance. If our hypothesis is correct, it may be that men are more responsible for divorces than women. It has long been suspected that women make the greater adjustment in mariage.[50]

PHYSICAL, MENTAL, AND PERSONALITY TRAITS. Among the factors of homogamy or assortative mating are physical characteristics. In the Burgess and Wallin research on engaged couples there was some mutuality in physical traits. The subjects rated themselves similar to their selected mates beyond what would be expected by chance on the present state of health, weight in relation to height, and physical attractiveness. However, complexion (blondness, brunetteness) did not show any correlation or similarity between the mates.[51] It is hardly a revolutionary thesis that those considered good looking have a bargaining power working in their favor. The process of mate selection becomes the supreme market place with a variety of factors, i.e., age, physical beauty, bank account, and varied status symbols, working through devious routes, but in an assortative fashion.

In view of the educational and occupational similarities of husbands and wives, there is, not surprisingly, positive correlation of slightly above .50 on intelligence, or approximately that correlation that exists among siblings or parents and their children. Surveys have yielded re-

[49] Paul H. Jacobson, *American Marriage and Divorce*, Holt, Rinehart and Winston, New York, 1959, pp. 66–74.

[50] Ernest W. Burgess and Paul Wallin, *Engagement and Marriage*, J. B. Lippincott, Philadelphia, 1953, p. 614.

[51] *Ibid.*

sults ranging from .42 to .74 in the correlation between the intelligence quotients of husbands and wives.[52] Of course, it must be realized that the I.Q. as such has limited meaning when applied to adults, and among the varied populations tested the disparity of results is not unexpected.

Research points to a small positive relationship in certain personality traits, particularly introversion-extroversion. Burgess and Wallin found 14 out of 42 items in their personality scale to show a homogamous relationship beyond chance. This finding is extremely moderate compared to the similarity between the partners on family backgrounds, life values, and leisure pursuits.[53] As we shall see in Chapter 13 certain personality backgrounds, for example, childhood as a "happy memory" and lack of hostility toward parents are related to marital happiness and appear to be homogamous. Individuals with these traits tend to find each other and marry significantly beyond what might be expected by chance. Social attitudes have also been positively correlated between marital partners.[54]

In explaining intellectual and temperamental homogamy the first and obvious answer lies in its relation to our needs for responsiveness and marital cohesiveness. Second, there is some ego-gratification in having our traits or attitudes duplicated in another individual. Third, there may be during the courtship and marriage a mutual learning experience by which some psychological coalescence occurs. Fourth, we cannot ignore the matter of endogamy and a common environment. If we marry within our social class, religion, national origin, and neighborhood, a common frame of reference is inescapable, and the fabric of personality develops along reciprocal lines. At the same time, in the almost mysterious process of locating a mate, homogamy is not necessarily the final theory.

COMPLEMENTARY NEEDS: A NEW APPROACH

Robert Winch and his colleagues have constructed a contradictory theory to homogamy, namely that we choose in marriage a personality

[52] Meyer F. Nimkoff, *Marriage and the Family,* Houghton Mifflin, 1947, Boston, pp. 421–423.

[53] Ernest W. Burgess and Leonard S. Cottrell, Jr., *Predicting Success or Failure in Marriage,* Prentice-Hall, Englewood Cliffs, 1939, pp. 344–345.

[54] E. Lowell Kelly, "Psychological Factors in Assortative Mating," *Psychological Bulletin,* 1940, **37**, 473.

structure opposed to our own.[55] This approach was partially suggested in an early study of 271 married couples who were personality opposites as based on the Jungian types.[56] Winch's theory with its neo-Freudian tone maintains that we tend to complete ourselves in the love process, which means |we must find an individual who fulfills the inadequacy or void in our own personality structure. We may marry homogamously by class, occupation, religion, etc., but within these categories we are looking for a kind of self-fulfillment (or in some cases a self-defense) against guilt or anxiety.[57] Specifically, the theory is oriented around Murray's list of 12 needs and general personality traits (anxiety, emotionality, and vicariousness).[58] For example, among other needs a woman may have nurturance, that is, a desire to lend sympathy to a defenseless person. She may then be looking for a young man who has a high dependency need, and who enjoys being aided by a kindly, sympathetic person. Some people are dominant or submissive, and rely on each other to complete their respective psychological equilibria.

In an intensively studied sample of 25 cases, Winch found 17 couples that fit this theory, with the remaining 8 neither proving nor disproving his theory. The 17 complementary cases belong to two classes: the husband dominant, and the wife dominant. The first group is composed of Ibsen's *Doll House* type where the husband is a decisive, paternalistic individual married to a passive or occasionally childlike wife (at least in the husband's image). In this same vein there is a suggestion of a Pygmalion concept with the male molding his wife. On the other hand, we see the less frequent "Master-Slave Girl" having a traditionalistic flair for male hyperdominance. Female dominance is expressed in the "Mother and Sons," the highly domestic big-sister type who enjoys mothering her husband; he in turn is happy with the mother substitute. There is also the Thurberian genre, the stereotypes created by the cartoons in which the strong female is married to the dependent male.

[55] Robert F. Winch, *Mate Selection: A Study in Complementary Needs*, Harper and Row, New York, 1958.

[56] Horace Gray, "Psychological Types in Married People," *Journal of Social Psychology*, 1949, 29, 189–200.

[57] Further evidence of this type of neurotic choice of mate can be found in Victor W. Eisenstein (ed.), *Neurotic Interaction in Marriage*, Basic Books, New York, 1956, especially in Ludwig Eidelberg, "Neurotic Choice of Mate," pp. 57–64.

[58] Henry A. Murray, *Explorations in Personality*, Oxford University Press, New York, 1938.

The theory of complementary needs has been criticized for lack of statistical evidence. Relatively few cases have been offered, and it is still questionable whether they are actually a random sample of the population. In terms of personality tests and the results of factor analysis the evidence is inconclusive. The theory has also been questioned in terms of its illogical character. Reasoning from this theory, how do some people select individuals so unlike themselves if a harmonious marriage is what they wish?

A partial corroboration of Winch's theory is provided by Kerckhoff and Davis of a sample of women at Duke University who were either engaged, pinned, or in some way "seriously attached." [59] Over a period of several months two variables were observed: the degree of consensus between the man and woman on family values and the degree of need complementarity, with the hypothesis that both variables were related to permanency of the union. As it turned out, those engagements or unions that dissolved were those that showed value consensus, but whose partners were least likely to attribute negative personality traits to each other.

It appears that couples in the initial phases of courtship often tend to idealize each other, and then arrive at a period of disillusionment followed by breakup of the union. Thus, both homogamy and heterogamy are supported. We attempt to choose among a set of individuals with characteristics like our own, including attitudes and values, who, even then, may have different personality needs. What Kerckhoff and Davis call "filtering factors" may operate at various stages of the selection process. In the earliest period status variables such as class or religion predominate, then consensus on values develops later, and finally need complementarity. Whether a courtship with accentuated differences in personalities survives in marriage varies with the individual, but there is some reason to suspect that need complementarity may be a relevant factor. |

THE IDEAL MATE: PATTERNS OF ACCEPTANCE AND REJECTION

The complementary needs approach cautions that marriage is not necessarily the meeting ground of individuals who have consciously

[59] Alan C. Kerckhoff and Keith E. Davis, "Similarity of Beliefs and Complementarity of Needs in the Choice of Mate," *American Sociological Review*, 1962, **27**, 295–299.

looked for the type of mate they eventually find. However, it is valuable to examine some of the expressed motives of young people who are seeking a mate.

One approach to this aspect of mate selection is to determine what individuals have stated as a standard for a marital candidate. It is apparent, from our discussion of homogamy, that people desire to marry someone like themselves, at least in broad social terms. On the other hand, according to research, no preconceived notion of what the bride or groom should be necessarily exists. However, Strauss found that an extremely large number of his sample had ideals concerning physical and cultural traits. Generally temperamental traits were stressed slightly less, but were still important. About half the sample mentioned consciously comparing the real with their ideal. The engaged couples reported making this comparison more frequently than the married, which may indicate memory loss about the process of mate selection once involved in the work-a-day world of marriage itself.[60]

A study conducted in Los Angeles was concerned with the problem of choosing mates: What traits would be most critical in a potential marital partner? The results shown in Table 10.1 reflect, on a five-point scale, the ratings ranging from "greatest importance" to "no importance." As can be seen from the Table, the preferred characteristics, in order, were making a good parent, similarity of interests, and enjoyment of home life. The next most important qualities showed some variation between the sexes, but they were in descending order: desire for children, even disposition, neatness in dress, intelligence, conversational ability, education, physical attractiveness, sociability, and proper religious attitudes. The men were more concerned with esthetic and physical aspects, and the women more with intelligence and religious orthodoxy. Both sexes down-rated age proximity and popularity with the opposite sex. The unmarried were more interested in similarity of interests, intellectuality, being attractive to the opposite sex, and parental competence. The married respondents seemed to be generally less identified with the whole process of mate selection, and consequently were less demanding. Similar results were obtained in comparing those who were in or had been to college with those who

[60] Anselm Strauss, "The Ideal and the Chosen Mate," *The American Journal of Sociology;* 1946, 52, 204–208.

Table 10.1

IMPORTANCE OF GIVEN CHARACTERISTICS IN A POTENTIAL
MATE *

	Men Single N = 134	Men Married N = 79	Women Single N = 162	Women Married N = 78
Having similar interests to yourself	84.2	68.4	89.4	78.2
Enjoying home life	76.1	79.7	80.9	84.6
Being very sociable	45.5	41.8	38.1	41.0
Good conversationalist	44.8	48.1	57.1	50.6
Popular with opposite sex	27.3	16.7	22.4	14.9
Physical attractiveness	49.3	46.2	21.6	27.3
Neatness and smartness in dress	60.4	62.0	49.7	57.1
Closeness in age	25.4	25.3	26.1	31.2
Even disposition	64.2	61.5	70.9	64.9
High intelligence	56.0	43.0	67.1	53.2
High education	32.6	17.7	56.8	50.6
Desire for children	67.9	68.4	69.8	66.7
Would make a good parent	82.6	79.7	87.0	74.0
Proper and conventional religious attitudes	33.6	48.7	60.2	40.8

* Per cent of respondents who stated these characteristics were of "considerable" or "greatest" importance. Figures based on the ratings of 492 Los Angeles college and noncollege respondents.

had not.[61] Of course, some differences were found when such questions were asked regarding preferences in dating.[62]

A similar approach to assessment of verbalized marriage ideals is seen in the following: "To what degree would you *reject* individuals as choices in marriage who had certain characteristics?"[63] For the males the traits in ideal mates most subject to rejection were physical handicaps, followed by deviant religious beliefs, and dependent parents. The women respondents listed in decending order: agnosticism, other religious differences, and drinking and smoking habits "very

[61] Williamson, unpublished research, cf. also "Dating, Courtship and the 'Ideal Mate': Some Relevant Subcultural Variables," *Family Life Coordinator*, 1965, 14, 137–143.

[62] A good presentation of this distinction is found in Harold T. Christensen, *Marriage Analysis* (second edition), The Ronald Press, New York, Chapter 11.

[63] Robert C. Williamson, *op. cit.*

different from one's own." Of least importance to both sexes was the possibility of marrying a widow or a person with diverging political outlook. On the whole, the women respondents were more critical or rejecting than the men. Women were generally more conventionality oriented, that is, more rejecting of candidates of lower-class background, religious and political deviants, and divorcees.

Subcultures also affected some of the views about mate preferences. Protestants placed emphasis on church attendance and religious propriety. Catholics demonstrated preferences for the desire for children, proper religious values, and were especially rejecting of divorcees, but less negative toward an individual of lower-class background. Jews, who were almost entirely a college sample, were more liberal in regard to their potential marital candidates: religious deviance, divorce, along with drinking and smoking habits, were of marginal importance.

THE PARENTAL IMAGE. The ideal mate may be patterned after the parent, especially the one of the opposite sex. This has been brought into the complementary needs theory indirectly. As explained in Chapter 5, a person frequently has very positive, and in some instances negative, feelings toward his parents; these are as likely to be unconscious as conscious. The close association with the mother through the formative years leaves an especially indelible stamp. Consequently the Oedipal tendency is relevant in this discussion even if unproved. Each of us is looking to some extent for a parent surrogate in marriage. According to another study of Strauss, we are generallly more concerned with personality characteristics than with physical resemblances.[64]

The extent to which parental relationships may be a negative influence is illustrated by the following case: A senior college student was contemplating marriage to a young man who, although several years older in age, was inferior in mental ability. She experienced considerable conflict about her relationship to this physically attractive and gregarious man. Conversation revealed that her father had been a research scientist completely absorbed in his work. She and her mother had been unable to communicate with him through the years to the degree that she had wished. This young woman in searching for her own marriage partner apparently wanted a male who would be more vigorous and less detached.

[64] Anselm Strauss, "The Influence of Parent-Images upon Marital Choice," *American Sociological Review*, 1946, 11, 554–559.

MISSED DESTINIES: OR HOW DO WE MEET?

THE CAMPUS SETTING.   Possibly the greatest problem of mate selection is *finding* the partner. Somehow our society does now always provide opportunities to meet the opposite sex. Even on the campus the selection may be somewhat disappointing. Age differences in dating and mate selection disfavor the male freshman and sophomore and favor the upper classman. On the other hand, the girl senior's chances of meeting a mate are reduced, because many of her classmates have already made their choices. Both sexes are disfavored as time goes on as the reduced marital market is partially composed of those who may be "rejects" in some respect.

On our urban campuses the student has a marginal commitment to the university or college. His day is divided between studies and a part-time or perhaps full-time job, and social life and dating may be curtailed. In comparing a student sample with a noncollege group, it was found that the students had roughly the same total number of social events or dates as the noncollege people. However, the students were involved in more institutional social events, such as those affiliated with religious groups and school. The noncollege group was more inclined to patronize bars, cocktail lounges, and public dance halls. There were also certain sex differences: for both the college and noncollege samples, women were more likely to report a kind of organized social life in the homes of friends and in religiously sponsored affairs, whereas men were more frequently found in public recreational facilities.[65]

THE OCCUPATIONAL SETTING.   In an economic enterprise where an almost equal number of each sex is employed, there may be few unmarried individuals with whom to make contact. Certain occupations have a low sex ratio, and women are likely to meet only other women. Teaching is most frequently mentioned in this category, although there has been some change in recent years. Library positions have been almost a monopoly held by women. Nursing and secretarial positions are almost exclusively the women's occupations, but usually offer a somewhat better chance to meet male prospects than, for example, teaching and library services. The male, too, may find his place of employment an important influence on the number of women he en-

[65] Robert C. Williamson, unpublished research.

counters. Nonetheless, our culture permits him more freedom, mobility, and self-assertion in the search for a mate.

MATRIMONIAL INTRODUCTION FACILITIES

Romanticism, particularly by contemporary American standards, implies choosing a mate for love. However, not all people are able to enjoy this opportunity. Consequently, various means of marriage introduction have evolved, especially in this country.

MARRIAGE ADVERTISEMENTS. Throughout most of the Western world, and particularly in Europe, marriage advertisements may be found. Even in Europe, however, they are not regarded as an ideal or prestigeful means of locating a marriage partner. A study of matrimonial ads in a Dutch newspaper revealed that individuals who advertised were generally over twenty-five years of age. Religion was one of the most frequently mentioned qualifications. Men were more inclined to mention income or occupational self-descriptions, whereas women were more likely to specify their physical traits and to request information about education or intelligence. Men, more frequently than women, requested a photograph.[66] A typical advertisement of this type from a German newspaper reads as follows: "Blonde woman with chic and charm, neither ugly, stupid, nor poor, is looking with matrimonial intentions for an affectionate and intelligent man, well groomed and widely traveled. He should be around fifty and, please, not too short." [67] "My Daughter—for whom I wish a husband, is 32, 5' 3", attractive and charming. Her self-confidence and exceptional education conceal a most friendly and humane heart. She also has property." [68]

To be sure, most advertisements are less flamboyant, but these represent a more direct or explicit statement of assets and goals than would probably be found in this country.

LONELY HEART CORRESPONDENCE CLUBS. These clubs have developed over the last half century or so. They are less direct than newspaper advertising, and therefore perhaps a more attractive means of locating a prospective mate. The marriage broker found in some parts of Europe and Asia may also prefer such means.

[66] Jetse Sprey, "Matrimonial Want Ads in Holland," paper presented at Eastern Sociological Society meetings, Philadelphia, April, 1962.

[67] *Süddeutsche Zeitung*, Munich, August 26, 1962.

[68] *Süddeutsche Zeitung*, Munich, September 12, 1964.

A number of conditions in American life make services of this type almost inevitable. For some people lack of primary group life, inability to find close contacts because of the depersonalization of urban residential life, and the range of mass activities in recreation and leisure pursuits prevent sufficiently close contact with appropriate or eligible members of the opposite sex. Although rural life is less depersonalized, the number of contacts the ruralite is able to make is, if anything, smaller.

An especially important factor in Western society is the unequal sex ratio: a surplus of men between the early twenties and mid-thirties and a surplus of unmarried women and divorcees in the age group over thirty-five and especially over fifty-five. These various social factors, combined with lack of aggressiveness or requisite personality skills, make the use of an agency as an avenue of mate selection valuable for some people.

MATRIMONIAL INTRODUCTION AGENCIES. In the late 1930's Joseph Clawson utilized various tests in a New York dating bureau (personality, general intelligence, social intelligence) to aid in assortative mating, which he did on a questionnaire-matching basis. After some months, however, he found that the technique had certain drawbacks among the better educated group from whom his clients were drawn. They disliked the scientific method, because they felt it was too "cold and calculating," they did not like the anxiety of being caught in a "blind date," and resented the charge made for the service.[69]

A more recent approach was seen in the Personal Acquaintance Service of Karl Miles Wallace, which involved 6,000 applicants. The data from these applications and the results of the personality tests were punched into cards for analysis; it is the largest research to date of its kind. Among other things, the Research Club, as it was known, sent a handbook to its members concerning certain realities of mate selection. At the same time, the machine could provide assortative mating on an organized or "scientific basis."

In matching two persons for an introduction, the electric card sorting machine selected for any of the thirty-five characteristics. For example, if a thirty-five-year-old engineer wished to meet women between the ages of thirty and thirty-seven, who were Catholic, with college education, living in California, under 5'6" tall, not divorced, who had outdoor life recreational in-

[69] Joseph K. Folsom, *The Family and Democratic Society*, John Wiley, New York, 1943, pp. 541–543.

terests, and who were compatible with him on the basis of the five personality traits measured, the machine could sort out all women in the active membership meeting these specifications in approximately fifteen minutes. An attempt was made to discourage the concept of the one-and-only or perfect mate. The objective was merely to enhance mate selection opportunities.[70]

The socio-economic backgrounds of the individuals revealed a higher than average type of clientele as compared to most correspondence clubs. Anonymity was assured by various techniques, and the language of the mailed material was on a more or less intellectual basis. Over 30 per cent of the clientele had some college education, and professional and upper-class white collar individuals were in the sample. Men outnumbered women two to one. The male preponderance was especially high under the age of thirty-five, but the sex ratio was reversed after age fifty. Part of the problem in matching was that the median age for the men was thirty-five, and for the women was forty-six, which points to age discrepancy as a basic problem in mate selection. Analysis of the personality items indicated that the clients were less sociable or more retiring, less neurotic, more religious, more conforming, more rigid and demanding than the average population (a control group). In other words, individuals who are shy and hard-to-please are possibly more likely to select a correspondence club approach. The service of the Club is demonstrated by the 640 individuals (more than 10 per cent of the total membership) who obtained a mate through its activities. Thus we may speculate about the future of electronic devices in the quest for matrimony.

We have in this chapter attempted to outline some of the choices involved in mate selection. Cultural tradition leans to in-group marriage or endogamy, although there are occasional suggestions of change. In the broad sense, we appear to desire a lifetime mate with traits similar to our own. The proponents of homogamy present a well-documented picture of selection in this direction. The complementary needs theory has tended to destroy this simple homogamous picture of the mate selection process. Still, evidence points to a vague "ideal mate," the set of specifications varying for different subcultures and personalities.

Unquestionably one of the most difficult problems in our society is providing an opportunity for young people to meet each other. For this reason many social clubs, church groups, and the like present various

[70] Karl M. Wallace, "An Experiment in Scientific Matchmaking," *Marriage and Family Living,* 1959, **21**, p. 344.

events to fill this gap. Most Americans, particularly those of college or white collar background, have been rather hesitant about utilizing commercial or rationalized agencies of mate selection.

As we shall see in Chapters 13 and 19, decisions occupying us in the choice of a mate are viewed in a different perspective in later years. The bases on which we select our life partner may shift with the adjustments of various phases of the family life cycle.

Supplementary Readings

Barron, Milton L., *People Who Intermarry: Intermarriage in a New England Industrial Community,* Syracuse University Press, 1946. In addition to being a more than satisfactory survey of the field, it presents a bibliography of interethnic marriages.

Blood, Robert O., Jr., *Marriage,* The Free Press of Glencoe, A Division of Collier-Macmillan, New York. Chapters 2 and 3 are an insightful introduction to mate selection.

Christensen, Harold T., *Marriage Analysis* (second edition), The Ronald Press, New York, 1958. Chapters 12–13 are valuable for some of the author's own research on preferences in mate selection.

Farber, Bernard, *Family: Organization and Interaction,* Chandler Publishing, San Francisco, 1964. Chapter 5 is a theoretical approach to mate selection.

Gordon, Albert I., *Intermarriage,* Beacon Press, 1964. An extensive study of the subject illustrated with case studies, particularly of Jewish-Gentile marriages.

Kerckhoff, Alan C., "Patterns of Homogamy and the Field of Eligibles," *Social Forces,* 1964, **42,** 289–297. The "field of availables" and the tendency toward assortative mating. The article by Dwight Dean in the same issue is also relevant.

Kirkpatrick, Clifford, *The Family as Process and Institution* (revised edition), Ronald Press, New York, 1963. Chapter 13 presents social psychological analysis into mate selection.

Mayer, John E., *Jewish-Gentile Courtships,* The Free Press of Glencoe, A Division of Collier-Macmillan, New York, 1961. An interesting documentation of inter-religious dating and courtship.

Nimkoff, Meyer F., *Marriage and the Family,* Houghton Mifflin, Boston, 1947. Chapter 13 contains a summary of a number of studies on endogamy, homogamy, and the like.

Simpson, George, *People in Families,* Thomas Y. Crowell, New York, 1960. Chapter 7 includes a summary of a wide scope of subjects, from sex ratio to "lonely heart" clubs.

Sussman, Marvin B. (ed.), *Sourcebook in Marriage and the Family,* Houghton Mifflin, Boston, 1963. Articles 16–20 in Chapter 2 present five important studies in mate selection.

Wallace, Karl Miles, *Love Is More than Luck: An Experiment in Scientific Matchmaking,* Wilfred Funk, New York, 1957. A popular treatment of the IBM approach to mate selection as based on the author's reasonably successful study.

Winch, Robert F., *Mate Selection: A Study of Complementary Needs,* Harper and Row, New York, 1958. An absorbing set of case histories, in addition to the theory of heterogamy.

Winch, Robert F., *The Modern Family* (revised edition), Holt, Rinehart and Winston, New York, 1963. Chapters 10, 18 and 19 deal with love, complementary needs and mate selection.

Chapter eleven

Society, Law, and Marriage

Law, the despot of making, often compels us to do many things which are against nature.

Plato, Protagoras.

Unnecessary laws are not good laws, but traps for money.

Thomas Hobbes, Leviathan, *1651.*

In a thousand pounds of law there's not an ounce of love.

John Ray, English Proverbs, *1670.*

. . . viewed in the light of society's interest in having people marry and stay married, the over-all picture of our laws affecting marriage and the family seems rather haphazard. The statute books and court reports are heavy with laws whose purpose and utility disappeared a hundred years ago.

Harriet F. Pilpel and Theodora Zavin, Your Marriage and the Law, *Holt, Rinehart and Winston, New York, 1952, p. 351. Used by permission.*

To have and to hold from this day forward, for better, for worse, for richer, for poorer, in sickness, and in health, to love and to cherish, till death us do part.

Solemnization of Matrimony from the Book of Common Prayer.

I believe marriages would in general be as happy, and often more so, if they were all made by the Lord Chancellor, upon a due consideration of the characters and circumstances, without the parties having any choice in the matter.

Samuel Johnson, Boswell's Life of Samuel Johnson, *March 22, 1776.*

The Doll and the Monster by Guy Pène du Bois
Courtesy of The Metropolitan Museum of Art,
Gift of Mrs. Harry Payne Whitney, 1921

Society has a strong commitment to marriage; our social and legal institutions are a testimonial to this. Religion, particularly, has regarded marriage as an extension of its own domain, but historically legal institutions have had an equal stake in the institution of marriage. Moreover, marriage laws reflect the cultural heterogeneity of American history. Each state determines its own laws and licensing procedures. Despite their diversity, these laws have their roots in ancient and medieval antecedents of Western society, as we have seen in Chapter 2.

There were three different streams in the development of marriage and family laws in the United States: New England, the Middle Colonies, and the South. For example, Plymouth in 1646 passed the first New England statute requiring that all marriages be solemnized before a justice of the peace or similar magistrate, even though religious ceremonies were later provided for. In the Southern colonies, marriage was considered an exclusively religious affair onto which civil legislation was later appended. The Middle Colonies took various positions according to the relevant sect.[1]

However, in almost all cultures it is agreed that society is the final arbiter of the way in which individuals are to be married or on what constitutes a valid marriage. Societies agree to varying degrees that marriage is by its very nature a privilege bestowed on people. It is true that some societies (the Samoans, for example) regard marriage ceremonials as somewhat more casual than in our society. Nevertheless, the marital relationship is subject to a number of regulations, implicit and explicit. The mores of any society indicate that marriage provides a relationship fundamental for control of the sex urge, continuation of the species, and socialization of individuals. Consequently, a set of regulations surrounds the functioning of marriage and family. The incest taboo is possibly the most universal of these, but there are others as well.

Society's stake in marriage is interwoven with religious, legal, and biological considerations. When the sharp division of church and state became increasingly apparent after the Protestant Reformation, the social order asserted its control through a rule of law. The strength of social sanctions on deviations in the marital behavior of its members is demonstrated in the reaction to the discovery of a renegade group of

[1] Helen I. Clarke, *Social Legislation* (second edition), Appleton-Century-Crofts, New York, 1957, Chapter 4.

Mormon polygynists in Northern Arizona in the late 1950's. Severe penalties were meted out to several of these bigamists.

LEGAL STIPULATIONS

THE QUESTION OF VALIDITY.   Legally, the basic question about marriage is "What is a valid marriage?" From a negative point of view there are two varieties of marriage that have dubious status. The first of these is marriages which society is determined to prevent. "Those marriages which may not be valid no matter how much the partners want them to be." [2] Incest and bigamy belong to this category. These marriages are void, for as far as the state is concerned they do not exist. Second, there are *voidable* marriages. These are not in and of themselves objectionable to the institution of marriage, but are subject to termination if one of the marriage partners does not meet the standards or norms society expects in the performance of married life. Such causes as fraud or a physical inability (for example, impotence—which in a sense is fraud if the male pretends to be normal before marriage) might be grounds for voiding the marriage or for annulment in most states. Society may feel a marriage such as this did not exist but, unlike the void marriage, court action would be required to end the "marriage."

From the legal viewpoint a marriage contract may be invalid for three reasons. First, an individual belonging to a given category cannot be married to someone from another group, as is the case concerning interracial marriage in some states. Second, certain situations impede the act of marriage; the individual already married cannot contract the same relationship with another individual. Third, certain mental or physical defects may make the marital state impossible.[3] The most articulate concern is with the categories of individuals who can marry. Certain requirements must be fulfilled if marriage is to take place.

AGE.   In most preliterate societies, and in the ancient civilizations, marriage occurred generally at puberty. Rural and peasant societies, too, accept marriage at an early age. But in our rationalistic industrial society, age at marriage has risen. Marriage is usually in the twenties

[2] Pilpel and Zavin, *op. cit.*, p. 255.
[3] Fowler V. Harper and Jerome H. Skolnick, *Problems of the Family* (rev. ed.), Bobbs-Merrill Company, Indianapolis, 1962, p. 81.

for the male. However, the danger of young marriages resulted in the provision of minimum ages of marriage in most countries and in all the fifty states of the United States. Even these ages are seen as minimal, and marriage is not encouraged.

State laws differ in age requirements depending on whether the candidate is male or female or whether he has parental consent, as Table 11.1 suggests. The most frequent marriage age is twenty-one for the male and eighteen for the female; whereas with parental consent it is eighteen for the male and sixteen for the female. In certain states the courts together with parental consent can alter or lower these age limits when pregnancy is involved. Most marriages below the legal age are subject to annulment. The marriage is void or voidable depending on the age of the couple. Where age is misrepresented or the official is derelict in his duty, penalties can be attached although the marriage may be held valid. There has been some agitation for raising the marriage age limits. Yet it is questionable whether this situation can be changed by legislation. Instead, a campaign might be mobilized with the help of education and the mass media.

RACE.   In most cultures endogamy of one variety or another becomes all-important. The Union of South Africa gives strict and ceremonious attention to the question of racial purity. Equally stringent were the laws of the Third Reich in Germany, which decreed "Aryan" blood was not to be defiled by mixture with "non-Aryan" blood. However, we need not travel outside the United States to discover taboos on miscegenation. In most Southern states as well as in Indiana, the Dakotas, and Montana, mixed marriages are regarded as a felony. Generally, the Southern and Mountain states have the least permissive laws regarding miscegenation. While in the South the ban is directed toward Negroes, in the West, American Indians and Orientals are the principal targets. However, there is interstate inconsistency in this respect:

Negroes are not the only people with whom marriage of whites is prohibited. Marriages between whites and Indians are prohibited in North Carolina and South Carolina. Mongolians, Chinese or Japanese may not marry whites in Idaho, Mississippi, Missouri, Nebraska, Utah and Wyoming. A white may not marry a Malayan in Utah and Wyoming.[4]

[4]Pilpel and Zavin, *Your Marriage and the Law*, p. 27. Copyright © 1964 by Harriet F. Pilpel and Theodora Zavin. Published by Holt, Rinehart and Winston, Inc. and Collier Books.

Table 11.1

MARRIAGE LAWS

(as of July 1, 1964)

State or Other Jurisdiction	AGE AT WHICH MARRIAGE CAN BE CONTRACTED WITH PARENTAL CONSENT		AGE BELOW WHICH PARENTAL CONSENT IS REQUIRED		Common-Law Marriage Recognized	PHYSICAL EXAMINATION AND BLOOD TEST FOR MALE AND FEMALE		WAITING PERIOD	
	Male	Female	Male	Female		Maximum Period Between Examination and Issuance of Marriage License	Scope of Medical Examination	Before Issuance of License	After Issuance of License
Alabama	17(a)	14(a)	21	18	*	30 days	(b)	.....	.....
Alaska	18(c)	16(c)	21	18	.....	30 days	(b)	3 days	.....
Arizona	18(c)	16(c)	21	18	.....	30 days	(b)	.....	.....
Arkansas	18(c)	16(c)	21	18	.....	30 days	(b)	3 days	.....
California	18(a,d)	16(a,d)	21	18	.....	30 days	(b)	.....	.....
Colorado	16(d)	16(d)	21	18	*	30 days	(b)	.....	.....
Connecticut	16(d)	16(d)	21	21	.....	40 days	(b)	4 days	.....
Delaware	18(c)	16(c)	21	18	.....	30 days	(b)	.....	(e)
Florida	18(a,c)	16(a,c)	21	21	*	30 days	(b)	3 days	.....
Georgia	18(c,f)	16(c,f)	21(f)	21(f)	*	30 days	(b)	3 days(g)	.....

Hawaii	18	16(d)	20	20	....	30 days	(b)	3 days	......
Idaho	15	15(d)	18	18	*	30 days	(b)	....	......
Illinois	18	16	21	18	....	15 days	(b)	....	......
Indiana	18(c)	16(c)	21	18	....	30 days	(b)	3 days	......
Iowa	18(c)	16(c)	21	18	*	20 days	(b)	3 days	......
Kansas	18(d)	16(d)	21	18	*	30 days	(b,h)	3 days	......
Kentucky	18(a,c)	16(a,c)	21	21	....	15 days	(b)	3 days	......
Louisiana	18(d)	16(d)	21	21	....	10 days	(b)	72 hours	......
Maine	16(d)	16(d)	18	21	....	30 days	(b)	5 days	72 hours
Maryland	18(c)	16(c)	18	21	....	....	....	48 hours	......
Massachusetts	18(d)	16(d)	18	21	....	30 days	(b)	3 days	......
Michigan	(i)	16(c)	18	18	....	30 days	(b)	3 days	......
Minnesota	18(a)	16(j)	18	21	....	....	....	5 days	......
Mississippi	17(d)	15(d)	21	21	....	30 days	(b)	3 days	......
Missouri	15(d)	15(d)	18	21	....	15 days	(b)	3 days	......
Montana	18(d)	16(d)	18	21	*	20 days	(b)	5 days	......
Nebraska	18(c)	16(c)	21	21	....	30 days	(b)	....	......
Nevada	18(a,d)	16(a,d)	18	21	....	....	....	....	......
New Hampshire	(k)	(k)	18	20	....	30 days	(b)	5 days	......
New Jersey	18(d)	16(d)	18	21	....	30 days	(b)	72 hours	......

Table 11.1 (*Continued*)

State or Other Jurisdiction	AGE AT WHICH MARRIAGE CAN BE CONTRACTED WITH PARENTAL CONSENT		AGE BELOW WHICH PARENTAL CONSENT IS REQUIRED		Common-Law Marriage Recognized	PHYSICAL EXAMINATION AND BLOOD TEST FOR MALE AND FEMALE		WAITING PERIOD	
	Male	Female	Male	Female		Maximum Period Between Examination and Issuance of Marriage License	Scope of Medical Examination	Before Issuance of License	After Issuance of License
New Mexico	18(c)	16(c)	21	18	.....	30 days	(b)	.....	24 hours(1)
New York	16	16(d)	21	18	.....	30 days	(b)	.....	.....
North Carolina	16	16(c)	18	18	.....	30 days	(m)	(n)	.....
North Dakota	18	15	21	18	.....	30 days	(o)	.....	.....
Ohio	18(c)	16(c)	21	21	*	30 days	(b)	5 days	.....
Oklahoma	18(c)	15(c)	21	18	*	30 days	(b)	(p)	.....
Oregon	18	15	21	18	.....	30 days(q)	(r)	7 days	.....
Pennsylvania	16(d)	16(d)	21	21	*	30 days	(b)	3 days	.....
Rhode Island	18(d)	16(d)	21	21	*	40 days	(s)	.....	(t)
South Carolina	16(c)	14(c)	18	18	*	.....	.....	24 hours	.....
South Dakota	18(c)	16(c)	21	18	.....	20 days	(b)	.....	.....
Tennessee	16(d)	16(d)	21	21	.....	30 days	(b)	3 days(u)	.....
Texas	16	14	21	18	*	15 days	(b)	(p)	.....
Utah	16(a)	14(a)	21	18	.....	30 days	(b)	.....	.....
Vermont	18(d)	16(d)	21	18	.....	30 days	(b)	.....	5 days

Virginia	18(a,c)	16(a,c)	21	21	......	......	......	30 days	(b)	......
Washington	17(d)	17(d)	21	18	......	......	......	......	(o)	3 days	......
West Virginia	18(a)	16(a)	21	21	......	......	......	30 days	(b)	3 days	......
Wisconsin	18	16	21	18	......	......	......	20 days	(b)	5 days	......
Wyoming	18	16	21	21	......	......	......	30 days	(b)	......
District of Columbia	18(a)	16(a)	21	18	*	......	......	3 days	......

* Indicates common-law marriage recognized.

(a) Parental consent is not required if minor was previously married.

(b) Venereal diseases.

(c) Statute establishes procedure whereby younger parties may obtain license in case of pregnancy or birth of a child.

(d) In special circumstances statute establishes procedure whereby younger parties may obtain license.

(e) Residents, 24 hours; nonresidents, 96 hours.

(f) If parties are under 21, notice must be posted unless parent of female consents in person, but if female is under 18, consent of parent is required.

(g) Unless parties are 21 years or more, or female is pregnant.

(h) Feeblemindedness.

(i) No provision in law for parental consent for males.

(j) Parental consent and permission of judge required.

(k) Below age of consent parties need parental consent and permission of judge.

(l) Marriage may not be solemnized within 3 days from date on which specimen for serological test was taken.

(m) Subject to uncontrolled epileptic attacks, idiocy, imbecility, mental defectiveness, unsound mind, infectious tuberculosis, and venereal diseases.

(n) Forty-eight hours if both are nonresidents.

(o) Feeblemindedness, imbecility, insanity, chronic alcoholism, and venereal diseases. (Also in Washington, advanced tuberculosis, and, if male, contagious venereal disease.)

(p) Three days if one or both parties are below the age for marriage without parental consent.

(q) Time limit between date of examination and expiration of marriage license.

(r) Venereal diseases, feeblemindedness, mental illness, drug addiction and chronic alcoholism.

(s) Infectious tuberculosis and venereal diseases.

(t) If female is nonresident, must complete and sign license 5 days prior to marriage.

(u) Does not apply when parties are over 21 years of age.

Source: The Book of the States, The Council of State Governments, Chicago, 1964–1965, p. 439. (Note: This table presents the basic legal regulations but does not include certain restrictions that many states have adopted, as is apparent from the discussion in the text.)

The legal definitions of what constitutes a Negro differ from state to state: Nebraska, Indiana, Florida, and Utah, among other states, define a Negro as a person having one-eighth or more Negro blood. Oregon has defined a Negro as one with at least a fourth of his blood of that race. North Carolina draws a legal nicety: in prohibiting the marriage of a white and a "Negro or Indian, or person of such descent to the third generation or a Cherokee Indian of Robeson County and a Negro, or any person of such descent to the third generation." [5] In at least one state, there are sex differences regarding legality of intermarriage: in South Carolina men are prohibited from marrying an Indian, Negro, Mulatto, Mestizo, or half-breed; whereas women are prevented from marrying "anyone except a white man." [6]

While these miscegenation laws remain in force in a number of Western and Central states, mixed unions contracted in another state are recognized. On the other hand, in certain Southern states the marriage of a white to a Negro even when performed in another state is regarded as a serious offense. Sooner or later, laws on miscegenation probably will be tested by the Supreme Court of the United States. In fact, there has been an appreciable decline of these laws in the last few decades. The decision of the California Supreme Court in 1948 is viewed as the death knell of the interracial marriage ban. The California court ruled that such laws were contrary to the Constitution, because no racial superiority could be demonstrated, and consequently forbidding such marriages would be an unnecessary invasion of the privacy and freedom of individuals to contract marriage.

CONSANGUINITY. The laws of all states forbid the marriage of close relatives. The *incest taboo* is universal, and in our society it carries the highest penalty of any of the "sex crimes" with the exception of rape. How much the interdict of consanguineous marriage is due to the incest taboo cannot be known. Essentially this taboo serves to outlaw sex relations with those who are in the immediate family group, who are usually those with whom we live in close day-to-day contact under the same roof. Freudians maintain that we have extremely strong unconscious, if not conscious, desires for the members of our family. Consequently controls must be severe. Another influence on the restriction of consanguineous marriages is an outworn nineteenth-century approach to biology; for centuries is has been believed that

[5] Harper and Skolnick, *op. cit.,* p. 97.
[6] *Ibid.*

many mental and physical weaknesses are ascribable to inbreeding. Although this theory is valid for a limited number of defects carried by recessive genes, evidence shows that most individuals do not carry such defects; if they do, the probability that they would marry an individual with similar recessive genes is low. There have been few incidences of this sort through the centuries. The same may be said of the close in-breeding of villages in Sicily or Vermont, for example, where laws on consanguinity are not violated, but where marriage of closely related individuals frequently occur. Nonetheless, all states prevent marriages within not only the immediate family but between aunts and nephews, uncles and nieces, and grandparents and grand-children. Over half the states prevent the marriage of first cousins. Many of these laws date back to a period in which large families lived together or they are hangovers from English common law in which incest may have been a greater threat than it is today.

As we mentioned in Chapter 2, in addition to consanguinity, the principle of affinity (relatives by marriage) prevents marriage of in-laws. These laws seem a further affront to individual freedom in marital selection. However, they illustrate the societal implications of the marital act. In a sense, society is protecting the previous claimant. The "older male is thus warned that the fresher charms of the step-daughter can never legally replace those of the wife in the marriage bed. It would certainly surprise the purveyor of the mother-in-law jokes to learn that it seemed necessary in a dozen states to prohibit marriage with the wife's mother." [7] Without the pressure of the incest taboo members of society might need legal reinforcement to preserve the marriage contract.

FURTHER RESTRICTIONS ON THE CHOICE OF A MARITAL PARTNER. Certain physical or personality defects may be grounds for preventing marriage. At least five states prevent the marriage of chronic alcoholics. Two states, Delaware and Oregon, reject the marriage of a drug addict. North Dakota, Virginia, and Washington specify an "habitual criminal" as unmarriageable. Thirteen states disqualify the epileptic marital candidate. Other diseases, notably tuberculosis, are also legal grounds for blocking marriage. Mental deficiency, which poses a number of problems in definition, is another legal reason for denying marriage. Insanity is a similar factor, partially because a mental disorder

[7] Clifford Kirkpatrick, *The Family as Process and Institution* (revised edition), The Ronald Press, New York, 1963, p. 422.

might make it impossible for the individual to give his lawful consent to the marriage contract.

LICENSING PROCEDURE

The legal procedure of getting married demonstrates cultural and regional inconsistencies in the selection of a mate. For instance, Catholic canon law is in contradiction to many state laws. New England tends to be stricter about licensing formalities than the South. In a few states it is still possible to marry an individual whom one has known only a few hours. In no state or country is there any attempt to assess the individual's ability to be an effective marital partner or parent other than meeting several routine specifications about age and the like. Generally, authorities in the field of marital relations have urged stricter but more rational laws on licensing procedure. Tradition has played the major role concerning these questions. In comparison with the legal requirements about the choice of a marital partner, the machinery of getting married is a modern historical product.

PHYSICAL EXAMINATIONS. The most common type of physical examination legally required for marriage is a blood test for venereal disease. No fewer than 18 per cent of the states require this examination to secure a license. Among the variations in the states' requirements, Washington does not require the male applicant to have a test but insists that he sign an affidavit to the effect that he has no venereal disease. An infected wife can sue for perjury and fraud. In a few states the partners may still marry if one of the partners is contaminated, provided the disease is not in a contagious or transmissible state. In other states if the wife is pregnant, or has borne a child by the suitor, the requirement can be waived. Still other states permit the official to omit the examination in an "emergency."

As with other requirements, the obvious escape from this physical test is to cross a neighboring state line where there is no required physical examination. Maryland has been a favorite retreat for this reason (Table 11.1). In recent years much progress has been made in venereal disease control, and the test may eventually become unnecessary. Some authorities argue that this test tends to be superficial and nonstandardized. Sometimes only the male is required to take the examination, a discrimination for which there is no sound reason.[8]

[8] Clarke, *op. cit.*, p. 73.

WAITING PERIOD.   As can be seen in Table 11.1, at least two-thirds of the states require some kind of waiting period either before or after the issuance of the license, in addition to whatever delays may be incurred because of the physical examination. The waiting period varies between one and five days with three days being the most common requirement. A few states have different requirements for residents and nonresidents. Delaware stipulates one day for residents and four days for nonresidents. Certain states, notably Georgia and Tennessee, permit the waiting period to be waived when the applicants are over twenty-one. Again, the waiting period can be curtailed in case of emergency, Georgia permitting pregnancy as an exception. Nevada is the most accommodating with neither waiting period nor serological test. At best, waiting periods act as a brake on what might be a hastily devised marriage. Licensing bureaus have indicated that in a number of instances applicants never return to complete the procedure. In a negative sense, waiting periods pay off, but more stringent procedures are needed to impress individuals with the significance of marriage and allow a deeper acquaintance with their mate-to-be.

Approximately 2 per cent of the applicants applying for a marriage license do not complete the specifications within the given period or do not return for the remaining requirements for licensing. In a study of Milwaukee County nonreturnees, Shipman found that lower economic status, poor occupational adjustment, youthful age, wide age discrepancies between the partners, parental objections, and former marital instability were among the factors characterizing most of the sample. In other words, the individuals who do not carry out their marriage plans are those who are the poorest statistical risks for marital success.[9]

LICENSING AND THE CEREMONY.   A license must be procured to have a valid marriage, and it must meet the legal stipulations of the particular state. The agent issuing the license is responsible both for obtaining the correct information and for meeting the requirements for age, race, and status of the individuals involved. For various reasons marriage contracts are regarded as more permanent than other forms of contracts: (1) they cannot be rescinded or have their basic character altered by agreement between the two parties; (2) the marriage itself becomes a type of legal status which in most cases cannot be dissolved;

[9] Gordon Shipman and H. Yuan Tien, "Non-Marriage and the Waiting Period," *Journal of Marriage and the Family,* 1965, **27,** 277–280.

(3) the legal requirements governing the ability to enter into a marital state are different from those permitting entry into ordinary contracts.[10] Marriage is a civil contract of maximum finality.

Even the nature of the ceremony itself is stipulated in some states in that an officiant, religious or lay, must preside at the marriage. Three states (Delaware, Maryland, and West Virginia) demand that a cleric be present (although in Delaware the Mayor of Wilmington may perform the ceremony). In a number of states, notably Pennsylvania, members of the Society of Friends (Quakers) may marry each other without an officiant. The marriage is a contract between two individuals contracted in the presence of their peers. The witnesses, including the committee which has been appointed to supervise the act of marriage, sign the marriage document. The union is as formalized as those made under a lay or religious official.

There has been marked controversy about proxy marriages, particularly during World War II. At that time conditions made it necessary for occasional marriages to be performed by mail or telephone with another person representing the absent male. Among the religious groups only the Roman Catholic Church recognizes this type of marriage, and the majority of the states are cautious about accepting its validity.[11] Marriages performed in a state or country where such a ceremony is legal may also be valid in another state. Generally the states recognizing common-law marriages are the ones most hospitable to proxy marriages.

IRREGULARITIES IN THE MARRIAGE PROCEDURE

BREACH OF PROMISE SUITS. As early as 1639, common law provided for payment of damages to women who were victims of broken promises to marry; this law was extended to cover males by the end of the century.[12] This type of suit was possibly justified in the days when marriages were more related to economic security, and even survival, than they are today. More important, the woman felt that she had been deprived of her marriageability. Implicit in these suits was the recognition that sexual intercourse frequently occurs among engaged

---

[10] Chester G. Vernier, *American Family Laws*, Vol. I, Stanford University Press, 1931, p. 51; also Clarke, *op. cit.*, p. 75.

[11] Pilpel and Zavin, *op. cit.* (1952) p. 45.

[12] Ray E. Baber, *Marriage and the Family* (second edition), McGraw-Hill, New York, 1953, p. 53.

partners, and that an engaged woman was to some extent damaged goods.

The practice of these suits continued into the present century. In fact, the 1920's were the high-water mark of lavish settlements, when a millionaire might confer on a young lady a fifth or more of his wealth for the pleasure of being engaged for a matter of several months. These suits provided voluminous newspaper copy in this last gasp of that golden age. By the less glamorous 1930's, a movement to outlaw such suits gained momentum, and at present at least fifteen states prohibit "heart balm" cases. Most European countries have similarly terminated this form of exploitation.

A major problem of breach-of-promise suits is that they contradicted the general conception of engagement as a testing period. They also permitted a woman to place a man in the position of paying a financial penalty rather than enter a less-than-appealing marriage. In addition to the sensationalism of the trials, the decision by the jury was often based on sentimentality rather than justice. Yet there are instances in which a breach-of-promise suit is justifiable. A woman may be victimized if she had been promised marriage, gave up her position, and invested in a trousseau only to find that the marriage did not materialize. Similarly, a man may occasionally be the loser in a broken promise, although men are freer agents with more marital opportunities awaiting them. Women find their chances for securing a mate distinctly more limited with the passing of years. In any case, most women would be reluctant to expose their emotional lives in court, and the motives immediately become suspect in such a case, even though there may be a legitimate grievance.

It has been suggested that if breach-of-promise suits were to continue, certain conditions must be enacted: (1) a written proof of promise to marry should be produced; (2) separate suits in case of seduction; (3) corroborating evidence for all claims; (4) limitation of damages "to material loss incurred on the faith of the promise"; (5) an arbitrary limit of, perhaps $1,000 should be placed on any suit.[13]

The converse case of victimization is demonstrated in the case of a lavishly generous male whose succession of gifts to his bride-to-be is not followed by her acceptance of marriage. Statutes of some states demand that such property be returned in the case of a broken engagement. In some instances distinction is made between "absolute" and

[13] Vernier, *op. cit.*, p. 29.

"conditional" gifts referring respectively to gifts bestowed out of friendship and those given in the expectation of marriage. The principal example of this second type is the engagement ring itself, which is traditionally returned to its donor.[14]

ANNULMENT. The discussion of annulment is related to the distinction between void and voidable marriages, which we have discussed briefly earlier in the chapter. Void marriages are in most cases automatically annulled, often without court action, because they are nonexistent marriages as in the cases of bigamy or the marriage partners being under age. Voidable marriages are also annulled, but the process is more complex: a judge must determine whether fraud or some other situation has prevented a valid marriage from occurring. Again, judges may vary in their interpretation of whether a marriage contract freely made between two parties has been fulfilled. Of course the time factor itself is an important variable. It would be considered presumptuous to annul a marriage of five or ten years duration. The consummation of the marriage is another critical matter: if sex relations have not taken place, the marriage is not regarded as complete, and therefore is technically more dissoluble. States vary in their grounds for annulment. New York with its strict law on divorce—even today restricted to adultery—is inclined to be more liberal in this matter.[15] On the other hand, in "easy-divorce" Western states, there is almost no consideration given to annulment as a way out from an impossible or invalid marriage.

The history of annulments is deeply rooted in Christian doctrine. Roman Catholic canon law recognized certain grounds for divorce and the Ecclesiastical Courts of England were also inclined to dissolve a marriage outright only under the most restricted grounds. In the nineteenth century, and especially in recent decades, annulment usually has been restricted to three grounds: bigamy, duress, and fraudulent representation. An example of duress is the case of Margaret, who is pregnant and persuades John that he is the father. Should Margaret's truculent father urge John's entrance into marriage by brandishing a firearm, he is likely to succumb with little delay. A court may later permit him to dissolve the marriage as he did not enter the marriage

[14] For further discussion of this problem, cf. Pilpel and Zavin, *op. cit.*, pp. 14f.

[15] England also has been relatively flexible in granting annulment, and this history may be influenced by its strong stand on divorce. C. E. P. Davies, "Matrimonial Relief in English Law," in R. H. Graveson and F. R. Crane (eds.) *A Century of Family Law, 1857–1957*, Sweet and Maxwell, London, 1961, p. 311.

freely. The marriage contract is not binding unless based on mutual consent.

Fraud as grounds for annulment may be illustrated by the case of the woman who turns out to be frigid even though she has given her husband-to-be the impression of complete normality. Another case of fraud is the situation in which Doris claims pregnancy, and Carl marries his plaintive victim. After the marriage Doris may prove not to be pregnant, or her amorous adventures may indicate that Carl's paternity might be disputable. In this instance he may not receive all the sympathy from the court that he would desire. Traditionally courts regard philandering as a calculated risk. Besides, the marriage contract is a permanent agreement except in extreme circumstances. There has been some relaxation in the attitude toward the adventuresome male during the last decade or two, because premarital intercourse is regarded as somewhat less serious than it was earlier. Generally, the courts, at least in most states, consider marriage as *sui generis*, or as basic to societal welfare, and not at the convenience of the individual. We have only to compare the harsher interpretations of Massachusetts with those of New York and California, which two states have accounted for nearly two-thirds of the annulments of the United States.[16]

Fraud is possibly the most common ground for annulment, and includes misrepresentations of age, sexual capacity, character, financial status (to a lesser extent), occupational status, and refusal to have children. Courts have the obligation to distinguish genuine cases of fraud from those that arise out of lack of judgment on the part of one or both marriage partners. Because the husband fails to produce the large bank account he promised is not necessarily sufficient cause for dissolution of the marriage. The judge would assert that it is the fiancée's obligation to investigate the financial standing of the suitor.

Annulment may be for causes other than those we have just mentioned. In some states insanity is regarded as grounds for annulment if there is a record of such an ailment for, say, five years before the marriage, which itself occurred in one of the normal phases. In still other states insanity is covered by divorce. Occasionally annulment has dissolved a marriage contracted as an adventure or as the outcome of a party spree, a possibility continually less frequent with the tightening

[16] Paul H. Jacobson, *American Marriage and Divorce*, Holt, Rinehart and Winston, New York, 1959, p. 14.

of marriage laws in most states. Generally, unless one of the partners was below the legal age, the "I-dare-you" type of marriage is valid. In other words, the partners who the next morning wish to dissolve a hastily devised marriage are likely to regret their adventure. Again, the judge must decide whether the offense is greater to the institution of marriage or to the individual. As a representative of the law he generally favors the "overall societal interest." [17] In a sense, where the societal welfare is affected it becomes a void marriage; where an individual's interest has been assaulted it is a voidable marriage. It is exceedingly arbitary to argue whether more harm results from casual treatment of the institution of marriage or from an unhappy partner in marriage.

Legitimacy of children is one of the problems of annulments. According to English common law, offspring of annulled marriages were illegitimate. Over forty states have adopted the principle that such children are legitimate, but in some states only certain types of annulment permit this privilege. The states that discourage or outlaw legitimization of children in annulments are those where courts are reluctant to grant annulments to their parents. In reality, the majority of annulments are granted to couples without children, and two-thirds of the annulments occur within the first two years of marriage.[18]

COMMON-LAW MARRIAGES. Common-law marriages are those in which a man and a woman agree to enter into a living arrangement resembling marriage without benefit of licensing or ceremony. They were frequently found in Europe until the Council of Trent outlawed them in 1563. Britain abolished the common-law marriage two hundred years later, but this type of union had found a function in the colonies of the Atlantic seaboard and remained with the frontier of the United States through the nineteenth century. The distance from governmental and ecclesiastical authorities meant that marriages could not always be performed legally. States began progressively to abolish common-law marriages, and today such a marriage is recognized in fifteen states (Alabama, Alaska, Colorado, Florida, Georgia, Idaho, Iowa, Kansas, Montana, Ohio, Oklahoma, Pennsylvania, Rhode Island, South Carolina, and Texas) and the District of Columbia.[19]

[17] William M. Kephart, *The Family, Society, and the Individual*, Houghton Mifflin, Boston, 1961, p. 410.
[18] Baber, *op. cit.*, p. 72.
[19] Will Bernard, *Law for the Family*, Charles Scribner's Sons, New York, 1962, p. 15.

This practice is somewhat more accepted in the rural rather than more industrialized states. Generally, a common-law marriage which is valid in the state where it was consummated is recognized in all states. Yet if a resident of a state not recognizing common-law marriages migrated to another state for the purpose of entering into such a marriage, the home state would consider it invalid.[20]

We may well ask why the common-law marriage has remained valid within nearly a third of the states. It complicates "questions pertaining to property rights, inheritance, legitimacy of children, etc. The courts have a recognized basis for making equitable decisons. Common-law marriages—devoid as they are of documentary proof—tend to snarl the machinery of the court and upon occasion to penalize the innocent." [21] In the interest of consistency of legal procedures, legal authorities have urged the abolition of the common-law marriage.

"RUN-AWAY" MARRIAGES. The varying restrictiveness of state marriage laws provides a suggestion of Gresham's law in economics. The cheaper currency drives out the harder. The individual seeking an easy marriage tends to cross the line into a state where possibilities exist for a quick, and perhaps glamorous, ceremony. The passage by Parliament of the Hardwicke Act of 1753 illegalized marriages which were not solemnized in the church where the banns had been published. With the doors closed to an easy marriage in England, couples eloped to Gretna Green, a town across the border in Scotland. For that reason the term "Gretna Green" has been attached to marriage-market towns the world over, even though changes in British law eliminated the "run-away" marriage.

In the United States there are or have been several well-known Gretna Greens: Crown Point, Indiana; Kahoka, Missouri; Reno and Las Vegas, Nevada; Yuma, Arizona; and Elkton, Maryland. The last of these, in particular, was utilized by the residents of the more populous Northeastern states until Maryland changed the law to a forty-eight hour waiting period in 1937. Some of the glamour and appeal of a Gretna Green marriage lingered on after laws were changed. As late as the 1950's it was estimated that fifty-seven towns in twenty-nine states offered commercialized marriages.[22] Some of these have had a declin-

---

[20] Martin J. Ross, *Handbook of Everyday Law*, Harper and Row, New York, 1959, p. 183.

[21] Kephart, *op. cit.*, p. 417.

[22] Baber, *op. cit.*, p. 65.

ing business, but a grandiose enterprise still flourishes in Las Vegas. A minister or justice of the peace offers marriage ceremonies at any hour of day or night, even though responsible denominations have discouraged or forbidden their ministers to enter into such practices. There is usually a price schedule that varies with services performed including the provision of witnesses, elaborate display of flowers and photography, "hushing-up" of publicity, etc. In fact, the function of these marriage-market towns is partially to provide a refuge for individuals desiring an elopement or secret marriage.

Kephart studied the longevity of marriages contracted in Elkton (and in Media, a suburb of Philadelphia located, however, in Delaware County where licensing procedures were slightly more relaxed than in Philadelphia County). He found a small but significant difference in the divorce rate for couples married in these towns as against those married in Philadelphia.[23] A similar study was made in Tennessee, where marriages contracted in the home state were more durable than those contracted in the neighboring states, Georgia, Mississippi, or Kentucky, which have more lenient marriage laws.[24] The mean for lasting Tennessee marriages was 11.9 years, whereas for Tennesseans married in Georgia it was 4.5, and for Arkansas 8.5, with Mississippi and Kentucky falling between the two means. While these figures are based on data now more than a decade old, changes in marriage laws have apparently only partially removed these differences.

SOME FUTURE TRENDS. It is clear from our discussion that some regulations regarding marriage need to be overhauled or abolished. State laws govern marriage although family life in many social, economic, and even legal respects is governed by the Social Security Administration and a number of federal agencies (particularly those within the Department of Health, Welfare, and Education). However, the entry of the federal government into increased services to family life has not prevented the states from expanding their control over marriage and the family; for example, the prohibition in recent decades of marriage with or between mental defectives and drug addicts.

One aspect of limited federal control is the lack of central registra-

---

[23] William M. Kephart and Rolf B. Strohm, "The Stability of Gretna Green Marriages," *Sociology and Social Research*, 1952, **36**, 291–296.

[24] Arthur Hopson, "The Relationship of Migratory Marriages to Divorce in Tennessee," *Social Forces*, 1952, **30**, 449–455.

tion of data. Seven states do not maintain central files of marriage records, although the National Vital Statistics Division has remedied this hiatus to an appreciable extent.[25] Attention has been given to the problem of uniform federal marriage laws. Federal legislation would have the advantage of reducing the confusion and contradictions in state laws. However, one neutralizing if inconsistent aspect of the present system is possible escape across the state line. There is also the danger that any law that could be passed in the majority of states might be extremely conservative.

Should an individual applying for marriage be required to pass a test, or a battery of tests, regarding his or her fitness for entering matrimony? The minimum move toward such an end, that we might legitimately expect, is more rationalized procedure in our licensing laws. As Shipman points out, the emphasis of governmental and private agencies has been on divorce procedure—often because of the intense feeling in religious circles regarding the dissolution of marriage—rather than on the critical point of marital selection.[26] Another possibility for regulation is to encourage a person to seek counselling if severe personality flaws are detected. It is hardly necessary to state the objections that might be raised to this type of regulation, however desirable such requirements might be. Only by way of a broad program of education through the family, school, pulpit, and mass media can some progress be effected.

Supplementary Readings

Baber, Ray E., *Marriage and the Family* (second edition), McGraw-Hill, 1953. Chapter 3 is an entertaining and informative presentation.

Harper, Fowler V. and Jerome H. Skolnick, *Problems of the Family* (revised edition), Bobbs-Merrill, Indianapolis, 1962. Chapter 3 contains a number of case studies and legal briefs on mate selection.

Jacobson, Paul H., *American Marriage and Divorce*, Holt, Rinehart and Winston, New York, 1959. A classical statistical approach to the subject, although the data (mostly of the 1950 census) are now slightly outdated.

Kephart, William M., *The Family, Society and the Individual*, Houghton Mifflin, Boston, 1961. Chapter 14 is an excellent review of marriage laws.

[25] Kephart, *op. cit.*, p. 964.
[26] Gordon Shipman, "A Proposal for Revising Marriage License Procedure," *Journal of Marriage and the Family*, 1965, **27**, 281–284.

Kephart, William M., "Legal and Procedural Aspects of Marriage and Divorce," in Harold T. Christensen (ed.), *Handbook of Marriage and Family*, Rand McNally, Chicago, 1964, pp. 944–968.

Pilpel, Harriet and Theodora Zavin, *Your Marriage and the Law*, Holt, Rinehart and Winston, New York, 1952. Chapters 1, 2, 3, 4, and 17 are most relevant and complete. A revised paperback edition became available in 1964.

Ploscowe, Morris, *Sex and the Law*, Prentice-Hall, Englewood Cliffs, New Jersey, 1951. A discussion of a number of topics among others: annulments, and common law marriages.

Vernier, Chester G., *American Family Laws*, vol. 1, Stanford University Press, 1931–1938. The most thoroughgoing, if not altogether up-to-date, presentation of marriage laws.

Chapter twelve
The Threshold of Marriage

What *was* behind the human botch of mating? . . . it seemed to get worse from generation to generation, as the gulf between the sexes widened until it threatened to become fatal. Was there something inherent in the sex bond itself that made a mate an adversary? Or was Mind the culprit, the overintellectualization of what should remain an emotional and instinctive link? Was it a failure to be romantic—a refusal to embrace the illusion to which nature invites us, and which we circumvent to our cost? Not even the poets romanticized women any more. Who would any longer regard their breasts as doves, or their hands as lilies? But did women themselves any longer invite such comparisons, women with their shirts and slacks, their well-stocked minds and their rude language, and the other competitive proofs of their equality with men? And this din of talk about their Ordeal. What a racket they had going, what a lobby they controlled. They now had a corps of trained anthropologists filling the magazines with the discovery that housework is tedious, as though office work were anything else. Was housework any more stultifying than the clerical tasks to which their husbands daily set forth without benefit of journalists advertising their lot or psychologists mourning it? Well, perhaps that wasn't quite fair: the offices and factories looked good from the kitchen but not the kitchen from the offices and factories. . . . One thing was certain. When it comes to sex we talk a good game, but that's about all. We're no better off with our freedom than the Victorians were with their tyranny. Ours seems a world in which the Individual prospers at the expense of the Pair. Maybe the price of the one is the decline of the other.

Peter DeVries, Reuben, Reuben, *Little, Brown, 1964, pp. 433–434. Copyright 1956, 1962, 1964 by Peter DeVries.*

The gods gave man fire, and man invented fire engines. They gave him love, and he invented marriage.

Anonymous

The Proposal by an unknown sailor
Courtesy of The Whaling Museum, New Bedford, Massachusetts

Most young people greet their wedding day with elation. This momentous event has been preceded by a complex process of socialization from infancy to adolescence culminating in the discovery of heterosexual interest, as expressed in dating and courtship. A partner has been chosen, either as a result of a whirlwind romance (which does exist despite the remonstrations of textbooks!) or a sustained, meticulous courtship.

Though this sequence of events may appear simple, and perhaps for a few it is, generally the prelude to marriage is intensely complicated. After the wedding ceremony itself come the equally exciting, but sometimes awkward and intimate, adjustments of the honeymoon. It is of course impossible to detach these phenomena from psychological and other developments in the individual's life pattern.

TO MARRY OR NOT TO MARRY

If an individual approaches life decisions impartially he may well ask, "Why marry?" There are many reasons for remaining single. Some argue against marriage on the following bases: desire to devote oneself to a cause, a career, or a relative; the almost complete freedom of dating and sex relations in our culture. Consequently, it may be said by some that there is no necessity to enter marriage when affectional and sexual bonds are possible in single life. Variety rather than the monogamy of married life may be more appealing for some individuals. Self-sufficiency and economic independence are possible in modern life, and this is perhaps another argument for the single life. Women especially have experienced a far-reaching revolution in this respect. The risk of divorce and widowhood may make a few pessimists pause before entering matrimony.

Nevertheless, others might claim that a less-than-ideal marriage is still more satisfying than single life. The experimental approach is not what Tennyson had in mind in his now almost trite words, "It is better to have loved and lost than never to have loved at all." Or in the words of today, it is better to be a "has been" than a "never was." Most of us prefer the "great adventure" to the uncertainty and near emptiness of bachelorhood. The arguments against marriage are likely to appeal only to those who are without affectional and emotional maturity or to those for whom circumstances prevent marriage.

Within certain cultural periods or areas arguments against marriage can be convincing. The author's research on family life in certain Central American communities revealed many consensual unions (common-law marriages), which were defended by the interviewee—often the female household head—on the grounds that she was better off in a union that could be terminated rather than in assuming the irrevocable responsibilities of supporting a husband in a male-dominated culture. Traditionally, most Western women might have argued in the same direction. A woman in nineteenth-century America could question the desirability of marriage in a world in which legal institutions supported the other sex. However, the lower marriage rate of that period is not explained by such reticence. Rather, spinsterhood had even more negative status than it has today. The lower marriage rate of the nineteenth century was largely a product of the transitional economy of the time, a high sex ratio, and, it is presumed, the less attractive appeal of marriage to both sexes. Today, marriage, despite its tenuous quality, is more attractive and universal than it has ever been before.

RITES OF PASSAGE: ENGAGEMENT

A ceremonious relationship between the two potential marital partners even before the nuptials take place is common in Western history. The betrothal was known to both the Mediterranean and Germanic people, as Chapter 2 indicated. However there is variation in Western culture regarding the degree of ceremony surrounding formal betrothal, publishing the banns, or conferral of the ring. (For the Romans engagement was highly formalized with the "placing by the groom of the ring on the fourth finger of his bride's left hand." [1] This practice is retained today in certain European and Latin American countries, with the ring being transferred to the right hand during the wedding ceremony.) A wider variation is apparent in primitive societies. The ceremonies surrounding nuptials are more formalized, for example, among some Bantus of South and East Africa as compared to the Samoans, where only a gradual transition is made from experimental love-making to the marriage itself.

The United States in particular has witnessed a far-reaching change in engagement practices. Traditionally in rural culture, with its deep

---

[1] Panos D. Bardis, "Family Forms and Variations Historically Considered," in Harold T. Christensen (ed.), *Handbook of Marriage and the Family*, Rand McNally, New York, 1964, p. 433.

religious ties and unvarying monogamy, engagement was indeed a formal announcement tantamount to marriage itself, and was seldom broken. In our urban, highly mobile culture, engagement means different things to different people depending on individual expectations and needs; for many, it is an informal testing period.

SIGNIFICANCE OF ENGAGEMENT. The engagement has several vital functions that have changed with time and place, but are deeply entrenched in Western, particularly American, culture.

First, the formal engagement announces to the world a forthcoming marriage. For roughly half the women and two-thirds of the men marriage follows the engagement.[2] The engagement ring in most cases (83.9 per cent of engagements in which neither partner has been married before)[3] symbolizes the status of engagement. The ring is in most instances a diamond, however any ring or pin will do. The formal announcement along with newspaper accounts and the succession of showers and prenuptial parties all confer status on the bride and give public sanction to the couple. In a deeper sense the engagement bestows a feeling of achievement on the two individuals. There is a sense of relief in knowing one has fulfilled expectations. Society may gaze on the lover who is now the conqueror.

Second, engagement commits the couple to a monogamous relationship. Former boy- and girl-friends are notified that extraneous dating is of the past. "Burning one's bridges" may be traumatic, but this is the process by which monogamy is assured.

Third, the engagement allows the marital candidates to be on display. It serves primarily as a testing period, of which one aspect is the opportunity of friends and relatives to examine the candidate, and allows both parties to assess the appropriateness of their choice. If this interpretation seems calculated to dull romantic ardor, it is precisely the function of a formal engagement to provide an experimental phase.

Fourth, the dyadic relationship of love and associated emotional shadings have a chance to develop.[4] Before the engagement period

[2] Ernest W. Burgess and Paul Wallin, *Engagement and Marriage*, J. B. Lippincott, Philadelphia, 1953, p. 273.

[3] August B. Hollingshead, "Marital Status and Wedding Behavior," *Marriage and Family Living*, 1952, 14, 308–311.

[4] Manford H. Kuhn, "The Engagement: Thinking about Marriage," in Howard Becker and Reuben Hill, *Family, Marriage and Parenthood* (second edition), D. C. Heath, Boston, 1955, pp. 276–304.

love relationships were generally public in one sense; dating was likely to have been multiple both in terms of varying from one partner to another, or in double-dating. In engagement, love is necessarily exclusive, and is permitted the opportunity to develop the rich and full sensitivity it deserves. At the same time, there is some anxiety in the realization that the escape routes are closing. More than that, if we accept the notion that love is ambivalent, anxiety in the intense love and hate situation is possible. For some individuals the feeling of mental and physical distress as the wedding day approaches generally signifies to the individual the momentous step he is taking.

Fifth, and most important, the engagement provides a climate in which various problems may be sifted. Again this reciprocal discussion and questioning is the essence of the premarital test period. The young lovers are experiencing a give-and-take relationship in which interests, values, and feelings are examined in the other individual and in the self on a more intensive basis than ever before.

THE ENGAGEMENT PROCESS.   About half of the engaged couples date a year or more before becoming engaged. In one sample 53 per cent were engaged within the first twelve months of dating, 27 per cent were engaged in less than five months.[5]

The most detailed study of engagement is Burgess and Wallin's [6] sample of some 900 engagements and marriages. They report that nearly half the sample (51 per cent of the men and 42 per cent of the women) consulted no one as to the wisdom of their choice in becoming engaged.[7] The other half of the subjects consulted an average number of 1.9 persons. Mothers accounted for over 60 per cent of these referrals, and fathers were the second choice or confidant.

In regard to the degree of involvement they found that approximately a fourth of the sample claimed to be "head over heels" in love, whereas less than 10 per cent felt "somewhat or mildly" in love. Forty-one per cent of the men and 48 per cent of the women experienced some hesitation about marrying their betrothed. It would be surprising indeed if there were no doubts during the engagement, despite the folklore surrounding this supposedly ecstatic event. Marriage is too tremendous an undertaking for a majority of people to be unshakably certain of their decision and choice.

---

[5] Judson T. Landis and Mary G. Landis, *Building a Successful Marriage* (third edition), Prentice-Hall, Englewood Cliffs, New Jersey, 1958, p. 272.

[6] Burgess and Wallin, *op. cit.*

[7] *Ibid.*, pp. 170f.

Length of Engagement. The act of engagement is found to be a positive factor in the success of the marriage, and so is the length of engagement. Burgess and Cottrell[8] found that the ratio of couples with "poor" adjustment declined from 50 per cent for engagements of less than three months to 11 per cent for those of twenty-four or more months in duration. In Terman's sample a longer length of engagement and of total acquaintance favored marital happiness.[9] In the Locke study the average length of engagement for his married men and women was 9.5 months and 11.1, respectively; for the divorced sample, it was 3.5 and 5.4 months.[10]

These results emphasize the role that engagement plays in marital happiness. Of course, the length of marriage cannot be separated from the degree and length of previous dating and courtship. Naturally, in the case of more mature individuals long engagements are not necessarily desirable. In cases of remarriage engagements are distinctly shorter than with first marriages.[11] At its very least, the length of courtship should provide the couple with the chance to maximize their socialization and communication, to explore the other's personality, to see one another as they really are.

PROBLEM AREAS OF ENGAGEMENT

Most important, engagement permits the couple to face reality. Without the intense relationship of engagement this problem-solving activity might not occur in the approach to marriage.

Techniques of Resolving Tensions. The popular image of the engaged couple is one of two people in ecstatic agreement on all issues. Consensus is indeed enjoyed to a considerable extent as reported by Burgess and Wallin. In a list of twelve areas of agreement, a fifth of the sample agreed or "almost always" agreed in all areas. Yet 28 per cent asserted they disagreed in five or more areas, which were in descending order: ways of dealing with the families, matters of conven-

---

[8] Ernest W. Burgess and Leonard S. Cottrell, Jr., *Predicting Success or Failure in Marriage*, Prentice-Hall, Englewood Cliffs, 1939, p. 167.

[9] Lewis M. Terman, *Psychological Factors in Marital Happiness*, McGraw-Hill, New York, 1938, p. 198.

[10] Harvey J. Locke, *Predicting Adjustment in Marriage: A Comparison of a Divorced and a Happily Married Group*, Holt, Rinehart and Winston, 1951, p. 92.

[11] William J. Goode, *After Divorce*, The Free Press of Glencoe, A Division of Collier-Macmillan, New York, 1956, p. 250.

tionality, philosophy of life, religion, and money matters. Arrangement of dates with each other, demonstration of affection, and details of the marriage ceremony seemed to cause the least conflict.[12]

The mechanisms of accommodation can be acquired to some extent in the deepening of communication during engagement. How many children to have, reactions to friends, means of resolving recreational differences, the career of the wife, are all problems to be solved. Religion, in particular, is an area of difficulty, especially if the marriage is mixed. There may be problems of birth control, extent of church participation, or the choice of religion for the children. Doubts and uncertainties unresolved before marriage often become more pressing after the honeymoon. Moreover, certain conflicts during the engagement period may reflect deep-seated tensions, which can become more pronounced after marriage. On the other hand, for some these tensions may decline in vigor when the security of marriage releases the individual for other activity. The preoccupation of two individuals about the launching of their marital career can itself promote tensions.

The means of resolving these tensions can be as varied as the personality of the two individuals involved. Disagreements are likely to be resolved by many of the same techniques used by married couples: "talking-it-out" and attempts at role-taking, more commonly known as "trying to see it from the other person's viewpoint." In some instances the couple may gain a clearer perspective of the problem by discussing the situation with a friend or relative. In some engagements the two individuals may have been seeing each other with such intensity that their perspective is limited. Each of the partners may benefit from developing a temporary sense of detachment by arranging not to see each other for a night or two, with an opportunity to test the absence and to "think it over."

PARENTAL RESISTANCE. Frequently the opposition of parents is a conflict area of sufficient magnitude to warrant special attention. In fact it appears that this problem is of increasing importance. In three successive generations of Ohio courtships, parents shifted from majority approval to majority disapproval of the style of courtship and especially the choice of boyfriend.[13] A relationship that is not atypical is described by a member of Burgess and Wallin's sample of fiancées:

[12] Burgess and Wallin, *op. cit.*, pp. 246–247.
[13] Marvin R. Koller, "Some Changes in Courtship Behavior in Three Generations of Ohio Women," *American Sociological Review*, 1951, **16**, 366–370.

The only thing we argue about is my family. My fiancé always speaks out of turn. One evening my parents said they didn't think he was the person for me and suggested I break up with him. I told him I thought I should see other fellows for a while, that my folks thought it better. He talked to my parents. He told me to choose between my family and him. He said we should put our cards on the table.[14]

A fourth of the Burgess and Wallin sample disagreed with their spouse-to-be on the subject of the family. Brothers and sisters may also become involved in this situation. Families are involved with their children's happiness, and the offspring have an emotional commitment to their families. Class, ethnic, religious, moral, and even political differences may accentuate this potential gulf. Documentation from marital surveys supports the desirability of parental cooperation with the forthcoming marriage. For instance, Locke found a higher incidence of approval by the parents in his happily married sample as opposed to his divorced sample.[15]

SEX EXPRESSION. Perhaps the most compelling question engaged couples may have to resolve is the problem of sex relations. It is a foregone conclusion that the expectation of sex is more pressing as one proceeds from steady courtship into the intimate stages of engagement and the increased frequency of being together. A married California sample demonstrated that as couples proceeded from casual to steady dating, to "going steady," "engaged to be engaged," and then engaged, there was a steady increase of physical intimacy in these last three stages.[16]

A number of research studies provide evidence of the degree to which the affianced enter into sex relations before marriage. For instance, Terman found a decrease of virginity at marriage among women from 86.5 per cent (women born before 1890) to 31.7 per cent for those born after 1910, similarly a decrease for the men from 50.6 to 13.6 per cent.[17] However, of the women born after 1910, more than half reported that coitus was reserved for their fiancé. Kinsey reports almost identical results.[18] For engaged couples the effect of sexual

[14] Burgess and Wallin, *op. cit.*, p. 250.

[15] Locke, *op. cit.*, p. 118.

[16] Jack R. Delora, "Social Systems of Dating on a College Campus," *Marriage and Family Living*, 1963, **25**, 81–84.

[17] Terman, *op. cit.*, pp. 321–323.

[18] Alfred C. Kinsey, Wardell B. Pomeroy, Clyde E. Martin, and Paul H. Gebhard, *Sexual Behavior in the Human Female*, W. B. Saunders, Philadelphia, 1953, pp. 298–302.

intercourse on later marital adjustment is not conclusively negative or positive. Burgess and Wallin found that the length of engagement was related positively to premarital intercourse: two-fifths of the couples who were engaged eight months or less so indulged as compared to roughly half for those engagements of sixteen months or more. Age was not a significant determinant of the occurrence of coitus in an engaged couple; in fact, the younger ones tended to have more sex than the older ones, although Terman found no consistent relationship between age of the couple and sex relations. Summarizing some of the differences between those disposed for and against premarital sex relations, Burgess and Wallin write:

> Couples are most likely to have sex relations before marriage if couple members have had sexual experience with some other person, if they have been engaged 16 months or longer at the time of marriage, if couple members have different religious affiliations (or none at all). Couples are least likely to have premarital intercourse if neither couple member had sex relations with some other person, if at the time of marriage they are engaged eight months or less, if couple members are both Catholic, and if the woman has had some college education and the man has not.[19]

Since Chapter 8 focused on premarital sex relations, sex in the present context is treated only as it refers to the engagement period. The effects of premarital coitus on marriage are not altogether conclusive. Locke found no consistent difference between the married and divorced sample on intercourse between fiancés although he did discover proportionately more promiscuous individuals among his divorced sample.[20] The subjects in the Burgess and Wallin study who deferred sex until marriage did so because they, or at least the fiancé(e), did not "consider it right." Other reasons given were in decreasing order of importance: "fear of pregnancy, possibility of weakening the relationship, fear of hurting parent's feelings, fear of social disapproval, conditions did not permit." Recent studies indicate that the majority of young people prefer to defer sex relations until the more favorable environment of the honeymoon. More explicitly they feel that the wedding ceremony and the honeymoon will otherwise not have its traditional value. For them, especially the girl, virginity at marriage has special meaning. In some cases the girl has been engaged previously, or in a serious and lengthy courtship with the expectation

[19] Burgess and Wallin, *op. cit.*, p. 341.
[20] Locke, *op. cit.*, p. 133.

that the relationship would terminate in marriage. As it failed to do so, she is all the more cautious in bestowing her favors in the next love union. In the matter of premarital sex relations, each individual must make the decision for himself. Much depends on his age, background, education, and value system.

BROKEN ENGAGEMENTS. Among the middle class, approximately one-third of the men and one-half the women break their engagements.[21] For most of these individuals the rupture is a tragic event. In fact some dubious engagements probably continue almost until the wedding before they are broken, rather than the couples facing the trauma of discontinuing the relationship. Sympathy for the other party is partly the cause of this reluctance, and fears about his or her reaction may result in a delay in announcing the parting of ways. However, engagement is a hypothetical stage, and the young person must be prepared for this tenuousness. Burgess and Wallin find five reasons for broken engagements:

1. Slight Emotional Attachment. One or both parties find their emotional involvement to be superficial or inconsistent. Generally love, despite the folklore to the contrary, develops slowly or at least may need some careful nurturing. Too, when we speak of engagement as a testing period, literally the partners are examining love to determine if it is a consistent process. The ambivalence of the love relationship has already been mentioned. What seemed like strong attachment may turn out to be a partnership based on a common social environment. Sometimes campus romances, the round of fraternity dances, and other campus ceremonials may only provide the illusion of a strong affinity. Being "in love" may have no deeper significance than a prolonged habit association.

2. Separation. This may permit the individuals to find other love interests or may lead to a sobering evaluation of the romance. For example, engagements in which the couple had had at least thirteen or more hours together weekly were significantly less likely to be broken than those in which less hours were spent together. Although separation can be used as a means of testing the depth of one's feelings, there is no reason to avoid some separation during the engagement. Yet in terms of statistical probabilities absence is a risk. Other things being equal, the more time spent together the greater the likelihood of inti-

---

[21] Burgess and Wallin, *op. cit.*, pp. 273f.

mate knowledge of each other. The larger the "exposed area," to use LeMasters' term, the less probability of those famous or infamous remarks, "if only I had known him better before." [22]

3. *Cultural Differences.* Subcultures of class, religion, and national background operate to draw individuals apart. If class boundaries, for instance, fade in the moonlight, they are plainly visible the next morning. These subcultures are fortified by parents and peers.

4. *Personality Problems.* Questions of maturity, compatibility, affectionateness, and a number of personality syndromes are relevant in this context. Today our heterogeneous life, fast-moving urban tempo, and scattered segmental roles involving contacts with a continuing round of people place a strain on the individual. This situation becomes more complicated in the marital situation, when two personalities must somehow harmonize in their relation to each other and the outside world. It is not that interpersonal, and particularly marital, relations were easier in the past, but the quasiunified roles of, for example, a Kansas farm family of the 1890's with its relative homogeneity of contacts suggests less conflict than the series of interpersonal episodes a married couple confronts today. Even though in contemporary America the individual enters marriage with more formal education and possibly more extensive knowledge of mental hygiene, he cannot escape the problems of personalities in conflict. The engagement period enables the individual to discover his relationship to the other party and to determine their potential of interplay with a fairly wide social universe. The age of the "other-directedness" gives an interpersonal significance to a marriage-to-be that did not exist for the "tradition-directed" or "inner-directed" man.[23]

5. *Parental Opposition.* Parental disapproval occurred twice as often in cases of broken engagements as compared to unbroken ones. As already suggested, parents are more likely to interfere today than formerly partly because of their concern with upward mobility and general welfare of the daughter or son. The fact that families are smaller today than in the nineteenth century suggests more parental involvement in the activities of the offspring until the time of their marriages.

[22] E. E. LeMasters, *Modern Courtship and Marriage,* Macmillan, New York, 1957, p. 160.

[23] David Riesman, *The Lonely Crowd,* Yale University Press, New Haven, 1951.

The following case history of a broken engagement illustrates some of the problems that may arise during the engagement period:

Dorothy started dating Bill in the last year of college, and by the spring of graduation they were engaged. They both came from upper-middle class homes. Although she was Protestant and he was Catholic, their religious differences on the surface did not appear to be a problem since they were both liberal, and their parents did not object to the idea of an interfaith marriage. They had similar interests, both enjoyed reading, although for Bill, athletics was a stronger interest than books. The college atmosphere in which Dorothy and Bill dated was conducive to the full aura of romantic courtship. They were both handsome, radiated charm, and were popular at parties. At one point they planned to have a summer wedding, but parental opposition caused the marriage plans to be deferred.

After commencement Bill obtained a position in Dorothy's home city where she had a teaching position. They planned a wedding for the late fall. During the summer they spent much time together taking country drives, attending tennis matches, the theatre, and became closer companions. However, as plans for the marriage developed, Dorothy noticed for the first time significant aspects of Bill's personality. He was limited in his depth of feeling; he seemed to be more concerned with material possessions, and was increasingly more self-involved. An example of this was his reluctance to discuss their own plans for a family. His scruples about having children were in part based on religious differences, but she wondered if his reluctance stemmed from a fear of becoming emotionally involved with children or accepting the responsibility of parenthood. Dorothy insisted that they not see each other for a while and think over their relationship.

Bill returned and offered declarations of complete devotion with the recommencement of their engagement. For a time it seemed that his affection was more complete, and he accepted the idea of marital and family responsibility. But within a few weeks there was the suggestion that marriage for him was to be patterned after his own parents'. In the meantime, after repeated visits to Bill's home, Dorothy realized that he, as the youngest child of the family, was catered to by both parents, and that within the home his father was the dominant figure imposing his influence on the mother. Within several weeks Dorothy became painfully aware that Bill's own personality inadequacies were probably not likely to change, and she consequently suggested a permanent breakup.[24]

This history illustrates a number of possible areas of difficulty in a serious courtship or engagement. Although there was no outstanding cultural difference between the two individuals—the religious difference was inconsequential—there was also no consensus between Bill and Dorothy regarding life values. The ability to perceive personality

[24] From the author's files.

factors in the other person requires a lengthy period of time. The dynamics of the love relationship can shift during a period of months. Bill's case demonstrates the degree to which the family structure can influence not only the personality but the kind of relationship into which the marriage can evolve. Bill's use of religious differences to cover his reservations about having children shows how conscious reasons may differ from unconscious motives.

MARRIAGE

For those couples whose relationships survive courtship and engagement, marriage, in the form of a twenty-minute formal wedding ceremony, usually follows. Marriages themselves have a pattern of their own. They occur most frequently in the month of June throughout most of the United States; although in the Northeast April is a favorite period because of the close of the Lenten season. Southerners prefer late fall and December as do many couples in agricultural areas. Canadians tend to avoid winter weddings.[25]

The type of ceremony is influenced by a number of variables. Church weddings are less frequent during periods of depression or wartime because of expense, time, and inaccessibility. Regionally, church ceremonies are most preferred in the North Central and Northeastern United States, and are less frequent in parts of the South and in the mountain states. Remarriages more often tend to be civil ceremonies than first marriages. Conversely, younger couples are more likely to prefer religious rites.

ELOPEMENTS AND SECRET MARRIAGES. In some cases the desire for anonymity, privacy, or haste to contract marriage may lead to an elopement. Or, as explained in Chapter 11, the desire to evade the laws of one state by going to another may be a reason for eloping. A recent study of Michigan secret marriages showed that age differences were influential factors. The wife being older than the husband or a large age discrepancy in the opposite direction often resulted in secret marriage. In addition, males of upper occupational status and females in the service and clerical areas were more attracted to secret marriages suggesting some fear of job loss. There was not as great a tendency as might be expected to get married far from home nor was there any

[25] Paul H. Jacobson, *American Marriage and Divorce*, Holt, Rinehart and Winston, New York, 1959, pp. 37f.

significant tendency for secret marriages to be civil ceremonies rather than religious.[26] Or in some cases the elopement or secret marriage may be followed by a more traditional ceremony. The evidence obtained of the runaway marriage points also to its nonpermanence.

THE WEDDING. The wedding as a ritual has enormous symbolic importance not only for the two people most directly involved but for their families. The day really belongs to the young bride. Our marriage subculture is female oriented as demonstrated by the succession of showers and other elaborate rituals surrounding the female in the wedding itself—bridesmaids, trousseau, flowers. This feminine priority probably is attributable to the change of status for the woman. More than for the male, her way of life—and name—changes. The festivities of marriage are historically regarded as a compensation for her last vestiges of "absolute" freedom. In Western tradition she moves from the parental home to that of the husband.

The wedding ceremony is surrounded by considerable legend. For instance, the ring which dates from Egyptian antiquity signifies eternity. The practice of throwing rice is supposed to induce fertility, although it was once considered as a means of giving food to evil influences so as to coax them into a benign state.[27] Carrying the bride across the threshold also has an ancient heritage. Today the wedding ritual has become a major event of "do's" and "don'ts," conspicuous consumption, and attention to protocol. The harassed bride's mother must guarantee that the wedding and the reception following be perfect. Such an understanding may require professional help and the American entrepreneurial world has taken advantage of this opportunity. A wedding director may be hired so that all arrangements from the choice of stationery for the invitation to the registering of the silver pattern are managed with sophistication.[28] However, the flexibility of American culture permits individual styling of the nuptial ceremony. For instance, even though some traditional half dozen songs are usually preferred, the selection of music may be quite varied, as one minister reflects:

. . . Once our organist, an austere man, a devotee of Bach, came to me in great perturbation. The groom, it appeared, was a member of a certain learned

[26] Sherman L. Ricards, Jr., "The Secret Marriage," *Marriage and Family Living,* 1960, **22,** 243–247.

[27] Ernest Crawley, *The Mystic Rose,* Macmillan, New York, 1902, p. 325.

[28] Arthur H. Cole, "The Bride System and Rites of Passage," *American Quarterly,* 1962, **14,** 527–544.

society in tribute to which the bride requested that the organist play "The Sweetheart of Sigma Chi." "Do I have to play that?" he asked wrathfully. "No!" I answered, "we've got to make a stand somewhere. It may as well be here." Once a young woman of fine taste and breeding had the organist play the love-death music from *Tristan und Isolde*. It seemed to me a little jarring to have played, as a prelude to a wedding, music which set forth (as only Wagner could) the consumption of physical passion, and that not between man and wife (King Mark was Isolde's husband, remember?) but between a married woman and her lover. But recently our organist has been cheered by requests for Bach chorales. . . .[29]

Of course, marriage can be performed in a fairly simple ceremony in a church or by a religious officiant in the home. Sometimes the minister's study serves for the family and immediate friends with the broader socialization confined to the formal reception. In any case, over 80 per cent of the American public marrying for the first time choose a religious ceremony (Table 12.1). Locke found that being married by a judge or justice of the peace was a significantly more frequent practice among his divorced than his happily married sample.[30]

The type of ceremony and the associated rituals are partially a function of the previous marital status, as Hollingshead determined in a sample of 900 couples in New Haven (Table 12.1). The sample included: type I, both individuals marrying for the first time; type II, the man but not the woman marrying for the first time; type III, the reverse of type II; and type IV, both individuals having been married before.[31] The elaborate wedding was found among types I and III; types II and IV tended to resemble each other in their simplicity. Type IV had the lowest amount of display. It is not surprising that types I and III had had a lengthier engagement and a more expensive ring. Of course, in interpreting the New Haven 1949 data, some allowance must be made for inflation since the study is for the year 1949–1950. The average outlay for a wedding is probably upwards of $1,000 at the present time. In fact, a 1956 study of University of Cincinnati students reported a "small family wedding" as costing $188; a medium size one of 150 guests, $944; and a large country club dinner and reception variety with 300 guests costing $3,509.[32]

[29] "Of Weddings and Funerals," anonymous, *Harper's Magazine*, December, 1945, p. 498.

[30] Locke, *op. cit.*, p. 238.

[31] August B. Hollingshead, "Marital Status and Wedding Behavior," *Marriage and Family Living*, 1952, 14, 311.

[32] United Press news release, July 20, 1956, of a study by Margaret J. Syndam, as cited by Robert O. Blood in *Marriage*, The Free Press of Glencoe, A Division of Collier-Macmillan, New York, 1962, p. 182.

Table 12.1

SELECTED BEHAVIORAL TRAITS ASSOCIATED WITH THE
WEDDING AND ATTENDANT FESTIVITIES SUMMARIZED
INTO MEANS OR PERCENTAGES BY MARRIAGE TYPE

	MARRIAGE TYPE			
Behavioral Trait	I	II	III	IV
Per cent who had bachelor party	33.7	31.1	13.8	4.6
Per cent who had showers	81.0	27.4	56.9	32.3
Number of showers	1.6	0.4	1.0	0.4
Per cent with formal wedding	69.7	4.8	29.3	6.2
Per cent with church wedding	81.3	22.6	44.8	24.6
Per cent with single ring	26.4	54.8	55.2	60.0
Number in bridal party	7.2	4.1	4.9	3.5
Number of wedding guests	172.0	34.0	77.0	30.0
Per cent of cases where bride's family paid for wedding	45.7	14.8	23.1	3.1
Per cent having a reception	87.7	51.6	79.3	44.6
Number of guests at reception	166.0	42.0	82.0	23.0
Cost of wedding	$948.0	$348.0	$571.0	$176.0
Value of cash gifts	$527.0	$168.0	$271.0	$ 70.0
Value of other gifts	$978.0	$336.0	$505.0	$182.0
Per cent taking wedding trip	94.5	75.8	79.3	61.5
Number of days on trip	9.0	6.0	9.0	6.0
Cost of wedding trip	$320.0	$254.0	$371.0	$174.0

Source: August B. Hollingshead, "Marital Status and Wedding Behavior," *Marriage and Family Living*, 1952, 14, 311.

THE HONEYMOON. Honeymooning has a lengthy tradition in Western society. Variations of this practice are also found in preliterate societies, at least in terms of permitting the newly married some sense of demarcation from their previous status. Among the Amish people of East Central Pennsylvania, the first weeks of married life are spent in making extended visits to friends who were wedding guests, and during these visits the newlyweds receive their wedding gifts. This circuit only reinforces their belongingness within the society and seems to indicate a different status from the single life they knew with their family of procreation.[33] As Pitts points out, the honeymoon harmonizes with the atmosphere of the Christian tradition in which "marriage

[33] William M. Kephart, *The Family, Individual and the Society,* Houghton Mifflin, Boston, 1961, p. 209.

makes man and woman of one flesh." Historically, it tends to emphasize the separateness of this new dyad. Even where the couple returned to live with the extended family, the fact that they had spent some time together alone, gave the marriage a certain reinforcement.[34]

In contemporary society the most euphoric aspect of the marriage process for young people is the wedding trip or honeymoon. The term itself suggests a rhapsodic note. Among its functions are:

1. Festiveness and Glamour. The unreality of the honeymoon is partially justified, because it is an expected period of celebration. Thus it extends and intensifies the enjoyment initiated by the wedding which was both brief and public. Commercial interests, such as the advertising of honeymoon suites, encourage this euphoria. Even entire hotels are designed exclusively for the honeymoon trade to appeal to the "resorty," pleasant, and quiet atmosphere.[35]

2. Intimacy. For practically all married couples the wedding trip signifies living together and the exploration of each other's personality with no limits on time. The process has to be a gradual one, because intimacy in emotional and physical behavior can easily be traumatic.

3. Adjustment. The first few days of married life permit the couple to work at the process of give and take which is basic to marriage. A whole set of practices—sharing the same bed and bathroom, dressing and undressing, ordering or preparing breakfast—introduce flexibility in roles and habit alterations so necessary to marriage.

4. Sex Experience. For most couples the honeymoon offers the first opportunity for coitus with each other, and for those who previously have had sex intimacy this period is the possibility for an extended sex relationship in an atmosphere more conducive to enjoyment. For some women, especially those from a sheltered environment, there may be a degree of traumatization, and unless this type of person has received some counselling from a physician or other reliable source of sexual information, such a woman may find that some basic adjustments are necessary. The wife preferably should choose a date for the nuptials in accordance with the menstrual cycle. But often excitement surrounding the wedding upsets the schedule.

[34] Jesse R. Pitts, "The Structural-Functional Approach," in Harold T. Christensen (ed.), *Handbook of Marriage and the Family,* Rand McNally, Chicago, 1964, p. 81.
[35] Cole, *op. cit.*

In many cases coitus is not successful the first or second time the couple engages in sexual relations. Young people may be counselled to avoid sexual relations the first night of the honeymoon, if for no other reason than the fatigue of the nuptial ceremonies themselves. It has even been suggested that the young couple avoid coitus for several days, if necessary, until living together and physical intimacy are sufficiently advanced to permit relaxation for sex.[36] Most males are unlikely to hold off their desires very long. On the other hand, impotence of the male during the early phase of the honeymoon is not unknown.

In an assessment of married women's recollections of reactions to their honeymoon, two-thirds considered the period emotionally satisfying, but 48 per cent asserted they failed to reach sexual satisfaction during this period, and 68 per cent agreed that a honeymoon is not essential to a happy marriage.[37] Honeymoons have become traditional, although they are not always as blissful as a couple might expect. Some suggestions for a successful honeymoon might be the following: (1) anonymity in the choice of location; (2) relaxation and enjoyment should be the theme; and (3) realization that sexual relations are only a part of the total enjoyment of the honeymoon period.

The significance of engagement and marriage has altered drastically since great-grandmother was a girl. Once engagement was a formalized betrothal; today it is to some extent an informal process during which values and emotions are examined. However, engagement and marriage remain critical events and should involve insightful assessment of personal feelings about the degree of maturity and readiness for marriage. Psychological counselling and testing services are available to aid in this examination if needed.

The pattern by which the individual proceeds from engagement, to the wedding, to the honeymoon is in our secular age largely left to his discretion, with ample suggestions from those about him. Yet despite the materialistic façade of our culture the marriage ceremony itself remains a sacred rite. Finally, it is in the days following this event that behavior patterns are more important than the style of ceremony that brought the two individuals together.

---

[36] Ray E. Baber, *Marriage and the Family*, McGraw-Hill, 1953, pp. 170–171.
[37] Stanley R. Brav, "Note on Honeymoons," *Marriage and Family Living*, 1947, **9,** 60.

Supplementary Readings

Bell, Robert R., *Marriage and Family Interaction*. The Dorsey Press, Homewood, Illinois, 1963. Chapter 10 introduces the student to some of the problems of the engagement, wedding, and the honeymoon. (See also Chapter 8.)

Blood, Robert O., Jr., *Marriage,* The Free Press of Glencoe, A Division of Collier-Macmillan, New York, 1962. Chapters 6–8 treat, although somewhat didactically, the problems of "readiness for marriage" and the ceremonies themselves.

Burgess, Ernest W. and Paul Wallin, *Engagement and Marriage*. J. P. Lippincott, Philadelphia, 1953. The classic study of engagement and its problems.

Jacobson, Paul H., *American Marriage and Divorce*. Holt, Rinehart and Winston, New York, 1959. The early chapters give the statistical picture with interesting explanations of the trends and causes involved.

Martinson, Floyd M., *Marriage and the American Ideal*. Dodd, Mead, New York, 1960. Chapters 12–16 are a sensitive approach to the subject. Chapter 16 presents some religious aspects to the wedding ceremony.

Merrill, Francis E., *Courtship and Marriage,* Holt, Rinehart and Winston, New York, 1959. Chapter 11 treats most adequately the psychological and sexual aspects of engagement.

Simpson, George, *People in Families*. Thomas Y. Crowell, New York, 1960. Chapters 5 and 9 turn, among other things, to the psychoanalytical aspects of the prelude to marriage.

Winch, Robert F., *The Modern Family* (second edition). Holt, Rinehart and Winston, New York, 1963. Chapters 20 and 21 describe our subject in a theoretical framework.

Part four
Relations in Marriage

Let us now turn to the marital experience itself. This book is based on the idea that the process of marriage interaction is understandable in terms of roles, and that marital adjustment can be studied empirically. The nature of marital roles and the study of adjustment are the focus of Chapter 13. The premise that marital problems can be discussed on a scientific basis is followed into the study of sex behavior (Chapter 14) and economic problems (Chapter 15).

The final chapters of Part Four are concerned with the challenge of parenthood in a broad context. Here the psychological frame of reference is emphasized, particularly in regard to parent–child relations. The concentration on childhood underscores the important influence it represents in our lives.

Chapter thirteen

Roles, Personality Dynamics, and the Adjustment Process

A good marriage (if there be any) refuseth the company and conditions of love; it endeavoreth to present those of amity. It is a sweet society of life, full of consistency, of trust, and an infinite number of profitable and solid offices, and mutual obligations.

Michel De Montaigne: Essays, III, 1588.

It may be useful to apply the distinction between role and personality to a diachronic view of American middle-class marriages. In the first, or mate-selective, stage the emphasis is on the personality of the prospective spouse, and love (complementariness of needs) is an important selective principle. To regard role characteristics (e.g., a man's occupational prospects or a woman's cooking) as more important in mate-selection runs counter to subcultural values. Then after the wedding comes a rapid succession of tasks: the wife's task of keeping a house, of bearing children and of having major responsibility for rearing them; the husband's task of "getting ahead" and of providing the financial means for the family's level of living. It seems reasonable that the pressure of these responsibilities would give greater emphasis to role. Then twenty to thirty years later the pressure is off. The children leave home, and the mates turn back to each other. The wife's domestic duties are reduced, and probably the husband has either achieved or has adopted a somewhat philosophical attitude toward his modest accomplishments.

Robert F. Winch, Mate-Selection: A Study of Complementary Needs, Harper and Row, New York, 1958, p. 309.

In every marriage, husband and wife act out individual variations of the traditional cultural roles. Some husbands do most of the shopping, take an active part in the cooking, and clean the house. Others act like permanent guests at a moderately well-run hotel, where they pay the bills and appear for meals with reasonable regularity. In some households, emptying the ashtrays is the entire male contribution to the domestic economy, whereas in others he may act as a virtual substitute housekeeper.

Francis E. Merrill, Courtship and Marriage (revised edition), Holt, Rinehart and Winston, New York, 1959, p. 177.

James and Sarah Tuttle by Joseph H. Davis
Courtesy of The New-York Historical Society, New York City

Two questions preoccupy young people contemplating matrimony: "Who will I marry?" and "How will it work?" We have already discussed the first question, although it is difficult to separate the two. It is also presumptuous to indicate that the quality or style of marriage is set by the first few weeks or months. Adjustment is a highly intricate process; yet the initial adjustments are immensely critical. They necessitate the acquisition of new roles, habit systems, techniques of communication, household skills, careful financial planning, and among other expectations, adjustments to the arrival of an infant. Two people often have to redefine their needs and values, even though much of the thought process is implicit. For some, all the intricate adjustments occur in a background of ambivalent emotional involvements so that considerable strain is likely. For others, the adjustments in the early months of marriage may develop naturally and easily.

The major emphasis of this chapter is on marital roles, their definitions, dimensions, and relation to other role commitments. These roles can hardly be met by universal specifications; yet most individuals entering marriage have standards not acutely different from those of their neighbors. Our discussion includes the problem of role variability in marriage and the degree to which roles are modified by marriage.

The second major purpose of this chapter is to attempt to define and measure marriage adjustment; we review the findings of several studies in this area. In other words, what are the factors that are predictive of marital success? To what degree can we study marriage adjustment by the use of testing instruments? And how can we relate the concept of marital adjustment to the question of roles?

THE GREAT EXPERIMENT AND THE EARLY ADJUSTMENT PHASE

THE INITIAL ADJUSTMENTS. The honeymoon is over and two people take up the process of being partners in a fascinating and conceivably perilous adventure, namely, welding two distinct personalities into a near-lifetime of intimate interaction. Even in the honeymoon, shock and unreality may have left an occasional blemish on an emotionally glamorous interlude. Successful or not, coitus may have left unconscious traces of guilt. In some instances, the posthoneymoon return to the round of day-to-day activities may even provide the newlyweds with a sense of relief. As the days and weeks pass after the wedding, the delight at feeling part of a tremendous experiment is secondary only to an awareness that one has found a life companion. The sense of security is the stronger for the status enhancement that marriage brings; the realization that one has satisfied another expectation of society; and most important of all, the security of emotional sharing. For most newlyweds it is a euphoric state.

Adjustment in marriage can mean entirely different experiences for different individuals. There is the excitement of becoming acquainted with another person to a degree that was not possible in engagement. A contemporary novelist captures some of this enjoyment of discovery in the following passage:

> On one of my trips through Illinois I met a girl and she was pretty and shy and a little confused, but shapely with a wishful knack for attractive positions, whether it be sitting on a swing or in a car, walking, running, or on a couch with her knees up under her chin.
>
> Dark eyes she had and dark hair and a wide warm face, and on the third date I knew she loved me because she told me so, her arms around my waist, her face pressed to my chest, and she said she needed me as much as she knew I needed her, and when I heard this my brain almost popped with the urgency of finding a place where we could be alone with a rug and chairs and a kitchen and a bedroom and a phonograph and a coffeepot. She agreed on what we needed, although she had endless additions to make, silverware, sheets, blankets, towels, dishes, lamps, tables, bedspreads, pots and pans, and a lot of names I had never heard before, like "a spatula" for pancakes and a "noodler."
>
> For months, my happiness was her smile and her pleasure, a kiss at night, her warm voice and her hand, as she lured me quite gently but deeper into love and more love, until if I couldn't look upon her I was in painful misery and there was no sight or face that could substitute for her void. So I proposed marriage and she accepted. There was a brief talk with her fat father while her birdlike mother hovered in the shadows; there was a ring, a rehearsal; then a tense, stomach-jangling ceremony before grinning strangers and friends, there to remind us of our vows forever; and then there was escape to a lodge for a weekend, where all her mysteries were solved and where warmth built cascading up to wildness, a frenzy of envelopment, of heart-stopping plunges, and then hard real capturable joy—the real ceremony of marriage, the pleasurable not the ritual, the ring of flesh rather than of silver, the actual union, the physical give and take. It was more than I imagined, or ever knew; not sex, but an expression of what we felt, and since I had never had anything to express before, and never felt love just relief, it was a first time for me, too, and I felt just as much a virgin as she.
>
> We house-hunted and found a white place just three blocks away from the finance company, within walking distance and an easy access for lunch

when I was in town. She was a vision, yet she was cruel sometimes as I was to her, but we swore out our arguments without ever assuming that they would not end. We were together for good, and we never assumed anything else, no split was possible, tolerable, except for moments. We were each other's only alternative.

How can I describe her laugh, her look, her contentment, her love, her play and her labor of cooking and cleaning, her happiness and her sour pensive anger at slights, insults and crudity, her conceits, her abilities strange and common. I give up ever transmitting the exact magic of her walking, talking, thinking loveliness to paper, and I say just that I got more than I bargained for, depths I could not even see, grace I would never have imagined was there, secret talents for pleasure which shocked even me, and a defiance which could bend, flex, change, capitulate, without once losing its rigidity or its insistence on being considered. I began to pity other men, because of their less lustrous prizes, for mine was the black earth, the blue sky, the why and what of all comfort, the beat that enhanced my melody, the pressure that surrounded my push, the practical reason for my ideas, and it seemed my poor friends had nothing in comparison. As the months went on, I felt luckier and luckier, and I could only justify the correctness of my original blind choice by manufacturing some superior instinct which I supposed had made me pick her for reasons I came to discover were plainly superficial and did not touch the magnificence of her offering in the least. How had I done it? I had simply deserved her, I concluded, and I never thought of it again for fear of not measuring up.

. . . She never judged me; I suppose she believed she had made one massive judgment when we were married and it was useless to consider standards at this late date, and I think she was only interested in discovering the whole nature of what she had won, since I must have been as unknown to her at the moment of that legal union as she was to me. I perceived this because she always asked her questions of me with a little fear as to what I might answer, since she had to accept any answer that came, and I felt the responsibility to her of making my speeches, if not good, at least true and certain and confident and thoughtful and workable. I avoided the easy, the pompous, the dangerous, the terror, the fright, the impossible, whenever I could. . . Sometimes I realize that women are question marks, at their happiest, in search of exclamation points, and if men deny them there is no dialogue for marriage, there will always be something missing. A man cannot counter with another question mark but must counter all interrogation with an answer and the courage to make one up.[1]

THE ADJUSTMENT POTENTIAL. At the same time, there are a number of initial adjustments to be made: does one sleep with or without pajamas, with the window up or down, the way the bathroom is to be

---

[1] James Drought, *The Secret*, Norwalk, Connecticut, Skylight Press, 1963, pp. 119–122. Used by permission.

shared, the degree of intimacy in living habits, plus the fact that the habits of one spouse may disturb the equilibrium of the other. The cap on the toothpaste is not replaced, dirty dishes are on the sink, the thirty-minute phone conversation with "Mom" and "Dad" each night. Not least there are the assignments of tasks between the two participants, in addition to the first attempts of learning to solve differences of opinion.

Much of the ability of two individuals to meet the challenge of marital living depends on their capacity for adjustment. This adjustability is a product of a lifetime of behavior and experience and their acquired reaction tendencies. The two personality systems have been developing for two decades or more, and the events transpiring in the opening weeks or years of marriage interaction cannot be detached from most of the previous learning experience. Through the chain of events that took place in infancy, childhood, and adolescence spontaneity and discipline, permissiveness and restraints all have made the individual into the final product. Perhaps the most obvious example is the tendency of the adult male to find in his wife the mother surrogate and relate her attentions to the succourance he once knew in his mother's arms. The more recent episodes of adolescence and early adulthood have left traces no matter what experiences a person may have had. For many newly married persons there are periodic attacks of nostalgia for a return to the independence of being single or the attentions of multiple admirers of the opposite sex.

The adjustment potential thus depends on maturity and is a product of highly involved origins. Its complexity is a primary reason for recommending a lengthy and deep acquaintance with the chosen mate before marriage.

THE ROLE OF EMPATHY. Possibly the most important ingredient in the marriage adjustment process is the capacity for empathy, which we discussed earlier. Empathic responses are fundamental to "taking the role of the other," [2] and consequently are basic to social relationships in a democratic social order. One of the aspects of maturity is, of course, the acquisition of a capacity for empathy. And even for the individual who supposedly has acquired an empathic type of response, practice is necessary. It is all too easy to look at the marital picture only through one's own eyes.

[2] Nelson N. Foote and Leonard S. Cottrell, Jr., *Identity and Interpersonal Competence*, The University of Chicago Press, 1955, p. 54.

Burgess and Wallin's married couples reflected on the necessity of seeing into each other's problems, although frequently on an implicit basis: "That is just like a woman" or "Men behave that way." Yet much of this training in identification depended on the ability of each person to communicate his own thoughts.[3] Another study of a married college sample suggests that empathy and communication are highly interrelated. This study disclosed that it is especially crucial for the wife to have her antenna focused on the needs of the husband because she makes the major adjustment in marriage.[4] It is difficult to detach empathy from other factors, such as the strength of the love relationship. In other words, a necessary prelude to empathy in the marital setting is monogamous affection. Only with a deep affectionate relationship can there be the degree of tolerance and understanding to provide for complete, or nearly complete, identification. Yet, there are other conditioning agents: a degree of detachment, objectivity, and sense of humor. Thus what may be defined as the "ability to shift the frame of reference" varies with changing marital situations. The opening weeks are likely to be characterized by an all too intense relationship followed by increasing insight and then periods of disenchantment, all of which influence empathy as well as other aspects of the marital situation.

SECURITY AND THE NEEDS SYSTEM.   As already implied in the preceding section, success in marriage depends on the maturity and degree of security in the self. Empathy and the process of adjustment depend on a reasonably high level of emotional security. A variety of response mechanisms reflect this potential. Does the individual have access to the channels by which he can ventilate and neutralize his conflicts? Does he have a sufficiently consistent affectional relationship with the loved one? Are accommodative processes generally available to one or both of the parties? Will either or both partners be sufficiently free of anxiety and at the same time have the ego strength to confide in others, such as a counsellor, who may be able to lend some insight into a given marital conflict that is already an emotionally loaded situation? It is clear that these adjustive techniques are not available to all

[3] Ernest W. Burgess and Paul Wallin, *Engagement and Marriage*, J. B. Lippincott, Philadelphia, 1953, pp. 624–626.
[4] Charles W. Hobart and William J. Klausner, "Some Social Interactional Correlates of Marital Role Disagreement and Marital Adjustment," *Marriage and Family Living*, 1959, **21**, 256–263.

people, and that the same person may have unequal periods in his interpersonal behavior. Moods, fluctuating needs, and the chance events of the day determine the particular equilibrium of the moment and the relationship to the other person. The reaction of the mate may either reinforce or divert the mood of the self.

Everyone has conflicts, but the individual who is not burdened with an excess of conflict has a markedly easier task in making the marriage work. The individual who is free of extravagant rationalizations and projections, that is, the need to interpret reality in terms of his own satisfaction, and one who does not shift his inadequacies on to another person, is better adjusted to marriage. Clinical literature points also to displacement, the wreaking of emotional frustration on the mate, as an undesirable characteristic for a good marriage. Examples of this behavior are flirtation and extramarital adventures or the wife's assignment of extensive window cleaning to her husband on alternate Saturdays. The woman may be one who needs to protect or aggrandize herself by reducing the stature of the male, or the male may be one who needs the attention of his wife to support his weak ego structure. Many of the verbal battles of two people are in a sense a futile attempt by each to bolster their own self-images. An attack on any part of the self-values, attitudes, even the clothes a person wears, can have extensive emotional overtones.

Another aspect of ego strength and security is the degree to which the *idealized* self is detached and fantasy-oriented as compared to the *real* self. Our ego tends to move in different directions. Very often it is the woman who must support the husband in his efforts to maintain his equilibrium and often his masculinity. Although the husband's insight into his wife's problems is equally important, he tends to take her for granted since he regards his economic support as his major contribution. Mowrer refers to the process of "emulation" by which one partner looks up to the other, giving a sense of pride to both spouses.[5] Although this mechanism is a normal and desirable aspect of marriage, it can in some instances become exaggerated. Occasionally marriages and family structures become mutual admiration societies; the fallacious security of this buildup may prove disastrous when the individual is threatened by an external force, for example, if the mar-

---

[5] Harriet R. Mowrer, "Getting Along in Marriage," in Howard Becker and Reuben Hill (eds.), *Family, Marriage, and Parenthood* (second edition), D. C. Heath, Boston, 1955, p. 349.

riage partner does not receive the acclaim outside the home that the mate has led him to believe he deserves.

ROLE PATTERNS AND THE ADJUSTMENT PROCESS

Throughout this book we have discussed roles and role behavior. Role characterizes the majority of occupants of a specific position; role behavior refers to the action of a given individual in the enactment of the role. However, the terms are nearly interchangeable.[6] Roles may be behavior patterns associated with a given social status. Role behavior only serves to emphasize that roles are dynamic, that is, changing and motivationally oriented. From the earliest months of our lives we are indoctrinated into a variety of roles based on identification and reciprocal relations. Thus, we interact in complementary fashion: husband to wife, father to son, teacher to student. We accept or reject the role behavior of another individual or *role model.* Our father and mother, a brother or aunt, the family doctor, along with the friends and neighbors become models or countermodels for our marital conduct.

We may define a role as a set of social obligations that group members, including those of the marital unit, utilize in their interaction with each other. Roles confer order, continuity, and predictability on the social world. We may look on roles as either mandatory, expected, or optional. The wife is *obligated* to regulate the household and prepare the meals; she is *expected* to be interested in his career and serve as hostess when he entertains his prospective clients, and as an alternative or *optional* form of behavior may accompany him to the opera. He, too, has a complementary set of behaviors, affectional, sexual, economic, etc. Roles depend on identification, which, as we have discussed, is understanding the place of another person. Identification may be *similar, opposite,* or *reciprocal* in relation to the roles of the other person. In most instances, roles are reciprocal or complementary: our role exists only to the degree that some other individuals call for it. The role of husband is meaningless without the role of the wife. Roles may be explicit, conscious or unconscious.

It is understandable, in view of these complexities, why role dis-

---

[6] Theodore M. Newcomb, *Social Psychology,* Holt, Rinehart and Winston, New York, 1950, p. 330.

crepancies and conflicts occur. In some cases the inability or failure to carry out a given role or a number of roles proves disastrous to the marriage. Differences in role perception are illustrated when the husband prefers the patriarchal pattern, and the wife looks forward to an equalitarian one. Divorce may be the only outcome for these role discrepancies. On the happier side, it is the depth and richness of role sharing that becomes the core of marriage.

PERCEPTION OF ROLES. As implied earlier in this chapter, empathy is itself a form of role taking. One question is the degree to which the husband and wife are capable of perceiving their personality and role. In regard to the decision making process, one study of 25 married couples revealed that neither mate was extraordinarily perceptive or conscious of what role he or she performed in making the major decision.[7] Perception of roles in the average person is apparently ill-defined and more likely implicit. The individuals were able to indicate who had done more of the talking, yet it was not readily apparent which had convinced the other in the dispute. Still more difficult for subjects to determine was who in their marriage was more capable of guiding the discussion and decision making. Role situations remain relatively inarticulate for a major share of the population. For this reason, it might be expected that the college-level spouse is more successful in perceiving his role entanglements.

Further documentation of the limitations on role awareness is found in an investigation of 32 married college students in which responses to a questionnaire indicated only limited perceptual sensitivity to marital roles. If we may judge from this small sample, the typical husband, and to a lesser extent the wife, only partially succeeded in assessing the level of role consensus between them or the adequacy of role performance. There was a small but irregular relationship between the length of marriage and the consensus of role perception. Interesting sex differences were noted. Women were more likely to perceive *affective* or emotional roles in the spouses, whereas the men were more inclined to perceive an instrumental role, that is, economic or household duties. Husbands tended to rate their wives as performing their roles adequately, but a similar tendency was not found in the wives. On the other hand, men married more than two years evaluated the wife's role performance on a lower basis than did the more recently married husbands. With the arrival of children the

[7] William F. Kenkel and Dean K. Hoffman, "Real and Conceived Roles in Family Decision Making," *Marriage and Family Living*, 1956, 18, 311–316.

demands placed on the wife increase, which probably tends to decrease the husband's satisfaction.[8]

However, we cannot assume that most couples are necessarily unable to verbalize role situations. In fact, it has been suggested that marriage success depends on the congruence in role perception between the two spouses.[9] Luckey proceeded to test this theory by hypothesizing a positive relation of marital adjustment when there was congruence between the perception of the self and perception of the partner's self by the spouse. This relationship proved to be tenable. Supporting Freudian theory, it was found that perception of the self might be related to the perception of the parent, and perception by the spouse of the parent of the opposite sex, both of which were apparently associated with marital satisfaction.[10] The unconscious dynamics of role behavior are documented in the study of complementary needs, which was discussed in Chapter 10. According to this theory, marital interaction may tend toward completing the inadequacies the person has experienced in his relationship to the opposite sex and to the parents.[11] In any case, perceptual sensitivity to these more indirect pressures and needs might be expected to have predictive value for marital success. The ability to perceive subtle personality nuances is valuable in a variety of interpersonal relationships.

Stating our problem in a somewhat different fashion, a basic question is the degree of similarity with which the two partners perceive roles in marriage. Do they perceive marriage more as a general role or as a number of specific roles? To what degree are these factors related to marital adjustment? Do the performances of roles differ from their initial expectations? A partial answer is given in a study of 50 randomly selected Milwaukee couples who were given a questionnaire. It was found that the wife's perception of the husband's concepts and expectations of roles was more accurate than his perceptions of her role concepts and expectations.[12] Among several factors measured in connection with marital adjustment, the similarity in role concepts of

[8] Carl Couch, "The Use of the Concept 'Role' and Its Derivatives in a Study of Marriage," *Marriage and Family Living*, 1958, **20**, 353–357.

[9] A. Raymond Mangus, "Family Impacts on Mental Health," *Marriage and Family Living*, 1957, **19**, 256–262.

[10] Eleanore B. Luckey, "Marital Satisfaction and Its Association with Congruence of Perception," *Marriage and Family Living*, 1960, **22**, 49–54.

[11] Robert F. Winch, *Mate Selection: A Study of Complementary Needs*, Harper and Row, New York, 1958.

[12] Robert P. Stuckert, "Role Perception and Marital Satisfaction—A Configurational Approach," *Marriage and Family Living*, 1963, **25**, 415–419.

the two spouses was among the most critical factors. Where there was agreement on the roles themselves, inaccurate perception was of secondary importance. The generalization made by Stuckert, that "marital satisfaction is a function of the mutual interaction," refers especially to role perceptions surrounding marriage. The results of this study indicate it is the husband who determines the success of the relationship, particularly in the early stage of marriage; consequently, his capacity for role perception is the more critical.

ROLES, COMMUNICATION, AND EXPEDIENCY. In the immediate or the ultimate sense roles depend on communication. It is impossible to disentangle the communication process from the perceptual one. How we perceive our roles determines how we verbalize them, and conversely the language process determines perception: words and syntax selected, the tone of voice, the emotional depth of the discussion, and variations in mood. Also, much depends on the purpose of the communication. Is it affectional or emotional—namely having to do with personal relations within the family—or is it institutional in scope, that is, oriented to basic values within the marital or family unit? [13] In determining the quantity and quality of communication, especially in the marital setting, there is the question of *feedback,* the degree to which the individual receives communication from the spouse.[14] For instance, the term "love" and its relationship can convey many different meanings between two individuals. The problem of communication is occasionally more critical in the later phases of marriage than in the earlier ones. If the "fit" or the harmony between two individuals declines in the succeeeding years of marriage, communication can suffer.[15] As a person's needs change, there is less agreement on the similarity of role expectations, and consequently more discrepancy in the role behaviors, which can be considerably complicated by the failure to communicate.

One problem is the phenomenon of *masking.* People often fail to communicate in the courtship process. According to one study of role conflicts in single women, there has been a tendency to "play dumb," to avoid exposure of ability by "misspelling an occasional word in a letter,"

[13] Bernard Farber, *Family: Organization and Interaction,* Chandler Publishing, San Francisco, 1964, p. 291.

[14] William G. Dyer, "Analyzing Marital Adjustment Using Role Theory," *Marriage and Family Living,* 1962, **24,** 371–375.

[15] Peter C. Pineo, "Disenchantment in the Later Years of Marriage," *Marriage and Family Living,* 1961, **23,** 3–11.

or avoiding the discussion of classical music, or to give the "clinging vine" stereotype, the dependency on the strong male.[16] The boy friend may create the image of successful masculinity, whether in the dating complex or on the football field. In marriage this masking is "toned down" in the realities of deeply involved marital living. The outer self is too easily "de-masked," unless he has a highly developed ability for manipulability. Still, the individual continues to disclose the deeper core of himself. It is reported that in French families there is a tendency for various family pairs, such as father-daughter, father-mother, etc., to have their own separate universes of confidence, which the other family members respect.[17]

Communicative patterns generally tend to become streamlined. Consequently facial expressions and gestures are increasingly more important communicative media as marriage interaction continues through the years.[18] Youth and higher education, which suggests the importance of extensive socialization, permit the couple a deeper level of communication. Marital adjustment depends on the mental resources of the partners. As with marital roles themselves, culture—including social class—places limits and norms on our verbalizations.

Roles by their very nature are manipulative, and there also exist role incompatibilities about which the subject must make certain choices. Illustrative of this problem is a now classical study of school administrators in which role behavior depended on how the administrator perceived a given situation and communicated aspects of his relationship to the electorate or the classroom teacher. The decisions were generally made according to three types: (1) "moralists," who resolved conflicts in roles by choosing the more legitimate of alternatives of behavior; (2) "expedients," who in role incompatibility or conflict selected the more convenient behavioral outlet; and (3) "moral-expedients," those who select a compromise of the two alternatives.[19] Some of these same role enactments occur in marriage. A husband with the temptation for extramarital relations may verbalize his

[16] Mirra Komarovsky, "Cultural Contradictions and Sèx Roles," *American Journal of Sociology*, 1946, **52**, 184–189.

[17] Joseph K. Folsom, "Communication in Marriage and Marriage Counselling," *Marriage and Family Living*, 1958, **20**, 113–116.

[18] E. Dorothy Brownfield, "Communication—Key to Dynamics of Family Interaction," *Marriage and Family Living*, 1953, **15**, 316–319.

[19] Neal Gross, Ward S. Mason, Alexander W. McEachern, *Explorations in Role Analysis*, John Wiley and Sons, New York, 1958, pp. 289–295.

role in terms of some balance of loyality, morality, and the strength of his sex desires. He may have a complex rationalization by which he communicates his roles. Folsom discusses a husband who did not communicate to his wife about his own promiscuity, although he hoped that she was faithful. However, during the lengthy periods that his career kept him out of town he carefully avoided asking her about her fidelity. To insure his ignorance on the subject he would call her a half hour before returning home.[20]

A factor analysis of marital interaction found that a kind of "mutual altruism" operated in role definitions between husbands and wives; that is, a habitual altruism that was oriented to each other's demands, yet was coupled with deference to middle-class norms of respectability, based on reference groups outside the family.[21] Deference to the needs of the mate is interlaced with self-interest. Altruism can be worked only so far. In a number of instances the husband, but more often the wife, did not insist on deference displayed by the partner: "For example, the husband says, 'My wife and I are at a party. She becomes bored and wants to leave. I'm having a good time, but would reconsider and tell her, we'll leave, since you want to go.' The high scoring wife would solve the problem by saying, 'I'll stay. He's enjoying himself.' This pattern is one of mutual altruism." Although a recent study comparing adjusted and maladjusted couples questioned the degree to which mutual altruism is an integrative factor in the marriage, there is little doubt that marital partners engage in elaborate reciprocal relationships.[22]

SOME DIMENSIONS OF ROLES. Roles tend to be covert and overt, inclusive or exclusive, totalistic or segmental depending on the setting, the person, and the values that are most relevant. Roles, in addition, are integrative or instrumental depending on whether they are oriented toward efficiency of household duties or are concerned with personal relations.[23] An instrumental role is more directed toward getting things done, whereas the integrative leader aims at reducing

---

[20] Folsom, *op. cit.*

[21] Jack V. Buerkle, Theodore R. Anderson, and Robin F. Badgley, "Altruism. Role Conflict, and Marital Adjustment: A Factor Analysis of Marital Interaction," *Marriage and Family Living*, 1961, **23**, 20–26.

[22] G. Levinger, "Altruism in Marriage: A Test of the Buerkle-Badgley Battery," *Journal of Marriage and the Family*, 1965, **27**, 32–33.

[23] Talcott Parsons and Robert F. Bales, *Family, Socialization, and Interaction Process*, The Free Press of Glencoe, A Division of Collier-Macmillan, New York, 1955.

the strain brought on by the instrumental leader or personality. In the family constellation roles take on the flavor of the personality as the person involved "defines the situation." Trial and error, of course, play a major role by determination of acceptable and unacceptable roles. Notwithstanding the psychological sophistication with which the sociologist and psychologist approach roles, the young person probably has an implicit definition of specific roles connected with the husband and wife.

Role dimensions have been approached in a factor analysis study by Tharp in which a large number of separate items were reduced to five factor clusters.[24] Particular emphasis was focused on the separation of role expectations and role enactments. We have redefined these variables (the original factors and subfactors appear in parentheses):

1. Social Adjustment. (External Relations—Social Activity and Community Affairs) or the family's gamut of relations, whether neighbors, the grocer, or the PTA.

2. Household Role Efficiency. (Internal Instrumentality—Wife Adequacy and Work Performance) or the efficient management of the household, the degree to which the performance meets the expectation.

3. Power Equilibrium. (Division of Responsibility—Role Sharing, Social Influence, Masculine Authority, and Division of Influence), the analysis of decision making of the distribution of power structure within the marriage or family.

4. Sex Relations. (Sexuality—Premarital Chastity, Sexual Fidelity, and Sexual Gratification) or the interrelations of sexual factors in the marriage.

5. Emotional Relations. (Solidarity—Intimacy, Social and Emotional Integration, Togetherness, Understanding, and Companionship) composed of several diverse dimensions but with some complex interrelationships. One of the surprising results was the relation of Sexuality to Intimacy for the male but not for the female. It had been taken for granted that a close affectional tie was markedly more essential for the woman than for the man. The fact that the sample was in the middle years may be relevant. A younger male sample might be more motivated toward physical expression.

[24] Roland G. Tharp, "Dimensions of Marriage Roles," *Marriage and Family Living*, 1963, **25**, 389–404.

The point of this discussion of Tharp's study is the complexity of role relationships and the variation between the two sexes. For instance, the role of parenthood was associated with intimacy for women but not for men. Moreover, differences in role expectancy and role performance were apparent, for example, Participation in Community Affairs differed between the ideal and actual roles and the perspectives of the two spouses. (Factors in some instances might be complementary, the expectation factor being labeled as Role Sharing, the enactment factor as Division of Influence, each composed of somewhat different items.) In broad interpretation, role definitions, both in ideal and performance, are subject to change.

THE POWER STRUCTURE AND EQUILIBRIUM. A central problem in role relations is the distribution of power and the arrangement of the decision making process. The solution to this question hinges on the balance of power between the two people, which itself may become a habit system, and not least on the "psychology of the sexes." The male who has inherited an image of superiority and the woman who uses her wiles as effectively as possible may have established a traditional solution within their respective domestic spheres. As has been implied, other aspects of the problem include the cultural background of both parties, that is, a set of attitudes based on social class and a number of other subcultural reference points. In the Blood and Wolfe Michigan study, power balances were found to be slightly in favor of the husband with little difference between farm and city families and none between white Protestants and Catholic. Older subjects showed patriarchalism in their decision making. On the other hand, Negroes leaned toward the matriarchal pattern. Variability seems to be more visible in the power structure of the contemporary marital dyad than was true a generation ago.[25] The drift toward equalitarianism is observable generally in Western culture.

Power structure or equilibrium can also break down, and complimentary role behavior can function in a fairly unbalanced manner. Disagreement about role definitions or enactments means that the two individuals involved may have to restructure their role functions, often painstakingly. Spiegel outlines certain of the mechanisms involved. Among the techniques, which may be used alternatively,

[25] Robert O. Blood, Jr. and Donald M. Wolfe, *Husbands and Wives; The Dynamics of Married Living*, The Free Press of Glencoe, A Division of Collier-Macmillan, New York, 1960, pp. 22f.

simultaneously, or successively are: coercing, coaxing, evaluation, masking and unmasking, postponing, role reversal or taking the alter-position of the ego, joking referral to a third party, exploring, compromising, and consolidating. Through these mechanisms we manipulate others or reequilibrate our roles.[26] This jockeying and reshaping of the immediate social structure is necessary. If the wife desires employment or the father-in-law needs a loan, if the wife enters the menopause, or if the husband is suspected of philandering, these events will make highly probable a major or minor readjustment of roles.

A METHODOLOGICAL NOTE. In the discussion of roles, there is question regarding the validity of attempts to observe and measure role behaviors. In the problem of role taking, decision making, and similar behaviors a number of research tools have become available. For example, Vidich made tape recordings with couples in an upstate New York village, and encountered a wide range of reactions between the spouses as well as toward the interviewer. In the presence of the interviewer, public discussion encouraged some measure of objectivity. Occasionally one partner forced the other into an agreement which possibly could never have occurred privately. Perhaps the most fundamental generalization regarding the use of recording instruments is their inability to reproduce a genuine marital setting in which normal communication takes place. Some artificiality in laboratory methods is inevitable.[27]

In the laboratory culture applied to a middle-class American milieu, Buerkle adopted a Marital Interaction Battery to measure decision making by posing a series of dilemmas requiring settlement. The results indicate that the "democratic-equalitarian" approach is not the exclusive model assuring marital stability. At least, as the authors point out, we need to have a considerably greater amount of information about marital interactional processes before we can determine the formula of decision making in the average American couple.[28]

Similarly, the work of Kenkel gives us relatively little empirical assurance as to what process may be involved in decision making. Using a hypothetical situation regarding the way in which to spend a

[26] John P. Spiegel, "The Resolution of Role Conflict within the Family," *Psychiatry*, 1957, **20**, 1–16.

[27] Arthur J. Vidich, "Methodological Problems in the Observation of Husband-Wife Interaction," *Marriage and Family Living*, 1956, **18**, 234–239.

[28] Jack V. Buerkle and Robin F. Badgley, "Couple Role-Taking: The Yale Marital Interaction Battery," *Marriage and Family Living*, 1959, **21**, 53–58.

gift of three hundred dollars, and with an interaction process analysis (the observation of solidarity, tension, tension release, suggestion, etc.), tapes were used to record the exchange of a sample of 25 married student couples. Various hypotheses, such as "traditional family ideology" or conventionalism, exaggerated masculinity and femininity, or "authoritarian-submission" relationships did not prove to be particularly fruitful as guide lines. While traditional roles were hypothesized by the investigator, there was sufficient dispersion in the results to indicate that there is no consistent pattern.[29]

Another study pointed to cross-cultural comparisons in marital interaction. The means of giving opinion, evaluation and analysis, or the methods of handling marital disagreements were found to differ in three Southwestern frontier cultures: a group of Texans, Mormons, and Navahos. Role equilibria, especially the tendency toward wife or husband dominance, differed for the three cultures.[30]

THE MEASUREMENT OF MARITAL ADJUSTMENT

There are two general approaches to assessing marital happiness or adjustment: one is the *case-study* approach, in which a given sample of marriages is investigated according to a longitudinal viewpoint by examination of the dynamics, unconscious motivation, analysis of the two personalities, and their needs and crises. The other is the *questionnaire-interview* approach in which a larger number of marriages are examined cross-sectionally according to a marital adjustment score, although the actual label may be "happiness," "success," or "adjustment." Most frequently, the subjects are divided into a "happy" or "unhappy" sample that is selected on the basis of the adjustment scores: the two samples in turn are compared with each other for background and personality traits and for any given criteria. These criteria of items may include such diverse factors as the amount of stocks and bonds possessed, the enjoyment of playing bridge, or preference for sleeping in the nude; although more frequently basic patterns, such as decision making or affectional relations, are selected for their relevancy to marital adjustment.

[29] William F. Kenkel, "Traditional Family Ideology and Spousal Roles in Decision Making," *Marriage and Family Living*, 1959, **21**, 334–339.

[30] Fred L. Strodtbeck, "Husband-Wife Interaction over Revealed Differences," *American Sociological Review*, 1951, **16**, 468–473; also Florence R. Kluckhohn and Fred L. Strodtbeck, *Variations in Value Orientations*, Harper and Row, New York, 1961.

This statistical technique is utilized in this chapter, whereas the clinical or nonquantitative outlook is used in Chapter 19 where interest focuses on the problem of conflict. The clinical method is considered the more fruitful approach for analyzing the causes, and possibly the solution, of tension areas. However, the problem of causation should be approached most cautiously, because in neither method is it possible to determine precisely what causes what. We find clusters of variables, but the exact proportion of causative influence has generally eluded us. The difficulty, however, has not diminished the value of these studies for understanding the general operation of basic factors in marital adjustment.

MARITAL ADJUSTMENT STUDIES. During the past several decades there have been published a number of statistical studies of "successful" and "unsuccessful" marriages with a mass of data concerning the influences favorable or unfavorable for marital happiness. In 1929 Hamilton combined a questionnaire and interview method in the investigation of 200 marriages placing considerable stress on social and psychological factors.[31] The same year Davis published a survey of 2,000 women, and found marriage to be happiest when no neurotic factors were reported, the woman was college educated, and had had no sex experience before marriage.[32] Dickinson and Beam were also pathfinders in their exhausive study of sexual factors and marriage adjustment.[33] Another pioneering attempt was made by Kirkpatrick, who through his graduate students distributed questionnaires to subjects who had been identified as happily and unhappily married. The two samples were designated by the physical form of the questionnaire so they could be scored according to this breakdown, and the two groups were compared for family and background data.[34]

One of the more definitive studies, having broader interest than the earlier investigations, was made by Burgess and Cottrell using couples selected from the Chicago area. Part of the limitation of this study was in the selectivity of the sample: 7,000 questionnaires were distributed unsystematically, of which only 1,300 were returned, resulting in only 526 essentially usable replies. The respondents were largely of the

[31] George V. Hamilton, *A Research in Marriage,* Boni, New York, 1929.

[32] Katherine B. Davis, *Factors in the Sex Life of Twenty-Two Hundred Women,* Harper and Brothers, New York, 1929.

[33] Robert L. Dickinson and Laura Beam, *A Thousand Marriages: A Medical Study of Sex Adjustment,* Williams and Wilkins, Baltimore, 1931.

[34] Clifford Kirkpatrick, "Factors in Marital Adjustment," *American Journal of Sociology,* 1937, 43, 270–283.

upper-middle class, and represented an educational bias; many were graduate students and their acquaintances. Still, as a broad survey of social background factors the study revealed some significant trends. Socialization, in terms of the childhood and adolescent backgrounds of the individuals, as well as participation in the community were found to be critical factors.[35] In other words, the psychological health of the family milieu had positive predictive value for marital adjustment. The contribution of sexual factors to marital adjustment was found to be influenced by cultural and psychological factors. One questionable aspect of the study was the failure to find a clear-cut influence of economic variables on the adjustment scores. This apparent difficulty led this author to raise the same question with a more extensive array of items among a heterogeneous sample in Los Angeles, which yielded different results.[36]

Terman, in still another study, used 792 couples from an original 1,250 who were largely of the San Francisco and Los Angeles areas, from upper-class white collar backgrounds, of whom 43 per cent were college trained, and their average ages in the upper thirties.[37] Happiness as the criterion of a "successful" marriage raises certain semantic problems. As in other studies, there was piling up of high happiness scores on the continuum, which has sometimes been interpreted as reflecting some possibly spurious or *halo effect*. However, it is probable that a higher percentage of unhappy marriages are terminated. Although Terman's interest was directed mainly to personality and sexual factors, he did explore a number of background factors. He confirmed the generalization that neuroticism was hardly calculated to insure marital bliss. Of his many sex items, only two had strongly predictive value: the partners' near equality of sex drives and the orgasm adequacy of the wife.

A study by Locke [38] was based on two unique features. One was the fact that the unhappily married group was a divorced sample, and

[35] Ernest W. Burgess and Leonard S. Cottrell, Jr., *Predicting Success or Failure in Marriage*, Prentice-Hall, Englewood Cliffs, 1939.

[36] Robert C. Williamson, "Socio-economic Factors and Marital Adjustment in an Urban Setting," *American Sociological Review*, 1954, **19**, 213–216; also "Economic Factors in Marital Adjustment," *Marriage and Family Living*, 1952, **14**, 298–301.

[37] Lewis M. Terman, *Psychological Factors in Marital Happiness*, McGraw-Hill, New York, 1938.

[38] Harvey J. Locke, *Predicting Adjustment in Marriage: A Comparison of a Divorced and a Happily Married Group*, Holt, Rinehart and Winston, New York, 1951.

consequently the validity of the responses was more secure than in studies that simply represented the low end of the marital adjustment scores. The other feature of this study was that the sample was more nearly representative of the general population, having been selected from semirural Monroe County in central Indiana. The happily married sample numbered 400, and the divorced sample 525. Both groups were early middle aged, and the average educational level was 8.9 years for the divorced and 9.5 for the married. Slightly more than half were of rural upbringing. Unlike certain other studies, the results were secured by interviews rather than by questionnaires. In some instances interviews are more valid than questionnaires, although the value of either approach depends on the representativeness of the sample and the validity of the questions. Often the interview permits a depth not found in the usual questionnaire study. In addition, the investigator has some control over the interview situation, which may also mean he has the possibility of indirectly influencing the interviewees, but at the same time may enable him to pick up clues regarding the validity of the response. Locke's study provided a great number of statistical findings. The generalizations of previous studies concerning socialization, adaptability, and conventionality were vindicated. As it was perhaps the only investigation to include a divorced sample, some conclusions were derived about the process of alienation.

Very likely the most ambitious study and one that combine the statistical and longitudinal approach was made by Burgess and Wallin.[39] It began with a study of 1,000 engaged couples, and followed these subjects for from three to five years after marriage. The study of the engagement period was performed in the late 1930's, and a subsequent questionnaire was administered in the early 1940's. In view of residential mobility and other problems the percentage of successful follow-ups was indeed remarkable. As with a number of other studies, the sample was largely college educated, Protestant, and employed in business or professional occupations. The average age at the time of the first interviews was in the upper twenties. Besides being the most searching study on engagement, the findings concerning marriage pertain to background, personality, and to a lesser extent sexual factors. In addition, prediction tests were possible because of the linkage between the questionnaire results in both the engagement and in the

---

[39] Burgess and Wallin, *op. cit.*

marriage periods. Follow-ups of the subjects in the middle years have been useful in determining the adjustment over a long term.[40]

THE CRITICAL DIFFERENCES BETWEEN THE HAPPILY AND UNHAPPILY MARRIED. Let us examine in partial detail the findings of the foregoing studies in addition to some others also studying marital adjustment. As suggested by Kirkpatrick, it is most useful to consider these studies in two categories: premarital and postmarital variables. The following are factors favorable to marital adjustment, as judged by several studies:

I. *Factors Associated with Premarital Situation of the Individual:* [41]
   A. Social and family background
      1. Higher socio-cultural background of the parents (Burgess and Cottrell, Burgess and Wallin, Roth and Peck, et al.)
      2. Similarity of family backgrounds (Burgess and Cottrell, et al.)
      3. Religious atmosphere in the home (Burgess and Cottrell, Terman)
      4. Presence of siblings (Burgess and Cottrell, Terman)
   B. Psychological relations within the family
      1. Happiness of the parents' marriage (Burgess and Cottrell, Schroeder, Terman, et al.)
      2. The respondent's personal happiness in childhood (Locke, Terman, et al.)
      3. Degree of attachment to the parent (in some studies notably the parent of the opposite sex) and the absence of strong con-

[40] Peter C. Pineo, "Disenchantment in the Later Years of Marriage," *Marriage and Family Living*, 1961, **23**, 3–11; and Paul Wallin and Alexander L. Clark, "Religiosity, Sexual Gratification, and Marital Satisfaction in the Middle Years of Marriage," *Social Forces*, 1964, **42**, 303–309.

[41] This list is only a partial one in terms of the type of statistical findings, and the number of references cited. A more complete documentation may be found in Kirkpatrick, *op. cit.*, pp. 665–678; and Burgess, Locke, and Thomas, *op. cit.*, pp. 547–569. The term et al. refers to at least two other sources, often ones specializing in the type of relationship mentioned. The sources specifically mentioned are: Burgess and Cottrell, *op. cit.*; Burgess and Wallin, *op. cit.*; Davis, *op. cit.*; Dickinson and Beam, *op. cit.*; Hamilton, *op. cit*; Kirkpatrick, *op. cit.*; Mirra Komarovsky, *Blue-Collar Marriage*, Random House, New York, 1964; Judson T. Landis, "Length of Time Required to Achieve Adjustment in Marriage," *American Sociological Review*, 1946, **11**, 666–677; Locke, *op. cit.*; Clarence W. Schroeder, *Divorce in a City of 100,000 Population*, Bradley Polytechnic Institute Library, Peoria, Illinois, 1939; Terman *op. cit.*; Lewis M. Terman and Melita H. Oden, *The Gifted Child Grows Up*, Stanford University, Press, 1947; Wallin and Clark, *op. cit.*; Williamson, *op. cit.*

flicts (Burgess and Cottrell, Hamilton, Kirkpatrick, Locke, Terman)

4. Lack of severe discipline at home (Terman)

C. Sex knowledge and experience

1. Healthy presentation of sex knowledge, especially from parents (Burgess and Wallin, Davis, Schroeder, Terman). On the other hand, there is no conclusive evidence that masturbation, sexual exploration, or sexual shock are necessarily harmful (Terman et al.)

2. Lack of petting, at least on part of women (Davis, Terman— although Terman and Oden found no relationship)

3. Lack of or extremely limited premarital sex intercourse, particularly in the case of women (Burgess and Wallin, Davis, Hamilton, Terman—on the other hand, Locke found a less clear relationship)

D. Personality and socialization

1. Moderate relationship with certain personality or physical traits (Burgess and Wallin, et al.)

2. Conformity to sex role: masculinity and femininity (Burgess and Wallin, Terman)

3. Social participation, both on an individual and organizational basis, the former with special reference to the opposite sex (Burgess and Cottrell, Burgess and Wallin, Locke, Terman, et al.)

4. Conventionality of attitudes, for example in regard to religious training and Sunday School attendance during the formative years (Burgess and Cottrell, Burgess and Wallin, Locke, Schroeder, Terman)

E. Place and circumstances of acquaintance

1. Favorable setting of first meeting, that is not a dance hall, nor nor a "pickup" (Terman)

2. Length of acquaintance of one, two, or more years (Burgess and Cottrell, Burgess and Wallin, Locke, Terman, et al.)

3. Length of engagement of six months or preferably longer, depending on the study (Burgess and Cottrell, Locke, Terman, et al.)

4. Approval of the marriage by close friends and relatives (Burgess and Cottrell, Burgess and Wallin, Locke)

F. Miscellaneous Factors

    1. Age at marriage: mid- to late twenties for the man, early to mid-twenties for the woman (Burgess and Cottrell, Terman et al.). No consistent findings in regard to age differences except suggestion that extreme differences may be unfavorable (Kirkpatrick, Locke)

    2. Upper educational and occupational status (Burgess and Cottrell, Komarovsky, Schroeder, Terman, Williamson)

    3. Favorable financial situation in employment, income, savings (Burgess and Cottrell, et al.)

    4. Ethnic and religious similarity (Landis, et al.)

II. *Postmarital Factors*

A. Nature of the marriage ceremony: church wedding or home wedding with religious officiant instead of a civil officiant (Burgess and Cottrell, Locke, Schroeder)

B. Sex adjustment

    1. First experience as pleasant (Davis, Terman)

    2. Relatively brief period required for adjustment (Landis)

    3. Similarity of sex drives (Hamilton, Terman, et al.)

    4. Adequacy of response orgasm capacity in female (Hamilton, Locke, Terman, Wallin and Clark, et al.)

    5. Sophistication in sex techniques, including use of contraceptives (Davis, Hamilton, Locke, Terman)

C. Consensus on attitudes and adjustment capacity

    1. Agreement on a variety of attitudes: finances, recreation, religious matters, amount of time spent together, friends, intimate relations, ways of dealing with in-laws, conventionality, ultimate values in life (confirmed by more than a dozen studies, however, since it is usually part of the adjustment score it has built-in bias)

    2. Favorable attitudes toward the mate and the marriage relationship (which again is endemic to the situation and supported by innumerable studies)

    3. Favorable attitudes toward in-laws (Burgess and Wallin, Locke)

    4. High social and community participation (Burgess and Cottrell, Kirkpatrick, Schroeder, et al.)

    5. Adequate emotional adjustment (Burgess and Cottrell, et al.)

6. Desire for, but not necessarily presence of, children (Burgess and Cottrell, Burgess and Wallin, Locke, Williamson—results vary but the desire is for children highly favorable, yet presence of children has ambiguous results)

D. Status and security factors

1. Upper residential area and above-average household situation (Burgess and Cottrell, Locke, Williamson, et al.)

2. Higher income and standard of living (Burgess and Cottrell, Komarovsky, Locke, Williamson, et al.)

3. Security, regularity of employment, occupational satisfaction, presence of savings and absence of debts (Williamson, et al.)

These critical differences by no means exhaust the findings, but they point to some areas which have support of empirical tests, notwithstanding the methodological complications, in the following section. Undoubtedly some problems may require further research, especially where results are contradictory or have been supported by only one or two investigations. Occasionally we encounter curious findings, such as a situation where one or both parents are deceased, and this operates as a favorable factor on the respondents' marital adjustment.

By combining the strength of the statistical test with the number of studies supporting a given generalization, Kirkpatrick makes the following resume in order of decreasing dependability:

Early and adequate orgasm capacity.
Confidence in the marital affection and satisfaction with affection shown.
An equalitarian rather than a patriarchal marital relationship, with special reference to the husband role.
Mental and physical health.
Harmonious companionship based on common interests and accompanied by a favorable attitude toward the marriage and spouse.[42]

CRITICISMS OF THE ADJUSTMENT TESTS. Despite general acceptance of studies in which an adjustment scale was used as the means of comparing happy and unhappy marriages, there has been extensive criticism of this technique of assessing marriage. This criticism is frequently in relation to: (1) the meaning and validity of concepts underlying the adjustment scale: happiness and adjustment, for instance; (2) the representativeness of the sample; (3) bias in the responses. (An explanation of these objections as well as a discussion of

[42] Clifford Kirkpatrick, *The Family as Process and Institution* (second edition), The Ronald Press, New York, 1963, p. 394.

other theoretical and methodological issues, is found in the Appendix.[43]) In defense of the studies the statistical approach offers a more systematic means of studying marital adjustment than those results available through the impressionistic or anecdotal methods. Such statistical studies conform reasonably well to our insistence on empirical evidence. The case-study approach, by which a limited number of marriages are viewed in terms of their development, is of equal value, and throughout this book findings based on this technique have been reported. However, the case-study, or longitudinal approach, also raises questions about the choice of sample or the scientific validity of its concepts.

In summary, it can be said that the use of the adjustment scale, the question–interview method, or prediction studies, as the statistical approach has been variously labeled, offer some useful generalizations. In spite of certain methodological weaknesses, the findings are based on pretested questionnaires applied to samples of middle-class populations under relatively controlled conditions. The results should be applied on an actuarial basis, that is, they can be applied to individuals only with caution. If too many of the characteristics of one or both partners, or of the marriage itself, are in conflict with the findings of the studies, some question can be raised, in the case of premarital factors, as to the advisability of the marriage or to the necessity of restructuring the marriage in the context of the postmarital situation. Counselling resources are relevant in both instances.

THE RELATION OF ROLES AND THE ADJUSTMENT PROCESS

CULTURES, SUBCULTURES, AND THE INDIVIDUAL.   The roles with which we are born and those we acquire later reflect our cultural pattern and the individual style of our marriages. There are a number of subcultures determining our roles and the pattern of interaction within marriage. The husband's occupation, especially, may operate to structure the quality of his marital adjustment. For instance, an artist's work may involve a more intense emotional life and irregular

---

[43] Additional discussion on the theoretical and methodological problems of the statistical approach is found in Charles E. Bowerman, "Prediction Studies," in Harold T. Christensen (ed.), *Handbook of Marriage and the Family,* Rand McNally, Chicago, 1964, pp. 215–246.

hours and income than a business man's. Only a flexible wife may be capable of the necessary adjustment. Religion and education are other subcultures that have particular significance for the roles a person plays. A medical doctor married to a Christian Scientist may find his marital role strained in view of the gulf in certain values. Such situations require clear recognition of the roles of the other person, and a conscious determination to accept his viewpoint. The more perceptive marital partners are able to subordinate a number of roles to the marital one.

PERCEPTION, ROLE CONFLICT, AND MARITAL ADJUSTMENT. As just implied, a basic factor in role conflict is the situation in which particular role behavior may bring forth both reward and punishment: an artist may have difficulty in pursuing his talent and at the same time meeting the ideal demands of his wife and family. We make certain compromises in our multiple roles to find a balance between, for example, breadwinner and husband.

Undoubtedly one aspect of the husband and wife relation is the similarity with which the partners apparently perceive each other, especially when the traits measured are rated as socially desirable, or when a subject's perception of the person with whom he interacts is an "extension of his self-concept." [44] Another aspect of roles and the adjustment level within the marriage is the question of role and personality changes in time.[45] The needs—intellectual, emotional, social, and sexual—are altered as a person's own personality pattern shifts, however gradually; adjustment in the occupational orbit is one example. The wife will note some changes, particularly with the arrival of children. Both spouses are redefining their roles, which in turn shift the adjustment potential between them. At the same time, marital satisfaction is inseparable from the perception they have of each other's roles. The interplay of relationships with relatives, the perception of roles in an upwardly mobile community, and the satisfaction partners derive in each other's company seem to be isolated factors, but each could relate to the marital adjustment and be at least marginally related to the definitions of the respective roles of both partners.

ROLES AND THE ADJUSTMENT SCALE. We may ask whether the mar-

---

[44] Kate L. Kogan and Joan K. Jackson, "Perceptions of Self and Spouse: Some Contaminating Factors," *Journal of Marriage and the Family,* 1964, **26,** 60–64.

[45] Robert F. Winch, *The Modern Family* (rev. ed.), Holt, Rinehart and Winston, New York, 1963, pp. 674–680.

ital adjustment scale is not in a sense a test of role behavior. By our definition of roles it would have to be. In fact, a factor analysis approach was applied to the marital adjustment scale to determine the critical variables. These critical variables may be defined as *role behaviors*.[46] (The twenty items constituting the scale are found in the Appendix.) The factor analysis was applied to the results of a sample of 210 married couples of lower and middle-class social status and revealed five factors, or clusters, of items:

1. *Companionship* or "couple sufficiency" contained several items, among which were engaging in outside activities together and agreement by mutual give and take.

2. *Agreement* or consensus, that is, agreement on various areas (choice of friends, religion, etc.) in addition to "never wishing one had not married" and "marrying the same person if one had his life to live over."

3. *Affectional intimacy* or emotional adjustment, "never or rarely getting on each other's nerves," agreement on sex relations, and other items emphasizing an emotional relationship.

4. *Masculine interpretation* or wife accommodation, the tendency of the wife to adjust to the husband. On certain agreement items the husbands were more positive than the wives indicating an accommodative attitude by the wives.

5. *Euphoria* or halo effect. The tendency to perceive the marriage as ecstatically happy or to give the appearance of superlative satisfaction: "always confiding in the mate," the marriage being rated as "very happy," kissing every day. For some couples romanticism or the honeymoon halo whether genuine or rationalized, appears to persist into marriage.

These various roles of companionship, consensus, affection, accommodation, and romanticism are of course interrelated. Most items appeared in more than one factor cluster. It is equally true that marital roles are not to be conceived of as a specific number of panels or that marital happiness depends on, for example, five or six isolated factors.

Social psychology in the 1920's and 1930's saw a tradition developed in which the behavior of individuals was regarded as consisting of

[46] Harvey J. Locke and Robert C. Williamson, "Marital Adjustment: A Factor Analysis Study," *American Sociological Review*, 1958, **23**, 562–569.

roles. This theory has been coupled with the concepts of identification and socialization. We acquire a social self early in life, as was pointed out in Chapter 5, and role taking remains a fundamental process throughout life. For the symbolic interactionist, who adheres to role theory and its extensive implication for communication, marriage is in largely a trial-and-error process, marked, hopefully, by more than occasional insight. In our review of a number of studies on roles we can conclude that marriage involves multiple roles, even though there is at times a fumbling consciousness of or an inadequate enactment of roles among married partners. Certain other investigations have pointed to more sophistication. In any case, the early months and years of marriage are probably the more difficult ones. For an apparent minority of marriages the later years may bring difficulties concerning role accommodation. Disenchantment may set in, and the marriage may become vulnerable to a crisis situation with the possibilities of role readjustment or a breakup of the marriage as a result.

Modern marriage and the family institution have been often portrayed as evolving toward a unity based on companionship and affection or toward a *Gestalt* of interacting personalities. In this context the theory of marital behavior as revolving about a number of roles is entirely plausible. Remaining problems include such questions as: What kinds of companionship does our society intend? Are family sociologists likely to have developed different theories or philosophies regarding the basis of marital and familial roles? Suggestive of this approach, Farber interprets the work of Parsons and of Blood and Wolfe as indicating that our roles are organized about community, vocational, and other instrumental considerations. On the other hand, Burgess conceives of marriage and the family as a means of companionship and as an end in itself. For him the *raison d'être* of the modern family may be interpreted as promoting congeniality, interstimulation, and informality.[47] In Chapter 5 we mentioned that the goal of the family had shifted from an almost neurotic striving toward socio-economic status and the norms this status demanded to a comfort and welfare-oriented type of family regime.[48] In other instances we have evidence of role strain in our inability to meet the institutional and personal demands of roles. The role conflicts of the woman in our

[47] Farber, *op. cit.*, pp. 291–302.
[48] Daniel R. Miller and Guy E. Swanson, *The Changing American Parent,* John Wiley, New York, 1958.

society also have been well documented. It has been noted the male finds himself somewhat inhibited in his associations with women outside his marriage, because of the possibility of his wife's misunderstanding or perhaps by his own masculine interests or occupational necessities.[49] This remark is partly inspired by the realization that innumerable members of our society have only partially analyzed their behavior and motivations in regard to interpersonal relations including their own marriages. It is worth noting that counselling, marital or otherwise, and psychotherapy are means of assessing and attempting some rearrangement of a person's roles.

The final portion of this chapter was devoted to the problem of measuring marital adjustment. Many feel that these studies are superfluous because they repeat what common sense already tells us. However, this argument is not entirely pertinent. First, the results do not always agree with popular folklore (for example, the belief that children make happy marriages—however much the desire for children may have salutory effects, or the belief that sex experience before marriage *necessarily* cheapens the marriage). Second, in science we are not content to rest our case on common sense. Yet we may repeat our warning about the difficulty of applying findings of the group to a given individual. This admonition should not discourage us from taking the engagement adjustment scale and the various marriage prediction scales either before or after marriage.

Supplementary Readings

Bell, Norman W. and Ezra F. Vogel, *A Modern Introduction to the Family,* The Free Press of Glencoe, A Division of Collier-Macmillan, New York, 1960. Part Three of this select collection of readings treats role relationships.

Bell, Robert R, *Marriage and Family Interaction,* The Dorsey Press, Homewood, Illinois, 1963. Chapters 10 and 11 are a review of major problems in roles from an interactionist viewpoint.

Blood, Robert O. Jr. and Donald M. Wolfe, *Husbands and Wives: The Dynamics of Married Living,* The Free Press of Glencoe, A Division of Collier-Macmillan, 1960. Decision making and the power structure in a large-scale Michigan study of marital relationships.

[49] Talcott Parsons, "Age and Sex in the Social Structure of the United States," *American Sociological Review,* 1942, **5,** reprinted in *Essays in Sociological Theory, Pure and Applied,* The Free Press of Glencoe, A Division of Collier-Macmillan, New York, 1949, p. 228.

Burgess, Ernest W., and Paul Wallin, *Engagement and Marriage*, J. B. Lippincott, Philadelphia, 1963. Although the entire book is relevant to the problem of predicting marital adjustment, Chapters 14–19 are concerned with personality and roles.

Christensen, Harold T. (ed.), *Handbook of Marriage and the Family*, Rand McNally, Chicago, 1964. Chapters 6, 14, and 17 especially are all well documented and up to date.

Farber, Bernard, *Family: Organization and Interaction*, Chandler Publishing, San Francisco, 1964. A theoretical work in which the contrasting viewpoints of Parsons and Burgess are examined. Chapters 8 and 9 are most relevant.

Foote, Nelson N. and Leonard S. Cottrell, Jr., *Identity and Interpersonal Competence*, The University of Chicago Press, 1955. The authors present a number of hypotheses about identification and the problem of role behavior within the family and its relation to the social context.

Kirkpatrick, Clifford, *The Family As Process and Institution* (revised edition), The Ronald Press, New York, 1963. Chapter 15 on measurement of marital adjustment and Chapter 18 on adjustment itself go well beyond the usual textbook approach to the problem.

Locke, Harvey J., *Predicting Adjustment in Marriage: A Comparison of a Divorced and a Happily Married Group*, Holt, Rinehart and Winston, New York, 1951. Locke's approach is typical of the adjustment studies, but has the advantage of comparing a "happily married" and a divorced sample.

Merrill, Francis E., *Courtship and Marriage* (revised edition), Holt, Rinehart and Winston, New York, 1959. This scholarly text is oriented around the concept of roles. Chapters 12–15 would be among the most pertinent ones.

Parsons, Talcott and Robert F. Bales, *Family, Socialization and Interaction*, The Free Press of Glencoe, A Division of Collier-Macmillan, New York, 1955. A theoretical and laboratory approach in the small groups tradition to family structure and roles.

Terman, Lewis M., *Psychological Factors in Marital Happiness*, McGraw-Hill, New York, 1938. Another classic in the statistical approach to marital adjustment.

Winch, Robert F., *The Modern Family* (revised edition), Holt, Rinehart and Winston, New York, 1963. Chapters 12 and 21 present our subject in terms of functional theory—and with considerable insight.

Chapter fourteen

Sex Adjustments in Marriage

Marriage is possible because it combines the maximum of temptation with the maximum of opportunity.

George Bernard Shaw, Maxims for Revolutionists, *1903.*

Detail of *Three A.M.* by John Sloan
Courtesy of the Philadelphia Museum of Art

For practically all men and a majority of women a central motive in marriage is sexual satisfaction. In fact, a marriage does not exist legally unless it is sexually consummated. In this respect all societies are essentially alike. Historically, Western ideas about the function of sex in marriage have changed markedly. The basic change has been in the tendency to regard sex as an activity to be enjoyed in an atmosphere marked by respect and affection. The feeling today is that sex is to be treated honestly and at the same time love is to be the basis of any sexual relationship. Implicit in this outlook is the idea that the individual acquires behavior patterns on the basis of a wide and intricate array of stimuli and that as with other phenomena he should maintain, insofar as possible, an objective approach toward sex.

The reasons for this transition toward an affection-oriented sex hedonism have been explained in Chapter 8: secularization, rapid mobility, and individualization. These changes have had more impact on women than on men. In our Judeo-Christian patriarchal culture men have been expected to indulge in sex, although what were considered acceptable opportunities for this indulgence varied with the times. In Western culture women traditionally have been denied freedom of sex expression. The Victorian period is often cited as the acme of man's sexual asceticism, as reflected in this passage from Hunt:

> What became of these purified and chaste sentiments on the bridal night and thereafter is not easy to discover; we are forced to imagine the quality of Victorial conjugal love on the basis of tangential hints. One woman, for example, who was married in the middle of the Victorian era and had borne several children, told Havelock Ellis when she was seventy that she had never seen a naked man in her life, and even those superlative lovers, the Brownings, are said never to have seen each other entirely nude.[1]

By the 1920's woman's right to sex enjoyment was fully vindicated, at least among certain urban circles. Besides the liberation of women, a second change was the novel idea that both parties might regard marriage as a continuation of sex exploration, which they experienced either much or little of in the period before marriage. However, the Kinsey findings maintain (Chapter 8) that sex inhibition still obtains for both sexes among the upper white collar world except as expressed in "necking" and "petting." The fundamental alteration and the one

[1] Morton M. Hunt, *The Natural History of Love*, Alfred A. Knopf, New York, 1959, p. 318.

357

most pertinent to this chapter is that women are now encouraged to enjoy sex, preferably within the marital situation.

The third change has been the scientific inception of birth control. Although limitation of births has been practiced since the ancient Egyptians, it is only in our century that we have had reasonably dependable methods. Moreover, these methods do not seriously interfere with the pursuit of sexual enjoyment. This shift probably has had greater effect on the sexual behavior of the female than of the male. After all, the woman worries more about the problem of pregnancy since she bears the major emotional and physical burden and has even less financial independence than the man. The woman is also less strongly motivated toward sexual release, and consequently more likely to be aware of marginal anxieties.

THE PHYSICAL PICTURE

Although an advanced physiology or anatomy textbook provides more detailed knowledge, this presents a review of essential material on the physical aspects of sex.

Male Sex Organs. The male genitalia are mainly external: the penis and scrotum, in addition to certain internal organs, such as the vas deferens and the seminal vesicles (as shown in Figure 2). The *penis* is the copulatory organ, and under erection enlarges $\frac{1}{4}$ in diameter and $\frac{1}{5}$ in length, attaining on the average $6\frac{1}{4}$ inches in length and $1\frac{1}{4}$

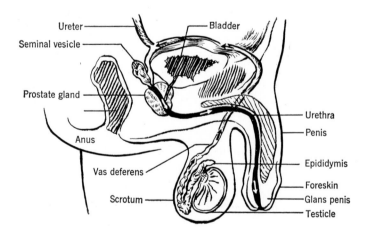

FIGURE 2   MALE SEX ORGANS.

inches in diameter at the base. Erection is mainly a property of the central nervous system, as controlled by the sympathetic nervous system, although it is under partial voluntary control. The erectile tissue in the penis is a spongelike system of irregular vascular spaces interspersed among arteries and veins. In the flaccid state they are more or less collapsed, but during erection they resemble large cavities distended with blood, which accompanies the action of skeletal muscle.[2] The skin surface, especially the head of the penis, is richly endowed with sensory nerve endings. Since the foreskin is extensively supplied with nerve endings, circumcision may reduce some sexual sensation.[3] However circumcision may also delay orgasm, thereby adding to the pleasure of the act, especially for the female partner.

The *testes* are about the size of a small walnut, and are $1\frac{1}{2}$ inches long and about $\frac{3}{4}$ to 1 inch thick.[4] They have two functions; the production of androgen (the male hormone) and spermatozoa. These functions are controlled by the hormones of the pituitary gland. The glandular pattern is particularly evident at puberty and throughout most of adulthood maintains, in contrast to the female, a fairly regular output and noncyclic level until the twilight years. The production of *spermatozoa* is carried on in the seminiferous tubules (in contrast to the interstitial cells where the hormones are produced). The spermatozoa measure roughly 1/500th of an inch in length, and their high mobility is produced by a tail-like structure. At each normal male ejaculation two hundred to four hundred million spermatozoa may be released, a demonstration of the prodigious margin associated with human reproduction. The spermatozoa are released into the seminal fluid, which is a combination of secretions of the prostate gland and the seminal vesicles. Ejaculation, or the release of semen from the penis, depends on two actions: [5] emission or the sudden contraction of the smooth muscle of the internal genital organs delivering semen into the *urethra* and the expulsion of seminal fluid from the urethra, which

[2] Charles W. Hooker, "Reproduction in the Male," in John F. Fulton, *A Textbook of Physiology*, W. B. Saunders, Philadelphia, 1955, pp. 1238–1239.

[3] Edgar S. Gordon, "Taking Physical Factors into Account," in Howard Becker and Reuben Hill, *Family, Marriage and Parenthood* (second edition), D. C. Heath, Boston, 1955, p. 309.

[4] Hans Lehfeldt, "Medical Aspects of Marriage," in Herman R. Lantz and Eloise C. Snyder, *Marriage*, John Wiley, New York, 1962, p. 358 and Gordon, *op. cit.*, p. 308.

[5] Fulton, *op. cit.*, pp. 1239–1240.

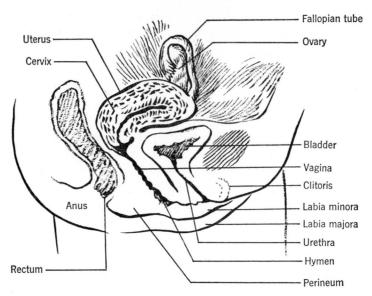

Uterus
Cervix
Fallopian tube
Ovary
Bladder
Vagina
Clitoris
Labia minora
Labia majora
Urethra
Hymen
Perineum
Anus
Rectum

FIGURE 3   FEMALE SEX ORGANS.

is the more immediate sensation although both acts are generally perceptible.

The reproductive machinery is designed to deposit semen in the vagina of the female and consequently impregnate an ovum. Release of the semen is a pleasurable act in itself. Men may achieve this response through *nocturnal emission* or wet dreams, masturbation, petting to a climax, or some other outlet (as in homosexuality) besides intercourse. On the whole, the male tends to react directly to sex stimuli, and his sexual pleasure is more immediately associated with orgasm than the woman's. Nonetheless, like the female, he has *erogenous zones* which make for a diffuse sexual excitability.

FEMALE SEX ORGANS.   The female organs are predominantly internal. The most important ones are the vagina, uterus, ovaries, and Fallopian tubes. In addition, there are the vulva, consisting of the labia, major and minor, the clitoris, the openings of the urethra, and the hymen (shown in Figure 3). The entire system is designed to receive the semen from the male, to produce the ovum, and to carry out the task of embryonic and fetal development of an infant. This function of reproduction involves an enormously complex hormonal system, some aspects of which are discussed in Chapter 16.

In sexual intercourse the vagina and labia are most important. The *labia majora* (large lips) consist of folds of tissue, somewhat covered by hair, extending from the fatty pubic area to almost the rectal area. The *labia minora* are the inner folds, less readily visible, and more sensitive. At the upper joining of the labia minora is the *clitoris*. It is an organ similar structurally and functionally to the penis of the male. It consists of erectile tissue and with its intensive covering of nerve endings can be stimulated to partial erection during the sex act. For most women the clitoris represents the chief, but not the exclusive, area of sexual pleasure.

The *vagina* is a membranous collapsible tube of variable length, five to seven inches long, which serves three functions: (1) as the passage-way of the menstrual discharge, (2) as the copulatory area, and (3) as the major part of the birth canal.[6] It is supplied with a lubricant and its elasticity permits it to adjust to the varying dimensions of the erect penis. It has been suggested that the emotionally mature woman may secure sexual pleasure from the vagina, whereas among the emotionally immature the clitoris is the relevant center of excitation. There probably is not sufficient evidence to substantiate this psychoanalytic theory.[7]

The *hymen* is a membranous fold, perhaps a half inch in diameter, which partly closes the opening to the vagina. It is ruptured during the initial intercourse, if this has not already occurred as a result of masturbation or some other cause. In connection with premarital examinations, which may include the fitting of a contraceptive device such as a diaphragm, stretching of the hymen has been recommended.

In structure and function the woman is more complex and subtle than the man. Orgasm is not as sharply defined as the ejaculatory act of the male. Although there is some concentration of sensation in the clitoris and the vagina, much more of the female body is brought into play as compared to the male. The setting, the approach, and the timing become more crucial. The erogenous zones play a still larger role than they do with the male. These sensitive areas include the ears, neck, shoulders, arms, and especially the breasts.

SPECIFIC CONDITIONS OF SEX ADJUSTMENT

For generations folklore has been a source of information about the ways in which to conduct sex relations. Although not completely

[6] Gordon, *op. cit.*, p. 315.
[7] George Simpson, *People in Families*, Thomas Y. Crowell, New York, 1960, pp. 175–176.

diffused among the public, many of these interesting notions have found their way into print. This citation from a 1925 book written by a physician offered advice on "How to Hold Your Husband" for disconsolate wives during that rebellious decade: "Wives (and husbands) should realize that electrical and chemical laws are the source of attraction . . . due to opposite magnetic qualities (positive and negative forces). When these magnetic currents meet and blend in certain proportions the sexual union becomes satisfying and sex attraction is lost." [8] Marriage manuals with more technical information concerning sex relations have been available for several decades. This approach may be of some value. However, some of these books contain misinformation and have a rather sensationalist tone.[9] It is a fair guess that the majority of young people still acquire their information through less formal sources from their peers and in more direct experience.

The major emphasis on sex relations is the direction of mutuality; both members should enjoy coitus, its prelude, and afterglow to the maximum. For those who enter marriage with prior initiation the meaning of intercourse is different from what it was before marriage. First, the affectional involvement is much greater. A number of new behaviors confront the individual. Nudity may be a shock to some brides. There may be nervousness and self-consciousness. In a few cases during the initial weeks there is overconcern with anatomical details. All these factors can cause impotence or frigidity. Most critical, the husband may not yet have acquired techniques by which he can make the experience enjoyable for the wife. On the other hand, individuals may have adequate sex relations in the first night or two of marriage and yet feel that they were in some way let down. Overanticipation may be the problem here.

There is conflicting evidence on the effect of initial sex relations. According to Terman, wives who found sex initiation either shocking or very painful reported less happy marriage adjustment.[10] Although this finding relates to what is possibly a more extended situation than the initial coital act, it indicates that sex initiation may be predictive of later marital happiness although we must be cautious in suggesting

[8] Simon L. Katzoff, M. D., *How to Hold Your Husband,* The Dollar Book House, San Francisco, 1925.

[9] William M. Kephart, *The Family, Society, and the Individual,* Houghton Mifflin, Boston, 1961, pp. 468–471.

[10] Lewis M. Terman, *Psychological Factors in Marital Happiness,* McGraw-Hill, New York, 1938, p. 344.

any chain of cause and effect. Another study discovered that in comparing agreement in the first months of marriage, agreement about income, in-laws, religion, choice of friends, and social activities was greater than that concerning sex adjustments. Only 52 per cent of the subjects were satisfied with their sex relations from the beginning, whereas two-thirds or more were satisfied, for example, with in-law relationships.[11] Such evidence seems to point to the fact that love and sex is an art to be cultivated, as some have said.

THE SETTING. Unquestionably sexual enjoyment is a variable dependent on mood, physical condition, and the psychology dividing the sexes and the particular individuals. Sex is an area of marriage that reflects the entire marital pattern. Most marriage studies indicate that, first, we are unable to isolate sex from other aspects—emotional, intellectual, and cultural—of marital life. Second, the presence of tension interferes with the quality and quantity of sex relations. However, some conflict-ridden marriage partners may engage in more intercourse than well-adjusted couples, as a means of tension release. Third, the arrival of children is another factor that may complicate sex relations. Children naturally reduce privacy. Fear of pregnancy is not conducive to sex enjoyment.

Although contraceptive techniques have substantially decreased this anxiety among women, probability of conception is reduced, but an anxiety-ridden wife may worry since fertility still exists. Contraceptive devices themselves may be a minor irritant. The douche, in popular use in the 1930's and occasionally used today, does not provide a restful postlude to the sex act. The condom, a male contraceptive device, is the second most commonly used form of contraception after the diaphragm, but it is not welcomed by most males as it reduces sensitivity. But, on the positive side, the condom has the advantage of slowing down the male's ejaculation and orgasm which is of benefit to the wife, whose reactions are usually slower than his. Religious scruples are another factor influencing sexual enjoyment in terms of stipulations about contraception. Finally, the presence of children increases the parental work load and their fatigue, which in turn may reduce the sex drive of the parents.

Despite these negative aspects, a more honest attitude toward sex has benefited marital relations. We have come to regard sex as a cul-

[11] Judson T. Landis, "Length of Time Required to Achieve Adjustment in Marriage," *American Sociological Review*, 1946, 11, 666–667.

mination of the blending of two personalities. Communication about sex is now more direct. Husbands and wives talk about their sexual problems and determine ways in which they can be solved. We are less inhibited in our sexual exploration, and young people enter marriage with more intellectual, scientific, and popular knowledge. The range of literature from the drugstore to the medical library provides a storehouse of information against which personal experiences can be compared with those of others. The fact that Freud and Kinsey are household terms is the index of a more relaxed attitude toward sex. It may remain mysterious and challenging, but is no longer an unassailable topic of conversation. There are those who maintain that the attention contemporary society gives to sex makes it both tawdry and commonplace and by implication a chief end of existence. Yet there is reason to believe that the lack of attention to the subject a generation or two ago had less salutary effects.

Several factors influence the atmosphere in which sex relations take place. Nudity between marital partners has increased resulting in less inhibited sexuality. Nudity during coitus varied from 43 to 92 per cent among Kinsey's subjects depending on the age and class of the partners.[12] Sleeping in the nude showed a similar increase. In addition, the diffusion of lubricating jellies and other aids have decreased the association of pain with sexual intercourse. More important, the psychological shift toward an objective attitude has reduced the fear reaction. This neutrality of feeling has also extended toward the problem of menstruation. A more healthy attitude toward one aspect of sexual behavior has an effect on all others. In addition, the removal of many of the religious rigidities about sex and a more objective feeling about bodily processes have reduced the neurotic aspects surrounding sex activity. Even so, for some, the fact that organs of elimination are also the site of sexual relations makes for a squeamish attitude toward sex relations. Child rearing should provide a realistic outlook in the early home environment so as to counteract unnecessary apprehension. Parent education has been urged in this direction, and it is hypothesized that children reared in a neutral setting are better prepared for marital living.

FREQUENCY.   One of the criteria by which the average person is inclined to measure the success of a marriage is the frequency of coitus.

[12] Alfred C. Kinsey, Wardell B. Pomeroy, Clyde E. Martin, and Paul H. Gebhard, *Sexual Behavior in the Human Male,* W. B. Saunders, Philadelphia, 1953, p. 372.

In reality, Terman found only a limited positive correlation between frequency of intercourse and marital happiness.[13] Like most other sexual behavior, the frequency of intercourse varies markedly among various societies.[14] Unfortunately we have little accurate information except for the present century within our American culture.

Kinsey reports that married couples under age twenty have a mean frequency of 3.9 copulations per week. The rate drops to 2.9 at age thirty, to 1.8 at age fifty, and 0.9 at age sixty.[15] The data for the female was almost identical. Dickinson also reports great variation in this area: 16 per cent engaging in intercourse daily, and 24 per cent less than weekly.[16] Even in his relatively young sample Terman found a difference of 8 or 10 copulations per month between the 10th percentile and the 90th percentile (roughly between the lowest and highest tenth). Social background may affect these differences; the rural rate of copulation frequency tends to be less than that of the urban population—probably because of heavier work loads, less knowledge of techniques, and some religiously inspired inhibitions.[17] Yet evidence might support the notion that the more intellectual the occupation, the less the frequency of sex. Semiskilled and clerical workers were found to have a slightly higher rate of intercourse than professional workers; however, this difference may be attributable to inaccuracies in estimation.[18]

Several generalizations may be made about sexual frequency. Husbands and wives have different definitions of their own sexual needs, and the majority of men desire intercourse more often than women. This is especially evident in the early years of marriage after which the gap closes somewhat. (In fact, Kinsey points to a reversal in sex desire between the early and late years of marriage.)

The reasons for these differing needs can be explained by deep-seated psychological needs, energy level, freedom from conflict, day-to-day variations in fatigue, state of health, and emotional crises. For the female, the menstrual cycle may be related to sex desire. Reports differ

[13] Terman, *op. cit.*, pp. 275ff.
[14] Clellan S. Ford and Frank A. Beach, *Patterns of Sexual Behavior*, Ace Books, New York, 1951, p. 122.
[15] Alfred C. Kinsey, *op. cit.*, p. 569.
[16] Robert L. Dickinson and Laura Beam, *A Thousand Marriages: A Medical Study of Sex Adjustment*, Williams and Wilkins, Baltimore, 1931, p. 57.
[17] Kinsey, *op. cit.* (Male), p. 455.
[18] Terman, *op. cit.*, p. 275.

regarding which phase of the cycle is marked by highest desire. One study reports the strongest desire just before and after this four to five-day period.[19] Others speculate that the period of ovulation is one of stronger desire, which places excess strain on premarital relations or the rhythm method. The length of time married is not a reliable index of the satisfaction derived in intercourse, as some of the foregoing factors indicate. Frequency of coitus may increase for a particular couple as both individuals acquire more adequate techniques or resolve conflict within their marital interaction. Sexual roles are intertwined with all others. The man who is a dubious success as a foreman, dean, or short-story writer may attempt to achieve compensation for this failure in his sexual role, or his failure in the world of men may reduce his sexual drive. The sex drive may change in strength depending on a person's general mood. We cannot overemphasize the danger of using frequency of intercourse as the barometer of marital success. The inadequacy of this measure of happiness is demonstrated, for example, by a couple for whom divorce is imminent. The couple may have a higher rate of sex activity in the hope of recapturing something of their shattered marriage or may be clinging to the only bond that they have in common—perhaps the primary motive that attracted them to marry one another. In a well-integrated marriage, sex becomes one of several objectives. A good marriage almost assures an enjoyable sexual life, but the converse does not hold. The presence and frequency of enjoyable sex relations does not guarantee a solid marriage or its survival.

A NOTE ON SEX DIFFERENCES.   Much of the success of the physical side of marriage depends on the knowledge of and the sensitivity of each partner to the needs of the other. For many generations the man has been accused of being unaware of the woman's emotional and sexual differences. A few of these include:

1. Amount and Onset of Sex Behavior.   Kinsey presents ample evidence to document more extensive activity on the part of the male. For instance, 93 per cent of the male sample has masturbated as opposed to 62 per cent of the female. Similar percentages for nocturnal sex dreams were approximately 100 and 70 per cent; for premarital coitus was 98 to 68 per cent for the male (depending on educational level), and 50

---

[19] George V. Hamilton, *A Research in Marriage*, Albert and Charles Boni, New York, 1929, p. 161.

per cent for the female with minor variations (depending on educational level).[20] The female not only has fewer total sexual outlets, but also fewer outlets that permit orgasm. The male's high percentage also includes, in the total number, homosexual and extramarital contacts. Despite his later puberty, sexual activity occurs earlier for the man than for the woman.

2. Responsiveness to Stimulation. Men generally can be stimulated sexually by visual means, as well as physical, and are more susceptible to visual stimuli than women. A comparison of stimulatory values has been documented by Kinsey, as shown in Table 14.1.

Table 14.1

SOURCES OF SEXUAL AROUSAL FOR MALES AND FEMALES

Stimulus	PERCENTAGE EVER SEXUALLY AROUSED BY PARTICULAR STIMULUS	
	Male	Female
Fantasies about opposite sex	84	69
Portrayals of sexual activity	77	32
Observing opposite sex	72	58
Burlesque and floor shows	62	14
Reading books	59	60
Nude photographs	54	12
Hearing erotic stories	47	14
Watching commercial movies	34	48

Source: Kinsey, *op. cit.* (*Female*), as summarized in Robert O. Blood, Jr. *Marriage*, The Free Press of Glencoe, A Division of Collier-Macmillan, New York, 1962, p. 359.

3. Freedom of the Male. In our patricentic culture, the male has been able to choose when and whom he wishes. Because the reproductive burden falls on woman, his feeling of independence, if not his actual superiority, has been supported by biology as well as culture. A good deal of humor has been institutionalized for men and markedly less for women. The man's mobility, physical freedom, and economic priority have all operated to accentuate a freer sexuality.

[20] Kinsey, *op. cit.* (*Female*), pp. 173, 215, 330.

4. Emotionality in the Male and Female.   For the man the sex act can be a direct physical release dissociated from love. Evidence of this is the ancient economic institution of prostitution. For women sex generally is identified with a deeply affectionate and erotic relationship —as it usually is with the more highly educated male. The romantic aura adds enormously to the coital act for the man, but is not indispensable for its success. Generally, the woman's sexual relationships are fraught with larger interests, because her anatomy and physiology are more intricately constructed, that is, for the production of a new human being.

Kephart labels this supposed differential drive as the "female myth." [21] He points to evidence that indicates the female when aroused may have equal or stronger sexual needs than the male. This heightened female sexuality seems to be the exception rather than the rule, but it is difficult to detach the problem from Western society's taboo of sex expression for the woman. In addition there has been a coalescence of sex roles, as we have discussed. Certainly subcultures enter the picture.

In a study of a Philadelphia college sample girls looked to marriage with more idea of erotic or physical satisfaction than did boys. This sex difference was especially noticeable for the Catholic sample.[22] The answer may be that our cultural order, and especially the remnants of a paternalistic Catholic tradition, permit sex exploration for the male. The girls, and again particularly the devout Catholics, can properly find this outlet only in marriage. Among the sex differences in relation to the goals of marriage, it was found that men look to marriage as a relief from loneliness and women see it as economic security. This differential perception may affect the way in which each partner views sex. In fact, women through the ages have been forced to confer sexual favors because they were not sufficiently self-dependent economically to refuse them. This status may be in a socially acceptable role such as marriage, or in a less respectable one of courtesan or prostitute.

THE DIMENSION OF TIME.   The sex act includes four phases: the prelude, love play, sexual union, and epilogue or afterglow.[23] The

---

[21] Kephart, *The Family, Society, and the Individual,* Houghton Mifflin, Boston, 1961, p. 457.

[22] Robert C. Williamson, "Dating, Courtship, and Mate Selection: Some Relevant Subcultural Variables," *Family Life Coordinator,* 1965, **14,** 137–143.

[23] Theodore H. Van de Velde, *Ideal Marriage: Its Physiology and Technique,* Random House, New York, 1926, p. 145.

first phase might be described as the psychological readiness with rather diffuse stimulation; the second is mostly exploratory and manipulative, yet can be either spontaneous or deliberate. Love play or petting is preparatory to the coital act, and is highly emphasized by the marriage manuals as necessary for timing in connection with the wife's orgasm, a theory not entirely supported by research.[24] Intercourse, the third phase, is itself not altogether distinguishable from the second in the sense that stimulation of the erogenous zones continues during coitus, and rather extensive stimulation may have to be provided in order to insure maximum pleasure or orgasm to both partners.

In fact, even minimal enjoyment, for the woman, depends on sensations well beyond the clitoric and vaginal. The more highly educated the two partners, the more likely they are to engage in auxiliary actions that maximize sexual pleasures. Considerable variability rests in feeling, both in the prolongation of the experience and the extent of sensation. Kinsey calculated on the basis of his female sample, which reflected a middle-class outlook, that practices such as manual stimulation of the genitalia by both sexes and deep kissing were engaged in by roughly 90 per cent of the sample. According to Kinsey socio-economic class is a definite determinant in this behavior. Manual stimulation of the female breast is practiced by 96 per cent of the males at the upper-class level, but by only 79 per cent in the lower level.[25] Consideration of timing and variations in sex technique are less frequently reported by lower-class married couples. A study of "blue-collar" marriages indicated the consequences of this lack of sophistication: only 30 per cent of the wives "expressed high satisfaction with their sexual relations." [26]

The coital act itself represents a variable. As stated in our discussion of petting, it is a mistake to be too literal in interpreting the marriage manuals. The reaction of both spouses depends on a number of factors: the speed of response of both partners, the degree of erotica witnessed, the amount of alcohol consumed in the evening, and whether a baby is whimpering in the next room. Again, the timing of the act becomes very important. Furthermore, two intelligent people

---

[24] Kinsey, *op. cit. (Female),* pp. 384–385.
[25] Kinsey, *op. cit. (Male),* p. 367.
[26] Mirra Komarovsky, *Blue-Collar Marriage,* Random House, New York, 1964, p. 85.

are likely to work out their own techniques; whatever information they have acquired may serve as a point of departure, occasionally in the wrong direction, but sex relations are a trial-and-error learning process, and a good deal more.

Duration itself represents a varying dimension. In one study, 40 per cent of the subjects estimated intercourse as lasting less than five minutes; 34 per cent, five to ten minutes; whereas 26 per cent maintained the act was fifteen minutes or more.[27] There has been no proof that the length of coitus has any relation to marital happiness. However, in view of the slower reaction of the woman, more cultivated couples prefer a lengthier period unless the woman is particularly responsive. Coital positions are subject to variation in preference, with nearly half of the sample replying that positions other than the conventional were used (female above, "frequently," 45 per cent; side by side, "frequently," 31 per cent; other positions "less frequently.")[28] Again, youth and upper education and social status were critical variables in this more experimental outlook. There is evidence that after some experimentation a given position or technique becomes stabilized.

ORGASM.   Let us recall Terman's generalization that of the many factors he investigated, only two (the equality of sex drive between the spouses and the orgasm adequacy of the wife) were consistently predictive indices of marital happiness.[29] For the male, orgasm is assured, although in less than 1 per cent of coitus, orgasm was not forthcoming despite the continuance of erection. There may be pseudoorgasms, such as the feeling of arrival of semen in the urethra but with no ejaculation. Multiple orgasms may be experienced by males,[30] although this occurs more frequently among women; 14 per cent reporting that they regularly responded in this fashion.[31] However, the serious problem is the failure of the wife to reach orgasm.

In the Dickinson and Beam survey, 26 per cent of the wives never had reached orgasm, but these were not the most typical marital cases.[32] According to Kinsey, the ability to achieve orgasm was related to the length of marriage: in the first year 63 per cent of coitus resulted

---

[27] Dickinson and Beam, *op. cit.*, p. 59. Comparable figures are found in Kinsey's females; estimates were three minutes or less, 11 per cent; four to ten minutes, 36 per cent; eleven to twenty minutes, 31 per cent; over twenty minutes, 22 per cent. Kinsey, *op cit. (Female)*, p. 393.

[28] *Ibid.*

[29] Terman, *op. cit.*

[30] Kinsey, *op. cit. (Male)*, p. 215.

[31] Kinsey, *op. cit. (Female)*, p. 375.

[32] Dickenson and Beam, *op. cit.*, p. 62.

in orgasm; by the fifth year, 71 per cent; and by the twentieth year, 85 per cent.[33] Kinsey's evidence indicates that educational level of both partners is positively related to the ability of the wife to have orgasm. His data also show that premarital practices, whether masturbation, petting or in coitus, are beneficial to marital coitus or post-marital orgasm. Selective factors are probably involved; according to Kinsey the kind of girl most likely to enter into premarital sex practices of one variety or another can be predicted to enjoy sex relations in marriage. The marital adjustment studies find no consistent pattern between these two sets of variables.

The orgastic capacity of the wife depends on a number of factors: freedom from guilt and anxiety, relaxation and lack of fatigue, and various subtle forms of stimulation. The length of time spent in fore-play has been regarded as a crucial variable but as pointed out in the preceding paragraphs, the Kinsey evidence is not conclusive on this point. However, foreplay may be enjoyable as an end in itself. For that matter, sexual intercourse can be pleasurable, if less exciting, in the absence of orgasm. In any case, most upper-level subjects indulge in petting. Petting varies from three minutes or less for a tenth of the Kinsey female sample, with roughly a third spending four to ten minutes, with another third at eleven to twenty minutes, and a fifth petting beyond twenty minutes, perhaps an hour in a few cases.

In foreplay, during, and after intercourse itself caressing is very critical for producing the orgasm and adding pleasure to the act. The distraction of the male in manual and oral stimulation tends to delay him from reaching his climax too soon. Deep kissing and oral stimulation of various erogenous zones become important to both parties. Stroking with both light and heavy pressure on various parts of the body may enhance the woman's pleasure, and her stimulation of his erogenous zones heightens his sensations. There can be no formula in sex accompaniment, and each couple has to work out their own patterns. The quality of petting probably varies from one occasion to another.

SOME PERSISTENT SEX PROBLEMS

Our cultural traditions, stretching from the Old and New Testaments to the value judgments of twentieth-century America, require more than a neutral attitude toward sex. Moreover, the combination

[33] Kinsey, *op. cit. (Female)*, pp. 375f.

of biology, culture, and the psychology of each human being operate in affecting the direction and control of sex activity. Finally, and most crucially, there are accumulations of experience in the private world of each individual, some of which act to direct our sex motives, sometimes causing blockages and a number of negative attitudes. This section discusses some of the sexual difficulties most frequently encountered by young couples.

IMPOTENCE.   The initiation and physical capacity of the sex act usually depends on the male. In one survey 15 per cent of the sample mentioned problems of potency on the part of the husband.[34] *Potency* is identified as the ability of the male to have an erection and carry through the coital activity to completion; *erectile* impotence is the common type, and this itself is a differential. *Partial* impotency is the more common form of this type of difficulty. *Absolute* impotency is extremely rare. Partial impotency means the man may occasionally lose the erection. For some males erection is more or less unpredictable. *Differential* impotency refers to the man who may be impotent in extramarital affairs but potent with his wife. The reverse may occur when deep marital conflict causes the husband to be unable to perform successfully with his wife. *Ejaculatory* impotency is another means by which the male may retain an erection, but is unable to have an orgasm, which, although rare, does exist. *Premature ejaculation* is more common, and from the viewpoint of some wives is as frustrating as impotency. The ability to withhold the ejaculation has been related positively to the social and educational level of the male.[35]

Causes of impotency vary from day-to-day nervous tension and physical fatigue to deep-seated conflict and guilt. As with any neurotic problem the history of this difficulty is traced back to childhood and early socialization. Homosexuality, overt or latent, is another cause. Again, in most instances impotence is a relative rather than an absolute phenomenon. Completely impotent husbands are rarely found, at least in marriages contracted under forty years of age, except when a distinctly abnormal situation exists (as when a male and female homosexual marry for convenience). Except for the occasional change in the life situation almost the only cure for impotency is psychotherapy, because few cases of impotency result from physical causes.

FRIGIDITY.   In a certain respect frigidity is less serious than im-

[34] Hamilton, *op. cit.*, p. 163.
[35] Kinsey, *op. cit.* (*Male*), p. 580.

potency, because sex relations may take place even when this condition exists. However, frigidity is the more prevalent difficulty, and consequently interferes with the enjoyment of sex. Of course the problem cannot be detached from the difference in the drives of the two sexes. The following quotes from the Burgess and Wallin sample serve to indicate the way in which this type of problem affects some couples:

Husband: Our sex life is terrible. That is our main source of trouble. Now we don't have intercourse more than once a month. She does not like to make love any more. She gets no satisfaction from it. I would like intercourse two or three times a week. A lot of tension arises from this, though we don't mention it. When she is not satisfied it leaves her irritated and frustrated. It makes me feel inadequate to the situation.

Husband: I am not completely satisfied. I have tried to adjust to her nature. She needs less than I would like. It is not so powerful a factor with me that I become discontent or melancholy. We have intercourse about three times a month. It is not too much for her. I would like to have it more often—maybe six times, but I adjust to her needs. In the early part of our marriage I had to meet the problem of timing. Because I had premature orgasm she would get no relief. This lasted two to four months. I used to feel that sex played a part of major importance in marriage—about seventy-five per cent. Lack of complete sexual compatibility has assured me that it is of much less importance than I thought before. I suppose that if I were very highly sexed or demanded it say two or three times a week and the female only wanted it once or twice a month that it would end in divorce.

Wife: I do not feel I've achieved good sex adjustment. I have orgasm sometimes. I am by no means warm and do not particularly enjoy it and am just as glad not to be bothered by it. There seems to be something bestial about it. I would prefer marriage without it.

Wife: I did find the sex adjustment rather difficult. I do not like the physical aspects. It seemed animal-like. I don't care especially for sex relations. I wouldn't miss sex if it was removed from marriage.[36]

Frigidity can be defined in different ways: (1) as the inability of the vagina to expand and the contraction of the musculatory entrance on insertion of the penis, thus making penetration impossible; (2) to the inability to have orgasm—the sense in which the term is used most frequently; (3) in loose terms, it refers to general disinterest in the sex act. In some instances, the husband's role may be involved in the wife's frigidity, and there is the problem of his own emotional state, as exemplified by this quote: "Our sex adjustment was extremely diffi-

[36] Ernest W. Burgess and Paul Wallin, *Engagement and Marriage,* J. B. Lippincott, Philadelphia, 1953, pp. 684–685.

cult. I felt a sense of inferiority while she probably felt frigid since her needs and desires were far less than mine. And it was not infrequent for me to experience pre-ejaculation. Thus the first two years were rough ones for our sexual life." [37]

If we accept Kinsey's figures which state that 20 to 30 per cent of copulations in marriage result in failure to reach orgasm for the female, and that perhaps 7 per cent of the wives in his sample never experienced orgasm (at least by age fifty), we may say that this form of frigidity seems to be a serious, although declining, problem.[38] This difficulty may be more widespread than the figures indicate; it is hard to know, however, because of the reluctance of lower class couples to admit this maladjustment.

In some instances the causes of frigidity have similarity to those of impotency: anxiety, shame, deep emotional conflicts, latent homosexuality are all causes. However, the girl's culture and socialization processes involve a number of problems that the boy is spared. Girls are warned of the results of intercourse, such as pregnancy out of wedlock. The high school girl has more to lose than the boy. Her sociosexual life is more carefully watched than his. Early fears such as these may be the basis for later frigidity.

Some insight into the causative framework of frigidity may be derived from a recent study of one thousand unconsummated marriages in the United States.[39] The respondents had a mean age of twenty-eight, and the marriages had a mean length of eight years. Inasmuch as failure to consummate a marriage suggests the existence of frigidity among other causes, a review of the findings is pertinent (Table 14.2). Other causes of frigidity, all under 4 per cent, made up the remainder including distaste for intercourse unless pregnancy is intended, and religious belief opposed to coitus. Among these couples as compensation for frustration, substitute activity occurred, such as mutual masturbation or self-relief on the part of the husband. In some cases total abstinence was reported by each partner. In spite of the atypical nature of the sample, the findings point to a basic problem that exists among a wider population. Phobias develop through earlier conditioning. Freudian literature abounds in case studies of frigidity and impo-

[37] From the author's files.
[38] Kinsey, *op. cit.* (*Female*), p. 392.
[39] John A. Blazer, "Married Virgins: A Study of Unconsummated Marriage," *Journal of Marriage and the Family*, 1964, 26, 213–214.

Table 14.2

Cause	Complaints by Wives in Unconsummated Marriages
Fear of pain in the initial intercourse	20.3%
Disgust with the sex act	17.8
Impotent husbands	11.7
Fear of pregnancy or childbirth	10.2
Small size of the vagina	8.2
Ignorance	5.2
Preference for a female partner	5.2
Distaste for male genitalia	4.6

Adapted from John A. Blazer, "Married Virgins: A Study of Unconsummated Marriages," *Journal of Marriage and the Family*, 1964, **26**, 213–214.

tence, which are often the result of traumatization; for such people sex activity or sex organs sometimes symbolize a conflict situation.[40]

EXTRAMARITAL ACTIVITY. There is a degree of universality in the monogamous pattern—61 per cent of the 139 preliterate societies studied in one survey disapproved the notion of extramarital liaisons.[41] In Western tradition with a few exceptions, the wife was expected to be faithful to the husband and vice versa. Among Kinsey's male subjects 50 per cent (until age forty) had to some extent indulged in extramarital coitus; the comparable figure for the woman was 26 per cent.[42] Between the ages of twenty-one to twenty-five, extramarital relations comprised 7 per cent of all male outlets and 3 per cent of all female; from ages twenty-six to forty the respective per cents were 8 and 10. These figures indicate extramarital behavior decreases relatively for the male as he gets older and increases for the female.

As compared to premarital sex behavior, there is a less clear-cut relation to social class in extramarital behavior. In the early years the lower class male tends to continue his premarital habits, which subside in later years. In the middle years there is a tendency for the upper class male to increase his extramarital activity and surpass that of the lower class male, even though the total lifetime outlets remain

[40] Helene Deutsch, *The Psychology of Women: A Psychoanalytic Interpretation* (vol. 1), Grune and Stratton, New York, 1945, pp. 81–90.

[41] Ford and Beach, *op. cit.,* p. 122.

[42] Kinsey, *op. cit.* (*Female*), p. 437.

lower.[43] For the lower class female low incidence is retained, whereas the better educated female has a slightly higher rate, and gains in the middle-upper years.[44] Again, the single standard is more apparent in the more highly educated group. There was a large discrepancy for both sexes in extramarital incidence between the religiously active and inactive.

Not all those in the Kinsey sample who indulged in adultery did so promiscuously. Forty-one per cent of the female sample had limited their extramarital pursuits to 1 man, 40 per cent maintained relations with from 2 to 5 men, and the remainder were freer with their favors. For many the experience was episodic; 42 per cent had confined their activities to one year or less. Although less detail was recorded for the male, it is assumed that his activity was broader in the number of contacts and the period of time involved. Although we have no reliable information, it is felt by many that there has been an increase in adultery, and as we have seen, the data on the female regarding later age groups indicate a sharp upward rate. It is not altogether clear whether extramarital interest is on the increase or whether there is simply a difference in samples. A study conducted by Terman found 28 per cent of the males and 73 per cent of the females replying that they had never had any desire for extramarital intercourse. He did find, however, that among those subjects (but especially among the men), the marital happiness rating decidedly declined.[45] It is difficult to dissociate the increase of adultery from the rising divorce rate.

The degree of acceptance or rejection of extramarital behavior within our culture has been open to conjecture. In discussion of the degree of disapproval from their husbands 42 per cent of Kinsey's wives noted that they encountered serious difficulty, 42 per cent faced no censure, and 16 per cent experienced only minor disapproval. Since only well under a third of the wives ever practiced extramarital intercourse, it appears that less than a sixth of the total sample found approving husbands. Roughly half of the wives who were involved in extramarital engagements thought that their husbands knew or suspected.[46]

SEXUAL DECLINE.   In our society, with its high premium on time and youth, we are caught in the self-consciousness of the passing years. A

---

[43] Kinsey, *op. cit. (Male)*, p. 382.

[44] Kinsey, *op. cit. (Female)*, pp. 421ff.

[45] Terman, *op. cit.*, pp. 335f.

[46] Kinsey, *op. cit. (Female)*, p. 434.

husband and wife may decide to have another child to prove that they can or to show they can place themselves in a younger age category. A husband may flirt with his secretary or seek the gratification or appreciation of any young women to enhance his ego as a reminder of his virility. In a culture that rewards the young the struggle against time is a fair one.

Kinsey discovered that the highest number of sexual outlets takes place in the late teens, whether measured by masturbation or coitus. (Premarital coitus did not reach as high a quantitative level.) At the other extreme is age seventy, by which time 30 per cent of the males he studied were totally inactive.[47] Individual variations were marked. One aspect of the female aging process is the *menopause,* which ordinarily occurs during the mid-forties to mid-fifties. In many cases this is a severe period of readjustment, and sex patterns may be temporarily affected. Occasionally a woman passing through the menopause or ovarian surgery may for an extended period deny intercourse if she was never particularly interested.[48] However, the menopause seldom has an effect on the sex drive. In some instances the woman may be happier in her sex relations during this time than she had been previously, because pregnancy is no longer a threat. For the male there is no menopause as such, but there is a gradual ebbing away of sexual interest. In the late years after fertility has disappeared, the male may still have a "morning erection" as a last suggestion of potency.

Aging is as much a psychological and social process as it is a physical phenomenon. Marital tension is reflected in the inability to accept the aging process. Aging may be used by one partner as an excuse for refusal or reluctance to engage in sexual activity. On the positive side life events, such as health recovery, change of mood, new motivations may renew sexual interest. Remarriage or the discovery of a new partner often introduces a new enthusiasm for sex. On the sexual side, there need be no crisis in later years, if the two partners accept the inevitability of aging, if they can adjust, and if the marriage is soundly constructed.

THE SIGNIFICANCE OF SEX IN MARRIAGE

Society tends to place marked emphasis on the sexual factor in marriage. The release from the Victorian mold provided a natural vacuum

[47] Kinsey, *op. cit. (Male),* p. 219f.
[48] Kinsey, *op. cit. (Female),* p. 736.

in which exaggeration could easily occur. It has been difficult for many observers to discuss this topic objectively. In some respects we have a freer attitude toward sex, but inevitably there is marked self-consciousness about the concept. By its nature sexual behavior is individualistic and private. For instance, if we were forced to eat in private and discuss nothing of our eating habits, to read only in private, or travel only in private these behavior patterns would also be fraught with self-consciousness. In addition, sexual behavior is complicated by its deep emotional involvement and years of conditioning within the individual. People are probably more comfortable about sex today than they have been for some generations. Yet there are some unresolved problems.

CONFUSION IN SOCIETY. The enormous transition in society during the last half century has increased rather than decreased ambiguity of feeling in regard to sex. Probably the most dramatic, if not notorious, aspect of this situation was illustrated by the Kinsey report, which pointed out that more than half the married couples of upper white collar and professional classes engaged in "unnatural" practices, as defined by certain states—for example, oral-genital contacts and could, if apprehended, be punished by extremely severe laws. Yet these same practices are fully recognized by psychiatrists, marriage counsellors, and other competent authorities as legitimate sex play. Masturbation is practiced by husbands under certain conditions, such as temporary incapacity of the wife during menstruation and pregnancy, or simply as a result of their stronger sex drive. Although not specifically a crime, in several states one spouse may point to masturbation on the part of the other as a petition for divorce on the grounds of "unnatural behavior." [49]

SEX RELATIONS IN THE MARITAL PROCESS. Sex differences continue to operate within the marital context. For instance, Locke found 54 per cent of his husbands responding that sex relations were "very enjoyable," 39 per cent as "enjoyable"; for the wives, the responses were 33 and 58, respectively. Or a total of 93 per cent of the husbands and 91 per cent of the wives were to some degree satisfied with sex relations. These figures were in contrast to the divorced sample, where only 68 per cent of males and 53 per cent of females expressed satisfac-

[49] Harriet F. Pilpel and Theodora Zavin, *Your Marriage and the Law*, Holt, Rinehart and Winston, New York, 1952, p. 220.

tion.[50] Even if we allow for the halo effect that influences the rating in the direction of sex satisfaction, the point remains that there is a sex differential in responses, but that the majority of women still find sex satisfying.

It is idle to argue that "marriage manuals" or courses of instruction are the answer to the problem of sex adjustment. Nor is premarital experience. What is called for is a freedom of prejudice, an affectionate relationship, and a more or less experimental outlook. As one writer states, the two individuals should look upon the matter of techniques:

Any act or expression that furthers the process is acceptable and desirable, provided that (1) it does not cause injury, pain, or disgust to either party; (2) it does not indicate or produce a fixation at a low level of adjustment; (3) it does not make either person feel guilty; (4) it does not become a permanent and regular substitute for normal sexual intercourse; (5) it leads up to and eventuates in normal sexual intercourse.[51]

In a study of marital adjustment Burgess and Cottrell were convinced that sex relationships of the husband and wife were determined by factors other than the biological—affectionate, social, and cultural.[52] There seems to be no reason to contradict this viewpoint. In a similar perspective, sex relations in marriage are a continuation of what occurred to two people before they were linked in matrimony. That is, the emotional atmosphere and even certain taboos are not completely abandoned. Two young people working out their sexual problems may not necessarily be the source of anxiety that some observers indicate. It is frequently said that with the successive years of marriage sex may become continually more enjoyable. A recent analysis

[50] Harvey J. Locke, *Predicting Adjustment in Marriage: A Comparison of a Divorced and a Happily Married Group,* Holt, Rinehart and Winston, New York, 1951, p. 145. The Terman study found 61 per cent of the husbands as compared to 46 per cent of the wives reported "entirely complete" satisfaction with intercourse. Terman, *op. cit.,* p. 308. To the question of Burgess and Wallin, "How much relief from sexual desire do you usually get from sexual intercourse with your spouse," 73 per cent of the husbands and 61 per cent of the wives replied "entirely complete." Burgess and Wallin, *op. cit.,* p. 669. The younger sample may explain this more thorough satisfaction.
[51] Henry A. Bowman, *Marriage for Moderns* (fifth edition), McGraw-Hill, New York, 1965, p. 506.
[52] Ernest W. Burgess and Leonard S. Cottrell, Jr., *Predicting Success or Failure in Marriage,* Prentice-Hall, Englewood Cliffs, New Jersey, 1939.

of the Burgess and Wallin sample, however, indicates that the woman's responsiveness increases through the years only if the quality of the marriage is satisfactory.[53] Habit systems and the growing together of two marital partners can have considerable significance.

Supplementary Readings

Bell, Robert R., *Marriage and Family Interaction*, The Dorsey Press, Homewood, Illinois, 1963. Chapters 7 and 12 represent clear thinking on the subject, a refreshingly objective outlook in textbook fashion.

Chesser, Eustace, *Love Without Fear*, Roy Publishers, New York, 1947. Now available in paperback (Signet). A discussion by an English physician of various techniques.

Duvall, Evelyn M. and Sylvanus M. Duvall (eds.), *Sex Ways in Fact and Faith*, Association Press, New York, 1961. Articles of varying quality in the more orthodox tradition, among the better treatments of the subject.

Ehrmann, Winston, "Marital and Nonmarital Sexual Behavior," in Harold T. Christensen (ed.), *Handbook of Marriage and the Family*, Rand McNally, Chicago, 1964, pp. 585–622. A research-oriented discussion of sex behavior with attention to certain of the psychological aspects.

Ellis, Albert, *The American Sexual Tragedy*, Twayne Publishers, New York, 1954. Not as grim as the title, but in a different vein from Duvall, although an equally competent authority.

Gordon, Edgar S., "Taking Physical Factors into Account," in Howard Becker and Reuben Hill (eds.), *Family, Marriage and Parenthood* (second edition), D. C. Heath, Boston, 1955. Marital sex relations and reproduction as explained by a physician.

Kephart, William M., *The Family, Society, and the Individual*, Houghton Mifflin, Boston, 1961. Chapters 15 and 16 constitute an excellent textbook presentation of sex in marriage.

Kinsey, Alfred C., Wardell B. Pomeroy, and Clyde E. Martin, *Sexual Behavior in the Human Male*, W. B. Saunders, Philadelphia, 1948.

Kinsey, Alfred C., Wardell B. Pomeroy, Clyde E. Martin, and Paul H. Gebhard, *Sexual Behavior in the Human Female*, W. B. Saunders, Philadelphia, 1953. Chapter 18 of the *Male* and Chapter 9 of the *Female* discuss marital coitus. Chapter 16 of the *Female* contains data on the sexual differences of males and females. Despite criticism Kinsey reports the only relatively complete data on the subject.

[53] Alexander L. Clark and Paul Wallin, "Women's Sexual Responsiveness and the Duration and Quality of Their Marriages," *American Journal of Sociology*, 1965, **71**, 187–196.

Simpson, George, *People in Families,* Thomas Y. Crowell, New York, 1960. Chapter 10 is recommended for a psychoanalytic treatment of sex adjustment in marriage.

Terman, Lewis M., *Psychological Factors in Marital Happiness,* McGraw-Hill, New York, 1938. In his questionnaire approach to marital adjustment Terman concentrated on sexual and psychological items, next to Kinsey perhaps our best survey of the question.

Van de Velde, Theodore H., *Ideal Marriage: Its Physiology and Technique,* Random House, New York, 1926. This pioneering work, despite its extravagant language, is like Chesser's a worthwhile approach to marital coitus.

Chapter fifteen

The Family and the Economy

The greatest sacrifice in marriage is the sacrifice of the adventurous attitude toward life: the being settled.

George Bernard Shaw, Preface, Androcles and the Lion, *1912.*

Perhaps no family in history has been so puny in home production and so conspicuously a consuming group as the American middle-class family. It is likely that future studies of the family will view it increasingly as a consuming group. . . . The family, not the individual, is the unit of consumption, and this applies clearly to our emerging democratic middle-class urban family. One of the major activities in this family is organizing and effectuating the consumption of goods and services. The effects which this shift in activities has had on family form show clearly the close relationship between changes in the economic system and changes in the structures of individual families.

Willard Waller, The Family: A Dynamic Interpretation *(revised by Reuben Hill), Holt, Rinehart, and Winston, New York, 1951.*

Family life has always required a multitude of skills of its practitioners, so that a husband or wife must necessarily perform many different tasks. Nevertheless, as long as the wife stuck to her cooking and the husband to his hunting, some of the advantages of specialization accrued. Such advantages would be lost if husband and wife were to merge their work completely.

Robert O. Blood, Jr. and Donald M. Wolfe, Husbands and Wives: The Dynamics of Married Living, *The Free Press of Glencoe, A Division of Collier-Macmillan, New York, 1960.*

Panel from *Society Freed Through Justice* by George Biddle
Courtesy of the Public Buildings Service and National Archives

Although strong affectionate and sexual bonds make a marriage, the economic structure is no less a foundation. In a broad cultural sense economics is as basic to the family as biology. It is through the family that most cultures assign their economic roles to individuals. In nomadic, peasant, and feudal societies the family is the central economic unit. Even in modern societies, there should be a strong financial base for marriage and the family. Yet a fourth of American citizens are considered to have incomes inadequate for satisfactory marital and family life.[1] In fact, in 1964, at a time when the United States reached a peak with the highest standard of living in its history, per capita income was roughly $2,600 per year; however, the income range among various regions and economic classes was enormous. From the viewpoint of the family sociologist, still more serious than a lack of an economic base is an inability to manage finances.

Several economic factors underly marital adjustment and family functioning. One of these is occupation and income. To what extent is the husband adjusted in his economic role, and how does this affect the marriage? Is the wife able to perform in the economic market place as earner or consumer? How does her (and his) role in household management develop out of joint decision making? As many marriages appear to fail because of the spouses' inability to organize and control expenditures as are threatened by inadequate income. There are a number of aspects to be considered: economic security—including insurance—economic planning, and investment. Many of the economic factors of family life are influenced by crises and transitions in the life cycle, such as the coming of old age. First, we discuss the nature of the American economy, thus setting the stage for specific economic problems that preoccupy family members.

THE AMERICAN ECONOMIC SETTING

In today's urban world the individual is caught in a web of interlocking relationships. Marriage is launched with an entirely different set of economic perspectives from those our forebears knew. These changes involve the size and complexity of the economic operation;

[1] Harrington may be high in his estimate of one-fourth of the nation to be below a minimal standard of living. However, it is likely that this proportion of the nation's population feels some economic frustration. Michael Harrington, *The Other America: Poverty in the United States,* Macmillan, New York, 1963.

the problem of security; the transition from production to consumption; the revolution in marketing, distribution, and services; and the expansion of credit.

The young person initiating his occupational and marital careers encounters a multitude of interrelated economic enterprises. In addition, the individual may own property that needs legal protection, drive a car that must be insured, may be a member of several organizations ranging from labor unions to fraternal orders, and must participate in the other complexities of an urban environment. In contrast, the young couple of 1850 had new land to be conquered and tilled, and the husband and wife constituted a self-sufficient economic unit. Each additional child, if it survived, was an economic asset. Even for the minority who lived in the city, life in many respects was grimmer than today, but man's socio-economic relationships were less extended. It is possible that the kinship group provided more of a cushioning effect, although recent data suggest that kinship relationships still function, for example, parents aiding young people to initiate their marriage and family responsibilities.[2] Certainly the expectations of 1850 were less extravagant, and there was a stability to life, that is, the rate of social change was slower. These reflections on nineteenth-century life are not meant to be sentimental, but simply to show how several aspects of marital life have changed.

Today the couple who marries without some economic foundation is indeed jeopardizing their future. Most important, the husband and possibly the wife must have a particular skill to provide a livelihood. They have to take their places in a society where more than 40 per cent of our labor supply is either professional, managerial, or white-collar.[3] In contrast to the labor force a hundred years ago, salaried employees constitute the bulk of our labor force; yet even today about a fifth of our workers are self-employed. The ever-expanding income and the climb upward cannot be detached from the marital and family role.

In our economic society we have become consumers instead of producers. Per capita income has passed the two-thousand dollar mark (median family income was $5,660 in 1959).[4] The outgoing distribu-

[2] Marvin B. Sussman and Lee Burchinal, "Kin Family Network: Unheralded Structure in Current Conceptualizations of Family Functioning," *Marriage and Family Living*, 1962, **24**, 231–240.
[3] U.S. Bureau of the Census, *Statistical Abstract of the United States*, Government Printing Office, Washington, D.C., 1965, pp. 228f.
[4] *Ibid.*, p. 343.

tion of this income, consumption, has altered markedly over the last generation. Indicative of the change is the amount of national income which finds its way into savings. During World War II, 28.3 per cent, or more than a fourth, of the national economy was converted into savings. Today less than 10 per cent is so channeled. Over the last quarter of a century less of the income has been diverted into food and clothing and more into housing, recreation, transportation, and medical care. Even in the period between 1950 and 1962 the proportion of the consumer's budget allocated for food (including beverages and tobacco), and clothing dropped from 42.8 per cent of the budget to 36.0 per cent.[5]

At the same time, the nature and distribution of services has shifted. Mass production has created goods having greater range in quality and quantity. To a greater extent than the individual of a few generations ago, we have difficulty in relying on the proprietor of a small retail business to guarantee the product. At one time the shelves of the general store constituted the range of the buying opportunity. These products were more stable and dependable and usually their serviceability was well known. In any case, the decision about what to buy was simpler to make. We become susceptible more and more to the appeals of the advertising media, the middle man, the chain store, and the mail order house. We are confused over what to buy with limited funds because of the intricacies of pricing, the sizeable array of items, the yearly change of models, all of which discourage any close scrutiny. The limited time available to some consumers discourages comparative shopping.

Along with these marketing processes have occurred large-scale changes in the handling of credit. Installment buying has become almost a national characteristic. The extension of credit has been abetted by the transition toward an inflationary economy. Where at one time incurring debts for a dwelling and/or for an automobile was the limit of individual credit, today it is not uncommon to procure credit for any number of luxury items including travel and dining out.

Inflation can be ascribed to expansion of credit and the elaboration in the standard of living made possible by war and postwar prosperity. Interest costs increase the price of the item, whether an automobile or an office building, which indirectly lowers the value of the dollar. A rise in monetary and real wages resulting from unionization and effec-

[5] *Ibid.*

tive bargaining power, along with the unprecedented rise in productivity, have accomplished this upward shift in consumer prices. Nor have the advertising media been inactive in this upsurge of buying habits. Except for the patriotic fervor engendered by World War II, with the lack of available stocks of commodities, our national psychology has been consumption rather than savings oriented. Generally man spends or "consumes" on the average more as his income grows, but not as much as the increase in his income.[6]

OCCUPATIONAL ROLES AND MARITAL ADJUSTMENT

The most important consideration, at least for the male at the end of the adolescent period, is the choice of an occupation. Some roles such as sex, nationality, or race are ascribed. Even a "free" choice of role such as getting married or remaining single is only *relatively* voluntary, and is in fact a combination of *ascription* and *achievement*. But occupation is an achieved rather than an ascribed role; we do not inherit roles from our fathers to the extent our ancestors did in the colonial period. Upward occupational mobility on an intergenerational basis has been documented in recent decades, and if it has not been accelerated, neither has it been suspended.[7]

Western society has increasingly differentiated between occupational and family roles. The demands of an occupation or career vary in the commitment required of the individual. Professional and entrepreneurial roles, in particular, compete with family considerations (for example, the lengthy preparation to become a doctor or long work hours that may be required of the business man). At the same time, there is a certain similarity between the socialization process and transition phases of both work and family experience: training and choice of career may be compared to the courtship and engagement periods in terms of being learning situations, and the establishment of one's career has something in common with adjustment to marriage.[8] Adjustments and transitions in the work area may, or may not, complicate those of the marriage, and vice versa.

[6] George Katona, *Psychological Analysis of Economic Behavior*, McGraw-Hill, New York, 1951, p. 134.

[7] Seymour M. Lipset and Reinhard Bendix, *Social Mobility in an Industrial Society*, University of California Press, Berkeley and Los Angeles, 1959.

[8] Robert Rapoport and Rhona Rapoport, "Work and Family in Contemporary Society," *American Sociological Review*, 1965, **30**, 381–394.

What has been remarkable in the occupational arena of the nineteenth and twentieth centuries is the opening up of new vocational roles. There has been a tremendous expansion of the educational system, which has furthered the equalization of opportunity and upward mobility, notwithstanding the social and economic limits imposed by intelligence, bank accounts, kinship, and the like. School facilities, including courses on occupational selection as well as the services of vocational counsellors, indicate the stake society has in this process. The purpose of discussing occupations here is to assess its significance in relation to marital adjustment.

VOCATIONAL AND MARITAL ADJUSTMENT. Occupational roles cannot fail to affect marital adjustment to the extent that a person's life work has unmistakable effects on personality. For instance, a minister has a different set of role attributes and values as compared to a bartender's, barber's, accountant's, or a school teacher's, even though there would be overlapping of innumerable traits. The physician or surgeon is generally credited with being devoted to his duties, rigorously methodical, with high manual dexterity, flexible in his role of diagnostician and practitioner, necessarily impersonal in his relationship to other people, and scholastic in his capacity to absorb large amounts of technical information. He is in all probability motivated by both the promise of high economic return and the knowledge that he enjoys high status in the community. In contrast, we might expect an artist to be emotional and esthetic in his value system, to be less interested in technical and routine duties, and to be motivated by the rewards, both internal and external, associated with creativity. Popular stereotypes might consider the artist as being less "masculine" than a doctor, who in turn may be thought to be less masculine than a policeman. While personality traits are hypothesized for occupations, with limited applicability to an individual, the woman contemplating marriage is advised to consider the behavior expected in certain vocational roles. She might guess what effect these traits will have on the pattern of marital adjustment. The question of occupation and personality are not irrelevant to the young man making his choices. There is evidence that women tend to elect given occupations on the basis of role expectancies which will determine whether they choose life-long interest in the career or whether they consider a vocation as merely transitional. The ways in which individuals make decisions can have long-lasting influence on both marriage and career.

It is no accident that nurses have married doctors to a disproportionate degree, partially because they work together, the community of
interests and values that bring them together, and the resources these
characteristics can contribute to the marriage. The folklore of marriage
has often claimed that marriage can lose its sparkle if the partners "talk
shop," a conjecture not supported by fact. There may be potential
danger when both partners work in the same office or business. Psychoanalysts point out that in most marriages some need exists for the partners to have an occasional escape from each other. However, on the
whole, occupational overlapping is apt to bring more to a marriage
than it detracts.

Occupations often demand individual performances that are in conflict with marital roles. In Lang's study of a sample of 17,000 men,
certain of their occupations were more likely to involve marital discontent: traveling salesmen, musicians, druggists, and laborers of various
categories. On the other hand, engineers, college professors, and ministers were among those occupations correlated with marital happiness.
Physicians, architects, and lawyers were intermediate.[9] If there are
common factors in these occupations it is in the stability, or lack of
physical mobility, along with a higher than average educational preparation, both of which are related to marital happiness. Too, irregular
hours are significant in this interrelationship as in the case of the
musician, druggist, and the doctor. Both the causes and effects of
marital adjustment in regard to specific occupations can be very complex, and a replication of Lang's investigation is desirable. In another
study, the rating of the husband's occupational adjustment, given by
the wife (both at the time of the marriage and at the time of the
interview), was more significant to marital adjustment than was the
rating given by the husband. White-collar occupations were found to
be related statistically to happy marriages. Other factors of negative
predictability were low interest in fellow employees, little opportunity
for responsibility and initiative, fatigue at the end of the day, and a
long work week (forty-seven hours or more).[10] Although some of these

[9] Richard O. Lang, "The Rating of Happiness in Marriage," unpublished M.A.
thesis, University of Chicago, 1932, as cited in Ernest W. Burgess and Leonard S.
Cottrell, Jr., *Predicting Success or Failure in Marriage*, Prentice-Hall, Englewood
Cliffs, 1939, pp. 139–146.

[10] Robert C. Williamson, "Socio-economic Factors in Marital Adjustment in an
Urban Area," Ph.D. dissertation, University of Southern California, 1951; cf.,
"Economic Factors in Marital Adjustment," *Marriage and Family Living*, 1952,
14, 298–301.

tests of significance revealed only low negative relationship, they were in a consistent direction. The criticism that certain individuals who are low in assessing their marital adjustment would also be low in rating their occupational adjustment is relevant but questionable. In other words, the finding that both marital happiness and occupational adjustment registered low is not a lack of discrimination on the part of the interviewee, but rather occurs because adjustment in one area affects adjustment in the other. The halo effect may exist, but it is not a serious impediment in determining the variables underlying marital success.

There is corroborative evidence from other sources, such as Locke, who found a higher incidence of professionals among his happily married group, and of unskilled and semiskilled in the divorced sample.[11] He ascribes this difference as partially due to the sensitivity of white collar and professional individuals to conformity needs and the desire to appear respectable in the public eye. In fact, respondents were asked to contribute the names of happy persons, which often included the names of community leaders and key professional individuals, consequently a bias in the sample was possible. The wife's occupation at marriage was also found to be predictive in the same direction. Another study suggests that upper mobile occupations are correlated with marital happiness; there is a relationship between marrying above the present family rank, which was found to be especially important for the girl.[12] Although this description of mobility was defined as "the distance which a subject moved from his parents in terms of social class level," there was no rigid distinction between occupation and social class.

Still other evidence regarding class and occupational influences or subcultures comes from data on divorce.[13] Divorce seems, in general, to be related inversely to social class, by combining income and education (except for some discontinuities within the Negro population). Occupations also showed an inverse correlation with social class; yet some manual laborers had a lower divorce rate than certain white collar and professional categories. Goode interprets these data as im-

[11] Harvey J. Locke, *Predicting Adjustment in Marriage: A Comparison of a Divorced and a Happily Married Group*, Holt, Rinehart and Winston, New York, 1951, pp. 272–273.

[12] Julius Roth and Robert F. Peck, "Social Class and Social Mobility Factors Related to Marital Adjustment," *American Sociological Review*, 1951, **16**, 478–487.

[13] William J. Goode, *After Divorce*, The Free Press of Glencoe, A Division of Collier-Macmillan, New York, 1956, pp. 52–68.

plying that problems of role relationships, moral norms, and psychological strain enter into occupational demands, and that the commitments are not the same for both sexes at all levels on the socioeconomic and occupational scale.

THE MANAGEMENT OF INCOME

Aside from the problem of acquiring money, the most critical aspect of household management is the control and distribution of income. The problem of making the money stretch, along with a constant struggle to find new sources of money, adds tension to the marriage. Locke found "the efficiency of home management" to be highly predictive of marital success, as were the husbands' regularity of employment and "efforts to provide." [14] Other studies discovered limited but consistently favorable relationships between economic stability and the happiness of the marriage.[15]

In terms of role behavior, the management of the economic affairs of a home has in recent decades become more of a dual or reciprocal affair. Namely, husbands and wives have altered the somewhat traditional division of labor and merged social and economic tasks. An example of this mutually responsible behavior role between husband and wife is the problem of socialization of the child. Wives now contribute to the standard of living through outside employment, and husbands are more likely to play a part in the buying and consumption aspects of the marriage than was true in the days of the fifty- to sixty-hour week when there was stricter dichotomization of household tasks. Blood and Wolfe found a number of reaction tendencies in regard to the problem of getting ahead: (1) The "collaborative pattern" was especially conspicuous among commercial or entrepreneurial families. (2) The "working wife pattern" was usually found among manual workers, in which both spouses had to pool their earnings to get ahead. (3) The "supportive pattern" belonged to the upper status households in which the wife saw her role as an auxiliary to her husband in a professional or business function. (4) In the "peripheral pattern" the wife perceived little if any economic or mobility function.[16]

---

[14] Locke, *op. cit.*, pp. 282–288.

[15] Williamson, *op. cit.*

[16] Robert O. Blood, Jr. and Donald M. Wolfe, *Husbands and Wives: The Dynamics of Married Living*, The Free Press of Glencoe, A Division of Collier-Macmillan, New York, 1960, p. 94.

LIFE CYCLE. To an appreciable extent, the marital and familial economic setup is focused on the life cycle. The age of the parents in relation to the generational pattern, or the ages of the children and the status of their educations, determine the climate of thinking on present and future economic matters. Generally, during the early years of marriage, if the wife is working, income is larger than expenditures. Once the furniture and other provisions are assembled the more provident couple should show a surplus. The first child usually arrives into a balanced budget economy. In the middle-class family, increases in the father's wages or salary, and an awareness of college years facing the children, results in accrual of limited savings followed by depletion of these assets during the child's college years. When the young adult children enter their own vocational lives, the parents attempt to accumulate savings to add to their retirement years. The years following age sixty-five are generally accompanied by a large drop in income. However, the stress in recent years on social security, in addition to the emphasis of unionized labor on fringe benefits and pension outlays, has drastically changed the situation from what it was a generation ago. At the same time, inflation since World War II has itself played havoc with retirement, and individuals have been forced to diversify their savings and investments to cope with this upward spiraling trend of prices. Fortunately, since the mid-1950's inflation has slowed down: between 1945 and 1950 consumer prices increased more than three times as fast as they did between 1960 and 1965.[17]

Postwar prosperity and spending habits reflect the family life cycle. The earliest months and years of marriage are mainly consumption-oriented during the setting up of a household. The middle years may be oriented toward spending or investment depending on the economic level and the success of the husband in his vocation. The motivation toward consumption or investment depends on the particular couple's philosophy of life. If the effort to secure a financial foundation was sufficiently successful there is no need, except for the individual's psychological security, for further investment and the trend shifts to consumption. Almost always consumption needs decline in the later years.

Besides age there is the economic climate of the moment, the question of health, size of the family, occupational level, and geographic considerations. Individual needs for "conspicuous consumption," to cite Veblen's term for the more elaborate display of wealth, are psycho-

[17] *Statistical Abstract, op. cit.,* p. 361.

logically necessary at middle- and upper-class levels. The restriction of
the number of children became popular in the 1920's because of the
discovery of contraceptive methods combined with a desire for a
higher standard of living. The economic depression of the 1930's further intensified this decline of the birth rate. The shift of wartime and
postwar prosperity, and the need for expressing affection as theorized
in the neo-Freudian philosophy created a new desire for parenthood
with the result that the birth rate moved upward. An inflationary
economy permitted large families with no noticeable barriers to the
standard of living as long as credit was available for deficit financing.
In the 1960's stress on the overpopulation theme as well as other
variables may drive the birth rate downward.

The economic health and style of living of the community is
another determinant of spending. The depressed areas of the South or
pockets in the Appalachians contrast with the flourishing centers of
the Southwest, and the great Northeast is intermediate. Too, the
suburban trend has given vent to diversified avenues of spending. In
some areas the second car may be a necessity, whereas the metropolitan
couple or family may find even a single automobile superfluous.

Credit expansion points to the interpretation that most individuals
are not concerned with financial security. In 1963 the average American family was $860 in debt for various installment purchases. By
March 1965 the nation was involved in $52 billion of consumer install-
ment buying.[18] The Federal Income Tax cut of 1964 inspired a new
wave of consumption expansion in the philosophy of "buy now, pay
later."

MANAGEMENT OF INCOME. Various methods have been suggested
by which the husband and wife can apportion the family finances. The
traditional pattern has been for the husband to make economic decisions, but the necessity for the wife to handle most of the purchases
because of her homemaking role and his long work week gave her the
practical role by default. Four different possibilities in the handling of
income have been suggested by Nichell and Dorsey.[19]

1. The Family Finance Budget. Here arranging a budget in terms
of given compartments (food, clothing, etc.) is the ideal. The budget
approach is suitable to some families, but generally its time-consuming

[18] *Statistical Abstract, op. cit.,* p. 470.
[19] Paulena Nichell and Jean M. Dorsey, *Management in Family Living* (third
edition), John Wiley, New York, 1959, pp. 226–230.

aspects and inflexibility, together with the unpredictability of financial outlay makes it cumbersome, however attractive it is ideally.

2. *The Allowance Method.* This approach permits the family to allocate a given amount for living expenses retaining an equal or larger amount for long-term expenses such as mortgage payments, insurance, etc. This method is especially appealing when business or professional expenses make for a somewhat irregular income.

3. *The Equal Salary or Fifty-fifty System.* The husband and wife share a salary or salaries, but beyond what is needed for the common pool of basic expenses may be spent on their own needs in whatever direction they wish. Generally, however, this surplus is divided on an equal basis. A variation of this method is the maintenance of separate accounts and meeting all expenses on a fifty-fifty basis. These systems, particularly the second, are adopted when the wife desires maximum independence, and when there are no children.

4. *The Handout Method.* Such a practice may be followed with the husband or wife in control depending on the degree of patriarchal character in the family setup. It is the antithesis of the more democratic budget system. Sometimes this system reflects lack of family unity, simply an inability to plan, or it may be attributed to ignorance about the financial aspects of the family.

Most modern marriages utilize budgets in a very approximate fashion. There is also a vague deference to the allowance method. In many instances the couple operates on a basis of calculation in broad terms that a certain number of dollars are for the essential needs of housing, food, taxes, insurance, family health needs, with a balance of a certain number of dollars to be used for recreation, travel, and social pursuits. In other words, except in the tightest family economies budgeting is flexible and not particularly articulate. Or budgeting may be followed very meticulously by the family members for a while, then relaxed until they are caught in a crisis and must return to precise economic planning. There is value in having all the family members cooperate. The child may better understand the meaning of finances if he is experienced in the ways of budgeting. Furthermore, it can be a means of bringing the members of the family closer together.

THE MAJOR OUTLAYS AND THEIR MEANING. Most families find it advantageous, and probably necessary, to analyze the allocation of their economic obligations. In the broadest sense, we can assume that

Table 15.1

AVERAGE EXPENDITURES, INCOME, AND SAVINGS OF ALL URBAN FAMILIES AND SINGLE CONSUMERS IN INDIANAPOLIS, INDIANA, 1960 AND 1950

Item	AVERAGE PER FAMILY		Per Cent Change, 1950 to 1960	PER CENT OF EXPENDITURES FOR CURRENT CONSUMPTION	
	N = 173 1960	N = 217 * 1950		1960	1950
Expenditures for current consumption †	$4,902	$3,561	37.7	100.0	100.0
Food and beverages	1,279	1,102	16.1	26.1	30.9
Tobacco	95	69	37.7	1.9	1.9
Housing, total	1,540 +	944	63.1	31.5 +	26.5
Shelter, fuel, light, refrigeration and water	960	566	69.6	19.6	15.9
Household operations	322	163	97.5	6.6	4.6
House furnishings and equipment	258	215	20.0	5.3	6.0
Clothing, materials, services	489	413	18.4	10.0	11.6
Personal care	148	80	85.0	3.0	2.2
Medical care	282	189	49.2	5.8	5.3
Recreation	195	155	25.8	4.0	4.4
Reading and education	115	51	125.5	2.3	1.4

Automobile purchase and operation	585	466	25.5	11.9	13.1
Other transportation	79	60	31.7	1.6	1.7
Other expenditures	95	32	196.9	1.9	0.9
Gifts and contributions	236	132	78.8	—	—
Personal insurance	321	156	105.8	—	—
Money income before taxes	6,502	4,260	52.6	—	—
Money income after taxes	5,652	3,863	46.3	—	—
Other money receipts	125	12	941.7	—	—
Average family size	3.0	2.8			
Per cent nonwhite families	15	15			
Per cent homeowners	53	48			
Per cent auto owners	72	59			

Source: U.S. Department of Labor, "Consumer Expenditures and Income," *BLS Report*, January, 1963, p. 2.
* From the Survey of Consumer Expenditures in 1950. See *Study of Consumer Expenditures, Incomes and Savings, Statistical Tables, Urban U.S., 1950*, University of Pennsylvania, 1956–57.
† The classification of items in the two surveys is not strictly comparable.
‡ The total may exceed the sum of the three subclasses because it includes items not listed separately in this table.

we have three basic areas of expenses: (1) consumption goods: items that will be consumed immediately, including the major outlays of food, clothing, and shelter; (2) production goods: those items contributed by the labor of the husband and wife. In former times these were the predominant economic endeavors of the family, and even today they exist, as witness the "do-it-yourself" movement. The equipment and supplies for these activities become an item of expenditure. (3) Institutional services are expenses dedicated to larger structures outside the family. Especially included are tax outlays, insurance, donations to churches and charities, and education.

As Table 15.1, based on data from a Midwestern city, suggests, housing—especially if we include furnishings, equipment, and operational expenses—has now displaced food as the major item in the American family budget. As we proceed into upper brackets the differential increases. Transportation is the third item, although not in New York, for example, because of the cheap public transportation system. Clothing may become the second or third entry in the budget if there are a large number of growing children with a heavy winter expense. Recreation is generally next. Taxes for certain income brackets can surpass all other outlays. In Table 15.1 the tendency toward deficit spending is indicated in the net change in assets and liabilities. A study of changes in the household budget over the last generation or two indicates that although all items have increased, certain allocations, such as housing and transportation, have risen at several times the rate of food and clothing.

THE ROLE OF THE CONSUMER. Today as never before, the individual can be armed with information about products and their comparative values. The *Consumer's Research Bulletin* and *Consumer Reports* contain analyses of given items in both their monthly publications and annual cumulative reports. These range from automobiles to motion pictures. The testing and rating of the various products contained in these publications may be limited to a specific model or type, but the purchaser can feel relatively confident, or at least he has some objective information on which to base his decision. Even consumer guides do not always provide the final decision, since they sometimes disagree on a given product. The place at which he makes his purchase may vary from a neighborhood store to a large discount house, which depends on quantity sales to relatively unknown customers rather than the more traditional type of business in a smaller community.

Still another factor determining consumer behavior is the analysis of costs, the desirability of separating fixed charges from operating expenses.[20] In the purchase of a car the customer should be clear on the difference between such structural items as the expected life of the car, cost of insurance, license fees and taxes as against gasoline and other ingredients, along with repairs, replacements, and parking. What seems like cheap transportation may not be far from the mileage of nine or ten cents allowed on expense accounts. Again the customer must determine, for any item, the amount of use he is likely to derive in order to know whether purchasing it is really worthwhile.

PURCHASE OF A HOUSE. Certain purchases by their very nature require considerable thought. House purchases, for example, are subject to long-term planning. Governmental insuring agencies such as the Federal Housing Authority (FHA), as well as certain state agencies, have stipulated relatively low-cost interest rates on mortgages.[21] The attractions of home owning have to be balanced with the disadvantages in a nation where one family out of five moves every year.[22] Renting has the advantage of permitting maximum mobility for the job market or the changing needs of the family. Rent is a relatively fixed sum, and is least affected by the shifting values of real estate or the increases in taxes and repairs. Owning a home provides greater pride and stability to the individual and in most communities permits a more varied selection of residences in which to live. In addition, the owner is making an investment, whereas the renter has only receipts to show for his money. Thus, barring high residential mobility, he tends to get more for his money. The majority of the nation's population own their own homes. However, among the disadvantages of home ownership are less occupational mobility, the possible deterioration of a neighborhood, and high maintenance costs. A house also may become a burden if mortgage payments do not adjust downward during depression or deflation. In almost uninterrupted prosperity (the exceptions being a few minor recessions) threatened loss of real estate values is remote. On the other hand, it is an exaggeration for the home owner to claim that

[20] Howard F. Bigelow, "Financing the Marriage," in Howard Becker and Reuben Hill, *Family, Marriage, and Parenthood,* D. C. Heath, Boston, 1955, p. 400.
[21] For particulars the reader may refer to publications of the Housing and Home Finance Agency obtainable through the Superintendent of Documents, U.S. Government Printing Office, Washington D.C.
[22] Donald J. Bogue, *The Population of the United States,* The Free Press of Glencoe, A Division of Collier-Macmillan, New York, 1959, p. 376.

once the mortgage is paid off he has free or nearly free rent. He has to determine what the value of his original investment of $15,000 or $25,000 would be if it had been gaining 4½ per cent interest through the years. By calculating total cost he is probably ahead.

Some of the considerations in purchasing a home are style, floor plan, quality of construction (for which technical advice should be sought), and cost of maintenance. Other questions include the following: What is the character of the neighborhood? Care should be exercised not to select a home overbuilt for its neighborhood as some loss will probably be incurred on resale. Does the house really meet the long-term needs of the family? The needs for the children are not the same at eight years as they are at eighteen. A whole set of questions arise about the developmental needs of the children. Is there a satisfactory school in the area? What kind of children, if any at all, may be his playmates? The socialization of the child should be carefully considered, and too isolated an area may prove to be confining or require considerable transportation service on the part of the parent. Finally, in the acquisition process, besides carefully investigating the true worth of the house—"asking prices" are often notoriously inflated— the potential buyer should be very cautious in his search for the best financing. Again, "shopping around" for credit may be a good idea. Among other things, he should check as to whether there is a penalty clause for prepayment of the loan.

CREDIT. Because of the amount of borrowing in our society, this topic invites a note of caution. The average person tends to live on a risky margin. Three alternatives for purchasing on credit are: (1) *open* charge accounts and *credit cards,* which are without cost to the consumer except for interest at fairly high rates on the unpaid balance; (2) *revolving* charge accounts, or setting up a budget beyond which the individual may not go (20 per cent of total income); (3) *installment credit,* which is the most familiar type of purchasing. To receive any of these, the individual must establish a *credit rating.* Although the advantages of these facilities are enormously tempting, extension of credit is dangerous. For example, with the revolving charge account some consumers feel that they must use up the maximum even when the item purchased is not essential.

Credit instruments, in addition to the installment-sales contract, can be divided into the following: [23]

[23] Nichell and Dorsey, *op. cit.,* pp. 292–295.

1. The Promissory Note. This represents an unconditional promise to pay an individual or organization within a given date (most frequently with a 60 or 90 day limit) and rate of interest specified.

2. The Collateral Note. A tangible asset as a security is provided, and the note usually runs for a longer period than the promissory note.

3. Real Estate and Chattel Mortgages. These are also defined as types of mortgage secured with a deed to property or to "goods and effects," respectively. In other words, security may be in the form of certain jewelry or an automobile. Incidentally, we may mention the possibility of bonds, which are loans to an established enterprise or the government. Although they function in the family as investments, they are technically a credit instrument.

For the purpose of most individuals and families alternate methods of securing loans come from several sources, such as the following:

1. Small Loan Companies. The disadvantage of these is the high interest rate, which varies from 2 to 3 per cent interest per month in most states, or 24 to 36 per cent per year.

2. Illegal Loan Companies. These companies charge still higher rates of interest and, to a greater degree than the legitimate loan companies, do not allow for reduction of the principal. Seldom are interest charges satisfactorily explained to the purchaser, as the purchase of a new or used car so often demonstrates. In certain states laws are sufficiently lax that abuses by quasilegal loan companies approach criminal behavior.

3. Bank Loans. These have a more favorable rate of interest, often 5 to 8 per cent per annum, particularly when collateral is available. For a promissory note a cosigner is usually required. Where no collateral or cosigner is offered, bank loans are discounted, that is, interest is deducted in advance. This amounts to a higher rate of interest, because it is based on the entire amount of the loan throughout the loan period. The rate of interest will often amount to between 12 and 20 per cent. Still, the bank is a more favorable source than most commercial lending agencies.

4. Life Insurance Loans. Such loans are made with an insurance policy as collateral. In most respects these loans function in the same way as a bank loan. The maximum interest rate is 5 per cent in most states, as opposed to higher rates permissible some years earlier. The major problem here is the reduction of the effective insurance by the size of the loan consequently entailing risk to the beneficiary. Findings indicate that most policy loans are never repaid, but rather are ultimately deducted from the amount payable on maturity of the policy.[24]

5. *Credit Unions.* These institutions have been the most helpful development over the last third of a century. The average credit union is small—the median for these is less than $100,000 in assets—yet in the United States there are more than 1,500 million-dollar unions.[25] Through various institutions—the corporation, labor union, governmental agency, church, club—members are invited to participate in a cooperative approach to credit facilities. In the most efficient credit unions the borrower may secure money at 5 or 5½ per cent interest, with the lender receiving 4½ to 5 per cent return on his investment. As nearly as possible, profit and overhead are eliminated with mutual advantage to both debtor and creditor. Credit unions now number 21,000, with some 13 million members, and hold more than 10 per cent of all installment credit outstanding.[26] There could be twice the number of unions in the country with no danger of saturation.

These methods of securing credit have been listed to introduce the variety of sources available. When a major loan is contemplated the variety of fees, interest rates, and length of payment should be investigated. In addition, the individual in need of funds may or may not have other sources, such as salary advances or loans from friends or relatives. The precariousness of certain procedures is obvious.

THE PROBLEM OF ECONOMIC SECURITY

Evidence shows with little doubt that a minimum of economic tension provides a healthy framework to marriage. In a study of 210

---

[24] Milton J. Goldberg, "Nonforfeiture Values and Policy Loans," in Davis W. Gregg (ed.), *Life and Health Insurance Handbook,* Richard D. Irwin, Homewood, Illinois, 1959, p. 119.

[25] John T. Croteau, *The Economics of the Credit Union,* Wayne State University Press, Detroit, 1963.

[26] *Ibid.*

couples in Los Angeles this generalization was well established. Among the indices reflecting this relationship were: [27]

1. Average Monthly Income of $445 or More.   This and other figures should be interpreted in light of the year of the investigation (1950). Individuals with higher incomes are apparently more able to cope with life's problems. Also a higher income may mean that individuals of a more secure economic level have a higher educational attainment that makes possible both higher marital adjustment and larger income.

2. Residential Area.   Middle- and upper-middle class neighborhoods were marked by happier marriages than lower class areas. As with other factors, these possibly are contingency rather than causative relationships.

3. Home Ownership as Opposed to Renting.   Residential stability versus mobility; mobility is interpreted as moving two or more times during the last three years.

4. Amount of Savings of $600 or more.   Indebtedness of less than $300.

5. Life insurance of over $5,000.   These findings imply that security provides a milieu in which marriage and family relationships are less anxiety ridden.

Other studies have shown a relationship between the security and management factors and marital success. Among these is Locke's report of a happily married sample and a divorced one. Home ownership, life insurance, savings, and the presence of appliances and status symbols (from a radio to an electric washer) produced a positive relationship. The regularity of the husband's employment, adequacy of income, and ability to borrow, that is, satisfactory credit rating, were all favorable factors.[28] Again, variables making for divorce may be the same ones that cause financial mismanagement. Yet the evidence remains that a sound economy is propitious to marital contentment.

Economic security or insecurity itself may be a kind of personality syndrome. There is clinical literature on the compulsive spender who is unable to control what he spends. And there is the psychopathic

[27] Williamson, *op. cit.*
[28] Locke, *op. cit.,* pp. 275–288.

gambler who may lose his money over the poker table or choose the slightly more long-range policy of unwise investments or speculative binges. Consumption may also take the form of an impulsive buyer who reaches too high with the installment plan or the credit card. Other variations include the ritualistic buyer who ponders infinitely over each acquisition—found almost exclusively among women. Some people cannot spend because of frugal impulses. The hoarder may feel insecure unless he has savings or investments far beyond the norm of his income bracket.

These labels point to personality variations that determine our habit systems of spending and saving. Unfortunately most people find the role of the freely spending consumer more pleasurable than the conservative pattern. Yet the married couple must give some attention to future security. On the investment side, the alternatives include depositing funds in credit unions, buying "blue chip" stocks and mutual funds, and property acquisition in expanding parts of the country (or ideally, a combination of all these). The average person finds this kind of an investment program difficult, or at least too ambitious for meeting emergencies. Insurance becomes the most practical means of protecting the family against catastrophe.

THE "LOWEST FOURTH" AND ECONOMIC DURESS. Although middle-class family economies function with relative security and no overwhelming problems, possibly a fourth of the population cannot hope to achieve minimal standards in the use of their incomes. Minimal budgets include: [29]

1. Basic subsistence, no movies or recreational expenditure, practically a meatless diet, no medical or dental budget, little new clothing, slum existence, etc. In 1965 this included incomes averaging around $3,300.

2. Minimum health and decency—an occasional movie, lower cuts of meat periodically, limited medical and dental care, extremely modest housing, etc., incomes above $4,000.

3. Minimum comfort—adequacy of diet, occasional recreational or culture outlets, etc., incomes of $5,500, still below the $6,200 median of the nation for the year 1963. More than 10 per cent earned in 1962 only enough to meet basic subsistence levels; approximately 30 per

[29] Robert Bierstedt, Eugene J. Meehan, and Paul A. Samuelson, *Modern Social Science,* McGraw-Hill, New York, 1964, p. 442; also *Statistical Abstract, op. cit.,* p. 344.

cent earned less than the needs of the minimum comfort budget. The greatest number of these families are found among the urban proletariat of unskilled manual workers, marginal farmers, and migratory workers. They are usually individuals who have been deprived of normal opportunity because of skin color and educational or health reasons.[30] The argument that the stagnation or lower mobility of these individuals is partially due to lack of incentive begs the question of the causative process. Social deprivation is a fact that cannot be escaped. That the socialization process, personality training, or education might have been different for these people can be argued, but the point remains that the middle-class bias is irrelevant.

Although the causation of economic disorganization in the family has been elusive, some suggestion of the factors involved are given by a study of stable versus unstable families within a housing project.[31] The unstable families were younger, married fewer years, and had 3.9 children versus 2.7 for the stable. However, a basic problem among the unstable families was the "lack of commitment to significant values of society." [32] The behavior of certain low-income families appears to be different from the kinds of cooperation and discipline expected of members of most social organizations. This is exemplified in the tendency toward early marriages, having children, followed by marital separation and still more children. "They pledge little, if any, allegiance to any reference group." [33] Their lives are relatively unregulated and uncontrolled.

The effects of poverty on married and family life were acutely apparent in Komarovsky's "blue collar" sample of 58 families. Among those families making less than $3,500 there was anxiety and self scrutiny about why they had failed. Bills constantly plagued them, and major disagreements resulted from decisions on priority of payment for the milk bill so that the children could eat or whether to pay the electricity bill so as not to be without light. The threat of illness was another preoccupation. Other strains were fear of pregnancy, sharing residence with relatives so as to make ends meet, and retreat of some

[30] Harrington, *op. cit.*
[31] Charles V. Willie and Janet Weinandy, "The Structure and Composition of 'Problem' and 'Stable' Families in a Low-Income Population," *Marriage and Family Living*, 1963, 25, 439–447.
[32] *Ibid.*, p. 443.
[33] *Ibid.*

husbands to a bar or tavern apparently as a means of escape from the sense of frustration.[34]

Research has shown that these families tend to pool all their wages, including the adolescents, beyond the usual degree expected in the middle-class family. Only rarely does one member retain his earnings for his exclusive use.[35] Studies of the Depression of 1930–1935, which reached its lowest point in late 1932, showed the varieties of adjustment a family might have to make to the complete loss of earnings. Angell found in his study that there were two variables enabling these 50 families to weather the economic catastrophe: *integration,* the degree to which the family members were interdependent and unified, and *adaptability,* the capacity for adjustment to change, which proved an even more important characteristic.[36]

LIFE INSURANCE

Disability, death, or old age are problems we must all face. Insurance is expensive, but there is no alternative except other investments that may provide a ready means of income in case of a financial crisis. In fact the individuals who claim they can least afford insurance are those who need it the most, which is the greater part of the United States population. The average American family has only sufficient insurance to provide continuance of the wage earner's salary to the family for one year in case of death.[37] The basic types of life insurance (Table 15.2) include

1. Term Insurance. This form of insurance represents the cheapest form of protection but also the least permanent in regard to security. The disadvantage of term insurance is that it must be renewed every five years at progressively higher rates. The only obligation the insurer has to the client is the payment to the beneficiary, in contrast to the advantages of investment type of policy. An advantage of term insurance, however, is temporary protection in the early years of marriage.

---

[34] Mirra Komarovsky, *Blue-Collar Marriage,* Random House, New York, 1964, pp. 288f.

[35] Hazel Kyrk, *The Family in the American Economy,* The University of Chicago Press, 1953, p. 101.

[36] Robert C. Angell, *The Family Encounters the Depression,* Charles Scribner's Sons, New York, 1936.

[37] Kyrk, *op. cit.,* pp. 191–194.

Table 15.2

PREMIUM RATES PER $1,000 CHARGED BY A LEADING
NONPARTICIPATING INSURER FOR SOME REPRESENTATIVE
CONTRACTS

Age	Five-Year Term	Straight Life	Paid up at 65	Twenty-Pay Life	Endowment at 65	Twenty-Year Endowment
25	$ 6.31	$15.73	$17.43	$17.43	$20.59	$46.12
35	7.32	21.30	25.03	32.92	29.82	46.88
45	11.76	31.08	41.51	41.51	49.57	49.57
55	23.97	47.32	88.23	54.51	. . .	56.42

Source: C. Arthur Williams, Jr., "Contracts," in Davis W. Gregg (ed.), *Life and Health Insurance Handbook,* Richard D. Irwin, Homewood, Illinois, 1959, p. 34.

Later, when the insured has sufficient assets or investments or when the house is nearly paid for and the children have about completed their education, the policy may be canceled. In fact, its very disadvantage is heavy cost with the advancing years of the insured. Generally the cost of term insurance is less than half that of ordinary life policies, and at age twenty-five, as can be seen in Table 15.2, it is only a sixth of what a twenty-year endowment policy would cost, but there is no cash value to the policy. Much of the decision to continue term insurance or any form of insurance may depend on the degree to which the individual has built up profitable investments. Some men who are successful in finding securities yielding a high per cent of return may prefer to buy term insurance rather than more expensive insurance, and consequently place more funds in their investment program with growth securities. In other words, the husband can take care of the basic family emergency and yet realize more profit and growth through some other economic program.

Most term insurance is convertible under certain circumstances; the client does not have to submit to another physical examination. As a macabre note, it may be added that term insurance is the most economical for one who is certain he will die during the term of the insurance. Curiously, the mortality rate is 13 per cent higher with term policies than with other forms of life insurance.[38] Most group policies

[38] William T. Beadles, "Contracts—Term Insurance," in Gregg, *op. cit.,* p. 27.

are term, because the interested company wants to secure maximum protection for its employees and obtain preferential group rates.

2. *Whole, Straight, or Ordinary Life Insurance.*   Such a policy represents the most economical and the common permanent policy. The face value and the premium remains the same throughout the life of the policy. Unlike term insurance, the policy has loan and cash surrender values and more flexible convertibility. As with all policies, premiums are determined on the basis of the Table of Mortality and are carefully regulated by law in at least forty-five states. In fact, the insurance industry is governed by the Federal Trade Commission in cases where state laws are not sufficiently stringent.

3. *Limited Payment Life.*   This type of policy emphasizes the saving aspects more than the straight life policy does. It stipulates an end to the premiums after ten, twenty, or thirty years, generally at age sixty-five, but the policy remains in effect. In other words, limited payment policies are designed to provide for protection in the years when the income is reduced. As interest accruing on the savings component is not taxable for the year in which it is credited; this policy is especially useful for men of above average income. It is primarily a savings type of contract and is more expensive than the ordinary policy, as suggested in Table 15.2.

4. *Endowment Policies.*   Such policies are for the purpose, if the insured survives, of providing funds after a given period—usually twenty years. Yet they may be for shorter or longer periods. These policies combine insurance with endowment but as two separate functions. They function more frequently as a form of retirement income than as insurance. One variation is a juvenile endowment policy maturing at a designated age, such as eighteen, for educational purposes. In some instances the premiums may be on the limited payment plan although they generally are on a straight-line plan.

As an investment the endowment policy has its merits, but with the inflationary tendency since World War II insurance now serves essentially an emergency function. More dynamic programs such as stock acquisition or even some building and loan concerns offer a higher return on the investment. On the other hand, if a person is inclined to spend, he may find an "enforced" savings plan like endowment insurance the discipline he needs.

HEALTH INSURANCE

A major problem in contemporary American society is the high cost of health protection and care. With steeply rising medical and hospital costs through the years, many feel that the United States has not met the challenge of successful plans in other countries. Governmental aid to provide health and medical security to the low-income groups, or at least to those over sixty-five, seems to many observers to be quite necessary. Except for Blue Cross and Blue Shield plans, which offer only limited coverage, medical and health plans are few and far between.

For years there has been medical, hospital, and accident insurance. However, all but the most expensive policies cover only limited situations, and because of high cost they have been prohibitive to that part of the public most in need. Contributory group plans have long existed in the United States. The Southern Pacific Railroad had a plan as early as 1868, which provided doctor's care for their employees at home, in the company's offices, or in a hospital.[39] Since that time a growing number of corporations have offered their employees health services for considerably reduced fees. Much of the impetus for health plans have come from labor unions. Generally labor organizations have insisted on the following four phases of care: preventive, diagnostic, therapeutic, and rehabilitative.[40] At the present time twenty million workers receive protection although plans do not have all the features that are ideally desirable. Blue Cross and Blue Shield, organized by the American Hospital Association and the American Medical Association respectively, dominate the scene nationally, often under contracts originally made to labor affiliates.

By 1962 there were seventy-eight Blue Cross plans, organized mostly on a geographic basis, operating in the United States. Blue Cross is designed to relieve the family of large hospital bills and primarily functions on a group basis through employers or unions. Blue Shield, or the physician service, offers three kinds of plans: (1) full service contracts entitling the subscriber to complete payment directly to the physician, (2) cash benefits to the subscriber for a designated sched-

---

[39] Nickell and Dorsey, *op. cit.*, p. 492.
[40] Joseph F. Follmann, Jr., *Medical Care and Health Insurance*, Richard D. Irwin, Homewood, Illinois, 1963, p. 474.

ule of procedures, (3) a combination of these plans partially dependent on the individual's salary limits. The advantage of these
plans is that they are an attempt to deal with the extreme emergency
costs. Because the scheme is countrywide the subscriber can enjoy the
service anywhere in the United States. The problems are: established
ceilings for each type of surgery or service, lack of services not covered
by the plan, coverage only for certain types of services, and inattention
to preventive care. The patient also generally has to be treated three
times by a given doctor before his coverage begins. Fortunately many
employers contribute supplementary help through "major medical"
plans. Although both Blue Cross and Blue Shield offer family coverage, they do not include children of nineteen years or more.

COMMUNITY AND INDUSTRIAL HEALTH PLANS.   A number of communities of the United States have health plans oriented around industry group facilities, which are also generally available to individual
subscribers and their dependents. The largest and most famous of
these is the Kaiser Foundation Health Plan which began during the
war in connection with Kaiser shipyards. In 1964 it had over 900,000
members on the Pacific Coast, most of whom subscribed as members of
government agencies, labor unions, and professional organizations.
One advantage of such a plan is the diversity of services (often in a
single building) and the total coverage by both medical care and hospitalization to the subscriber and his dependents. In addition to the
annual, quarterly, or monthly fees, which, in many other health plans
can be deducted from the pay check, there is a nominal fee of $2.00
collected at each visit. The Kaiser Foundation insists that organizations presenting the plan to their employees offer rival plans (such as,
for instance, the Ross-Loos Medical Group or Blue Cross–Blue Shield)
and some variation in the extent of coverage for the client and his
family. Most subscribers, according to one informal survey, were satisfied with the service despite a certain impersonality implicit in any
group approach to medical care.

Other variations include the Health Insurance Plan of Greater New
York for both group and individual memberships. There are certain
cooperative ventures, such as the Group Health Association in Washington, D.C. or the Group Health Cooperative of Puget Sound.

PRIVATE HEALTH INSURANCE.   For decades various kinds of medical,
hospital, and accident insurance policies have been available to the
public. Two principles have been incorporated into these programs,

whether in the same policy or separately: (1) funds for major medical expense, especially hospital, and (2) compensation for employment loss. The provisions and the premiums of the policies vary according to the length of hospitalization, for the limits of surgeons' fees, number of visits by the physician, the amount of physiotherapy, and cost of medicines covered. Accident policies stress hospitalization costs and often include lump sums for certain varieties of injuries and reimbursement for lost wages or salary. In some instances the policy is "permanent" with no increase in the cost premium, more often to age sixty-five; in other instances it is renewable intermittently with higher premiums. Certain very inexpensive policies require periodic physicals to qualify. The lengthier and more complete the coverage, the higher the premium. The difficulty with any satisfactory policy is its expense and, as we have already noted, individuals with the most critical need are the ones least likely to be able to afford the policy. As with all insurance policies, the consumer must be especially wary of the product that promises too much, is sensationally advertised, or where high advertising or publicity costs point indirectly to potential high profits. A few states are lax in licensing procedures regarding health and life insurance. Fortunately, the growth of community health plans and the Blue Cross and Blue Shield, despite their limitations, have made the practice of holding private policies less of a necessity.

HEALTH PROGRAMS FOR THE AGED. As of 1960, 16.5 million (or 9.2 per cent) of our population were sixty-five years or older, a proportion that will become higher with increased longevity due to the continuing rise in standards of health and medicine. One of the most unpleasant aspects of old age is the inadequacy of medical care. In a California study of persons sixty-five or older it was found that more than a third of the sample received no medical attention, presumably because of the inability to pay for such services.[41] Another study revealed that for persons over age sixty-five, 6.8 visits to the doctor per person were reported annually.[42] Elderly people become progressively more incapacitated. For example, whereas patients of between sixty-five and seventy-five years of age were more predictably found in hospitals, those from ages seventy-five to eighty-five were more often in nursing homes. In the age bracket over sixty-five there is a higher incidence

---

[41] Peter O. Steiner and Robert Dorfman, *The Economic Status of the Aged,* University of California Press, Berkeley and Los Angeles, 1957, pp. 142–145.

[42] Follmann, *op. cit.,* p. 155.

of chronic disabilities, and as these people become long-term care problems they are more often shifted to custodial care.

With the amendments to the Social Security Act in 1965, the federal government adopted a program of health insurance for those individuals of sixty-five years or older. The services include a maximum of 60 days of hospitalization for a given illness—in addition to visits or day care by nurses—physicians' and surgeons' services, diagnostic tests, and certain types of medical aids. This insurance is voluntary, and each recipient pays $3.00 monthly.

The problem of old age has not yet been solved either sociologically or economically or perhaps even adequately faced by the law makers of the United States. Although retirement benefits have been increased within private enterprise and as a result of the social security system, inflation means that a lag is inevitable. The interest in senior citizens has been well focused on the provision of facilities, but long-range education to cope with this problem has been only partially success-ful. Even with the almost insurmountable barriers of the rigidity of old age, some means will have to be found to train elderly people in social and recreational skills by which some life direction in old age can be found. Even then, the basic problem of inadequate economic provision remains for that time of life when health problems are the most acute and society furnishes little status or role. The solutions to this problem go well beyond the purpose of this textbook. At the family level it is difficult to resolve this dilemma and to make this age group feel wanted, and yet not have them interfere with the activities of the younger generation.

SOCIAL SECURITY AND THE FAMILY

Probably no single action has had as much effect on the relationship of the family to the elderly as the adoption of old age benefits and other social security services by federal and state governments. Social welfare legislation has symbolized the extent to which we have rede-fined the significance of old age and of all individuals with disabilities. The philosophy of *laissez-faire* economics is dead. However, the obliga-tion of society and the individual family to the aged is a problem that has not been truly resolved.

In 1935 Congress voted the Social Security Act which became effec-tive on January 1, 1937, some fifty years after Western European countries had adopted a similar program. There are several aspects of this program, but of greatest interest is Old Age and Survivors Insurance. Its original purpose was to protect the individual worker, but by 1939 the purpose shifted to the family as a unit. In fact, several major changes, in addition to innumerable minor ones, have occurred since the plan's inception. The focus of these changes has been on protecting the widest number of individuals as compared to the original eight million people who first came under the act in 1937. The amendments have brought under the provisions of the act employees of educational and religious associations, agricultural workers, servants; in fact all self-employed individuals who earn a net profit of at least $4,000 per year, including personnel firms, businesses, and the professions. As of 1963, 14.2 million Americans received Social Security benefits.[43] For a male retiree the monthly check may be as high as $135, and with a wife and dependent children the maximum is $312. Under the 1965 revision these amounts will be increased in future years.

Despite its universality, many Americans are unaware of the stipulations of the act. Each employee has 4.3 per cent deducted from his earnings up to a maximum of $6,600. In addition, his employer makes an equal contribution. This amount will eventually increase to more than 5 per cent. The self-employed individual currently pays 5¼ per cent. As a governmental commitment, the Security Act has been modified to include disability benefits at age fifty in lieu of the normal retirement benefits at age sixty-five; wives, widows, or female workers may apply at age sixty, and children (under twenty-two years of age) of the deceased parent may receive benefits. There are aid programs for the various age groups including a number of disabilities, blindness among others.

In addition to the federal government program, practically all the states have a program of old age assistance. Much of the impetus of the federal act was inspired by programs within twenty-eight states and the two territories.[44] Presently the federal government subsidizes the state jurisdictions in aid to the aged. Generally the laws have been liberalized so individuals no longer have to depend exclusively on their relatives, nor are they ineligible for aid simply because of the presence of relatives who might contribute. However, support by the children is highly encouraged and is deducted from the amount of

[43] *Statistical Abstract, op. cit.,* p. 288.
[44] Kyrk, *op. cit.,* p. 220.

state aid. In a number of states relatives no longer have legal responsibility. Cash payment is based on a "budget-deficiency" basis, and in a few states the dollar amount is actually stated in the law. In others an administrator or case worker may use discretion, so there is a large chance for error and bias. Of particular interest to the welfare of the family is federal government aid to children with physical, intellectual, emotional, or social handicaps, in addition to judicial protection.[45] Since 1944 Canada has had a major family allowance program by which aid is given to lower income families to meet the costs of rearing children. Approximately a third of Canadian families have received help (the monthly allotment for the average child amounted to $6.69 in 1953) from birth through age 15.[46] For Canada the system has meant not only an increase in schooling and a decrease in child labor, but an expanded birth rate and reduced infant mortality.

This discussion of various economic problems suggests that the couples entering marriage today find many positive economic features as compared to those encountered by their great grandfathers. America has less of an economic frontier than it did in 1870, yet there are problems within a quasiwelfare society. A tremendous range of occupational roles is available, in which the individual must place himself. How successfully he does this is relevant to marital adjustment.

Levels of income and the pattern of consumption habits determine the degree to which a given family may feel economic security. Some balance between insurance for basic security and investments for economic growth is the goal of most families. Health and medical care and provision for the aged remain major problems. All these questions are more acute if there are children in the family or on the way, a subject to which we now turn.

Supplementary Readings

"American Poverty in the Mid-Sixties," *Journal of Marriage and the Family*, 1964, 26, 389–497. Various marital and family problems resulting from economic stress.

[45] Dorothy Zietz, *Child Welfare: Principles and Methods*, John Wiley, New York, 1959.
[46] Bernice Madison, "Canadian Family Allowances and Their Major Social Implications," *Journal of Marriage and the Family*, 1964, 26, 134–141.

Angell, Robert C., *The Family Encounters the Depression*, Charles Scribner's Sons, New York, 1936. An intensive study of the adjustment of 50 families to economic stress.

Bigelow, Howard F., *Family Finance* (revised edition), J. B. Lippincott, Philadelphia, 1953. A discussion of, among other things, consumption habits, insurance possibilities, and the family life cycle.

Blood, Robert O. Jr., and Donald M. Wolfe, *Husbands and Wives: The Dynamics of Married Living*, The Free Press of Glencoe, A Division of Collier-Macmillan, New York, 1960. Chapters 3 and 4 report the occupational and financial problems of a Detroit sample.

Cavan, Ruth S. (ed.), *Marriage and Family in the Modern World* (second edition), Thomas Y. Crowell, New York, 1965. Chapters 2, 12, and 13 contain some excellent readings on family income and finances.

Croteau, John T., *The Economics of the Credit Union*, Wayne State University Press, Detroit, 1963. An exploration of the economics of a most important social invention for borrowing or investment.

Gregg, Davis W. (ed.), *Life and Health Insurance Handbook*, Richard D. Irwin, Homewood, Illinois, 1959. Although occasionally on the technical side, this work is possibly the most complete treatment of the subject available to the student.

Komarovsky, Mirra, *Blue-Collar Marriage*, Random House, New York, 1964. A report of depth interviews with 58 lower status workers and their wives.

Kyrk, Hazel, *The Family in the American Economy*, The University of Chicago Press, 1963. Income, social security, consumption, and living costs are covered in a thoroughly scholarly fashion.

Nickell, Paulena and Jean M. Dorsey, *Management in Family Living* (third edition), John Wiley, New York, 1959. Two home economists write of the management of income and the household. Part 3 is especially relevant.

Packard, Vance, *The Waste Makers*, David McKay, New York, 1960. Consumption in contemporary society as seen by this prolific writer of best sellers.

Troelstrop, Arch W., *Consumer Problems* (second edition), McGraw-Hill, New York, 1957. A textbook on questions of budgeting, efficient buying practices, insurance, and credit.

"Women and Work," *Marriage and Family Living*, 1961, **23,** 325–387. A series of articles on the occupational roles of women and the relation of work to marriage.

Chapter sixteen

Becoming Parents

Man is for woman a means: the end is always the child.
> *Friedrich W. Nietzsche,* Thus Spake Zarathustra, *XVIII, 1885.*

No man is so virtuous as to marry a wife only to have children.
> *Martin Luther:* Table-Talk, *CCLVII, 1569.*

A woman's body belongs to herself alone . . . and [she] has the right to dispose of herself, to withhold herself, to procreate or suppress the germ of life.
> *Margaret Sanger, as cited by Morton M. Hunt,* The Natural History of Love, *Alfred A. Knopf, New York, 1959, p. 348.*

The Bath by Mary Cassatt
Courtesy of The Art Institute of Chicago; Robert A. Waller Fund

M ost married couples want children. In 1962 only 14.8 per cent of married women in the age group of fifteen to forty-four were childless. In fact, 90 per cent of women in their thirties, who reflect the high marriage and birth rate of the immediate postwar period, were mothers.[1]

Society regards procreation and socialization as the major functions of the family. In most societies the family is highly organized and controlled regarding this reproductive function. The family guarantees to society the replacement of its population. In this chapter we first discuss the social factors involved in procreation so as to understand the significance of reproduction in its broader societal perspective. *Fertility*, in sociological terms, refers to the actual procreation of offspring, whereas the term *fecundity* is the capacity for procreation.

Family planning is also examined in conjunction with the controversial question of contraception, the physical process of reproduction —encompassing both pregnancy and the birth process itself—and the psychological and social reactions to this event. Among other problems, infertility, artificial insemination, and adoption are relevant. This chapter treats the concepts of reproduction, pregnancy, parenthood, and contraception as varied and critical roles in marriage.

TRENDS IN REPRODUCTION

Western society has been moving in the long-term direction of a reduced childbirth rate despite occasional irregularities resulting from depression and postwar prosperity. There was a marked increase in birth rate of the mid- and late 1940's, which was preceded by a slight upturn in 1936. It surged further upward during and after World War II, and remained unexpectedly high for more than a decade after the war. By the late 1950's it became stabilized and in the 1960's a slight decline was perceptible. However, to get a perspective on the birth rate, let us move backward in time.

Historically, the American birth rate has been on the decline for at least a century and a half. For example, birth rates were three and a half times as high in 1800 as in 1930.[2] The average white woman in

---

[1] *Statistical Abstract of the United States,* U.S. Bureau of the Census, Washington, D.C.: Government Printing Office, 1964, p. 54.

[2] Conrad Taueber and Irene B. Taueber, *The Changing Population of the United States,* John Wiley, 1958, p. 251.

1910 had produced 5.4 children as compared to approximately 8 for Colonial times.[3] We have no accurate data on births before the census of 1910. However, it is estimated that the birth rate was 40 live births per thousand population in 1800 and dropped to approximately 30 in 1900. The process of industrialization and urbanization during the nineteenth century was a major factor in this transition. Children were no longer economic assets in the city. We must remember, too, that an enormous decline in the death rate occurred during the nineteenth century, the rate being estimated at 17.2 per thousand for the United States in 1900.[4] Infant and childhood mortality also declined markedly. As the death rate decreased, there was less need to replace the infants and children who had died. Concurrently, the number of potential mothers increased. Consequently, from the viewpoints of the individual and society replacement needs were less stringent. Moreover, church records point to a moderate upgrading of the age at marriage during the nineteenth century. The later age at marriage had a negative effect on the birth rate, as it reduced the number of productive years during which women could give birth. Other miscellaneous factors also operated to reduce the birth rate, for example, vulcanization of rubber in the middle of the nineteenth century, making possible mechanical contraceptive appliances, was a contributing factor.

Following the turn of the century another visible decline in the birth rate took place. The birth rate for 1910 was 30.1, dropping to 21.3 in 1930, to 18.4 in 1933, to generally above 23 for the years beginning with 1946.[5] Several factors account for this process of decline: (1) Industrialization and urbanization, initiated in the nineteenth century, increased at a rapid pace. (2) The diffusion of birth control methods reached a high point during the years following World War I, permitting reasonably "safe" intercourse. (3) The style of the times encouraged small families. For instance, the trend toward apartments and other multifamily dwellings, as in the city flat or duplex, became popular. (4) The strongly downward trend of the 1920's plunged even further in the Depression when acute economic stress required limitation in family size.

[3] Wilson H. Grabill, Clyde V. Kiser, and Pascal K. Whelpton, *The Fertility of American Women*, John Wiley, New York, 1958, p. 22.

[4] Donald J. Bogue, *The Population of the United States*, The Free Press of Glencoe, A Division of Collier-Macmillan, New York, 1959, p. 174; Taueber and Taueber, *op. cit.*, p. 271.

[5] Grabill, et al., *op. cit.*, p. 26.

The birth rate reached its lowest point in 1933, and by 1936 there was a significant rise. It is intriguing to speculate about whether the increase in births was attributable only to the improvement in economic conditions or whether part of the upsurge was due to the suspicion of population decline and the fear of extinction of certain family lines. In any case, it seems that when the birth rate reaches a certain low point there is only one direction it can take, and that is upward (although in the case of Ireland a hundred-year decline seems only now to be interrupted).

The outbreak of war in Europe in 1939 was reflected perceptibly in the birth rate of the United States. As we became economically, and to a lesser extent, militarily involved during 1940 and 1941, the birth rate jumped higher. After Pearl Harbor further increase was registered, reaching 22.7 in 1943. With complete participation of the American people and the movement of troops into foreign areas during 1943 and 1944, the rate dropped to 20.4 in 1945. After the cessation of hostilities and return of troops in late 1945 and early 1946 the birth rate reached its highest point in decades, namely 26.6 in 1947.[6] It remained relatively high on account of the postwar prosperity and the predilection for large families. The idea of three or possibly four children was considered desirable instead of the Depression limitation of one or two. Whether the current concern over the "population explosion" will become a deterrent factor remains to be seen. It is difficult to know whether young people or potential parents are motivated by abstract and seemingly remote factors. Living space will also become a problem if we are to maintain present standards. It does appear that family planning is affected by peer groups. If our friends have three children there is psychological pressure to equal their family size.

DETERMINANTS OF FERTILITY

Social, economic, and various cultural factors—quite as much as individual preferences—influence reproductive trends. In many directions our behavior is shaped consciously but more often unconsciously or indirectly by traditions within Western culture. In fact, we have already alluded to the historical configurations influencing the birth rate according to the situation in which society finds itself (peace or war,

[6] *Ibid.*

prosperity or depression, or the psychological style of the times). Ideologies are relevant; Fascist Italy and Nazi Germany emphasized reproduction for national aggrandizement and military programs. The present trend is toward checking population growth as a means of raising the standard of living and reducing national and personal frustration. Japan offers perhaps the most dramatic example of restraining population growth. Approximately half of the conceptions in that country terminate in legal abortions.[7]

In this section we are interested in a few determinant influences on reproduction in the broad socio-cultural context.

CLASS DIFFERENTIALS. It has been known for many decades that socio-economic status is a determining factor in child-birth rates. A study of a county in the New York State Census of 1865 revealed that birth rates could be patterned according to given socio-economic categories. White-collar workers had a higher rate than skilled workers, who in turn outproduced the unskilled. A similar situation prevailed among the rural population, farm owners having more children than their tenants.[8] The twentieth-century surveys have emphasized the influence of such differentials as education, occupation, and income. Evidence now indicates that these differentials are waning but still visible; the 1950 data, for instance, pointed to clerical and service workers falling below professionals, for instance.[9]

Some of the long-term changes in the relation of occupations to birth rates can be seen in Table 16.1. The working class discovered the principles of family limitation in the postwar years, and the upper white-collar class has perceived larger families as being desirable. Although birth rates are not yet equal between the classes, these differences have been reduced. There has been some merging of our socio-economic culture, especially in the last twenty years.

An educational differential also exists. For example, there is an inverse relationship between finishing high school and the number of children anticipated.[10] The number of children born per 1,000 mar-

[7] Yoshio Koya, "Why Induced Abortions in Japan Remain High," in Clyde V. Kiser (ed.), *Research in Family Planning*, Princeton University Press, 1962, pp. 103–110.

[8] Wendell Bash, "Differential Fertility in Madison County, New York, 1865," *Milbank Memorial Fund Quarterly*, 1955, 33, 161–186.

[9] Grabill, et al., *op. cit.*, p. 160.

[10] Ronald Freedman, David Goldberg, and Doris Slesinger, "Current Fertility Expectations of Married Couples in the United States," *Population Index*, 1963, 20, 366–391.

Table 16.1

NUMBER OF CHILDREN EVER BORN PER 1000 MARRIED
WOMEN, 15–44 YEARS

Categories of Occupational Groups *		*1910*	*1940*	*1957*
Upper white-collar workers	Professional	1818	1266	1939
	Managerial (except farm)	2164	1459	2085
Lower white-collar workers	Clerical and kindred	1887	1325	1920
	Sales workers	—	—	2029
Upper blue-collar workers	Craftsmen, foremen, and kindred	2575	1842	2282
Lower blue-collar workers	Operatives	2765	2001	2454
	Service (including private household)	2256	1645	2229
	Laborers	3131	2283	2699
Farm workers	Farmers and farm managers	3727	2826	3023
	Farm laborers	3522	2803	—
	TOTAL	2915	1927	2313

* Age has been standardized for the various occupational samples. *Source:* Adapted from Robert F. Winch, *The Modern Family,* (revised edition), Holt, Rinehart and Winston, New York, 1963, p. 207.

ried white women with a college education in 1950 was 1,296; for high school, 1,569; for elementary school, 2,421; and nearly twice that of the woman with a B.A. degree.[11]

ECONOMIC INDIVIDUALISM. An important determinant of fertility is the economic climate. If we accept the long-term trend of a declining birth rate (except for the short-term upsurge from the early 1940's to the late 1950's) a major factor is that of changing economic roles in our society. Women now have an opportunity to work outside the home, which implies a reduction in child-birth rates. This employment possibility does not explain the short-term shifts, for instance, the lowering of the birth rate in the Depression and the spectacular rise of the birth rate after the war period, when employment opportunities were, respectively, low and high for women. It is the number of children

[11] Grabill, et al., *op. cit.,* p. 201.

under five years of age which most determines the employability of the wife.[12]

Ever-increasing urbanization influences reproduction. The city offers a wider range of experience, and employment opportunities must be considered in the light of high consumption aspiration on one side and the availability of day nurseries on the other. There is evidence that the length of time after marriage, before the birth of the first child, has increased over the last two decades.[13] On the whole, several factors affect the questions of child spacing and shifting of roles of family members: the sharing of roles between husband and wife, the lengthened school hours and year for the child, and the diversified job arena available to women over the last twenty years or more—signifying employment once the children are in school—have permitted a relatively high birth rate, especially if planning is the norm for the respective couple. More important, a higher proportion of the population being married and the younger age at marriage have tended to contribute to high fertility. On the other hand, high urbanization and geographic mobility have tended to decrease the birth rate.

RACIAL FACTORS. Inevitably a discussion of racial factors in the United States refers to Negro-white differentials. The birth rate for Negroes is higher than for whites; in 1963 the rate was 20.7 for whites and 29.7 for Negroes.[14] In the North the birth rate for both Negroes and whites is larger than in the South, and in the North the Negro birth rate is subject to the same set of factors (that is, class, occupation, and education) as the white.[15] Actually, the high birth rate of the Negro slackened in the period after World War I as contraceptives were discovered and migration to the cities flourished. It appears that the rate again moved upward in the 1950's. Among the factors influencing this rise were increased prosperity for the Negro and eradication of sterility connected with venereal diseases.[16] It is likely that with integration and the movement toward equality the white and Negro birth rates will approximate each other over the next several decades.

[12] Grabill, et al., *op. cit.*, p. 268.

[13] Ronald Freedman, Pascal K. Whelpton, and Arthur A. Campbell, *Family Planning Sterility and Population Growth,* McGraw-Hill, New York, 1959.

[14] *Statistical Abstract, op. cit.* (1965), p. 47.

[15] Everett S. Lee and Anne S. Lee, "The Differential Fertility of the American Negro," *American Sociological Review,* 1952, **17**, 437–447.

[16] Everett S. Lee and Anne S. Lee, "The Future Fertility of the American Negro," *Social Forces,* 1959, **37**, 228–231.

RELIGION. Catholicism is generally associated with high fertility, a situation that has come to be qualified. The opposition of the Catholic Church to birth control methods is well known. However, the stringent position taken by Pope Pius XII seems to be in a gradual process of change, at least among the liberal wing of the Church. The development and support of oral contraceptives, by a Catholic physician in Boston in particular, with the tacit approval of the local cardinal is a case in point.[17] However, the birth rate for Catholic white women in the United States was 46 per cent higher in 1940 than for non-Catholic white women.[18] By the late 1950's certain studies indicated that the difference between Catholics and non-Catholics was approaching the vanishing point.[19] Yet a sample of Protestants, Catholics, and Jews matched on several factors indicated a sharp cleavage between the Catholics and Protestant-Jews.[20] First, Catholics show less differentiation by occupational or educational grouping than do the Protestants and Jews. Possibly this is a reflection of the fact that many upper-level Catholics are educated in Catholic schools and colleges. Catholics characteristically desire and have more chidren than Protestants and Jews.[21] The degree of religious participation affects contraceptive patterns. As might be expected, Catholics show a negative relationship in this respect. On the other hand, the more faithful Protestants in Westoff's 1960 study leaned toward restriction of births possibly because of the emphasis on the "moral theme of responsible parenthood." [22] No clearcut relationship appeared between fertility and religious belongingness in respect to Jews. There is a suggestion that Catholics use contraception for limiting family size, whereas non-Catholics employ it for both family limitation and child spacing.[23]

[17] John Rock, *The Time Has Come: A Catholic Doctor's Proposal to End the Battle Over Birth Control,* Alfred A. Knopf, New York, 1963.

[18] Dudley Kirk, "Recent Trends of Catholic Fertility in the United States," in Current Research in Human Fertility, *Milbank Memorial Fund Quarterly,* 1954, New York, **32,** 93–105.

[19] Freedman, et al., *op. cit.,* pp. 277–278.

[20] Ronald Freedman, Pascal K. Whelpton, and John W. Smit, "Socio-Economic Factors in Religious Differentials in Fertility," *American Sociological Review,* 1961, **26,** 608–614.

[21] Charles F. Westoff, Robert G. Potter, Jr., Philip C. Sagi, and Elliot G. Mishler, *Family Growth in Metropolitan America,* Princeton University Press, 1961, pp. 179f.

[22] Charles F. Westoff, Robert G. Potter, Jr., and Philip C. Sagi, *The Third Child: A Study in the Prediction of Fertility,* Princeton University Press, 1963, p. 238.

[23] N. Krishnan Namboodiri, "The Wife's Work Experience and Child Spacing," *Milbank Memorial Fund Quarterly,* 1964, **42,** 65–67.

There has been some suggestion that Catholics use the rhythm method (the officially approved method of the Church) until they have the number of children they desire and then shift to the nonapproved mechanical devices.

OTHER VARIABLES.   In addition, various cultural and regional factors influence fertility. The urban birth rate tends to be lower than the rural rate. Yet cities may vary among themselves. Pittsburgh, in 1940, had a rate roughly 70 per cent higher than that of San Francisco, both predominantly Catholic cities; however, Pittsburgh is primarily an industrial city and San Francisco is oriented toward commerce and transportation.[24] Because of a decreasing heterogeneity in our national culture these differences between cities were substantially diminished by the 1960's. Rates may vary within the city, and are frequently attributable to ethnic strains.

Similarly, if we go beyond the borders of the United States, national cultures assume distinct patterns of fertility. Ireland is an example of a traditional culture in which low fertility is conditioned by a number of situations: out-migration, an economic system of primogeniture (inheritance exclusively by the eldest son hardly encourages large families), late age of marriage, absorption of large numbers of the population into the clergy. In the United States, however, Catholics of Irish descent tend to have larger families than those of Italian and other nationalities.[25] It is assumed that the higher the birth rate among Catholic groups, the greater the adherence to Catholic norms. In this country, as compared to other ethnic groups, the Irish have been credited with more faithful devotion to the Church.

In a different fashion from Ireland, France has suffered a lengthy demographic deficit. The population increased little in the one hundred fifty years between the French Revolution and World War II. During this time most of her neighbors trebled their populations. The system of family bounties and a change in family styles and ideology has permitted France to gain nearly 20 per cent in a decade and a half.

The upper class generally is known for its low birth rate, although we might expect the situation to be just the reverse because of the facilities at their disposal. The desire to consolidate wealth acts as a deterrent to a high birth rate in this class. Evidence suggests that there

[24] Grabill, et al., *op. cit.*, p. 91.
[25] Westoff, et al., *op. cit.* (1963), pp. 102f.

is a curvilinear relationship between social class and fertility, although fertility is generally inversely related to social class. However, at some point in the upper-middle or upper class the pattern shifts and the higher income or other factors permit a larger birth rate.[26]

PLANNED PARENTHOOD

If more than 90 per cent of young people look forward to children, they are also determined to control the number they produce. In this section we regard the question of birth from the viewpoint of the individual rather than society. Here we are viewing the motivation underlying the birth rate.

Anticipation of children varies for certain of the factors we have examined. A Detroit study found that the preferred average number of children was 3.52 for grade-school educated wives, 3.34 for high school, and 3.31 for college graduates.[27] Five per cent of the grade-school group, 2 per cent of the high school, and none of the college group replied that they desired no children indicating that education may be correlated with family size restriction but not with the absence of children. In terms of religious affiliation we find that Catholics prefer 3.4 children; Protestants, 2.9; and Jews, 2.4.[28] On the whole, studies of the early 1960's have shown some preference for reduced size in families as compared to the late 1940's and the 1950's. Throughout the 1950's the birth rate remained close to 25, but declined to 21.7 in 1963.[29]

LEVELS OF FECUNDITY. In discussing planned parenthood, the first factor to consider is the reproductive capacity of the couple in question. As we have already noted, fertility, in the sense used here, refers to the *reproductive rate,* and the term fecundity defines the biological *capacity to reproduce,* which is more difficult to measure. There are

[26] Robert F. Winch, Robert McGinnis, and Herbert R. Barringer, "Patterns of Fertility in the United States," in *Selected Studies in Marriage and the Family,* Holt, Rinehart and Winston, New York, 1962, pp. 194–203; cf. also H. Yuan Tien, "The Social Mobility Fertility Hypothesis Reconsidered: An Empirical Study," *American Sociological Review,* 1961, **26,** 247–257.

[27] Robert O. Blood, Jr. and Donald M. Wolfe, *Husbands and Wives: The Dynamics of Married Living,* The Free Press of Glencoe, A Division of Macmillan-Collier, New York, 1960, p. 122.

[28] Freedman, et al., *op. cit.* (1959), p. 287.

[29] *Statistical Abstract, op. cit.,* p. 47.

different and rather arbitrary degrees of fecundity with no absolute separation among them: [30]

1. Definitely Sterile. Those known to be unable to reproduce or conceive; the majority of these cases are because of an operation. In most cases these individuals have already had a family.

2. Probably Sterile. Those for whom medical evidence indicates little likelihood of successful conception. There may have been a history of miscarriages, fetal deaths, or conception may be a health risk for the wife.

3. Semifecund. Individuals who demonstrate apparent sterility shown in a history of abstaining from preventive measures, representing a period of three years for those who have been pregnant before, and two years for those who have never been.

4. Indeterminate Cases. Those for whom evidence is inconclusive, that is, their habits cannot be classified for fecundity.

Sterility, or certainly fecundity, is a relative term, because two semifecund individuals married to each other are not predicted to have children, whereas if either were married to a highly fecund individual there would be little likelihood of sterility.

ANTICIPATED PARENTHOOD. A major decision or series of decisions involve the couple's attitudes toward the amount and distribution of children through the years. Westoff lists more than a score of possible variables that influence the couple's decision to have children and under what conditions. Along with our general categories of race, status (including occupation, income, and education), and religion, there are variables such as type of housing, neighborhood and community, degree of credit buying, in addition to a number of family and individual variables.[31] However, not all of these influences revealed significant statistical differences.

Generally young people have in mind an ideal number of children that is usually greater than their money and energy can support. In a study of six Philadelphia colleges and universities, a difference was found between the number of children desired and expected (Table 16.2). An even greater difference was found between the males and

[30] Freedman, *op. cit.*, pp. 21f.
[31] Westoff, *op. cit.* (1961), p. 164.

Table 16.2

NUMBER OF CHILDREN DESIRED AND EXPECTED
AMONG A SAMPLE OF PHILADELPHIA COLLEGE
STUDENTS

		Desired Number of Children	*Expected Number of Children*
Single men	236	3.44	3.2
Married men	36	3.03	2.75
Single women	186	4.37	3.8
Married women	21	3.43	2.86

Source: Robert C. Williamson, unpublished data.

females in terms of family aspirations; women theoretically are interested in a large family, but their more realistic attitude toward the
anticipated size was not markedly different from that of the males.
Part of the sex difference was a reflection of a disproportionately large
Catholic female sample, but the difference between the Protestant-
Jewish and the Protestant sample was not as large as that for men and
women.[32]

The desire to have children is regarded by many observers as a sign
of maturity. Most of us no doubt know couples who elect not to have
children because one or the other partner prefers the independence
and freedom from responsibility that a childless marriage brings. If we
look below the surface we very likely encounter an individual who
may have been scarred psychologically in childhood. Or it may be a
woman or occasionally a man who may have career aspirations that
would suffer by the distraction of children. Not least is the possibility
that financial burdens of one kind or another operate to forestall
parenthood, and when the situation is eased conception may no longer
be possible.

An attempt by Westoff to correlate several personality characteristics
with the size of family and the child spacing desired did not produce
findings clearly above the level of statistical significance.[33] These relationships are probably too subtle to decipher on the basis of most
psychological tests. Yet the difference between the woman who desires

[32] Robert C. Williamson, "Dating, Courtship and the 'Ideal Mate': Some Relevant
Subcultural Variables," *Family Life Coordinator*, 1965, **14**, 137–143.

[33] Westoff, et al., *op. cit.*, pp. 316–319.

two, three, or four children and the one who desires none unquestionably rests on a deep-seated personality orientation. In reality, few women reject the idea of children altogether. In Blood and Wolfe's sample only 3 per cent of the urban women and 1 per cent of the rural women preferred to remain childless.[34]

CHILD SPACING. If the wife continues her employment for two to three years after marriage, preventive measures usually are taken from the beginning of the honeymoon onward if any real chance for contraceptive success is to be attained. Of course, a double income may become a kind of need system in the marriage so that parenthood is delayed longer than intended; or an accident in birth control techniques might cause the birth of a child before it is intended. The average time elapsing between marriage and the first birth has been reported as 27 months for Protestants and 23 months for Catholics.[35] The interval was naturally shorter for the fecund than for the subfecund. Most of the mothers in Westoff's study seemed content with the arrival time of their first child: 66 per cent of them indicated it was "just right," 22 per cent asserting it was "too soon," for 10 per cent it was "too late," and 3 per cent were not concerned with the timing.[36] In cases of birth before 18 months of marriage, a majority of the wives complained that the child was too early in view of their financial situation, and interfered with their "enjoyment of things" with their husbands and with marital adjustment itself.

On the other hand, the first child may arrive several months after the marriage. Among one Ohio sample of brides under 20 years old, 13 per cent had their first births within the first six months of marriage, and 55 per cent had their first births within the first year of marriage, as compared to 4 per cent and 31 per cent, respectively, for those brides of 20 years or older.[37] Besides age, Christensen found nonreligious weddings and lower social class related to accelerated parenthood. Generally, however, delayed parenthood has become increasingly popular over the last several decades.

For the Protestant sample the second child arrived 36 months after

[34] Blood and Wolfe, *op. cit.*, p. 118.
[35] Freedman, et al., *op. cit.*, p. 279.
[36] Westoff, et al., *op. cit.*, pp. 116f.
[37] Harold T. Christensen, "Child Spacing Analysis Via Record Linkage: New Data Plus a Summing Up from Earlier Reports," *Marriage and Family Living*, 1963, **25**, 272–280.

the first; for the Catholic, 33 months.[38] There was apparently a wide latitude of choice on the matter of spacing; 85 per cent of the mothers who fell within the span of 19 to 36 months considered the interval as satisfactory.[39] Child spacing, in theory at least, depends on the relative strength of variables or motives that are not altogether consistent with the number of children. On the side of close intervals, two years or less is desirable for maximum companionship between the siblings. Parents may prefer to concentrate the difficult child-rearing years in as brief a period as possible. On the other hand, many prefer to spread the work load and energy resources, that is, to enjoy relief from diaper changing and other exhausting tasks before the cycle of infant and child-rearing recommences. Sibling rivalry generally is reduced when children are separated in age by three or more years—especially if they are of the same sex—even though in the early years the older sibling is more perceptive and perhaps more resentful of the younger child. For some parents the advantages of avoiding a heavy cluster of college expenses must be another motivating factor in spacing their children. Finally, there may be a great deal of pleasure for the parent who can observe the series of stages of infancy and childhood at spaced intervals. For example, if one child is separated from his older sibling by four years, his parents may find further enjoyment in witnessing the younger child's physical, mental, and personality growth because they have forgotten some of these events that they enjoyed with their older child.

One other question affecting family planning is the sex of the child. Most couples have a slight preference for a male first, but generally there is a desire for children of both sexes. On a chance basis roughly 50 per cent of two-child families, 75 per cent of three-child families, and 88 per cent of four-child families have children of both sexes.[40] Thus, in the two-child family there is only a fifty-fifty chance of reaching the usual ideal of a child of both sexes. It has been shown that one reason for planning a third, fourth, or fifth child is the hope of having a child of different sex. This seems to be slightly more predictable of Protestants than of Catholics, who apparently plan larger families anyway.

Unquestionably, some of the findings and predictions about norms in family planning have to be reexamined from to time, because there

---

[38] Freedman, et al., *op. cit.,* p. 279.
[39] Westoff, et al., *op. cit.,* p. 121.
[40] Freedman, et al., *op. cit.,* p. 199.

are fashions or cycles in expectations about family size. Demographers were unprepared for the postwar "baby boom" partly because they had no theory of fertility and consequently had to depend on the trends of the past to make predictions. The last two decades have seen considerable research directed toward the theory underlying fertility rates. However, we are at this point uncertain whether the present birth rate will continue to decline slightly, whether it will be stabilized, or even rise again. We can only repeat that many variables affect fertility.

METHODS OF CONTRACEPTION

For the greater part of the marriage, at least until the wife's menopause, contraception is probably of more interest to the couple than conception. In the broadest sense the methods can be classified as the following:

1. Rhythm or "Safe Period." This method involves abstinence from intercourse during the period immediately before and after *ovulation,* that is, the depositing of the egg in the uterus. Ovulation occurs at a modal point thirteen or fourteen days after the onset of menstruation. Nevertheless, there are sufficient variations in the cycle that any very secure generalization can be misleading. Although ovulation usually occurs between the twelfth and sixteenth days of the cycle, normally the period in which intercourse is to be avoided, for a few women the event can occur at any point between the eighth and twentieth days.[41] The method, as is well known, is the only type of modern birth control officially approved by the Roman Catholic Church, and that only in recent years. Many Catholics who use this method also use a douche following coitus, ostensibly for cleansing, but also for contraceptive effects. The rhythm method is satisfactory for those who are ambivalent about the prevention of conception. There is a popular school of opinion that sex relations are more enjoyable when conception is possible, that is, in cases in which the family maximum size has not been reached. Accordingly, sex is still more pleasurable when conception is intended. Possibly on these counts the rhythm method can be recommended, but it cannot be regarded as completely reliable.

[41] Nicholson J. Eastman and Louis M. Hellman, *Obstetrics* (twelfth edition), Appleton-Century-Crofts, New York, 1961, p. 66.

Besides stressing the need for remembering the calendar, the rhythm approach can include observance of temperature readings. Ovulation produces a rise in temperature; consequently, sex relations are permissible only when temperature is "normal." Aside from the disadvantage of nonspontaneity, the method places a good deal of responsibility on the wife in record keeping.

2. *Coitus Interruptus.* The withdrawal of the penis immediately before ejaculation is a method used almost exclusively in the blue-collar class.[42] It is unreliable, since it is not always possible for the male to accurately anticipate ejaculation. Besides, the method acutely limits the pleasure of sex both physically and psychologically. Historically it has no doubt been a major means of restricting conception.

3. *The Condom Method.* This is probably the most common one of the methods. It was used by a third or more of the Westoff sample of 1,165 couples.[43] The use of this sheath of rubber or animal membrane, which fits over the penis, has been extensive. Use of a condom is regarded as a safer method than some others, unless the condom breaks, but it is generally resented by the male partner because it seems a more conspicuous barrier to natural union and diminishes some of the sensation. However, the thinner animal membranes interfere less with sensitivity. From the woman's viewpont it has the advantage of prolonging coitus and helping insure her orgasm.

The condom is more commonly used among the less educated because it somehow seems safer. In a study of working-class men and women in the Midwest nearly half of the successfully contraceptive sample used the condom and somewhat less of the nonsuccesful sample. There was some feeling among this group that direct contact with each other's genitals was unpleasant or dangerous.[44]

4. *The Douche.* This method places the responsibility of contraception on the wife. It consists of a mildly acid solution, which washes out the sperm presumably before they have entered the critical area. The popularity of the douche has continually dwindled since the 1930's when it was used by over 40 per cent of respondents versus 15 per cent in recent

[42] Freedman, et al., *op. cit.,* p. 190.
[43] Westoff, et al., *op. cit.,* p. 761.
[44] Lee Rainwater and Karol K. Weinstein, "A Qualitative Exploration of Family Planning and Contraception in the Working Class," *Marriage and Family Living,* 1960, **22**, 238–242.

studies, and is now used principally among a less-educated group.[45] Psychologically, the douche is a less than ideal method, because it requires the wife to get out of bed and consequently disrupts the postcoital emotional relationship. This is also not an altogether reliable method, since the solution can reach only the upper end of the vagina and may fail to act on spermatozoa that have passed beyond this area. The lack of assurance implied by this method may interfere with the desired coital relationship.

5. *The Diaphragm.* This device is being used with increasing popularity. It is a rubber dome, approximately two inches in diameter, worn at the upper end of the vagina to prevent entrance of the semen into the uterus. Among the non-Catholic population it is widely used, and is the most common contraceptive method in upper-educated levels. It has the advantage of not interfering with the sex act and is generally more trustworthy than the douche or the rhythm method. It can be inserted some hours before intercourse and can be removed hours later. The size usually requires adjustment after childbirth, and a qualified doctor can arrange for a fitting. In the lower-class sample slightly over 10 per cent used this technique; an equal number had tried it and given up.[46] Some women resist using a diaphragm, because insertion may be unappealing, especially if they have emotional conflicts about sex. The lower-class repugnance to masturbation may have some effect, and Rainwater and Weinstein also found that there may be distaste for placing a foreign object into the body.

6. *Vaginal Jellies.* These are used both with and without mechanical birth control techniques. Some gels are noncontraceptive and serve only as lubricants. Other types of creams and foams are used primarily as contraceptives, are chemically prepared for use with or without the diaphragm, and at the same time serve as a lubricant. In other words, combined with a diaphragm, gels provide some degree of mechanical and chemical protection.

7. *The "Pill" and the Control of the Ovarian Cycle.* For a number of years experimentation has been directed toward the hormonal changes in the ovaries as a means of controlling conception.[47] For

[45] Freedman, et al., *op. cit.*, p. 177.

[46] Rainwater and Weinstein, *op. cit.*

[47] Richard L. Meier, *Modern Science and the Human Fertility Problem*, John Wiley, New York, 1959, pp. 112f.

instance, progesterone, a female hormone, is released by the body just prior to ovulation to facilitate fertilization. By administering a progesterone compound at an earlier period in the cycle, fertilization is inhibited. In 1960 the oral contraceptive or pill was approved by the Food and Drug Administration and the Planned Parenthood Federation. By 1964 at least ten different kinds of contraceptive pills were on the market. Almost all of them required a medical prescription and daily usage. They apparently had satisfactory results. Because of the expense (currently approximately $2.50 per month), pills may have only limited usage among the lower class. However, assuming that reports continue to be favorable in regard to its reliability and a minimum of side effects, oral contraceptives may prove to be the ideal solution to the problem of family planning. One of the advantages of the pill is that ovulation may be regulated and, consequently, the rhythm method can be made more reliable.

8. Intrauterine Devices. A plastic device may be inserted into the uterus for an indefinite period of time to act as an inhibitor to conception, in contrast to the diaphragm, which blocks passage of the sperm and is placed outside the uterus. Such an internal device acts as an irritant inside the uterus and prevents the fertilized egg from attaching itself to the uterine wall. It probably offers a more realistic solution to contraception than the pill for use in underdeveloped countries because of its low cost and the simplicity with which it may be used. Like the pill, its effects cannot yet be fully assessed, but in a study involving 1,800 women, the pregnancy rate was less than one per cent.[48] However, approximately 6 per cent of the women had excessive bleeding and had to suspend usage of the device.

9. Vasectomy. This method involves severance of the *vas deferens,* but because of its permanent effect it cannot be considered in the same sense as the previously mentioned techniques. In fact, in some states voluntary sterilization is not legal. In Poffenberger's study of 2,000 men who underwent a vasectomy, 71 per cent were manual laborers, and only 15 per cent were white collar.[49] Presumably, most of these men were fearful of more children for economic reasons.

[48] *The Wall Street Journal,* November 1, 1963.
[49] Thomas Poffenberger, "Two Thousand Voluntary Vasectomies Performed in California: Background Factors and Comments," *Marriage and Family Living,* 1963, 25, 469–474.

It has been suggested that vasectomy is selected because of some personality deviation, since eliminating a person's reproductive capacity might indicate a masochistic form of self-laceration or destruction, or at least an expression of hostility toward the self. However, a study of a limited sample of 48 upper white-collar workers revealed no precise personality deviation on the basis of the Minnesota Multiphasic Personality Inventory. Rather, the men selected this solution because more conventional methods like the condom and the diaphragm had interfered with the spontaneity of the act.[50] Rationalization may also have been a factor, because although the men overwhelmingly expressed satisfaction with their choice of a vasectomy, some reported a decline in sexual activity. More research probably is necessary to determine the complete motives and personality syndromes underlying vasectomies.

CONCEPTION

The act of conception depends on a complicated series of events, particularly within the female. Basically the process is the fertilization of the *ovum* (egg) by a spermatozoon. This fertilized egg will multiply itself over two hundred billion times between conception and birth.

OVULATION. The ova are produced in the ovaries, two flattened, almond-shaped organs (see Figure 2, Chapter 14), the principal functions of which are the manufacture and extrusion of ova and the elaboration of hormonal secretions. The ovaries remain active from the menarche to the menopause. During this period they are normally from 1 to 2 inches in length. The production of ova depends on an intricate pattern of endocrine activity initiated in the pituitary gland. An ovum is ordinarily produced every 28 days and migrates toward the surface of the ovary forming a follicle shaped like a blister. From the ovary the ovum is emitted into the Fallopian tube. In the meantime, the *corpus luteum,* which provides progesterone and prepares the uterus for a fertilized egg forms in the ovary at the location of the ruptured follicle. The golden pigmentation accounts for its name,

---

[50] David A. Rodgers, Frederick J. Ziegler, Patricia Rohr, and Robert J. Prentiss, "Sociopsychological Characteristics of Patients Obtaining Vasectomies from Urologists," *Marriage and Family Living,* 1963, **25**, 331–335. See also, David A. Rodgers, Frederick J. Ziegler, John Altrocchi, and Nissim Levy, "A Longitudinal Study of the Psycho-Social Effects of Vasectomy," *Journal of Marriage and the Family,* 1965, **27**, 59–64.

which means "yellow body." The corpus luteum degenerates if fertilization fails to take place, menstruation eventually removes the new spongy lining of the uterus, and the cycle recommences. If fertilization occurs, degenerative changes within the corpus luteum are postponed for the greater part of pregnancy.[51]

FERTILIZATION. The sperm is a "modified cell" consisting of three parts: the head containing nuclear material, the tail, and an intermediate portion. More often only the head and intermediate portion enter the ovum. The sperm passes the *cervix* (neck), which connects the vaginal and the uterine areas. Ascent of the sperm is approximately one inch in eight minutes. The sperm may even intercept the ovum in the Fallopian tubes during its journey of several days to the uterus. Of course the act of fertilization depends on a normal egg, which is not always encountered by the sperm. However, the timing is especially critical as the life of both the ovum and the sperm is perhaps anywhere from several to 48 hours or 72 hours, which is actually a rare maximum of longevity.

For the sperm to make a successful union with an ovum depends on: (1) sufficient number of healthy spermatozoa to be able to achieve the statistical probability of locating the ovum; the range of production may vary from well under 80 to more than 200 million; (2) sperm transport, the vigorousness of movement of the sperm once in the insemination process (the process of entering the female genital area); (3) ability to pass through the cervical area. Chemical factors within that area may in some instances be hostile to the sperm.[52] In addition, there are various endocrine factors in the uterine area that determine the success of fertilization.

In view of these limitations Westoff found that the average time between cessation of contraceptive measures and successful conception was between 4 and 6 months.[53] With a subfecund individual the gap could be much longer. According to medical practices, the term *primary sterility* is used when conception fails to take place after one year or more of normal coitus. *Secondary sterility* refers to the condition in which a successful pregnancy is followed by a year of involuntary barrenness.[54]

[51] Eastman and Hellman, *op. cit.*, p. 71.

[52] S. Leon Israel, *Diagnosis and Treatment of Menstrual Disorders and Sterility,* Paul B. Horber, Medical Book Division of Harper and Row, New York, 1959, pp. 450–451.

[53] Westoff, *op. cit.*, p. 110.

[54] Israel, *op. cit.*, p. 447.

PREGNANCY

The advent of pregnancy generally brings positive feelings to both spouses. In these days of contraceptive measures, a third to perhaps half of pregnancies are specifically planned.[55] The overwhelming majority of married couples anticipate parenthood, and even an unplanned pregnancy is usually well received. In most societies motherhood is the apex of the female role.

On the negative side, pregnancy may entail considerable anxiety for both wife and husband. According to one medical report, 75 per cent of expectant mothers studied experienced strong fear reactions [56] and all these expectant mothers showed some anxiety expressed through restlessness, wakefulness, and depression. Specific fears may arise from the possibility of miscarriage, especially if there has been a history of this condition in the individual or her family. There may be fear of pain, distress, or various complications. In addition, concern arises as to whether the infant will be normal. Despite abundant scientific evidence to the contrary, certain superstitions concerning ideas such as the mother seeing a dead rat possibly having some unhappy esthetic effect on the baby may worry her. Rising educational standards have decreased the extent of this misinformation.

ADJUSTMENT IN PREGNANCY. Pregnancy demands a number of shifts in roles in the anticipation of the coming child. Economic adjustments as well as adjustments to the physical changes are required. Psychologically, along with the pleasurable anticipation, there is the realization, although somewhat vague, that the responsibility of being a parent is tremendous. Both spouses may feel anxiety symptoms if they are not sufficiently mature and are reluctant to give up the freedom they have had.

Research about the marital interaction of 212 young expectant parents at Michigan State University revealed that the husband's role during pregnancy was an all-important factor in the wife's psychological welfare. The majority of the husbands studied were more concerned than previously with their wives' well being, and assumed some of the household chores in order to reduce her strain. The husbands'

[55] Freedman, et al., *op. cit.*, pp. 70–78.
[56] Leo Kanner, "Psychiatric Aspects of Pregnancy and Childbirth," in Eastman and Hellman, *op. cit.*, pp. 354–372.

own sexual desires tended to decrease as the wives did. Among the more difficult adjustments were suspension of the wife's employment, especially when financial burdens were evident. Even more resented was the abrupt end of her studies. On the whole, the wife's reaction was highly related to the marital adjustment itself. For approximately half of the women, pregnancy was less distressing than they had anticipated.[57]

Marked resentment toward pregnancy more often results from marital conflict or economic crises. In many cases where resentment occurs there has been a history of laxity in the use of contraceptives. A study of 55 "failures" among the clients of one affiliate of the Planned Parenthood Federation indicated that some crisis, such as unemployment or illness of the husband, was associated with the advent of an unplanned child.[58] On the other hand, the personality characteristics that make for eager, planned parenthood appear to be opposite from those characteristics accompanying shaky and irregular use of contraceptives. It has been pointed out that among other things, family planning rests on the ability to "delay gratification of impulses" and to demonstrate cooperation.[59] Except for a severe economic or health problem, marked unhappiness and depression by either prospective parent at the onset of pregnancy is symptomatic of emotional immaturity or of a tension-laden marriage.

PHYSICAL CHANGES IN PREGNANCY. The female organism is conditioned to accept the physical changes in pregnancy with a minimum of discomfort. In fact, it is some time before it is known for certain that pregnancy has occurred. Among the signs of pregnancy are the following:

1. Absence of Menstruation. When a woman who has had sexual intercourse fails to menstruate for ten days or more after the expected date, it is a fair guess that she is pregnant. However, it is possible for a woman to be pregnant even though she menstruates following intercourse.[60] Moreover, after conception there may be a bloody discharge, or "spotting," at the menstrual period. Failure to menstruate may

[57] Judson T. Landis, Thomas Poffenberger, and Shirley Poffenberger, "The Effects of First Pregnancy upon the Sexual Adjustment of 212 Couples," *American Sociological Review*, 1950, 15, 766–772.

[58] Nicholas Babchuk and Angelo LaCognata, "Crises and the Effective Utilization of Conception," *Marriage and Family Living*, 1960, 22, 254–258.

[59] Westoff, et al., *op. cit.*, pp. 175–177.

[60] Eastman and Hellman, *op. cit.*, p. 275.

occur for reasons other than pregnancy, for example, under various kinds of psychological stress including worry about pregnancy, extreme changes in climate, or certain physical diseases.

2. *Changes in the Breasts.* Due to hormonal action the breasts become more sensitive and there may be some tingling feeling. At approximately the fourth week of pregnancy some enlargement occurs and *colostrum* (a fluid associated with milk production) may be apparent around the twelfth week, but on the other hand, may not appear until delivery.

3. *Illness Symptoms.* Nausea may occur particularly from the end of the first month until some six or eight weeks later. More often than not, it is experienced early in the day, and is a symptom that varies widely from one woman to the next.

4. *Urination.* The enlarged uterus places pressure on the abdomen and especially on the bladder, which causes a change in urination habits.

5. *Fluttering Movements in the Abdominal Area.* During the fourth or fifth month of pregnancy, fetal movements are perceptible; however, this condition, known as "quickening," shows high individual variation.

There also will be growth changes, and occasionally there may be pigmentation changes. A feeling of fatigue is common, and a pregnant woman requires considerable rest.

Pregnancy is generally counted from the first day of the last menstrual period, or approximately 280 days or 10 lunar months until birth. Since ovulation follows menstruation by roughly 13 days, the period from conception to birth averages 267 days. For the first two weeks of this period the organism is identified as an *ovum;* for the next six weeks, as an *embryo;* for the next seven months, as a *fetus.* The early human embryo is hardly distinguishable from that of other animal species. At the end of the second month the embryo measures 1¼ inches in length, and its appendages have begun to take shape. In the third month ossification commences, and the arms and legs are developed including the appearance of nails. The head portion continues, however, to dominate the total organism. During the fourth, fifth, and sixth months the heart beat becomes audible with a stethoscope; fetal movements, generally in the form of kicking, are observable by the mother. The skin is less transparent, and eventually becomes somewhat wrinkled, with some fatty tissue developing below the skin surface. At the end of the sixth month the fetus measures slightly over 13 inches in length and approaches 2 pounds in weight. The breathing apparatus is not sufficiently developed at this period to permit survival if birth should occur. Beginning with the seventh month the fetus has some chance of existence if born prematurely. During this period a tremendous gain in weight occurs. At full term, or nine months, the infant is on the average 20 inches in length and weighs 7 pounds, with variations from 5.5 to 10 pounds.

FETAL NUTRITION AND PROTECTION. A whole set of metabolic changes occur during pregnancy. For instance, the water content of the mother's body increases enormously accounting for the average gain in weight of 24 pounds, of which nearly half occurs in the last three months of pregnancy.[61] These metabolic and weight changes are carefully watched by the doctor or obstetrician.

The greatly enlarged uterus develops various membranes. Principal among these is the *amnion,* which contains amniotic fluid. This fluid serves several functions: maintenance of the fetus at a constant temperature, protection from possible injury, and provision of a medium in which the fetus can live. Furthermore, the fertilized ovum plants roots in the wall of the uterus. From these roots the disk-shaped *placenta* develops and by the latter part of pregnancy measures 7 to 9 inches in diameter and one inch in thickness. The placenta is covered by thousands of rootlike projections or *villi,* through which the infant receives its physical requirements. This membrane-like arrangement means that there is a minimal connection between the blood stream of the mother and the infant.

There are several cautions that must be observed. First, the mother's weight should be carefully maintained. Frequently obstretricians prescribe a salt-free diet to hold women below a twenty-pound increase. Her diet should be rich in protein, potassium, iron, calcium, vitamins, and especially in vitamin A. Bizarre appetites are experienced by some pregnant women; however, the prescribed diet of the physician should be followed. Desire for sexual intercourse is likely to diminish during pregnancy, and is not recommended in the early stages if there has been a history of miscarriages. In fact, many obstetricians suggest that coitus be avoided if it coincides with what would be the normal menstrual period. Because of physical danger and general awkward-

[61] Eastman and Hellman, *op. cit.,* p. 235.

ness, intercourse is completely suspended during the last six weeks of pregnancy.

The early period of pregnancy is more precarious than the later portion. One danger during the initial months is *miscarriage,* which occurs in roughly 13 per cent of all pregnancies. Or in other words, in 1957 some 640,000 miscarriages occurred as compared to the 4.3 million births.[62] Most miscarriages occur at the end of the second or third month. This possibility of spontaneous abortion is worrisome to a number of women, and a program of medication including glandular extracts, in addition to rest, is recommended. Most miscarriages are thought to be due to a faulty embryo or fetus.

Another danger is *rubella* or German measles. If a mother who has never contracted rubella is exposed to the disease during the first twelve weeks of pregnancy, she may develop symptoms which could affect her unborn infant. It has been estimated that 60 to 70 per cent of babies born to mothers who had German measles during pregnancy have blindness, cardiac disease, deafness, and other defects,[63] although recent reports point to less risk than earlier surveys, possibly only 10 to 20 per cent of the infants of mothers suffering from rubella are affected.[64] The question of the advisability of *therapeutic abortion* in these cases is debatable. Preventive medication, like gamma globulin, may be given in case of exposure to rubella. However, symptoms due to the medication may be confused with the disease.

CHILDBIRTH

Toward the end of nine calendar months the anticipation becomes almost unbearable, but eventually the day arrives when the mother begins labor. A few weeks before the onset of labor the fetus moves to a lower position in the pelvis. The descent of the uterus, accompanied by the movement of the head into the *pelvic inlet* is known as *"lightening."* [65] Occasionally this causes what is known as *false labor.* False labor pains can be distinguished from true uterine contractions because they are not at regular intervals, do not increase in intensity, nor are they intensified by exercise.

There is no predictable pattern in the onset of labor and childbirth.

[62] Freedman, et al., *op. cit.,* p. 31f.

[63] Joseph B. DeLee and J. P. Greenhill, *The Principles and Practice of Obstetrics,* W. B. Saunders, Philadelphia, 1947, p. 431.

[64] Eastman and Hellman, *op. cit.,* p. 786.

[65] Eastman and Hellman, *op. cit.,* p. 419.

The *first* stage of childbirth is marked by short slight pains, usually separated by lengthy periods (10 to 15 minutes) as the cervix, which is a band of circular muscles, dilates. The *second* stage involves the descent of the infant, usually head first, through the genital area and vagina. There are recurrent pains of a minute or more in duration.

As labor progresses pains increase in frequency and sometimes in intensity separated by intervals of two to three minutes. A major problem during this phase is to get the mother to relax. In some hospitals the husband is encouraged to be with her during this period to comfort her. The childbirth process, including labor, lasts on the average of 13 hours for first babies and approximately 8 hours for subsequent births.

During the birth process an anesthetic is generally administered. Traditionally, a general anesthetic has been used, but there has been an increasing trend toward spinal or caudal anesthetic. The doctor may occasionally elect to do an *episiotomy,* obstetrical surgery to widen the opening of the birth canal. This hastens delivery of the baby and protects the mother from injury due to tearing of the parts. The obstetrician may also occasionally use forceps to facilitate the egress of the baby, but usually these methods are not necessary. For most women birth proceeds with no major difficulty.

The *third* stage occurs after the birth itself, and is marked by contraction of the uterus and discharge of the placenta and various membranes and cords. Over the next six weeks the woman recuperates and must take care to prevent infection. The period in the hospital ordinarily varies from 3 to 6 days.

VARIATIONS IN CHILDBIRTH. Certain irregularities are possible in the birth process. In about 5 per cent of births there is a *breech* extraction in which the infant arrives feet first. If the descent is by the infant himself it is called a *spontaneous breech delivery,* it may be a *partial* or *total* breech extraction depending on the degree of assistance rendered by the obstetrician. In some instances, the doctor may turn the infant around in the uterus to elicit a head presentation.

Other problems include *anoxia* in the fetus, or breathing problems either before or after birth. Birth injuries are still a possibility, and obstetricians are trained to avoid any type of cranial stress. Other possible dangerous situations are prolonged or precipitous labor, various malpresentations of the fetus, and multiple pregnancies.[66]

[66] Robert E. E. Nesbitt, Jr., *Perinatal Loss in Modern Obstetrics,* F. A. Davis, Philadelphia, 1957, pp. 202–203.

Caesarean Section. The name supposedly was derived from the circumstances surrounding Julius Caesar's birth, but it is also interpreted as coming from Roman law by which a dying mother in an advanced period of pregnancy might be operated on in the hope of saving the life of the child. As with breech extractions, the rate for frequency of Caesarians approaches the 5 per cent mark. This type of abdominal surgery occurs when dimensions within the pelvic region do not permit normal birth or when there is some other irregularity in the birth canal. Inasmuch as a Caesarean constitutes an unnatural birth, it involves greater risk than the natural process. Not too many years ago obstetricians urged sterilization after the second Caesarean birth, but medical improvements indicate a more favorable outlook at present. One out of 2,700 Caesarean births prove fatal for the mother, yet the rate might be five times as high and still be a minor risk.

In recent decades interest has been focused on reducing the painful aspects of childbirth. (Some physicians believe that anesthetics are unnecessary.) Emphasis is placed on educating the wife so that birth can be a more pleasant experience. Other medical authorities may especially emphasize the training and educative approaches to delivery. One study points to reduction of 20 per cent or more in delivery time for mothers who have acquired the techniques of relaxation.[67] Relaxation during labor appears to help the dilation of the cervical muscles, and with the appropriate mental attitude derived from sufficient training a woman may observe the birth process. One doctor reports that a mother may feel closer to the child whose birth she witnessed than to siblings born under conventional circumstances.[68]

MOTHERHOOD—A NEW ROLE. The four or more days that the mother spends in the hospital with her new infant prepare her for tasks ahead as well as providing a recuperative environment. The majority of hospitals provide separate facilities for the mother and infant to insure maximum care for both. However, some hospitals permit *rooming-in,* an arrangement in which the mother has the infant in a bassinet or drawer-like arrangement beside her bed. This gives her the opportunity, that is, to the maximum potential of her strength, to acquire the techniques of being a mother. The advantage of rooming-in is that she may participate in the baby's care.

[67] Herbert Thoms, *Training for Childbirth,* McGraw-Hill, New York, 1950.
[68] Ida M. Brechtel, M.D., "The Growth and Birth of a Baby," in Ruth S. Cavan, *American Marriage,* Thomas Y. Crowell, New York, 1959, p. 448.

Various factors, such as the question of family planning and the mother's response to pregnancy, affect readiness for the mother role. In one sample of some 200 pregnant women and their subsequent births, only 32 per cent had planned the pregnancies, although interestingly enough 67 per cent of the mothers "believed" in planned parenthood. The study explored the expectant mother's expressed fear of harming the baby—the assumption of the investigators being that this anxiety reaction would indicate unconscious rejection. The mothers expressing anxiety had significantly more behavior problems with their infants (feeding irregularities and other forms of distress) than did the less anxious or accepting mothers. Although the test was in no way a final answer, it does suggest that unconscious factors in regard to acceptance or rejection may affect pregnancy and the subsequent mother role.[69]

ADOPTION

There were 127,000 adoptions in the United States during 1963. About half these children were from homes broken in some way by death, desertion, divorce, or some other type of familial dissolution, with almost half of adoptions made by other relatives, principally by step-parents.[70] Of the remaining 67,000, the majority (44,000) were arranged by adoption agencies; the remaining thousands were distributed through the black market at exorbitant fees. It is estimated that roughly a million applications are made for adoption every year; thus thousands of couples must remain childless.

Much of the market of infants for adoption depends on the unwed mother. Possibly 150,000 infants are born out of wedlock in a given year.[71] Of these more than half are offered for adoption. Evidence suggests that the severity or punitiveness of the social environment in which the girl lives, as well as her personality needs, determine the degree to which she may elect to keep the child or place it for adoption. The psychologically insecure girl, it seems, is more likely to retain her child,[72] as is the Negro mother, who is disproportionately represented

[69] Antonio J. Ferreira, "The Pregnant Woman's Emotional Attitude and its Reflection on the Newborn," *American Journal of Orthopsychiatry,* 1960, **30,** 533–561.
[70] *Statistical Abstract, op. cit.,* p. 312.
[71] Helen I. Clarke, *Social Legislation,* Appleton-Century-Crofts, New York, 1957, p. 366.
[72] Clark E. Vincent, "Unwed Mothers and the Adoption Market: Psychological and Familial Factors," *Marriage and Family Living,* 1960, **22,** 112–118.

in cases of illegitimacy. One reason for the tendency of the Negro mother to retain her child is the difficulty of finding a family to adopt it. In general, the penalties society places on illegitimacy make it possible for the childless couple to find a child to adopt—a curious paradox where the nonsolution of one social problem may contribute to the solution of another.

The shortage of children for adoption results in stringent regulations for prospective adoptive parents regarding their race, age, religion, intelligence, and economic responsibility. Considering the law of supply and demand and the welfare of the child, some of these standards can be justified on the grounds of equality and of humanitarianism. However, many a potentially excellent parent is turned away because of age. Still more restrictive are religious requirements. Couples of mixed religious background, for example, Protestant-Catholic marriages, find adoption agencies closed to them even if the infant in question is only a few hours old. These difficulties explain the prevalance of the very expensive black market in adoption. At the same time, many illegitimate or parentless children are not adopted because of a physical defect, an emotional problem or "inappropriate" racial parentage.

Other vexing procedural matters are the endless delays while the parents are being investigated and the social agency decides which parents to choose. Legal delays may be another factor. Laws differ among the various states, and the adopting parent should be certain that the proper legal authorities have been consulted so that there is no chance the child may be reclaimed by its natural mother. It must be remembered that laws are designed to protect the rights of three parties: the natural parents, the adopting parents, and the child. The desires of the natural mother are especially considered in the court. However, increasingly states have been inclined to favor the rights of the adopting parents and child in that a special birth certificate is made out in cases of adoption. The certificate states that there is no indication of irregular or illegitimate birth. Certain states provide that all records regarding an adoption are sealed and only opened on court order, a protection that the adopting parents should request.[73]

Adoption becomes the only possible course for those individuals who

[73] Lee M. Brooks and Evelyn C. Brooks, "Adoption: Some Legal and Social Procedures," in Morris Fishbein and Ruby Jo R. Kennedy (eds.), *Modern Marriage and Family Living*, Oxford University Press, New York, 1957, pp. 442–456.

are sterile. The love a parent has for an adopted child can be as strong as for his own. However, the individual who wishes to adopt should carefully examine his motives—the adoption agency will undoubtedly ask him to do so—to determine whether the child is to fulfill his need for normalcy, to give a companion to an only child already in the family, or whether the interest is primarily directed toward the child. What kinds of ego involvement are relevant to the adoption of the child? It is strongly recommended by adoption agencies that the adopting parents inform the child that he is adopted. Honesty is indispensable in any parent-child relationship.

ABORTION AND STERILITY

ABORTION. Abortions can be divided into three categories:

1. Spontaneous Abortion. The fetus is discharged by natural processes, and in most cases is defective as a result of faulty germ plasm; there are biological causes over which the individual has no control. Roughly one-seventh of all pregnancies are believed to end in a fetal death.[74]

2. Therapeutic Abortions. These are abortions performed under legal medical guidance for the sake of the mother's health—mental or physical. In a study of causes of abortions in one New York hospital, psychiatric reasons were first followed by contraction of German measles. Among other physical causes were organic diseases of various kinds, tumors, circulatory or renal problems, as well as a history of excessive Caesarean deliveries. The rate of therapeutic abortions is not more than 2 per cent of live births, and a possible 5 per cent of induced abortions.[75]

3. Induced or Criminal Abortions. The term is relative since so-called criminal abortions, if performed by a well-trained, conscientious, and once-licensed physician, may not be essentially different from the therapeutic abortion, at least in regard to the woman's physical security. States and localities differ in their definitions and especially in the interpretation and execution of the law. It is impossible to estimate the extent of induced abortions in this country; calculations vary be-

[74] Freedman, et al., *op. cit.,* p. 31.
[75] Mary Steichen Calderone (ed.), *Abortion in the United States,* Paul B. Hoeber, Medical Book Division of Harper and Row, New York, 1958, p. 93.

tween 200,000 and 1,200,000.[76] Induced abortions are dangerous, since they are generally performed by unqualified persons operating outside the law and for whom the safety of the client is of marginal significance. Several thousand women suffer permanent disabilities every year as a result of these abortions.[77] The teenager, the unmarried, and the nonwhite are particularly vulnerable.

A greater number of abortions are performed on white women than on Negroes for whom sanctions of illegitimacy are less severe. College women are more likely to have an abortion than those who have not gone beyond high school. Protestants and Jews accept abortion in an inverse relationship to their interest in religion. Catholics consider abortions even more abhorrent than contraception. For all religious groups abortion signifies the taking of a life.[78] Surprisingly, married women have more abortions than single girls.[79] The more children a woman has, the less she resists the idea of abortion with successive pregnancies. The criminal abortionist finds his largest market among those women who physically, psychologically, and especially financially, cannot cope with one more pregnancy.

Abortion for any of these reasons predictably affects the woman negatively. Aside from the loss of her child-to-be, she must face the hostile reaction of the public and of religious authorities toward the taking of a life. Her own emotional reaction is especially severe in the case of a first or second pregnancy, but is less marked, although not absent, when family size was the situation that led her to abortion. Regarding the unwed mother, a more understanding attitude about illegitimacy may tend to encourage the girl or woman to carry the fetus to full term. While this shift in moral attitudes does not imply the solution to the problem of illegitimacy, it is debatable which is more traumatic, an abortion or giving birth to a fatherless child. However, as long as abortion is not legalized the individuals selecting this solution to their problems are faced with grave risks to health and even life.

STERILITY AND ARTIFICIAL INSEMINATION. As already mentioned, over a tenth of our marital population is, for all practical purposes, unable to conceive. One authority places the estimate as high as 15 per

---

[76] Freedman, et al., *op. cit.*, p. 32.

[77] Russell S. Fisher, "Criminal Abortion," *Journal of Criminal Law, Criminology, and Police Science*, 1951, **42**, 242–249.

[78] Ray E. Baber, *Marriage and the Family* (second edition), McGraw-Hill, New York, 1953, p. 616.

[79] Calderone, *op. cit.*, pp. 50–59.

cent.[80] Absolute sterility, in which there is no possibility whatsoever of conception, might be 8 per cent. For centuries the woman was considered completely responsible for infertility and she was subject to divorce. Yet in over 40 per cent of the cases of sterility the male is the major contributing factor. Possibly half or more of these sterile or subfecund marriages, or what is labeled as relative sterility, can be aided medically.

Another solution for sterility is artificial insemination. This technique is called *homologous* when the sperm of the husband is utilized to counteract a low sperm count or some other barrier. It is termed *heterologous* when an anonymous donor is selected, and in this case the doctor must secure the approval of all parties concerned.

In artificial insemination, a number of factors must be checked, including the Rh factor. The ovulation period of the wife has to be carefully noted, as in all subfecund couples when conception is desired. The donor is generally selected in view of similarity of traits to the husband and as most of the cases involve upper white-collar population, a professional male is chosen, not infrequently a physician. In some instances the husband's spermatozoa are mixed with those of the donor to allow for some possibility of his becoming the father. The spermatozoa must be collected and injected into the genital tract of the woman while they are still motile as even the most sensitive storage techniques are limited in time. Immediately prior to the insemination process the married couple is expected to have intercourse to prepare the wife's genital area for the sperm, to provide a favorable psychological feeling for her, and particularly for the husband.[81]

Legitimacy is a problem, especially in certain states. The donor must indicate in writing that he is surrendering all rights to the child. The status of the infant from AID (artificial insemination, donor, as opposed to AIH, artificial insemination, homologous or husband), may be brought into question, an example being the obligation of the husband to support the child in case of a divorce.[82] In one Canadian case artificial insemination was considered by the court to be adultery.[83] In a British court a wife was granted an annulment of the marriage for her husband's impotence even though her psychologically

[80] Israel, *op. cit.,* p. 446.

[81] *Ibid.,* p. 600.

[82] Walter J. Reich and Mitchell J. Nechtow, *Practical Gynecology,* J. B. Lippincott, Philadelphia, 1950, pp. 400–401.

[83] Helen I. Clarke, *Social Legislation* (second edition), Appleton-Century-Crofts, New York, 1957, p. 181.

impotent husband was father of her AIH child.[84] Generally, American legislature and courts have been sympathetic to the husband. In New York the wife in a divorce case wished her husband to be denied visitation rights on the grounds that the child was a product of AID. The court ruled her petition as invalid.[85] Because of the infrequency of court petitions it is difficult to determine the disposition of AID cases for the various states and localities. In some instances doctors and judges have urged the destruction of records of artificial insemination to prevent entanglements, such as attempts by relatives to deny inheritance rights to such a child. It may be added that certain religious groups have been opposed to artificial insemination on moral grounds.

This chapter has presented several aspects of the ways in which a marriage becomes a family. One of the points covered was the degree to which fertility reflects socio-economic, ethnic, and religious variables. There is speculation about possible future effects of the population explosion on fertility and family planning. Will people restrict their family size in view of the unprecedented rise in the population of the United States (projected to rise to 260,000,000 by 1980)? Family planning and child spacing are subject to styles, as are approaches to child rearing.

A modest revolution in birth control methods is taking place. The shift to contraceptive pills or injections appears imminent because they offer a more convenient and safer procedure than traditional methods. Whether pregnancy and childbirth practices can be improved is more doubtful in view of the medical progress already accomplished in this area.

Abortion, including the question of its legalization, remains a serious problem. Sterility is a severe misfortune for some couples. A solution has been found in artificial insemination, but adoption is the more frequent solution. The availability of infants for adoption constitutes one of the unsolved problems of our time.

Supplementary Readings

Becker, Howard and Reuben Hill, *Family, Marriage and Parenthood* (second edition), D. C. Heath, Boston, 1955. Chapters 14 and 15 discuss, respectively, heredity and problems surrounding childbirth and care of the infant.

[84] *Ibid.*
[85] Harriet F. Pilpel and Theodora Zavin, *Your Marriage and the Law,* Holt, Rinehart and Winston, New York, 1952, p. 123.

Blood, Robert O. Jr., *Marriage,* The Free Press of Glencoe, A Division of Collier-Macmillan, New York, 1962. Chapters 19 and 20 offer a sound discussion of the problem of family planning and the process of pregnancy and birth.

Calderone, Mary S. (ed.), *Abortion in the United States,* Paul B. Hoeber, Medical Book Division of Harper and Row, New York, 1958. This report of a conference of specialists treats a number of phases concerning this difficult problem.

Freedman, Ronald, Pascal K. Whelpton, and Arthur A. Campbell, *Family Planning, Sterility, and Population Growth,* McGraw-Hill, New York, 1959. This report provides considerable theoretical and statistical information based on a sample of 2,700, in regard to child spacing, and the problem of sterility.

Gebhard, Paul H., Wardell B. Pomeroy, Clyde E. Martin, and Cornelia V. Christensen, *Pregnancy, Birth, and Abortion,* Harper and Row, New York, 1958. The results of an extensive study by the Kinsey staff of the Institute for Sex Research.

Guttmacher, Alan F., Winfield Best, and Frederick Jaffe, *The Complete Book of Birth Control,* Ballantine Books, New York, 1963. A contemporary guide to contraceptive techniques and their respective reliability.

Rainwater, Lee, *And the Poor Get Children,* Quadrangle Press, Chicago, 1960. A study of the problem of family planning in the lower class.

Rock, John, *The Time Has Come: A Catholic Doctor's Proposal to End the Battle Over Birth Control,* Alfred A. Knopf, New York, 1963. This controversial book by a Boston physician is one of the factors changing the position of the Church on contraception, at least in the case of the pill.

Simpson, George, *People in Families,* Thomas Y. Crowell, New York, 1960. Chapter 17 offers an excellent review of birth-control methods.

Spock, Dr. Benjamin, *Baby and Child Care* (revised edition), Pocket Books, New York, 1957. The alltime classic and best seller on the physical aspects of infancy care.

Thoms, Herbert, *Training for Childbirth,* McGraw-Hill, New York, 1950. Representative of the books on easier childbirth techniques.

Westoff, Charles F., Robert G. Potter, Jr., Philip C. Sagi, and Elliot G. Mishler, *Family Growth in Metropolitan America,* Princeton University Press, 1961. A 1957 study of attitudes and other data surrounding child planning among 1,165 couples.

Westoff, Charles F., Robert G. Potter, Jr., and Philip C. Sagi, *The Third Child: A Study in the Prediction of Fertility,* Princeton University Press, New Jersey, 1963. A 1960 follow-up with 905 couples chosen from the original sample.

Winch, Robert F., *The Modern Family* (revised edition), Holt, Rinehart and Winston, New York, 1963. Chapter 7 and 8 examine the demographic and societal aspects on reproduction.

Chapter seventeen
Parental Roles

Children begin by loving their parents; after a time they judge them; rarely, if ever, do they forgive them.

Oscar Wilde, A Woman of No Importance, *Act II, 1893.*

Now what does direct observation of children, at the period of object-choice before the latency period, show us in regard to the Oedipus complex? Well, it is easy to see that the little man wants his mother all to himself, finds his father in the way, becomes restive when the latter takes upon himself to caress her, and shows his satisfaction when the father goes away or is absent.

Sigmund Freud, A General Introduction to Psychoanalysis (*1915–1917*), Permabooks Edition, New York, 1953, p. 341. By permission of Liveright, Publishers, New York. Copyright © R, 1963, by Joan Riviere.

Thus sex and birth order of children, mothering and fathering behavior, and relationships between parents influence the course of socialization. In addition, however, various cultural trends are achieving prominence in family relations. Notable among these are the emphasis upon equality in the family and pressure by parents for children to achieve certain social-status goals in life. These changes in cultural emphasis are probably related to various events in the past quarter century that have generated much interest in the welfare of all family members. With these changes, a focus on competence in interpersonal relations has emerged, especially among middle-class families.

Bernard Farber, Family: Organization and Interaction, *Chandler Publishing, San Francisco, 1964, p. 474.*

. . . It also appears that, at least in relation to sons, mothers are very central figures in lower-level families but become decreasingly significant in the higher levels. The complement to this is that fathers become less significant as one moves down the classes—they have less authority, play less significant parts in the emotional life of the family, and seem to be generally less involved in the family. . . .

Donald G. McKinley, Social Class and Family Life, *The Free Press of Glencoe, A Division of Collier-Macmillan, New York, 1964, p. 152.*

He is a little bored. He would rather be with men and girls his own age, but his mother has supported him and defended him so he finds some security in her company. She has been a staunch and formidable protector. She can and has intimidated the headmaster and most of the teachers at his school. . . . He is timid about competitive sports, about the whole appearance of organized society, as if it concealed a force that might tear him to pieces; but why is this? Is he a coward, and is there such a thing? Is one born a coward, as one is born dark or fair? Is his mother's surveillance excessive; has she gone so far in protecting him that he has become vulnerable and morbid? But considering how intimately he knows the depth of her unhappiness, how can he forsake her until she has found other friends?

He thinks of his father with pain. He has tried to know and love his father, but all their plans come to nothing . . . He learned to cast with a fly rod, feeling that, cast by cast, he might work his way into the terrain of his father's affection and esteem, but his father had never found time to admire him . . . His shoulders droop. He looks childish and forlorn, and his mother calls him to her.

John Cheever, "A Miscellany of Characters" in Some People, Places and Things, That Will Not Appear in My Next Novel, *Bantam, 1963, pp. 116–118. Originally appeared in* The New Yorker. *Permission by Harper and Row. Copyright © 1960 by John Cheever.*

April Snow, Salem by Maurice Prendergast
Collection, The Museum of Modern Art, New York. Gift of
Abby Aldrich Rockefeller.

The difference between marriage and a family is children. In the key function of the marriage-family institution, namely the reproduction and socialization of a new generation, our society is oriented toward a nuclear family with occasional trappings of a kinship system. The intimate family consisting of the parents and the children stands in marked contrast to the extended and patriarchal form so characteristic of most cultures of the world. This book has provided abundant evidence of the peculiar variety of roles the nuclear family expects, but most critical is the prescribed behavior of a parent toward his child.

No sooner is the baby born than the parents launch a career that seldom lasts less than two decades. As a result of this experience, probably the supreme challenge of marriage, a remarkable adjustment takes place in the lives of two people. For most married couples the responsibility is accepted in stride, although with differing degrees of enthusiasm and sophistication. For some, especially those who have more children than planned, the negative aspects of accommodating to children apparently outweigh the positive. Adjustment surveys have pointed out the ambivalent contribution of children to marital happiness. The strain and expense, the burdens and frustration are blended with a feeling of pride and creativity. And the sense of incompleteness of childless couples is not a welcome prospect for most of us.

Chapter 5 discussed childhood in the context of the individual's personality development, especially in respect to his preparation for courtship and marriage. This chapter is more directly concerned with the specific obligations, roles, and problems of parents in providing for adequate socialization of the child.

THE MOTIVES OF PARENTHOOD. Psychologically, parenthood operates as a motive before it becomes an actuality. It is an acquired motive and not an instinct. It is not easy to disentangle the motives but they include:

1. Ego Expansion. The child gives the self a greater sense of importance and immortality. In the child the ego is projected and a person's own traits and attitudes, good and bad, are represented. In some instances the aspirations for the child may be compensatory for the parent. (The father who did not get to college insists that his son have that privilege.) Or strain may be created if impossible or unrealistic demands are placed on the child. Whatever its consequences, pride in parenthood provides a sense of continuity.

2. *Creativity and Achievement.* These universal social drives act as powerful motivators toward parenthood, possibly more in terms of the maternal than the paternal role. First, the birth process itself constitutes something of a miracle, despite its biological inevitability. If the average expectant father prefers a son, and the wife a daughter, the creativity motive has merged with the identification process. The creative desire may become overly intense, and the parent, as has just been suggested, may try to mold his offspring according to some preconceived plan.

3. *Status and Conformity Needs.* The status of the male and female in most societies is enhanced by proof of fertility; in fact in certain cultures divorce is required of the wife who cannot give birth. For the male, virility receives tangible proof in the act of biological fatherhood, the *machismo* (emphasis on masculine values) cult in Latin America being only one example. In our society parenthood provides status among peers because of meeting expectations in reproduction, conformity in another direction. Moving to the suburbs or saving for the son's college education are less likely possibilities for the family with a higher birth rate.

4. *Control and Authority.* A universal social motive is the need for power.[1] For most people the desire for dominance over others cannot be practiced anywhere as easily as through the direction of their own offspring. To what degree the power motive influences desire for children cannot be known. The decision to assume parenthood is seldom a very articulate process. However, in the family constellation the struggle for control may be observed. Family members vary in their permissive or restricting behavior toward one another.

5. *Love or Affectional Needs.* According to W. I. Thomas, man has four basic needs or "wishes": security, response, recognition, and new experience.[2] Unquestionably parenthood meets all of these, but the need for affection or response is a key one. The desire to give

---

[1] Gardner Murphy, "Social Motivation," in Gardner Lindzey, *A Handbook of Social Psychology* vol. 1, Addison-Wesley, Reading, Massachusetts, 1954, pp. 601–633.

[2] William I. Thomas, *The Unadjusted Girl*, Little, Brown, Boston, 1923.

nurturance to a defenseless creature, the intense emotional involvement between parents and their children is the reason psychologists from Aristotle to McDougall considered the urge for parenthood an inborn drive, a theory now out of fashion.

6. *Hedonic Tone or Happiness.* The degree of satisfaction a parent derives from parenthood comes from a combination of factors: creativity, pride, etc. Whatever its ingredients, rarely does the new parent fail to feel a euphoric state. One component of parental satisfaction is esthetic: babies are pleasant to look at. Finally, toward the end of the family life cycle, there is the role of grandparenthood, which proverbially has most of the advantages of parenthood and few of its disadvantages. Related to the matter of hedonic tone is optimism, which accompanies parenthood. In an upper white-collar sample the number of children desired was positively correlated with scores on an Optimism Scale.[3]

These motives do not exclude others such as an attempt to preserve a marriage that is tenuous or unsound. A precarious marriage may not be strengthened by the arrival of a child; the responsibilities and emotional strain of parenthood may only complicate the marital situation. Often counselling and psychotherapy can determine how realistic parenthood is for such couples. The arrival of children may also serve to extricate the partners from other obligations; the couple preoccupied with children have less time for their own parents. Frequently, grandparents-to-be or others may feel some anxiety about their roles in the new family.

The pressures for and against parenthood are indeed complex. For many individuals too much extra energy and time are involved, and the emotional and financial burdens are too great. The additional work and responsibility, the anxieties of decisions about discipline, and the worry of "how the kid will turn out," act as inhibitors. The desire for procreation seems to be an ambivalent one. The reasons for this ambivalence may lie in the lack of preparation for parenthood that exists in our culture, the romantic notions we have toward the arrival of children without proper understanding of the roles expected, the fact that interaction and understanding between the two

[3] John C. Flanagan, "A Study of Psychological Factors Related to Fertility," *Proceedings of the American Philosophical Society*, 1939, **80**, 513–523.

marital partners is disturbed, if not shattered, by the arrival of a third member.[4] Motherhood may become a trial-and-error experiment with a developing sense of guilt as mothers think of themselves as performing below their preconceived standards. Fathers vary in their emotional reaction between feelings of neglect or guilt for not being of more help to their wives, and at the same time resent the attention and time given to the infant.[5]

PARENTAL TASKS AND THE DEVELOPING CHILD

INFANCY. The parent suddenly finds himself with a set of expectations regarding his obligations to his child. The arrival of the child poses basic problems. First, the mother has to decide whether to bottle feed or breast feed. In a study of a small New England community, 10 out of 24 mothers nursed their infants, the length of time ranging from a few days to five months. The decision not to breast feed was attributable to inability or, in some cases, distaste for the physical act. On the other hand, those who nursed found it difficult to discontinue the practice.[6] There is also the question of a feeding schedule and the currently preferred method of demand feeding. In a number of households a compromise is worked out between demand and schedule feeding, since demand feeding poses the problem of middle-of-the-night feedings.

Although he shows himself to be a unique individual, in the earliest months of the infant's life his functions are largely biological. He arrives in a highly dependent state and well below the performance standards of his mammal relatives. In his early weeks the infant sleeps most of the time, and is unable to react to visual or auditory stimuli in any refined fashion. Gradually he becomes aware of the world about him, recognizes a few essential faces, and commences the initial phases of his psychomotor development. However, only after the first few months is personality readily distinguishable. Even in the second year the child's biological needs seem fairly potent to an overworked

[4] E. E. LeMasters, "Parenthood as Crisis," *Marriage and Family Living*, 1957, **19**, 352–355. See also Daniel F. Hobbs, Jr., "Parenthood As Crisis: A Third Study," *Journal of Marriage and the Family*, 1965, **27**, 367–372.

[5] Katharine W. Taylor, "The Opportunities of Parenthood," in Howard Becker and Rueben Hill (eds.), *Family, Marriage, and Parenthood* (second edition), D. C. Heath, Boston, 1955, pp. 454–492.

[6] John L. Fischer and Ann Fischer, "The New Englanders of Orchard Town, U.S.A.," in Beatrice B. Whiting (ed.), *Six Cultures: Studies of Child Rearing*, John Wiley, 1964, New York.

mother, although his intellectual and personality behavior become increasingly more stimulating. The child's demands on the parent are heavy until the third year when he is fully toilet trained and the most precarious phases of accident prevention are passed.

The parents have to bear in mind the total dependence of the infant and young child on them. To what degree the type of socialization or handling of the infant by the parents affects later personality has not been fully assessed (as pointed out in Chapter 5). Certainly, the evidence supporting a narrowly Freudian interpretation seems inconclusive on this point, as a review of the literature might reveal.[7] On the other hand, there is extensive evidence that meeting the physical needs of infancy and early childhood—indeed the administration of physical security in the first months of life—is part of the process of socialization.

CHILDHOOD. In the early years of childhood a number of growth changes occur from the control of motor and verbal behavior to sex identity. Parents are not always aware of the overwhelming role they play in the child's life. The parent controls the child's behavior through various manipulative channels, not least of which is punishment. For one, punishment, whether actual or threatened, can have many different meanings for the child: a painful attack, an act of vengeance, or the withdrawal of love.[8] On the positive side, warmth and affection are correlated with the child's independence, according to a number of studies.[9] Children and adolescents who have been without sufficient emotional and affectional attention in the first five years of their lives are later found to demonstrate anxiety symptoms and behavior problems.[10] Regardless of the emotional tone that pervades a home, certain universal processes occur in all social situations, including the parent-child relationship.

COMMUNICATION. Human beings communicate with each other,

[7] See Chapter 5 for references.

[8] Daniel R. Miller and Guy E. Swanson, *Inner Defense and Anxiety*, Holt, Rinehart and Winston, New York, 1959.

[9] E. L. Horowitz, "Child-Adult Relationships in Preschool Years," *Journal of Social Psychology*, 1940, 11, 41–58, cf. also, Robert R. Sears, Eleanor E. Maccoby, and Harry Levin, *Patterns of Child Rearing*, Harper and Row, New York, 1957, pp. 477–488; Lois W. Hoffman and Ronald Lippitt, "The Measurement of Family Life Variables," in Paul H. Mussen (ed.), *Child Development*, John Wiley, New York, pp. 973–985.

[10] A considerable amount of literature exists on this, the classic statement being found in Ribble, Spitz, and other references noted in Chapter 5.

beginning with the infant's early awareness of the mother's breast. By the second and third year, communication becomes predominantly verbal. In the psychological and physical act of acquiring speech, girls learn earlier than boys, as we have already mentioned. The ability of the child, parents, and siblings to interpret words, gestures, facial expressions, and other symbols contribute to smooth functioning in the home and in the school.

The relationship of the parent to the child is a function of the honesty with which the two parties can maintain open channels of communication. In the family it is not possible to isolate one member's needs from another's. The neo-Freudian literature documents the degree of importance attached to intrafamily relationships regarding the child's personality development.

IDENTIFICATION.   Identification and *introjection* refer to the deep emotional empathy between two people, in this case parent and child. Parent-child relationships are certainly more meaningful when the child can have a fully positive attachment to both parents and not just one.

The tendency of the child to incorporate parental values and attitudes may be ascribable to a process by which personal loyalty toward parents is developed in the child and reaches its maximum point at perhaps eight years of age, which is before the peer group makes its full impact on the child.[11] The success of this process depends on the parents' own receptivity and their involvement with the child. The child's growing self-esteem is a function of the identification process between parent and child. Generally it has been noted that both boys and girls tend to spend most of their time with the mother in the early years. Less hardship is placed on the boy if he can identify with the father, and if a male figure is not available, a *cultural stereotype,* such as a teacher, uncle, etc., might serve as a substitute.[12] However, there is no proof that the variety of modeling is dependent on the sex of the parent. According to a recent study, the child may identify equally or differentially with the parent of like or different sex with little danger to his own ego identity.[13] The critical question is what kinds of identi-

[11] D. P. Ausubel, *Ego Development and the Personality Disorder,* Grune and Stratton, New York, 1952.

[12] David B. Lynn, "A Note on Sex Differences in the Development of Masculine and Feminine Identification," *Psychological Review,* 1959, **66,** 126–135.

[13] Rae Carlson, "Identification and Personality Structure in Preadolescents," *Journal of Abnormal and Social Psychology,* 1963, **67,** 566–573.

fications or introjections take place. Are they positive or negative? Is the relationship marked by free interchange of communication? How insightful is each member of the family into the needs of the others? To what degree can the parent take the role of the child and vice versa? Personality characteristics, motivations, and life wishes of the parents become, to some extent, apparent to the child. Intelligence and emotional sensitivity are among the relevant factors.

In this context identification may be paraphrased as the intensity of interest the parent has in his child. In an ingenious experiment the degree of parental interest was examined in three kinds of situations: knowledge of the child's friends, the tendency to react either approvingly or disapprovingly in reference to the child's grades, and the degree of interest in the conversation of the child at mealtime. It was found that the child's self-esteem was lower for parental disapproval of these behaviors than for parental approval, but the lowest self-esteem was for children who reported parental disinterest in their activities.[14]

THE SOCIOCULTURAL SETTING OF CHILDHOOD

It is impossible to detach the parent-child relationship from the society in which it operates. Socialization, including communication and the kinds of identification occurring within the home, depends on the sociocultural experiences of the partners and children as they develop. The child finds himself being indoctrinated into a set of behaviors defined by society. Indeed, it is during this critical period of childhood that culture impresses the individual with lifelong values. While society is structuring the child, the child is at the same time manipulating the social world around him.

A study of one Kansas town pointed to the quantitative significance of the children in the total activities of a community. Childhood was central in the social action and in the transmission of culture in the town. For instance, one-fourth of all social behaviors or interpersonal responses were by children. The behavior of children in relation to that of adults was broken down into categories of dominance, aggression, resistance, submission, nurturance, appeal, and avoidance.[15]

[14] Morris Rosenberg, "Parental Interest and Children's Self-Conceptions," *Sociometry*, 1963, **26**, 35–54.
[15] Roger G. Barker and Herbert F. Wright, *The Midwest and Its Children*, Harper and Row, New York, 1954.

Children may attack, refuse, struggle against, submit, offer help, ask for help, or walk away, depending on the situation. The child learns to react in certain socially acceptable and expected categories of response, and these norms of behavior persist throughout life. Whether the social environment is a quiet Midwestern community or the streets of Manhattan, the behavior can be systematically investigated. Although the quality and range of interpersonal behavior may be different in the farm community than in the large metropolis, the same basic ingredients remain. The child may have freer range in a rural environment since the territorial range of the child in this Midwest locale included 60 per cent of the town's settings, increasing to 79 per cent in adolescence.[16]

The particular sociocultural norms governing these types of behavior are the products of the various situations inevitably found where human beings live together. For instance, the child becomes angry when his older brother takes his toy away, or the sister may resent the attention her mother gives to Daddy. Irrespective of the Freudian dynamics governing these situations, the expression of resentment or aggression to an appreciable extent depends on the way the parents handle a particular situation and on the reactions of the siblings. These behavior patterns are not constant for all cultures. To choose one example, a German father may be harsher toward his children, or more controlling and punitive about sibling rivalry than an American. In the Latin American home the "absent father" is common, a problem that has been only partially assessed.

THE SCHOOL.   Although the home is the primary social medium by which the child is initiated into the refinements of cultural patterns, the educational institution is the next most influential. Our schools emphasize the values associated with Anglo-Saxon culture: cooperativeness, some competition, punctuality and other norms of time-consciousness, a number of symbolic and motor skills, and the basic fabric of the American values system, such as humanitarianism combined with an awareness of economic success. Family cultures may not always be in harmony with the philosophy of the school. For example, the Southern white or Negro community, the urban depressed area, or certain rural zones each have particular cultural values of their own, aside from those of the classroom. Certain subcultures may conflict with the schools' value systems.

[16] *Ibid.*, pp. 460–461.

Whatever the family heritage, success in school is the criterion for success in society. Even in a relatively homogeneous Midwestern city of 45,000, considerable pressure was placed on the child to conform to the norms of academic achievement. About 20 per cent of the school children failed one or more grades prior to their entry into high school. Three kinds of failures were noted. The first category was mainly composed of boys who showed aggressive social maladjustment and who often drifted into delinquent or semidelinquent careers. The second type of failure, in which case there were more girls than boys, was the emotionally maladjusted child who was generally withdrawn and shy. The third was the student who was disinterested. This form of behavior became particularly apparent during the high school period.[17] Motivational problems are taxing both to the teacher and to the parent.

Some notion of the child's lack of adjustment to the school regime is indicated in the report that over four million students between the ages of eight and eighteen were retarded in their age-grade placement as of 1950.[18] In view of population growth, the problem undoubtedly has been aggravated. According to one critic, a basic problem of the school is its failure to consider the preference of the lower class or marginal child for the physical and visual versus aural stimuli, external reality versus the introspective, content versus form, concrete versus abstract problems, space versus time. In other words, the "culturally deprived" child prefers to look at pictures rather than read or listen to a lecture, likes to be involved in active movement rather than remain passively at his desk, and favors a vocational course over an academic one. The reluctance to administer tests using symbols other than those of the middle class proves to be another deterrent. Intelligence tests and other inventories are predominantly geared to school information.[19]

It is important to examine the degree to which the teacher functions as a parent substitute. Teachers are expected to take on the following responsibilities or roles: goal definition, moral training, development of self-identity and character formation, in addition to attention to a number of personality attributes. The teacher must become an ade-

[17] Robert J. Havighurst, Paul H. Bowman, Gordon P. Liddle, Charles V. Matthres, and James V. Pierce, *Growing Up in River City,* John Wiley, New York, 1962, pp. 36f.
[18] Eleanor H. Bernert, *America's Children,* John Wiley, New York, 1958, p. 65.
[19] Frank Riessman, *The Culturally Deprived Child,* Harper and Row, New York, 1962, pp. 63–80.

quate model for identification.[20] The gamut of problems, from discipline and ethical training to medical and dental exams, implies that the role of the teacher or school has merged with that of the parent.

THE PEER GROUP.   As childhood fuses with adolescence, the full impact of the peer group is felt and becomes more important than the parents in the determination of behavior. A number of sociometric tests have been administered to children to examine their preference and rejection of other children in the schoolroom and on the playground. The peer group becomes the major avenue by which adults-to-be are tested in regard to their ability to get along with social equals. Much success in school and relationships with parents are determined by the child's acceptance by his peers, his ability to develop satisfactory relationships with contemporaries, and to eventually withdraw from the influence of the peer group and become an individual. Parents may be encouraged if their culture is similar to that of the parents of their children's peers. For example, the Jewish child may not be able to easily establish satisfactory peer group relationships in a Gentile neighborhood, although increasing attention has been given to the improvement of ethnic relations. Or the lawyer's son may not be as successful as his peers in a block where they are the sons of blue-collar workers, and the criterion of success is physical skill rather than intellectual achievements. Generally, however, children are more flexible in crossing the boundaries of class and ethnic origin than are their parents.

SOCIAL CLASS.   In this section we are concerned with the socio-economic status of parents as a factor in socialization of the child. Undoubtedly, the principal determinant of behavior, beyond age and sex status, is social class. This subculture, so abundantly researched by the sociologist over the last forty years, exercises interesting and variable influences on child-rearing practices. As pointed out in Chapter 5, studies carried out in the prewar period indicate a tendency toward more indulgence in the lower class. As compared to the middle class, more lower-class infants were breast-fed and weaned later, toilet training was less stringent, and as the child grew up he was permitted more

---

[20] Eunice Clarke, "In Loco Parentis," in Robert R. Bell (ed.), *The Sociology of Education: A Sourcebook*, The Dorsey Press, Homewood, Illinois, 1962, pp. 352–358.

freedom to roam the streets, attend movies, and generally allowed more permissive attitudes toward sex and aggressive behavior.[21] Postwar studies reversed the findings and suggested that the middle class was more permissive. How much of this shift can be attributed to postwar socio-economic changes, which have favored the working class and the relaxation of middle-class standards on upward mobility, and how much is a result of the age level of the sample, is conjectural.[22]

It may be recalled that the 1930's remained in the twilight of behaviorism and the publications of the United States Children's Bureau at this time emphasized discipline, self-reliance, and the achievement of normative, predictive behavior of infants (scheduled versus demand feeding). The middle class became attuned to shifts in child-rearing practices as a result of the new developments in professional literature. This social class used as a guide for its child training a variety of informational sources, such as Karen Horney and Margaret Mead, who eventually found their way into the syndicated columns of the newspapers. In the same period there was some blurring of class lines. Bronfenbrenner maintains that these changes were more psychological; that is, middle-class parents were more inclined to have their child self-reliant and were likely to appeal to his reason, guilt, and threaten removal of love. The postwar middle-class parent was also inclined toward a more spontaneous demonstration of affection and wider tolerance of the child's motives and desires. Thus, the middle class seems to be concerned with the intent or motivation of the child's conduct, whereas the lower class parent is interested in the immediate effects of behavior. The middle-class parent has more exacting aspirations for his child's academic behavior and preparation for a superior adult role. An example of this attitude is seen in River City, where in a substandard school less privileged students had 4.5 times the absences of those in an upper middle-class school.[23] However, as a study in an Eastern city has indicated, a distinction must be made between

[21] Richard A. Littman, Robert C. A. Moore, and John Pierce-Jones, "Social-Class Difference in Child Rearing: A Third Community," *American Sociological Review,* 1957, **22**, 694–704.

[22] Urie Bronfenbrenner, "Socialization and Social Class Through Space and Time," in Eleanor E. Maccoby, Theodore M. Newcomb, and Eugene Hartley (eds.), *Readings in Social Psychology* (third edition). Holt, Rinehart and Winston, New York, 1959, pp. 400–425.

[23] Havighurst, et al., *op. cit.,* p. 37.

the lower-lower and upper-lower class.[24] Large differences were apparent in the stability of individual and family behavior, affectional relations between the parents and the child, and responsiveness to the school environment.

The relationship between a child's social status and social development is not completely settled. Some substantiation for Bronfenbrenner's position is found in two recent investigations, which do not have altogether consistent results. An experimental study with preschool children indicated that the middle-class mother, more than the lower class ones tended to direct, help, and interfere by lending cooperation, and by these modes of behavior to structure the play situation. The middle-class mother also played interactively with her children.[25] In other words, the middle-class world as demonstrated in an unstructured laboratory situation, tended to be parent dominated—a finding in harmony with the majority of previous studies. Another study with a sample of third graders focusing on the problem of aggression and punishment found few reliable class differences. However, contrary to the findings of previous research, middle-class, more than lower-class, parents were inclined under given circumstances to use physical punishment.[26]

Some of the contradictions in studies of child rearing as it is related to social class may be the result of not only merging class lines, but the specificity with which the child's behavior is punished or ignored. Whereas the working-class parent tends to act in terms of the immediate behavior, the middle-class parent is likely to treat the response in terms of his interpretation of it. For instance, middle-class parents may punish an angry outburst when they consider it to be a loss of self-control, but refrain from punishment for an outburst interpreted as an emotional release.[27] Even though the middle-class parent is more inclined to read the literature on child rearing, some aspects of faddism or styles of child training must necessarily be selective. Parents do not

[24] Eleanor Pavenstedt, "A Comparison of the Child-Rearing Environment of Upper-Lower and Very Low-Lower Class Families," *American Journal of Orthopsychiatry,* 1965, **35,** 89–98.

[25] James Walters, Ruth Connor, and Michael Zunich, "Interaction of Mothers and Children from Lower-Class Families," *Child Development,* 1964, **35,** 433–440.

[26] Leonard D. Eron, Leopold O. Walder, Romolo Toigo, and Monroe M. Lefkowitz, "Social Class Parental Punishment for Aggression, and Child Aggression," *Child Development,* 1964, **34,** 849–868.

[27] Melvin L. Kohn, "Social Class and Parent-Child Relationships: An Interpretation," *American Journal of Sociology,* 1963, **68,** 471–480.

always apply all the guidance on socialization they receive. Also, besides class differences there are sex differences and the specific day-to-day relationships between the child and his parent.

The whole problem of class and child rearing needs more attention. Social psychological theory may have to be restructured to account for these inconsistencies. But despite the discontinuities in this research area, middle-class norms provide for the maximum of communication and identification in the parent-child relationship.

THE PARENTAL ROLE

MATERNAL ROLES. The new mother's daily activities undergo drastic changes. During her child's infancy and early childhood the mother often feels she has inherited a twenty-four hour work day. Her physical roles become extensive and may place a strain on the marital relationship. Yet despite the responsibilities motherhood entails, most mothers regard the care of their infant as the proper role for a woman. In Sears' sample of 61 mothers, the majority of which had given up work before the arrival of the infant, 71 per cent were happy or at least not dismayed at abandoning other pursuits in order to turn to motherhood.[28]

The mother's role is extremely important for she, perhaps more than the father, determines the shape of the child's personality. It would not be an exaggeration to state that the origin of love depends upon the first contact with the mother, specifically with the mother's breast or with its nearest substitute, the bottle. Winch comments: "This recognition of the mother or mother-substitute as the agent of the pleasurable sensation of tension reduction provides the basis for the infant's positive feeling (or positive affect) toward the mother figure. It is the writer's view that the earliest form of human love is the positive affect that coincides with tension reduction, and that is associated with the mother figure." [29]

The mother also necessarily becomes the primary punitive agent for the child. The development of a superego or conscience (the words are not synonymous, but sufficiently overlapping to be regarded as a unit

[28] Robert R. Sears, Eleanor E. Maccoby, Harry Levin, *Patterns of Child Rearing*, Harper and Row, New York, 1957, pp. 44–50.
[29] Robert F. Winch, *The Modern Family* (revised edition), Holt, Rinehart and Winston, New York, 1963, p. 444.

in this context) depends on the mother. Although the father may come to have more potency and visibility and use more persuasive methods in discipline, it is the mother who has laid the foundation for the socialization of the child. In some instances the mother may find herself in a dilemma, especially when there are the rival needs of siblings:

> I try to be understanding about it—I realize he needs an awful lot of security. I try to give him as much as I can, but there are limitations—it gets to a point where I just can't do any more than I have already done. He is very much inclined to say, "You don't love me," and of course it kills me, it breaks my heart, but I really don't know quite what to do about it; and yet I feel that I give him more than his share of love and affection. He gets much more than the other children do, and I really feel that I have neglected the baby terribly for him. I have ignored the baby completely for him, but I think that there would be no limit to what he would want from me. I think he would want me to be around whenever he wanted me, so he could sit in my lap and I could tell him a story, or I could play a game with him, or talk to him.[30]

As we have suggested in Chapter 5, the mother functions at two levels: the *instrumental* role by which essential family functions are provided, particularly the economic ones, and the *expressive* functions, including affection, love, and personality growth. Both parents demonstrate this dual function, but the mother is particularly oriented toward the expressive role. She frequently moves from her familial, parental, or instrumental role to the more expressive one of being "mother-to-this-child" role.[31] The mother is related to the child in a way that fathers cannot duplicate.

Duvall points to the *traditional* versus the *developmental* type of role played by both mothers and fathers.[32] Traditional roles focus on the physical well being of the child, his basic disciplines, and efforts to make him conform to the needs of society. Development roles concern the more subtle psychological aspects of parent-child relationships: personality growth, relations with the peer group, and preparation for adult roles. For instance, the traditional approach—in reference to the adolescent, for example—refers to the mother's need to mold her son or daughter in the given "stereotypes of socially acceptable behavior" using her experience as a guide to conduct and generally to dissociate

[30] Sears, et al., *op. cit.*, pp. 168–169. Permission of Harper and Row, Publishers.

[31] Talcott Parsons and Robert F. Bales, *Family, Socialization and Interaction Process*, The Free Press of Glencoe, A Division of Collier-Macmillan, New York, 1955, p. 204.

[32] Evelyn M. Duvall, *Family Development* (second edition), J. B. Lippincott, Philadelphia, 1962, p. 300.

herself, as much as possible, from her own personal reactions. In the developmental sphere her attitude is one of insight and of providing somewhat flexible models, but attempting to avoid overreacting to the actions and emotions of the adolescent.

THE FATHER ROLE. The American male is conditioned to the idea that he is mainly responsible for the instrumental role, namely, providing a living for the family, and that the mother is responsible for care and socialization of the child. Contemporary culture has been moving away from the dichotomization of husband and wife roles, but some essential differences still obtain. Parental roles in our society are loosely prescribed: Duvall found that fathers could be either traditional or developmental in their orientation according to the way in which they perceive their role. Developmental fathers are inclined toward play with the children, guidance, and the like.[33] To the child there is an aura about the father that emerges from an image based on his size, strength, and remoteness in the child's life. This impressiveness is particularly apparent until the ages of seven or eight. A father may be able to obtain high status with the child's peer group to a degree that the mother cannot.

Some pitfalls of fatherhood have been alluded to in Chapter 5. The father may detach himself from the child by his career involvement or in the pursuit of his own pleasure. The entrepreneurial and professional world often demands a sixty-hour week, not to speak of community obligations and recreational outlets in the suburban middle class. These demands are not conducive to his role as father. Regarding the relation of class to the paternal role, a Detroit nursery school study of working-class fathers points to an authoritarian image of their roles. The family role of such a father was more power oriented than that of the mother, as compared to the more equalitarian situation, or at times a maternal domination, of the middle-class home. The lower-class father is inclined to make the basic decisions.[34]

In some instances there may be a cultural basis for the power structure of the family. In a study conducted in New Haven, Connecticut it was found that in Italian families the father exercised more dominance than in Jewish families. These power relationships have differ-

[33] Evelyn M. Duvall, "Conceptions of Parenthood," *American Journal of Sociology*, 1946, 52, 193–203.
[34] Martin L. Hoffman, "Personality, Family Structure, and Social Class as Antecedents of Parental Power Assertion," *Child Development*, 1963, 34, 869–884.

ent effects in later life, namely, the more dominant father may indirectly create a passive type of personality which in turn makes for less achievement in the son. Consequently, the Jewish mother with her stronger role in the household has been interpreted as influencing a more mobile aspirational level in the son, and consequently a higher sense of achievement, whether in academic or vocational pursuits.[35]

In the day-to-day round of activities the father may find himself in conflict about how far he can enter into the child's universe. He wants to be a pal, and yet may find himself in an awkward position in his determination regarding the role he can play as he approaches his child and the peer group. At the work bench he can easily overwhelm the youngster with his superior capability. The parent's aid in homework is another example of subtle domination. The child can be embarrassed before his peers by the father's domination of a situation. A birthday party can be built around the children or can be a gala event in the preconceived notions of the parents, perhaps representing more a need of status seeking by the mother than of the father. All in all, the father may find himself in an ambiguous position with one end of the continuum being overinvolvement and domination and the other end remoteness and passivity.

In the father's adjustment to his role a major problem seems to be the inability to coordinate his occupational role with his paternal role.[36] In a middle-class sample of fathers who were concerned with personality problems of their children, actual or potential, there was extensive self-scrutiny about their ability to prepare their children for the kind of world they had known. They questioned their own and their wives' lack of positive knowledge and consequent ambivalence regarding child-rearing practices. In other words, technical information is subject to change and the middle-class parent finds himself confronted by fashion emerging from research findings, namely, restraint in one decade and spontaneity in another. This confusion only highlights the need for exhausting investigations from which more valid generalizations can be made. It is clear that for some generations children have been reared with a variety of practices, and perhaps the damage done is less a result of the particular training regime than of the personalities of the parents.

[35] F. L. Strodtbeck, "Family Integration: Values and Achievement" in David C. McClelland, et al. (ed.), *Talent and Society*, Princeton University Press, 1958.
[36] David F. Aberle and Kasper D. Naegele, "Middle-Class Fathers Occupational Role and Attitudes Toward Children," *American Journal of Orthopsychiatry*, 1952, **22**, 366–378.

Supplementary Readings

Aries, Philippe, *Centuries of Childhood: A Social History of Family Life.* Alfred A. Knopf, New York, 1962. Although the emphasis of this work is more on education than on psychological development, it is an excellent perspective on childhood in Western cultures.

Bernert, Eleanor H., *America's Children,* John Wiley, New York, 1958. The demography of childhood, especially dependency, schooling and work history.

Bossard, James H. S. and Eleanor S. Boll, *The Sociology of Child Development* (third edition), Harper and Row, New York, 1960. By far the most complete handling of the family setting and the development of the child.

Buhler, Charlotte, *Childhood Problems and the Teacher,* Holt, Rinehart and Winston, New York, 1952. The question of psychological development as it is shared between the parent and the teacher.

Dager, Edward Z., "Socialization and Personality Development in the Child," in Harold T. Christensen (ed.), *Handbook of Marriage and the Family,* Rand McNally, Chicago, 1964. An insightful and theoretical approach with the concepts well documented by research studies.

Havighurst, Robert J., et al., *Growing Up In River City,* John Wiley, New York, 1962. Chapters 1–7 describe childhood and adolescence in a small Midwestern city.

Kirkpatrick, Clifford, *The Family as Process and Institution* (second edition), The Ronald Press, New York, 1963. Chapters 8–10 are the insightful discussion of problems of child rearing.

Miller, Daniel R. and Guy E. Swanson, *The Changing American Parent,* John Wiley, New York, 1958.

Miller, Daniel R. and Guy E. Swanson, *Inner Defense and Anxiety,* Holt, Rinehart and Winston, New York, 1959. These two works deal with the Detroit study, respectively with changing styles in parental training, including the role of childhood, and the inner psychological reactions.

Simpson, George, *People in Families,* Thomas Y. Crowell, New York, 1959. Part Four is in the psychoanalytic tradition and treats development from infancy to adolescence.

Sussman, Marvin B. (ed.), *Sourcebook in Marriage and the Family* (second edition), Houghton Mifflin, Boston, 1963. Part Four contains nine outstanding articles on infancy and childhood.

Whiting, Beatrice R. (ed.), *Six Cultures: Studies of Child Rearing,* John Wiley, New York, 1963. A study of six cultures, including New England, which is illuminating for one reason, among others, in that it points out that child rearing is a relative matter and culturally determined.

Winch, Robert F., *The Modern Family* (revised edition), Holt, Rinehart and Winston, New York, 1963. Part Five, particularly Chapters 13–15, is a penetrating analysis of the socialization process.

Chapter eighteen
Problems in Parent-Child Relationships

The first question in psychiatry becomes: why do human beings behave as they do, or what makes people tick? The infinite variation in human personality, even within groups of people who are brought up in much the same manner—indeed, the wide difference between members of one family—calls for explanation beyond the old belief, "They were born that way." With due respect to the importance of inheritance, psychiatry is more concerned with what *happens* to individuals. When something goes wrong, the psychiatrist tries "to do something about it."

> Helen Ross and Adelaide M. Johnson, "A Psychiatric Interpretation of the Growth Process in the Early Years," Journal of Social Casework, *1949, 30, 87.*

Looking back over our survey of sexual development in childhood and adolescence, we may trace a parallel between learning the heterosexual pattern and learning any other complex performance. In our society, because of the social barriers interposed between the individual and the goal, there is much trial and error. . . . The learning would be more insightful were the young people given as careful preparation in sex living as in reading, writing, and arithmetic. For a proudly literate society consciously to evade the responsibility of education in this important area is difficult to understand and impossible to excuse.

> Georgene H. Seward, Sex and the Social Order, *McGraw-Hill, New York, 1946, p. 186. Permission of McGraw-Hill Book Co.*

A continuously expanding body of experience and knowledge offers a challenge to all parents, teachers, child welfare workers, and citizens to see that what the best and wisest parent wants for his child, the community assures to all children. It is the responsibility of the state to furnish special facilities for a decent standard of well-being for the specially handicapped child and to provide other services, such as universal education and public health protection, for all children.

> Helen I. Clarke, Social Legislation *(second edition), Appleton-Century-Crofts, New York, 1957, p. 307. (Copyright © 1957, Appleton-Century-Crofts, Inc.)*

The Untilled Field by Peggy Bacon (1937. Pastel.)
Collection of the Whitney Museum of American Art, New York;
Gift of Mr. and Mrs. Albert Hackett (19⅛ x 25¼)

This chapter may be regarded as a continuation of the theme of the broad problem of socialization which was discussed in Chapter 17. In this chapter we are particularly concerned with atypical parent-child relationships: the one-parent family, the retarded child, and other family irregularities. However, we shall first examine a question that affects all parents.

SEX EDUCATION

Our society has not solved, nor is it likely to solve completely, the problem of how knowledge, attitudes, and standards regarding sex are to be communicated to the younger generation. One study pointed out that of an upper middle-class male sample in a Midwestern city, only 45 per cent had received any sex instruction from their parents by the time they entered college.[1] Daughters apparently fare somewhat better; 71 per cent of the girls in an Oregon sample were given information by their mothers.[2] Even so, in an Iowa high school sample, over a third of the group had to depend on sources other than their mothers for information about menstruation and to a still greater degree on sexual topics.[3] There has been negligible improvement; in a prewar nationwide sample, 66 per cent of the boys and 40 per cent of the girls depended on their peers for their knowledge of sex.[4] The reasons for parental neglect in this area are probably a hangover of Victorian prudery, the awkwardness of introducing the subject, and in some instances, the ignorance of the parents.

Of course, the lack of any systematic information from parents hardly means that children grow up without some structured attitudes and feelings about sex. Even at the age of three or four, claims Kinsey, the child can discern certain judgments, namely the ease or embarrassment with which the parent approaches anatomical features, sex functions, etc.[5] Most of us have some memory of early impressions we

[1] Glenn V. Ramsey, "The Sex Information of Younger Boys," *American Journal of Orthopsychiatry*, 1943, **13**, 347–352.

[2] Margie R. Lee, "Background Factors Related to Sex Information and Attitudes," *Journal of Educational Psychology*, 1954, **43**, 467–485.

[3] Lee G. Burchinal, "Sources and Adequacy of Sex Knowledge among Iowa High School Girls," *Marriage and Family Living*, 1960, **22**, 268–269.

[4] Howard M. Bell, *Youth Tell Their Story*, American Council on Education, Washington, D.C., 1938, p. 40.

[5] Alfred C. Kinsey, Wardell B. Pomeroy, and Clyde E. Martin, *Sexual Behavior in the Human Male*, W. B. Saunders, Philadelphia, 1948, pp. 441–443.

received concerning the differences between the sexes, the sense of objectivity or of unnaturalness with which our parents or other family members approached our bodies or biological functions. Sears records various methods by which parents provided modesty as studied in a sample of young children: (1) Prevention of stimulation, guarding the child from awareness of sexual symbols, or avoiding the topic of sex, as in requiring the child to knock before entering the parents' room; buying underclothing a size too large to prevent irritation and consequently eliminate stimulation. (2) Distraction, that is, giving the child a toy while he was on the toilet seat so he would be unconcerned with his anatomy; avoiding labels, that is, referring to the genitalia as "it" or "there." (3) Use of borrowed sanctions, such as telling children to keep dressed to avoid catching cold, or "we mustn't touch 'it' for it is 'dirty' " (because *it* is "what we go to the toilet with").[6]

In Chapter 5 the strategic significance of the early years was indicated in structuring our motivation about sexual and affective processes. The child who grows up in a home in which genitalia are associated with purely negative responses is at a considerable disadvantage. These experiences can be further confused by contacts with peers from whom most children secure the limited, and often distorted, knowledge they acquire about sex. This is not to say unhealthy sex attitudes acquired in childhood seriously endanger a person's future courtship and marriage, but they are hardly an asset and generally have to be relearned.

STRUCTURAL SUPPORTS OF SEX INFORMATION. Our sociocultural structure does not permit the same freedom to girls as to boys. Girls are less curious about sex, as may be recalled from Chapter 6. Burchinal found reluctance on the part of girls to discuss sex with their parents: 71 per cent never approached their fathers, and 21 per cent failed to ask their mothers.[7] Of those who did venture a question, only about half were supplied with any knowledge that could be considered adequate.

There are other structural factors in determining the amount of sexual knowledge at different class levels. Using the McHugh Sex Knowledge Inventory in a family life college class, a pretest discovered that masculinity, upper age level, and upper education of the parents

---

[6] Robert R. Sears, Eleanor E. Maccoby, and Harry Levin, *Patterns of Child Rearing*, Harper and Row, New York, 1957, pp. 185–192.

[7] Burchinal, *op. cit.*

were factors associated with more extensive sex knowledge. There were no significant differences, however, between rural and urban environments nor between single and engaged students. A follow-up at the end of the course revealed a marked improvement in knowledge and the erasure of subcultural differences.[8] The significance of sex education was further substantiated by members of a biology class, where again comparable differences in information had been found between men and women. Weekly panel discussions, lectures, and films greatly increased knowledge.[9]

It is important to give correct sex information early—during the elementary and secondary school years. Systematic sex instruction must be geared to the age level of the child or adolescent. In the early years curiosity is oriented toward anatomical differences and birth when interest is directed first toward the mother and the events of pregnancy, followed by interest in the role of the father. The adolescent has specific questions regarding puberty changes and approaches and techniques of heterosexual relations.[10]

Relatively few communities have a systematic sex education program. However, at the high school level various courses do offer some approach to the subject in classes in the biological sciences, physical education, social studies, and in home economics, but rarely are these presented in an integrated and relatively complete fashion. Among the exceptions is Pittsburgh, where a coordinated course is taught within the high school. Students may come with consent of their parents, of whom 97 per cent are reported to give permission.[11]

THE PARENTAL ROLE. The parent usually feels self-conscious about his role in creating healthy sex attitudes. Part of the problem is lack of an adequate precedent for the parent, as his or her parents failed to impart this information. A few generalizations that possibly may be helpful to parents are:

1. Discussion of sexual matters should as nearly as possible be presented in their natural setting, namely, as the child expresses curiosity

[8] Panos D. Bardis, "Influence of Family Life Education on Sex Knowledge," *Marriage and Family Living*, 1963, **25,** 85–88.

[9] Edward V. Perkins, "Reproduction in a College General Biology Course," *Marriage and Family Living*, 1959, **21,** 41–42.

[10] Georgene H. Seward, *Sex and the Social Order*, McGraw-Hill, New York, 1946, pp. 186–189.

[11] Charles E. Manwiller, "Sex Education and the Child," in Morris Fishbein and Ruby Jo R. Kennedy, *Modern Marriage and Family Living*, Oxford University Press, 1957, pp. 476–883.

and begins to question. As the years pass and few if any specific questions are asked, the parents usually can find some oblique item in the child's conversation or some stimulus in the child's world on which to launch an explanation.

The advantages of a farm environment have frequently been pointed out, since the child observes the reproduction of animals. The city offers house pets and zoological gardens, not to mention a considerable range of reading material.

2. At most age levels it is necessary to take a neutral stand on certain sexual data. Most important, any sense of embarrassment should be avoided. If the adult feels uncomfortable about conversation in this area, a very enlightening or profitable session is unlikely.

3. The choice of vocabulary is often a definite stumbling block. It is more satisfactory to use words like vagina, penis, or navel than the vulgar or vernacular equivalents. In the end this is less confusing, and once the child has adjusted to this language and its neutrality, he is better equipped both conceptually and emotionally to handle the terms he will acquire from his peers.

4. Questions should be answered as they arise. Any relevant question deserves an answer; the response should be geared as nearly as possible to the conceptual level of the child. If the answer seems remote to the child, it is also innocuous. Often the parent must judge how much the child can profitably absorb at one time; he can return to the subject at the next appropriate opportunity.

5. The positive, permissive approach will have more favorable after-effects than a negative, forbidding outlook. The older beliefs in the necessity of warnings about masturbation, venereal disease, pregnancy —and at one time lectures delivered to girls about the dangers of being alone with a boy—have now been revised. The factual approach, stressing the subordination of sex to affectionate relationships, is calculated to benefit the later sexual adjustment of the individual.

6. The question of environmental supports must be constantly reexamined. For instance, there is no agreement on the question of nudity among family members. Certainly embarrassment on the part of the husband or wife about exposing the body is not beneficial to the child's acquisition of healthy attitudes. On the other hand, a natural feeling about the body and implication about sex can be cultivated even at a fairly young age.

In later years when sex has acquired some meaning for children parents are concerned about the child's viewing the parent or sibling of the opposite sex in the nude. While this practice is strictly disfavored by the lower class, opinion is divided in the upper educated classes. Apparently we are anxious to retain a sense of privacy about our bodies. It would be interesting to have more information about this point, that is, whether those who accept nudity in the home have a different set of premarital sex morals. If, as Kinsey reports, there is less nudity among the lower class and yet more premarital heterosexual coitus, nudity may prove to be of questionable relevance in connection with sex education.[12] Nudity is an individual matter. For some people nudity between the sexes should be reserved for marital life or for that approximation of marital life occurring among fiancés.

THE ONE-PARENT FAMILY

Among the problems of child-parent relationship is the incomplete or broken family in which one parent, probably the mother, rears the child alone. More than a tenth of all children are reared in homes in which a parent is missing, either because the parent has not married or as a result of separation, divorce, or death.[13]

THE UNWED MOTHER. Of the pregnancies occurring before marriage, the largest percentage terminate in marriage. It is the minority that do not, with some 100,000 illegitimate births among the white population of the United States in 1963, and a greater number among Negroes, 150,000 or a ratio of well over ten to one.[14] Here we are interested primarily in pregnancies not followed by marriage, especially when the mothers prefer to retain their infants after birth. Illegitimacy under these conditions seems to be particularly associated with both social background and personality factors.

One social worker reports that a disproportionately large number of unmarried mothers come from broken homes and have been reared by one parent.[15] According to her analysis, the girls generally came from

[12] Kinsey, et al., *op. cit.,* p. 365–367.

[13] Donald J. Bogue, *The Population of the United States,* The Free Press of Glencoe, a Division of Collier-Macmillan, New York, 1959, pp. 277f.

[14] U.S. Bureau of the Census, *Statistical Abstract of the United States,* Government Printing Office, Washington, D.C., 1965, p. 51.

[15] Leontine Young, *Out of Wedlock,* McGraw-Hill, New York, 1954, p. 40.

a mother-dominated home. Most of the girls were disinterested in the father of their infant. The man was often little more than "a necessary biological accessory who served only one purpose—to make her pregnant." [16] A certain degree of corroboration of this viewpoint is provided by another study, in which girls, who were willing to permit their baby to be adopted, were compared with those who elected to keep the illegitimate child. The girls who retained the children demonstrated less mature personality traits—more passive, impulsive, and retiring behavior—as reflected on a personality scale. They also had unfavorable intrafamily relationships and unconventional and impoverished social ties. On the whole, the girls preferring to maintain the child had less to lose in the status system of our society. They were in need of a primary relationship in which they would feel needed and able "to receive and return that love in their own way." [17]

These characterizations do not apply to all categories of unwed mothers. As we noted in Chapter 16 in our discussion of adoption, there are insufficient Negro adoption facilities. It has also been traditional, or at least acceptable, for a rural or lower class Negro woman without a husband to rear her own child. But, the middle-class Negro girl, if we may judge by a college sample, has a typical middle-class disapproval of illegitimacy similar to that of her white counterpart. Both lower class Negroes and whites are more tolerant of unmarried parenthood.[18]

Illegitimacy does not necessarily rest on personality disturbances either in lower or middle-class backgrounds. Vincent prefers to categorize several different personality types among unwed mothers: (1) the girl whose training in the traditional mores is deficient, often because of parental disinterest; (2) the immature or suggestible girl who is more interested in the peer group than in her home and often lacks in ego strength; (3) the immature, impulsive girl, often of average or below average intelligence, unsuccessful in school; (4) the lonely girl, frequently from an unhappy home. Personality and social factors accounted for still other types.[19] In view of the social and per-

---

[16] *Ibid.*, p. 50.

[17] Clark E. Vincent, "Unwed Mothers and the Adoption Market: Psychological and Familial Factors," *Marriage and Family Living*, 1960, **22**, 112–118.

[18] Joseph S. Himes, "Some Reactions to a Hypothetical Premarital Pregnancy by 100 Negro College Women," *Journal of Marriage and the Family*, 1964, **26**, 344–347.

[19] Clark E. Vincent, *Unmarried Mothers*, The Free Press of Glencoe, A Division of Collier-Macmillan, New York, 1961, Chapter 6.

sonality factors involved, he points to the "hush-up," hypocritical social policy in regard to illegitimacy, and feels that a more explicit appraisal of the causes would be a step toward solving the problem.

Another study, focusing on background factors, casts doubt on the evidence that illegitimacy and the decision to retain the infant are primarily related to internal stresses. In a New York sample of 290 white illegitimacies, youthfulness, non-Catholicism, and higher educational attainment were associated with the decision by the mother to surrender her baby. There is no readily apparent reason for Catholicism to operate as an encouraging factor for retention of an infant, except perhaps because of "strong religious beliefs associated with sex, marriage, and motherhood, or with retribution and responsibility." [20] A good deal of the conflict revealed in the personality tests of unwed mothers was partially a product of the anxiety of having a baby. After birth both the surrendering and retaining samples manifested less maladjustment.[21]

Whatever the motivations for the woman who chooses to rear her child alone, the problem of establishing a satisfactory relationship with her child is not easy. First, although there has been considerable improvement over the last few decades, the position of society is generally hostile. In many states the unwed mother is not able to receive social security benefits, and she generally has a severe economic struggle. Necessarily she must have sympathetic and financially able relatives or have considerable resources of her own—psychological and economic. Having to face various problems and crises alone—from measles to homework to discipline—places an enormous strain on her nervous system. Most important, the girl or woman will no doubt eventually be prepared to encounter the questions her child will raise as to his paternity and the attitudes he confronts in regard to his status. Such a child will miss the socialization of the father (however, this factor is no more serious than in some other broken families, and is partially resolvable if an uncle or some other male figure can be substituted).

THE BROKEN HOME. A child may be deprived of a parent through desertion, divorce, or death. In the majority of homes where there is

---

[20] Wyatt C. Jones, Henry J. Meyer, and Edgar F. Borgotta, "Social and Psychological Factors in Status Decisions of Unmarried Mothers," *Marriage and the Family,* 1962, **24**, 224–230.

[21] *Ibid.*

only one parent it is usually the father who is missing. However, the man may lose his wife through death or, as is true in relatively few cases, he may receive custody of the children following a divorce. Almost invariably the father of a motherless family solves his problem by remarriage or by the aid of relatives who take over and act as mother surrogates. In the more common situation in which the woman is forced to rear the child alone, the problem revolves about the capacity of the child to make a satisfactory adjustment in the one-parent environment. In Goode's study of women divorcees who did not remarry, when asked about the situations in which their children were most difficult to handle, they replied as follows: [22]

	Per Cent
Always about the same	55
Most difficult during the marriage itself	13
Most difficult during the separation and around the time of the divorce	18
Most difficult at present	14

Apparently, these women felt the one-parent family was not an unsurmountable problem, although their replies may indicate some bias. In comparison, three-fourths of the women who remarried thought their children had improved during the second marriage. According to another study, children of divorcees who did not remarry were even more isolated from the other parent than those whose parent remarried.[23]

Irrespective of remarriage, findings have not indicated any extreme traumatization in the psychological and social adjustment of children from broken homes. In some instances the divorce produces minimal effects, because the child was too young to remember the home situation before the divorce. Much of childrens' reactions seems to depend on the image of the home before the divorce. Generally it is desirable for the child if the parent remarries.[24]

Another report, using several indices, indicates that children are not any more handicapped in personality development as a result of di-

[22] William J. Goode, *After Divorce*, The Free Press of Glencoe, A Division of Collier-Macmillan, New York, 1956, p. 318.

[23] Jesse Bernard, *Remarriage: A Study of Marriage*, Holt, Rinehart and Winston, New York, 1956, p. 316.

[24] Judson T. Landis, "The Trauma of Children When Parents Divorce," *Marriage and Family Living*, 1960, **22**, 7–13.

vorce than children from unbroken but unhappy homes.[25] However, evidence remains that frustration and isolation are perceived and resented by the only child.[26] In addition to disturbance of the affectional relationships within the family, the loss or absence of a parent also alters the communication and power structure in the home.[27] The range of discussion and decision making between the children and the parents becomes highly constricted when only one parent is present. The infrequent visits or absence of the father, the overinvolvement of the child with the mother (which lacks the balancing effect of a father substitute), and the general emptiness and isolation of the home, all stand in contrast to the homes of friends and neighbors.

THE MENTALLY RETARDED CHILD

In the United States it is estimated that between 8 and 15 per cent of children are mentally or physically handicapped, the largest portion of these are mentally retarded (defined as those with an I.Q. below 70) or those for whom schooling is confined to the achievement of only the most rudimentary skills. Not all these children represent a problem to their parents as they are educable to a limited extent, and standards of achievement are not excessively high for those in lower socio-economic groups. Other kinds of physical handicaps include cerebral palsy, muscular dystrophy, spasticity, severe injuries, and sensory deprivation.

Mental retardation is an acute problem. However, school facilities for these children have improved over the last few decades, and more accurate diagnoses of mental deficiency are being made. Classrooms and curricula have been designed for the child with less ability and retraining is now possible. The National Association for Retarded Children, with approximately 700 local units of lay and professional people, have attempted to improve educational facilities and establish clinics, recreational and other programs for the mentally retarded. Retardation is now believed attributable to more than a score of illnesses or irregularities, which should lessen the sense of inferiority and disgrace that has in the past disturbed parents of retarded children.

[25] F. Ivan Nye, "Child Adjustment in Broken and in Unhappy Unbroken Homes," *Marriage and Family Living,* 1957, **19**, 356–361.

[26] James H. S. Bossard and Eleanor S. Boll, *The Sociology of Child Development,* (third edition), Harper and Row, New York, 1960, pp. 422–428.

[27] Paul Glasser and Elizabeth Navarre, "Structural Problems of the One-Parent Family," *Journal of Social Issues,* 1965, **21**, 98–110.

Yet the birth of a retarded child constitutes a tragedy for all members of the family, especially those with typical middle-class aspirations.

EFFECTS ON FAMILY RELATIONSHIPS. Parents' reaction to the handicapped child varies, particularly in the case of mental retardation, and we find these tendencies: (1) disguise of the facts and refusal to accept mental deficiency; preferring to consider the child lazy or uncooperative or continual changing of doctors in the hope that an operation or the administration of drugs or hormones can change the situation; (2) denial, by which the parent simply rejects the diagnosis; and (3) acceptance of the condition.[28]

For most parents and other family members major readjustments have to be made in view of the time involvement, financial outlay, and the emotional drain. Marital and family roles must be redefined, and a social readjustment is necessary. The family tends to become isolated from the community. In an English study, about half of the families with a retarded child in the home were more confined in their social contacts than families with normal children.[29]

According to Farber, reorganization within the family generally elicits two kinds of general response: the "tragic crisis" and the "role-organization crisis."[30] In the tragic crisis, the goals and aspirations of a normally functioning family become disorganized; some blame is consciously and unconsciously placed on the child. This reaction is especially observable in families with higher social status. In the role organization crisis, the problem is perceived more as a challenge to organize family roles. This type of response is more frequent in the working class, where long-range family goals are less conspicuous. The tragedy is seen as being within the "realm of what is regarded as controllable by the family members."[31]

The size of the family may be a determinant of the degree of crisis the family experiences when a child becomes disabled. According to one study, small families (having a mean of 2.0 children) reacted more dysfunctionally to incapacitation of a child than did large families (mean of 4.4). Undoubtedly the explanation lies in a greater emotional involve-

---

[28] Max L. Hutt and Robert G. Gibby, *The Mentally Retarded Child*, Allyn and Bacon, Boston, 1958, pp. 245–246.

[29] J. Tizard and Jacqueline C. Grad, *The Mentally Handicapped and Their Families*, Oxford University Press, 1961, New York.

[30] Bernard Farber, *Family: Organization and Interaction*, Chandler Publishing, San Francisco, 1964, p. 416f.

[31] *Ibid.*, p. 417.

ment with the child and the disruptive effects on the more closely knit structure of the smaller family.[32]

Let us note the parent-child and teacher-child relationships as regards retarded children. First, the problem of discipline is a stumbling block for the teacher as well as the parent; limits set for the retarded child must be flexible. Second, the child's level of understanding is restricted, and therefore he suffers a considerable amount of frustration. Third, for a brain-damaged child and related problem cases, whether he can participate in activities outside his home depends on fluctuations of mood. Fourth, there is often the temptation to pamper a handicapped child as "the baby" of whom little can be expected. This overprotective role may be psychologically unfortunate for handicapped children who want, realistically or unrealistically, to be treated as equal.[33] The problems noted in this chapter represent some major abnormalities that can occur in the family situation. Some of these problem relationships are less likely to be found in families who have had college educations than in the average population, but either a broken marriage or a handicapped child may occur at any educational or social level. In addition, there are other possible dislocations in the parent-child relationship.

OTHER VARIATIONS OF THE PARENT-CHILD RELATIONSHIP

STEPPARENTS AND OTHER SUBSTITUTE PARENTS. A fairly common problem in our society, since nearly a tenth of the divorces involve children, is the question of stepparents and the remarriage of parents. We may legitimately ask what kind of generational relationships have been established. Perhaps the most systematic study has come from Bowerman and Irish, who surveyed some 2,000 stepchildren in three parts of the United States: Washington, Ohio, and North Carolina.[34] The mother-stepfather combination was encountered more frequently than the father-stepmother because of the established method of awarding custody. The child's affection for the real parent varied: the

[32] Thomas E. Dow, Jr., "Family Reaction to Crisis," *Journal of Marriage and the Family,* 1965, **27,** 363–366.

[33] Harriet E. Blodgett and Grace J. Warfield, *Understanding Mentally Retarded Children,* Appleton-Century-Crofts, New York, 1959, pp. 98–99.

[34] Charles E. Bowerman and Donald P. Irish, "Some Relationships of Stepchildren to Their Parents," *Marriage and Family Living,* 1962, **24,** pp. 113–121.

strongest bond was between the young female and her mother; the
weakest between the older female and her father. Few consistent relationships based on sex or age could be found. Generally, the child was
less close to a real parent when the other parent was a stepparent as
compared to completely intact homes. At the same time it was found
that the child's relationship with the stepparent was more remote, suggesting that there is no substitute for a completely unbroken, happy
home. Stepfathers fared better than stepmothers in terms of affectional
bonds. Children were also happier with stepparents where divorce
rather than death caused the remarriage of the real parent. The explanation may lie in the deep attachment of the child for the parent lost
through death, the younger age of children in the situation of divorce,
the more rapid occurrence of remarriage after the termination of the
marriage, and—if a triangle was involved—some acquaintance has
paved the way for the readjustment. In a large-scale survey of remarriages, Bernard reports comparable results. Over 50 per cent of the
children favored the remarriage of their widowed or divorced parent,
providing it was the parent with whom they were living (usually the
mother). Only 36.3 per cent of the children in the sample favored the
divorced father's remarriage.[35] Generally, the stepfather was reported to
be more favorably disposed toward the child acquired by marriage than
was the stepmother.

There is also the situation of children who are reared by other
relatives. One variation of this is a *polymatric* situation where an older
sibling, an aunt, and/or a grandmother may all tend to the needs of
the child. One study of a comparison of polymatric to *monomatric*
(one mother) rearing of infants pointed to the advantages of a surplus
of mothering.[36] There may also be substitution of the mother by an
older sibling when the mother is removed from the family situation by
illness, death, or long hours of employment. As with other kinds of
parent-child relationships, much depends on the warmth, affections,
and stability of the household.

LONG-TERM ILLNESS OR ABSENCE OF THE PARENT.   Another problem
is the parent who is unable to give the children an adequate upbringing due to an illness. Sometimes the parent may be in the home but
not able to perform adequately. In other cases prolonged or repetitive

[35] Bernard, *op. cit.*, p. 319.

[36] Bettye M. Caldwell, et al., "Mother-Infant Interaction in Monomatric and
Polymatric Families," *American Journal of Orthopsychiatry*, 1963, **33**, 654–664.

hospitalization may occur. Still another problem is the parent suffering from alcoholism or drug addiction, which would cause maximum disturbances in a home. Generally family resources, a grandmother or older sibling, counteract the greater part of the potentially damaging effects of an irregular home situation or a psychotic mother, for example.[37] In many instances the wife's mental illness brings an almost irremedial disruption of the family. Withdrawal from interaction and role performance and threats of violence and self-destruction by the patient find most family members, including the husband, unable to cope with the situation.[38] The onset of a psychosis in the father may not be as immobilizing as that of a mother's, but can place emotional as well as financial strain on the mother and children.[39]

The father's occupation may necessitate his complete absence from the home for long periods of time. An interesting report comes from Norway in which merchant marine service removes fathers from their families for as long as two years in some instances. An investigation showed that the children are often immature, have a high level of dependence, and frequently tend to overidealize their fathers. The overanxious mothers were more overprotective and ego involved than the control mothers. The boys had marked difficulty in their sex identification, which led to compensatory masculinity. Compared to normal children, there was poorer adjustment to peers and a general indication of anxiety.[40] Perhaps the length of absence is a variable. As compared to a control group, children whose fathers were absent for periods of three months at a time did not show any deleterious changes in their image of either parent. Further research is desirable regarding the effects of the absent parent.[41]

[37] James N. Sussex, Frances Gassman, and S. C. Raffel, "Adjustment of Children with Psychotic Mothers in the Home," *American Journal of Orthopsychiatry*, 1963, 33, 849–854.

[38] Harold Sampson, et al., "The Mental Hospital and Marital Family Ties," in Howard S. Becker (ed.), *The Other Side: Perspectives on Deviance*, The Free Press of Glencoe: A Division of the Collier-Macmillan Co., New York, 1964, pp. 139–162.

[39] Marian R. Yarrow, "The Psychological Meaning of Mental Illness in the Family," *Journal of Social Issues*, 1955, 11, 12–32.

[40] David B. Lynn and William L. Sawrey, "The Effects of Father-Absence on Norwegian Boys and Girls," *Journal of Abnormal and Social Psychology*, 1959, 59, 258–262; and P. O. Tiller, "Father-Absence and Personality Development in Sailor Families: A Preliminary Research Report," in Nels Anderson (ed.), *Studies of the Family*, vol. 2, Vandenhoeck and Ruprecht, Gottingen, 1957, pp. 115–133.

[41] A. J. Crain and C. S. Stamm, "Intermittent Absence of Fathers and Children's Perceptions of Parents," *Journal of Marriage and the Family*, 1965, 27, 344–347.

THE LEGAL STATUS OF CHILDHOOD

Throughout most of this chapter we have been concerned with the psychological and social aspects of parenthood and childhood. It is significant that parenthood and childhood are legal entities. However much the family seems a unit, in and of itself, the final arbiter is the state. In Chapter 11 we showed that law determines who we may marry and under what conditions the ceremony can be performed. A variety of problems from adoption, to drawing up a will, to the rights of inheritance sooner or later bring family members into contact with a legal advisor.

CUSTODY. In regard to childhood the most frequent legal question is the matter of custody. Custody should be distinguished from adoption, which implies, in addition to custody, a change of name and certain inheritance rights. It is also different from a guardianship which refers to "a way of fulfilling public responsibility for children." [42] *Guardianship* is generally of more limited scope than custody and refers to property or financial matters. Custody is both a privilege and an obligation of the parent, and may be removed for a number of reasons: (1) separation or divorce, (2) neglect by parents, (3) delinquency on the part of the child or parent, (4) mental or physical disablement on the part of the child or parents, and (5) death of one or both parents. [43] Custody is not an inalienable right of parenthood. For instance, a parent cannot give away his child and release himself from the obligation of support. There may also be a number of circumstances in which the court must decide between foster parents and natural parents. For example, following the death of the mother, the court may place an infant in the custody of an unrelated couple until the father can provide for the child adequately. After the father has remarried and improved his economic situation, the court is likely to return the child to him on the theory that a parent has a natural right to his child.

In more than forty states the husband and wife share equally in the custody of the child, although courts generally consider the mother to

[42] John S. Bradway, "What Family Members Should Know About Law," in Howard Becker and Reuben Hill (eds.), *Family, Marriage and Parenthood* (second edition), D. C. Heath, Boston, 1955, p. 589.

[43] Helen I. Clarke, *Social Legislation* (second edition), Appleton-Century-Crofts, New York, 1957, pp. 223f.

be the most competent parent to assume rearing of the child. However, until recently, in the wake of Western patriarchalism, several states gave preference to the husband.[44] Most states regard the mother as having exclusive right to an illegitimate child until she provides custody to the adopting parents.

Recently there has been a movement to allow more flexibility in the custody arrangements following divorce. The interest of the child will continue to be the basis of decision, but more emphasis will be placed on the individual needs of each child. It is proposed that if the parents cannot agree, they should submit the question of custody to a committee composed of professionals (a child psychiatrist, an educator, a lawyer, for example). If such a committee procedure were adopted, the court would ordinarily be bound by their findings.[45]

RIGHTS AND OBLIGATIONS. Parents assume a number of responsibilities when they have children; one of these is financial support. At the time of the establishment of the colonies, English law was somewhat equivocal about the duties of parents. By the nineteenth century the legal interpretation in the United States held the father responsible for maintenance of his children. Consequently following divorce the husband is liable for his child's expenses until the child reaches the age of twenty-one, although financially able mothers may share in this obligation.[46] Among the items for which parents are responsible are a child's food, clothing, shelter, and medical attention. Parents have responsibility for the education of their child. Although parents have only statutory obligation to send their child to school until the compulsory attendance age has been reached, there has been a challenge in some courts for parents to provide as much education as could be profitable to the child and within the financial ability of the parents.[47] Provision for a college education, according to this interpretation, could be required of parents of a given income bracket. Court interpretations also permit the parent to have prerogatives concerning the religious education of their children.

If the parent has obligations to the child, he also has privileges. According to the laws of most states parents are entitled to the services

[44] Chester Vernier, "American Family Laws," in Fowler V. Harper, *Problems of the Family,* Bobbs-Merrill, 1952, p. 487.
[45] Lawrence S. Kubie, "Provisions for the Care of Children of Divorced Parents: A New Legal Instrument," *The Yale Law Journal,* 1964, **73,** 1197–1212.
[46] Clarke, *op. cit.,* p. 243.
[47] *Ibid.,* p. 249.

and earnings of their children.[48] Some states stipulate what usage the
parents may make of the income. Rights and responsibilities are reciprocal; inheritance, for instance, implies that the children (including those who are adopted) share equally with the mother the estate of
the deceased father.

The law generally states that the parent is not responsible for delinquencies or crimes committed by the child, except when the parent has
been negligent. Too, the parent or child or both have the right to
claim redress when the child has been injured in any respect. Miscon-
duct, as in encouraging drinking or sexual behavior on the part of
minors, is subject to penalties. Legal processes may differ somewhat as
to whether such protection of the minor applies to cases of custody and
guardianship to the same extent as they do to natural parenthood. In
respect to injuries, either physical or moral, to the child, the threatened loss of earnings is the traditional legal justification. A more
modern interpretation would rest on the "wounded feelings" of the
parent.[49]

As suggested, a child may bring civil action for mistreatment, even
against his parents. The child may sue a third party for injuries done
him. It is possible that he would receive a fairly sympathetic treatment
in the courts as he is less likely to be labeled as guilty of contributory
negligence. The degree of caution required of a child is less than the
law might demand of an adult.[50]

Parenthood is possibly the most critical role of a lifetime. In our
study of the parent and the child we have considered some of the more
salient problems. Many questions cannot at this point be answered.
The parent, often on the basis of insufficient knowledge, has to
make decisions regarding what he should do when his child refuses to
cooperate, when he won't eat certain foods, when he "sasses back," or
seems to have a number of arguments with the neighbor's son. Probably most of these day-to-day events are not as serious as they seem at
the time. The parents' treatment of the child is no doubt more meaningful when the motives underlying the conduct are considered and
discussed. The weighing of alternatives is a never-ending process in the
discipline of the child. In Chapter 5 we maintained that discipline
administered in an affection-oriented relationship has a greater pros-

[48] Vernier, *op. cit.,* p. 488.
[49] Clarke, *op. cit.,* p. 236.
[50] Bradway, *op. cit.,* p. 589.

pect of establishing constructive behavior than in a negative environment in which the child does not feel loved. In this chapter this
position has been reaffirmed. The fact that not all studies of class have
produced identical findings does not detract from the consensus of
results; namely, that the middle class is strongly oriented toward
warmth and affection in the parent-child relationship. Nor can we
pretend to have infallible answers to all emotional and discipline
problems arising during the course of a child's development.

As this chapter has indicated, parenthood is markedly more complicated by the arrival of an atypical child or an irregular family setting.
However, the central ingredient of parenthood is maturity and competence. Competence does not refer to a specific trait nor to any
inborn capacity of the individual, but refers to capabilities to adjust
constructively to change. In terms of the family setting, it denotes a
kind of adaptability by which children can be compared with their
own potential rather than with "extraneous competitive norms." Foote
and Cottrell have described competence as the principle by which
adequate interpersonal relations are conducted.[51] The child or adolescent may be compared with his own previous stage of development,
or possibly with that of his peers, but not with some artificial image
that may be the parent's conception of ideal or perfect development.

The components of competence as we have described it are somewhat hypothetical, but they include: (1) health, which means, among
other things, the mother who is not overworked physically or emotionally; (2) intelligence, both in marital relations and in child guidance,
the ability to consider alternatives, and to verbalize and understand
consequences; (3) empathy, taking the role of the other, which is
central to all interpersonal relations; (4) autonomy, the clarity of the
individual's conception of self (identity) or the maintenance of a
stable set of internal standards by which he acts—the parent who is
secure and consistent in his behavior; (5) judgment, the ability to
make decisions, preferably correct decisions, which ability to a great
extent depends on experience; (6) creativity or flexibility, the ability
to arrive at imaginative decisions, to find new perspectives, and impro-
vise novel roles.

These various factors of course overlap. They refer not only to the
capacity for parenthood but for all interpersonal relations. Usually the

[51] Nelson N. Foote and Leonard S. Cottrell, *Identity and Interpersonal Competence,* The University of Chicago Press, 1955, p. 50.

individual who is capable of handling other people and is sympathetic in close relationships is likely to carry over that ability into his role as a parent. As the therapist or teacher detaches himself from the situation, the parent must be able to do the same.

In this chapter, even more than in Chapter 5, we have emphasized the role of the middle-class parent as oriented toward communication and empathy, and a role based on affectionate directiveness combined with permissiveness. Although the findings of hundreds of research studies are not completely in agreement, the observer may still conclude that most parents consider their experience challenging, if not always pleasurable. The rewards are in a series of rich experiences.

Supplementary Readings

Ayrault, Evelyn W., *You Can Raise Your Handicapped Child*, G. P. Putnam's Sons, New York, 1964. Popular in approach, the author presents data on the recent improvements in education, social welfare, and medical advance surrounding the defective child.

Clarke, Helen I., *Social Legislation* (second edition), Appleton-Century-Crofts, New York, 1957. Part Two, "Parent, Child, and the State," offers a relatively complete treatment of the legal status of the child.

Farber, Bernard, *Family: Organization and Interaction*, Chandler Publishing, San Francisco, 1964. Chapters 8–11 deal with different phases of socialization. Chapter 10 includes some findings in regard to the family's reaction to a handicapped child.

Harper, Fowler V. and Jerome H. Skolnick, *Problems of the Family* (revised edition), Bobbs-Merrill, Indianapolis, 1962. Chapter 3 treats problems in parenthood, such as "fertility control," adoption, and parental obligations, largely through a review of legal cases.

Smith, I. Evelyn (ed.), *Readings in Adoption*, Philosophical Library, New York, 1963. More than forty articles by various writers, particularly social workers, regarding this serious problem.

Vincent, Clark E., *Unmarried Mothers*, The Free Press of Glencoe, A Division of Collier-Macmillan, New York, 1961. One of America's unsolved problems as analyzed in terms of an incisive survey.

Zietz, Dorothy, *Child Welfare: Principles and Methods*, John Wiley, New York, 1959. An authoritative presentation of the handicapped child, with emphasis on welfare programs.

Part five

Conflict, Crisis, and Dissolution

Not all married couples live happily ever after. The final part of this book is concerned with the problem of marital conflict, family crises and breakdown, and some of the ways in which these problems may be resolved. Chapter 19 discusses the bases of marital conflict and the means of meeting these tensions. A discussion of internally and externally caused family crises concludes the chapter.

The societal, historical, and legal aspects of the termination of marriage are presented in Chapter 20. The psychological processes and role involvements in marital conflict and dissolution are considered, as well as the effects of divorce and the topic of remarriage. Chapter 21 describes the contribution of the marital counsellor.

Chapter nineteen
Marital Conflict and Family Crises

Marriage: The state or condition of a community consisting of a master, a mistress and two slaves, making in all, two.
> *Ambrose Bierce,* The Devil's Dictionary, *1906.*

Love without marriage is like a bird of passage alight upon the mast of a ship at sea. For my part, I prefer a fine green tree with its own roots, and room in its branches for a nest.
> *Jean Paul Richter,* Titan, *CXXV, 1803.*

Marriage *is* corrupting, he thought to himself with redoubled emphasis. In the complex, hundredfold daily emotional transactions of which it was formed, shrewd bargaining was inevitable—with dishonesty close on the heels of that. Mopworth's beef in a nutshell was that he was not appreciated. For think. He did his own work and a third of his wife's, dropped his moods to attend to hers, ministered to her humors and humored her wishes—and it was all taken for granted. In common with her generation she took as a matter of course an amount of distaff drudgery by the male that would have appalled a previous generation.
> *Peter De Vries,* Reuben, Reuben, *Little, Brown, Boston, 1964, pp. 409–410. Copyright 1956, 1962, 1964 by Peter De Vries.*

Christina's World by Andrew Wyeth
Collection, The Museum of Modern Art, New York. Purchase.

It would be strange indeed to find a marriage without disagreement or conflict. The psychologist might well ask the couple who says, "We've never had a quarrel" whether this is *really* the case. However, some individuals may repress or internalize their disagreements; an outward calm and cheerfulness may conceal conflict and hostility. If we accept the universality of marital conflict and the probability of tension, we shall have a more realistic basis for judging marriage. It is possible for conflict to be minimal if certain conditions are fulfilled in the marriage. Conflict can be handled constructively. Marital conflicts arising from exterior forces must be distinguished from those that spring from interpersonal relations within the family.

In this chapter we review some of the specific bases of conflict, such as the so-called in-law problem and economic and sexual ones. However, the main emphasis of the chapter centers on the psychological processes, both conscious and unconscious, and on the critical question of roles. This book has stressed the analysis of marital and family behavior in terms of a multiplicity of roles, and the area of conflict is no exception. In the interaction between family members it is unlikely that full agreement can be reached about role behaviors. And agreement reached on ideal roles or role models is not necessarily translated into action in a specific situation. Both ideal roles and role enactments may get in the way of each other, especially when two or more people are involved. Minor differences in the values and roles of two individuals may, with certain triggering, become escalated into major tensions. Or perhaps there may be no single area sufficiently far-reaching to jeopardize the relationship, but a number of minor conflicts may pile up so that a major crisis can develop. The change of the marital relationship over the years may also engender conflict. Other situations may influence the marital or family setting, such as an outside catastrophe or a disability on the part of the two central figures. The socio-cultural milieu may also be an important factor. A common example of such a situation today is the family whose head is in military service, representing a case of culturally induced conflict which could assume crisis proportions.

SOME RECURRENT SOURCES OF CONFLICT

In the modern world complex stimuli demand equally complex responses. It is impossible to say whether the pressures surrounding marriage are more demanding today than they were a century ago. However, it is a general assumption that today there exist more distractions operating on the unity and integrity of the home. It is also possible that roles were more static and the channels of verbalizing discontent were more limited in the past. Today, family life literature and counselling facilities illuminate the labyrinths of marital living. Yet the problems surrounding present-day marriage would have a familiar ring to the husbands and wives of previous generations.

Consequently the tensions of contemporary society, such as the in-law problem, financial strains incumbent upon the nuclear family in urban life, changes in the pattern of the wife's employment, and sex adjustment are not entirely new. The sequence of our discussion will proceed from specific areas of disagreement, to the basic patterns of marital conflict.

THE IN-LAW PROBLEM. The mother-in-law situation has long been the source of a good deal of joking, along with some anxiety, in many marriages. Probably the situation is not as alarming as popular sources imply, and in recent years this type of humor has decreased. A number of events have reduced the significance of in-law relationships. First, the nuclear family is more firmly entrenched than ever before. Individual families now live almost entirely in separate households. Family life education and the popularization of information regarding mental health have affected the behavior in relation to in-laws. Finally, the mobility of the postwar age has reduced the scope of interfamily associations. At least it is easier now to escape an unpleasant in-law situation. Perhaps the mother-in-law has never really been as ubiquitous as popular folklore indicates.

In a study of 276 husbands and wives, Landis found that 60 per cent of the subjects complained of the mother-in-law, the remainder naming another in-law their chief source of complaint.[1] It seems from this study, that women are more conspicuous as the source of in-law difficulties. Some years after the first Landis study Duvall discovered in a sample of 1,337 subjects that although mothers-in-law figured dominantly (37 per cent found her to be the most perplexing in-law) the sister-in-law was so indentified by 20 per cent of the sample, with other

---

[1] Judson T. and Mary G. Landis, *Building a Successful Marriage* (third edition), Prentice-Hall, Englewood Cliffs, New Jersey, 1958, pp. 405–406; see also Judson T. Landis, "Length of Time Required to Achieve Adjustment in Marriage," *American Sociological Review*, 1946, 11, 666–677.

in-laws being listed by smaller numbers of subjects. The remainder, a fourth of the sample, reported they had no difficulty with in-laws.[2]

The older an individual is at the time of marriage, the less likely is he or she to encounter in-law trouble. Landis found difficulties three times more likely to occur with in-laws if the age of the wife was under twenty as compared to those over twenty-three. Most important, a doting mother seems to feel more self-conscious about intrusion if the newlyweds are well into their twenties.

Causes. In analyzing the causes of in-law friction we come to the generalization that the individual's reaction to his or her parent affects the spouse's responses. In a study of married university students, mother-in-law problems were more likely to be reported by men whose wives had a close dependence on their mothers. However, in the case of husbands whose wives were deeply attached to their fathers, the husband was more favorably adjusted to their wives' fathers.[3]

There are several reasons for the difficulties the wife's mother may represent to a marriage in the cases where such a situation exists. She may be very sensitive to the way in which her daughter is treated, because the daughter symbolizes herself to some degree. She also becomes a mother-in-law at the time her own child-rearing career has practically ended, because her children are now married. Climacteric difficulties may complicate her own life. Moreover, such a mother-in-law no doubt perceives her role as one of helpfulness, and the failure of her newly acquired son to express gratitude may only enhance her own emotional reaction. There may be cultural complications. Perhaps the difference in social-class backgrounds, the son-in-law's occupation as compared to the father's, the difference in style of living may tend to freeze social relations between the two households once the nuptials are over or to force a grudging acceptance of the new couple at best. Interfaith marriages are expecially vulnerable to in-law difficulties. Religious differences can be extremely sensitive, and the son-in-law's or daughter-in-law's actions may be carefully scrutinized to determine the degree of progress in this situation.

The underlying dynamics of in-law relations are no less intricate and explosive than those encountered in other areas of marital rela-

[2] Evelyn M. Duvall, *In-Laws: Pro and Con,* Association Press, New York, 1954, p. 188.

[3] Sheldon Stryker, "The Adjustment of Married Offspring to their Parents," *American Sociological Review,* 1955, **20,** 149–154.

tions. Parents frequently cannot adjust to the "loss" of their child through marriage. They may accept the union at the conscious level, but not at the unconscious. If there has been a history of overprotection, the son or daughter may be oversolicitous to the parents, who may retain the prerogative of decision making. For instance, an overprotecting mother may convince herself that she must continue to protect her son or daughter and may possibly extend the same devotion to the newly acquired relative. The parent who has been rejecting of the child perhaps finds himself with feelings of guilt and loneliness and a consequent urge to be helpful, which often may be interpreted as manipulative and dominating. Parents who are reluctant to regard their children as separate entities deserving of self-respect probably will not prove to be more enlightened when their children are grown.

We may ask why some young people are unable to withstand the intervention of their parents. The in-law problem may often result from the fault of one of the spouses, who lacks maturity and insight and is unable to identify with an older individual who has had to make a major adjustment. Children may grow up with a fear reaction toward their parents which only disappears after marriage, if at all. If such an individual lacks ego strength in maintaining a respectful and affectionate alliance between his family of procreation and the family of orientation, such a person by his or her own action can influence the in-law relationship. Husbands and wives frequently read into the behavior of in-laws a number of motives that may not be relevant. Most married couples face the problem of maintaining both independence in their marriage and an acceptable relationship with their parents. Can the partners achieve a degree of detachment or withdrawal and at the same time reassure their parents? One solution to the problem is for the spouse affected to learn to select a number of behavior alternatives in associations with the mother-in-law that may smooth over rather than disturb the relationship.[4] The parents on both sides are often weaned away over a period of months. Serious situations may occur when an only child is concerned, where an excessively strong tie has been formed, or if the parent is widowed. More often it is the mother who is involved. Marriages contracted by individuals in their thirties especially encounter the problem of the widowed mother-in-law.

In-law conflicts may be marked by a number of unconscious or

[4] Landis and Landis, *op. cit., pp.* 416–421.

semiconscious motives. Self-directed hostility or hostility directed toward the spouse may shift toward the in-law who is a safer target or less dangerous adversary. The relation to one's in-laws may rest on frustrations or substitute reactions toward a new stimulus. A middle-aged woman who poses a mother-in-law threat may be making the new son-in-law into a love object, as Simpson describes:

> The wife's mother may cause discord because she leads the daughter to demand of the husband what she herself would like to have if she could live her life over again—this time with him. Her demands are aimed to elicit from the son-in-law some form of obeisance toward her daughter which she then takes as a sign of love for her. The husband's mother may demand of the daughter-in-law that she treat him the way he would have been treated if he had married his mother, his first love, from whom he has been stolen.[5]

The same situation may occur in reverse with a father-in-law. However, only 5.0 per cent of the subjects in Duvall's study complained of the father-in-law.

Effects. There is little question that in-law difficulties can diminish the happiness of some marriages, and, conversely, approval of in-laws was expressed more frequently by the happily married than the divorced sample in a study by Locke.[6] Burgess and Wallin found that the problem situation can, however, be eased by a number of techniques from changing residence to a tacit agreement to avoid certain areas of discussion. Most critical in handling the difficulties is the couples' attempt to place themselves in the mental framework of the other person.[7] Generally, accommodative processes solve most severe in-law entanglements, except in the instances of deep ego involvements or basically immature personalities on the part of either spouse. Parenthetically it can be added that a number of our generalizations apply to relationships with friends; the partners often come to marriage with deep loyalties to friends which may be inappropriate to those of in-laws. The difference is that relatives have a greater claim on the individual and one extending over a longer period of time.

As a final note, let us emphasize the *positive* aspects of in-laws, who may give much in the way of moral support to the young couple. Rela-

[5] George Simpson, *People in Families*, Thomas Y. Crowell, New York, 1960, p. 204.
[6] Harvey J. Locke, *Predicting Adjustment in Marriage: A Comparison of a Divorced and Happily Married Group*, Holt, Rinehart and Winston, New York, 1951, p. 119
[7] Ernest W. Burgess and Paul Wallin, *Engagement and Marriage*, J. P. Lippincott, Philadelphia, 1953, pp. 603–607.

tives have given extensive financial aid to their married children in the postwar period. This phenomenon is most common in the middle class, is especially heavy in the early years of marriage, and declines noticeably by the tenth year of marriage. The working class usually gives more in the way of services, on the other hand. The wife's parents are more likely to give aid by indirect means (that is, nonreciprocal gifts) so as not to interfere with the son-in-law's traditional status as provider.[8] The most frequent service given by in-laws is that of baby-sitting. It seems that there are styles of grandparenthood. A recent middle class study found the more "distant figure" or formal role as opposed to the "fun seeker," usually among grandparents over sixty-five.[9] In addition to the roles of alternate parents and socializers of the children, the in-laws may serve as confidants to the new parents.

Several factors during the more recent past have operated to make the role of in-laws less formidable. With younger marriages during the past thirty years, intergenerational age differences have been reduced creating more possibility for mutual understanding. Better health standards have made for a happier outlook among people who are in upper age levels. The emphasis on preparation for retirement and education in the use of leisure time, including the cultivation of hobbies, have introduced the older generation to pursuits that distract them from manipulating their children.

FINANCIAL STRAIN. Since the beginning of history economic problems of one kind or another have placed strains on marriage. But the prosperity of the postwar years has reduced the number of married couples who have serious economic problems. Only 1 per cent of the white sample in Blood and Wolfe's Detroit study felt they "were really missing out" on the world's goods, although 17 per cent stated that "it would be nice to have more." [10] This study pointed to a comparative lack of acute economic problems, but it may be recalled from Chapter 15 that the "blue collar world" presents a different picture. A lack of future orientation, an inability to set limits to behavior, and deficient commitment to the "significant values of a society" are among the

[8] Bert N. Adams, "Structural Factors Affecting Parental Aid to Married Children," *Journal of Marriage and Family,* 1964, **26,** 327–331.

[9] Bernice L. Neugarten and Karol K. Weinstein, "The Changing American Grandparent," *Journal of Marriage and the Family,* 1964, **26,** 199–204.

[10] Robert O. Blood, Jr. and Donald M. Wolfe, *Husbands and Wives: The Dynamics of Married Living,* The Free Press of Glencoe, A Division of Collier-Macmillan, New York, 1960, p. 108.

predisposing factors leading the family toward financial distress. For example, teenage marriage, uncompleted education, inability to carry on successful family planning, and lack of discipline in consumption habits are sources of trouble.[11] Some antisocial habit system, such as alcoholism, of course, severely complicates the family's economic pattern and marital adjustment.

Among 46 urban low-income families, Koos found that 15 families complained of illness, and 12 families, with some overlapping, had difficulties in economic management. These financial problems generally were not as serious as interpersonal problems in threatening the happiness of the home. In only a few cases were financial difficulties a prolonged threat to the family.[12] The surveys and literature of the 1930's present a much grimmer picture, although economic stress was more likely to elicit family disorganization than marital conflict as such. In fact, of 100 depression families studied by Cavan and Ranck, 27 had developed a sense of responsibility which apparently increased marital and family solidarity. It was possible to distinguish families in which *some* worry led to effective planning and organization, but where excessive worry was related to distress and consequent reorganization in family roles.[13]

PATTERNS OF MARITAL CONFLICT

The Nature of Conflict. We have already had occasion to examine conflict in relation to marital roles and adjustment, particularly in Chapter 13. However, in this section we are specifically concerned with an analysis of conflict itself.

When two people have conflicting desires, the needs of one individual may get in the way of the other. A healthy marriage based on deep love between two people does not preclude hostility. There are also more extreme instances as when a husband and wife are frightened of

[11] Charles V. Willie and Janet Weinandy, "The Structure and Composition of 'Problem' and 'Stable' Families in a Low-Income Population," *Marriage and Family Living*, 1963, 25, 439–447.

[12] Earl L. Koos, *Families in Trouble*, King's Crown Press, New York, 1946, pp. 63–64; see Chapter 15 for further discussion of the problems of the lower income family.

[13] Ruth S. Cavan and Katherine H. Ranck, *The Family and the Depression: A Study of One Hundred Chicago Families*, The University of Chicago Press, Chicago, 1938, pp. 55f.

being separated from each other for even brief periods. Their self-enforced togetherness may arise from unconscious hostility that prevents them from risking their relationship by absence from each other. We may conclude that conflict can be covert or overt, latent or active, unconscious or conscious, intermittent or chronic.[14]

Much marital conflict is amorphous and fluctuating, although of continuing character. Perhaps the husband wants to further his career, but at the expense of family obligations; attention to his bowling score necessitates his absence from home. Or maybe there is conflict over whether the wife will buy a new fur-trimmed coat or the husband will have a new set of golf clubs. These "tremendous trifles," as Baber calls them, may become the verbal substance of marital relations.[15] Often their value is more symbolic than actual. Minor conflict may become highly important for the two partners, because these day-to-day events are blown up to serve some unconscious need. Apparently trivial but meaningful stimuli, such as a husband's demand that his wife have dinner ready on time, may be the conscious material for a deep-seated conflict he cannot face. Neurotic conflict may be attached to a number of free-floating anxieties (that is, those anxieties having no apparent particular cause) and aggressions, which could be the cause of any minor tension between two partners.[16]

THE EXPRESSION AND TYPES OF CONFLICT. Conflict may be expressed in different ways. Frequently manipulative strategies are used. A person may control his marital partner by appealing to sympathy or praise, and through comparisons with others, all of which are a curious mixture of flattery and deflation. In some instances, the behavior resembles the strategies of two contestants in a game. The players are husbands and wives with conflicting aims, each with alternative techniques by which victory or an "anticipated outcome" may be achieved. Each outcome has a certain value or payoff to each contestant.[17]

Similarly, a laboratory study of 75 married couples showed different strategies of resolving role conflicts. The couples were presented with

[14] Willard Waller, *The Family, A Dynamic Interpretation* (revised by Reuben Hill), Holt, Rinehart and Winston, New York, 1951, pp. 296–297.

[15] Ray E. Baber, *Marriage and the Family*, McGraw-Hill, New York, 1953, p. 221.

[16] Ludwig Eidelberg, "The Neurotic Choice of Mate," in Victor Eisenstein (ed.), *Neurotic Interaction in Marriage*, Basic Books, New York, 1956, pp. 57–64.

[17] Jesse Bernard, "The Adjustments of Married Mates," in Harold T. Christensen (ed.), *Handbook of Marriage and the Family*, Rand McNally, Chicago, 1964, pp. 695–696.

a hypothetical role situation and the decision of whether the husband should accept a more satisfying job—although it paid less than his present one—and whether the wife should continue working, despite her pregnancy. Three modes of resolving the problem were discovered: (1) egocentric or self-centered, namely the winning by overcoming the partner's viewpoint; (2) cocentric, or consideration of both the self and the other, with consequent disarming effects on the other person; and (3) altercentric or total consideration of the partner, which indirectly forces the latter to "give in." The egocentric approach was the most frequently used and the most successful, the concentric the least. To what degree this model applies to real life settings is questionable, but it is noteworthy that the husbands did most of the talking and won most of the arguments.[18]

Marital and family conflict may be farreaching without the members being aware of the pattern of expression they have chosen. In an intensive study of 25 middle-class families, Naegele reports that hostility was expressed in several subtle or unconscious ways: (1) bristling tension masked through the use of "Dear" before each sentence; (2) sulking—silence demonstrating hostility; (3) explosive scenes with family members "blowing up" periodically.[19] These responses hold good for parent-child and intersibling relationships as well as for husbands and wives. When these conflicts approach long-term neurotic needs in which insecurity, anxiety, or guilt is persuasive, counselling or psychotherapy is likely to be the only promising means of assuring the marriage adequate satisfaction or probability of continuance. Yet in many hostility-ridden homes it is extremely difficult to convince the relevant family members of their need for treatment.

In certain marriages, two candidates may perceive in each other a resolution of psychological deficiencies or complementary needs. Some individuals marry in the hope of encountering someone to reduce or counteract their anxiety level, as we have already discussed in Chapter 13. Winch's theory of complementary needs, it will be recalled, presupposes two individuals who unconsciously realize in each other a completion of themselves, usually involving very different or opposite

---

[18] Harold Feldman and Martin E. Rand, "Egocentrism-Altercentrism in the Husband-Wife Relationship," *Journal of Marriage and the Family*, 1965, **27**, 386–391.

[19] Kasper D. Naegele, "Some Problems in the Study of Hostility and Aggression in Middle Class American Families," in Norman W. Bell and Ezra F. Vogel (eds.), *The Family*, The Free Press of Glencoe, A Division of Collier-Macmillan, New York, 1960, pp. 417–434.

personality structures. These personality tendencies underpin reciprocal role relationships: the boy looking for a mother, the male with
dominance needs desiring a girl who loves to serve her master. Generally, the dynamics of motivation for a couple is more complex than
implied by these overly simplified examples, but two partners in a
marriage based on complementary needs are in some way supportive of
each other. These types of marriages can be as successful as the more
homogamous variety.

EFFECTS OF CONFLICT ON THE CHILD.   In some situations the child
may become a scapegoat if his parents are unable to resolve their tensions, as one study of disturbed children and their families has shown.[20]
Several explanations have been offered. First, the child is in a relatively powerless position vis-a-vis his parents. Second, the child may
symbolize the conflict between the husband and wife, particularly as
illustrated in the older male child, who may represent the father in the
eyes of the mother. The scapegoat may be any child who physically
represents one of the parents. Third, there may be disappointment
with the child. He may be an underachiever who then becomes the
focus of tension, which hampers his capacity even more. The child with
a physical or emotional defect can be another subject for parental
conflict.

Such behavior illustrates the mechanisms by which parents may in
subtle and unconscious ways allow the child to displace their own
inadequacies. In some instances one parent may frustrate the spouse
by punishing the child. The child may occasionally present more problems than the parents are able to cope with. Sometimes the presence of
a child prevents or makes more difficult the dissolution of the marital
union. Thus he poses an even greater threat and consequently the
situation may become intensified.

THE RESOLUTION OF CONFLICT.   Conflict itself may be therapeutic
or clarifying; the term *constructive quarreling* has been used to describe the exploration of alternatives when marital partners are in
disagreement with each other. Presumably, constructive conflict is
delimited in scope, and in time and becomes aimed at producing
positive results; it is thus a variety of decision making.[21] In the jargon

---

[20] Bell and Vogel, "The Emotionally Disturbed Child as a Family Scapegoat," *op. cit.*, pp. 382–397.

[21] Waller, *op. cit.*, p. 311.

of the sociologist, *accommodation* is the process of conflict resolution by which two or more individuals or groups solve their problems. Mowrer has outlined several mechanisms by which tension with the married pair may be reduced or two individuals acquire techniques by which they learn to interact in marriage: [22]

Identification. The individual places himself in the situation of the other and may perceive the area of conflict in a different way.

Differentiation of Marital Roles. (The assumption of a variety of roles.) The ability of the couple to develop a series of interlocking roles points to flexibility in personality. This flexibility occasionally borders on inconsistency—the wife who may be a social climber at the expense of her responsibilities to her husband. Individual roles of the partners may be sufficiently rigid in some cases as to be on the margin of deep conflict.

Emulation. This interaction technique often functions in a marriage where there is a cultural gulf between the partners. In this context, emulation refers to the spouse who cultivates the traits of the other partner.

Idealization. This process probably functions more in courtship than in marriage. It occurs when one partner vests the other with given desirable qualities. The individual so idealized may respond by attempting to capitalize on the traits with which he has been endowed. Mowrer believes that in marriage idealization can be a means of developing an "affectional role relationship in which the parts played by husband and wife are complementary and equally satisfying."

Enhancement. Here a questionable trait in one partner is selected by the other and reworked or transposed into a socially acceptable one. This mechanism is most likely to appear when there are cultural differences between the two individuals. The woman disliking the gruff masculine exterior of a socially inferior husband reshapes him into the mental and physical image of an enterprising sportsman, an image she can accept.

Interhabituation or Interlocking of Habits. Partners may develop a set of mutually interdependent practices, such as doing the dishes together, shopping, or playing bridge. Unquestionably, the solidity and continuity of a marriage depends on the establishment of habit

---

[22] Harriet R. Mowrer, "Getting Along in Marriage," in Howard Becker and Reuben Hill (eds.), *Family, Marriage and Parenthood* (second edition), D. C. Heath, Boston, 1955, pp. 347–352.

systems which are indispensable to the individual; and their termination would be one of the more painful aspects of marriage dissolution.

The processes which Mowrer cites are related to the resolution of conflict, but success depends on insight and trial-and-error. They certainly presuppose a minimal rather than maximal level of internal conflict. Such response mechanisms exist in practically all marriages although seldom as articulate processes. Perceptive partners are probably conscious of the use of these techniques, and are quite as aware of the satisfaction their application may bring to the marriage as they are conscious of the risk involved if utilized to an exaggerated degree.

ROLE INVOLVEMENT AND CONFLICT

In analyzing the process of conflict and its resolution in marriage, the definition and enactment of roles is pertinent. Spiegel found that role reciprocity broke largely because of the failure to achieve satisfaction on several fronts: [23] (1) Insufficient acquaintance with the roles required by one or both partners (*cognitive discrepancy*). The individual is not familiar with expected sex or age roles, for instance, and cues are misunderstood: the husband does not realize that his wife expects flowers on anniversaries. The gap in understanding is still greater during a crisis as in the role of the husband during a period of unemployment. (2) Confusion and misinterpretation of motives (*goal discrepancy*). One spouse sets up ideals or ends the other considers unacceptable. The husband expects his wife to be the party hostess when her own life ideal is simply to be a traditional homemaker. (3) The problem of communicating the particular or individualistic role we wish to assume (*communicative discrepancy*). The spouse may be misled by information, intentional or unintentional, given by the partner, and consequently, may feel cheated. This type of discrepancy is more subject to individual variation than more traditional role expectancies. (4) The failure to provide the means by which marital functioning can occur (*instrumental discrepancy*). The most important prop is probably economic, but many other factors may enter the picture, such as questions of residential stability, transportation adequacy, or health level. (5) The discontinuity of class, ethnic, and religious subcultures within the United States may prevent husband

---

[23] John B. Spiegel, "The Resolution of Role Conflict within the Family," in Bell and Vogel, *op. cit.,* pp. 361–381. This list is an adaptation of Spiegel's model.

and wife from developing a consensus in perception, communication, and role behavior (*discrepancy in cultural values*). The movie version of the heiress who marries her chauffeur and lives happily ever after is an extreme example of this situation.

The discrepancies just listed are, of course, not mutually exclusive. Discrepancies of several types may occur within the same marriage. The theory that divergent definitions or roles constitute a barrier to marital adjustment has been confirmed in a number of studies. Comparing 100 divorced couples with an equal number of happily married couples in Chilicothe, Ohio, Jacobson discovered in the divorced sample greater disparity between the husbands and wives regarding preferred roles.[24] Presumably divorce was a more likely outcome for couples with conflicting ideas of sex roles, for instance, the insistence of the husband on a traditional authoritarian role for himself and a passive, subordinate one for his wife. Recently, Betty Friedan's protest in *The Feminine Mystique*[25] pointed to the conflict engendered by what she considered the underprivileged role relegated to women —the wife's discovery of herself caught in a dreary set of household chores, which, even if they fill her day, rarely measure up to her aspirations. Her search for status and meaning may pose conflict for her husband as well as for herself.

Value and role conflicts will continue to influence interpersonal relationships, including marriage, in a society that encourages opposing social behavior such as romanticism on one side and practical success on the other, social cohesiveness and individualism, and equality and cultural heterogeneity. Roles have to be adjusted to a number of contingencies. Definitions of roles are caught in communicative barriers. Among 354 "unhappy" marriages—compared to 630 "happy" ones (as determined by a marriage adjustment score) the most common complaints were problems in communication and empathy: "We don't think alike on many things"; the mate "has little insight into my feelings"; "We say things that hurt each other."[26] These complaints reemphasize lack of identification, the unwillingness to see one's responsibility in the marriage, and the inability to respect the self-image of the other party.

[24] Alver H. Jacobson, "Conflict of Attitudes Toward the Roles of the Husband and Wife in Marriage," *American Sociological Review*, 1952, 17, 146–150.

[25] W. W. Norton, New York, 1963.

[26] Vincent D. Mathews and Clement S. Mihanovich, "New Orientations on Marital Maladjustment," *Marriage and Family Living*, 1963, 25, 300–304.

THE PROCESS OF DISENCHANTMENT

A phenomenon of marked consequence to many marriages is the process of aging in the broad connotation of that term. Both the middle and upper years of marriage reflect change. Disenchantment may set in. Using the Burgess and Wallin sample, Pineo analyzed the disenchantment process twenty years after the engagement period and discovered three indices of romantic decline: a drop of marital satisfaction; loss of intimacy, as in confiding, kissing, and consensus; and diminution of certain activities, most notably sexual relations.[27] Since personal adjustment did not decline, the loss of interest could be accounted for by changes in time rather than by the process of aging. Pineo's statement that the "fit between the two individuals which leads them to marry reduces with time," [28] calls for certain explanations.

Decline of Romantic Impulses. The idealized premarital relationship suffers some reality consciousness after marriage.[29] The ensuing years of marriage register a further drop in romantic attitudes, particularly among the male population, as a comparison of non-daters, couples in serious courtship or engagement, and a married population indicated.[30] The fact that the male may be more inclined to romanticize before marriage seems to imply that the female is more realistic in the marriage market place, since she is on the defensive and is trained to be more calculating in her courtship process. This practicality may survive into marriage even though her emotional outlook is traditionally subject to romanticism.

Monotony or Lack of Change. Any individual becomes weary of an unchanging source of stimulation or a situation that fails to offer the same degree of interest it may have had at one time. However, the store house of common memories and many shared events provides an emotional tie for the partners.

Sex Roles. These may lead to disenchantment as men find other

[27] Peter C. Pineo, "Disenchantment in the Later Years of Marriage," *Marriage and Family Living*, 1961, **23**, 3–11.

[28] *Ibid.,* p. 7.

[29] Clifford Kirkpatrick and Charles W. Hobart, "Disagreement, Disagreement Estimate and Non-Empathetic Imputations for Intimacy Groups Varying from Favorite Date to Married," *American Sociological Review*, 1954, **19**, 10–19.

[30] Charles W. Hobart, "Disillusion in Marriage and Romanticism," *Marriage and Family Living*, 1958, **20**, 156–162.

interests, such as poker or deer hunting, for example. For the woman especially the home situation may not be altogether stimulating. With her children partially or fully grown, the woman may attempt to find release and self-importance in organizational work, but these activities may not provide sufficient outlets for her needs.[31]

The Psychological Bases of the Marriage. These factors are altered through time. If some marriages exhibit a growing dependency of the spouses on each other, others find their interests moving in different directions. Individuals change psychologically, and the relationship between spouses shifts with time. According to the complementary needs theory, the attraction of the opposite person, for example, in terms of nurturance or succorance or in fulfillment of some other need may change. The man who marries a forceful woman for support may later become more secure and no longer find his original choice meaningful. Waller mentions the case of Sinclair Lewis, who found considerable ego-gratification in his first wife, Grace Hegger Lewis, since she recognized his work before the rest of the world did. Once Lewis was famous, her words of praise or solace were no longer necessary. Her autobiographical novel reflects some bitterness on this point; equally insightless was Lewis's attack on her in *Dodsworth*.[32]

Differential Rate of Aging. Husbands and wives may not grow old at an equal rate, physically or mentally. Moreover, two people shift their interests during the years, and what brought them together as newlyweds may seem less compelling in later years.

Coalescence and the Marital Situation. Marital interaction has different effects on people. Whereas certain couples may move in somewhat opposite directions during their marriages, others may begin to act, think, and superficially even look alike. Speech, gestures, movements, and interests may appear alike. In these marriages a closer relationship may develop between the partners; yet this coalescence may cause or reflect an indifference, dullness, and even an unconscious aversion. This hypothesis of coalescence, whereby two individuals feel more secure by developing or concentrating on their similarities, has not been adequately tested. However, it poses an interesting comparison to the theory of complementary needs.

Disengagement is related to the disenchantment process. In the

---

[31] Robert R. Bell, *Marriage and Family Interaction,* The Dorsey Press, Homewood, Illinois, 1963, p. 283.
[32] Waller, *op. cit.,* p. 280; cf., also, Robert F. Winch, *Mate-Selection: A Study of Complementary Needs,* Harper and Row, New York, 1958, pp. 301–302.

later years of marriage, there is a withdrawal from a number of activities. A sample of 211 men and women between the ages of fifty and seventy revealed a tendency toward constriction of activities. With aging the individuals were found to become more self-involved.[33] Physical limits themselves operate to prevent widescale recreational and social pursuits.

Often the strain of parenthood is a principal cause of disengagement and disenchantment, and relief is felt when the parent role is completed. In a study of a limited number of middle-aged parents who had seen their children launched in a career or marriage, over a third considered the postparental period as "better" than preceding phases of marriage. At the time of the interview the subjects frequently felt that they had an opportunity to develop their relationship with their mates which could not be adequately realized during the parental years of their marriage.[34]

Whatever the negative generalizations regarding disenchantment, the advancing years of marriage may bring a feeling of greater solidarity and a deepening of love. Romantic notions become somewhat diminished with time, and the quality of the experiences may change. Some marriages may grow stronger through the years, others weaker, but the bases change in either case. If there is disenchantment on one hand, loyalty and other emotional tendencies, as well as a common set of experiences, add more to the love relationship than the physical changes in age can take away.

TOWARD A MORE ENDURING RELATIONSHIP

The following points furnish some guidelines for an enduring marriage.

The partners should examine their needs and question what the marriage means to them. To what extent are the ego needs of both fulfilled. An articulation of these questions may be beneficial in determining the strengths and weaknesses of the union.

What are the levels and types of communication in which they engage, and how do these function in comparison with other couples?

[33] Elaine Cumming, Lois R. Dean, and David S. Newell, and Isabel McCaffrey, "Disengagement—A Tentative Theory of Aging," *Sociometry*, 1960, 23, 23–35.

[34] Irwin Deutscher, "The Quality of Postparental Life: Definitions of the Situation," *Journal of Marriage and the Family*, 1964, 26, 52–59.

For example, does the husband return home bored, tired, and non-communicative? To whom does the wife turn most for confiding her feelings? Is there really free expression of emotional reactions? Is communication purely verbal, or is there an attempt to use other channels, love-making, periodically coming home with flowers, or having an occasional candlelight dinner? Kissing itself may be largely ritualistic—a peck on the cheek, or a warm embrace implying much deeper significance. Of course, either can be important. Some families have devised a set of informal signals to which its members are attuned. Often certain family members are so absorbed in their own emotional problems that they are unconscious of the need signals of other members that warn of an approaching crisis.[35]

What is the quality of the relationship between the husband and wife and between the parents and children? How does the power structure operate? Under what conditions do the husband or wife appear to be dominant? To what extent is there respect for the identity of the other? The transition within the marriage years should be optimally—and this cannot be true at all phases of the marriage—a growth situation of economic, social, or other goals. Perhaps we can describe one criterion of marriage adjustment as progression toward interpersonal competence. In other words, the husband and wife should be able to respect each other as an "end" rather than as a "means." Each partner should demonstrate, or be capable of demonstrating, a satisfactory level of identity.[36]

Does each partner perceive the marriage as a habit system, both in the positive and negative aspects of that term? The sense of interdependence may be of more significance than any unhappiness they may experience. Most individuals probably place security over change, if a choice between the two had to be made. Marriage is satisfying for its predictability, except for that minority who suffer chronic indecision and conflict. However, within this collective habit system there must be recognition of the need for privacy. The wife must have a chance to be liberated from the children, with a periodic day off, and spouses may even entertain the possibility of separate vacations.

Do the marital partners both recognize the variations of human

[35] Otto Pollak, "Issues in Family Diagnosis and Family Therapy," *Journal of Marriage and the Family*, 1964, **26,** 281.

[36] Nelson N. Foote and Leonard S. Cottrell, Jr., *Identity and Interpersonal Competence*, The University of Chicago Press, *Chicago*, 1955, p. 225.

nature, including sex differences? Does each perceive the spouse in view of his or her upbringing, including the pressures of children, parents, in-laws, and the job? The husband may be irritable on returning home because he is unable to get back at the boss, or the wife may be irritable because of one too many diaper changes. Not least, there must be a recognition of the sex differences within our culture. For instance, women enjoy a maximum of explicit verbal communication; they want to be told how much they are loved, and their sexual receptivity depends on a more total communicative approach.[37]

The ability to use outside resources, such as counselling and therapy may be important in some cases. In the broader sense, guidance may be available in the responsiveness of other members of the family. The sensitivity of the husband is necessary for him to recognize when he should take his wife out to dinner, or knowing which morning to bring her a cup of coffee in bed. She must be similarly aware, for example, of his desire to go on a fishing expedition with the office crew. But equally important, and preferably before the marriage reaches a complete impasse, both partners should appreciate the desirability of seeking an objective viewpoint from an impartial source, if needed—a topic covered more fully in Chapter 21.

CRISIS AND FAMILY READJUSTMENT

Chapter 19 discussed the matter of crisis and readjustment, as it pertained to specific causes. Here the discussion centers on the problem of analyzing crisis in terms of what generalizations might be significant in the middle-class frame of reference. In the broader perspective, family crises can be described as arising from the following sources:

EXTERNAL EVENTS. These can be described as disasters resulting from natural catastrophes such as tornadoes, floods, wars, etc. Other external events might be severe economic depression (1931–1935, for example) and political movements and revolutions. As the studies of the effects of the depression have shown, not all effects of these events are shattering to the family, but they can be temporarily highly disorganizing. A third type of external (or socio-cultural) event may function as a crisis: wartime separation, a demotion, change of job, or temporary unemployment of the head of the family. The birth of the

[37] Bernard, *op. cit.*, p. 715.

first infant may constitute a sort of crisis.[38] Possibly the degree of planning explains the difference in reaction.

INTERNAL EVENTS. This category includes, for example, personal disaster, as in the prolonged illness or death of a member of the family. The removal of the sick person into a hospital setting minimizes the disruptive effects on the family.[39] However, the financial and emotional drain and accompanying role discontinuities may be very disorganizing. Death in the immediate family is usually very traumatizing, not to speak of its social and economic impact.

A family disgrace (illegitimacy, suicide, alcoholism, delinquency resulting in a conviction) has tragic consequences for middle-class individuals. An internal crisis may result from a neurosis or severe maladjustment of one family member or from the inability of the husband and wife to manage their economic affairs. The borderline between these situations is arbitrary, as a neurotic symptom may be the result of external stress. Economic problems are, of course, enormously complicated by failures of family planning, the death of the breadwinner, or a chronic illness. Strongly neurotic trends may make the breadwinner unemployable, or as in the case of the compulsive gambler or speculator, may keep the family in a continuous state of economic peril. In a number of respects the impact of crisis on the family requires redefinition of statuses and roles. The family must regain its equilibrium.

How the crisis event is interpreted depends, among other things, on the family structure, the interrelationships of its members, and their definition of the situation. The "crisis-proneness" of a family may be a result of educational background, degree of ability to make decisions, and levels of ego strength of the relevant individuals, as well as certain uncontrollable factors (whether the son returns from the war, or the question of whether work will commence on the new industrial plant, etc.).

As one approach to the problem of family disorganization, Hill studied war separation and reunion crises. He found that the situation could be identified at diverse levels: (1) an objective definition by the social worker or other appropriate professional person, (2) a cultural

[38] E. E. LeMasters, "Parenthood as Crisis," *Marriage and Family Living*, 1957, **19**, 352–355. See also Daniel F. Hobbs, Jr., "Parenthood As Crisis: A Third Study," *Journal of Marriage and the Family*, 1965, **27**, 367–372.

[39] Talcott Parsons and Renee Fox, "Illness, Therapy, and the Modern Urban American Family," *Journal of Social Issues*, 1952, **8**, 31–44.

definition as the community might perceive the event, and (3) a subjective definition by the individual himself.[40] An important determinant of the family's ability to meet the crisis was the mobilization of resources, particularly psychological and financial.

REORGANIZATION FOLLOWING A CRISIS—THE CASE OF MENTAL ILLNESS. The processes of reorganization following and accompanying a family crisis may be illustrated in the case of mental illness. Somewhat over 180,000 persons are admitted to mental institutions each year for the first time, and approximately 80,000 are readmitted with recurring psychoses.[41] Roughly half of these individuals are married adults between the ages of twenty-five and sixty, implying a heavy toll in terms of family responsibility.

In an intensive study of 33 male mental patients, Clausen and Yarrow found several stages of readjustive behaviors by family members, particularly the wife. Among these were:

1. The family, or at least the wife, perceives certain symptoms which, although not immediately comprehensible, often have somewhat traumatic effects, and as a result family disorganization occurs.

2. The wife attempts to interpret her husband's behavior, but only reluctantly accepts it as deviant. Generally there is a desire to "normalize" the situation with certain defenses, as "the hallucinations he hears happen to other people, too." Gradually and reluctantly she accepts the psychiatric diagnosis when she cannot cope with the problem.

3. Once hospitalization occurs he and other members of the family are forced to readjust their roles. In view of the stigmatization applied, the psychological reactions are often complex, and a feeling of inadequacy and disgrace may make for disorganized responses even when the situation is stabilized.[42]

Similar results were encountered in research with families in which the wife was hospitalized for psychiatric reasons. The husband experienced considerable difficulty in comprehending the breakdown and the disorganizing effect on the family. In many situations the hospitalization was delayed until a serious overt act had occurred, such as attempts of violence toward a member of the family. "Alienative acts" during the prehospitalizational period made the return to given marital

---

[40] Reuben Hill, *Families Under Stress*, Harper and Row, New York, 1948.
[41] John A. Clausen and Marian R. Yarrow, "The Impact of Mental Illness on the Family," *Journal of Social Issues*, 1955, **11**, 3.
[42] *Ibid.*, pp. 16f.

roles after recovery from the illness more difficult.[43] On the whole, various factors, such as blocking out the unpleasant experiences, a skillfully handled visitation program, and aid of the social caseworker can be highly beneficial for the restoration of the former patient to the home.

Family adjustment to crisis is outlined by Hill as a sequence of crisis: disorganization, recovery, reorganization—especially in reference to disaster experience. In internal family maladjustments a roller-coaster or wave-like effect may occur as successive peaks of crisis.[44] The ups and downs of mental illness, successive admissions and releases from the mental hospital, bouts with alcohol and recovery, or taking risks in inordinate business operations all produce alternate despair and relaxation.

MARRIAGE AND THE FAMILY IN MILITARY SERVICE

Crises can be regarded as an inevitable phase of the socio-cultural order in which we live. Military service, in particular, is now accepted by most observers as a legitimate or inevitable phase of our culture.

COURTSHIP PRACTICES. The tempo and quality of dating and premarital courtship were drastically altered during World War II. The male population was recruited into military service and concentrated in restricted areas. In the urgency of wartime, the more reserved moral outlook of peacetime dating was no longer appropriate. War strengthened the tendencies that had been underway since the 1920's. An "emerging single standard" governed several aspects of dating: the arrangement of the date by the girl, the sharing of expenses, and the weakening of the "double standard" of morality.[45] There was an unhealthy polarization of the sexes into two worlds, the male contingent in army bases in the United States and overseas, and the female in civilian communities.

MARRIAGE PATTERNS. War tends to accelerate the marriage rate. In fact, one of the minor dangers of war is the frequency of hasty and ill-advised marriages. The "marry-and-run" marriages of World War II

[43] Harold Sampson, Sheldon L. Messenger, Robert D. Towne, "The Mental Hospital and Marital Family Ties," in Howard S. Becker (ed.), *The Other Side Perspectives on Deviance*, The Free Press of Glencoe, A Division of Collier-Macmillan, New York, 1964, pp. 139–162.

[44] Reuben Hill and Donald A. Hansen, "Families in Disaster," in George W. Barker and Dwight W. Chapman (eds.), *Man and Society in Disaster*, Basic Books, New York, 1962, p. 196.

[45] John F. Cuber, "Changing Courtship and Marriage Customs," *The Annals of the American Academy of Political and Social Science*, 1943, **229**, 30–38.

often led to a brief cohabitation, followed by service obligation for the male; the separation only served to terminate the relationship. More serious, this type of marriage did not have the extensive courtship desirable for preparing the couple for a successful married life with its emotional growing together and techniques of give-and-take.[46] Even when there was an adequate affectional base, the separation and other experiences of wartime produced a certain rupture or reevaluation.

The absence of the loved one and the anxieties about the welfare of family members both subjected marriage to farreaching strain. Many men, by writing frequently to their wives, maintained bonds that symbolically, at least, were nearly as powerful as if they were living under normal circumstances. For others, correspondence was immensely difficult as many were unable to write letters either with sufficient frequency or depth to sustain the affectional aspects of a marital relationship. In addition to the separation, sometimes an extramarital affair or a succession of amorous adventures, affected the emotional involvement.

As a result of marital conflict during wartime the divorce rate rose precipitously in the immediate postwar period. In 1920 the divorce rate in the United States was 7.7 per thousand existing marriages, one third above the 1917 rate, which in turn was higher than pre-1914 levels.[47] In England, France, and Germany similar increases were sustained. World War II demonstrated an even greater wave of divorces. In the five-year period from 1941 to 1945 the largest percentage of accumulation of divorces in our history occurred. In 1946 no less than 629,000 marriages were dissolved by divorce and annulment. The Korean war itself created more than a mere ripple in the rate; however, by 1955 the divorce rate declined to 9.3. This rate was still higher than that of the 1920's and 1930's.

FAMILY RELATIONSHIPS.   The emotional havoc that war brought to children has been well documented.[48] The most disastrous situations

---

[46] James J. S. Bossard, "War and the Family," *American Sociological Review,* 1941, **6**, 330–344.

[47] Paul H. Jacobson, *American Marriage and Divorce,* Holt, Rinehart and Winston, Inc., New York, 1959, p. 92.

[48] Reuben Hill, *Families under Stress: Adjustment to the Crisis of Separation and Reunion,* Harper and Row, New York, 1949; and Lois M. Stolz, et al., *Father Relations of War-Born Children,* Stanford University Press, Stanford, 1954.

occurred outside the United States, especially during World War II. In our own country the fatherless homes represented one of the major casualties. For as long as three years, great numbers of children were separated from their fathers except for one or two brief periods. Some never saw their fathers again.

Moreover, the number of working wives complicated the problem. More than three million women were employed in war industries during World War II. This situation combined with high residential mobility, inadequate housing, and overcrowded transportation, was responsible for family tensions, and large-scale frustration in many cases. The lack of supervision of children along with other problems seemingly served to increase juvenile maladjustment and delinquency. In addition, children and adolescents were confronted by an inordinate amount of violence in the newspapers, radio, and on the screen. Hate compaigns were directed toward the enemy, which left the child confused. The teacher shortage complicated the strain placed on parents. Substitute or inadequately trained teachers could not provide either the requisite academic skills or emotional guidance.

Undoubtedly the aftereffects of war, at least for the younger generation were vital. Father-child relations have been studied in a sample of 19 first-born children, born while their fathers were in uniform. The average age of the child was eighteen months at the time of the father's return. The reaction toward the returning father was shyness, complicated by the father's partial rejection of the child. Neurotic symptoms such as anxiety, lack of appetite, insomnia, and faulty elimination were apparent in the children.[49] In view of the size of the sample some caution in full acceptance of the figures is justified. However, there was sufficient consistency in the results to lend support to the theory that the presence of the father is highly desirable in the socialization process of the infant.

Present-day servicemen, and particularly their wives or wives-to-be, face essentially the same questions as in wartime, although fortunately on a reduced scale: Shall we marry or wait? Shall I follow my husband to his new camp? Shall I defer family planning until the return of my husband? Shall I take a job? With children the problems become even more complex. A psychiatric study of 15 children of naval officers revealed severe behavior problems apparently as the result of residen-

---

[49] Stolz, et al., *op. cit.*

tial mobility and absence of the father.[50] Even though the armed services are making more satisfactory provisions for the families of servicemen, the basic problems remain. In addition, most peacetime military situations have cultural and psychological disadvantages. Foreign residence can assume the form of cultural enclaves supporting ethnocentrism instead of broadening cultural horizons. But the most serious problem is still mobility.

Family crises, in comparison to marital conflicts, are often attributable to events beyond the control of the individual and have a more disruptive effect, if only temporary, on the marriage and family setting. They are similar to marital conflicts in that they involve problems in role definitions and enactments, as well as difficult problems in communication, and definition of the situation. In both conflicts and crises, marital partners and family members can learn to develop techniques for handling tensions and, hopefully, resolving them. However, there are a number of conditioning factors: most notably, the psychological resources of the individual or the family, which includes attitudes, feelings, and insight. Also critical are health factors, cultural factors of class and ethnic backgrounds, individual family background, and the total socio-economic setting. Not all married couples are able to resolve their conflicts and crises and the marriage may be dissolved, a problem to which we now turn.

Supplementary Readings

Becker, Howard and Reuben Hill (eds.), *Family, Marriage and Parenthood* (second edition), D. C. Heath, Boston, 1955. Chapters 11 and 12 by Harriet R. Mowrer explain the processes of conflict and adjustment.

Bernard, Jesse, *Remarriage, A Study of Marriage*, Holt, Rinehart and Winston, New York, 1956. Part Four, "Solidarity, Competition, and Conflict," describes the adjustments of second marriages, which have something in common with first marriages.

Bernard, Jesse, "The Adjustments of Married Mates," in Harold T. Christensen (ed.), *Handbook of Marriage and the Family*, Rand McNally, Chicago, 1964, pp. 675–739. A presentation of the role dimensions in adjustment and of the techniques of bargaining and conflict.

[50] Genevieve, Gabower, *Behavior Problems of Children in Navy Officers Families: as Related to Social Conditions of Navy Family Life*, Catholic University of America Press, 1959, as cited in Ernest W. Burgess, Harvey J. Locke, and Mary M. Thomes, *The Family* (third edition), American Book Company, New York, 1963, p. 494.

Duvall, Evelyn M., *In-Laws: Pro and Con,* Association Press, New York, 1954. A very readable report of the author's survey of the in-law question.

Farber, Bernard, *Family, Organization and Interaction,* Chandler Publishing, San Francisco, 1964. Chapter 10 is a penetrating analysis of family crises.

Hansen, Donald A. and Hill, Reuben, "Families Under Stress," in Christensen, *op. cit.* The authors approach the problem of crisis in terms of both theoretical concepts and major research findings.

Kirkpatrick, Clifford, *The Family As Process and Institution* (second edition), Ronald Press, New York, 1963. Chapter 18 is a well-documented presentation of the subject.

Lantz, Herman R. and Eloise C. Snyder, *Marriage,* John Wiley, New York, 1962. Chapters 13 and 14 are an introduction to the subject as based on the experience of counselling.

Levy, John and Ruth Monroe, *The Happy Family,* Alfred A. Knopf, New York, 1938. The book treats with some useful insights the problem of the resolution of conflict.

Rogler, Lloyd H. and August B. Hollingshead, *Trapped: Families and Schizophrenia,* John Wiley and Sons, New York, 1965. A study of mental disorders and their impact on the nuclear and extended family system of Puerto Rico.

Sussman, Marvin B. (ed.), *Sourcebook in Marriage and the Family* (second edition), Houghton Mifflin, Boston, 1963. Chapters 6 and 7 contain some excellent readings.

Waller, Willard, *The Family, A Dynamic Interpretation* (revised by Reuben Hill), Holt, Rinehart and Winston, New York, 1951. Chapters 13–17 and 21 are probably the most psychologically mature discussion of conflict and its resolution.

Winch, Robert F., *Mate Selection: A Study in Complementary Needs,* Holt, Rinehart and Winston, New York, 1958. Although the final assessment of complementary needs is still in doubt as to the bases of mate selection, the study still presents some interesting aspects of conflict and accommodation.

Chapter twenty

Bereavement, Separation, and Divorce

What therefore God hath joined together, let not man put asunder.
> *Mark X, 9 c. 70 (Cf. Matthew XIX, 6 c. 75)*

Marriage is a romance in which the hero dies in the first chapter.
> *Arab Proverb, in H. L. Mencken,* A New Dictionary of Quotations, *Alfred A. Knopf, New York, 1946, p. 765.*

It seems to us legitimate to interpret the recent and, to what extent we do not know, continuing, high level of the divorce rate in this light. It is not an index that the nuclear family and the marriage relationship are rapidly disintegrating and losing their importance. The truth is rather that, on the one hand, the two roles have been changing their character; on the other, their specific importance, particularly that of marriage, has actually been increasing. Both these aspects of the process of change impose additional strain on family and marriage as systems, and on their members as personalities. We suggest that the high rates of divorce are primarily indices of this additional strain. When the difficulty of a task is increased it is not unreasonable to expect that a larger proportion of failures should result until the necessary adjustments have been better worked out. In this case we feel that the adjustments are extremely complex and far-reaching.
> *Talcott Parsons and Robert F. Bales,* Family, Socialization and Interaction Process, *The Free Press of Glencoe, A Division of Collier-Macmillan, New York, 1955, pp. 24–25.*

The one charm of marriage is that it makes a life of deception necessary for both partners.
> *Oscar Wilde:* The Picture of Dorian Gray, *G. Munro's Sons, New York, 1895.*

Jerusha Williams' Mourning Picture by an unknown artist
Courtesy of The American Heritage Collection,
Colby College, Waterville, Maine

Since most marriages within Western society are terminated by death rather than separation or divorce, this chapter first explores the topics of death and bereavement, followed by a discussion of separation and desertion, and finally turns to examine divorce. Attention is given to the historical, social, and psychological factors influencing the decision to divorce involved in the divorce process. We also examine the complexities of divorce and the law. The chapter concludes with the subject of remarriage.

DEATH AND BEREAVEMENT

In the United States widows outnumber widowers; there are approximately 3.5 times as many widows as widowers.[1] During the early years of marriage, statistics indicate that divorce exceeds death as the terminator of marriage, but after the thirteenth year of marriage death becomes the major reason for marital disruption.[2] As the number of years married increases, the proportion of marriages terminated by the death of one partner steadily mounts. However, age is not the only factor influencing widowhood. Nonwhites and members of lower occupational strata are subject to a higher incidence of mortality.[3] One reason for the high recorded rate of widowhood among these groups is that frequently unmarried women with children list themselves as widows in order to escape stigmatization. However, let us begin with an examination of the adjustive processes required by the death of a spouse.

First, the cultural norms regarding bereavement can be of considerable value to the person experiencing the loss of a member of the family. Proper mourning attire and the funeral ritual are among the socio-cultural norms surrounding death. As Waller points out, the individual is told "how he shall react to death, how he shall arrange for burial, and what he shall say and think, and it provides hints as to how long he shall mourn"[4]—not excluding the respectable period of a year before he may remarry. Moreover, bereavement becomes a "collective process,"[5] and reliance on estab-

[1] Paul H. Jacobson, *American Marriage and Divorce,* Holt, Rinehart and Winston, New York, 1959, p. 140.

[2] *Ibid.,* p. 145.

[3] Paul C. Glick, *American Families,* John Wiley, New York, 1957, p. 153.

[4] Willard Waller, *The Family: A Dynamic Interpretation* (revised by Reuben Hill), Holt, Rinehart and Winston, New York, p. 489.

[5] *Ibid.*

lished habits, both social and cultural, give some sense of continuity to the individual during his grief.

BEREAVEMENT AS A PSYCHOLOGICAL PROCESS. For the surviving relative, death has severe psychological effects. Three general stages of bereavement and adjustment appear in the reactions of a person to the death of the spouse: [6]

Traumatization. The emotional shock is one of disbelief and unreality and especially acute when the death is a sudden one. Absorption in the first few days after the tragedy may prevent feeling the full effects of grief until after the services are over. The attention of relatives and friends may be a support in this initial period. But for days and weeks thereafter there may be a numbing effect until the individual can manage to comprehend the loss. The traumatization may also be accompanied by loss of appetite, insomnia, and other physical symptoms. As with any critical event in life no two people react identically in the face of loss. Agee in a well-known novel portrays the reaction of shock in a young widow who has lost her husband in an automobile accident:

> When grief and shock surpass endurance there occur phases of exhaustion, of anesthesia in which relatively little is left and one has the illusion of recognizing, and understanding, a good deal. Throughout these days Mary had, during these breathing spells, drawn a kind of solace from the recurrent thought: at least I am enduring it. I am aware of what has happened, I am meeting it face to face, I am living through it. It had of course occurred to her that this happens to many people, that it is very common, and she humbled and comforted herself in this thought. She thought: now I am more nearly a grown member of the human race; bearing children, which had seemed so much, was just so much apprenticeship. She thought that she had never before had a chance to realize the strength that human beings have, to endure; she loved and revered all those who had ever suffered, even those who had failed to endure. She thought that she had never before had a chance to realize the might, grimness and tenderness of God. She thought that now for the first time she began to know herself, and she gained extraordinary hope in this beginning of knowledge. She thought that she had realized all that was in her soul to realize in the event, and when at length the time came to put on her veil, leave the bedroom she had shared with her husband, leave their home, and go down to see him for the first time since his death and to see the long day through, which would cover him out of sight for the duration of this world, she thought that she was firm and ready. She had refused to "try on" her veil; the mere thought of approving or disapproving it before a mirror was obscene; so now when she came to the mirror and drew it down across her

---

[6] The author's interpretation is borrowed heavily from Waller, *op. cit.,* pp. 478f.

face to go, she saw herself for the first time since her husband's death. Without either desiring to see her face, or caring how it looked, she saw that it had changed; through the deep, clear veil her gray eyes watched her gray eyes watch her through the deep, clear veil. I must have fever, she thought, startled by their brightness; and turned away. It was when she came to the door, to walk through it, to leave this room and to leave this shape of existence forever, that realization poured upon and overwhelmed her through which, in retrospect, she would one day know that all that had gone before, all that she had thought she experienced and knew—true, more or less, though it all was—was nothing to this. The realization came without shape or definability, save as it was focused in the pure physical act of leaving the room, but came with such force, such monstrous piercing weight, in all her heart and soul and mind and body but above all in the womb, where it arrived and dwelt like a cold and prodigious, spreading stone, that she groaned almost inaudibly, almost a mere silent breath, an *Ohhhhhhh,* and doubled deeply over, hands to her belly, and her knee joints melted.[7]

Mourning. The death of a loved one is, of course, always traumatic, and each person reacts to and handles death in his own way, some finding it easier to adjust than others. A study of the bereavement process in a sample of widows of early middle age in East London indicated that three-fourths of them suffered from difficulty in sleeping and were apathetic toward social activities and life in general.[8] Less frequent reactions were unrealistic attitudes, such as the feeling that the dead husband was still alive or present, psychosomatic disorders, and hostility toward specific individuals, particularly the physician. However, when a marriage partner dies, the widowed spouse must reorganize his or her patterns of living to compensate for the loss.

Stabilization and Role Behaviors. Eventually the individual accepts the idea of death, and rationalizes the event to a point where a continuance of normal activity can occur. Readjustments are made in various habits, in relationships with other members of the family, and new roles are taken in social and economic life. Sexual needs, too, have to be met or sublimated.

The low status assigned to older age groups is one of the complicating factors of widowhood. The widowed person experiences a loss of identity, especially the woman who has seen her children grow up and, who may have no, or limited, interest outside of her family. Since wid-

---

[7] James Agee, *A Death in the Family,* McDowell, Obolensky, New York, 1957 (Avon Books Edition G1034), pp. 229–230.

[8] Peter Marris, *Widows and Their Families,* Routledge and Kegan Paul, London, 1958.

owhood is usually a problem in later years, health problems and certain forms of personal disorganization are related. The rigidity of old age is another factor in the readjustment process. The adjustment worked out over many years with a spouse is shattered when the partner is no longer present.

Yet the adjustment process is in some respects easier for the widowed than for the divorced. Society has been accustomed to widowhood for a longer period than to divorce, and the role is less ambiguous. Widowhood is less likely to lead to the sense of failure than is divorce, although there is sometimes greater guilt feeling for not having made the late spouse happier during his lifetime.

The question of whether the widow or the widower makes the better adjustment is frequently raised. In the home a woman is thought to be more self-sufficient than a man, accustomed to a variety of roles and more likely to receive attention from her children, who usually are fully grown by the time of her widowhood. On the other hand, a woman is usually more emotionally identified in the marriage, and consequently the death of her husband can be a great personal loss. The death of a man in terms of his role as breadwinner can be quite serious, especially if there are dependent children. Conversely, the widower has greater mobility and employability. Yet the male, widowed or divorced, is known to have a higher death rate, especially by suicide, than the widowed or divorced female.[9] The married individual of both sexes has a more favorable adjustment in regard to personal organization than the single, divorced, or widowed person. We might hypothesize that at least in the early or middle years the widow has a greater adjustment problem than the widower. The widower has a higher statistical chance of remarriage than the widow.[10] For both sexes the surviving spouse's chances for remarriage are reduced if there are children, but the widower is more likely to find another spouse.

SEPARATION AND DESERTION

Besides death and divorce, there are three ways of terminating a marital relationship: annulment, separation, and desertion.

Annulment. As we discussed in Chapter 11, annulment refers to severance by a court of a void or voidable marriage.

---

[9] Jesse Bernard, *Remarriage: A Study of Marriage,* Holt, Rinehart and Winston, New York, 1956, p. 83.

[10] Jacobson, *op. cit.,* p. 68.

Separation. There are two kinds of separation; legal and non-formalized agreement. Legal separation or *partial divorce* was derived from English common and canon law. Possibly half the states permit such a procedure. In fact, in Louisiana an absolute divorce is possible only when preceded by a year of partial or limited divorce.[11]

Usually separation refers to a mutual agreement by the husband and wife to live apart. Although this kind of situation may be unacceptable to the people involved, it is a frequent solution to marital incompatibility. Separation usually occurs when the trauma of a divorce is too much for the two partners to face, where moral or religious scruples forbid divorce, or in instances of economic pressure which forestall the expense of divorce. A business relationship between the husband and wife involving such complexities as property ownership can be another deterrent. In some instances an individual may be wary of a divorce simply because being single would only make him free for another marriage. A threat to the image of respectability in the eyes of one's relatives, friends, and business associates may become another obstacle. But the most important reason people separate rather than divorce is usually the obligation to the children.

In 1940 a fourth or more separations, legal and informal, occurred because one spouse, more often the male, was confined to a prison or mental hospital or was engaged in an occupation requiring absence from home as in certain branches of the armed service or merchant marine.[12] The extent of separation is indicated by the Census of 1960, which reported no less than 1,903,000 men and 1,304,000 women as separated.[13] Probably more than half of these separations were because of psychological difficulties between the two mates. The gap of 600,000 between the sexes indicates differential perception and definition as to what constitutes separation. Also, male migration and other occupationally determined variables account for some of the differences.

Desertion. Desertion has a lengthy history in Western culture and remains a major cause of divorce. Some idea of the extent of desertion is indicated in the estimate of the Philadelphia Municipal Court that

[11] William M. Kephart, *The Family, Individual and Society,* Houghton Mifflin, Boston, 1961, p. 584.
[12] William F. Ogburn, "Marital Separations," *American Journal of Sociology,* 1943, **49**, 316–323.
[13] Bureau of the Census, "Marital Status and Family Status: March 1960," *Current Population Reports,* 8.

more than 175,000 desertions occurred in that city between World War I and the year 1960. In one nationwide estimate more than half (54.5 per cent, or 330,000 families) of the applicants for aid to dependent children were families in which separation had occurred.[14]

The variables underlying desertion are:

1. *Socio-economic factors.* At one time desertion was known as the "poor man's divorce," which in itself is something of a legal misnomer. In any case, the data indicate that lower status individuals are also more prone to other kinds of family disorganization, including divorce. Traditionally, the lower class has the least commitment to conventional morality and a marginal interest in conformity. Also, economic duress makes the economically depressed population more vulnerable to catastrophe so that continuity of the marriage does not have the same priority it has in the middle class.

However, in recent decades the picture has changed somewhat. In a study of Philadelphia desertions, 43.6 per cent were found in the upper half of the occupational ladder.[15] Lower and middle-class subcultures have tended to merge somewhat in the postwar world.

2. *Race.* With his lower educational background, unequal bargaining power in the labor market, and less rigorous norms of behavior, the Negro is disproportionately represented in desertion cases. In Philadelphia in 1950, two-fifths of the desertions were reported among non-white families even though they constituted less than a fifth of the population.[16]

3. *Religion.* In view of the caution which governs reportage of religion in various censuses, it is difficult to obtain satisfactory data on this aspect of desertion. Reports from Chicago, Baltimore, and Philadelphia suggest that Catholics are slightly overrepresented and Protestants and Jews underrepresented.[17] Catholics have a higher rate of desertion, since divorce is forbidden, and escape from an untenable marriage is possible only by separation or desertion. Jewish desertions tend to be concentrated in upper occupational strata. A probable explanation is that with upward mobility conflict develops between the two mates. In addition, the higher the status of a given group,

---

[14] Kephart, *op. cit.,* 1961, pp. 547–548.

[15] William M. Kephart and Thomas P. Monahan, "Desertion and Divorce in Philadelphia," *American Sociological Review,* 1952, **17,** 719–727.

[16] *Ibid.*

[17] Kephart, *op. cit.,* 1961, pp. 554–555.

behavioral traits, including divorce proneness, tend to resemble the larger population.

4. *Personality factors.* Desertion stems from neurotic and emotional difficulties within the individual. As we have seen, desertion often results from a reluctance to terminate the marriage formally, yet an inability to continue the relationship. Several factors are relevant: immaturity, restlessness, and unconscious conflicts. Many separations are temporary, often a desperate response to what the individual regards as a hopeless situation. In the lower class the anticipation of one more birth has often triggered off the so-called "pregnancy desertion," for example.

THE BACKGROUND OF MARITAL DISSOLUTION

Divorce probably appeared first among the Babylonians, where it was stipulated in the marriage contracts of women who married without a dowry. The Hebrews, Greeks, and Romans granted divorce under varying conditions. For the Hebrews and, to a lesser extent, the Greeks and Romans, marriage was an alliance between two families rather than between two individuals. Consequently, certain controls existed to reduce the probability of divorce. With the advent of Christianity, marriage, as well as divorce, became religious and, in a sense, individual matters. As Kirkpatrick says regarding marriage, the "essence of the contract is consent, with full expectation of exclusiveness and indissolubility." [18] In other words, the idea of marriage as sacramental made it indissoluble. However, by ruling that marriage was subject to human strains and stresses, and by declaring the sacrament as invalid, the Church provided for annulment as a means of terminating marriage, particularly among the upper classes, for such causes as defect of consent, impotency, disparity of worship, and consanguinity.[19] Even today the Roman Catholic Church permits annulment, in theory at least, for several grounds related to the position of the medieval Church.

After the Protestant Reformation, legitimacy for marriage and divorce passed to the civil authority. In addition, in contrast to the ancient period, marriage became a contract between individuals,

[18] Clifford Kirkpatrick, *The Family as Process and Institution* (second edition), The Ronald Press, New York, 1963, p. 573.

[19] Jacobson, *op. cit.,* p. 89.

which indirectly facilitated divorce. However, in England marriage and its dissolution remained under the jurisdiction of the ecclesiastical courts. Through the royal authority it was possible for an advantageously placed husband to terminate a marriage with an unfaithful wife. In the American colonies, where Protestantism was deeply entrenched, divorces were granted in some colonies by courts and in certain others by legislature, in accord with the English system. For instance, in Pennsylvania 304 legislative decrees were granted between 1769 and 1873.

During the latter half of the nineteenth century divorce became institutionalized in the United States. Unquestionably, the woman's rights movement was a factor in this development. The Census Bureau maintained divorce statistics beginning with the Civil War period. Between 1866 and 1876 a total of 122,261 divorces were granted.[20] With industrialization and urbanization, divorces gradually increased (Table 20.1).

Table 20.1

DIVORCE RATES FOR THE UNITED STATES

Date	Event	Per 1,000 Existing Marriages
1860	Pre-Civil War	1.2
1866	Post-Civil War	1.8
1913	Pre-World War I	4.7
1919	Post-World War I	6.5
1929	Prosperity	7.9
1932	Depression	6.1
1938	Pre-World War II	8.3
1946	Post-World War II	18.2
1961		9.6

Source: Adapted from Paul H. Jacobson, *American Marriage and Divorce*, Holt, Rinehart and Winston, New York, 1959. p. 90; and U.S. Bureau of the Census, *Statistical Abstract of the United States: 1964*, Government Printing Office, Washington, D.C., 1964, p. 63.

Like marriage and birth rates, the divorce rate reflects the social climate of the times. War, in particular, increases the number of mar-

[20] Mabel A. Elliott, "The Scope and Meaning of Divorce," in H. Becker and R. Hill (eds.), *Family, Marriage and Parenthood* (second edition), D. C. Heath, 1955, p. 672.

riages and divorces. The Civil War, both World Wars, and the Korean conflict all reflected a fundamental trend: an irregular movement of divorce rates during the hostilities and a sharp rise with the return of men from the front. For example, during World War II the rate increased, reaching an unprecedented high after the war.[21] In April 1946, the divorce rate reached its highest point in American history— 59,500 divorces in one month.[22] By the mid-1950's the rate returned to its pre-World War II level.

Divorce also reflects economic conditions: the stock market crash of 1929 and the resulting depression noticeably decreased the divorce trend. Depression marriages were associated with longer periods of courtship and engagement, and consequently were less subject to term- ination.[23]

DIVORCE: DISTRIBUTION AND THE CAUSATIVE PATTERN

This part of our discussion of divorce is oriented toward the social factors operating to cause divorce.

In the United States, as we have seen, one-fourth of all marriages terminate in divorce (259 out of 1000 marriages in 1959).[24] The rela- tively high American divorce rate, as compared to lower European ones, is frequently explained by the fast tempo of American life in- cluding the centrifugal tendencies within the home, as outlined in Chapter 3. Just as important in assessing the problem is the hetero- geneity of culture, race, religion, and national origin found in this country. The tendency toward upward mobility also places a strain on the relationship between two individuals, who may not always per- form in the newly acquired marital role as the other partner deems appropriate. In fact, divorce may be considered basically as the out- come of role conflicts. There is a breakdown in the image of the other person and in his or her ability to personify the role desired. This point is discussed more fully when we turn to psychological reasons for divorce. Not least in the problem of roles are the differing aspects of aspirations for men and women and the growing independence of women in the economic world.

With the secularization of society, both religious and kinship ties are

---

[21] Jacobson, *op. cit.*, p. 92f.

[22] *Ibid.*

[23] *Ibid.*

[24] William J. Goode, *World Revolution and Family Patterns,* The Free Press of Glencoe, A Division of Collier-Macmillan, New York, 1963, p. 82.

less demanding than in previous generations. The effect of divorce, for instance on one's relatives, is regarded more as a psychological blow than as a violation of the mores. Again, divorce as an institution cannot be detached from the social structure in which we live. Although moral norms have been subject to change over the last few generations, explanations of divorce in terms of weakening ethical principles is grossly oversimplified. In reality, for the majority of couples who divorce the decision is very difficult. They tend to regard their action as both psychologically and morally undesirable. Yet the ready availability of divorce does have some connection with the secularization of values in our society. In fact, divorce has an ambiguous status in our contemporary culture partly because of a blend of both religious and secular values. Most members of our society regard divorce as a necessary evil, inevitable in a marriage strained with conflict.

Divorce is influenced by culture as can be seen in the following example. A recent comparison of Australian divorce rates with those of the United States showed our rate to be more than five times theirs at the turn of the century, but by 1960 the ratio was roughly 2.5 to 1.[25] In other words, Australia is experiencing the same influences as the United States: mobility, urbanization, and impact of the mass media. The Australian divorce rate also reflects relatively higher financial cost and the legal difficulties of obtaining a divorce in the first three years of marriage. Moreover, certain structural aspects of the culture may explain the difference in rates between the two countries. There is a difference in the psychological availability of divorce. Americans are more used to divorce as a way out of marriage. Not less important is the degree of institutionalization of sex roles. In Australia the male may retire to a pub or to the local unit of a veterans organization, which offers him an acceptable means of escape from excessive marital involvement. Australians with their closer relationship to European traditions are more conscious of the obligations to kinship and the effects of divorce on the extended family structure. Too, the Australian may expect less from marriage than does the American. Consequently, marriage may be less likely to be a disappointment.[26] More research is desirable to determine whether certain cultures encourage a safety-

[25] Lincoln H. Day. "Patterns of Divorce in Australia and the United States," *American Sociological Review*, 1964, **29**, 509–522.
[26] *Ibid.*

valve effect in marital relations, consequently reducing the disposition toward divorce.

A number of variables in our culture are specifically associated with higher divorce rates:

Regional Distribution. Geographic variations in divorce rates exist within the United States. The most liberal laws are found in the Western states because of a freer frontier condition. The most conservative part of the country is the Northeast, which has a higher percentage of Catholic population. To what degree this regionalism affects the propensity toward divorce is difficult to say, since migratory divorce erases the differences in state laws. On the whole, regional differences reflect other variables mentioned here.

Rural-Urban Factors. Divorce is predominantly an urban phenomenon. This is one reason the United States has a higher divorce rate than Canada, and why, for instance, the rate is higher in Denmark than in Norway. This difference is probably attributable to the large number of distracting influences within the city environment, both in the possibility of diversions and the greater availability of an alternate mate. There are more legal facilities in the urban setting. Not least, the divorced wife finds employment more easily in the city.

Race. Negroes have a higher rate of divorce than whites, although not to the extent that occurs with desertion. In Goode's study of 425 Detroit divorced women, 81 per cent were white and 19 per cent were Negro, even though at the time of the study 15 per cent of the population was Negro.[27] A similar discrepancy occurs on a national scale, where divorces are approximately a fifth higher among Negroes than among whites.[28] This differential is explained by the same racial variables that operated in connection with dessertion. However, as Goode points out, a number of variables must be considered: values within the Negro culture of the South and of the North, the socioeconomic status, and other barriers placed on the Negro's mobility. With future improvement in education and job opportunity, the Negro divorce rate can be expected increasingly to resemble the white rate. However, levels of education determine the specific relationship: the Negro divorce rate varies positively with education through the

[27] William J. Goode, *After Divorce,* The Free Press of Glencoe, A Division of Collier-Macmillan Company, New York, 1956, p. 38.
[28] Kephart, *op. cit.* (1961), p. 606.

high school level, but decreases with college education.[29] That is, the Negro of grade school background is more likely to be a deserter, of high school background is more subject to divorce, and of college training has more stability in his marital relations.

Religion. Divorce is highest for the less religious, next highest for interfaith marriages, followed by Protestants, and least for Catholics and Jews.[30] Goode found Catholics had a much greater reluctance to accept the idea of divorce, they sought outside advice more than non-Catholics, in the hope of finding a solution to their marital problems.

Social Class. Contrary to the popular notion, data have supported a tendency toward a higher divorce rate among lower occupational strata. In a Philadelphia sample of divorces Kephart found semiskilled workers overrepresented and professionals and proprietors underrepresented.[31] Other studies have confirmed this finding. The reasons for higher marital stability among higher occupational strata and the upper educated are not difficult to understand in view of older age at marriage, more adequate economic return, and greater personality and role flexibility. All in all, the middle class has a larger stake in the status quo. Still if the present financial cost of divorce were reduced, the differential in marital dissolution between social classes might be still wider.

Age and the Duration of Marriage. Despite the legendary account of the difficult 40's and the "seven year itch," the majority of divorces occur in the early years. The most hazardous period of a marriage is the first year. The duration of a marriage can be determined by two methods: separation itself and the formal granting of the decree. In a Philadelphia sample more than 25 per cent of the marriages eventually terminating in divorce indicated separation before the end of the second year, although less than 6 per cent of the decrees were granted by that time.[32] Table 20.2 indicates the time difference between separation and the formal divorce. With only minor variations,

---

[29] Glick, *op. cit.*, pp. 154–155.

[30] Thomas P. Monahan and William M. Kephart, "Divorce and Desertion by Religious and Mixed-religious Groups," *The American Journal of Sociology*, 1954, 59, 454–465.

[31] William M. Kephart, "Occupational Level and Marital Disruption," *American Sociological Review*, 1955, 20, 456–465.

[32] William M. Kephart, "The Duration of Marriage," *American Sociological Review*, 1954, 19, pp. 287–294.

Table 20.2

MEDIAN DURATION OF MARRIAGE:
PHILADELPHIA COUNTY SAMPLE,
1937–1950
$(N = 1,434)$

	Separation in Years	Divorce in Years
First marriages	5.4	10.4
Remarriages	3.4	7.1

Source: William M. Kephart, "The Duration of Marriage," *American Sociological Review*, 1954, **19**, 287–294.

each succeeding year becomes less vulnerable in a marriage. The peak of decree granting is between the second and fourth year.

Since marriages ending early are assumed to involve basic personality difficulties, emotional and sex conflicts are necessarily relevant. In an analysis of divorces caused by sexual maladjustments Kephart found that the average length of marriage was 7.7 years and for non-sexual complaints, 10.1 years.[33] Of course, as he indicates, even if the partners attribute their marital breakdown to sexual maladjustment, there is no evidence that this diagnosis is correct. Sexual difficulties probably reside in personality conflicts.

The Presence of Children. Roughly 60 per cent of divorces involve childless couples. However, if we consider that the highest rate of divorce is in the early years of marriage, we can see that there is a spurious factor. By the sixth year of marriage the ratio of divorces among childless couples, as compared to those with children, is 3.5 to one. By the thirteenth year of marriage the two rates are equal.[34] The prevalence of divorce among childless couples points more to a situation of convenience or availability of dissolution rather than to a causative relationship.[35] We recall from Chapter 13 that the presence of children

[33] William M. Kephart, "Some Variables in Cases of Reported Sexual Maladjustments," *Marriage and Family Living*, 1954, **16**, 241–243.

[34] Jacobson, *op. cit.*, pp. 134–135.

[35] Thomas P. Monahan, "Is Childlessness Related to Family Stability?," *American Sociological Review*, 1955, **20**, 446–456.

had no consistent relationship with marital adjustment, although the desire for children was highly favorable.

ALIENATION AND THE PROCESS OF DIVORCE

Divorce is a product of society and the individual. The dissolution or retention of a marriage may be considered the resultant of opposing forces.[36] Certain factors operate in the direction of cohesiveness: esteem for the spouse, desire for companionship, home ownership, approval of relatives and friends, etc. Other factors act as repulsions, such as interest in another person, desire for economic independence on the part of the wife, or religious conflicts. Whether one chooses to remain married or to divorce depends on the balance of these forces of attraction and repulsion.

We have discussed the historical and cultural factors influencing marital dissolution. Let us now turn to the psychological processes associated with it. We focus particular attention in this section on the effects of divorce on the individual and his adjustment.

THE PSYCHOLOGICAL DENOUEMENT. Divorce can be understood as a process of role change or breakdown. Alteration in the perception of the images of each other held by husband and wife, as well as changes in the self-image, are related to the undercurrent of recrimination, hostility, and guilt accompanying divorce. In attempting to analyze the divorce process it should be kept in mind that many marriages ending in divorce are no more inadequately structured or integrated than those that remain weakly together. One distinguishing feature between the two kinds of marriages, is that the first is characterized by a strong desire for escape—"a desire strong enough to involve a willingness to face the penalties of divorce." [37] More often this decision to break is made by the male, at least within the experience of Goode's sample of divorces. The reason for this is the lesser emotional involvement of the male in the house, the availability of the job market, and greater economic security.

Unquestionably, divorce may be considered as a continuation of the strategy-type of conflict mentioned in Chapter 19. If we accept the

---

[36] George Levinger, "Marital Cohesiveness and Dissolution: An Integrative Review," *Journal of Marriage and the Family*, 1965, **27**, 19–28.

[37] Willard Waller, *The Family: A Dynamic Interpretation* (revised by Reuben Hill), Holt, Rinehart and Winston, New York, 1951, p. 511.

near universality of conflict in marriage—and for the psychoanalytical interpretation, conflict at the unconscious level—the divorce process may be viewed as a portrayal of conflict in which the stakes are the survival or termination of the marriage. The couple in conflict reckons with divorce as a possible outcome. If a third party is involved, one or both of the partners may weigh the alternatives of continuance or termination of the marriage.[38] Not least, divorce is a breakdown of roles: The problem of John and Barbara illustrates role and value conflicts. The deterioration of their relationship results in divorce:

John, age 27, and Barbara, age 26, both college graduates, were married six years at the time of their divorce. They met in high school and became steady daters in college with engagement and marriage in the senior year. The first three years of marriage presented little difficulty. Later with their two children, four and two years of age, they were settled in a suburban housing tract of a West Coast city. In the fourth and fifth years of marriage conflicts developed that proved irreparable. John's attention to a girl he had met in an evening class at the university was the precipitating cause of the marital breakdown, but a number of other problems had appeared.

John's father was the son of an engineer who himself had come from a broken home and had occasionally been on the alcoholic margin. His parents' marriage was not satisfactory, and John had grown up in a home marked by a good deal of tension, which apparently caused him and his older brother a certain degree of insecurity. The father was not overly communicative with the mother or the sons, and the mother had had to assert her rights, whether regarding the use of the family car for herself or the boys, or her use of the pocketbook. These favors were only grudgingly bestowed. Moreover the father was somewhat withdrawn from the family and emotionally unresponsive.

Barbara's home life had been more secure; however, her father, a police sergeant, was somewhat rigid in his relationships within the family; and Barbara, who was perhaps even more intelligent than John, reflected some of his rigidity and set very high standards for herself and for those with whom she came into contact. The father had little regard for John, which John realized. This impasse disturbed their marital relations since Barbara was devoted to her family. Barbara criticized John for his lack of tact with the father.

John's erratic success as a sales representative depended on the vagaries of the market and possibly his own drive. This occupation and financial problem seemed to lower his usual warmth, affectionateness, and inner security. The first years of his business had been successful. Installment purchases of a house, furniture, and car added to the financial burden in the following, less successful years. Occasional drinking bouts were likely a result of various pressures, particularly the reduced income when sales began to fall off. There were

[38] Jessie Bernard, "The Adjustments of Married Mates," in Harold T. Christensen (ed.), *Handbook of Marriage and the Family,* Rand McNally, Chicago, 1964, p. 723.

disagreements over finances, care and training of the children, and relations with the in-laws. Part of the problem may have been Barbara and John's close association with each other through high school and college, which meant little opportunity to have courtship experiences with other members of the opposite sex. Both implicitly felt that they had been a little cheated by their monogamous relationship for so many years.

John had determined to complete a master's degree in business administration and began taking courses in the third year of marriage. Barbara also took an occasional course. Two years later John met a girl on campus and began clandestine dating. What significance he found in this date is not certain, but his own security appeared to be bolstered by the attentions of a girl who was extremely attractive and affectionate and less demanding than his wife. When Barbara learned of his dating activities, she threatened separation and John suspended his relationship with the girl. Afterwards he became defensive and argumentative about his wants and critical of Barbara's roles as homemaker and mother and especially her attention to her parents. His drinking was an occasional problem and her attempts to persuade him to find help in counselling were not heeded. In the meantime he resumed interests in dates. Consequently three months after her mention of a separation and divorce she felt the situation to be hopeless and returned to her parents' home.

John continued to live in their home and six weeks later with the approach of the Christmas holidays Barbara returned to her husband, but their values, attitudes, and feelings toward each other were still too far apart to permit a successful relationship. Two months later at the urging of John, who promised to seek therapy, and her own feeling of conflict she returned to the home and the marriage. She felt the marriage would somehow have to succeed. John began his therapy but as bills began to pile up, he canceled further appointments with the counsellor, rationalizing that he had gained sufficient insight into his problem. For five months the marriage was probably better than it had been for two or three years. However, as his sales began to slip, basic conflicts reappeared and he lapsed into drinking. Six months later Barbara and John separated again.[39]

This case study is not necessarily representative of all divorces, as each marital situation is unique. Here, the underlying causes appear to be the insecurity of the husband and his need for obtaining ego strength in extramarital involvement and alcohol. The marriage was also complicated by financial pressures. It is probable that the wife herself may have lacked the warm, affectionate personality necessary for John. As it turned out, a final separation followed by divorce made for an extremely unhappy period for both of them. But eventually both remarried, John to a girl with a more flexible personality who played up to his needs, and Barbara to an individual who was more

[39] From the author's files.

self-reliant. To what degree their second marriages have proved successful is not known. But each apparently was determined to profit from
the experience of the first marriage. John found a more responsive partner, and with the completion of his master's degree has had a promo-
tion in business. He himself has apparently acquired maturity,
something he did not have in his twenties.

In Goode's tabulation, the "causes of divorce" range over a variety
of reasons, as seen in Table 20.3. The causes listed reflect problems in

Table 20.3

CAUSES AS REPORTED BY 425 DETROIT DIVORCEES

Complaint Theme	Responses	Respondents
Nonsupport	13%	33%
Authority	12	32
Complex of "drinking, gambling, and helling around"	12	31
Drinking	12	30
Personality	11	29
Home life	9	25
Values	8	21
Consumption or economic	8	20
Triangle	6	16
Desertion	3	8
Relatives	2	4
Miscellaneous	4	12
TOTAL	100%	
Number of items enumerated	1,110	

Source: William J. Goode, *After Divorce*, The Free Press of Glencoe, A Division of
Collier-Macmillan, New York, 1956, p. 123.

definition and enactment of roles as the terms "non-support," "authority," and "complex-drinking, gambling, and helling around" indicate. A sample of Idaho lawyers classified the "real" causes, as opposed
to the legal grounds, of 282 divorces. The major causes were, in declining order: financial problems (including support), infidelity, drunkenness, and basic incompatibility.[40] Of course, causation is far more
complex than the enumeration of complaints. One predictable rela-

[40] Harry C. Harmsworth and Mhyra S. Minnis, "Non-Statutory Causes of Divorce:
The Lawyer's Point of View," *Marriage and Family Living*, 1955, **17**, 316–321.

tionship of cause and effect is premarital pregnancy and subsequent divorce. A study of divorce in an Indiana sample county assessed the association of pregnancy and divorce. Most prone to divorce were, again in declining order, those: (1) who delayed marriage until late stages of pregnancy; (2) early marriage following pregnancy; (3) early pregnancy following marriage; and (4) delayed pregnancy following marriage. In the first group, "delayed marriage following pregnancy," other factors predisposing toward divorce were: young age at marriage, wide age discrepancy between the spouses, urban background, lower level occupation, nonreligious wedding ceremony, and second or subsequent marriage.[41]

The foregoing studies are drawn from both lower and middle class population. An analysis of the process of divorce as reflected in the experience of marital counsellors, clinical psychologists and psychiatrists effecting a middle-class bias point less to problems of economic strain and excessive drinking and more to the role relationships and emotional conflict as a basis of estrangement in divorce decision.

STATES IN THE DIVORCE PROCESS. *Alienation* is a complex process involving an irregular movement toward dissolution of the marriage. Since divorce is usually regarded as a last resort by one or both of the partners, considerable ambivalence usually exists about the decision to divorce. The thought of divorce may preoccupy one or both partners over many years. In a recent novel a middle-aged husband reflects on his motives regarding a possible divorce, which never came to pass:

Well, it's too bad. It's too bad for me as well as for Maude. I haven't any pity for her. She was a grown adult woman when she married me, and she promised she'd be a loving wife, and one hell of a loving wife she's been. Maybe I hurt her. So what? What kind of a marriage would it be if you had to worry every minute about hurting your wife? She hurt me too. It hurt when she backed out on me, looking at me like I was dirt. It still hurts.

I stood up then because I was surprised. I hadn't known Maude could still hurt me, now, in the present, Poor Old Maude, shabby and out of date. But I suppose it's so. I'm not free of her even now. Why didn't I divorce her years ago if I was free of her? Why did I go on living there, going home to dinner with her, keeping up some kind of marriage? It's true that it's convenient to *be* married sometimes, if only because it means you don't have to *get* married to somebody else—but that's not enough of a reason.

Think, man, I said to myself, and poured a drink. This comes into it some-

---

[41] Harold T. Christensen and Hanna H. Meissner, "Studies in Child Spacing: III. Premarital Pregnancy as a Factor in Divorce," *American Sociological Review*, 1953, 18, 641–644.

how. Why should you stick with Maude? Why have you stuck with Maude?

I could have divorced her. I had girls, but I wasn't the only one who played around. Maude did too.

.   .   .

Why didn't I divorce her then, twenty years ago, when I was young? Did I still want her then? I stirred the ice in my drink and tried to remember. I hadn't wanted anybody else, I knew that. That is, I'd wanted anybody and everybody, and I got them. . . .

I didn't take it seriously, you see. And I was right. I mean—

Well, I mean she didn't leave me. None of it came to anything. As for me leaving her—

Maybe I was sorry for her. I don't know. She had a bad time when she broke off with Steinholt. That was all very high-minded too. He had three daughters just growing up. He was a pillar of her community. I don't know whether he'd have thrown it all over for her in the end, maybe not. But she broke it off without letting him. . . .

.   .   .

I hadn't gone to Maude any more than she'd come to me. Neither of us broke up that limping marriage, but neither of us tried to fix it. If guilt matters, we were both guilty. But guilt doesn't matter, that's the point, even if it seems sometimes as if it matters, there on the way down.

I'll tell you about guilt. It's like bursitis. It's an inflammation in a joint. The joint is where you connect with someone. Well, you never will connect perfectly. That's in the nature of things. Guilt is nothing to be concerned about, it is simply the inflammation set up by the faulty connection. The more you worry about it and try to manipulate the joint with the other person, to get it to work as if it were a natural automatic thing, the two of you one by nature, the worse it gets. Let it go, let it go. Don't try to get inside it, you may never get out. The human race has got as far as it has—let's not argue about how far that is—by gritting its teeth and enduring pain, including guilt. Let's not forget it. Write guilt off.

I let my marriage get to be a habit. Maybe that was stupid, but it's nothing to be guilty about. The truth is, I never had any particular reason to want to break it up. It didn't seem to me that important. The guys who care about marriage are the ones who get divorced, I guess. They keep thinking it will work out. If it doesn't, it must be something wrong with the girl. So get rid of her and try again. They're optimists, they're romantics. Why bother? If it goes bad on you once, why try again? That's the way it had seemed to me.

To tell you the truth, I don't think I wanted to get as mixed up with anybody again as I had been with Maude. Too much time and energy, and what came out of it? [42]

As we have already discussed, there is no set pattern of events, since no two divorces are exactly alike. Waller suggested certain phases of

[42] Elizabeth Janeway, *Accident*, Harper and Row, New York, 1964, pp. 69–72. Copyright © 1964 by Elizabeth Janeway.

the relationship between two people and the development of their perception regarding the meaning of their relationship:

1. A disturbance appears in the affectional-sexual life of the pair. A lack of rapport develops, and although their sexual relationship may have been most satisfactory at first, it gradually diminishes in satisfaction or frequency or both. The sexual impasse probably reflects a fairly involved emotional situation.

2. Mention of the possibility of divorce constitutes a definitive and painful break in the psychological linkage between the spouses.

3. The appearance of solidarity is shattered and considerable censure of the other person occurs, seldom of the self. Goode's wives placed almost the entire blame on the husband, who, although undoubtedly the more responsible of the two, probably was not as reprehensible as the wives judged.

4. Although divorce is often mentioned in jest or anger, the final decision comes after a lengthy period of thought and discussion. Goode found that the median time for the serious consideration up to the time of final decision was 4.6 months, and the median time from this point to the filing of the divorce was 3.2 months.[43]

◦5. Separation, with its breaking up of roles, habit systems, and loyalties signals traumatization for both partners. The sense of shock and despair is probably at its maximum at the time of the final separation, rather than at the moment the decree is granted.

The capacity to make the needed psychological readjustments during divorce decision varies greatly between individuals. For some, it is accepted as are other critical adjustments in life. For a greater number of persons there is a frantic attempt to lose oneself in hard work, long hours, social activities, or in drinking. Even the thought of suicide is not infrequent. The degree to which outside resources, notably counselling, may be sought during this period of adjustment depends on an individual's readiness to recognize a problem as needing attention. Unquestionably the sensitive individual who "goes it alone" finds himself carrying an especially heavy burden.

SOCIAL AND PSYCHOLOGICAL EFFECTS OF DIVORCE

Divorce means a profound rearrangement of roles for the two people involved. What probably began as an ecstatic marriage has failed.

[43] Goode, *op. cit.,* p. 138.

There may even have been anxiety at the time of marriage about whether it would work out. In either instance, the marriage, with its social and emotional interlocking of two personalities, and the respective role expectancies and behaviors is terminated. The readjustment for the individual is farreaching and complicated by the confused status of divorce in our society. If the social sanctions against divorce were greater, the number of divorces might be smaller. If, on the the other hand, divorce were more explicitly accepted, the divorced person might feel less self-conscious and rejected. However, an important aspect of marital disruption from the viewpoint of the individual is the sense of failure, wounded self-pride, and the feeling of futility, because many months or years have been invested in what turned out to be a lost cause. The major commitment of one's life is now shattered. There are several areas of adjustment that are especially vulnerable in a marriage.

Affectional-Emotional Adjustment. The impact of the divorce is, of course, related to the degree of emotional involvement in the marriage. It is difficult to ignore the relationship of relatives and friends to the marital adjustment during and after the divorce process, specifically in terms of the emotional support or understanding they give. Still more important is the presence of children. It appears that the higher the number of children, the greater the trauma in the divorce action.[44]

Certain social factors may also be relevant in this context. The age of the individual and duration of the marriage, with some exceptions, are positively related to the emotional trauma. As stated earlier in this chapter, religion is, for example, a factor: Catholics proceed into divorce with a deeper sense of guilt and consequently are slower to arrive at a decision than Protestants. An analysis of their parents' marriage by students would confirm the generalization that the religiously oriented individual is the least disposed toward terminating his marriage.[45]

Social Adjustment. One reason for the sense of discontinuity in marital disruption is the orientation of adult social life toward couples. Moreover, associations and friendships may frequently be dis-

[44] *Ibid.*, p. 192.
[45] Judson T. Landis, "Social Correlates of Divorce and Nondivorce Among the Unhappily Married," *Marriage and the Family*, 1963, **25**, 178–183.

rupted because of the awkwardness of appearing alone with the former group. If the social ties were to be continued or resumed, only one of the pair can be readily retained in the relevant group. Apparently the social readjustment can be effected by a number of factors. For one, Goode's divorced wives were more likely to seek a new set of friends if they found a new love relationship; whereas when it was the husband who had found other love interests, the wife was more likely to remain in her previous friendship group. A relatively large number of divorced persons within the group might be a factor that would encourage retention of ties with friends. Dating was available at least in the younger years; 84 per cent of the divorcees under age thirty dated, with the possibility of remarriage.

Sexual Adjustment. The reaction of the individual to a terminated marriage affects his or her sexual adjustment in widely varying respects. Involvement with a third party may be the factor precipitating the divorce, in which case the sexual pattern may continue in the same direction before and after the divorce. Sexual conflicts, often labeled as incompatibility, may be a primary cause of the divorce. Masturbation or even homosexual practices may occur in postdivorce adjustive experience. Indifference to sex often appears among a number of divorced women. Kinsey found the frequency of sexual outlets to be above the level of single women but below that of married women.[46] Ninety-six per cent of the previously married younger males he studied and 82 per cent of those at age fifty engaged in sexual intercourse.[47] Heterosexual activities accounted for 80 to 85 per cent of their total outlet.

EFFECTS OF DIVORCE ON CHILDREN. Roughly three-fifths of divorces involve children. This ratio would be larger if divorces were not concentrated in the early years of marriage. The proportion of divorces with children varies from 9 per cent in the first year of marriage to 64 per cent in the eighteenth year.[48] Approximately two-thirds of the children of divorcees are under ten years of age. Well over 300,000 children are affected per year. Regional differences are

[46] Alfred C. Kinsey, Wardell B. Pomeroy, Clyde E. Martin, and Paul H. Gebhard, *Sexual Behavior in the Human Female,* W. B. Saunders, Philadelphia, 1953, p. 533.
[47] Alfred C. Kinsey, Wardell B. Pomeroy and Clyde E. Martin, *Sexual Behavior in the Human Male,* W. B. Saunders, Philadelphia, 1948, p. 295.
[48] Paul H. Jacobson, *American Marriage and Divorce,* Holt, Rinehart and Winston, New York, 1959, pp. 129f.

conspicuous. In the Northeastern part of the United States the number of divorces with children is higher.

Custody of the children is given to mothers in almost 90 per cent of divorce cases. This practice is almost universal when the mother is the plaintiff, and amounts to perhaps half of the cases when the husband initiates the divorce proceedings.[49] In other words, even when the wife is at fault, court authorities regard the role of the mother as indispensable in rearing the children. In certain instances other relatives are appointed as guardians.

There is no agreement about the evaluation of the effects of divorce on the children. Evidence shows that the degree of psychological damage to children following divorce of their parents is no greater and probably not as great as in unbroken homes marked by tension.[50] Each divorce is an individual case. Each child has a different situation to recall and face. Remarriage probably is best for the welfare of the child. In the same vein, Despert writes of "emotional divorce," within a technically unbroken home as an even unhappier situation than actual divorce.[51] The tension and distance that are between two parents through an extended period of bickering, hostility, and alienation is so wearing that divorce in these instances may stabilize the situation despite the isolation from the father.

LEGAL ASPECTS OF DIVORCE

The legal framework for divorce presents one of the most curious cultural lags in modern society. With each of the fifty states of the United States having different machinery, an individual seeking a divorce finds himself in a dilemma. Grounds sufficient for a divorce in one state are meaningless in another. In addition, the problem raises certain moral questions. To what degree can a nation permit confusion in the ethics underlying divorce? However, of even deeper concern is the question as to what is the function of law in reference to marriage and particularly the legal underpinning of divorce. Divorce is, of course, a means of social control. As Litwak points out, the legal

[49] Morris Ploscowe, *The Truth about Divorce*, Hawthorne Books, New York, 1955, pp. 219–220.

[50] F. Ivan Nye, "Child Adjustment in Broken and in Unhappy Unbroken Homes," *Marriage and Family Living*, 1957, **19**, 356–361; Judson T. Landis, "The Trauma of Children When Parents Divorce," *Marriage and Family Living*, 1960, **22**, 7–13.

[51] J. Louise Despert, *Children of Divorce*, Doubleday, New York, 1953, p. 260.

system functions so as to control, not only obtaining a divorce, but a person's total attitude toward marriage.[52] He cites the law's latent functions:

1. Divorce law in a sense represents a certain degree of punishment, or the threat of punishment. First, divorce, which is possible because of our legal institutions, cannot basically change an individual's behavior, such as drunkenness, for instance. It also acts as punishment in that the "innocent" party suffers as well as the "guilty" one.

2. Divorce law also functions as therapy in that an indirect premise of the law presumes that clients seek a divorce because of serious emotional and personality conflicts. The therapist may attempt to keep the two individuals together, which suggests that in the total perspective the divorce process is a means of social control. The degree to which legal processes can act as therapy is limited. But whether a marriage stays together by means of therapy, instituted because of the threat of divorce, is beneficial or not, depends on the viewpoint of each partner or a neutral observer.

3. Divorce law, as with other phases of our legal system, has certain educational effects. In the broad context of socialization, divorce as well as marriage laws prescribe both the attitudes people should emulate and the norms of behavior by which they should conduct themselves.

The philosophy underlying our courts is that the granting of a divorce is both a privilege made possible by the theory of individual freedom and the commitment that marriage is a sacred institution. The basic premise is maximum freedom of the individual within the context of the law. Generally courts have been more generous than legislators. In the United States divorce lawyers and judges have taken it upon themselves to interpret the laws as freely as possible.

This problem has to be seen within a socio-cultural perspective. In a certain number of cultures the provision for divorce was liberalized only to be slowed at a later period. The Soviet Union offered such a case in its very liberal laws during the 1920's when divorces were readily procured by the application of one partner, although more often by both. With the tightening of divorce laws in the late 1930's and early 1940's divorce rates became comparable to those of the United States.

In Latin countries, divorce is forbidden or permitted only in the

[52] Eugene Litwak, "Divorce Law as Social Control," *Social Forces*, 1956, **24**, 217–223.

most limited circumstances. In these cultures there may be certain institutionalized escapes like the mistress system. In some cultures social class may determine the availability of divorce or other safety valves, whereas in upper social classes the spaciousness of living arrangements or the elaborateness of roles may permit a more tenuous interrelationship between the spouses. At this social level marital involvement, if frustrating to one of the partners, can be kept to a minimum.[53] At the same time, for social reasons both partners may find it desirable to maintain the appearance of an intact marriage.

The ambiguous or negative role divorce plays in many Western cultures has led to a marked degree of discontent with the legal procedure connected with marital dissolution. For instance, 35 per cent of Americans in a national sample complained that laws regarding divorce were not sufficiently strict; 9 per cent responded that the laws were too strict, and the remainder were either satisfied or uncertain. Similar responses have been found for several Western European nations.[54] With the American system and in most European countries, where divorce laws are no less confusing than in our own, there is a guilt-and-innocence underpinning to the processing of divorce. Necessarily this system means a reduction of psychological realities to a travesty of legal justice. Only 15 per cent of divorce suits in this country are contested, and for the greater part of a century there has been a maximum variation of 3 per cent in this rate.[55] As a result, the lack of investigative rigor and scientific objectivity in the courtroom suggests the style of a daytime television serial. The following dialogue derived from a desertion case indicates the depth of investigation:

Court. And you say your husband has been gone for twenty-six months?
Wife. Yes.
Court. Have you heard from him during this period?
Wife. No, not a word.
Court. Have you seen him at all?
Wife. Not since the day he left.
Court. Why did your husband leave you?
Wife. I've no idea. He just packed and left.
Court. You have no idea why he left?
Wife. None.

[53] Jesse R. Pitts, "The Structural-Functional Approach," in Harold T. Christensen. (ed.), *Handbook of Marriage and the Family,* Rand McNally, Chicago, 1964, p. 277.

[54] Goode, *op. cit.* (1963), p. 82.

[55] Jacobson, *op cit.,* p. 120.

Court.   Did you take care of the house properly?

Wife.   Yes, even the neighbors knew I was an immaculate housewife.

Court.   Did you cook his meals properly?

Wife.   I had hot meals ready for him every day, whether he came home or not.

Court.   Did you fulfill your wifely duties properly; that is, did you satisfy your husband's sexual needs?

Wife.   Certainly, unless I was sick.

Court.   Will you tell the court of the events leading up to his departure. . . .[56]

In most instances the husband is not in court. Thus, in many divorce cases the court procedure becomes a ritualized fiction.

Certain techniques have become routine in the establishment of guilt and innocence, which have little to do with the dynamics of the marriage in question:

Collusion.   This is the cooperative arrangement of both spouses in order to obtain a divorce, and is a well-known practice in cases of adultery. (A New York judge once prepared a leaflet on the procedure to expedite uncontested divorces.) "Hotel divorce" has been particularly prevalent in England, in New York, and in other areas which limit divorce to the grounds of adultery. This technique simply depends on the arrangement by the couple for a photographer and witnesses to convene at the appointed hour. Another type of collusion is desertion, which is an agreed-upon "leave of absence." In addition, there is the compartmentalization technique. Only one side of a case is presented, as in cruelty or drunkenness, which may be related to the behavior of the other party, but the lawyer asks that only the plaintiff appear in court.

Connivance.   In technical language this term refers to "the corrupt consenting by one married person to the marital offenses and acts of another." [57] It functions most frequently in connection with adultery. The defense uses it to challenge the truth of the accusations against the man or wife. "Yes, I committed this offense of which I am accused. But it happened because my spouse deliberately induced me to do it so that he could use it as a ground for bringing a divorce suit." [58] In other terms, from the viewpoint of the courts, the participation of an

[56] William M. Kephart, "Legal and Procedural Aspects of Marriage and Divorce," in Christensen, *op. cit.*, pp. 953–954.

[57] Helen I. Clarke, *Social Legislation* (second edition), Appleton-Century-Crofts, New York, 1957, p. 130.

[58] Harriet F. Pilpel and Theodora Zavin, *Your Marriage and the Law*, Holt, Rinehart and Winston, New York, 1952, pp. 292f.

agent, say, a detective acting in behalf of the wife, for "arranging the adultery" is sufficient reason to deny the divorce.

Condonation. This practice constitutes the forgiveness of an offense and consequently amounts to rescinding a plea for divorce. If adultery has been committed and the offended spouse continues to live with the partner, the court considers the resumption of marital relations as "conditional forgiveness." In some states the law referring to condonation may apply to a number of grounds—in others, only to adultery. In most courts reestablishment of sex relations with the spouse constitutes an acceptance of the status quo. Consequently, a wife could not sue for divorce on the grounds of the husband's desertion, if on the return of the husband she reestablished full marital living.

The effect of the statutes of limitations applies in certain states so that a divorce action cannot be brought on given grounds except within a designated period after the offense occurs. However, a divorce may be considered on new grounds. In contrast, New Jersey prohibits an applicant for divorce from filing suit for six months after the last act of cruelty specified. Although this law would not prevent a legal separation, the authorities consider a period of reflection is desirable to assess the motives regarding the divorce.

Recrimination. This term implies that the plaintiff has also been guilty of the offense which constitutes the ground for divorce. In other words, if both parties are guilty of adultery or cruelty, for example, neither party is entitled to the divorce. In certain states, the divorce may be granted to the party least at fault.

The foregoing legal mechanisms add to the difficulties of applying just or ethical principles to divorce procedure in the United States or in other countries which have similarly questionable practices. The legal profession is not at all satisfied with the subterfuge found in divorce legislation and litigation. Moreover, a number of lawyers prefer a panel composed of psychiatrists, social workers, and counsellors, as well as legal representatives, so that a more objective examination could be made of a marriage in trouble.[59]

GROUNDS FOR DIVORCE. In addition to the inconsistent legal philos-

---

[59] Richard H. Wels, "Psychiatry and the Law in Separation and Divorce," in Victor W. Eisenstein (ed.), *Neurotic Interaction in Marriage*, Basic Books, New York, 1956.

ophy underlying divorce, the specific grounds state by state complicate the situation even more. States vary enormously in the acceptable grounds for divorce. For example, "violent and ungovernable temper" (Florida); "any gross behavior or wickedness" (Rhode Island); and "husband leaves United States to become citizen of another country" (New Hampshire).[60] Adultery is sufficient for divorce in every state. Cruelty, although defined in varying ways, is acceptable in all but two states, New York and North Carolina. Other grounds with decreasing frequency in the number of states specifying are: impotence, felony conviction, negligence to provide, insanity, pregnancy at marriage, bigamy, separation, indignities, drug addiction, violence, and fraudulent contract.[61] The definition of most of these differs markedly. Of the twenty-seven states stipulating separation or absence, the time specified varies from eighteen months (Maryland) to five years (Rhode Island).[62] Finally, in contrast to New York with only one ground (adultery), Kentucky provides no less than twenty different grounds for divorce.[63]

Even if a client has apparent grounds for divorce, there is no assurance that he or she will obtain a divorce. In the case of a divorce petition based on adultery, certain circumstances may intervene. First, the individual must have entered into adultery of his or her own free will. Consequently, rape would not constitute adultery. Intoxication in the interpretation of some courts might conceivably be viewed as a mitigating circumstance. Insanity would almost be certain to constitute qualifying circumstances.[64]

Regarding the frequency of the use of given legal grounds for divorce, cruelty has been steadily rising in its relative importance. At the close of the Civil War desertion and adultery far outdistanced cruelty as a complaint for divorce. By 1800 cruelty had overtaken adultery and in 1922 outranked desertion. Today it accounts for three-fifths of the divorces, although in language varying from "extreme cruelty," to

---

[60] Fowler V. Harper, *Problems of the Family*, Bobbs Merrill, Indianapolis, 1952, pp. 658–659.

[61] *Information Please Almanac*, 1964, p. 284.

[62] *The Book of the States*, 1964–65, Council of State Governments, Chicago, 1964, pp. 440–441.

[63] Richard Mackay, *Law of Marriage and Divorce*, Oceana Publications, New York, 1959, p. 63.

[64] Harper, *op. cit.*, p. 706.

"repeated cruelty," "excesses and outrages," and "violence endanger-
ing life." [65] It is hardly necessary to spell out the subtleties in behavior to be gleaned from these terms in the divorce court. Incompatibility is specified in New Mexico and Oklahoma. For many observers this
term is used as a substitution for cruelty, as the reason for divorce may
be reasonably honest, if not very precise.

Desertion, which is grounds in all but five states, similarly varies in
the required duration from six months to five years, but most states
specify one year. Desertion accounts for roughly a third of all divorces.
However, the circumstances surrounding the desertion may be critical
in determining the legal appropriateness of divorce. For instance, the
wife who refuses to follow her husband to his new place of employment would not be charged with desertion if a doctor testifies that the
locality is dangerous to her health. Nor could he be considered a
deserter if he corresponds as an affectionate husband and provides for
her adequately. A nagging, neurotic wife is not always granted a divorce because her husband deserted her.

MIGRATORY DIVORCE. For several reasons many people prefer to
escape the difficult process of obtaining a divorce in their home state
and migrate to another. After establishing residence for the given
period of time stipulated by the state, the applicant becomes eligible
for a divorce. As we have seen in the case of New York residents, the
restriction to adultery for divorce grounds can mean a fictitious and
sordid arrangement. Going to another state may be less painful in
regard to the association with relatives and friends. Also, publicity
may be avoided. Too, because of the distance involved, the other party
may find it less difficult to contest the divorce. The vacation possibilities of Las Vegas, Miami, the Virgin Islands, or Mexico are added
incentives.

Nevada and Idaho permit a divorce after sixty days residence and
certain other mountain states have relatively short periods. Florida
and several other states require six months. This time factor makes the
divorce process considerably shorter than in the areas with one and
two year requirements. These more liberal states also have few stipulations about the time limit before the plaintiff is permitted to remarry.

Despite the attractiveness of these "quickie" divorces, the divorce
procured in one state is not always recognized in another. Supposedly

[65] Jacobson, *op. cit.,* p. 122.

divorces recognized by one state would have equal validity in another state; however, court decisions in the home state have considered that domicile established in another state simply for the purpose of abtaining a divorce does not constitute a bona fide residence. Consequently, such divorces have been occasionally ruled invalid. When divorces are acquired in other states, remarriage has in some instances been subject to bigamy charges.

ALIMONY AND RELATED SETTLEMENT.   States differ in the degree to which they permit alimony. Presumably the justification for alimony payments is based on the responsibility of the husband to the wife even if the marriage fails. In Pennsylvania, no alimony is allowed, although in all states support must be provided for minor children. Despite the economic independence or increased job market available to the woman, the courts have been increasingly disposed over the last several decades to grant alimony.[66] The Midwestern States are especially noted for alimony payments. The proportion of wives securing alimony payments varied in a given period from a fifth in Oklahoma to a half in Wisconsin.

The dilemma of alimony and property settlements, as well as the divorce itself, are reflected in a novelist's account of a professor on the eve of his divorce action:

There is no question but that there at our house Dorothy had attempted to show me the reward of right action . . . or right action as she saw it. And the reward was a well-run house, clean shirts with buttons sewed on, polished shoes, socks which had no holes. This she had pointed out graphically. And dramatically she had hinted at the punishment wrong action could bring. I was to be smashed. I was to be smashed. That was all. But how could this be done?

It seemed to me that my job at the university was secure. I had tenure; and if my book succeeded as it now seemed that it might, my academic position should, if anything, be more sure.

But about other things I was not so sure. I called my lawyer that night from the hotel and I was not so optimistic after I had talked to him. If Dorothy filed for divorce . . . which was a possibility even though she had said she would not . . . injunctions could be put on about everything I owned in order to guarantee that I would not sell out anything until the case was tried. And if Dorothy handled things cleverly, which she could be counted on to do, matters could be so prolonged that, financially at least, I would find myself smashed for a number of years. My salary, what stocks and bonds I owned, my share of my father's estate, even the royalties from my book, should it make any,

[66] Ray E. Baber, *Marriage and the Family*, (second edition), McGraw-Hill, New York, 1953, p. 480.

could all be enjoined. It was not a pleasant picture should Dorothy decide to carry matters to their furthest extremes.[67]

Courts are concerned with three problems in the distribution of property and the determination of alimony: the return of property to the individual to whom it originally belonged, the division of property accumulated during the marriage, the protection of the wife and children against economic difficulties, but with a view to avoid an unrealistic burden for the husband. Some states, like California, have a "community property" law by which the wife is considered to be making a direct financial contribution to the marriage, and property accumulated during the marriage is equally divided between them. In connection with these provisions, it appears that the "innocent" party often receives more than an equal share, as in the case of the occasional notoriously large alimony settlement. For example, community property settlements may force a movie star to sell his collection of paintings to comply with the court order regarding settlement.

REFORMS IN DIVORCE PROCEDURE. In surveying the background and legal framework of divorce it is apparent that reform is needed. Perhaps the most far-reaching innovation would be the passing of a federal divorce law. An amendment to the federal constitution was seriously proposed in the 1920's. In the meantime, changes within state jurisdictions have been suggested. These proposals relate to several aspects of divorce: the liberalization of divorce in order to eliminate lying, collusion, and fraud; use of interlocutory decree in order to discourage hasty divorces; abolition of discrimination between the sexes in grounds for divorce; disuse of the term "guilty spouse"; standardization of alimony procedures; and more uniform provisions between the states.[68]

We ask, "What implication will these changes have in our marriage system in the United States?" Presumably, certain changes would create a more honest approach to divorce. Whether reform would increase or decrease the number of divorces, and whether the degree of anxiety and guilt about divorce would be materially changed are basic questions. In reality, each of the reforms might have very specific effects. The fundamental question is whether any or all of these proposals will be adopted on a federal or interstate basis.

[67] Carl Jonas, *Lillian White Deer*, W. W. Norton, New York, 1964, pp. 235–236. Used by permission.

[68] Clarke, *op. cit.*, p. 150.

The one encouraging aspect has been the family-court movement.[69] The first family court was developed in Cincinnati in 1914, and the movement has spread to most major cities. Generally, family courts employ a varied staff including social workers, counsellors, and legal advisors. Ideally, the court is integrated, but in certain cities, as in New York, there is a division into separate courts regarding divorce proceedings, support, illegitimacy, delinquency and neglect, adoptions, and disorderly conduct within the family.[70] The expense of budgeting the large staff has discouraged most communities from providing sufficient court procedures. Consequently, the number of cases processed is limited, and waiting periods are long. Public opinion is not especially vocal in regard to either the expansion or integration of the courts.

REMARRIAGE

About one-fourth of the marriages in the United States are remarriages.[71] The declining age at marriage and the high ratio of the married population, combined with a relatively high rate of marital dissolution, are responsible for the highest rate of remarriages in history. Of course, social factors also influence the rate of remarriage. The divorce rate is higher for urban areas and so is the rate of remarriages.[72] As we might expect, Catholics have a lower tendency to remarry than Protestants. In addition to having higher rates of marital termination, individuals of lower education are more likely to remarry than those of higher.[73] Some sense of the frequency of remarriage can be seen when we examine the age bracket of thirty five to thirty nine, where 63.5 per cent of the marriages are for the second time, with increasing percentages for higher age categories.[74]

Three-fourths of divorced men and two-thirds of divorced women eventually remarry. Usually the groom is on the average six years older

[69] For a description of the courts as they operate in several cities, see Maxine B. Virtue, *Family Cases in Court*, Duke University Press, Durham, 1956.

[70] Kephart, *op. cit.* (1964), p. 956.

[71] Jacobson, *op. cit.*, p. 71.

[72] Paul C. Glick, "First Marriages and Remarriages," *American Sociological Review*, 1949, 14, 726–734.

[73] Paul C. Glick and Hugh Carter, "Marriage Patterns and Educational Level," *American Sociological Review*, 1958, 23, 294–300.

[74] Paul C. Glick, *American Families*, John Wiley, New York, 1958, p. 139.

than the bride, whereas in first marriages the difference is approximately three years. Yet remarriages for individuals under thirty resemble the age differences of marriages between single people, as reported in Chapter 4.

Approximately 90 per cent of single individuals marry homogamously in regard to marital status; about half of divorcees and widowed marry within their groups.[75] These rates are affected by age, sex, and geographic region. For instance, in 1948 first marriages accounted for 85 per cent of the marriages in the Northeast, but only 65 per cent of those in the Mountain states. For all parts of the country however, the rate of remarriage has been increasing on a long-term basis since the beginning of the century.

The probability of remarriage is highest in the period immediately following the divorce. One-third of divorced women remarry within a year, almost half within two years, and about two-thirds within five years. About three-fifths of divorced men remarry within five years.[76]

SUCCESS OF REMARRIAGES. The findings regarding the outcome of these marriages are not consistent. On an impressionistic basis one writer concludes that divorce is mainly a result of neurotic tendencies, including jealousies, hostility, aggressiveness, sex conflicts, anxieties, and power contests.[77] According to this theory, remarriage represents a frantic attempt to find a partner to complement one's weakness, to express retaliation, or to bolster an offended ego. If all remarriages were made on this basis, remarriages would not produce very satisfactory results. A sample of Iowa marriages, however, suggests partial support of this generalization.[78] Second marriages were of shorter duration than first marriages, and each later union was successively briefer.

On the whole, research has produced more hopeful findings regarding remarriage. Locke found widowed persons more likely to have a happier relationship on remarriage as compared to the divorced person. Yet even for the divorced, three-fourths of the subsequent remarriages were rated as "happy" or "very happy" by the subjects. The

---

[75] Jacobson, *op. cit.*, p. 71.

[76] Jessie Bernard, *Remarriage: A Study of Marriage*, Holt, Rinehart and Winston, Inc., New York, 1956, pp. 46–50.

[77] Edmund Bergler, *Divorce Won't Help*, Harper and Row, New York, 1958.

[78] Thomas P. Monahan, "The Duration of Marriage to Divorce: Second Marriages and Migratory Types," *Marriage and Family Living*, 1959, 21, 134–138.

divorced woman tended to have a more satisfying second marriage than did the divorced man.[79]

The most far-reaching study of remarriage has been performed by Jessie Bernard.[80] Over half of the divorced and nearly two-thirds of the widowed persons regarded their new marriages as happy or successful (Table 20.4). In contrast to Locke's findings, divorced men were slightly more positive in their ratings of the marriage than were divorced

Table 20.4

RELATIVE SUCCESS IN REMARRIAGE OF WIDOWED AND DIVORCED PERSONS

	Divorced Men (N = 779)	Widowed Men (N = 539)	Divorced Women (N = 816)	Widowed Women (N = 422)
Very happy (or extremely successful)	25.3%	32.3%	25.1%	34.0%
Happy (or above average)	28.8	29.0	25.5	30.0
Average	32.6	25.9	33.2	24.0
Unhappy (or below average)	8.5	7.8	9.9	5.0
Very unhappy (or unsuccessful)	4.8	5.0	6.3	7.0

Source: From Jessie Bernard, *Remarriage: A Study in Marriage,* Holt, Rinehart and Winston, New York, 1956, p. 111. *Note:* This table is based upon ratings by informants.

women, and widows were more positive than widowers. Goode in another study found that 92 per cent of his remarried wife sample considered their second marriages to be "better" or "much better" than the first.[81] In regard to these data, the same problems concerning self-ratings of marital happiness, which are found in Chapter 13 and in the Appendix, apply to the second marriage as well as to the first. Yet the rating of the second marriage has the previous one as a basis of comparison.

For both the widowed and divorced persons, remarriage calls for various problems of adjustment. The individuals may have been too

[79] Harvey J. Locke, *Predicting Adjustment in Marriage: A Comparison of a Divorced and a Happily Married Group,* Holt, Rinehart and Winston, New York, 1951, pp. 298, 309.

[80] Bernard, *op. cit.*

[81] Goode, *op. cit.,* p. 335.

young at the first marriage, but their experience in that marriage will benefit them subsequently. Eighty-four per cent of Goode's respondents claimed that their first marriage facilitated adjustment in the second. The second marriage often constitutes a determined effort in order to assuage wounded pride, to prove to oneself and the world that a successful marital adjustment can be accomplished. Bernard found that for the serious and determined type of individual the failure of a second marriage could be a greater blow than failure of the first. Among the several factors that Bernard found to be predictive of success in remarriage were:

1. Personality factors related to the question of maturity.

2. Class factors, as defined by both partners' college educational background and a professional or semiprofessional occupation of the husband.

3. The factor or role of the ex-spouse was significant. Divorced husbands had more tension with the ex-wife than the divorced woman might have with her former spouse, frequently around problems developing out of her custodial award of the children.

4. Approval of the remarriage by the children. Most of the children interviewed were happy in their new homes. There was a minority of children who were unhappy with their new fathers, often because of antipathies that developed before the marriage took place. Most difficult were the cases in which the wife had divided custody. On the whole, the step-parent problem appeared to be caused by the inability of the child to adapt rather than by deficiencies in the new parent.

In addition to these were pressures surrounding the remarriage, including attitudes of the former in-laws and the community, as well as economic problems, and the value system of the individual involved. Lingering roles and habits of the first marriage were a more serious problem in the marriage following bereavement than following divorce, but were present in both types of remarriages. "The wife calls her husband by her first husband's name, or prepares a dish for her second husband which her first husband considered a special treat." [82]

Frequently problems are in remarriages of divorced spouses to each other. A study of 200 cases indicated that approximately half of these were successful. The success in this type of remarriage depended on a number of factors: (1) whether there had been ambivalence and con-

[82] Goode, *op. cit.*, p. 336.

flict about securing the divorce;   (2) lessons learned in the first marriage, which may be of profit in diagnosing and solving problems in the
second—age or maturity being an advantage;   (3) whether the new-
found freedom following the divorce of the two partners did not prove
to be as profitable as had been anticipated;   (4) many pressures that
were no longer present in the remarriage; and   (5) recognition of psychological damage to the children.[83]

In this chapter we have recognized that statistically there is one
chance out of four that a given marriage will be dissolved by divorce.
However, this actuarial probability is reduced by the middle-class setting in which many of us live. College education and, in fact, enrollment in a course in marriage relations, act as inhibiting factors against
divorce. With the extension of higher education in the United States a
reduction in the present divorce rate is probable. At the same time,
with the individualism of our society and the complexity of institutions in our present age, a relatively high rate of marital disruption
will probably continue.

It is hoped that the institutional framework in our society may solve
certain problems in the surrounding marital crisis and divorce. The
need for revamping our legal norms and procedures was mentioned.
There is also need for expanding family life education and counselling
facilities. The question of marital and family counselling is our next
subject.

Supplementary Readings

Becker, Howard and Reuben Hill (eds.), *Family, Marriage and Parenthood* (second
edition), D. C. Heath, Boston, 1955. Chapters 22 and 23 are a discussion of
bereavement and divorce, respectively.

Bernard Jesse, *Remarriage: A Study in Marriage,* Holt, Rinehart and Winston, New
York, 1956. A study of 2,008 remarriages, with considerable research material
in addition.

Clarke, Helen I., *Social Legislation* (second edition), Appleton-Century-Crofts, New
York, 1957. Chapter 6 is exposition of the conflicts in state laws.

Despert, J. Louise, *Children of Divorce,* Doubleday, New York, 1953. An insightful
and relatively complete treatment of the subject.

[83] Paul Popenoe, "Remarriage of Divorcees to Each Other," *American Sociological
Review,* 1938, **3,** 695–699.

Goode, William J., *After Divorce,* The Free Press of Glencoe, A Division of Collier-Macmillan, New York, 1956. A searching study of practically all aspects regarding divorce, decision, and adjustment of 425 Detroit divorced women.

Goode, William J., *World Revolution and Family Patterns,* The Free Press of Glencoe, A Division of Collier-Macmillan, New York, 1963. Data is presented about marital dissoultion as well as other subjects in regard to several different cultures.

Jacobson, Paul H., *American Marriage and Divorce,* Holt, Rinehart and Winston, New York, 1959. A history and analysis of divorce data and remarriage. Chapters 6–11 are the most relevant.

Kephart, William M., *The Family, Society and the Individual,* Houghton Mifflin, New York, 1961. Chapters 19–22 are a well-documented review of desertion, divorce and related topics.

Kephart, William M., "Legal and Procedural Aspects of Marriage and Divorce," in Harold T. Christensen (ed.), *Handbook of Marriage and the Family,* Rand McNally, Chicago, 1964, pp. 944–968.

Pilpel, Harriet F. and Theodora Zavin, *Your Marriage and the Law,* Holt, Rinehart and Winston, New York, 1952. In Part Four the authors present in a popular style a number of aspects of the termination of marriage. (Paperback edition, 1964).

Sussman, Marvin B. (ed.), *Sourcebook in Marriage and the Family* (second edition), Houghton Mifflin, Boston, 1963. Part Six contains several significant discussions of the divorce question especially from the remedial viewpoint.

Waller, Willard, *The Old Love and the New: Divorce and Readjustment,* Liveright, New York, 1930. Partly autobiographical, this work is an insightful study of divorce and remarriage.

Waller, Willard, *The Family: A Dynamic Interpretation* (revised by Reuben Hill), Holt, Rinehart and Winston, New York, 1951. Chapters 22–24 are a penetrating analysis of the dissolution of marriage, more strengthened by case studies than by empirical data.

Winch, Robert F., *The Modern Family* (revised edition), Holt, Rinehart and Winston, New York, 1963. Chapters 22 and 23 provide considerable data as well as a theoretical framework on the subject.

Chapter twenty-one

Marriage
and Family Counselling

All happy families are alike, but every unhappy one is unhappy in its own way.
Leo Tolstoy: Anna Karenina, *I, 1876.*

All marriages, like all lives, must end. Some marriages are dissolved by divorce, some by death, and some gradually come apart, to exist for years as a mere formality. Since family life is suffused with emotion, those who are unhappy in their family relationships usually learn that this kind of misery, like a toothache, cannot easily be set apart, compartmentalized, or controlled by an effort of will. It affects much of their lives. Almost everyone will eventually experience one or another of the various forms of disorganization at some time in their lives; the patterns and processes of family disorganization deserve analysis.
William J. Goode, "Family Disorganization" in Robert K. Merton and Robert A. Nisbet (eds.), Contemporary Social Problems, Harcourt, Brace and World, New York, 1961, p. 390.

Thus interpersonal competence is neither a trait nor a state. Competence denotes capabilities to meet and deal with a changing world, to formulate ends and implement them. The incessant problem of equipping human beings to handle their affairs and to progress toward the discovery of new values and new means is not solved by authoritarian indoctrination of static attributes and beliefs. To rely upon such methods would not only be subversive of the most fundamental of American democratic values but would ultimately result in failure of the system which sought to maintain itself by these means.
Nelson N. Foote and Leonard S. Cottrell, Jr., Identity and Interpersonal Competence, *The University of Chicago Press, 1955, p. 49.*

House by the Railroad by Edward Hopper
Collection, The Museum of Modern Art, New York

The application of counselling and therapy to marriage and the family by psychologists, sociologists, and other professional personnel is a major development of this century. Its practical consequences are considerable for the average man. Although advice regarding marital relations from one's peers has ancient and certainly Biblical authority, scientific and professional emphasis is distinctly recent. Counselling, both in philosophy and technique, is central to the theme of this book; that is, the belief that scientific knowledge should be applied to individual and marital adjustment. Implied in counselling is a broad acceptance of the concept of normality. Judgments of success and failure, adjustment and maladjustment, become relative terms. An implicit notion is that the individual must recognize the desirability of seeking outside help in the solution of his problems.

The chapter traces the background of counselling. It also introduces the types of questions clients have about their problems. Counselling resources involve a number of professional services, and procedures, as well as the goals anticipated, constitute the core of the chapter. The emphasis is on marital rather than family counselling.

BACKGROUND. Formal marital counselling was introduced in the post-World War I period. Its establishment was related to social work and family services, which became organized during the 1920's. The first serious marital counselling began in Austria and Germany during that decade. Drs. Abraham and Hannah Stone inaugurated a clinic in New York in 1929. In 1930 Paul Popenoe organized the American Institute of Family Relations in Los Angeles, which has employed an extensive staff of varying professional qualifications. In 1932 Dr. Emily H. Mudd established the Marriage Council of Philadelphia at the University of Pennsylvania. Another important influence in the training of marital counselors was the program of Ernest R. Groves at the University of North Carolina.

In the last three decades counselling has come of age. The American Association of Marital Counsellors was formed in 1942. In addition, counselling and therapy resources depend heavily on and support other sources such as the clergy, social workers, clinical psychologists, and psychiatrists, among others. Marital counselling and therapy is not the exclusive domain of any given set of practitioners. In fact, a larger proportion of individuals is receiving guidance in their marital and family problems by psychotherapists than by marital counsellors.

THE CLIENT AND HIS PROBLEMS

Generally, three types of individuals seek the services of the marital counsellor and therapist. First, premarital counselling concerns itself with questions regarding the stability of a couple's engagement and readiness for marriage. The couple may desire knowledge as to the predictability of the success in the marriage-to-be. Second, tensions within the marital or family relationships require assessment or possibly extended treatment. Third, the married couple anticipating divorce may profit from counselling, and postdivorce adjustment could require attention.

Half to three-forths of the clients requesting marriage counselling are wives.[1] The reasons for this are the readiness of the wife to discuss marital problems, the freer time at her disposal, and the more strategic significance of marriage in her life. Consequently, it is no surprise that the husband is the more likely of the two partners to be considered the problem in the marriage. As we saw in Chapter 13, the husband tends to have traits, habits, or maladjustments that may be highly disturbing to a marriage.

An old adage in counselling and psychiatric practice is that the person most in need of therapy or treatment is the one least likely to recognize the problem or the need for treatment. Unfortunately, many individuals even today consider therapy in any form an acknowledgement of weakness, and consequently reject it. Much of this resistance stems from conflicts in the unconscious, a latent anxiety to confront certain hostile feelings, and a general fear of change in one's personality structure. Somehow psychological habits, despite the unhappiness they may cause in the marriage, are less terrifying to the individual than new kinds of affectional relationships, changes in marital roles, or shifts in the power structure of the family. Conflicts within the unconscious and immature reaction patterns are also significant in this resistance. Too, the influence of relatives, friends, and neighbors, especially the public admission of being a "failure" in the marriage, acts as a deterrent. There are the usual rationalizations: "It's too expensive," "I can't find time," "Things will somehow work out," and "I can develop my own insights."

---

[1] Robert G. Foster, "How a Marriage Counsellor Handles a Case," *Marriage and Family Living*, 1954, **16**, 139–142.

Counselling, or deeper techniques like psychotherapy, are most successful when the client has the following attitudes: (1) volition in seeking help or treatment. There must be a desire to be helped. Entering counselling purely at the request of another person—the wife or judge—is not likely to lead either to insights or changes in behavior; (2) recognition of one's own responsibility in the marital relationship. By implication, the individual acquires in the counselling situation the capacity to identify with another person; (3) honesty and openness in the counselling situation. Covering up, restraints in communication, and other blockages are impediments to a close relationship between the therapist and the client. Although no one can be completely objective about his marriage and its involvements, the capacity to develop a sense of detachment is essential for adjustment and necessary changes in roles; (4) confidence in the counsellor. The selection of a counsellor itself can be flexible: of a male or female, a minister or clinical psychologist. The choice may depend on both the nature of the problem as well as the individual's anticipation of rapport.

THE RANGE OF PROBLEMS. An idea of the motivation of individuals seeking marital counselling is found in the distribution of 2,566 cases from the Marriage Council of Philadelphia: [2] general preparation for marriage, 23 per cent; specific marital problems (parental relations, engagement decisions, etc.), 16 per cent; and problems of marital adjustment, 61 per cent. Within the marital adjustment area, 21 per cent of the total sample were of general adjustment problems: sexual difficulties, 15 per cent; specific problems, 15 per cent; and considering separation or divorce, 10 per cent.

Frequently the client complains of a given defect in the other partner or a lack of commitment in this person to the marriage. Problems in communication are particularly evident in counselling cases.[3] When sex or economic problems bring the individual to the counsellor, the deeper conflicts may be very different from the conscious ones. Consequently the role of the counsellor is to determine the

[2] Emily H. Mudd and Malcom G. Preston, "Contemporary Status of Marital Counselling," *Annals of the American Academy of Political and Social Science*, 1950, **272**, 102–109.

[3] Robert A. Harper, "Communication Problems in Marriage Counselling," *Marriage and Family Living*, 1958, **20**, 107–112; and Richard N. Hey and Emily H. Mudd, "Recurring Problems in Marriage Counselling," *Marriage and Family Living*, 1959, **21**, 127–129.

underlying nature of the tension. Not infrequently the reason for one or both partners coming to the counsellor is an impending divorce. In this situation earlier counselling might have prevented a marital crisis. However, the willingness or interest to seek outside guidance is indicative of a healthy attitude and of the inclination to explore the strengths and weaknesses of the marriage. Perception of role and value discrepancies can be illuminated in the sessions with the counsellor.

In some instances treatment of the case reveals the counsellor's own values regarding divorce.[4] At one time most counsellors felt that at all costs the marriage should be saved. More frequently today the counsellor objectively weighs the alternatives and attempts to look at the problem in terms of attitudes and needs of the individual. These attitudes and needs can be assessed in the process of counselling. Parenthetically, it may be added that in certain states the counsellor can recommend divorce only if he is a physician. Otherwise, he might become the correspondent in a divorce and could be sued for alienation of affection.

Other problems confronting the counsellor may involve various members of the family. *Family counselling* is the term applied to the treatment of more general interrelationships concerning parents and children. However, a family counsellor may begin with more than one member of the family but proceed to work intensively with one individual through a number of sessions. He may invite both spouses or all the family members into joint sessions later. The family is a miniature social structure representing three subsystems: marital, parent-child, and sibling relationships. These subsystems are sufficiently interlocked that a deterioration in one is almost inevitably reflected in another.[5] Consquently, individual and family problems merge, although some therapists may prefer to work exclusively with one client.

Frequently counselling is directed toward problems in deviance. An example is alcoholism. *Alcoholism* on the part of either or both spouses, more often the husband, is a major determinant of marital and family crises. The causes of alcoholism are complex, but there are three general types: [6] (1) *primary,* the habit appearing early and develop-

---

[4] Aaron L. Rutledge, "Should the Marriage Counsellor Ever Recommend Divorce," *Marriage and Family Living,* 1963, 25, 319–325.

[5] Otto Pollak, "Issues in Family Diagnosis and Family Therapy," *Journal of Marriage and the Family,* 1964, 26, 279–287.

[6] S. D. Bacon, "Alcoholism: Nature of the Problem," *Federal Probation,* 1947, 2, 3–7.

ing out of neurotic needs in insecurity, conflict, and anxiety; (2) *secondary*, alcoholic habits emerging from prolonged social drinking, establishing a compulsive habit system; and (3) *situational*, resulting from a prolonged stressful situation. Since the ratio of alcoholic husbands to wives has been reported as running from six to one, the complaint is more likely brought up by the wife.[7] A considerable amount of literature on the personality dynamics of the wife of an alcoholic husband points to a common situation in which she unconsciously enjoys the role of being protector to the weaker or more dependent spouse.

Counselling may focus on other problems, such as contraception and sterility, as we saw in Chapter 16. Mental health professionals and family planning agencies point to the need of extending counselling to include dissemination of contraceptive techniques. Areas covered by counselling range from childbearing to economic questions, but these problems can seldom be isolated from the effects of other discontinuities. Ethnic relations, religious differences, and occupational choice are still other possibilities.

COUNSELLING RESOURCES

The definition of *marital counselling* has been a moot question since the inception of this profession. Increasingly, a doctorate in clinical psychology or a related field is recommended for a counsellor. In addition, according to the standards set by the American Association of Marriage Counsellors, practitioners should have extensive casework experience under supervision before commencing certified practice.[8]

The practice of therapy is an art. The practitioner must be endowed with an affectionate attitude toward people, a capacity for empathy, and a receptivity to cues. This ability cannot be acquired in the classroom. Experience, including intelligent trial and error, counts heavily in conducting counselling and therapy.

A controversy persists as to whether the term marital counselling can be meaningful unless it implies a deeper relationship, that is, psychotherapy. Documentation of this viewpoint is found among a number

[7] Ruth Fox, "The Alcoholic Spouse," In Victor W. Eisenstein (ed.), *Neurotic Interaction in Marriage*, Basic Books, New York, 1956, pp. 148–168.

[8] Gerald R. Leslie, "The Field of Marital Counseling," in Harold T. Christensen (ed.), *Handbook of Marriage and the Family*, Rand McNally, Chicago, 1964, p. 938.

of writers in the field. Karpf maintains that the counsellor is not ordinarily equipped to work on the deep-seated problems. When he encounters psychotic or neurotic problems in the individual, he consults a clinical psychologist or psychiatrist.[9] A prerequisite for the counsellor is an ability to recognize the problems he can adequately handle, as opposed to the deeper disturbances. On the other hand, Ellis asserts that marriage dynamics inevitably involve unconscious factors and, therefore, counselling must be a form of psychotherapy, or as he terms his own technique, "rational psychotherapy." [10] In other words, the marital counsellor is, according to their viewpoint, a psychologist.

PASTORAL COUNSELLING. During the last generation the clergy has become oriented to the idea of counselling as one of its essential functions. Higher level divinity schools usually require courses in this area, which are generally taught by qualified psychologists or marital counsellors. With this training the minister, priest, or rabbi may acquire insight into marital problems and can offer assistance and particularly provide intelligent listening, which in itself may be of considerable reassurance to the individual in need of help. One professor of marital counselling in a seminary maintains that the minister must not refrain from recommending divorce when it is appropriate.[11] The clergyman is in a strategic position to make referral to other facilities. But one limitation to counselling members of his own church is the influence of friendship and personal involvement.[12] Consequently, some churches may prefer a separate staff for counselling purposes.

In an extensive community survey of mental health resources, 46 per cent of the subjects had turned to the clergy for help.[13] In another study, clergymen reported that 58.7 per cent of the cases which came to them concerned specific marital problems.[14] The remainder of the

[9] Maurice J. Karpf, "Marriage Counselling and Psychotherapy," *Marriage and Family Living*, 1951, **13**, 49–51.

[10] Albert Ellis, "Marriage Counseling With Demasculinizing Wives and Demasculinized Husbands," *Marriage and Family Living*, 1960, **22**, 13–21.

[11] Charles W. Stewart, *The Minister as Marriage Counselor*, Abington Press, New York, 1961.

[12] Wayne A. Oates, "The Pastor as a Marriage Counselor," *Marriage and Family Living*, 1955, **17**, 62–67.

[13] Gerald Gurin, Joseph Veroff, and Sheila Feld, *Americans View Their Mental Health*, Basic Books, New York, 1960.

[14] Reginald Robinson, David F. DeMarche, and Mildred K. Wagle, *Community Resources in Mental Health*, Basic Books, New York, 1960, p. 242.

problems focused, in declining order, on child-parent relations, juvenile behavior problems, problems of the aged, emotional problems, and alcoholism.

A number of progressive clergymen require premarital counselling before they perform a marriage ceremony. One Columbus, Ohio, minister asserts that of 1,100 premaritally counselled couples, only 9 terminated their marriages.[15] The couples offered practically no resistance to premarital counselling.

In a Syracuse study of severe social problems, including marital disruption, the probability of a clergyman functioning in a counselling role depended on his perception of other facilities in the community and on the educational level of the church membership.[16] If he considered a given problem to be beyond his competence, he generally referred the matter to another agency or a social worker, for example. Ministers in this study referred more cases than they received as referrals.

PSYCHOTHERAPY AND PSYCHIATRY. Certain marital problems require extensive exploration of an individual's deep-seated motives and often an investigation of the early development, which means a laborious probing into the unconscious for many months. This kind of analysis is very different from the type that is received in marital counselling. The interest of the counsellor is concentrated on the marriage, although not necessarily committed to preserve it; the marital counsellor is to some degree situation-oriented, whereas the psychotherapist or psychiatrist is almost exclusively individual-oriented. In addition to the use of insight and other counselling tools, the counsellor is particularly expert in his use of "working through" problems of the unconscious.[17] The psychotherapist is relatively less concerned with values as compared to marital counsellors.

There are a variety of marital and family counselling facilities: (1) social work agencies, which are directed toward the family under dependency or duress; (2) family court agencies, which handle prob-

---

[15] Roy A. Burkhart, "A Program of Premarital Counseling," *Pastoral Psychology,* 1950, p. 26, as cited by George Simpson, *People in Families,* Thomas Y. Crowell, New York, 1960, p. 518.

[16] Elaine Cumming and Charles Harrington, "Clergyman as Counselor," *American Journal of Sociology,* 1963, **69,** 234–243.

[17] An excellent introduction to these and related techniques is found in Harrington V. Ingham and Leonore R. Love, *The Process of Psychotherapy,* McGraw-Hill, New York, 1954.

lems of divorce, alimony, and custody of the children; [18] (3) student counselling at the university level—sometimes in connection with preparatory programs of masters and doctorates in marital counselling—as at the University of North Carolina, University of Pennsylvania, and the University of Southern California.

Counselling involves varied and interrelated groups of professionals with divergent approaches geared to different personality needs, life situations, and income levels. The individual client with severe economic pressures is not likely to be able to afford extensive individual psychotherapy. Short-term counselling or group therapy is recommended. Fortunately, state and local facilities, in addition to certain foundations and private agencies, have recognized the necessity for extending services to lower income groups. The mental hygiene movement stresses the need for expanding marital and family counselling.

Comparison with other countries is interesting. Britain, which initiated its first marriage guidance center in 1943, has at present a large program, relying principally on carefully screened "lay-counsellors." [19] Personality factors are as important as professional qualifications, although there is a training course for all individuals. Every counsellor is subject to standards set by the National Marriage Guidance Council. In contrast, the *laissez-faire* system of the United States encourages the development of high professional skills by most counsellors, yet it is possible for a quack to pose as a certified counsellor. Also, in Britian church-oriented marriage guidance works closely with the National Council.[20] In 1961 Australia passed the federal divorce law (Matrimonial Causes Act), which requires a lawyer to advise his client of marriage counselling facilities. As in Britian, counselling represents a coordinated civil and religious program there.[21]

METHODS AND PROCEDURES

The counsellor uses a number of different techniques, and he may also have a basic style or methodology. The specific tools of the

[18] Maxine B. Virtue, *Family Cases in Court,* Duke University Press, Durham, N.C., 1956.

[19] David R. Mace, "Marriage Counseling in Britain Today," *Marriage and Family Living,* 1958, **20**, 379–383.

[20] John Mogey, "Marriage Counseling and Family Life Education in England," *Marriage and Family Living,* 1961, **23**, 146–154.

[21] L. V. Harvey, "Marriage Counseling and the Federal Divorce Law in Australia," *Journal of Marriage and the Family,* 1964, **26**, 83–86.

counsellor depend on the problem presented in the particular case. For example, the approach is different for premarital counselling than it is for postmarital counselling. Although there is some overlapping of tools, in premarital situations an engagement-prediction scale is probably used. Various other tests or instruments can be used by the counsellor to determine the probability of success in marriage. A counsellor may use a battery of personality, intelligence, and interest tests depending on his assessment of the individual's situation. In the case of postmarital counselling, personality and related tests are useful in diagnosing problem areas in the marriage.

One difference between premarital and postmarital counselling is the question of permanence. Despite the pressure and urgency that exists when two people are anticipating marriage, the union has still not been completed. The situation is usally more fluid than the postmarital one, where an established marriage or family can be dissolved, making the situation less flexible. However, the counsellor must consider his neutrality and the limits with which he operates in both pre- and postmarital settings. Recommendations are to be made always in view of the total feeling state of the client and the reality that surrounds him.

A major distinction can be made between *directive* and *nondirective* counselling. The directive counsellor tends to dominate the counselling situation and is more inclined to make recommendations. This method particularly characterizes short-term counselling. Nondirective counselling or "client centered" therapy, advocated by Carl Rogers a generation ago, prescribes a less overt role for the counsellor.[22] This method requires the counsellor to do less of the talking and act more as a prompter in encouraging the client to form his own insights. The advocates of this type of counselling assert that the client makes a greater personality change as a result. They hold that his decisions will come from his own conviction and, therefore, be more meaningful. In either case it is strongly recommended that the counsellor be a listener, especially in the early phases so as to permit *catharsis,* by which the client may find a necessary release through talking out his problems.[23] The counsellor must be nonjudgmental and maintain an objective attitude whatever his personal opinion might be. In most instances he will no doubt prefer, at least in the early phases, to confer

[22] Carl R. Rogers, *Client Centered Therapy,* Houghton Mifflin, Boston, 1951.
[23] Maurice J. Karpf, "Some Guiding Principles in Marriage Counselling," *Marriage and Family Living,* 1951, **12**, 49–52.

with both parties to obtain a clearer understanding of the marital conflict involved.

In both types of counselling, but especially in the nondirective variety, the therapist is likely to encounter *resistance* on the part of the client. Resistance refers to the hostility and blockage the client feels toward the counsellor or therapist. In Freudian or psychoanalytic theory, love and hate may alternate in the client's attitude toward the therapist, who functions unconsciously or consciously as an alterego. In a sense, the therapist becomes internalized within the client. As treatment continues, an opposite reaction sets in, and the counsellor may become a kind of love object; the therapist may become a substitute for the spouse. This process is called *transference* and means the love feeling is directed toward the therapist. Falling in love with the therapist temporarily disrupts the therapy process, but as the sessions continue the task is to neutralize the ambivalence of love and hate. Although resistance, transference, and neutralization particularly characterize the process of deep therapy, they are not unknown in marital counselling.

INDIVIDUAL, CONJOINT, AND GROUP COUNSELLING.   Although marital counselling is oriented mainly toward an individual, conjoint counselling is also practiced. The more frequently used individual approach is designed to concentrate on the problem and the development of one person's feelings, roles, and his attempts in decision making during treatment. On the other hand, conjoint therapy has been gaining ground. Working with both spouses has certain advantages. The counsellor can make an interpretation to one spouse even though it is more pertinent to the other. Interpersonal behaviors and feelings also may be observed, which is difficult in individual counselling or therapy. The counsellor is able to "attend to a far broader range of stimuli" and can "reflect the emotional communication of both partners" when conjoint counselling is used.[24] Techniques of accommodation acquired in the counselling process can be applied in other settings. This joint approach is especially important when conflict between the spouses and resistance toward the therapist become acute during the counselling period. Initiation of counselling can lead to more intensified or overt hostility than was present before.[25] Problems

[24] Andrew S. Watson, "The Conjoint Psychotherapy of Marriage Patterns," *American Journal of Psychotherapy*, 1963, **33**, 912–922.

[25] Norman B. Henderson, "Married Group Therapy: A Setting for Reducing Resistances," *Psychological Reports*, 1965, **16**, 347–352.

can be viewed by the therapist in the context in which they arise. On the whole, a less passive relationship occurs in this triad than in the more usual counsellor-client relationship. If the problem is one of divergent attitudes about disciplining the children the conflict can be "worked through" in the counselling in a more effective manner than if the other spouse were not present.

In view of the shortage of counsellors and the even more critical problem of cost, the joint method is especially attractive. However, for certain neurotic types of individuals the method may not be successful.

Psychodrama is another variation in the group technique. This method was devised by Moreno to permit role protrayals in which a marital partner may act out with another individual the types of problems encountered in the marriage.[26] To what degree this role flexibility can be acquired and transferred to a person's own marriage depends on his intelligence and insight, as well as on the counsellor's training and experience. *Sociodrama* is a variation of this method, focusing on social and cultural situations.

THE CONTRIBUTION OF COUNSELLING

The degree of improvement possible as the result of a counselling program may be seen in a follow-up of 72 cases of the Marriage Council of Philadelphia and is modestly encouraging (Table 21.1). Signifi-

Table 21.1

OUTCOME OF PRE- AND POST-MARITAL
COUNSELLING

(Marriage Council of Philadelphia, $N = 72$)

Improvement or "positive movement"	58%
No improvement	32
Retrogression	7
Uncertain	3

Source: Emily H. Mudd and Malcolm G. Preston, "The Contemporary Status of Marriage Counseling," *Annals of The American Academy of Political and Social Science,* 1950, **272,** 107–108.

[26] Jacob L. Moreno, "Psychodramatic Treatment of Marital Problems," *Psychodrama Monographs,* **7,** Beacon House, Beacon, New York, 1945.

cantly, of the 58 per cent (42 cases) of the total sample which were
marked by "positive movement," only 1 case, or 2 per cent, showed
"considerable improvement"; 36 per cent showed "intermediate
movement" and 62 per cent, minimal improvement.[27] Although these
results do not seem overly encouraging, undoubtedly the divorce rate
was lower for this limited sample than if there had been no counselling.

The Legal Aid Bureau of the District of Columbia offered
counselling on a low cost basis ($1 fee charged for each visit) specifi-
cally for divorce or marital breakdown. Of 112 problem cases handled,
52 were apparently reconciled. Seventeen were referred to the mental
hygiene clinic or to a social agency, 11 went to Legal Aid attorneys,
and most of the remainder discontinued counselling because the other
partner refused to attend the counselling sessions.[28] Although this
study is limited in both the size of the sample and the scope of setting,
the results indicate a positive value in counselling.

The marital counsellor is concerned with several alternatives in his
goals. First, he may enable the client to be comfortable in an unalter-
able marital or family situation. In this instance the counselling
process focuses on the individual's motivational and perceptual system.
For instance, a man married to a woman less intelligent than himself
must be prepared to make adjustments in his social life or to perceive
her in a new frame of reference, which may include an inventory of
her less apparent, but more enduring, qualities. Second, the counsellor
may aid the client in *altering* the situation by changing roles or other
modes of behavior. The wife whose husband would like her to be more
demonstrative in her affections may be helped to change her behavior
unless there is a deep-seated hostility or some other emotional conflict.
Third, in certain marital situations the counsellor may support the
idea of divorce. (The decision for divorce may have a certain shock
value and may initiate a closer examination of the situation by the
client.) The decisison for divorce provides considerable material to
analyze for both client and counsellor. Fourth, when the individual or
marital problem is very complex, counselling may lead to the recognition of more farreaching therapy. A well-trained and insightful counsellor can detect neurotic and psychotic symptoms and make a referral.

[27] Mudd and Preston, *op. cit.*, p. 108.
[28] Patricia Schiller, "Marriage Counselling in a Legal-Aid Setting," *Marriage and Family Living*, 1960, **22**, 213–217.

Perhaps the major contribution of counselling is the improved communication that it provides between the partners. The security that an individual receives in counselling makes him more tolerant of the behavior patterns of others. Family interaction, role performance, and the power structure are subject to change with counselling. Counselling and therapy alter the decision-making process and unquestionably change the relations between the husband and wife, parents and children, and siblings.

Moreover, most counsellors assume that problems emerging from a marriage are embedded in the personalities of the marriage partners. By adjusting the personalities to make a better "fit," the counsellor thereby rescues the marriage. From a societal viewpoint the counsellor is convinced that the nuclear family has priority over and independence from other types of kinship relationships. Both the role of the counsellor and the family-life educator have acted to promote this kind of organization.

Counselling cannot be detached from other developments in our society, notably the mental hygiene movement in the community and family life education in the schools at all levels.[29] Despite the tensions confronting marriage and family life today, most students of the family regard the situation as markedly improved over what it was a century or even half-century ago. Although the tensions of modern living place varied strains on the family, educational and therapeutic facilities are meeting the challenge with at least moderate success.

Supplementary Readings

Ackerman, Nathan W., *The Psychodynamics of Family Life*, Basic Books, New York, 1958. A solid, analytically oriented report on therapy in various phases of family relations.

Buhler, Charlotte, *Values in Psychotherapy*, The Free Press of Glencoe, A Division of Collier-Macmillan, New York, 1962. A well-known clinical psychologist presents a theoretical framework on values in counselling, illustrated with case studies.

Burgess, Ernest W. and Paul Wallin, *Engagement and Marriage*, J. B. Lippincott, Philadelphia, 1953. Chapter 22 treats the question of prediction and adjustment tests and their use in counselling.

[29] Richard K. Kerckhoff, "Family Life Education in America," in Christensen (ed.), *op. cit.*, pp. 881–911.

Cuber, John F., *Marriage Counselling Practice*, Appleton-Century-Crofts, New York, 1958. A presentation of a variety of topics: interviewing, diagnosis and training.

Delliquadri, Fred (ed.), *Helping the Family in Urban Society*, Columbia University Press, New York, 1963. A collection of readings on various aspects of family welfare services.

Eisenstein, Victor W. (ed.), *Neurotic Interaction in Marriage*, Basic Books, New York, 1956. A psychoanalytic orientation to therapy by a variety of contributors.

Foote, Nelson N. and Leonard S. Cottrell, Jr., *Identity and Interpersonal Competence*, University of Chicago Press, 1955. Although the book is not specifically concerned with counselling, it provides a setting for family help and growth.

Leslie, Gerald R., "The Field of Marriage Counseling," in Harold T. Christensen (ed.), *Handbook of Marriage and the Family*, Rand McNally, Chicago, 1964. A review of background, concepts, methods and goals.

Mowrer, O. Hobart, *The New Group Therapy*, D. Van Nostrand, Princeton, New Jersey, 1964. An eminent research psychologist develops in readable form a theory of certain aspects of treatment.

Satir, Virginia M., *Conjoint Family Therapy: A Guide to Theory and Technique*, Science and Behavior Books, Palo Alto, California, 1964. A theoretically oriented work with extensive discussion of stress, communication, and roles, explaining the differences between individual and conjoint therapy.

Taft, Jessie, *The Dynamics of Therapy in a Controlled Relationship*, Dover Publications, New York, 1962. A detailed study of the therapeutic process in the case of a problem child.

Vincent, Clark E., *Readings in Marriage Counseling*, Thomas Y. Crowell, New York, 1957. An excellent selection of articles on all phases of the subject.

Glossary

The terms defined are those most useful for an understanding of the text. For specific technical terms the reader is referred to the Index.

affective. Refers to love or feeling, with a minimal erotic relationship.

affinity. A legal term usually referring to the prohibition of marriage with in-laws; cf. *consanguinity.*

alienation. The process of physical, emotional, or intellectual isolation of the individual from the group or culture. May also refer to estrangement between two partners in marriage.

ambivalence. The alternation of emotion or affectional tone, as in love and hate, toward an object or individual also fluctuations in mood or motivation.

annulment. The dissolution of a marriage because of nonfulfilment of a legal requirement such as age, etc.; cf. *void.*

anomie. The state of normlessness or conflicting norms on the part of the individual; isolation and personal disorganization resulting because of a shift in the life situation; cf. *alienation.*

anxiety. A generalized and continuing fear reaction in relation to an object or situation, usually resulting from unconscious conflict.

assortative mating. Mate selection in line with endogamy and homogamy; the more or less unconscious process by which "like mates like."

attitude. A potential or incipient response for or against a given stimulus and determining a person's future behavior.

birth rate. The number of live births per 1000 (or 100) of the population in a given area per year.

bureaucratization. The tendency toward regimentation, centralized authority, and a pyramidal structure or hierarchy in the large scale organization. See also traditionalistic-rationalistic.

catharsis. The "talking out" in counselling or therapy of pent-up or repressed emotional shock, anxiety or guilt; experience or participation in activities neutralizing or reducing the emotional state of the individual.

causation. The relation of anterior and posterior elements in a given phenomenon, or the analysis of cause and effect. When applied to human beings, causation is often refered to as motivation.

class (social). A category or division of society, usually into lower, middle, and upper, which constitutes to a marked degree the individual's social environment and reaction tendencies.

collusion. Techniques used in divorce proceedings by which a divorce is arranged through misrepresentation so as to conform with state law and judicial procedure; cf. Chapter 20.

common law marriage. A marriage not solemnized by formal ceremony but recognized in certain states.

communication. The transfer of meaning through gestures, speech, the printed page, or other medium.

complementary needs. A theory (Winch) of mate selection based on unconscious needs: the choice of a mate is unconsciously motivated and serves to complete a person's personality structure.

conjugal. Alternate term for marital; conjugal family is equivalent to nuclear family.

consanguinity. Blood relationship; a term used to indicate the prohibition of marriage between two related persons.

contraception (birth control). The prevention of conception by mechanical, chemical, or other means.

correlation. The degree of statistical relationship between two variables, symbolized by the *r*, which varies from a positive (or plus) to a negative (inverse or minus) relationship, with zero or near-zero as an intermediate relationship.

culture. The total social heritage defining accepted ways of behavior; the totality of objects, material and immaterial, identified with a society, as in American culture, Navaho culture, etc.

definition of the situation. The frame of reference in which the individual perceives the situation; the various factors influencing the individual in his assessment of alternative behaviors (Thomas).

deviance. The tendency to vary or deviate from the norm or average. The term may refer to personal or social disorganization.

disorganization. Partial or complete maladjustment of the individual or society, as in divorce, alcoholism, delinquency, for example.

dynamic. Refers to motivation or change; in psychoanalysis usually refers to unconscious motivation or causation.

ego. An alternate term for the self; psychoanalytical terminology, the more conscious, organizing and integrated part of the total personality; cf. Chapter 5.

ego-ideal. The personality one would ideally desire for oneself; an imaginative model toward which one may aspire.

empathy. The capacity to identify, or "feel in," with another person, or to perceive the situation of the other person; cf. *identification.*

endogamy. Mate selection within the group (race, social class); cf. *exogamy.*

exogamy. Mate selection outside the group (kinship, for instance).

extended family. In contrast to the nuclear or small family, represents the large family, usually sharing a common domicile with other relatives and organized on a patriarchal basis.

family of orientation. The present family in which a person lives and toward which he is oriented.

family of procreation. The family in which a person was originally socialized.

fecundity. The capacity to have children, or reproductive capacity, as opposed to the actual reproduction or fertility.

fertility. Cf. birth rate.

fixation. The tendency to become rigid in a given behavior pattern; attachment of the libido at a premature level.

folkways. Traditional practices within the society, such as shaking hands or presenting a corsage on a date. Noncompliance elicits only moderate sanctions.

function. The role or meaning underlying a unit or behavior sequence; the action it performs in relation to other units in the system.

Gemeinschaft and Gesellschaft. See traditionalistic-rationalistic.

guilt. Feeling of unworthiness and dejection often resulting from libidinal conflicts.

heterogamy. Mate selection according to dissimilarity of characteristics; cf. *homogamy.*

heterosexuality. Attraction between the two sexes; cf. *homosexuality.*

hierarchy. The orderly arrangement of articulation of statuses and values, into a pyramid-type structure by which certain items have priority over others.

homogamy. Mate selection according to similarity of characteristics such as in intelligence; "like mates like."

homosexuality. Physical attraction between members of the same sex.

id. The unconscious and primitive aspect or portion of the self or personality which expresses basic or sexual drives.

identification. The act of assuming the qualities of another person; emotional involvment with a person, group, or cause, as in the term "ego-involvement."

identity. The significance and integrity of the self; a feeling of self-importance.

in-group. A group with certain values and norms distinguishing them from other groups implying rejection of nonmembers.

instinct. Generally an inborn disposition to behave in a given fashion. Although there are different interpretations, it is an inborn complex behavior pattern universal in the species. The term instinctual usually refers to biologically determined behavior.

institution. A continuing, complex set of culturally defined organizations and behaviors by which the basic needs of society are fulfilled, for example, the family, state, and church.

integration. The unity resulting from diverse items, such as roles or values, as applied to the individual, group, or institution.

interlocutory degree. The period preceding divorce as granted in certain states, usually one year, following the initial court action.

intermarriage. Marriage between members of different racial, ethnic, or religious groups.

internalization (interiorization). The process of accepting or absorbing an experience, value, or role.

kinship. A relationship between individuals based on common ancestry.

latent. An unconscious or covert motive, thought, or emotion, as in latent homosexuality, for example. Latent may also refer to a function not readily discoverable and revealed only by scientific analysis, that is, a latent function in contrast to a *manifest* function.

mobility. Movement of individuals from one area or level to another. Social or vertical mobility refers to changes in social class; horizontal mobility refers to residential or geographic movement.

model. An ideal pattern, as in the term "ego-model."

mores. Social norms or behavior patterns severely sanctioned by the group; written or unwritten laws by which societal welfare is protected, for example, the taboo on sex relations before marriage; cf. *folkways.*

Neo-Freudian. Refers to the revision of classical Freudian theory; the instinctual and sexual emphasis is reduced.

norm. A standard of judgment generally resulting from social agreement by which behavior is regulated; "normative" in adjective form.

nuclear family. The small family consisting of the husband, wife, and children characterizing contemporary Western society; cf. *extended family.*

other-directedness. A concept (Riesman) of contemporary society pointing to the individual's need for social approval. In contrast are *tradition-directed* societies (behavior in terms of the mores) and *inner-directed* (behavior based on independently arrived at norms).

patriarchal. The type of family system in which the father is dominant.

peer group. The in-group composed of a person's associates or peers through which behavior is influenced.

polygyny. A form of marriage uniting a man with two or more wives, as compared to *monogamy* or to *polyandry* (plurality of husbands).

primary group. A small intimate group usually characterized by close affectional ties, especially favorable for socialization, the family being a principal example.

projection. The process of ascribing to another individual or to a group an unfavorable quality in oneself.

projective test. A personality test (Rorschach Ink-Blot, Thematic Apperception) in which the individual may project his deeper personality traits as opposed to the questionnaire-type of test.

psychoanalysis. A technique of personality analysis and therapy, based on the work of Freud, with emphasis on the deeper unconscious factors.

rationalization. The largely unconscious process of justifying one's behavior or faults; the invention of reasons or excuses in order to make reality more acceptable.

regression. The tendency to revert to some earlier level of adjustment.

repression. Driving of thoughts, motives, and conflicts into the unconscious, often with dynamic effects causing tensions or symptoms.

resistance. The tendency to avoid recall of unconscious and repressed memories, motives, and feelings; may also refer to the hostility of the client toward the therapist.

role. The function or behavior of an individual in a given status and group as defined by the culture or the individual. (*Role expectations* are the roles prescribed or anticipated by a given individual. *Role performances* are the actual behaviors attached to a given role. *Role model* is a normative or idealized conception often based on the behavior of another individual. *Ascribed* roles are in general inherited [race, for instance] by the individual. *Achieved* roles are acquired through a person's own effort, education, or accomplishment. *Reciprocal* roles are interlocking or complementary—husband-wife or student-teacher. *Role conflict* refers to cotradictions or inconsistencies of various roles because of the inability to represent all roles.)

sanctions. The application of reward or punishment for conformity or nonconformity with social norms.

secondary group. The larger, more impersonal, and often more temporary group characterizing urban life; cf. *primary group.*

sibling. Brother and sister.

socialization. The development of an individual from an organism into a functioning member of the society, emphasizing the acquisition of personality. (*Anticipatory* socialization refers to acquiring norms in preparation of a later or adult status, that is, courtship as anticipatory socialization for marriage. *Resocialization* is the process of a later stage of socialization, as in the acquisition of new roles in marriage.)

societal. Adjective for society.

society. A fairly continuous group of people having a common culture.

status. A social position as defined by society. Being a husband constitutes a status which has a number of expected roles.

subculture. A subdivision of culture based on a given characteristic of the members such as age, occupation, social class, etc.

sublimation. The redirecting of sexual interests or some other disapproved motive or emotion into socially acceptable channels; for instance, dancing, writing poetry, or even dating itself becomes a substitute for direct sexual activity.

superego. The part or aspect of the self or personality organization having to do with the regulation of behavior or acts as control of the id; roughly equivalent to the conscience, but more unconscious and dynamic in nature.

traditionalistic-rationalistic. A continuum on which given traits are measured. Rationalistic represents bureaucratic or standardized practices often identified with urban culture or large scale organizations. Often the rationalistic is equated with the scientific approach as opposed to an intuitive and highly personal outlook. Similar continua are the folk-urban, Gemeinschaft-Gesellschaft, sacred-secular, or particularistic-universal, although each continuum represents certain differences. The extended family system is generally, although not always, found at the traditionalistic or folk end of the continuum and the nuclear family at the rationalistic or urban end.

trait. An enduring and presumably measurable personality characteristic.

transference. The tendency toward fixating love or libidinal interest on another individual such as on the therapist.

traumatization. The state of shock (or trauma), usually emotional, arising from deep conflict or an emotional crisis.

urbanism. The style of life in the large city: impersonality, multiplicity of roles, and secondary group relationships. See also *traditionalistic-rationalistic.*

urbanization. The concentration of population in and around cities, including changes of behavior and attitudes associated with urban life.

value. A belief or commitment in an object, idea, or goal; also may be defined as the capacity of an object to satisfy a human desire.

void. A marriage that is legally not tenable, as in bigamy, or that is *voidable* by court action if marriage fails to provide the legal expectation of a marriage, such as sexual intercourse; cf. *annulment.*

Appendix

Methodological Notes on Marital Adjustment Research

Chapter 13 contained considerable discussion of the marital adjustment questionnaire or scale. Certain theoretical and especially methodological questions were not included in the body of the text because of their limited interest. Even here the discussion is only partial.[1] This exposition focuses on the question of criticisms, implications, and possible improvements of such scales.

Before assessing the significance of the adjustment scale, it is pertinent to introduce the process by which the scale or test is constructed. An example of a scale is found in Table A.1 at the end of the Appendix. This particular scale was used in a Los Angeles study and was adopted from the instruments developed by Burgess and Cottrell and by Locke.[2]

Ordinarily, the first step in the construction of such a scale is to select a number of items based on various criteria of marital happiness or adjustment. As is seen in Table A.1, the items concern the degree of satisfaction, affection, and consensus in the marriage and the amount of participation of husband and wife in joint activities. The researcher is expected to begin with more items than will be eventually used in order that overlapping or nonsignificant items may be eliminated. The second step is to choose a representative sample of the population to whom the scale is administered. The results of a marital adjustment scale yield a group of individuals with high scores who are presumably

[1] Books reporting various statistical approaches to marriage adjustment contain methodological presentations, two of which are Harvey J. Locke, *Predicting Adjustment in Marriage: A Comparison of a Divorced and a Happily Married Group*, Holt, Rinehart and Winston, New York, 1951; and Ernest W. Burgess and Paul Wallin, *Engagement and Marriage*, J. P. Lippincott, Philadelphia, 1953. Also useful is Harold T. Christensen (ed.), *Handbook of Marriage and the Family*, Rand McNally, Chicago, 1964, especially Chapters 6, 7, and 10.

[2] Ernest W. Burgess and Leonard S. Cottrell, Jr., *Predicting Success or Failure in Marriage*, Prentice-Hall, New Jersey, 1939; Locke, *op. cit.*

happily married, and a smaller group with low scores who constitute the unhappily married.

As a validating criterion of the test, an outside measurement should be obtained, such as Locke's—a happily married and a divorced sample. With the establishment of this validating procedure the instrument may then be used to determine the relevance of other characteristics and behavior to marital happiness, as was indicated in Chapter 13.

CRITIQUE OF ADJUSTMENT TESTS

In this textbook we discussed, primarily, studies in which adjustment scales were used as a means of comparing happy and unhappy marriages. However, there has been extensive criticism of this technique of assessing marriage. Criticism has centered on the following problems:

1. *The choice of the sample.* With few exceptions the results have referred to college populations or to individuals of more than average literacy and to those oriented to the "proper" values of the community. The inability or reluctance to study noncollege and lower class as well as other subcultures, remains a limitation in applying the data to the population at large.

There are a few exceptions, in particular, Locke's Indiana study, which included a partial rural sample.[3] At the high end of the social class and intelligence continuum is the research of Terman and Oden, which was directed toward marriages of a California sample of gifted persons after they reached maturity. This study revealed few differences as compared to other studies.[4] A Los Angeles investigation of 210 couples included an upper-middle, lower-middle, and upper-lower class population. The results pointed to less favorable adjustment with individuals of lower socio-economic status, but did not basically indicate a different set of principles governing marital adjustment.[5] More data would be useful in regard to this subculture of class.

2. *Arbitrariness of the concepts.* There is some doubt as to what characteristics are being measured. Ambiguity exists about the area

---

[3] Locke, *op. cit.*

[4] Lewis M. Terman and Melita H. Oden, *The Gifted Child Grows Up,* Stanford University Press, 1947.

[5] Robert C. Williamson, "Socio-economic Factors and Marital Adjustment in an Urban Setting," *American Sociological Review,* 1954, **19,** 213–216.

under study, namely marital "happiness," "adjustment," "success," "integration," etc. We are not certain what the various terms may mean individually or whether they may be used with near inter-changeability, even though the researcher may have defined the term or terms to his own satisfaction. It is probable that a G or general factor is operating. The G-factor refers to a common variable underlying a variety of items. Besides the overlapping of the items and responses of "happiness," "adjustment," etc., the discrete items of the scale, such as "kissing every day" and "never having regretted marrying," have some commodity or factor in common.

In particular regard to the question of validity of the scale, we may ask whether the respondent is clear as to what is meant by the abstrac-tions contained in the questionnaire. Of course, both the interpreta-tion of the assumptions or concepts underlying the scale and the wording of the items may affect validity. Most marriage adjustment scales have various ambiguous items, such as "Please indicate the degree of happiness you have achieved in your marriage." Or there is little adverbial constancy in the following or like items: "Do you ever wish you had not married: frequently, occasionally, rarely, never?" Although the difference is valid between the two ends of the con-tinuum, there is inevitably some blurring in the middle. Lack of validity is perceptible in the basic premises underlying the measure-ment of marital adjustment. Are the scales measuring what they purport to measure? It is claimed that adjustment becomes a depend-ent variable of questionable scientific status.[6]

3. *The "halo effect."* Individuals who rate one aspect of their experiential world as happy are likely to rate some other as pleasant or successful. If I say my marriage is happy, I am also inclined to rate my childhood similarly. Related to this problem is the "differential sub-group bias,"[7] or the "tendency of one biased subgroup of a sample population consistently to answer questionnaire variables in the direc-tion of *their* biases": thus leading to (partly or wholly) artificial corre-lations. The variation of scores between the prediction and the adjust-ment scale has been particularly subject to question. Whether biases or

[6] Robert F. Winch, *The Modern Family* (rev. ed.), Holt, Rinehart and Winston, New York, 1963, pp. 681–683.

[7] Albert Ellis, "The Value of Marriage Prediction Tests," *American Sociological Review*, 1948, **13**, 710–718; in rebuttal see Lewis M. Terman and Paul Wallin, "The Validity of Marriage Prediction and Marital Adjustment Tests," *American Sociological Review*, 1949, **14**, 497–504.

falsification of responses tend to lower or raise correlations depends on a number of variables. Research has indicated the probability of spuriously high correlation in such instances.[8] Many of the researchers are aware of these problems and urge the restrained interpretation of the results. This tendency toward bias does limit slightly the usefulness of the data.

4. *Middle-class respectability.* There is a tendency toward conventionality in the respondents—a penchant to state that their marriage is happy, that they attend church regularly, that they enjoy sex—which may be attributable to the desire for social approval and to appear proper and respectable.[9] This is not to imply that the interviewees are dishonest, but a stereotyped response is likely to be forthcoming in the average interviewing or questionnaire situation.

5. *The lack of reliability.* Besides questionable validity, the marriage adjustment test has been criticized on grounds of deficient reliability—the possibility of securing consistent results in retesting, or whether the individual's attitudes about the marriage and other situations may change over time. The claim of individuals responsible for marriage adjustment studies that attitudes do not vary greatly with the age or date of marriage only partially answers the question. In the words of Kirkpatrick, the group statistic may conceal individual variations in the peaks and troughs of marriage adjustment.[10] Perhaps reliability is less of a problem than validity, but there has been no genuine answer to either problem. The problem of lack of absolute validating criteria is unsolved. Outside rating of a marriage by friends hardly provides the ultimate solution. Bias and lack of control mean that the happiness of the couple cannot be measured. The consistency of husbands' and wives' responses, which has been relatively high among a number of studies, does not remove the possibility of two individuals developing the same reaction to the marriage.

6. *The lack of cross-cultural comparisons.* As marriage studies have concentrated on an urban middle-class college population, so it appears that studies have been confined to the American culture. One exception has been the research of Locke and Karlsson in Sweden,

[8] Bernard Farber, "Response Falsification and Spurious Correlation in Survey Research," *American Sociological Review*, 1963, **28**, 123–130.

[9] Clifford Kirkpatrick, *The Family As Process and Institution* (second edition), The Ronald Press Company, New York, 1963, pp. 380–384.

[10] *Ibid.*, p. 382.

which pointed to certain differences in equalitarianism and in the expression of affectionate and in other marital attitudes.[11] Further corroboration on cross-cultural use of this work has supported the findings within the white Anglo-Saxon American population. The study of a Southern Negro urban sample produced results substantially akin to those found in the white culture.[12] An investigation of Chinese families even though it extended to a broader range of problems than marital adjustment, led to conclusions that marital adjustment has certain universal features.[13]

In connection with a study of class values in two Central American cities, a study which included five of the adjustment items from the Burgess-Cottrell and Locke scale found two of them to be discriminatory of lower and middle social class, implying that lower class marriages tend to be less happy than those in the middle class.[14] This very partial attempt indicates a possibility for further investigation with the same instrument in other cultures. In fact, the marriage adjustment scale might be the means of testing the values underlying marriage.

In view of these criticisms, it is wiser to regard the findings in actuarial terms. Statistical generalizations should be applied with caution. Certainly most of the investigators themselves consider the findings to be of value in pointing to causal areas in broad terms rather than suggesting that John and Mary conduct their courtship or marriage on a point-to-point relationship with selected statistical findings. We have indicated that most of the samples are derived from individuals with a college background and upper white-collar or professional status, and for this reason represent a population similar to the world of the student. Those studies of a rural or worker sample do not necessarily point to results different from those of the middle-class urban sample in my own research among different levels of the population; however, communication was sufficiently disturbed that same

[11] Harvey J. Locke and George Karlsson, "Marital Adjustment and Prediction in Sweden and in the United States," *American Sociological Review*, 1952, **17**, 10–17.

[12] Charles E. King, "The Burgess-Cottrell Method of Measuring Marital Adjustment Applied to a Non-White Southern Urban Population," *Marriage and Family Living*, 1952, **14**, 280–285.

[13] Lewis S. C. Smythe, "The Success of Chinese Families as Families," *Marriage and Family Living*, 1952, **14**, 286–294.

[14] Robert C. Williamson, "Some Variables of Middle and Lower Class in Two Central American Cities," *Social Forces*, 1962, **41**, 195–207.

doubt must be placed on the results. It seems that generalizations derived from the marriage adjustment scale are primarily intended for at
least a high school intellectual level.

SOME IMPLICATIONS OF THE MARRIAGE ADJUSTMENT TEST

THE PROBLEM OF VALIDATION. As implied, the major question
regarding the marriage adjustment scale is its validity. One aspect of
this problem is the comparison of husband and wife scores. Correlation
coefficients reached a high point of .88 in the Burgess and Cottrell
subsample with 66 pairs of schedules being filled out separately by
husbands and wives.[15] On account of the noncontrolled nature of the
survey it is likely that husband and wife conferences were held in
connection with the responses to the questions. On the other hand, the
respective coefficients for the married and divorced subjects in the
Locke scale were .41 and .04. The Terman husbands and wives produced an *r* of .59. Among 210 couples in a Los Angeles survey, only
four showed marked divergence in their marital adjustment scores,
even though the two spouses were separated during the interviews.
Does this mean that there is near equality in the rating of the two
spouses on marriage success or happiness? Or is the scale of insufficient
sensitivity to discriminate these differences?

Another issue is the success of outside validation criteria for the
adjustment of the marriage. Burgess and Wallin relied in part on the
judgment of relations and friends in assessing the engagement and
marriage success. Another study obtained a sample from high school
seniors rating the marriage adjustment of their parents, to whom the
scale was administered. The correlation of husbands' and wives' scores
was .65; for the girls with the mothers was .58; with the fathers, .48; for
sons with both the mothers and fathers, .56. It appears that in this
particular sample of 70 families in a Southern California city that
there was some degree of consensus within the family regarding the
marital profile of the husband and wife.[16]

REDUCTION OF THE SCALE. Related to the problem of validation is

[15] The coefficient was a tetrachoric *r*, which is higher than a Pearsonian *r*,
consequently the significance of the finding must be reduced somewhat.

[16] Aubrey B. Harter, *Adjustment of High-School Seniors and the Marital Adjustment of Their Parents in a Southern California City*, Ph.D. thesis, University
of Southern California Library, 1950, pp. 65–71, as cited in Locke, *op. cit.*, p. 60.

the possibility of abbreviating the scale, which, varying with the study, may run to well above 50 items. A relatively common set of items has been developed through various studies, particularly those of Burgess, Cottrell, Terman, and Locke. In fact, Burgess and Wallin suggested a composite score by which several factors may be combined. Although this might provide for a more valid score, it would not necessarily permit a briefer test. In the factor analysis study by the author it was discovered that of the the 20 items used in the scale, the last one, number 20 (see Table A.1), "What things does your mate do that you do not like?" received no significant loadings. It also appeared that the items on agreement could be consolidated in the adjustment scale so as to reduce the overlapping. On the other hand, "marrying the same person if one had his life to live over" appeared in several clusters indicating a higher validity.[17] On the basis of statistical treatment Locke and Wallace found that the marital adjustment test could be shortened from 50 to 15 items without significant loss in validity.[18]

PREDICTION OF MARITAL ADJUSTMENT. From a practical viewpoint prediction perhaps remains the most intriguing aspect of the marital adjustment scale. Prediction is based on two sources: premarital and postmarital items, both of which have only actuarial relevancy. In several studies the attempt to discover predictability of marriage success led also to the prediction of engagement success.

Marital prediction tests generally tend to be longer than the marital adjustment test. In the Locke shortened marital prediction test, attention is focused on personality traits and the socialization process in the family as well as on the circumstances surrounding the courtship process. The Engagement Success Inventory of Burgess and Wallin is an adaptation of the marriage adjustment scale with most of the items relating specifically to the engagement relationship. Presumably, an individual in the not unusual premarital quandary might find both the engagement and marriage scales to be of value. It is pertinent to add that among the engagement success scores, twice the number of broken engagements were below a given cut-off point (130 points) as were those followed by a "successful marriage." Although this finding

---

[17] Harvey J. Locke and Robert C. Williamson, "Marital Adjustment: A Factor Analysis Study," *American Sociological Review*, 1958, **23**, 562–569.

[18] Harvey J. Locke and Karl M. Wallace, "Short Marital-Adjustment and Prediction Tests: Their Reliability and Validity," *Marriage and Family Living*, 1959, **21**, 251–255.

indicates the possibility of utilizing the test as a means of prediction, it also points to some risk in applying findings to individual cases. In other words, prediction tests are useful for locating areas of tension rather than providing the final answer to when to marry or not to marry. Of the Burgess and Wallin sample, the 123 couples who broke their engagements, as opposed to the 877 who did not, probably did not need the test to inform them. Yet in reviewing the items there was an opportunity for the subjects to verbalize and crystallize their doubts.

Table A.1

MARITAL ADJUSTMENT ITEMS, FAVORABLE AND UNFAVORABLE RESPONSES,
AND PER CENT RESPONDING FAVORABLY *

Item	Favorable Response	Unfavorable Response	Per Cent of Sample Responding Favorably
1. Check the place on the scale which best describes the degree of happiness of your present marriage. 1 2 3 4 5 Very Happy Very Unhappy Happy	Checking 4 or 5	Checking 1, 2, or 3	58
2. Check any of the following things which you think cause serious difficulties in your marriage: attempt to control my spending money, insincerity, excessive criticism, narrowmindedness, untruthfulness, paying attention to another person, being easily influenced by others, religious differences, different amusement interests, lack of mutual friends, ill health, constant bickering, lack of mutual affection, selfishness, adultery, etc.	0	1 or more	60

Table A.1 *(Continued)*

Item	Favorable Response	Unfavorable Response	Per Cent of Sample Responding Favorably
3. How often do you and your mate "get on each other's nerves?"	Never, rarely	Occasionally, frequently	49
4. Do you ever wish you had not married?	Never	Rarely, occasionally, frequently	36
5. If you had your life to live over, do you think you would:	Marry the same person	Marry a different person, not marry at all	88
6. When disagreements arise, they usually result in:	Agreement by mutual give and take	Husband giving in, wife giving in, neither giving in	73
State approximate extent of agreement or disagreement during marriage on the following items:			
7. Handling family finances	Always agree	Do not always agree †	40

8. Matters of recreation	Always agree	Do not always agree	32
9. Religious matters	Always agree	Do not always agree	65
10. Amount of time spent together	Always agree	Do not always agree	54
11. Choice of friends	Always agree	Do not always agree	44
12. Sex relations	Always agree	Do not always agree	45
13. Ways of dealing with in-laws	Always agree	Do not always agree	43
14. Conventional behavior	Always agree	Do not always agree	45
15. Aims, goals, and things believed important in life:	Always agree	Do not always agree	36
16. Do you confide in your mate?	Always	Almost always, rarely, almost never	36
17. In leisure time, husband and wife both prefer:	To stay at home	To be on the go, or one prefers to be on the go and the other to stay at home	42

Table A.1 (Continued)

Item	Favorable Response	Unfavorable Response	Per Cent of Sample Responding Favorably
18. Do you and your mate engage in outside activities together?	All of them	Some, very few, none of them	35
19. Do you kiss your mate?	Every day	Occasionally, almost never	86
20. What things does your mate do that you do not like?	Nothing, one thing, two things	Three or more things	64

* The data of Table A.1 refer to the Los Angeles sample of 171 husbands and 178 wives derived from the total sample of 420 spouses (since persons 50 years or older were eliminated to permit greater homogeneity). The original sample came from three social areas of Los Angeles: a lower class area with 63 couples, a lower middle-class area with 82 couples, and an upper middle-class area with 65 couples. The average age was thirty-three years, a median education of approximately twelve years, and occupationally the subjects were divided about equally between manual workers, lower white collar employees, and in upper white collar and professionals.

† Includes almost always agree; occasionally, frequently, almost always, and always disagree. *Source:* Harvey J. Locke and Robert C. Williamson, "Marital Adjustment: A Factor Analysis Study," *American Sociological Review*, 1958, **23**, 562–569.

Name Index

Aberle, David F., 472
Ackerman, Nathan W., 579
Adams, Bert N., 504
Adams, John B., 28, 29, 30, 33, 35, 37, 41
Adams, Romanzo, 254
Addams, Jane, 97
Agee, James, 529
Aldous, John, 126
Allport, Gordon W., 245
Altrocchi, John, 436
Anastasi, Anne, 148
Anders, Sarah, 66
Anderson, Nels, 489
Anderson, Theodore R., 162, 336
Angell, Robert C., 406, 415
Anshen, Ruth N., 3, 39, 40, 43
Appell, Clara, 55, 56
Aries, Phillippe, 249, 473
Arieti, S., 101
Arima, R. K., 110
Aristotle, 12, 27, 459
Ausubel, D. P., 462
Ayrault, Evelyn W., 494

Babchuk, Nicholas, 439
Baber, Ray E., 292, 296, 297, 299, 319, 448, 506, 556
Bacon, S. D., 570
Badgley, Robin F., 162, 336, 339
Bailyn, Lotte, 69
Bain, Read, 138, 246
Baker, Luther G., Jr., 68
Bakwin, Harry, 111, 112
Baldwin, James, 193
Bales, Robert F., 19, 22, 49, 109, 138, 336, 353, 470, 527
Bandura, Albert, 122, 125
Banks, Franklin, 262

Bardis, Panos D., 26, 40, 304, 479
Barker, George W., 519
Barker, Roger G., 463, 464
Barnett, Larry D., 256
Barringer, Herbert R., 427
Barron, Milton L., 259, 276
Bash, Wendell, 422
Bates, Alan, 190
Bauer, Alice H., 55, 56
Bauer, Raymond A., 55, 56
Beach, Frank A., 11, 153, 365, 375
Beadles, William T., 407
Beam, Laura, 341, 344, 365, 370
Becker, Howard, 27, 31, 36, 39, 40, 80, 96, 138, 246, 305, 330, 359, 380, 399, 451, 460, 489, 490, 509, 519, 522, 534, 562
Bee, Lawrence S., 138, 191
Beigel, Hugo, 227
Bell, Norman W., 352, 507, 508
Bell, Robert R., 40, 60, 66, 69, 138, 181, 219, 260, 320, 352, 380, 477, 513
Bendix, Reinhart, 388
Benedict, Ruth, 39
Bensman, Joseph, 69
Bergle, Edmund, 559
Bernard, Jesse, 219, 484, 488, 506, 516, 522, 530, 541, 559, 560, 561, 562
Bernard, Will, 296
Bernert, Eleanor H., 138, 465, 473
Best, Winfield, 451
Bierce, Ambrose, 497
Bierstedt, Robert, 404
Bigelow, Howard F., 399, 415
Blazer, John A., 374
Blitsen, Dorothy R., 40, 83
Blodgett, Harriet E., 487
Blood, Robert O., Jr., 93, 94, 172, 173, 182, 191, 219, 246, 262, 276, 316, 320,

338, 350, 352, 367, 383, 392, 415, 427, 430, 450, 504
Blos, Peter, 138
Blumberg, Leonard, 181
Bode, Boyd, 59
Bogart, Leo, 56
Bogue, Donald J., 75, 76, 78, 79, 399, 420, 481
Boll, Eleanor S., 117, 138, 473
Boni, Albert, 263
Boni, Charles, 263
Bora, Katherine von, 32
Borgatta, Edgar F., 483
Boskoff, Alvin, 46
Bossard, James H. S., 94, 117, 138, 252, 473, 485, 520
Bowerman, Charles F., 264, 348, 487
Bowlby, J., 111
Bowman, Henry A., 163, 379
Bowman, Paul H., 465, 467, 473
Bradstreet, A., 23
Bradway, John S., 490, 492
Brav, Stanley R., 319
Brechtel, Ida M., 444
Breed, Warren, 201
Brightbill, Charles K., 52
Broderick, Carlfred B., 168, 173
Bronfenbrenner, Urie, 467, 468
Brooks, Evelyn C., 446
Brooks, Lee M., 446
Brown, Daniel G., 199
Brown, Muriel, 67
Brownfield, E. Dorothy, 335
Browning, Robert, 227
Buerkle, Jack V., 162, 260, 336, 339
Buhler, Charlotte, 473, 579
Burchinal, Lee, 16, 74, 94, 117, 181, 182, 192, 257, 386, 477, 478
Burgess, Ernest W., 10, 17, 19, 20, 21, 101, 187, 192, 206, 210, 211, 225, 239, 240, 241, 244, 246, 265, 266, 305, 306, 307, 308, 309, 310, 311, 320, 329, 341, 342, 343, 344, 345, 346, 347, 353, 373, 379, 390, 503, 512, 522, 579, 587, 592, 593, 594
Burkhart, Roy A., 573
Burma, John H., 256
Byron, George Gordon, 3

Calderone, Mary Steichen, 447, 448, 451
Caldwell, Bettye M., 488

Calhoun, Arthur W., 34, 35, 36, 37, 40
Calvin, John, 32
Campbell, Arthur A., 428, 430, 431, 433, 434, 438, 442, 447, 448, 451
Campisi, Paul J., 84
Caplow, Theodore, 180, 187, 188, 190
Carlson, Rae, 462
Carpenter, George R., 202, 206
Carter, Hugh, 558
Catton, William R., Jr., 57
Cavan, Ruth S., 21, 177, 192, 415, 444
Centers, Richard, 263
Chancellor, Loren E., 260
Chapman, Dwight W., 519
Cheever, John, 71, 455
Chesser, Eustace, 380
Christensen, Cornelia V., 214, 451
Christensen, Harold T., 21, 22, 26, 40, 58, 67, 69, 88, 111, 138, 163, 176, 178, 180, 182, 192, 201, 202, 206, 215, 219, 257, 270, 276, 300, 304, 348, 353, 380, 430, 473, 506, 522, 541, 544, 552, 571, 579, 580, 587
Christopher, Victor A., 85
Clark, Alexander L., 344, 346
Clarke, Eunice, 466
Clarke, Helen I., 281, 290, 292, 445, 449, 450, 475, 490, 491, 492, 494, 552, 557, 562
Clausen, John A., 518
Clawsen, Joseph, 274
Clayton, Horace R., 78
Cochran, William G., 205
Cole, Arthur H., 315, 318
Cole, Charles W., 184
Coleman, James C., 61, 138, 174, 192
Connor, Ruth, 468
Cooley, Charles H., 108, 235
Coranti, Elio, 82, 83
Cottrell, Leonard S., Jr., 20, 101, 170, 229, 244, 266, 307, 328, 341, 342, 344, 345, 346, 347, 353, 379, 390, 493, 515, 565, 580, 587, 593
Couch, Carl, 333
Crain, A. J., 489
Crane, F. R., 294
Crawley, Ernest, 315
Creeley, Robert, 249
Crist, John R., 174, 190
Croteau, John T., 402, 415
Crutchfield, Richard S., 50

Cuber, John F., 519, 580
Cumming, Elaine, 514, 573

Dager, Edward Z., 138, 473
Darwin, Charles, 249
Davies, C. E. P., 294
Davis, Katherine B., 341, 344, 345, 346
Davis, Keith E., 268
Davis, Kingsley, 132
Day, Katherine H., 263
Day, Lincoln H., 536
Dean, Dwight G., 246, 276
Dean, Lois R., 514
Dedman, Jean, 66
DeLee, Joseph B., 442
De Lissovoy, Vladimir, 74
Delliquadri, Fred, 580
Delora, Jack R., 309
DeMarche, David F., 572
de Montaigne, Michel, 323
de Rougemont, Denis, 226, 247
de Sola, Ithiel, 56
Despert, J. Louise, 549, 562
Deutsch, Helene, 375
Deutscher, Irwin, 514
DeVries, Peter, 301, 497
Dewey, John, 59, 60
Dickinson, Robert L., 341, 344, 365, 370
Dinitz, Simon, 262
Distler, Luther, 118
Dobriner, William M., 60
Dollard, J., 124
Doob, J. Leonard, 124
Dorfman, Robert, 411
Dorsey, Jean Muir, 22, 394, 400, 409, 415
Doty, Carol N., 92
Douvan, Elizabeth, 95
Dow, Thomas E., Jr., 487
Dowell, Kathryn S., 94
Drake, St. Clair, 78
Drought, James, 327
Dunn, Marie S., 135
Durrell, Lawrence, 223
Duvall, Evelyn M., 8, 380, 470, 471, 501, 503, 522
Duvall, Sylvanus M., 380
Dyer, William G., 334

Eastman, Nicholson J., 432, 437, 438, 439, 441, 442

Ehrmann, Winston, 14, 180, 192, 202, 203, 206, 209, 218, 219, 380
Eidelberg, Ludwig, 267, 506
Eiduson, Bernice T., 62
Eisenstein, Victor W., 200, 267, 506, 553, 580
Elliott, Mabel A., 534
Elliott, William Y., 69
Ellis, Albert, 219, 239, 380, 572, 589
Ellis, Evelyn, 92
Empey, Lamar T., 17, 92, 160
England, R. W., Jr., 228
Eron, Leonard D., 468

Fairchild, Roy W., 66, 68
Falk, Laurence, 88
Farber, Bernard, 16, 67, 183, 231, 276, 334, 350, 353, 453, 486, 494, 523, 590
Farber, Seymour M., 69
Faulkner, William, 142
Feld, Sheila, 572
Feldman, Harold, 507
Ferreira, Antonio J., 445
Fischer, Ann, 460
Fischer, John L., 460
Fishbein, Morris, 446, 479
Fisher, Russell S., 448
Fitzgerald, F. Scott, 99
Flanagan, John C., 459
Foley, John P., Jr., 148
Follmann, Joseph F., 409, 411
Folsom, Joseph K., 240, 246, 274, 335, 336
Foote, Nelson N., 92, 170, 328, 353, 493, 515, 565
Ford, Clellan S., 11, 153, 365, 375
Ford, Mary E. N., 214
Foster, Robert G., 568
Fowler, Stanley E., 168, 173
Fox, Renee, 517
Fox, Ruth, 571
France, Anatole, 5
Frazier, E. Franklin, 77, 78, 79, 96
Freedman, Mervin, 63
Freedman, Ronald, 422, 424, 425, 427, 428, 430, 431, 433, 434, 438, 442, 447, 448, 451
Freeman, Linton, 257
Freud, Sigmund, 8, 101, 105, 106, 107, 108, 109, 112, 115, 118, 127, 203, 232, 236, 237, 238, 333, 453, 461, 464

Friedan, Betty, 71, 96, 511
Fromm, Erich, 238
Fulton, John F., 359
Funk, William, 277

Gabower, Genevieve, 522
Gans, Herbert J., 96
Gardner, Bruce, 117
Gassman, Frances, 489
Gebhard, Paul H., 14, 196, 198, 200, 204,
  206, 214, 309, 367, 369, 370, 371, 374,
  375, 376, 377, 380, 451, 548
Geddes, Donald P., 219
Geis, Gilbert, 179
Gibby, Robert G., 486
Gini, Corrado, 82, 83
Glassberg, B. Y., 210
Glasser, Paul, 485
Glick, Paul C., 75, 89, 527, 538, 558
Gold, Herbert, 71, 135, 136
Goldberg, David, 422, 424, 425
Goldberg, Milton J., 402
Golden, Joseph, 255
Goldsen, Rose K., 161, 210
Goode, William J., 10, 73, 91, 215, 225,
  230, 254, 307, 391, 484, 535, 537, 543,
  546, 547, 548, 551, 560, 561, 563, 565
Goodsell, Willystine, 24, 31, 40, 156
Gordon, Albert I., 276
Gordon, Edgar S., 359, 361, 380
Gover, Robert, 209
Grabill, Wilson H., 420, 421, 422, 423,
  424, 426
Grad, Jacqueline C., 486
Graveson, R. H., 294
Gray, Horace, 267
Green, Arnold W., 139
Greenhill, J. P., 442
Gregg, Davis W., 402, 407, 415
Gross, Neal, 335
Groves, Ernest R., 567
Gurin, Gerald, 572
Guttmacher, Alan F., 451

Habenstein, Robert W., 28, 29, 30, 33,
  35, 37, 41
Hamilton, George V., 263, 341, 344, 345,
  346, 366, 372
Handel, Leo A., 53
Hansen, Donald A., 519, 523

Harlow, Harry, 110, 232
Harmsworth, Harry C., 543
Harper, Fowler V., 282, 288, 299, 494,
  554
Harper, Robert A., 569
Harrington, Charles, 573
Harrington, Michael, 385, 405
Harris, Dale, 125
Hart, Lorenz, 223
Hartley, Eugene, 467
Hartley, Ruth E., 159
Harvey, L. V., 574
Haskins, George L., 35
Haveman, Ernest, 64
Havens, A. Eugene, 180, 186
Havighurst, Robert J., 465, 467, 473
Hawkes, Glenn R., 117
Heer, David M., 261
Heiss, Jerold S., 174
Heist, Paul, 63
Helfrich, Margaret L., 90
Hellman, Louis M., 432, 437, 438, 439,
  441, 442
Hemingway, Ernest, 167
Henderson, Norman B., 576
Herber, Will, 68
Herman, Robert D., 175, 184, 185
Hey, Richard N., 569
Hill, Reuben, 9, 27, 31, 36, 39, 40, 80, 96,
  138, 192, 240, 246, 247, 253, 305, 330,
  359, 380, 383, 399, 451, 460, 490, 506,
  508, 509, 518, 519, 520, 522, 523, 527,
  534, 540, 562, 563
Himes, Joseph S., 255, 482
Hitchcock, Mary E., 74
Hobart, Charles W., 183, 188, 329, 512
Hobbes, Thomas, 278
Hobbs, Daniel F., Jr., 460, 517
Hoeflin, Ruth M., 92
Hoffman, Dean K., 332
Hoffman, Lois W., 43, 89, 95, 97, 461
Hoffman, Martin L., 471
Hollingshead, August B., 61, 131, 139,
  173, 179, 192, 257, 262, 305, 316, 523
Hooker, Charles W., 359
Hopson, Arthur, 298
Horney, Karen, 109, 467
Horowitz, E. L., 461
Horton, Donald, 229
Howard, David H., 211
Howard, George, 32

Hunt, Morton M., 96, 225, 231, 247, 357, 417
Huschka, M., 113
Hutt, Max L., 486

Ingham, Harrington V., 573
Irish, Donald P., 116, 487
Israel, S. Leon, 437, 449

Jackson, Andrew, 47
Jackson, Joan K., 349
Jacobson, Paul H., 73, 75, 76, 96, 265, 295, 299, 314, 320, 511, 520, 527, 530, 533, 535, 539, 548, 551, 555, 558, 559, 563
Jaffe, Frederick, 451
Janeway, Elizabeth, 545
Johnson, Adelaide M., 475
Johnson, Miriam M., 118
Johnson, Samuel, 278
Jonas, Carl, 557
Jones, James, 193
Jones, Wyatt C., 483
Joubert, Joseph, 99

Kallman, F. J., 101
Kanin, Eugene J., 203, 210
Kanner, Leo, 438
Kardiner, Abram, 154, 219
Karen, Robert L., 203
Karlsson, George, 591
Karpf, Maurice J., 572, 575
Katona, George, 388
Katz, Alvin M., 253
Katz, Elihu, 57
Katzoff, Simon L., 362
Kell, Leone, 126
Kelly, E. Lowell, 266
Kenkel, William F., 40, 332, 339, 340
Kennedy, Ruby Jo R., 446, 479
Kephart, William M., 22, 41, 123, 219, 238, 296, 297, 298, 299, 316, 362, 368, 380, 531, 532, 537, 538, 539, 552, 558, 563
Kerckhoff, Alan C., 252, 268, 276
Kerckhoff, Richard K., 579
Keyserling, Count Herman, 18
Kilpatrick, William, 59
Kimball, Solon T., 59, 69
King, Charles E., 591
King, Edward, 261

Kinsey, Alfred C., 8, 14, 130, 132, 180, 196, 197, 198, 200, 204, 205, 206, 207, 213, 214, 219, 220, 309, 357, 364, 365, 366, 367, 369, 370, 371, 372, 374, 375, 376, 377, 378, 380, 477, 481, 548
Kirk, Dudley, 425
Kirkendall, Lester A., 135, 139, 206, 212, 219
Kirkpatrick, Clifford, 22, 32, 35, 41, 69, 89, 96, 136, 137, 163, 187, 188, 190, 192, 203, 276, 288, 341, 344, 345, 346, 347, 353, 473, 512, 523, 533, 590
Kiser, Clyde V., 420, 421, 422, 423, 424, 426
Klausner, William J., 329
Klein, Armin, 159
Kluckhohn, Florence R., 340
Kluger, Richard, 217
Knight, Arthur, 54
Knox, John, 32
Kogan, Kate L., 349
Kohn, Melvin L., 468
Koller, Marvin R., 225, 252, 253, 308
Komarovsky, Mirra, 49, 96, 161, 163, 335, 344, 346, 347, 369, 405, 406, 415
Koos, Earl L., 505
Kosa, John, 93
Koya, Yoshio, 422
Krueger, Marie N., 85
Kubie, Lawrence S., 491
Kuhn, Manford H., 36, 39, 80, 305
Kunz, Philip R., 81
Kyrk, Hazel, 406, 413, 415

LaCognata, Angelo, 439
Landis, Judson T., 67, 87, 124, 259, 260, 261, 306, 344, 346, 363, 439, 484, 500, 502, 547, 549
Landis, Mary G., 87, 306, 500, 502
Landis, Paul H., 175, 263
Lang, Richard O., 390
Lantz, Herman R., 220, 523
Larsen, Otto N., 57
Lazarsfeld, Paul, 229
Lee, Anna S., 424
Lee, Everett S., 424
Lee, Margie R., 477
Lefkowitz, Monroe M., 468
Lehfeldt, Hans, 359
Leik, Robert K., 261
Leites, Nathan, 50, 161, 228

LeMasters, E. E., 163, 184, 185, 186, 192, 312, 460, 517
Leslie, Gerald R., 571, 580
Levin, Harry, 125, 461, 469, 470
Levinger, George, 336, 540
Levy, John, 523
Levy, Nissim, 436
Lewis, Grace Hegger, 513
Lewis, Sinclair, 513
Liddle, Gordon P., 465, 467, 473
Lindzey, Gardner, 458
Linton, Ralph, 3, 228
Lippitt, Ronald, 461
Lippman, Hyman S., 119, 121
Lipset, Seymour M., 388
Littman, Richard A., 467
Litwak, Eugene, 16, 550
Llewellyn, Karl, 43
Locke, Harvey J., 8, 10, 17, 19, 20, 21, 101, 231, 244, 258, 261, 264, 307, 308, 310, 316, 342, 343, 344, 345, 346, 347, 350, 353, 378, 379, 390, 392, 403, 503, 522, 560, 587, 588, 591, 592, 593, 598
Love, Leonore R., 573
Lowrie, Samuel H., 174, 175, 215
Luckey, Eleanore B., 333
Luther, Martin, 32, 140, 417
Lyle, Jack, 56, 57
Lynn, David B., 118, 462, 489
Lysgaard, Sverre, 74, 204

McCaffrey, Isabel, 514
Maccoby, Eleanor E., 56, 64, 125, 461, 467, 469, 470
McClellan, James E., Jr., 59, 69
McClelland, W. J., 110
McCullers, Carson, 128
McEachern, Alexander W., 335
McGinnis, Robert, 20, 427
MacKay, Richard, 554
McKee, John P., 150
Mackeprang, Muriel, 20
McKinley, Donald G., 97, 453
Madison, Bernice, 414
Magoun, F. Alexander, 239, 247
Male, David R., 574
Mangus, A. Raymond, 333
Manwiller, Charles E., 479
Martin, Clyde E., 14, 66, 180, 196, 198, 200, 204, 206, 207, 213, 214, 309, 364,

365, 367, 369, 370, 371, 372, 374, 375, 376, 377, 380, 451, 477, 481, 548
Martinson, Floyd M., 220, 244, 245, 247, 320
Maslow, A., 113
Mason, Ward S., 335
Mathews, Vincent D., 511
Matthes, Charles V., 465, 467, 473
Matthews, Richard E., 64
Mayer, John E., 276
Mead, George H., 108, 235
Mead, Margaret, 129, 142, 151, 152, 163, 229, 230, 467
Meehan, Eugene J., 404
Meier, Richard L., 434
Meissner, Hanna H., 215, 544
Menander, 23
Mencken, H. L., 525
Merrill, Francis E., 183, 192, 247, 320, 323, 353
Merton, Robert K., 215, 254, 255
Messinger, Sheldon L., 519
Meyer, Harold D., 52
Meyer, Henry J., 483
Mihanovich, Clement S., 511
Miles, Catherine C., 149
Miller, Daniel R., 122, 133, 139, 350, 461, 473
Miller, Neal E., 124
Milton, John, 99
Minnis, Mhyra S., 543
Mishler, Elliot G., 425, 428, 429, 430, 431, 433, 437, 439, 451
Moberg, David O., 65, 67, 69
Mogey, John, 69, 574
Monahan, Thomas P., 244, 260, 532, 538, 539, 559
Monroe, Ruth, 523
Montagu, Ashley, 163
Moore, Robert C. A., 467
Moreno, Jacob L., 577
Morgan, Clifford T., 132
Morton, Anton S., 64
Mosteller, Frederick, 205
Mowrer, Harriet R., 330, 509, 510
Mowrer, O. Hobart, 124, 135, 139, 203, 580
Mudd, Emily H., Dr., 567, 569, 577, 578
Mullahy, Patrick, 150
Muller-Lyer, F., 226
Murphy, Gardner, 458

Murray, Henry A., 267
Mussen, Paul H., 118, 461
Mustacchi, Piero, 69

Naegele, Kasper D., 472, 507
Namboodiri, N. Krishnan, 425
Nash, Arnold S., 27, 28, 29, 31
Navarre, Elizabeth, 485
Nechtow, Mitchell J., 449
Nesbitt, Robert E. E., Jr., 443
Neugarten, Bernice, 504
Neumeyer, Esther S., 69
Neumeyer, Martin H., 69
Newcomb, Theodore M., 63, 331, 467
Newell, David S., 514
Nichell, Paulena, 394, 400, 409, 415
Nicholson, Samuel O., 182, 262
Nickell, Paulena, 22
Nietzsche, Friedrich, 417
Nimkoff, Meyer F., 22, 97, 171, 266, 276
Nisbet, Robert A., 215, 565
Nugent, Elliott, 140, 142
Nye, F. Ivan, 43, 89, 95, 97, 123, 485, 549

Oates, Wayne A., 572
O'Dea, Thomas, 80
Oden, Melita H., 344, 345, 588
Ogburn, William F., 22, 97, 531
Orlansky, Harold, 112

Packard, Vance, 415
Parker, Edwin B., 56, 57
Parker, Francis, 59
Parsons, Talcott, 19, 22, 40, 49, 109, 137, 138, 150, 189, 336, 350, 352, 353, 470, 517, 525
Pasmanick, Benjamin, 262
Pavela, Todd H., 255, 256
Pavenstedt, Eleanor, 468
Peck, Robert F., 391
Perkins, Edward V., 479
Peterson, Donald R., 123
Peterson, James A., 139
Philbrick, Robert E., 88
Pierce, James V., 465, 467, 473
Pierce-Jones, John, 467
Pilpel, Harriet F., 278, 282, 283, 292, 294, 300, 378, 450, 552, 563
Pineo, Peter C., 334, 344, 512
Pitts, Jesse R., 59, 147, 317, 318, 551
Plato, 278

Ploscowe, Morris, 300, 549
Poffenberger, Shirley, 439
Poffenberger, Thomas, 135, 139, 435, 439
Pollak, Otto, 515, 570
Pomeroy, Wardell B., 14, 66, 180, 196, 198, 200, 204, 206, 207, 213, 214, 309, 364, 365, 367, 369, 370, 371, 372, 374, 375, 376, 377, 380, 451, 477, 481, 548
Pope Leo XIII, 23
Popenoe, Paul, 562, 567
Potter, Robert G., Jr., 425, 426, 428, 429, 430, 431, 433, 437, 439, 451
Prentiss, Robert J., 436
Preston, Malcom G., 569, 577, 578

Queen, Stuart A., 28, 29, 30, 33, 35, 37, 41

Rachiele, Leo D., 93
Raffel, S. C., 489
Rainwater, Lee, 433, 434, 451
Ramsey, Glenn V., 477
Ranck, Katherine H., 505
Rand, Martin E., 507
Rapoport, Rhona, 388
Rapoport, Robert, 388
Ray, John, 278
Reevy, William R., 211
Reich, Walter J., 449
Reik, Theodore, 234, 241, 247
Reiss, Ira L., 147, 175, 195, 201, 203, 207, 208, 212, 218, 219, 220, 234
Ribble, Margaret, 111, 112, 113, 461
Ricards, Sherman L., Jr., 315
Richardson, Samuel, 227
Richter, Jean Paul, 497
Riemer, Svend, 85
Riesman, David, 49, 50, 51, 69, 160, 312
Reissman, Frank, 465
Pobinson, Reginald, 572
Rock, John, 425, 451
Rockwood, Lemo D., 214
Rodgers, David A., 436
Rogers, Carl R., 575
Rogers, Everett M., 180, 186
Rogers, Richard, 223
Rogler, Lloyd H., 523
Rohr, Patricia, 436
Roosevelt, Eleanor, 97
Roosevelt, Theodore, 47
Rosenberg, Bernard, 69

Rosenberg, Morris, 161, 210, 463
Rosenthal, Erich, 260
Ross, Helen, 475
Ross, Martin J., 297
Rossman, Jack E., 94
Roth, Julius, 391
Russell, Bertrand, 193
Rutledge, Aaron L., 570

Sabagh, George, 258
Sagi, Philip C., 425, 426, 428, 429, 430,
    431, 433, 437, 439, 451
Sampson, Harold, 489, 519   /
Samuelson, Paul A., 404
Sanger, Margaret, 417
Sarnoff, Irving, 200
Satir, Virginia M., 580
Sawrey, William L., 489
Scheinfeld, Amram, 163
Schermerhorn, Richard A., 31
Schiller, Patricia, 578
Schommer, Cyril O., 93
Schneider, Louis, 74, 204
Schramm, Wilbur, 56, 57
Schroder, Ralph, 87
Schroeder, Clarence W., 344, 345, 346
Sears, Robert R., 124, 125, 461, 469, 470
Seeley, John R., 90
Seidman, Jerome M., 139
Selfors, Sheila A., 261
Seward, Georgene H., 119, 146, 163, 475,
    479
Seward, John P., 126
Sewell, William H., 107, 108, 114, 115
Shakespeare, William, 99
Shaw, George Bernard, 355, 383
Sherriffs, Alex C., 150
Shils, Edward A., 49
Shipman, Gordon, 291, 299
Simenson, William, 179
Simpson, George, 115, 220, 276, 320, 361,
    380, 451, 473, 503, 573
Simpson, Ida H., 90
Simpson, Richard L., 90
Sirjamaki, John, 69
Skolnick, Jerome H., 282, 288, 299, 494
Slesinger, Doris, 422
Smit, John W., 425, 427
Smith, Ernest A., 184
Smith, Evelyn I., 494
Smith, William M., Jr., 201

Smythe, Lewis S. C., 591
Snyder, Eloise C., 220, 523
Sobol, Marion G., 91
Sorokin, Pitirim, 220
Spiegel, John P., 338, 339, 510
Spiro, Melford E., 112
Spitz, Rene A., 111, 461
Spock, Benjamin, Dr., 451
Sprey, Jetse, 273
Stamm, C. S., 489
Steinberg, Charles S., 69
Steiner, Gary, 56, 57
Steiner, Peter O., 411
Stewart, Charles W., 572
Stolz, Lois M., 520, 521
Stone, Abraham, 567
Stone, Hannah, 567
Strauss, Anselm, 241, 254, 269, 271
Strauss, Murray A., 132, 133
Strodtbeck, Fred L., 340, 472
Strohm, Ralph, 298
Stuckert, Robert P., 333, 334
Suchman, Edward A., 161, 210
Sullivan, Harry S., 109, 237
Sussex, James N., 489
Sussman, Marvin B., 16, 22, 192, 276, 386,
    473, 523, 563
Swanson, Guy E., 122, 133, 139, 350, 461,
    473
Symonds, P. M., 235
Syndam, Margaret J., 316
Szilagyi-Kessler, I., 113

Taft, Jessie, 580
Taueber, Conrad, 419, 420
Taueber, Irene B., 419, 420
Taylor, Katharine W., 460
Tennyson, Alfred Lord, 107, 223, 227
Terman, Lewis M., 8, 101, 149, 195, 210,
    237, 244, 264, 307, 308, 310, 342, 344,
    345, 346, 353, 362, 365, 370, 376, 379,
    380, 588, 589, 592, 593
Terrien, Frederic W., 60
Tharp, Roland G., 337
Thomas, John L., 258, 344
Thomas, William I., 458
Thomes, Mary M., 10, 17, 19, 21, 258,
    522
Thoms, Herbert, 444, 451
Thurber, James, 140, 142
Tien, H. Yuan, 291, 427

Tiller, P. O., 489
Tizard, J., 486
Toigo, Romolo, 468
Tolstoy, Leo, 565
Towne, Robert D., 519
Troelstrop, Arch W., 415
Tukey, John W., 205
Turner, Ralph H., 91

Updike, John, 167

Valentino, Rudolph, 228
Van de Velde, Theodore H., 368, 380
Vandiver, Joseph S., 85
Vernier, Chester G., 292, 293, 300, 490, 492
Veroff, Joseph, 572
Vidich, Arthur J., 339
Vincent, Clark E., 482, 494, 580
Virtue, Maxine B., 558, 574
Vogel, Ezra F., 352, 507, 508

Wagle, Mildred K., 572
Walder, Leopold O., 468
Wallace, Karl M., 274, 275, 277, 593
Waller, Willard, 13, 22, 172, 192, 240, 247, 383, 506, 508, 513, 523, 527, 540, 563
Wallin, Paul, 21, 187, 206, 210, 211, 225, 239, 240, 241, 246, 265, 266, 305, 306, 308, 309, 310, 311, 320, 329, 343, 344, 345, 346, 347, 353, 373, 379, 503, 512, 579, 587, 589, 592, 593, 594
Walters, James, 468
Walters, Richard H., 122, 125
Warfield, Grace J., 487
Watson, Andrew, 576
Watson, John B., 232
Webster, Harold, 63
Weil, Mildred W., 93
Weinandy, Janet, 405, 505
Weininger, O., 110
Weinstein, Karol K., 433, 434, 504
Wels, Richard H., 553

West, Patricia S., 64
Westermarck, Edward, 41
Westoff, Charles F., 425, 426, 428, 429, 430, 431, 433, 437, 439, 451
Whalen, Thelma, 235
Whelpton, Pascal K., 420, 421, 422, 423, 424, 425, 426, 427, 428, 430, 431, 433, 434, 438, 442, 447, 448, 451
Whiting, Beatrice B., 139, 460, 473
Whyte, William H., Jr., 69
Wilde, Oscar, 99, 453, 525
Wilensky, Harold L., 51
Williams, Arthur C., 407
Williams, Robin M., Jr., 3, 60, 69, 161, 210
Williamson, Robert C., 53, 65, 182, 231, 251, 255, 263, 270, 272, 313, 342, 344, 346, 347, 350, 368, 374, 390, 392, 403, 429, 542, 588, 591, 593, 598
Willie, Charles V., 405, 505
Wilson, Roger H. L., 69
Winch, Robert F., 10, 20, 22, 43, 69, 97, 127, 139, 168, 192, 230, 239, 241, 244, 247, 266, 267, 268, 277, 320, 323, 333, 349, 353, 423, 427, 451, 469, 473, 523, 563, 589
Wolfe, Donald M., 93, 338, 350, 352, 383, 392, 415, 427, 430, 504
Wolfenstein, Martha, 50, 133, 161, 228
Wood, Arthur L., 171
Wright, Herbert F., 463, 464
Wylie, Philip, 121
Wynn, John, 66, 68

Yarrow, Marian R., 489, 518
Young, Brigham, 97
Young, Kimball, 81, 97
Young, Leontine, 481, 482

Zavin, Theodora, 278, 282, 283, 292, 294, 300, 378, 450, 552, 563
Ziegler, Frederick J., 436
Zietz, Dorothy, 414, 494
Zimmerman, Carle, 18, 29, 39, 41
Zunich, Michael, 468

Subject Index

Abortion, 447–448
Absence of parent, 487–489
Accommodation, in in-law relations, 501–504
Adjustment, to divorce, 546–547
  marital, 323–353
Adolescence, 128–138
  dilemmas of, 134–136
  and family styles, 133–134
  and physical changes, 130
  in Polynesia, 129
Adoption, 445–447
Adultery, 375–376
Advertisements in mate selection, 273
Affinity and marriage laws, 289
  in mate selection among the Romans, 30
Agape, 237
Age, differences in marriage, 75–76
  and divorce, 538
  and extramarital relations, 375, 377
  and marital sex, 365
  and marital status, 263–264
  at marriage, 73–76
  and widowhood, 527, 529
Aged, health programs, 411–412
  social security, 412–414
Aggression in children, 124–126
Alcoholism, 235, 570–571
Alienation and divorce, 540–546
Alimony, 556–557
"Allowance method," 395
Ambivalence, 236–237
American Association of Marital Counsellors, 567, 571
American family, 33–40
  see also Family
American Hospital Association, 409

American Institute of Family Relations, 567
American Medical Association, 409
Amish, 317
Anaclitic love, 235
Annulment, 294–296, 530
Anxiety and socialization, 127
Arizona, University of, 85
Artificial insemination, 449
Attitudes and marital adjustment, 346–347
Australia and divorce, 536
  and counselling, 574
Autoeroticism, 196–197
Automation, 93–94

Behaviorism and home, 232–233
Bennington College, 63
Berdache, 153
Bereavement, 527–530
Biological factors in sex difference, 144–147
  sex organs, 358–361
Birth, see Reproduction
Birth control, among Mormons, 81
  methods of, 432–436
Birth rate, 419–432
  see also Reproduction
Blood test in marital examination, 284–287, 290
"Blue collar" families, 405–406
Blue Cross and Blue Shield, 409–411
Breach of promise, 292–294
Britain, 449, 574
Broken family, 483–485
  see also Divorce
Budgeting, family, 393–398

Bundling, 34–35
"Bureaucratic family," 133–134

Caesarean section, 444
Campus marriages, 85–88
Campus setting, *see* Colleges and Universities
Canada, and artificial insemination, 449
  intermarriage, 261
  social security, 414
Cardiac-respiratory theory, 239
Careers for women, 89–94
Case studies, broken engagement, 313
  divorce, 541–542
  faculty socialization and love, 234–235, 242
  and marital sex adjustment, 373
Catharsis, in counselling, 575
Catholic-Protestant marriages, 260–261
Catholicism, 64–68
Censorship, 54–55
Charge accounts, 400
Child bearing, 419–445
Child-parent relations, *see* Parent-child relations
Child spacing, 430–432
Childbirth, 442–445
Childhood, and socialization, 112–128, 461–462
  see also Parent-child relations
Childlessness, 427–428
Childrearing, *see* Parent-child relations
Children, and divorce, 539–540, 552
  and mother's employment, 94–95
  number desired, 428–432
  sex desired, 431
  and television, 56–57
  see also Parent-child relations, socialization
Children's Bureau (U. S.), 63, 467
Christianity, family life, 30–32
Church, relation to family, 65–68
Civil contract, 32–33, 35
Class, *see* Social class
"Client centered" therapy, 575
Climacteric, *see* Menopause
Clitoris, 361, 369
Coitus, *see* Premarital sex behavior and Sexual aspects of marital adjustment
College students, dating, 176–179
  marriage of, 85–88

Colleges and universities, campus life and mate selection, 272
Collusion and divorce, 552
Colonial period, marriage and family, 33–38
  sex roles, 157
Commercialization of leisure, 52
Commitment and dating, 183–184
Common-law marriages, 296–297
  among Romans, 28
Communication, and marital roles, 334–336
  and marital role conflict, 510
  in parent-child relations, 461–462
Competence and parent-child relations, 493–494
Complementary needs and mate selection, 266–268
Conception, 436–437
Concubinage, 26
Condonation in divorce, 553
Conflict, *see* Marital conflict
Conformity, 50–51
  in education, 60–61
  as motive for parenthood, 458
Conformity and dating, 170
Connivance in divorce, 552–553
Consanguinity, 288–289
Consumer reports, 298
Consumer's Research Bulletin, 398
Consumption, economic, 392–402
Contraception, 363, 432–436
Counselling, 565–580
  contribution of, 577
  directive and nondirective, 575–576
  and divorce, 570 f
  group, 576–577
  methods and procedures, 574–577
  pastoral, 572–573
  problems of the client, 568–571
  and psychotherapy, 573–574
  resources, 571–574
  results of, 577–579
  sex differences, 568
  training for, 574
Courts and divorce, 550–555
Courtship, 182–191
  in American history, 34–37
  changing norms of, 12–14
  and mate selection, 268
  and sex roles, 160–162
  and war, 519

Credit, 400–402
Credit unions, 402
Crisis, and family readjustment, 516–519
 in homes with retarded children, 486–487
Cross-cultural comparisons, 590
 see also Subcultures
Cultural patterns and marriage, 77–85
Custody of children, 490–491

Dating, 164–192
 in colleges, 176–179
 frequency, 176–178
 in high school, 173–176
 as mate selection, 182–184
 motives of, 170–172, 177
 and parental opposition, 175, 190
 problems of, 189–191
 subcultures and, 179–182
Death and bereavement, 527–530
Dependency and love, 232–237
Depersonalization of modern life, 45–51, 62–63
Desertion, 531–533, 555
Disaster, *see* Crisis
Disenchantment and marital conflict, 512–514
Disengagement, marital, 513–514
Disorganization, economic, 404–406
 family readjustment to, 516–522
Dissolution of marriage, 527–563
 see also Divorce
Divorce, 533–562
 as alienation, 540–546
 in American colonies, 35, 37, 38
 causative factors, 535–540, 543–544
 children, presence of, 539–540
 and child's reaction, 123, 483–485, 548–549
 and counselling, 570–571
 distribution of, 535–540
 and duration of marriage, 538
 among Greeks, 27
 among Hebrews, 26
 historical factors, 533–535
 and intermarriage, 259
 legal aspects, 549–558
 legal reforms, 557
 migratory, 555–556
 and occupations, 391–392
 as psychological denouement, 540–541
 psychological effects of, 546–549

Divorce, racial factors, 537–538
 rate, 535–540
 and role perception, 511
 and substitute parents, 487–488
Double standard, 207–210

Early marriages, 73–76
Economic aspects of the family and marital adjustment, 383–415
 life and health insurance, 406–412
 management of income, 392–402
 and marital adjustment studies, 406–408, 504–505
 occupational roles, 388–392
 security for the aged, 412–414
 social security, 402–414
Economic changes, 46–48
Economic factors and birth rate, 423–424
Economy, American, 385–388
Education, and birth rate, 422–423
 and childhood, 464–466
 in endogamy, 263
 and family, 58–62
 for marriage, 58–62
Educational level and premarital sex, 206
Ego, and childhood socialization, 127–128
 in Freudian theory, 105
Ego-ideal, 234–235, 241
Elopement, 297–298, 314–315
Emotion, and dating, 186–189
 and divorce, 547
 and romantic love, 239–240
Empathy, and love, 245
 role in marital adjustment, 328–329
Employment, *see* Economic aspects of the family
 of wife, 88–95
Endogamy in mate selection, 250–263
 and education, 263
 and nationality, 261–262
 and propinquity, 250–251
 and racial homogeneity, 251–252
 and social class, 262–263
 see also Mate selection
Endowment policies, 408
Engagement, 304–307
 broken, 311–314
 and dating, 186
 function of, 305–306
 history of, 304

Engagement, length of, 307
  problems of, 307–308, 311–312
  sex relations in, 310–311
Engagement Success Inventory, 593
Entertainment and the family, 53–58
"Entrepreneurial family," 133–134
Equalitarianism, in family power structure, 93
"Equal salary" method, 395
Erogenous zones, 105, 371
Eros, 237
Erotic love, 237–238
Ethnic differences, marriage, effect on, 77–85
  premarital sex behavior, 207–208
Euphoria, 231, 350
Extramarital sex relations, 375–376

Factor analysis and study of marital adjustment, 350
Family, background and marital adjustment, 344–345
  counselling, 570 f
  definitions of, 10
  economic aspects of, 383–415
  and education, 58–62
  and government, 62–64
  history of, 25–40
  and immigration, 82–85
  and leisure, 51 f
  Mormon, 79–82
  among Negroes, 77–79
  readjustment to crisis, 516–522
  recent changes in, 15–20
  and religion, 64–68
  social and institutional setting of, 43–70
  styles of, 133–134
Family court movement, 558
Family life cycle, 393–394
  in Italian family, 83
  see also Age
Fathers, *see* Parent-child relations
Fecundity, 419, 427–428
Federal divorce law, 574
Females, and concept of ideal mate, 269–271
  physical differences, 144–147
  sex organs, 360–361
  see also Sex differences

Fertility, 419–432
  careers and, 89–91
  see also Reproduction
Fertilization, 437
Financial aspects of the family, 383–415
  see also Economic aspects of the family
Financial problems and marital conflict, 504–505
Fraud, as grounds for annulment, 295
Freudian theory, 104–108, 114–115, 236–238
Frigidity, 372–375
Frustration, childhood, 124–126
Frustration-tolerance, 125
"Fun morality," 133–134

G-factor, 589
Gemeinschaft–gesellschaft, 45, 49
Germany, 73
Going steady, in college, 184–186
  in high school, 175–176
Government and the family, 62–64
Greece, ancient, marriage and the family, 26–27
  and sex roles, 155
Gretna Green marriage, 297–298
Grounds for divorce, 553–555
Group counselling, 576–577
Group health plans, 410
Guardianship of children, 490–491

Habits and marital adjustment, 509–510
Halo effect, 342, 350, 589
"Handout method," 395
Hawaii, 257
Health insurance, 409–412
Hebrews, marriage and family, 25–26
  sex roles, 154–155
Heterogamy as factor in mate selection, 252–263
High school dating, 173–176
Higher education, 61–62
  see also College students
Historical factors, in counselling, 567
  in divorce, 533–535
  in marriage and the family, 25–40
  of sex roles, 154–158
Hollywood, *see* Motion pictures
Home, purchase of, 399
Homogamy as a factor in mate selection, 263–266

Homosexuality, 197–200, 207, 226, 372
Honeymoon, 310, 317–319
Hopis and adolescence, 129
Hostility, 236–237
  parental, 124
Husbands, reaction to wife's working, 93
  see Sex differences
Hymen, 361

Idealization and love, 240–241
"Ideal mate" in mate selection, 268–271
Identification, in parent-child relations,
  462–463
  in resolution of marital conflict, 509
  in socialization, 108
Identity and adolescence, 128–138
Illegitimacy, 214–217, 481–483
  and annulment, 296
  among Negroes, 77–78
Illness, mental and family readjustment,
  518–519
Illness of parents, 488–489
Immigration and family life, 82–85
Impotence, 372
Incest taboo, 288–289
Independence and adolescence, 136–138
Industrial health plans, 410
Industrialization, 46–48
Infancy, 110–115, 460–461
  training practices, 112–114
Infatuation, 239–240
  in engagement, 306
In-group marriage, 250–263
In-laws, 500–504
Insanity as grounds for annulment, 295
Insurance, health, 409–412
  life, 406–408
Intelligence and mate selection, 265–266
Interaction, influence of in socialization,
  108–110
Intermarriage, racial, 253–257
  religious, 257–261
Introjection, 462
Italian family, 82–85

Japanese-American marriages, 254
Jewish-Christian marriages, 257–261
Jews, 64–68
  see also Hebrews

Kaiser Foundation Health Plan, 410
Kibbutz, 112

Latency period, 106
Law, *see* Legal aspects
Legal Aid Bureau, 578
Legal aspects, age criteria, 282–287
  of childhood, 490–493
  consanguinity, 288–289
  of divorce, 549–558
  of marriage, 281–300
  physical examinations, 284–287, 290
  and race, 283, 288
Legitimacy and artificial insemination,
  449–450
Leisure, 51–58
Libido, 105–106
Licensing procedures in marriage, 290–
  292
Life cycle, and economic adjustment,
  393–394
  in Italian family, 83
Life insurance, 406–408
  loans, 401
  in marital adjustment, 403
Loans, 401–402
"Lonely heart" clubs, 273–274
Love, 223–247
  definitions of, 238–239
  motivation of, 243–244
  nature of, 232–244
  parental and peer models, 235–237
  and the self, 234–235
  see also Romantic love
Low income families, 505
Lower class, *see* Social class

Male sex organs, 358–360
Males, and ideal mate, 269–271
  physical differences, 144–147
  see also Sex differences
Marital adjustment, 323–353
  capacity for, 327–328
  and communication, 334–336
  factors associated with, 344–347
  and occupational roles, 389–392
  post-marital factors, 346–347
  and power structure, 338–339
  prediction of, 593–594
  premarital factors, 344–346
  psychological adjustment, 325–340
  role behavior, 331–339, 348–351
  studies of, 340–348
  tests, 340–348

Marital adjustment, tests, criticisms of,
  348–349, 588–594
  see also Economic aspects and Sexual
  aspects of marital adjustment
Marital conflict, 497–516
  and disenchantment, 512–514
  effect of on the child, 508
  and military service, 519–520
  nature of, 505–506
  resolution of, 508–510, 514–516
  role behavior in, 510–511
  types of, 506–508
  see also Marital adjustment
Marital sex, 355–381
  see Sexual adjustment in marriage
Marital success, 344–348
  see Marital adjustment
Marquesans, 153–154
Marriage, age of, 73–76
  in American colonies, 33–38
  ceremony and licensing, 291–292, 314–
  316
  definitions, 9–12
  history of, 25–40
  legal aspects, 282–297
  and military service, 519–522
  motivation for, 1
  roles, 323–340
  secret and elopement, 314
  statistics, 75–76
  study of, 6–9
  systems, 11
  types of ceremony, 314–317
  see also Marital adjustment and Mate
  selection
Marriage Council of Philadelphia, 567,
  569, 577
Marriage manuals, 362, 369, 379
Masculinity and occupational roles, 389–
  390
  see also Sex differences
"Masking," 334–335
Mass media, 53–58
  in romantic love, 227–229
Masturbation, 196–197
Mate selection, 247–277
  and age, 263–264
  complementary needs, 266–268
  and dating, 182–184
  ideal mate concept, 268–271
  and personality traits, 265–272

Mate selection, and propinquity, 250–251
  and racial factors, 251–257
  and religion, 257–261
  and social class, 252–263
Maternal care, 110–112
  see also Parent-child relations
Matrimonial Causes Act, 574
Matrimonial introduction agencies, 273–
  276
Maturity, and love, 214–216
  see also Socialization
Menopause, 377
  as a factor in in-law problems, 501
Menstruation in pregnancy, 146, 439–440
Mental disorders and the family, 518–519
Mental retardation, 485–487
Methodology in study of marital adjust-
  ment, 339–340, 347–348, 587–598
Middle ages, family life, 31–32
  sex roles, 156–157
Middle class, *see* Social class
Middle class respectability, 590
Migratory divorce, 555–556
Military service, 519–522
Minnesota Multiphasic Personality In-
  ventory, 436
Miscegenation, 283–288
  see also Mate selection
Mixed marriage, 253–261
Monogamy among Greeks, 27
Mores, sexual, 200–219
Mormons, 79–82
Mother-in-law, 500–504
Mothers, *see* Parent-child relations
Motion pictures, 53–55
  and romantic love, 228
Motivation, for marriage, 303–304
  and premarital sex, 211–214
Mourning, 527–530
Music, popular and romantic love, 229

Narcissism and love, 239
National Association for Retarded Chil-
  dren, 485
National Industrial Conference Board,
  91
National Marriage Guidance Council,
  574
National Vital Statistics, 299
Navaho child rearing, 112

Necking, 200–204
Need fulfillment and love, 234
Negro, 77–79
Negro illegitimacy, 481–482
  see also Racial factors
Negro-white marriages, 254–256
Neo-Freudian viewpoint, 109–110
New England family, 34–35
New Guinea and sex differences, 152
Nocturnal emissions, 360
Nudity in marital sex, 362
Nursing, 113

Occupation and mate selection, 263–272
  of wife, 88–95
Occupational roles, 388–392
Oedipal tendency, 106, 115, 242
Old age, *see* Aged
Old Age and Survivors Insurance, 413–414
Orgasm, 370–371
Outlays, economic, 395–398
Overprotection, parental, 120–122
Ovulation, 436–437

Parent-child relations, 453–494
  in adolescence, 132–136
  communication in, 461–462
  hostility in, 124–126
  identification in, 462–463
  indecision in, 122–124
  maladjustments, 119–128
  and mother's employment, 94–95
  one parent family, 481–485
  and overprotection, 121–122
  personality formation in, 115 f
  rejection in, 119–120
  and social class, 467–469
  and socialization, 115–128
  theories of, 104–110
Parental image and mate selection, 271
Parental models in love relationship, 241–243
Parenthood, childbearing, 419–445
  see also Reproduction
  and engagement, 308, 309, 312
  motives for, 457–460
  see also Parent-child relations
Pastoral Counselling, 572–573
Pater potestas, 28–29

Patriarchalism, 25–26
Peer groups, in childhood, 117, 466
  effects on pre-marital sex behavior, 203
Peer models, and love, 235–236
Perception, of roles, 332–334, 349–350
Permissiveness, parental, 122–124, 466
  and sex education, 480
Personal acquaintance service, 274–275
Personality, as determined by adjustment studies, 345
  and early socialization, 110–115
  and love, 244–246
  and marital adjustment, 325–352
  and sex differences, 148–149
  theories of, 104–110
  see also Parent-child relations, *Roles,* Socialization
Petting, 200–204
  in marital sex, 369, 371
Physical defects, and mate selection, 289–290
Pinning, 186
Planned parenthood, 427–432
Planned Parenthood Federation, 435, 439
Polygyny, definition of, 11
  among Mormons, 80–81
"Poor man's divorce," 532
Poverty, 404–406
Power relations and marriage, 92–94, 338–339
Pregnancy, emotional factors, 438–439
  fetal changes, 441–442
  and marital licensing, 290–291
  physical changes, 439–441
Premarital sex behavior, 204–220
  in American colonies, 35
  and cultural differences, 206–207
  in engagement, 309–310
  homosexuality, 197–200
  and marital adjustment, 210–211
  moral arguments, 211–219
  necking and petting, 200–204
Professions and marital adjustment, 389–392
Progressive education, 59–60
Propinquity, as a factor in mate selection, 250–251
Protestant Reformation, and marriage, 32–33
  and sex roles, 157

Protestantism, 64–68
  in American marriage, 38–39
Psychoanalysis and early socialization,
    104–110, 114–115
Psychoanalytical theory, 104–106
  evaluation of, 106–108
Psychodrama, 577
Psychological needs and mate selection,
    266
Psychotherapy, 573–574
Puberty, 130
Punishment and child training, 125–126
Purchasing, 395–402
Purdue University, 87–88

Quakers, *see* Society of Friends
"Quickie" divorces, 555–556
"Quickie" marriages, 295–298

Racial factors, and desertion, 532
  and divorce, 537–538
  in marriage, 75
  and marriage laws, 283, 288
  in mate selection, 251–252
  and reproduction, 424
Radio, 55
Random dating, 184–186
Recreation, 51–58
Recrimination in divorce, 553
Regression, 106
Rejection, parental, 119–120
Reliability, 590
Religion, 64–68
  and dating, 180–182
  and desertion, 532–533
  and divorce, 538
  and the family, 64–68
  history of in American marriage, 32–38
  and "ideal" mate, 271
  and intermarriage, 257–261
  and premarital sex behavior, 206
  and remarriage, 588
  and reproduction, 425–426, 431–432
Remarriage, 558–562
  social factors of, 558
  success of, 559–562
Renaissance, and romanticism, 226
  and sex roles, 157
Reorganization by parents to crisis, 486–
    487, 516–519

Reproduction, 419–432
  class differentials, 422–423
  conception, 436–437
  determinants of, 421–427
  and economic factors, 423–434
  and educational level, 422–423
  historical trends, 419–421
  national factors, 426
  number and sex of children desired,
    428–432
  pregnancy, 438–442
  racial factors, 424
  religious factors, 425–426
  and sex differences, 146–147
Research Club, 274–275
Resistance in counselling, 576
Rhythm method, 432–433
Role conflicts, and marital adjustment,
    349–350
  and sex roles, 159–162
Role playing in socialization, 108
Roles, and adolescence, 131–137
  expressive, 470
  feminine, 89–91
  instrumental, 470
  and management of income, 392
  in marital adjustment, 331–339, 348–
    351
  in marital conflict, 510–511
  maternal, 469–471
  parental, 119–128, 469–472, 479–481
  segmentalization of, 48–50
  and wife's employment, 89–94
Roman Catholic Canon Law, 294
Romantic love, 223–247
  history of, 226–227
  in mass media, 227–229
  psychological bases of, 232–237
Romanticism, 226–232
  and marital conflict, 512
Rome, ancient, family, 27–29
  sex roles, 155–156
"Rooming-in," 444
Ross-Loss Medical Group, 410
"Run-away" marriages, 297–298
Rural-urban factors and divorce, 537

Samoa, 229
Sampling in marital adjustment studies,
    341–343, 347–348, 588–589
Scandinavia, 202, 206, 215

School and the family, 58–62
  see also Education
Science, effect on family, 45–48
  and study of the family, 7–10
Secret marriages, 314–315
Secularism, 48–51
  of education, 59
Security, economic, 402–406
  see also Economic aspects
Security, emotional in marital adjustment, 329–331
Self, and adolescence, 129–131, 137
  and marital adjustment, 328–336
  see also Ego
Self-love, 234–235
Separation, 531
Sex behavior, *see* Premarital sex behavior and Sexual aspects of marital adjustment
Sex differences, 140–163
  biological aspects, 144–147
  and career choice, 88–94
  in choice of "ideal mate," 269–271
  and culture, 151–154
  in dating, 177 f
  in dissolution of marriage, 530, 540 f
  and environmental influences, 149–151
  and extramarital relations, 375–377
  historical factors, 154–158
  and in-law problems, 500–504
  and marital coitus, 366–371
  in marital conflict, 510–516
  and mate selection, 269–271, 275
  in parental roles, 469–472
  personality traits, 148–149
  psychological aspects, 148–151
  in sex identity, 118–119
Sex education, 477–481
Sex identity, 118–119
  and homosexuality, 199
Sex organs, 358–361
Sex relations, in engagement, 310
  see also Premarital sex behavior and Sexual aspects of marital adjustment
Sex roles and Western history, 154–158
Sexual aspects of marital adjustment, conditions of, 361–366
  duration of, 370
  enjoyment of, 378–379
  extramarital relations, 375–376
  frequency, 364–366

Sexual aspects of marital adjustment, frigidity, 372–375
  in honeymoon, 318–319
  impotence, 372
  initial relations, 362
  legal aspects, 378
  male-female differences, 366–370
  orgasm, 370–371
  problems of, 371–377
  significance of, 377–379
  and social class, 369
  timing, 368–369
Sexual capacity and annulment, 295
  see also Frigidity and Impotence
Sibling rivalry, 116–117, 431
Social class and birth rate, 422–423
  and dating, 179–180
  and divorce, 538
  and endogamy, 262–263
  and extramarital relations, 375–376
  and marital coitus, 369
  and parent-child relations, 467–469
  and romantic love, 230
Social Security, 412–414
Social Security Administration, 298
Socialization, 103–139, 460–472
  and adolescence, 128–138
  anticipatory, 129
  identification in, 108
  political, 63–64
  role-playing, 108
  in the school, 58–61
  see also Parent-child relations
Sociocultural factors, *see* Subcultures
Society, changes in contemporary, 45–51
Society of Friends, 36–37, 292
South Pacific, and romantic love, 229
Southern Pacific Railroad, 409
Spermatozoa, 359
Stepparents, 487–488
Sterility, 427–428, 448–450
Subcultures, in childhood, 463–466
  in contemporary American family, 64–68, 77–85
  and dating, 179–182
  in history of American family, 33–40
  and mate selection, 252–263, 271
  see also Racial factors, Religion, Social class

Teachers and the child, 465–466

Television, 55–57
Term insurance, 406–407
Testes, 359
Therapy, *see* Counselling
Toilet training, 113–114
Traits, psychological and mate selection, 265–272
Transference in counselling, 576
Transvestism, 199
Traumatization and death, 528–529
Tristan legend, 226
Trustee family, 29

Unwed mother, 481–483
Upper class, *see* Social class
Urbanization, 46–51
and divorce, 536

Vagina, 361, 369
Validity, of marriages, 282–283
statistical, 588 f
Values, secularization of, 48–51
Vasectomy, 435–436
Vocations, and marital adjustment, 389–392

Void and voidable marriages, 282

Waiting period, 284–287, 291
War, and the birth rate, 419–421
and divorce, 534–535
effect on marriage and family, 519–522
Washington, University of, 85
Weaning process, 113
Weddings, 315–317
Widowhood, 527–530
adjustment in future marriage, 530
as a psychological process, 528–529
Wives, in career selection, 88–94
employed, 89–94
in marital role relations, 331 f
in marital sex relations, 366–371
and non-Western cultures, 151–154
and psychological characteristics, 148–149
in Western history, 154–158
see also Sex differences
Women, *see* Roles, Sex differences
Work, *see* Employment